REGNUM EDINBURGH CENTENARY SERIES
Volume 3

Edinburgh 2010: Mission Today and Tomorrow

REGNUM EDINBURGH CENTENARY SERIES

The Centenary of the World Missionary Conference of 1910, held in Edinburgh, was a suggestive moment for many people seeking direction for Christian mission in the twenty-first century. Several different constituencies within world Christianity held significant events around 2010. From 2005, an international group worked collaboratively to develop an intercontinental and multi-denominational project, known as Edinburgh 2010, and based at New College, University of Edinburgh. This initiative brought together representatives of twenty different global Christian bodies, representing all major Christian denominations and confessions, and many different strands of mission and church life, to mark the Centenary.

Essential to the work of the Edinburgh 1910 Conference, and of abiding value, were the findings of the eight think-tanks or 'commissions'. These inspired the idea of a new round of collaborative reflection on Christian mission – but now focused on nine themes identified as being key to mission in the twenty-first century. The study process was polycentric, open-ended, and as inclusive as possible of the different genders, regions of the world, and theological and confessional perspectives in today's church. It was overseen by the Study Process Monitoring Group: Miss Maria Aranzazu Aguado (Spain, The Vatican), Dr Daryl Balia (South Africa, Edinburgh 2010), Mrs Rosemary Dowsett (UK, World Evangelical Alliance), Dr Knud Jørgensen (Norway, Areopagos), Rev. John Kafwanka (Zambia, Anglican Communion), Rev. Dr Jooseop Keum (Korea, World Council of Churches), Dr Wonsuk Ma (Korea, Oxford Centre for Mission Studies), Rev. Dr Kenneth R. Ross (UK, Church of Scotland), Dr Petros Vassiliadis (Greece, Aristotle University of Thessalonikki), and coordinated by Dr Kirsteen Kim (UK, Edinburgh 2010).

These publications reflect the ethos of Edinburgh 2010 and will make a significant contribution to ongoing studies in mission. It should be clear that material published in this series will inevitably reflect a diverse range of views and positions. These will not necessarily represent those of the series' editors or of the Edinburgh 2010 General Council, but in publishing them the leadership of Edinburgh 2010 hopes to encourage conversation between Christians and collaboration in mission. All the series' volumes are commended for study and reflection in both church and academy.

Series Editors

Knud Jørgensen	Areopagos Foundation, Norway, MF Norwegian School of Theology & the Lutheran School of Theology, Hong Kong. Chair of Edinburgh 2010 Study Process Monitoring Group
Kirsteen Kim	Leeds Trinity University College and Edinburgh 2010 Research Coordinator, UK
Wonsuk Ma	Oxford Centre for Mission Studies, Oxford, UK
Tony Gray	Words by Design, Bicester, UK

REGNUM EDINBURGH CENTENARY SERIES
Volume 3

Edinburgh 2010

Mission Today and Tomorrow

Edited by Kirsteen Kim and Andrew Anderson

First published 2011 by Regnum Books International

Regnum is an imprint of the Oxford Centre for Mission Studies
St. Philip and St. James Church
Woodstock Road
Oxford OX2 6HR, UK
www.ocms.ac.uk/regnum

09 08 07 06 05 04 03 7 6 5 4 3 2 1

British Library Cataloguing in Publication Data
A catalogue record for this book is available from the British Library

ISBN: 978-1-506476-24-7

Typeset by Words by Design
Printed and bound in Great Britain
for Regnum Books International
by TJ International LTD, Padstow, Cornwall

Distributed by 1517 Media in the US and Canada

TABLE OF CONTENTS

Edinburgh 2010 Common Call

The Edinburgh 2010 Common Call emerged from the Edinburgh 2010 study process and conference to mark the centenary of the World Missionary Conference, Edinburgh 1910. The Common Call was affirmed in the Church of Scotland Assembly Hall in Edinburgh on 6 June 2010 by representatives of world Christianity, including Catholic, Evangelical, Orthodox, Pentecostal, and Protestant churches.

As we gather for the centenary of the World Missionary Conference of Edinburgh 1910, we believe the church, as a sign and symbol of the reign of God, is called to witness to Christ today by sharing in God's mission of love through the transforming power of the Holy Spirit.

1. Trusting in the Triune God and with a renewed sense of urgency, we are called to incarnate and proclaim the good news of salvation, of forgiveness of sin, of life in abundance, and of liberation for all poor and oppressed. We are challenged to witness and evangelism in such a way that we are a living demonstration of the love, righteousness and justice that God intends for the whole world.

2. Remembering Christ's sacrifice on the Cross and his resurrection for the world's salvation, and empowered by the Holy Spirit, we are called to authentic dialogue, respectful engagement and humble witness among people of other faiths – and no faith – to the uniqueness of Christ. Our approach is marked with bold confidence in the gospel message; it builds friendship, seeks reconciliation and practises hospitality.

3. Knowing the Holy Spirit who blows over the world at will, reconnecting creation and bringing authentic life, we are called to become communities of compassion and healing, where young people are actively participating in mission, and women and men share power and responsibilities fairly, where there is a new zeal for justice, peace and the protection of the environment, and renewed liturgy reflecting the beauties of the Creator and creation.

4. Disturbed by the asymmetries and imbalances of power that divide and trouble us in church and world, we are called to repentance, to critical reflection on systems of power, and to accountable use of power structures. We are called to find practical ways to live as members of One Body in full awareness that God resists the proud, Christ welcomes and empowers the poor and afflicted, and the power of the Holy Spirit is manifested in our vulnerability.

5. Affirming the importance of the biblical foundations of our missional engagement and valuing the witness of the Apostles and martyrs, we are called to rejoice in the expressions of the gospel in many nations all over

the world. We celebrate the renewal experienced through movements of migration and mission in all directions, the way all are equipped for mission by the gifts of the Holy Spirit, and God's continual calling of children and young people to further the gospel.

6. Recognising the need to shape a new generation of leaders with authenticity for mission in a world of diversities in the twenty-first century, we are called to work together in new forms of theological education. Because we are all made in the image of God, these will draw on one another's unique charisms, challenge each other to grow in faith and understanding, share resources equitably worldwide, involve the entire human being and the whole family of God, and respect the wisdom of our elders while also fostering the participation of children.

7. Hearing the call of Jesus to make disciples of all people – poor, wealthy, marginalised, ignored, powerful, living with disability, young, and old – we are called as communities of faith to mission from everywhere to everywhere. In joy we hear the call to receive from one another in our witness by word and action, in streets, fields, offices, homes, and schools, offering reconciliation, showing love, demonstrating grace and speaking out truth.

8. Recalling Christ, the host at the banquet, and committed to that unity for which he lived and prayed, we are called to ongoing co-operation, to deal with controversial issues and to work towards a common vision. We are challenged to welcome one another in our diversity, affirm our membership through baptism in the One Body of Christ, and recognise our need for mutuality, partnership, collaboration and networking in mission, so that the world might believe.

9. Remembering Jesus' way of witness and service, we believe we are called by God to follow this way joyfully, inspired, anointed, sent and empowered by the Holy Spirit, and nurtured by Christian disciplines in community. As we look to Christ's coming in glory and judgment, we experience his presence with us in the Holy Spirit, and we invite all to join with us as we participate in God's transforming and reconciling mission of love to the whole creation.

INTRODUCTION

Kirsteen Kim and Andrew Anderson[1]

The centenary of the historic and influential World Missionary Conference held in Edinburgh in 1910 presented a unique opportunity for the whole church worldwide to come together in celebration, reflection and recommitment to witnessing to Christ today. Edinburgh 1910 is recognised very widely across the Christian world as a key event in the ecumenical movement, as an empowering moment in world evangelisation, and as a landmark in the serious study of world mission. The Edinburgh 2010 project was first a celebration of the fruit of that event over the last one hundred years in mission and unity. This was referred to by the shorthand 'world Christianity' – the globally widespread, inter-connected and locally rooted nature of contemporary Christianity, which is present in all regions of the world and now finds its centre of gravity in the global South. Edinburgh 2010 also engaged in serious study and reflection on the current state of world mission and the challenges facing all who seek to witness to Christ today. The results of this research was presented and debated within the context of Christian fellowship and worship at the conference in June 2010, and this culminated in a Common Call to mission (see above). This record of that conference is intended to give the background to that Call, to share the spirit of the conference, and to stimulate informed and focused participation in God's mission in Christ for the world's salvation.

Preparations to celebrate the centenary began as early as the year 2000. In 2002 a small group based in Edinburgh, but drawing on the missionary community of the church worldwide, initiated a series of seminars under the heading 'Towards 2010'. These reflected critically and systematically on the eight commissions of the 1910 conference, and related them to the mission of the church today. From this there emerged the vision of a new study process covering a range of contemporary mission issues that would lead to a centenary conference in June 2010 in Edinburgh. Unlike 1910 which was a gathering of Western Protestant missionaries, Edinburgh 2010

[1] The editors of this volume. Dr Kirsteen Kim was Research Coordinator for Edinburgh 2010 and is Director of Programmes in Theology and Religious Studies at Leeds Trinity University College. Revd Andrew Anderson was Chair of the General Council of Edinburgh 2010. He is the minister of Greenside Parish Church in Edinburgh and from 2003-2006 he was Vice-convener of the Church of Scotland's World Mission Council.

would be ecumenical, and mindful of the shift in the centre of gravity of world Christianity to the global South, it would be representative of all regions of the world.

Thanks to the hard work of a small team led until March 2010 by Dr Daryl Balia, the International Director, and to many others who served voluntarily in different capacities, together with the generosity of many churches and mission agencies, the study process and conference took place as planned. The names of many of these individuals and organisations are listed in the Appendices of this volume. Particular acknowledgement should be made of Stephen Smyth who was seconded by ACTS (Action of Churches Together in Scotland) as Conference Manager for the months immediately before the Conference, of Jasmin Adam who successfully managed the communication and public relations strategy, and Amy Middlemass who with her team handled the complex practical arrangements at the Conference venue. Edinburgh 2010 proved to be a project of daunting complexity. Uniquely it brought together the main branches of the Christian 'family', Catholic, Evangelical, Orthodox, Pentecostal and Protestant, and it established an ecumenical study process in all the major centres of the Christian world which was unprecedented in its scope and depth. An international group met in 2005 and 2006 to discern current mission issues and define the themes to be addressed through the study process. The International Director was appointed in April 2007 and the University of Edinburgh agreed to act as host for the project, with the Church of Scotland also supporting it in many ways. A General Council of twenty 'stakeholders' was formed and met for the first time in Edinburgh that September. The study process began in 2008 – working collaboratively and in a polycentric way – and at the start of 2009 a small support staff was appointed.

Originally it was thought that the conference would be of about a thousand delegates, similar to the 1910 conference. But a lack of financial resources in the face of the world economic recession, together with other factors, led the General Council to decide on a smaller but highly symbolic conference limited to three hundred delegates. The theme would be 'Witnessing to Christ today'. In fine June summer weather the conference opened with the Pollock Halls, the University of Edinburgh's residential and conference facility, as the well-appointed venue. It brought together delegates sent by the stakeholders with representatives of the different study groups to explore what challenges the study process may bring to the life of the churches over the years to come. The 300 delegates came from 202 organisations/bodies representing 115 denominations or national churches. They were of 75 nationalities and 61 different mother tongues, and they travelled to Edinburgh from all continents.[2] About one in three

---

[2] The General Council of Edinburgh 2010 were concerned about the impact of the Centenary on the environment. In order to reduce its ecological footprint, they

were female and about ten percent were under the age of 35. On Sunday 6 June there was a much larger gathering, of some thousand and more people, designed to be a day of celebration, thanksgiving, penitence and re-commitment. This took place in the same Assembly Hall of the Church of Scotland in which the 1910 conference was held. In order to encourage as much as participation possible from churches worldwide, the project made use of electronic means (website, Facebook and Twitter). There was also an online conference and the final celebration was streamed 'live' through the internet.

Edinburgh 2010: Mission Today and Tomorrow is the official record of that conference. It contains selected highlights of the event: the spiritual life, the plenary sessions and the study process, together with messages to the conference, the Common Call, reflections and statements made by those who were there, and also some photographs. One concrete outcome of the conference was the Edinburgh 2010 Common Call (see the following pages). Each of the groups which worked in parallel on the study themes was asked to submit a short statement of their mission priorities. This material was compiled, edited and presented to the final plenary where further amendments and suggestions were received. The final version was affirmed by representatives including all the main branches of world Christianity during the final celebration. In the interests of unity, the appendices include two other significant mission documents produced in 2010 by centenary conferences: a précis of the *Cape Town Commitment* of the Lausanne Movement and the World Evangelical Alliance (which were also stakeholders of Edinburgh 2010), and the *Tokyo 2010 Declaration* made by a special gathering of members of Evangelical mission structures.

This volume is one of the ways in which the work of the Edinburgh 2010 conference is being disseminated more widely. It is being distributed to all those who attended the conference and to other partners and significant depositories. The publishers, Regnum Books International (Oxford, UK) are also co-publishing it through partners in the USA, India and South Africa. In addition to this volume, an even fuller record of the conference, including video material, is to be found on the Edinburgh 2010 website, www.edinburgh2010.org. The website also hosts the material generated by the study process which preceded the conference and links to many other organisations which marked the centenary.

This is the third of the Regnum Edinburgh 2010 Series, which when complete will have more than twenty volumes. The first is *Edinburgh 2010: Mission Then and Now*, edited by David A. Kerr and Kenneth R. Ross, which records the deliberations of the Towards 2010 seminars. The second, *Edinburgh 2010: Witnessing to Christ Today*, edited by Daryl Balia

---

invited sending agencies and individual participants to make a donation of £20 ($35, €25) per delegate to the Cool Carbon initiative of Mercy Corps, an international charity organisation, which supports climate-friendly projects in the developing world.

and Kirsteen Kim, contains the fruits of the study process and was the preparatory material for the conference. Other projected volumes in the series include publications by several of the groups that worked on the main study themes, books devoted to transversal topics, and volumes emerging from regional and confessional study processes.

There is no institutional continuation of the Edinburgh 2010 project, but that does not mean it is the end of the process. The 2010 conference, and this volume which records it, are not intended to be the last word on any of the issues but rather to renew mission spirituality, stimulate further reflection, and encourage common action by the churches at this unique point in history. The warm fellowship generated at the conference across ecclesial, cultural and economic boundaries, and the Common Call that it produced, demonstrate that, although expressed in many different ways, we can glimpse together the one mission in which all God's people share as we seek to follow Jesus Christ under the guidance of the Holy Spirit. It is now the role of the stakeholders and all those touched by the project to disseminate this vision, study its implications and work it out in our contexts in ways which encourage the churches and mission organisations towards renewed mission in unity.

With our forebears who gathered in 1910, and we hope generations to come, we rejoice that we are called share in the mission of the triune God. And we pray that in the power of the Holy Spirit we may faithfully and courageously witness together to Christ now and tomorrow – and until the reign of God comes in its fullness.

WORDS OF GREETING

The addresses by Rev. Dr Olav Fykse Tveit and Rev. Dr Geoff Tunnicliffe were given at the Opening Celebration at Pollock Halls on 3 June 2010. The address by Cardinal Keith O'Brien was given at the Opening Welcome on Wednesday, 2 June 2010.

Rev. Dr Olav Fykse Tveit, General Secretary of the World Council of Churches[1]

Dear sisters and brothers in Christ! There are some moments in our lives when we realise, in a very special way, that we are participating in the triune God's mission in the world. To be here in Edinburgh today is one of them. This makes me feel both humble and thankful.

Today in the World Council of Churches we give thanks to God for how this hundredth anniversary of the contemporary ecumenical movement brings us back to where we came from and sends us out to where we need to be. Whether you come from churches and mission movements linked to the WCC or not, together we can give thanks to the Holy Spirit for assembling such a wide spectrum of disciples of Jesus Christ in today's world.

We who are in Edinburgh today participate in the same prayer as those who were here 100 years ago. I read from the gospel of John, ch. 17, v.21 – and please take note of the poetic structure in these wonderful words:

> I ask not only on behalf of these, but also on behalf of those who
> will believe in me through their word, that they may all be one.
> As you, Father, are in me and I am in you, may they also be in us,
> so that the world may believe that you have sent me.

These words remind us why they were here then and why we are here now. Mission and unity belong together. To be one in Christ is to witness together to Christ. We have a foundation going deeper than ourselves, our institutions or our traditions. We have a call which spreads wider than our plans. We are called to witness that the crucified and risen Christ was sent by God for our salvation, that Jesus Christ really has the power to forgive sins, to reconcile and heal, to change lives, individually and collectively, to make the church one, and to bring peace and justice to the world. These words of Christ's prayer are not only a reminder to us. They also transform us as we are here together, drawing us together as churches into

[1] Representing the Stakeholders of the Conference. For a full list of the Edinburgh 2010 stakeholders, see Appendix 2.

communion with Christ in the triune God. 'May they all be one' is parallel to 'May they also be in us'.

What comes immediately after these words in John's gospel is the story of Jesus' passion and cross. This story is about how all the disciples left him – betraying, denying, and abandoning Jesus Christ. Yet these are the ones who will later receive these words from the risen Christ: 'As the Father has sent me, so I send you' (John 20:21).

This means that if there is to be a witness to Christ, there must be a mission movement of the cross. This means that if there is a will to be one in Christ, there must be an ecumenical movement of the cross. Nobody needs triumphalistic movements. The world needs faithful disciples of Christ, always carrying the cross in love and solidarity with the world for which Christ died.

Christ has called us to witness, to share the gifts of God with one another and with the world, in love and compassion for all human beings and for the whole of creation.

Christ has called us to carry the cross together, to bear the burdens of one another, to share the burdens of our failures and our shortcomings in being one and witnessing together, to learn and to take new steps forward together.

Christ has called us to be good neighbours to all human beings, wherever they are, whatever faith they might have, or not have, to be sensitive and respectful to all who are created in the image of God.

Christ has called us to be peacemakers, to share in the burden of suffering in this world and to fight against violence and injustice.

Many more sectors of world Christianity now take their inspiration from the deliberations of the 1910 Edinburgh conference than those who actually participated in the event. At its meeting in 1951 the WCC central committee stated: 'It is important to insist that [the word "ecumenical"] is properly used to describe everything that relates to the whole task of the whole Church to bring the Gospel to the whole world'.

Let me share a personal word with you. One of my deepest joys following my election as general secretary is that I was reminded just how much the meaning of the World Council of Churches is defined by God's mission. Among the greetings that came to me, I particularly remember one from some Christians in India and from Cardinal Kaspar of the Pontifical Council for Promoting Christian Unity, reminding me that they expected me to be a leader of the church's mission in the world. Among the visits I have received during these first months, I have very much appreciated those of the two leaders of the World Evangelical Alliance and the Lausanne Movement. It has been moving and inspiring for me to realise how deeply we share a holistic understanding of mission.

Let me also say that Unity and Mission were the two main streams which led to the formation of the World Council of Churches. This wisdom led the International Missionary Council ('the child of Edinburgh') and the

WCC to merge in 1961. It is important to keep a healthy dialectic and creative tension between the many dimensions of our calling. To witness to Christ is both evangelism and the prophetic stand for Christ's will for justice, peace and care of creation. Christian mission is called to offer reconciliation to humanity – with God, with fellow human beings and with creation – a life that has the quality of the eternal life. The churches can be witnesses of hope in times of injustice, of financial crises, of violence and tensions between peoples of faith, and of environmental threats.

We know that these calls can in themselves be a cross to carry. However, today as we come together in this place as a much wider constituency, we come to celebrate the progress of world Christianity over the last 100 years. We are also aware that many Christians do not feel represented here and we humbly acknowledge the limitations of this conference. Despite very positive developments, the past century has unfortunately witnessed much hostility in mission, and we know this all too well.

There have been many difficult lessons to learn. Our struggles with mission have included valid criticism towards different actors, a wide variety of reflections, as well as critical commentaries on the WCC's work. We have all learned about the links between mission and colonialism, about shameful power struggles, and about the need for renewing the response to the gospel in what used to be called Christian cultures. We are continuing to learn hard lessons about being sensitive to one another in mission. We cannot but reflect and wrestle with the problematic tensions mission can lead to, even with so many good intentions. We cannot ignore that mission is a challenging theme in our relations to people of other faiths.

In Edinburgh 1910 the world missionary movement already had a deep concern for common theological education as a joint task of all Christian churches. This is also a strategic question for the future of world Christianity in the 21st century. We are therefore grateful that we shall receive fruits of this work here in Edinburgh through a book which is to be presented to us[2]). One hundred years after the Edinburgh conference in 1910 we are challenged to launch together a new beginning for common mission in the 21st century. We need to discern together what the call to carry the cross of Christ means for us today, as we witness together and find different ways to make visible our call to be one.

This is the hope and prayer of the WCC for this conference.

It seems to me that the excellent work done through the study process offers common theological ground for such a call and hope.

May these days be moments when we realise in a new way that we are participating in God's mission in the world, to the glory of God, the Father, the Son and the Holy Spirit.

---

[2] Dietrich Werner, David Esterline, Namsoon Kang & Joshva Raja, *Handbook of Theological Education in World Christianity: Theological Perspectives, Ecumenical Trends, Regional Surveys* (Oxford: Regnum Books, 2010).

Rev. Dr Geoff Tunnicliffe, Secretary General, World Evangelical Alliance[3]

It gives me great pleasure today to speak to the Edinburgh 2010 conference on behalf of the World Evangelical Alliance and our close friends in the Lausanne Movement. The WEA brings together some 128 national evangelical alliances, linking together churches of many denominations, and one hundred international organisations, thirteen major global networks, one thousand Bible colleges and seminaries, representing around 420 million evangelicals worldwide. We are culturally and ecclesiastically quite diverse, and celebrate that with joy as a little foretaste of the worship drawn from every tribe and tongue and nation described in Revelation 5:9. But, as that scripture also tells us, at the heart of heaven is the crucified and risen Lamb of God, and it is he who unites us, in time and in eternity.

Today we are celebrating the centenary of the World Missionary Conference held in Edinburgh in 1910. Many of those who participated in the research for the eight commissions, and many of those who came to this delightful city as delegates, were evangelicals. They were serving missionaries, or home staff of mission boards, or leaders of churches from which so many went out to take the gospel around the world. They gathered around the conference theme, 'The evangelisation of the world in this generation', because this was their prayer, their action and their passionate commitment.

They did not do everything right, and with hindsight we can see many things that perhaps should have been done differently. They were flawed human beings, and children of their age and culture, just as we are. But their commitment and devotion is beyond question. And as today we rejoice that the church is now global in a way that they saw only by faith and not by sight, we notice that many of those churches in Asia and Africa and Latin America, unrepresented by national believers in 1910, but now so wonderfully vibrant and growing, are the fruit of their labours and lives. That is God's gracious doing, and we praise him.

I hope that in these few days we will not lose sight of the fact that we are celebrating the centenary of a ***missionary*** conference. This conference's theme is 'Witnessing to Christ today'. We are not talking about some vaguely theistic or humanist agenda, but bearing glad witness to Jesus Christ, the second person of the Trinity. This is the Christ to whom the Scriptures bear witness, and central in person and work to the good news of the gospel. There is no authentic Christian mission that does not bear witness to him in word and deed and character, both individually and corporately. And there is no authentic church that does not have a

[3] Representing the Stakeholders of the Conference.

passionate commitment to mission, reflecting the heart of Father, Son and Holy Spirit.

There is no corner of the world where the mission of the church is complete. God's calling to the whole church is to take the whole gospel to the whole world, and that call comes anew to us in every generation. There are still communities and people groups who have never yet had anyone bear witness to Christ among them. There are others, especially here in Europe, where a fresh re-evangelisation is desperately needed. I hope that in these few days we will ponder that, with humility and repentance, and with renewed commitment to bear witness to Christ, with the love of the Father and in the power of the Holy Spirit, in every corner of our globe.

Historically, there have been many things that have divided the different streams of the church. We would be foolish to think that in these few days all those often deeply-held and painfully fought-over differences could be resolved. But I hope that we can listen to one another with love and respect, build bridges rather than create chasms, pray together, learn together, establish new friendships. In WEA we have had fruitful long-term discussions in recent years with many of the constituencies you represent: the Pontifical Council of the Roman Catholic Church, the World Council of Churches, the Orthodox Churches, and others. We are committed to continuing these conversations, to furthering mutual understanding, and to finding ways of standing alongside one another wherever possible. We will look for ways to continue the theological discussions begun through the study themes. We remain, like our 1910 forebears, passionate about world mission in our broken and hurting world. We recognise with sorrow that the *dis*unity of the church makes it harder for the world to believe in Christ.

And we pray that God may visit us all in grace and power, renewing our faith and vision, our hope and our resolve, so that we can indeed bear witness to Christ in this generation and throughout his world.

Cardinal Keith O'Brien, Archbishop and Metropolitan of the Archdiocese of St Andrews and Edinburgh

I begin by saying simply: 'There is only one of me here – and there were none of me here in 1910!' I make that remark as an indication of the tremendous change which has occurred over the past 100 years since the Edinburgh Missionary Conference of 1910. Then, there were no Roman Catholics present at the conference; and the thought of a Roman Catholic Cardinal being invited to speak at the opening service would have been unthinkable. And, of course, I am not here as the only Roman Catholic. I had the privilege of welcoming the Catholic delegation for lunch in my home here in Edinburgh this afternoon, along with our own Archbishop, the Archbishop of Glasgow, Mario Conti, who is the President of the Commission for Christian Doctrine and Unity of the Bishops' Conference of Scotland; and also Bishop Brian Farrell, who is the Secretary of the Council for Promotion of Christian Unity in Rome, representing Cardinal Kasper, the President. Our delegation represents Catholics from literally all over the world actively involved in the work of promoting Christian unity. How things have changed!

A further indication as to how things have changed over the past hundred years is indicated in the fact that each year when the general assembly of the Presbyterian Church of Scotland takes place, there is a Roman Catholic delegate invited, who is invariably a bishop and now has the right to speak during any of the debates. This has been one of my privileges over my past twenty-five years as a bishop also. However, I took particular pleasure from the invitation extended to me shortly after my creation as a cardinal in October 2003, to address the General Assembly after a formal congratulatory greeting. On ascertaining that a reasonable dissertation would be welcomed, rather than a formal thank you, I brought with me to that General Assembly three particular visual aids:

I had with me a small compass made from Iona silver, which had been presented to me by the Very Reverend James Weatherhead, a previous moderator of the General Assembly and his wife, Anne. What was most moving was the inscription, which stated: 'May this compass point us on the way ahead and may the cardinal points on the compass help us on our journey!' The second visual aid was a little towel which represented the 'service' of this newly-appointed Cardinal. I indicated that the towel, according to the synoptic accounts of the Last Supper from Matthew, Mark and Luke, was an expression of Christ's service at the institution of the Eucharist. Thirdly, I produced my little set of wooden rosary beads as a pre-Reformation sign of prayer, which united us all, whatever the form of prayer we use today as members of our Christian churches.

The moderator of the Church of Scotland, the Very Reverend John Christie, has already spoken very eloquently of the 1910 conference and the missionary endeavour then, which was an important part of the life of the Scottish church – but he now points us forward. And I would emphasise that we all face new challenges as members of Christian churches in witnessing to Jesus Christ at this present time. The challenges are evident both in today's society and in the world. And the challenges facing us include trying to spread the gospel here at home in Scotland and in those countries where the Christian message has already taken root, far from home. Among these challenges are those to life in all its aspects, from the beginning of life to natural death; during life itself; with increased poverty in our land, homelessness, drink and drugs problems; and problems with trying to build up our young community, strong in our Christian faith.

However, there are indeed increasingly positive signs in what we Christians can and do together in witnessing to Christ today. In Scotland all the mainstream Christian Churches meet regularly as members of 'Action of Churches Together in Scotland' (ACTS) – bringing together representatives of our churches, discussing possible ways of working together and seeing to the implementation of decisions taken. And, of course, at local level there are increasingly practical experiences of our Christian witness.

I would also say at this present time the efforts of the Christian churches here in Scotland and the increasing value of what we say and do is recognised both by our Scottish government here at home and the United Kingdom government in Westminster. In Scotland the Christian leaders meet regularly with the First Minister of our government, discussing issues of common concern – which help both us and the government in formulating a policy which, hopefully, will coincide with Christian values. Similarly, in the Westminster parliament, through the secretary of state for Scotland, and our contact with Scottish members of parliament in Westminster, we are able to lobby, often successfully, with regard to Christian values. Further, here in Scotland we have a very valuable interfaith outreach through our Scottish Inter Faith Council. This ensures that at every level we have the concerns of our people at heart, whatever their Christian denomination or whatever world faith they belong to.

In our country at this present time, much has been made of the initials PC as standing for political correctness – an indication that perhaps everyone should observe their proper place and not speak out of turn! However, the Christian Churches would rather see PC as standing for proclaiming Christianity – and it is that that we are increasingly able to do together at this present time. I see this as a natural 'follow on' over the past one hundred years from what was tentatively beginning in 1910 – a magnificent Christian witness here at home to the message of Jesus Christ himself and, hopefully, our example extending throughout the world.

Spiritual Life of the Conference

Elizabeth Moran, SSC[1]

'Edinburgh 2010' was a conference of committed Christian men and women. From the start of the planning, there was the understanding that the programme of study and consultation would be surrounded by and based on a framework of shared spirituality. To prepare this, an international group, ten in number met and worked together as the Spiritual Life Committee through the months in preparation for, and during the days of, the Edinburgh Conference. Working together, the group had a shared concern for enabling an atmosphere of faith and trust, gratitude and hope. The spiritual life of the conference should be just that – the energy, the dynamism of the Spirit of Christ present among the members. More than an activity confined to set times of worship, it is a developing life of relationship in mission. Everyone present as a delegate was coming either from the experience of involvement in the study process or from an organisation or church that prepares, sends or supports missionary personnel. Yet everyone present was coming to listen, to respect, to contribute and to learn. Each was conscious of the changes in the hundred years of human history since 1910, and of the differences in the composition between the membership of the 1910 conference and of this one in 2010. Each was conscious of the need to recognise the many ways in which the call to witness to Christ is to be heard today, and of the need to work towards unity in response. It was on those realities of 'everyone present' that the spiritual life of these conference days could be built.

Welcome

The primary, deep need was for welcome, as always in human situations – the official welcome of recognition, of finding one's room, taking possession, the invitation to eat, to explore the territory, read the notices, find the fire escapes, walk in the garden, 'feel at home'. Whatever the culture, the message has to be the same. You belong, you have a part to take here, you are well come. The Pollock Halls residence reception staff

[1] By Sister Elizabeth Moran, SSC. Sister Elizabeth Moran, of the Columban Sisters, was a member of the Spiritual Life Committee. A substantial version of this article was first published in *One in Christ* v.44 (1), 2010 under the title "Reminiscences and Reflections on the Spirituality of a Conference".

and the supportive conference staff managed this well. It was a good entry into the first 'Songs and Welcomes' session which brought this phase of arrivals to a close.[2] The spirit of welcome, of gracious hospitality, finds deep resonance in the Christian understanding of life as life-in-relationship, a journey of meetings, a journey towards the final welcome. 'In my Father's house there are many rooms. Were it not so, I would have told you. I am going to prepare a place for you …' (John 14:2).

The most obvious feature of that opening welcome session was the presence of so many different nationalities, called together on this occasion by the insistent beat of the drums, and singing together to melodies from many countries of the world. 'God welcomes all' – they sang their truth. The introductory invitation to prayer brought a reminder of the gathering of missionaries one hundred years ago in this same city, and a recognition of the different era, the challenges today to Christian witness, and the hope for a new vision, new energy for the churches. Then came the opportunity to welcome one another – to greet someone as yet unknown, to share names, countries, church families, and hopes for the conference. Then, as individuals became part of the group, welcomed and welcoming, leaders from the nation's churches and the city's ancient university each offered a short welcome speech.

Ancient, inspired words illumined the reality of the gathering: 'all nations praise the Lord', 'you are my witnesses'; and encouraged hope: 'I am about to do a new thing'. The gospel proclamation brought the reminder 'I am the Vine: you are the branches'. Spoken prayers first gave thanks and asked protection for the lands and the churches from which the delegates came, and then, remembering with thanks the blessings that came with the 1910 conference, asked for the necessary graces for the here and now of this 2010 meeting. A few moments silence, then a quiet night prayer, the 'Our Father' together in various languages, and a simple blessing.

The day was over. The conference had started. Delegates had crossed the boundary, and, becoming members of this new population of an ecumenical missionary country, would waken in the morning into a new reality. The spiritual life of the conference is situated in the here and now, where we are, in relationship with the Father, the Son and the Holy Spirit, and where we are called, in that circle, into relationship with one another. Temporary, yes, but real, as is life on earth.

Was it all so clear, at that beginning moment? In that atmosphere of welcome and hope, with its invitation to participation, delegates tired from a long journey, experiencing the dislocation of time and place, separated from the familiar, also realised that they bring elements of the negative. On the path leading away from the Hall of Welcomes, I met an Asian woman and an African man, and the conversation highlighted two of the difficult areas of relationship ready to emerge in this gathering – so full of potential,

---

[2] See Wednesday Night Songs and Welcome, Appendix 7, 411ff.

so vulnerable. The question came: Where were the women speakers and leaders in that session? All those who welcomed the delegates were white, Western men. The feelings, rather than the facts and their explanation, were important here. They are indicators of a whole range of awareness of need for reconciliation, for dialogue on disturbing or painful aspects of reality. Would they prove to be possible sources of desolation, or entry points to a path to new hope, new energy, new cooperation?

Worship

Next morning, delegates were called into awareness of the present and its possibilities, in the simplicity of movement into a gathering in the garden.[3] The call was given by the sound of the Scottish bagpipes. It is almost impossible not to hear and be drawn by that sound! On that beautiful morning, of sunshine and green growth, it was a summons to hope, to exploration and discovery. In that great crowd, each one carried something of individual life and history, a pebble from home, stones of the ancient earth to be laid around the central cross in the worship space. The cross was the Celtic Cross, symbol and reminder of death and resurrection, redemption and remaking of all creation. All the earth was carried in the entry procession, with the chanting of Psalm 122, 'I was glad when they said to me: Let us go to the house of the Lord...'. Palm trees, with moving leaves made from the fabrics of many countries, provided a symbolic atmosphere of earth's growth and the worship of the nations, and the chant mounte to a unified 'Glory to God the Creator, to the Son and to the Holy Spirit...'.

There was no constraint in the singing that followed of 'All people that live on the earth, sing to the Lord with cheerful voice ...'. It was in truth the song of the moment. And the prayers that followed were also of the moment – thanksgiving for the privilege of sharing in this gathering of the church, with all its variety of culture and colour, and a prayer that being together in joy will bring surprise, new insights, new energy, new hope. A prayer too for wisdom that personal agendas may be set aside, that rehearsed speeches may not block the voice of the other. This prayer led to the invitation to converse for a while with 'the other' – to turn to someone as yet a stranger and to share a little of one's own faith history. The worship space came alive with the sharing of these life stories. Then the call to silence, to listen together to the Word of God in Scripture, drawn this time from the letters of Peter – the encouragement to come to Christ as living stones, to be built together into a spiritual temple. The response, framed in a hymn from Malawi, was one of dedication to the work of God.

Then representatives of the stakeholders stood to speak. These were the voices from the organisations and churches, some worldwide communions,

---

[3] See Conference Worship, pp.37ff.

some nationally based, which gave support and encouragement from the start for this conference. Approximately two out of every three of the participants were representing these organisations and churches. They spoke of the opportunities and the tasks of the conference, with its studies and its agenda of hope for unity and a renewal of missionary spirit. The study process should hear, support and energise the pastoral and practical experience of mission, from which came the questions, the case studies and the new perspectives.

Then together, delegates from the stakeholder organisations and delegates from the study process were called to listen to the Gospel – not to study but to listen and respond. In this time of opening celebration, three stories from the Gospel, each one about a person who encountered Jesus and was totally changed by that meeting, were dramatised by symbolic actions accompanied by a soliloquy from the person in the story. Black mud, a pottery water jug, and a bag of coins and bread recalled the blind man at the pool of Siloam, the woman at the well, and Zacchaeus. Most of us think we know these stories, and may even be prepared to explain their meaning. It is a little different to be asked which of these three you would most like to meet, and to share a little of your possible conversation. Each of these three became a disciple, each became a witness. What have they to say to us? So delegates moved out of the worship space to walk together in twos or threes, talking 'about all these things'.[4]

Gratitude

On the Friday morning[5] the Common Prayer was enlivened by children from a local primary school. They had prepared well, with their young, enthusiastic teacher, and with help from the pioneering schools' group, Fischy Music, and from members of the Spiritual Life Committee. In their classroom they had a very serious discussion about ways of helping these missionary people from all over the world to celebrate the great work that had been carried on for more than one hundred years. They would read the letter that St. Paul wrote to young Timothy telling him to treasure the gift of knowing Jesus and to guard it carefully, with the help of the Holy Spirit (2 Tim. 1: 2-11). They read from that letter as if they had just received it 'from our brother Paul who is travelling to tell people in far countries about Jesus'. They chose their favourite words from that letter and prepared three hundred small origami-style cards as gifts for the delegates, presenting

---

[4] This aspect of the Opening Celebration, as well as the form in which the three stories were presented in the dramatic script, was a conscious echo of the Emmaus Road theme of the 2010 Week of Prayer for Christian Unity (convened this year by Scotland) in which delegates, in different parts of the world, would already have participated.

[5] See Appendix 7, 414ff.

these efficiently and easily before settling down at the side of the room to work in silence at making cards for friends or relatives during the homily.

Prof. Dr. Metropolitan Nifon, who had carefully prepared his address to the delegates, had been a little surprised to realise that children were involved, and slightly apprehensive that they might be restless and noisy. It was quite a moving moment when, after the children had proclaimed their reading, and carried their letters to the delegates, he came to the microphone and began by a warm reference to 'my young partners in the gospel'. His address was one of warm encouragement to the churches to continue on the path towards fullness of life together with each other in common witness. A prayer of gratitude followed the address, giving thanks for good gifts received, for all that children bring and for the ways in which they remind us of the times when Jesus met with children. We were asked to become like children, which must mean listening to them, learning from them, encouraging them, as on this morning, so that we will find the kingdom of heaven. The closing blessing and song wished the delegates – and their young visitors – peace, hope and joy for this day. These were already tangible.

The Spiritual Life Committee from the start had looked for ways to provide opportunities for delegates to encounter Scripture as a living Word, and decided to offer times for 'Sharing Scripture'. Sharing Scripture followed Common Prayer on the Friday and Saturday. Groups had nine or ten members, one of whom was a guide who had an overview of the process to help the group to use the time well. On each of the two days, a particular story from the New Testament was offered for the group's exploration. At the start, after a moment of prayer to ask for the gift of the Holy Spirit, for wisdom and understanding, the group were asked to reconstruct the story together, as each one remembered and contributed to it. After ten minutes, the group divided into two smaller groups and each person received a copy of the Scripture text. This was read slowly, with the members listening from the background of the way it had been told earlier. There was then some time to reflect on the meanings, the emphases, what the group members had missed out – or added. The story on Friday was that of the meeting of Jesus with the Syro-Phoenician woman (Mark 7:24-30 and Matt.15:21-28), and on Saturday that of Philip and the eunuch on the Gaza road (Acts 8:26-39).

For those who were able to share fully in this short experience of working together with Scripture, there were important realisations and learnings for the conference itself. We hear and draw on the message of the Gospel as the persons we are and in the context of our present being. In such a rich and varied group as this conference membership, the stories are being told over and over again, rooted in and challenged by the Word of God in the Scriptures. To share this realisation can be a powerful experience. Not all the delegates were able to be in a group for this sharing each day. Some discovered other priorities. It is easy to see in hindsight that in a programme of such depth, time must be allowed for exploring books and resources, for establishing connections, for press conferences and one-to-one meetings, and, it might well be suggested, simply for 'free time' to allow for absorption of input and processing of experience. These are not just practical issues or matters of business. They are elements, surely, of the building of a community of faith and commitment.

Repentance

Saturday presented the theme of Repentance,[6] with the strong reminder at the start that the nature of God is love; repentance is far from the dark misery of despair. 'Know that God is good' was the song to gather the delegates together, and the constant theme echoing through the prayer was 'Kyrie Eleison', using settings from different areas of the world. Standing together as brothers and sisters in the presence of the Father of Mercies is perhaps one of the most powerful of ecumenical experiences. Here we can listen to the challenge of the truth, and this day it was read in minority languages. 'Are you not still of the flesh? There is quarrelling and jealousy among you. ... Neither the one who plants nor the one who waters is anything, but only God who gives the growth ... We are God's servants, working together ...' (1 Cor. 3:1-9).

All true, and standing together before the Father of Mercies in the freedom of the truth is perhaps the greatest relief. Humility is truth. In this atmosphere it is possible to begin to see ourselves, one another, the churches and the world from the point of view of Almighty God. The homily brought the reminder of Israel's stories of the beginnings and the Creator God who constantly comes looking for the children in crisis, opening the conversation, 'Where are you?', 'What have you done?' – up to the point where God has a pain in his heart and is almost ready to 'wipe them off the face of the earth' (Gen. 6:6-7). Instead, the Word Incarnate is sent to earth and our story begins. This conference needed to hear the missionary commission as it is given in the gospel of Luke, in the final lines of the closing chapter 24: 'In his name repentance and the forgiveness of sins is to be proclaimed to all nations, beginning from Jerusalem. You are to be witnesses to these things.' The writer Luke is himself witness to these things – his Gospel brings us into the company of those who need and receive forgiveness. "You are to be witnesses to these things." Looking out from the conference setting, delegates could see painful realities, and the common prayer that followed named some of them in truth and asked for forgiveness. Naming them in truth is already a healing, but in the silence that followed there was the call to witness, the beginning of renewed commitment.

[6] See Appendix 7, 417ff.

In the final study sessions, delegates prepared a 'Common Call' to the churches and the missionary organisations, which would be presented to a much wider gathering during the closing celebration in the Assembly Hall the next day, and is included in this Conference Report.[7] It is presented in nine short paragraphs, recalling the nine themes of the preparatory studies. Each paragraph starts with a declaration of attitude, an element of spirituality, shared among the participants of this conference. It is this attitude, each time, that generates the call to mission and to witness. Here the work of the Holy Spirit of God in this gathering can be heard and seen. One can only listen with respect, with the gratitude and repentance that informed the prayer of the gathering in these days:

Trusting in the Triune God and with a new sense of urgency...

Remembering Christ's sacrifice on the Cross and his resurrection for the world's salvation, and empowered by the Holy Spirit...

Knowing the Holy Spirit who blows over the world at will, reconnecting creation and bringing authentic life...

Disturbed by the asymmetries and imbalances of power that divide and trouble church and world...

Affirming the importance of the biblical foundations of our missional engagement and valuing the witness of the Apostles and Martyrs...

Recognising the need to shape a new generation of leaders with authenticity for mission in a world of diversities in the twenty-first century...

Hearing the call of Jesus to make disciples of all people – poor, wealthy, marginalised, ignored, powerful, living with disability, young and old...

Recalling Christ, the host at the banquet, and committed to that unity for which he lived and prayed...

Remembering Jesus' way of witness and service, we believe...

We are called....

---

[7] See pp.46ff.

HOMILIES

Prof. Dr Nifon, Metropolitan of Targoviste, Romania. Friday, 4 June 2010

We listened today to the first fourteen verses of the second Epistle addressed by St. Apostle Paul to his disciple Timothy. It is not the first contact between the mentor and his disciple and not even the first epistle addressed to him. That is why St Paul, who called himself 'an Apostle of Christ Jesus by the will of God', began immediately with the message he wanted to bring to his 'beloved child', the message which is clearly expressed in verses 13-14: 'Hold the standard of sound teaching that you have heard from me, in the faith and love that are in Christ Jesus. Guard the good treasure entrusted to you, with the help of the Holy Spirit living in us'.

But before we focus on this message, let us have a look on the verses in front of it and try to understand the context behind this epistle and of this message. It seems that St Paul wrote to Timothy in a difficult moment of his mission. St Paul recalls Timothy's 'tears' and makes mention of a 'spirit of cowardice' (v. 7), which is clearly present in this moment in Timothy's life. St. Paul knows that Timothy needs to be encouraged in his mission and he is ready to do it. His words of encouragement speak not only to Timothy, but also to all those who are called 'with a holy calling' (v. 9), to all those involved in spreading the Gospel of our Lord Jesus Christ throughout the centuries, to all the world.

The main strength of Timothy is 'the power of God' (v. 8) which lives in him. That is why St Paul reminds him 'to rekindle the gift of God that is within you' (v. 6). The rekindled power and gift of God was the source of strength helping the Apostles to announce the Resurrected Christ to the world. The power and gift of God made the Christians in the first centuries ready to die with joy confessing their belief in our Lord Jesus Christ. It is the same power and gift of God that brought strength to all those who preached the Gospel in these last one hundred years throughout the entire world. The power and gift of God supported Christians of all confessions while they suffered abuse from totalitarian and atheistic regimes, from intolerant ideologies, or even from other Christians, because of their witness and commitment to the Gospel.

Alongside the strength from God, St Paul also mentions and values the strength which may come from Christian to Christian through fellowship in

Christ. Timothy is encouraged by St Paul, who knows to appreciate his 'sincere faith', and to appreciate also the support and strong faith of his grandmother and his mother (v. 5). Preaching the Gospel is not an individual mission, but a communitarian concern, an ecclesiological charge. St Paul was aware of this reality. The Church throughout the centuries was aware of this. And last but certainly not least, those who called the Edinburgh Conference one hundred years ago were aware of it.

Timothy and all missionaries can and must be good guardians of the 'good treasure' entrusted to them because we are assured that it is guarded by our Saviour Jesus Christ to whom it actually belongs. He is the One who brought it into the world for our salvation. He is the One who appointed for its gospel heralds, Apostles and teachers like St. Paul, Timothy and all those called for this. He is the One who sent the 'Holy Spirit living in us' (v. 14) to help and assist us in holding and guarding the Gospel. Holding and guarding the Gospel does not mean hiding it or keeping it away from the world, rather it means preaching it in the way it has been entrusted to us; without changing, modifying or altering its nature. This is the challenge we have as missionaries: to bring the Gospel to everyone but to hold and keep it unmodified; to be aware that while preaching it we may suffer. More than this, we are called to suffer for it (v. 8), but in spite of this we are asked to be joyful. How is this possible? Humanly this is not possible. Or even more than that, it is nonsense; it is a frenzy; it is just 'not according to our words' (v. 9). But if we look to the words of St. Paul to his 'beloved child' then, yes, this is possible 'in our Lord Jesus Christ', 'with the help of the Holy Spirit living in us' (v. 14) Who brings us from God 'a spirit of power and of love and of self-discipline' (v. 7).

Dear friends, sisters and brothers, missionaries of our Lord Jesus Christ in the word today, let us not forget that the Lord Jesus Christ has stirred up in Christians a deep yearning for unity. He has enabled us to see that this longing is found among so many Christians of different traditions. It is a sign that this Spirit has been at work in all of us, prompting us to recognise that in this too we must obey his will. When we look up, we now see brothers and sisters, from other Christian communities, offering us gifts that are the fruits of grace. Painfully, often too slowly, we have acknowledged how much already unites us through our baptism into Christ and the faith we profess. Hesitantly, then with increasing confidence we have said to one another: let us not settle here, 'let us journey on our way, and I will go alongside you'. The Lord's own prayer is being answered: he has opened the way for us through his blood and his Spirit in guiding us along that way. His must precious gift will be when we do indeed dwell together in unity.

There is no turning back now. This road leads to the fullness of communion with one another and with the Blessed Trinity. Let us encourage one another to persevere in this search for full visible unity among Christians. Such a unity of faith and life will make possible a profoundly common witness, no longer marred by division, discord and rivalry. If there is one communion among Christians, who truly live and experience their healing and reconciliation, the world will see the truth of our words proclaiming Jesus Christ as the one the Father has sent, their Lord as well as ours. 'He who has promised is faithful', so we can hold fast to this hope without wavering. Even while the Lord has been revealing to us what we already share, he has been urging us to go the whole way with him, to be fully united in his truth and in his life with the Father and the Holy Spirit. We can rightly feel responsible for each other since we see that we are brothers and sisters. We can give encouragement, pray together, explore our differences and work for their healing, provoke one another to love and to hear afresh the call to deeper conversation.

Father, on the very night your Son offered for all time a single sacrifice for sins he prayed that we and all who would come to believe in him might be one, as you are in him and he in you. Hasten the day when your will is done and we are so completely one that the world may believe in Jesus Christ whom you have sent. So may all women and men know that you love them as much as you love your only Son. Help us by your Holy Spirit to persevere courageously and confidently along this way together, through Christ our Lord. Amen.

Sister Elizabeth Moran SSC. Homily at Common Prayer, Saturday, 5 June 2010

Before speaking about repentance, today's theme, we recall the introductory comment at the very start of our prayer together – that repentance is not sad and gloomy, it is rather an honest, grateful standing in the presence of the God of Mercy, and a willingness to accept the gift of forgiveness and all its demands. 'God only loves, as the sun only shines'. It is the nature of God to love. It might be a good exercise today to go outside, stand in the full light of the sun, and reflect on this truth.

I live in an eighteenth century stone house in the North-East of Scotland. The house is old, the winds are strong, the old floorboards creak from room to room. The house was for years the holiday home of a family with three growing sons – active, energetic, noisy youngsters. One day I asked the lady of the house if she had ever thought of doing something to mend the floorboards. She gave me a wonderful smile and said, 'Oh no! The floorboards were my friends. I always knew where the boys were'. That was the voice of the parent, listening, reluctant to interfere, watchful for impending crisis, ready to arrive if need be.

We can go back to Israel's stories of the beginnings, as we find them in the opening chapters of the Book of Genesis. We remember the stories of the Garden, of the crisis time when God came to the Garden and Adam and Eve were hiding. 'Where are you?' called the Creator God, and Adam came out from among the trees and they had a conversation about what had happened. A little further on in the story-telling, God comes again, this time to find Cain out in the field, 'What have you done?' says God, and once more there is the conversation. And then again there is the time when they are building a tower, to reach as high as heaven – instead of getting on with what they were made for (which was filling the earth and subduing it), and this time God comes down to break up the gathering and scatter them out over the earth. And, eventually, we come to that dreadful account in chapter 6 (vv. 6-7), where the Almighty looks down and sees how great is the wickedness of human beings upon the earth. God has a pain in his heart, and regrets bitterly that he ever made them. He says 'I will wipe them off the face of the earth. I should never have made them'. But we know that God did not 'wipe them off the face of the earth'. Far from that, when the time had come, the Most Holy Trinity decided to send the Second Person, to bring mercy and forgiveness, and new life, into the very life of humankind. The poet R.S. Thomas has a poem called *The Coming*. God holds in his hand a small globe. 'Look', he says to the Son. The Son looks. He sees a dried wasted land, with a slimy polluted river snaking through it. Thin people hold up sticklike arms helplessly in the hot air. The Son looks. 'Let me go there', he says. And our story begins.

The Gospel of Luke gives several accounts of the appearance of Jesus to his disciples after his resurrection, of his coming to them with the gift of peace, reassuring them that he, the one they have known as friend and teacher, is really with them. He opens for them the meaning of the Scriptures; he eats with them. And in his final reassurances in this Gospel, he gives them their commission, in these words: 'This is what is written: the Christ will suffer and rise from the dead on the third day, and repentance and forgiveness of sins will be preached in his name to all nations, beginning at Jerusalem. You are witnesses of these things.' (Luke 24:46-48) And then he tells them to stay in Jerusalem until they receive the gift that has been promised. As in this Gospel his own mission began with the Spirit coming down upon him at his baptism in the Jordan, so the continuing of his mission in the disciples starts with that gift, that confirmation.

And, in this Gospel, where does Luke bear witness to the repentance and forgiveness of sins that the disciples have seen and heard? Where are we being shown the Son doing what the Father wants? When we enter these scenes, the atmosphere is the Holy Spirit. What are the effects? Who are the ones who receive the gift? We go first to the key moment of the Gospels, to the death of Jesus on the Cross. Nearest of all to the Christ who has had to suffer and will rise again are the two who die on either side of him. We might call them hardened criminals; on the one side so hardened by life that in his last moments his speech is still filled with insults and bitterness. But go there, stand at the foot of the Cross and listen to the conversation on the other side. This one turns to see the face of Jesus, incarnate Mercy, and hears the words, 'this day you will be with me…'.

Step back from the Cross, in this Gospel, to return to the scenes of the Supper, and the Garden, and the Trial. Listen to Peter, brave dear Peter, insisting on his love and loyalty, not strong enough yet to draw on that power and love and self control that is to come (22:61). Luke tells us, 'The Lord turned and looked straight at Peter', and just then the cock crowed, and Peter remembered … and went out. He does not come in again in this Gospel until chapter 24. Then, with the Cross in the background, we hear that he has run to see the emptiness of the tomb – and then that 'the Lord has risen and has appeared to Simon'. How kind the Risen Lord is – of course he has gone to seek out Peter who went out weeping bitterly, to let him share his Lord's own joy, to bring him the healing that comes from the wounds.

Go back a little further in this Gospel and find Zacchaeus, small, unhappy, despised, cheating a bit (well, everybody does it!) to be a little better off – but just wanting to see this Teacher. Then suddenly he finds himself called, strangely confronted, all his own natural warmth and hospitality drawn out of the shell of business dealings. The direct look of love, and being asked for welcome, food, conversation, made it easy to return to keeping the Law – 'I will return my thefts fourfold' – and to being once more his own generous self.

Go further still, and find the woman in the Pharisee's dining room, being the bringer of welcome, the washer of feet, the one who understands forgiveness and renewal. Jesus says to the Pharisee, 'Do you see this woman?' 'Do you see?'

These scenes are not given to us only as remembered incidents from the past. Here is the repentance, the renewal of relationship, that we are asked to enable, to experience day by day. The story spreads backwards and forwards from the central story, back to the very beginning, forward to the very end. It is so good for us to meet together in it as disciples, to walk in it as our atmosphere – God's story, God's Mercy incarnate, God's atmosphere. And then to walk in the garden in the evening for a little and let him ask: 'Where are you? What have you done?'

The Most Reverend and Right Honourable Dr John Sentamu, Archbishop of York. Homily at the Closing Celebration, Sunday, 6 June 2010

Where in heaven's name is the Church Universal going? Some would say, 'Nowhere'. Others would say, 'All over the place'. And others, 'Backwards'. After all, the Church tends to move forward by looking backwards! As mission-minded people, what is our answer to the question, 'Where is the Church of Jesus Christ going'? As Teachers and Leaders in God's mission, we ought to know.

Beloved in Christ, we all need to be equipped, in the environment of Pentecost, to be, to see, to think, and to do mission. Bishop John V Taylor, in his award-winning book, *The Go-Between God, The Holy Spirit and the Christian Mission,* writes:

> The chief actor in the historic mission of the Christian Church is the Holy Spirit. He is the director of the whole enterprise. The mission consists of the things that he is doing in the world. In a special way it consists of the light that he is focussing upon Jesus Christ. This fact, so patent to Christians in the first century, is largely forgotten in our own. So we have lost our nerve and our sense of direction and have turned the divine initiative into a human enterprise. 'It all depends on me', is an attitude that is bedevilling both the practice and the theology of our mission in these days. That is precisely what Jesus forbade at the start of it all. They must *not* go it alone. They must *not* think that the mission is their responsibility. They were not invited to deploy their resources or plan their strategy. ... The very mandate to engage in this world-wide mission could only be given simultaneously with the gift of the Holy Spirit... If for Jesus himself both messiahship and mission were derived from his self-immersion in that flood-tide of the Holy Spirit, how could his followers possibly be involved in the same mission except through the same immersion?[1]

As Bishop Fison once said,

> The story of Acts is the story of the stupendous missionary achievement of a community inspired to make a continual series of creative experiments by the Pentecostal Spirit. Against a static Church, unwilling to obey the guidance of the Holy Spirit, no 'gates' of any sort are needed to oppose its movement, for it does not move. But against a Church that is on the move, inspired by the Pentecostal Spirit, neither 'the gates of hell' nor any other gates can prevail.[2]

'But', Taylor continues,

---

[1] John V Taylor, *The Go-Between God, The Holy Spirit and the Christian Missions* (London: SCM Press Ltd, 1972), 3-4.

[2] J. E. Fison, *Fire upon the Earth* (London: Edinburgh House Press, 1958), 79.

> while we piously repeat the traditional assertion that without the Holy Spirit we can get nowhere in the Christian mission, we seem to press on notwithstanding with our man-made programmes. I have not heard recently of committee business adjourned because those present were still awaiting the arrival of the Spirit of God. I have known projects abandoned for lack of funds, but not for lack of the gifts of the Spirit. Provided the human resources are adequate we take the spiritual for granted. In fact we have only the haziest idea of what we mean by resources other than human wealth, human skill and human character.... The relationship of the Spirit to the Christian believer and to the church is without precedent, and this fact must be central to our understanding of the Christian mission.[3]

The Spirit of God is given to a believer through faith in the incarnate Son of God, and that believer receives the Person, the Word and the Work of the Son of God. This is what makes them witnesses. And the crucial fact is that it is God's message and God's witness. In John 8:18, Jesus said, 'I bear witness to myself and the Father who sent me bears witness to me'. And in John 15:26, 'When the counsellor comes whom I will send you from the Father, the Spirit of truth who proceeds from the Father, he will bear witness to me'. In other words, God the Father, God the Son, God the Holy Spirit all bear witness to Jesus Christ because Jesus Christ is the message. Therefore all we can do in obedience to God the Father is to bear witness to God the Son in the power of God the Holy Spirit. It is God's work, God's witness, and God's message.

Next to worship, witness is the primary and urgent task of the Church. 'Come to Jesus', wrote Peter in 1 Peter 2:4-5, 'and like living stones be yourselves built into a spiritual house'. Why? First, 'to offer spiritual sacrifices acceptable to God through Jesus Christ'. That is worship. Second, 'to declare the wonderful deeds of him who called you out of darkness into his marvellous light'. That is witness. Therefore worship and witness in that order, and both in the power of the Holy Spirit, are the two most vital callings of the Christian Church, the body of Christ. Compared with evangelism, everything else happening in the Church is like re-arranging the furniture when the house is on fire. And tragically that is what is so often what we are doing in the Church. Re-arranging the furniture; reorganising the structures; arguing over words and phrases while humanity as a whole plunges suicidally into obscurity and meaninglessness and despair.

According to Leighton Ford in his book *One Way to Change the World*,[4] while the Russian Revolution was raging in Petrograd in 1917, the Russian Orthodox Church was in session a few blocks away reportedly having a warm debate about what coloured vestments their priests should wear. And so often the Church's activities and energies appear to be totally irrelevant to the needs of the world today.

---

[3] Taylor, *The Go-Between God*, 4-6.

[4] Leighton Ford, *One Way to Change the World* (New York: Harper & Row, 1970).

Not every follower of Jesus Christ is an evangelist; some are evangelists. But every Christian *is* a witness – like the Samaritan woman at the Well in John, chapter 4:

> 'Come and see a man who told me everything I have ever done! He cannot be the Messiah, can he?' Many Samaritans from that city believed in him because of the woman's testimony, 'He told me everything I have ever done'. They asked Jesus to stay for two days. And many believed because of his word. They said to the woman, 'It is no longer because of what you said that we believe, for we have heard for ourselves, and we know that this is truly the Saviour of the world.' (John 4:29, 40b–42)

In our witness, our task is to take people to Jesus and leave them there with him, and he knows exactly what to do with them. Every follower of Jesus Christ is a witness. 'You *are* my witnesses', said God through the prophet Isaiah in his day. And 'You *shall* be my witnesses', said Jesus when he promised his disciples the power of the Holy Spirit. And putting it bluntly, Jesus today is on trial in the court of the world by our lips and our lives. Jesus and his Gospel are being judged. And if we just warm ourselves by the fire and are not totally identified with him then we shall be guilty as Simon Peter was when he denied his Master.

It is a sobering thought that Nietzsche, whose philosophy greatly influenced Hitler and therefore in part was responsible for the horrors of the concentration camps, once said of Christ, 'His disciples have to look more saved if I am to believe their Saviour'. It is sobering that Freud, whose psychology has been one of the greatest anti-Christian influences over the last one hundred years, developed his hatred for Christianity when he saw some professing Christians ill-treating his Jewish father. It is a sobering thought that Karl Marx, whose political and economic theory brought about the most powerful revolution of this century, swallowing up one third of the world in fifty years, was spurred into action, partly when he saw the utter irrelevance of middle-class Christianity in Britain – in an industrial society. It is sobering too that many others have said the same kind of thing: for example, an Indian leader, after years of examining the lives of Christians, once said 'Christians claim that Jesus Christ is the Saviour of sinners, but they show no more signs of being saved than any one else'. Another person said, 'I would become a Christian if I could see one'.

Do you see the crucial importance of Christian witness? One way or the other, for the whole world, at this very moment, Christ is on trial. And what you do and say will make the most profound difference to those who are judging Christ now and who will be judged by Christ later. I cannot over-emphasise the importance of Christian witness.

Where in Heaven's name is the Church of Jesus Christ, throughout the world, going? The Prophet Ezekiel was confronted with a similar question about the Covenant people of God. In Ezekiel, chapter 37, we see humanity's helplessness and God's power. Ezekiel 37 gives us a picture of God's promise of the Life-giving Spirit coming as wind. The people of the

Covenant are set in a place of desolation. Ezekiel's vision is of a chosen people who are in a cemetery. Is there still hope? They are set in death. Ezekiel's vision reminds me of a notice I saw once outside a Parish Church. The background to the story was that the graveyard at the parish was slowly getting filled up by burials of the dead from surrounding parishes. Members of the Church Council wanted to put a stop to this, conscious that when their time came to be buried there might be no room left. So they passed a resolution to stop this neighbourly practice. A notice went up: 'The graveyard of this parish is full: restricted for burying the dead who live in the parish.' Some of our church gatherings often feel like graveyards. But, as followers of Jesus Christ, we should never give up on them – because God loves graveyards, as they are his greatest opportunity.

The prophet is asked, 'Son of man, can these bones live?' The prophet is sat in a graveyard. I wonder, as leaders in mission with a prophetic calling, what would have been our response? Some of us would have said, 'Yes, Lord, surely they can – you just sit back and I will show you how'. And then of course, planning hard to make it happen, and then plunging into despair when we discover that the Kingdom of God is very reluctant to come forth. Very often, how do we do it? Plan a series of sermons; return to biblical orthodoxy, yes, slabs of orthodoxy doled out; evangelism seen as a duty; pray hard to do it, go out into all the streets; start stewardship campaigns. This on its own is doing God's work in human strength. It is like a merry-go-round. We keep going round and we feel a bit giddy, but we are still in the same place. Planning and strategy are important. But we must not substitute them for God's Spirit and God's ways of doing things. Can these bones live? Yes Lord, you watch me, and I will show you how! A sort of computerised despair.

The second answer for some of us would go like this. 'Can these bones live?' 'No, Lord, they can't'. These are the disciples who have sussed it all out. They claim to know God's way of working. They have stopped being expectant. They have seen it all before. The sort of church-goers we have all met, who have seen off five ministers of the Gospel! 'We tried it under minister "so-and-so", and it didn't work. It is useless to try again.' Forgetting how our Lord transformed the failure and hopelessness of his tired fishermen disciples, when they listened to him and cast their nets into the deep. We need to learn to expect the unexpected. Otherwise we'll become what here in Scotland is referred to as the peely-wally no-hopers. People who are off-colour, pale and ill-looking, with no sense of hope or energy: 'He's a wee bit peely-wally this morning!'

Son of Man, can these bones live? The proper answer is what Ezekiel gives: 'Sovereign Lord, you know all things.' Ezekiel's answer wasn't a cop-out. He was open to God. Renewal is being open to God once we have discovered our need of God. It isn't activity, but a response. Our hyper-activity simply gets in God's way. Nor is it finding a guru who is eager to lay hands on you to let it happen. The prophet is open to what God longs to do. God wills life. All he asks of us is to be open. The sweet smell of the Gospel, such love, opening ourselves up and letting ourselves be kissed by God. It isn't like champagne in the night and great pain in the morning.

So we need the bones of Scripture and the breath of the Spirit to bring life. Renewal without Scriptural truths is merely a filtered human Christianity – it has no life. We need both the Word and the Spirit. If we build our life solely on Scripture, we will dry up; if we build our life purely on the experience of the Holy Spirit, we will blow up; if we build our life on Scripture and the Holy Spirit, we will grow up into the full stature of Christ. Human activity only begets human activity. The prophetic Word and the Spirit make us live. So to be filled with the Holy Spirit is grace experienced. It's a foretaste of the power of the age to come. It is to experience in time a glimpse of what life will be with God in all eternity. And then, as leaders in mission, making Christ visible together.

Can these bones live? 'Lord, you know all things'. Prophesy, speak, call upon the Spirit to do something. 'Lord, you know all things.' Three times, the word is 'They shall live, they shall live, they shall live.' God wills life: the Spirit gives life. The Holy Spirit comes to minister to each one of us. And the greatest healing to wholeness God offers is the healing of our memories, healing of our hurts, healing of our pain, healing of our sin. Forgiveness is the greatest gift and miracle of God in us. We physically may remain not whole, but inwardly we are being renewed by the Spirit as he renews our mind, our heart, our soul, our strength.

Where in heaven's name is the Church of Jesus Christ going? To the place of renewal and liberation by the Holy Spirit. And as Teachers and Leaders in God's Mission, our role is like that of Prophet Ezekiel. And if we followed in Ezekiel's footsteps, he would bring us to Chapter 47, which says to us that we all need a fresh vision of God and the desperate death-like condition of humanity, if we are not to follow the trends. In the midst of the place of worship there is a river that makes glad the City of God. And we need to follow the river of life by looking in three directions: First, look up it: the source, where it comes from. Secondly, look down it: where it is going. Thirdly, look on the sides of it: what happens as it flows down into the desert.

First, look up it: the source of the river. It's the temple – a place of worship – it stands for the presence of God. It's not private, nor merely a place of organised religion. The river stands in relation to God. The river flows from the temple. But notice, it is flowing from the altar, the place of sacrifice. It's not cheap. It comes from under it. For us, this is the place of Calvary. Where the power of the age to come was offered for us, with us, and without us. Look up and see afresh the source of the River of Life. See with the eyes of Super-man – light from within and not just from without.

As Archbishop Michael Ramsey said so powerfully, in *Be Still and Know*:

> In the Eucharist [also called Holy Communion and the Lord's Supper], with the Risen Jesus present as our food, we are worshipping with the saints and the angels in heaven. But the Risen Jesus who is the heart of the heavenly worship is also a Jesus who was crucified, and we share in heaven's worship only as sharing also in the Jesus who suffers in the world around us, reminding us to meet him there and to serve him in those who suffer. Indeed in the Eucharist we are summoned by two voices, which are really one voice: 'Come the heavenly banquet is here. Join with me and my mother and my friends in the heavenly supper'. 'Come, I am here in this world in those who suffer. Come to me, come with me, and serve me in them.'... Our wisdom as well as our folly faces the darkness of Calvary and the light of Easter. Jesus suffered outside the gate, and he summons us to go out to him bearing his reproach.[5]

Look up the River of Life: see its powerful redeeming source: Calvary.

Second, look down it – its destination. It deepens as it goes out of the temple into the desert. It gets deeper as it reaches its final destination. We are so accustomed in the Church to a picnic culture: all is frothy and bubble; it's shallow and we can easily paddle in infantile religion. We must start to swim by going where the river is deepest – when standing still is an impossibility. We can't stand in a deep river – we must take our feet off the ground and we are no longer carrying ourselves but are being carried by the river of life. We all know we never start to swim properly until we get our feet off the ground. Fear holds us back. But we can't stand and swim at the same time. To swim is to let go of our earth-bound tendency to control things. And of course it comes differently to different people, but we can't dodge it.

However, there are others who only sit in the shallows and never follow the river of life to its ultimate destination – in the desert – in the world. The river goes into the desert and life begins to spring up – even in the dead sea. Oh, yes, expect life in what is now regarded as dead. For when God's river of life goes into the deep places, we ourselves can't remain dry and dead. A river of life will refresh and give life. And we can't build canals, and dams to redirect it – a very common attempt in the Church. No. The river wants to flow down into the desert. We need to be filled with the Holy Spirit in order to engage with the world.

As Bishop Frank Weston, of Zanzibar said in 1923:

> You have your Mass, you have your altars ... now go out into the highways and byways and look for Jesus in the ragged and the naked, the oppressed and the sweated, and in those who have lost hope and those who are struggling to make good. Look for Jesus in them; and when you find him, gird yourselves with his towel of fellowship and wash his feet in the person of his brothers and sisters.

---

[5] Michael Ramsey, *Be Still and Know, A Study in the Life of Prayer* (London: Fount Paperbacks, 1982), 121, 122, 124.

Look up the river: See and be transformed. Look down it: Do as Christ promised, in the power of the promised enabler and strengthener. 'For we are what he has made us, created in Christ Jesus for good works, which God prepared beforehand to be our way of life.' (Eph. 2:10)

Third, look at the banks of the River and see what is happening. On the banks are fishermen and trees. Where God's river flows there will be fishermen. Evangelists and servants putting love where love isn't. Yes, people enabling us to enter into everything that the Gospel of God's love revealed in Christ sends to the world: the pursuit of justice, peace and care of creation, as well as the sharing of the Good News of God in Christ. Witnesses to the Love of God in Christ. Being and thinking in a Christ-like way. Charitable acts are easy but to speak and act in love is not easy. We need to identify ourselves as those who belong to a sending God of Love. Fishermen casting their nets.

Along the banks of the river we also notice, fruit trees. Fruit that is not just in season. The fruit is for all seasons and we need to bear the fruit of the Spirit as people for all seasons. Yes, fruit even in winter – when no one loves us. Joy when the going is hard. To the thirsty we give a drink. To the hungry we offer Christ the Bread of Life. As Revelation 22 reminds us, the river flows from the throne of God down the City and the trees provide medicine for the healing of the nations. Ours is the duty to pray, give and go, for the Lord gave us a commandment to love and a commission to go and he assured us of his presence and his power.

As leaders in mission we must help our Churches by acting prophetically, speaking out for freedom against injustice. Our forebears have done so in the past against slavery and more recently against apartheid, world debt, and poverty. We must continue to speak out against injustice shown to asylum seekers and all in need. Also, at a time where we face unprecedented crisis in our economic systems, we need to speak prophetically about the need for fraternity, fellowship and community – how to build together, in a system based on respect of the individual, and care for each other in the community; and to speak prophetically about the need to turn away from the culture of self-absorbed individualism and rediscover the benefit of service to one another. As we do this, we must remember that speaking prophetically is not the same as condemning other people's failures, but rather one of helping us all towards the acceptance of common goals which uplift the heart. To help lift the heart of a nation is an exciting challenge, and it is one which we can do together, because it is what God has called us to as part of our mission and discipleship.

Let us do it. Let us do it now. How? Flexibly, in the way in which the Early Church did it. The Acts of the Apostles tell us that they did it: through the Holy Spirit; through a loving and united Church; through Signs and Wonders; through united praise and prayer; through careful re-organisation; through suffering; through talking publicly and privately about Jesus; through social action; through the home.

Let me end by quoting from Antoine de Saint-Exupéry. He says,

> If you want to build a ship
> don't summon people to buy and collect wood
> prepare tools, distribute jobs,
> and organise the work;
> rather inspire in them a yearning for the wide boundless ocean.

That's our task as missional leaders. To teach and lead our people, by our being, seeing, thinking, doing, and longing for the endless immensity of the sea: the Kingdom Rule of God. Let us do it. Let us do it now.

WORSHIP, COMMON PRAYER AND CELEBRATION

Douglas Galbraith [1]

The services of worship at the Edinburgh 2010 event were the early morning confessional Eucharist, the Opening Celebration at Pollock Halls on Thursday 3 June, the Common Prayer at the opening welcome on the evening of Wednesday 2 June and on the mornings of Friday 4 and Saturday 5 June, and the Closing Celebration at the Assembly Hall of the Church of Scotland on Sunday, 6 June. These were prepared by the Spiritual Life Committee, led by John Bell of the Iona Community, Scotland, and coordinated by Douglas Galbraith, both ministers of the Church of Scotland.

It is not possible to include in this volume the full transcript of each of the services. These may be found on the website. Here you will find the order of service for the Opening Celebration, which conveys the nature of the worship services in general, and a short report of the Closing Celebration including reference to the music of the conference and the preparation of the gathering spaces. Orders of service for the daily common prayer are included in the appendices.

Two points are important to make, in order to explain the way the worship was prepared for this gathering of the world's Christians. The first concerns the languages used. The common prayer of the conference moved between the three official languages, with the occasional addition of minority languages. The material spoken or sung was printed on the left hand page, with parallel translations into the remaining languages on the facing page, including rubrics. Translations were by Adèle Djomo Ngomedje (French) and Pauline Moran (Spanish). For reasons of space, the order of service for the Opening Celebration which follows is an English language version of the event, but where either French or Spanish was the lead language at any point this is recorded. The second point is about the music. Over the whole conference, songs were sung in 11 languages. Although translations were provided of all the songs, these were mainly for purposes of comprehension and were not intended to fit the music. These translations are not reproduced here. Where a song, hymn or chant is easily accessible, it is listed only and at least one source given (even though it may be found in several). In the order of service that follows, musical items

[1] Revd Dr Douglas Galbraith, was Co-ordinator of the Spiritual Life Committee.

that would be less easy to find and those as yet unpublished are given in full. An account of the Closing Celebration follows thereafter.

Order of Worship for the Opening Celebration, Thursday, 3 June 2010

1. Gathering

Delegates gather to the sound of the Scottish bagpipes in the garden outside the South Hall

Opening responses

Leader How good and how lovely it is
All **to live together in unity.**
(Etc.) Love and faith come together;
justice and peace join hands.
If the Lord's disciples keep silent,
the stones would shout aloud.
Open our lips, O God,
and our mouths will declare your praise.

Hymn 'Lobe den Herren', sung in German, Spanish, French and English
Source: *Thuma Mina* Basileia Verlag, Basel/Strube Verlag, München-Berlin

Introduction

Delegates are invited to hold in their hands the stones they brought with them from their own country. The following was spoken by two voices in dialogue.

What I hold in my hand
is older than me ...
and older.
What I hold in my hand
is older than my name, my language, my culture...
and older.
What I hold in my hand
is as old as the human race ...
and older.
It is as old as the soil,
as old as the sea ...
and older.
It is as old as the earth,
but younger than God.
For this stone is part of God's creation.
God made and meant its shape, its colour,
its journey from below to above.
This stone bears witness to God's intention
to make a world which was loved and lovely

before humanity ever walked the earth.
And to us, who come from all over the world,
God has given the care of this planet,
to love, admire and preserve it for others.
So let us bring these stones from all over the world
and lay them together round the cross,
because it was for the world and not just humanity
that Jesus was born and lived and died and rose again.
And any theology, any spirituality, any worship
which does not take the world seriously
does not bear witness to Christ.

Procession

We now proceed into the hall. As we enter, we lay our stones upon the cross-shape on the floor. The unique circle at the head of the cross is an ancient Celtic symbol for the resurrection, and for Christ's supremacy over the world and all things. While moving into the hall, we sing:

'Halle, halle, hallelujah' (Caribbean traditional) (widely available)

Acclamation *based on Psalm 122* [spoken in Spanish]

I was glad when they said to me,
'Let us go to the house of the Lord.'
And look, now we stand in this place,
in the city beloved of God.
Jerusalem proudly is built
to gather all people together:
she welcomes the children of God
as they worship their Maker in unity.
Glory to God the Creator,
to the Son and the Holy Spirit,
as it was in the beginning is now,
and shall be forever. Amen.

Song 'All people who live on the earth' (Singapore/Scotland)

Music © Lim Swee Hong; paraphrase of Psalm 100 © WGRG Iona Community (unpublished)

1 All people who live on the earth,
sing to the Lord with cheerful voice;
serve him with joy, sing out his praise
and in this place rejoice.
2 Know that the Lord is God indeed
whose parenting is firm and fair;
God shepherds us, calls us his own
and shows us constant care.
3 Where we now stand is heaven's gate,
so enter in with songs of praise;
give thanks and bless God's holy name
in endless words and ways.
4 For God is good, God's love shall last;
God's faithfulness is always sure;
to generations yet unborn
God's kindness will endure.
5 Amen! Amen! Alleluia
Let praise to God be given
Amen! Amen! Alleluia
Let earth prepare for heaven.

Prayer *Chant in African-American tradition* (unpublished)

Cantor O Lord,
All **hear our prayer.**

Gracious and eternal God,
we praise you because we are here.
We look and listen and know that we are part of your church,
multi-coloured, multi -cultured, multi-lingual,
and all by your design.
We are privileged to be present.
We praise you.... **Chant**
If we have come with our minds full of rehearsed speeches,
if we are keener to hear our own voice
than those of our neighbours,
help us to lay our personal agendas aside,
so that we can be open to you and to each other... **Chant**
Help us to enjoy being together.
Help us to believe that you have great things in store –

new insights, new discoveries, new energy, closer solidarity.

Help us to find hope for your church and to cherish it… **Chant**

In the name of Christ, **Amen.**

Recognising and affirming each other

Last night, we recognised that we came from different parts of the world, and we know that we belong to different churches. But we are here also because we have been shaped by different people:

by teachers and writers,
by priests and pastors,
by parents and grandparents,
by close friends and those we have only met once,
by people who showed us what God was like,
and encouraged us to follow Jesus.

In a moment we will turn to someone we do not know and tell them about someone alive or dead who has helped to shape our faith. Now let us speak.

Conversation ends when drums are sounded

Scripture reading from 1 Peter 2 [read in French]

Come to him, the living stone,
rejected by mortals but chosen by God,
and of great worth.
As living stones,
you also must be built up into a spiritual temple
and form a holy priesthood
to offer spiritual sacrifices to God through Jesus Christ.
You are a chosen race.
You are a royal priesthood.
You are a dedicated nation.
You are a people claimed by God as his own.
You are to proclaim the glorious deeds of him
who has called you out of darkness
into his marvellous light.
Once you were no people,
but now you are God's people.
Once you were outside God's mercy,
but now you are outside no longer.

Song 'Humbly in your sight' (Malawi)

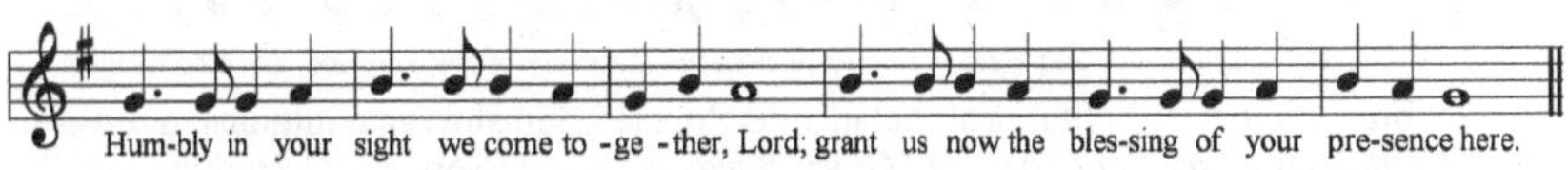

Humbly in your sight we come together, Lord;
grant us now the blessing of your presence here.
These, our hearts are yours, we give them to you, Lord;
purify our love to make it like your own.
These, our eyes are yours, we give them to you, Lord;
may we always see your world as with your sight.
These, our hands are yours, we give them to you, Lord;
give them strength and skill to do all work for you.
These, our feet are yours, we give them to you, Lord;
may we always walk the path of life with you.
These, our tongues are yours, we give them to you, Lord;
may we speak your healing words of life and truth.
These, our ears are yours, we give them to you, Lord;
open them to hear the Gospel as from you.
Our whole selves are yours, we give them to you, Lord;
take us now and keep us yours for evermore.

2. Hopes and Expectations

Representatives of the 'stakeholders' for the Edinburgh 2010 project look ahead to the opportunities and tasks of the conference

Rev. Dr Olav Fykse Tveit,
General Secretary, World Council of Churches

Rev Dr. Geoff Tunnicliffe
Secretary General, World Evangelical Alliance[2]

3. Listening to Scripture

Song '*Yakanaha Vangeri*' 'Listen now for the Gospel' (Zimbabwe)

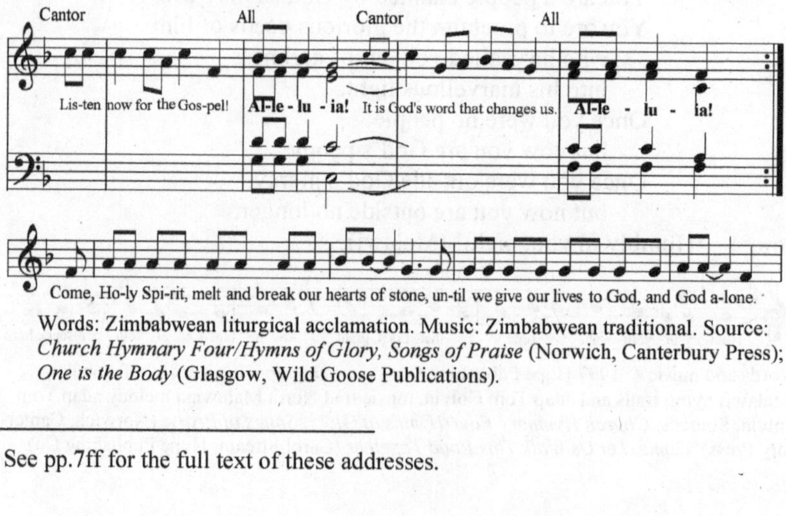

Words: Zimbabwean liturgical acclamation. Music: Zimbabwean traditional. Source: *Church Hymnary Four/Hymns of Glory, Songs of Praise* (Norwich, Canterbury Press); *One is the Body* (Glasgow, Wild Goose Publications).

---

[2] See pp.7ff for the full text of these addresses.

Cantor Listen now for the Gospel!
All **Alleluia!**
Cantor It is God's word that changes us!
All **Alleluia!**

Come, Holy Spirit, melt and break our hearts of stone,
until we give our lives to God, and God alone. …
Come, Holy Spirit, root in us God's living word,
that we may show the faithfulness of Christ our Lord. …
Come, Holy Spirit, bind the broken, find the lost,
confirm in us the fire and love of Pentecost. …

Three Gospel stories

We listen to three Gospel stories about people whose lives were changed after meeting Jesus, and became his witnesses.

[The dramatised script that follows was not translated, but it was presented with the use of enactment and symbol. The stories were of the Blind Man at the Pool of Siloam, the Woman at the Well, and Zaccheus. Each story was greeted by this chant -]

'*Loi nguyen cau*' (Vietnam) [origin not known]

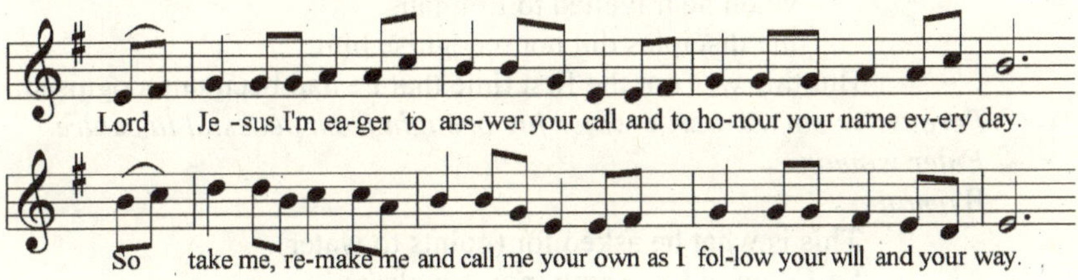

Telling of the Gospel stories

Three tall pedestals draped with cloth. On these, a large water jar, basin of mud, a bag of coins or loaf of bread.

Voices Reader, Jesus, prop carrier, woman (at well), blind man, Zaccheus

Chant 'Lord Jesus, I'm eager to answer your call'

Drum signal or gong

Narrator

On the day of Jesus' resurrection, people went on journeys:
women went to the tomb,
men went into hiding.
And two disciples travelled to Emmaus where their eyes were opened.
But this was not the first time that Jesus required a journey
in order that eyes could be opened.

Percussive sound. Basin of mud brought from pedestal to centre. Blind man (dark glasses and white stick) enters. Takes off glasses to show mud on cheeks.

Blind man

I don't need this (holds up white stick) any more.
This (puts hand in mud) is what cured me.
And also, going on a journey.

Jesus

Go and wash yourself in the pool of Siloam (repeated in main languages).

Blind man

So I went and washed,
though I had washed many times before.
And I was converted from blindness to sight.
I became a disciple.
And some people rejoiced for me
And some people still rejected me
And some people were angry with Jesus.

Chant

Drum signal or Gong

Narrator

On the day of Jesus' resurrection,
when he travelled to Emmaus,
the disciples did not recognise him.
But this was not the first time that he had been unrecognised.

Percussive sound. Large water jug brought from pedestal to centre.

Enter woman.

Woman

This is what he asked for (points to water).
So I poured him some (pours a glass).
But he never drank it.
He said something which I could not understand.

Jesus

I will give you the water of eternal life (repeated in main languages).

Woman

I did not understand him.
I did not recognise him
I did not know who he was.
But through conversation I was converted
from curiosity to faith.
I became a disciple.
And some people rejoiced for me.
And some people were curious.
And his disciples were annoyed with Jesus

Drum signal or Gong

Narrator

On the day of Jesus' resurrection,
when he travelled to Emmaus,
he sat at table and broke bread.
But this was only one of many times when he shared a meal in unusual circumstances.

Percussive sound. Bread brought from pedestal to centre. Zaccheus, dressed like a dandy, follows.

Zaccheus

This [*referring to food*] is what he wanted.
I did not expect to be his host.
I wanted to remain anonymous.
But he saw me, and said with great enthusiasm -

Jesus

I am coming to your house (repeated in main languages).

Zaccheus

So he came,
and he ate in my house.
And at the meal, I was converted
from meanness to generosity.
I became a disciple.
And some people rejoiced with me.
And some people suspected me.
And some people were disturbed by Jesus.

Chant

Narrator

Here we have a man whose illness kept him apart,
and a woman whose nationality kept her apart,
and a man whose occupation kept him apart:
all made whole and made believers
by the converting love of Jesus.

4. Walking with God and God's People

We now leave the hall in groups of three with people from the same language group, but - if at all possible - from a different nation or denomination. We walk outside wherever we wish. With them we share our answers to these questions:

1. *Which of the three people Jesus met would we most like to meet, and why?*
2. *What would we like to ask that person?*

We continue our conversation until coffee time.

Recessional song

'*Sarantañani* Let us walk together' (Bolivia)

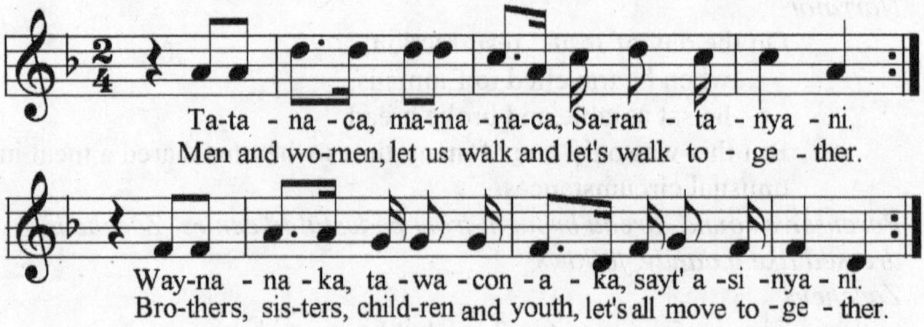

THE CLOSING CELEBRATION
SUNDAY, 6 JUNE 2010

The Closing Celebration was the only event to take place in the venue of the original 1910 conference, the Assembly Hall of the (now re-united) Church of Scotland. The change of venue also symbolised the fact that, while in a real sense it was the climax of the conference, it was also the point of rejoining the world church and announcing its discoveries. Assembling with the delegates were people from local churches, visitors from farther afield, and the many who watched the proceedings on line as they unfolded. The use of the historic venue also underlined the hope that, just as the original conference had changed the way the church approached mission, the new conference would offer new purpose and insight to the church in a different age.

Gathering

Continuity with the working days of the conference was provided in a number of ways, but none more so than the way the space was furnished. The approach (on a grey and wet Sunday afternoon) through the quadrangle dominated by the statue of the uncompromising Scottish Reformer John Knox was lightened by palm trees designed and constructed (by Carol Marples of the Scottish-based Soul Marks Trust) from colourful fabric from many nations. These palms (in early Christian history symbolising victory and celebration) also surrounded the people gathered inside the hall, complementing the costumes of the African choir and Indian dancers. Earlier in the week they had massed in the approaches and meeting spaces at Pollock Halls, creating, as here, a welcome and an expectation of beauty and variety. In addition, individual leaves with embroidered messages of peace, or recalling the titles of some of the songs (in several languages) which had been used in the common prayer and celebration of the conference, were randomly distributed round the hall, at ends of rows of seats, on lecterns and other surfaces. These leaves also were familiar to delegates as having been 'planted' in the foliage in the gardens surrounding the conference buildings, little glimpses of colour, so enticing that many did not survive more than a few hours!

That the congregation was surrounded and sheltered in this way supported the concept for the event, which was to be not so much a service of worship as a coming together of many different voices and approaches on common ground – less a building dedicated to one purpose, more like the centre of a village with all its variety and movement where contributions could be spontaneously made. The 'gathered' layout, with no-one far from the centre (as indeed in 1910), contributed to the feeling of being part of things. By the same token, there was no formal beginning. People entered and settled down to the exuberant singing of a fifty-strong choir from Edinburgh's African churches, colourfully garbed, during which Pastor Festus Olatunde of the local Mountain of Fire and Miracle Ministries congregation led in prayer. There was no 'presiding minister' as such, the initiative being passed from group to group, person to person. Thus Ganoune Diop, of the Seventh-day Adventist Church world headquarters, representing the Stakeholders of the conference, made the transition from working conference to celebrating church, followed by a reprise, this time in Spanish and given by Claudio Carvalhaes (a member of the 10-strong international team that planned the spiritual life of the conference), of the words which had called delegates to worship on their first night together – and indeed cemented the connection between this gathering and its famous predecessor.

A sequence of songs, led by John Bell and Mairi Munro of the Iona Community, echoed the fare of the previous four days. At Edinburgh 1910, delegates had sung only from the hymn books of the sending churches and organisations. At this conference, out of 39 items from 29 nations, the vast majority came from those who had in recent centuries received the Gospel and made it their own. These last were typically unaccompanied, often sung in parts which required minimal or no teaching, sounding themes of justice as well as celebration, and contributing to an immediacy and spontaneity during times of common prayer and worship. A small ensemble enhanced the sound, consisting of keyboard, guitar and flute. This was added to by special guest Peter Okeno Ong'are, a Kenyan musician pursuing doctoral studies at Durham University regarding the role of music in processes of reconciliation and healing after conflict in nations of Africa. His expertise enabled the drums to be used throughout the conference as signal as well as accompaniment.

Looking Back in Gratitude and Penitence

One hymn only was sung by both conferences, the stirring missionary hymn, 'Through midnight gloom from Macedon' by Samuel John Stone, placed in a sequence which, through interview, visual image and documentary, explored changes in understandings and strategies of mission over the intervening century. The interviews were conducted by Professor Brian Stanley, author of *The World Missionary Conference, Edinburgh 1910,* and the Rev. Dr. Ken Ross, one of those who took the first steps towards the planning of the present conference. Their guests included descendants of Korean and Indian delegates at 1910 as well as Bishop Devamani of Dornakal, the diocese of which 1910 Asian delegate V.S. Azariah ultimately was made the first bishop, reading parts of the latter's famous address. In the documentary section, voices from around the hall represented people in a number of 'mission contexts' who sought reconciliation, with creation, with each other, with God.

Dancing the Word

Contrasting with 'Macedon', the sequence closed with a more contemporary take on mission in the hymn 'As a fire is meant for burning' by leading American writer Ruth Duck. As people sang, the words were interpreted by the leader of a colourful group of Indian dancers, Jesica Sinniah, currently engaged in doctoral studies at Selly Oak Centre for Mission Studies, The Queen's Foundation, Birmingham, on the subject 'Enhancing Indian Christian Worship through Indian Dance'. The five dancers' main contribution was to the section on the Word when they vividly interpreted, without the passage being read, the story of the Woman at the Well, which had featured during the previous days. All except the leader were Hindu, including the portrayer of Christ. It ended by the dancers moving into the congregation and bringing converts from the ends of the earth. Also heard was Ezekiel's vision of the dry bones, read by Aftab Gohar from Pakistan, another member of the planning team, leading to a stirring address from the Archbishop of York, the Most Rev. John Sentamu.

Affirmation, Commitment and Sending

The response to the seeing and hearing of the Word took several forms. A section in which members of the conference shared turning points was curtailed because of time but the Common Call which had arisen out of the conference was heard in its entirety, published in many voices representative of the breadth of the nations, churches and stakeholding organisations. A Celtic peace was shared in common and the delegates sent out, to be clapped and cheered by the rest of the congregation lining the corridors and steps, to a resounding rendering of 'Now thank we all our

God', then to the sounds of the African choir. As they left, each received a pebble from the beach on the Isle of Iona where the missionary saint Columba landed in 563, replacing the stone that each had brought from their own country and placed on the Celtic Cross at the opening ceremony.

CONFERENCE STUDY PROCESS

Kirsteen Kim[1]

The 2010 conference in Edinburgh marked a new and important stage in the Edinburgh 2010 study process, which began in 2008. At the conference those taking part in the international study process engaged with representatives from the worldwide church to explore what challenges the study process may bring to the life of churches over the years to come.

The study process was centred on nine main themes, which were complemented by seven transversal topics, and supplemented by regional, confessional and other study processes. Studies and consultations took place in all continents and the process was as inclusive as possible of churches and Christian mission networks. Each of the groups working on the nine study themes produced a report which, together with contributions on the transversals relating to women and the Bible, formed the raw material for discussion at the conference. This was published as *Edinburgh 2010: Witnessing to Christ Today* (Oxford: Regnum Books, 2010), edited by Daryl Balia and Kirsteen Kim. All delegates to the conference were sent this book and urged to read it in preparation for the conference.

At the conference the material already disseminated was subjected to critique from various transversal perspectives and engaged with by church and mission delegates from around the world, and from various denominational perspectives. This was intended to open up the study process and move it forward, allowing each theme to be further developed and for cross-fertilisation of themes with each other.

In Edinburgh on 2-5 June 2010 study took place in the context of the spiritual life of the conference. The aims of the conference study process were to:

- Make clear the changes in mission thinking since 1910
- Create a new vision and spirituality of mission to inspire Christians in churches and mission bodies

[1] Dr Kirsteen Kim worked as Research Coordinator of Edinburgh 2010 from January 2009 until March 2011. Dr Kim is Associate Senior Lecturer and Director of Programmes in Theology and Religious Studies at Leeds Trinity University College, Leeds, UK.

- Encourage networks and alliances across regions (especially the North-South divide) and confessions for common witness
- Give guidelines on mission practice and identify priorities for church and mission leaders
- Highlight issues for further research and reflection
- Result in commitment to continue the spirit of cooperation

The tangible outcomes of the study process of the conference were intended to be:

- Shared ownership of common calls/commitments for the Sunday celebration
- A record of the key issues and priorities identified, with some indication of which are felt to be most urgent
- A listeners' report prepared by a listening group
- Reflections on the conference by three invited delegates
- Audio-visuals used in the conference which can be posted on the website
- A conference report, including presentations at the conference and a record of the discussions

The aims of the study process of the conference were realised through nine timetabled sessions over the three full days at the Pollock Halls. These comprised three plenary sessions and six parallel workshops in which delegates were divided into three.

The plenary sessions were organised as follows:

Plenary 1: 'Mission in long perspective', Thursday 3 June 2010, 11.00am-12.50pm

> This was to illuminate the conference theme (witnessing to Christ today) in the light of one hundred years of mission since 1910. The focus was on mission, and the complementary perspectives were intended to ensure that different histories and current contexts were recognised.

Plenary 2: 'Mission worldwide', Friday 4 June 2010, 11.00am-12.50pm

> This magazine-style event included four examples of contemporary initiatives in Christian witness. These were intended to offer real engagements in current contexts and comments were invited from the floor.

Plenary 3: 'Towards a common call', Saturday 5 June, 8.00-9.30pm

> The final plenary was a business meeting to conclude the study process, highlight the key issues and priorities for the churches. Three participant-reflectors gave their personal perspectives on the event and the conference listening group presented their report. Delegates were encouraged to reflect on the conference and look to its outworking in churches and mission agencies. A draft of Common Call arising from the work in the parallel and to be articulated in the following day's celebratory worship service was presented in plenary, and comments on it were received for further editing.

The conference study process was informed by presentations in the plenary sessions of the conference but it was focused on processing the results of the main study themes. Two consecutive sessions wee allowed for work on each theme, and these were arranged in three tracks according to the following table. Delegates were being asked before the conference to select the track they would like to follow.

Day	Sessions	Track 1	Track 2	Track 3
3 June	2.15-4.00pm 4.30-6.00pm	1 Foundations for mission	5 Forms of engagement	2 Mission among other faiths
4 June	2.15-4.00pm 4.30-6.00pm	8 Mission and unity	4 Mission and power	6 Theological education
5 June	11.15am-1.00pm 2.15-4.00pm	9 Mission spirituality	7 Christian communities	3 Mission and postmodernities

Each session followed a programme worked out by the conveners of the study groups in consultation with invited chairpersons. Each theme was approached in a different way, utilising different resource people representing transversal topics and regional, confessional and other studies.

The aim of the parallel sessions was to debate and refine the key issues and priorities raised in the pre-conference report by hearing diverse perspectives and working in small groups. Delegates were expected to have read the relevant reports before coming to the conference and were asked to bring their insights to share. Issues and priorities arising from each track were be reported briefly in the final plenary by members of the conference listening group. They were also passed to the Research Coordinator and used as the basis for the work of the committee tasked with drafting the Common Call.

The following sections of this conference report include the plenary presentations, reports of the proceedings of the parallel sessions and selected papers presented in those sessions. These give a snapshot of mission thinking in 2010, but more importantly the reports highlight key issues and identify priorities for action by the churches in the twenty-first century. The priorities have been summarised in the Common Call so that the study process may inform and inspire the churches in their witness to Christ today and in decades to come.

Plenary 1: Mission in Long Perspective
Thursday, 3 June 2010

Keynote Address

Dr Dana L. Robert, Truman Collins Professor of World Christianity and History of Mission, Boston University School of Theology, USA [1]

> After this I looked, and there was a great multitude that no one could count, from every nation, from all tribes and peoples and languages, standing before the throne and before the Lamb, robed in white, with palm branches in their hands. They cried out in a loud voice, saying, 'Salvation belongs to our God who is seated on the throne, and to the Lamb! (Rev. 7:9-10)

Since the early days of the persecuted church, this powerful Revelation vision has anchored Christian hope amid suffering and struggle. It carries prophetic significance for united Christian witness, as it points to the day when the followers of Jesus – called out from every nation, tribe, people, and linguistic group – together praise God. It promises that those washed in the blood of the Lamb will hunger and thirst no more, and 'God will wipe away every tear from their eyes'. (Rev. 7:16-17)

This Revelation prophecy grounds us in the history of God's mission. Over two hundred years ago, the first African seminarians in England became followers of Jesus. Against the powers and principalities of the African slave trade, then at the height of its brutality and global reach, they prepared to return to Sierra Leone as witnesses to the Gospel. At their baptismal service in 1805, the Reverend John Venn, a founder of the Church Missionary Society, charged them to herald the day 'when Africa shall embrace the Truth of Christ'. Venn described the vision of assembled believers from the ends of the earth, united in love with no racial or national divisions among them: 'Glorious day! Whose heart does not burn with the sacred prospect? Who does not, amid the desolation of war, the

[1] For further biodata, see Appendix 4.

tumult and destruction, the feuds and jealousies, which agitate the Earth – who does not cry, How long, O Lord, how long?'[2]

In 2010, the promises of Revelation 7 take on renewed meaning for united Christian witness. During the lifetimes of the people gathered in this room, Christianity has undergone one of the biggest changes in its two thousand year history. It is now a multi-cultural faith, with believers drawn from every inhabited continent. Today we rejoice in God's global mission as we gather to celebrate this moment in history! Yet as we look at our interconnected world today, we still cry with the psalmist and John Venn, 'How long, O Lord, how long?' For in God's timing, our work on earth has not finished. 'Witnessing to Christ today' means *both* inviting others to join us in following Jesus, *and* discerning the ways in which our promised unity challenges those things that enslave God's people in the twenty-first century.

Participants in the World Missionary Conference a century ago attempted to evangelise the world in their own generation. We who are alive in 2010 must bear witness to our own generation. It is our turn to point to the Revelation vision of believers called from all nations, in praise of the living God, who speaks to us through Jesus Christ and the Holy Spirit. Looking backward reminds us that continuity with the Edinburgh conference a century ago does not lie narrowly in the particular accomplishments or structures to which it gave birth. To take the 'long view' requires that we acknowledge that both Edinburgh 1910 and Edinburgh 2010 are proleptic moments. In other words, our gatherings derive their shared meaning from the certainty that the past and the future belong to God. The history of world mission is located somewhere along the road from Jesus' resurrection to the glorious day when believers from all nations will stand before the throne of the Lamb. Because we live within this larger narrative, witnesses to Christ are first and foremost ambassadors of hope: Today we witness to the Good News of what God has done, what God is doing, and what God will do through our Lord and Saviour Jesus Christ!

In this address, I will explore two turning points in twentieth century mission history, both of which light the pathway of our shared journey toward God's *shalom*. These moments show that despite our sins and limitations, the biblical promises beckon as a light in the darkness, and make united witness to Christ both *possible* and *necessary*.

---

[2] John Venn, quoted in Max Warren (ed.), *To Apply the Gospel: Selections from the Writings of Henry Venn* (Grand Rapids, MI: Eerdmans, 1971), 57-59. John Venn was a leader of the Clapham Sect, the evangelical antislavery group that both led the fight to outlaw slavery in the British Empire, and founded the Church Missionary Society. His son Henry Venn was Secretary of the CMS from 1841, and enabled the consecration of the first African bishop in the Church of England, Samuel Ajayi Crowther.

World Missionary Conference 1910

A century ago, over twelve hundred delegates from Protestant missionary societies came by ship and train from around the world to Edinburgh. For ten days, Protestant leaders discussed the key issues facing world missions in the twentieth century. For two years prior to the event, conference organisers had corresponded with missionaries and informants around the world to produce eight commission reports. The contemporary importance of the conference was such that the archbishop of Canterbury judged it to be without parallel in the history of Christianity.

The vast majority of delegates were European and North American men. Two hundred were women, an estimated nineteen were Asians, and one African.[3] They gathered under the assumption that missions operated in the context of western colonialism. But they departed with a prophetic glimpse of Christianity as a worldwide fellowship! In other words, the conference itself awakened them to the reality that discussions of mission policy could not be separated from the deeper meaning of the church as a worldwide community united before God. The depth of this discovery was expressed by the chairman John R. Mott, in his closing remarks:

> Gathered together from different nations and races and communions, have we not come to realise our oneness in Christ? ... It is not His will that the influences set forth by Him shall cease this night. Rather shall they course out through us to the very ends of the earth. ... Our best days are ahead of us because we have a larger Christ, even one who requires, as we have learned increasingly these days, all of us, and all nations, and races, and communions through which adequately to express His excellences, and to communicate His power to our generation.[4]

Mott's words show that conference delegates recognised that the Christ to whom they witnessed was 'larger' than that of western dominance and sectarian divisions. They cemented this bigger vision through united prayer and fellowship. It also broke into their consciousness through the witness of the non-western delegates at the conference, notably that of young V.S. Azariah, co-founder of the first Indian missionary society. Azariah gave a

---

[3] On the ethnic composition of the conference, see Brian Stanley, *The World Missionary Conference, Edinburgh 1910* (Grand Rapids, MI: Eerdmans, 2009), 91-107. After the publication of Stanley's book, I discovered the name of an 'Anglo-Indian', Miss Grace Stephens, as a delegate from the Woman's Foreign Missionary Society of the Methodist Episcopal Church. The addition of Stephens brings the number of Asian delegates to nineteen or twenty. On Stephens, see Dana L. Robert, 'Faith, Hope, Love in Action: United Methodist Women in Mission Yesterday, Today, and Tomorrow', unpublished address delivered April 29, 2010, at the Mission Forward event, UMW Assembly, St. Louis, Missouri.

[4] John R. Mott, in World Missionary Conference 1910, *The History and Records of the Conference together with Addresses Delivered at the Evening Meetings* (Edinburgh and London: Oliphant, Anderson, & Ferrier; New York, Chicago, and Toronto: Fleming H Revell, 1910), 347-348.

powerful speech calling for equality and friendship between missionaries and Indian Christians. Not only was cross-racial friendship practically necessary, but it was a spiritual imperative for faithful witness. He said, 'The exceeding riches of the glory of Christ can be fully realised not by the Englishman, the American, and the Continental alone, nor by the Japanese, the Chinese, and the Indians by themselves – but by all working together, worshipping together, and learning together the Perfect Image of our Lord and Christ'.[5]

The youngest delegate to the conference, Cheng Jingyi, pastor of an independent church in Beijing, made a strong impression on the conference when he declared that, in Chinese terms, the universal church was a family: 'The Church of Christ is universal, not only irrespective of denominations, but also irrespective of nationalities – "All one in Christ Jesus"'.[6] Cheng urged that as a full member of a universal family, Chinese Christianity should be united and become independent of foreign denominations. He appealed to the conference to take concrete action toward uniting the church in China: 'Let us go, with our Divine Master, up on the top of the Mount of Olives, and there we will obtain a wider, broader, and larger view of the needs of the Church and the world'.[7]

The courage behind Azariah, Cheng, and Mott's statements lay in their eschatological hope. Obviously in human terms they could not achieve the Revelation vision. Colonialism and racism continued unabated, and World War I broke out soon afterward. But they lived in courageous certainty of the 'long view' that God's love would ultimately prevail. Thus they refused to separate Christian mission from concrete work for unity among believers of different nations, ethnicities, denominations, and social classes.[8] The

---

[5] Azariah in World Missionary Conference 1910, *The History and Records of the Conference*, 315. See also Cheng Jingyi's vision of a unified Church of Christ in China – Stanley, *World Missionary Conference*, 107-111.

[6] Cheng Jingyi, in World Missionary Conference 1910, *Report of Commission VIII, Co-Operation and the Promotion of Unity* (Edinburgh and London: Oliphant, Anderson, & Ferrier; New York, Chicago, and Toronto: Fleming H Revell, 1910), 197. Stanley points out that 'All one in Christ Jesus' was the motto of the Keswick movement.

[7] Cheng Jingyi, in World Missionary Conference 1910, *Report of Commission VIII*, 197.

[8] None of these three leaders at Edinburgh 1910 could easily be slotted into a stereotype of evangelism versus social justice, or mainline versus evangelical. Their grounding in a bigger vision resisted such compartmentalisation. After the conference ended, Azariah continued his evangelism among the lower castes, supported the interracial partnerships that characterised the YMCA, and eventually was consecrated the first Indian bishop in the still colonial Church of England. Cheng returned to China and founded an interdenominational home mission movement to work in tribal China, and the China for Christ movement. He lived to see his plans come to fruition as the first moderator of the Church of Christ in China in 1927. After the conference, Mott travelled throughout Asia organising

commitments of Azariah, Cheng, and Mott cohered around their realisation that despite human brokenness, the followers of Christ do in fact constitute a worldwide fellowship. In retrospect what historians remember about Edinburgh 1910 is that it led to a number of important organisations and transnational Christian movements. But ticking off a list of organisations does not do justice to the deeper contribution of Edinburgh 1910 – namely, that it kindled an unquenchable longing for the realisation of God's kingdom in the hearts of those touched by it.

Another way the conference framed the challenge of living into a 'larger Christ' was that it named the complex problems of diversity within unity – issues that are still with us today. The Commission on Co-Operation and Unity asked the questions 'How is it possible to attain that unity for which our Lord prayed and yet to leave free play for the diversity which alone will give to the unity comprehension and life?' 'How can we help to lay the foundations of a Church that shall have its roots deeply planted in the national life, and which at the same time will not be so exclusively national in spirit as to forget its place and membership in the Church Universal?'[9] These questions raised not only the issue of sectarian divisions, but of what we now call 'inculturation' or 'contextualisation'. The report noted that the growth of Christianity in India, China, Japan, and Africa 'is presenting problems of great complexity and gravity'. And the delegates humbly admitted that their own comprehension was not adequate to envision the future of Christianity. 'Unity when it comes must be something richer, grander, more comprehensive than anything which we can see at present.... We need to have sufficient faith in God to believe that He can bring us to something higher and more Christ-like than anything to which at present we see a way.'[10]

Commission VIII's call for 'penitence and prayer'[11] over Christian divisions occurred amid what Commission I on 'Carrying the Gospel'

---

interdenominational and interracial mission councils. In each country, he met and mentored young national Christian leaders. Mott's assumption that missions required active work for unity was reflected in his long-term leadership both of the world's largest parachurch agency, the YMCA; and of organisations that led to the World Council of Churches.

[9] World Missionary Conference 1910, *Report of Commission VIII*, 137. Note that the term 'co-operation' gave way in the course of the century to the word 'ecumenical'.

[10] World Missionary Conference 1910, *Report of Commission VIII*, 138-139.

[11] 'The great issues which confront us in the modern situation are the concern of the whole Church of Christ; and the spiritual resources of the whole Church will be required to deal with them. The solution of problems so complex and difficult, and so vitally related to the advancement of the Kingdom of Christ, can be attempted only in a spirit of penitence and of prayer. Penitence is due for the arrogance of the past and for the lack of sympathy and of insight by which all of us have helped to create and perpetuate a situation that retards so seriously the advancement of

called 'the rising spiritual tide in many mission fields'.[12] This report noted the rapid growth of Christianity in China, Korea, Japan, India, Burma, Oceania, and Indonesia. The report also saw the growth of 'national and racial patriotism' as 'a most inspiring summons' for Christian missions to improve not only the lives of individuals but entire nations. For Christianity was 'universally indigenous' and needed to adapt to Asian and African peoples.[13]

From the vantage point of a century later, we see that the World Missionary Conference stood on the cusp of the greatest demographic shift in the history of Christianity. The subsequent growth of Christianity in Asia, Africa, and Latin America during the twentieth century no doubt would have delighted the delegates. After all, they were missionaries who had given their lives to make it possible.

What the delegates to the 1910 World Missionary Conference could not have imagined was the elimination of entire communities of ancient Christians in the Near East, nor the destruction of Orthodoxy under the Soviet Union, nor the decline of Christianity in the European heartland. Neither could they envision the radicality of the indigenisation that they called for, nor its often brutal suppression by colonial authorities. Even as the conference was meeting in Edinburgh, Liberian prophet William Wadé Harris was in prison receiving a call from God to evangelise throughout West Africa. This great missionary would convert an estimated 100,000 people before being re-arrested by the French in 1914. In Congo, African-American missionary William Sheppard had just been tried for libel, for exposing the atrocities perpetuated by Belgian companies against rubber gatherers.[14] In the Philippines, the first ordained Protestant minister Nicolas Zamora had just broken away from the Methodist mission, thereby founding one of at least twenty-five independent Filipino churches organised by the 1930s. The growing Korean Christianity praised in conference reports would soon be suppressed by Japanese annexation of Korea two months after the conference. In 1910 while denominational mission leaders met in Edinburgh, freelance faith missionaries were spreading the new Pentecostal movement from San Francisco and India

---

Christ's Kingdom.' World Missionary Conference 1910, *Report of Commission VIII*, 138-139.

[12] World Missionary Conference, 1910, *Report of Commission I, Carrying the Gospel to all the Non-Christian World* (Edinburgh and London: Oliphant, Anderson, & Ferrier; New York, Chicago, and Toronto: Fleming H Revell, 1910), 35.

[13] World Missionary Conference, 1910, *Report of Commission I*, 35.

[14] E.g. for cutting off the hands of people who did not gather enough rubber, including those of children.

into Chile, Norway, Sweden, South Africa, China, Russia, Germany, Australia, and elsewhere.[15]

Today when we identify the historical legacy of the World Missionary Conference of 1910, we must include the unintended consequences of what the delegates could only then see through a glass darkly (1 Cor. 13:12). The importance of grounding our work today in the Revelation vision of united witness to Christ is not only because we live in the certainty of Christian hope, but because we also know that the shape, timing, and achievement of God's kingdom is beyond human control. Just as witness and unity are inseparable in God's timing, so are Christian hope and humility. 'How long, O Lord, how long?'

Whole Church, Whole Gospel, Whole World 1963

Now let us fast forward a half century to another decisive turning point in the inseparability of mission and unity. Here I quote the conclusion of the final Message from the groundbreaking World Council of Churches mission conference in 1963, 'Witness in Six Continents': 'We therefore affirm that this missionary movement now involves Christians in all six continents and in all lands. It must be the common witness of the whole Church, bringing the whole Gospel to the whole world.'[16]

---

[15] While Brian Stanley's book is a superb introduction to the Edinburgh conference, much historical work remains to be done on its impact. For example, Darrell Whiteman has pointed out that the founding of the Kennedy School of Missions and training in missionary anthropology came from the conference. Another area ripe for investigation is the spread of conference ideals in Africa. Malawian Baptist John Chilembwe, for example, was one of the informants for the conference reports. Did the ideals of equality that came from the conference inspire him in his revolt against colonial authority a few years later? Another un-researched area is the way in which women's missionary societies immediately publicised the findings of the conference in women's mission magazines and then launched initiatives of their own. Women delegates commented that men did the talking, but that they 'acted'. Following the conference, the women's missionary societies of North America adopted a plan by conference delegate Clementina Butler to launch the Committee on Christian Literature for Women and Children in Mission Lands, in response to the problem of youth formation discussed at Edinburgh 1910.

[16] Ronald K. Orchard (ed.), *Witness in Six Continents. Records of the Meeting of the Commission on World Mission and Evangelism of the World Council of Churches held in Mexico City December 8th to 19th, 1963* (London: Edinburgh House Press, 1964), 175. The phrase 'whole Church bringing the whole gospel to the whole world' appears to have been written by J.C. Hoekendijk into the Rolle Declaration of the World Council of Churches in 1951, to define united ecumenical mission. 'We would especially draw attention to the recent confusion in the use of the word 'ecumenical'. It is important to insist that this word, which comes from the Greek word for the whole inhabited earth, is properly used to describe everything that relates to the whole task of the whole church to bring the Gospel to the whole world. It therefore covers equally the missionary movement and the movement

This statement, in a nutshell, reflected fifty years of missiological developments set into motion by Edinburgh 1910. In retrospect, we see that it marked the symbolic beginning of a postcolonial framework for mission – its liberation from captivity to western Christendom.[17] The articulation of a united world community – as opposed to western-dominated Christianity – emerged from struggles for Christian solidarity under the horrific conditions of the Second World War. The rescue of stranded allied servicemen by South Pacific Christians, international Lutheran support for orphaned German missions, missionary defence of the Chinese under Japanese occupation, Christian succour for enemy prisoners of war – these are but a few of the examples that validated hopes for the church as worldwide fellowship in the minds of those who lived through the war. In 1948, both the founding of the World Council of Churches and the passage of the Universal Declaration of Human Rights resulted from hard work by Christians to frame a global Christian ethic suitable to an interconnected world.[18]

During the 1950s and 1960s, nationalist movements gave birth to independent nations in Asia and Africa. Churches in postcolonial contexts threw off western control.[19] Independence movements added urgency to the conviction that mission was a task of the 'whole church', and not just the West. By the time delegates met in Mexico City in 1963, mission leaders hoped that a new egalitarian era of the 'whole church' was dawning.[20] This

---

towards unity, and must not be used to describe the latter in contradistinction to the former. We believe that a real service will be rendered to true thinking on these subjects in the Churches if we so use this word that it covers both Unity and Mission in the context of the whole world.' *Minutes and Reports of the Fourth Meeting of the Central Committee of the World Council of Churches, Rolle (Switzerland), August 4-11, 1951* (Geneva, Switzerland: World Council of Churches, 1951), 65. Keith Bridston attributes the phrase to Hoekendijk. See Keith R. Bridston (compiler), *Shock and Renewal: The Christian Mission Enters a New Era* (New York: Friendship Press, 1955), 10.

[17] At the time, ecumenical leaders stated this as the end of the 'missionary era' and the beginning of the 'ecumenical era'.

[18] See John Nurser, *For All Peoples and All Nations: Christian Churches and Human Rights* (Geneva: WCC Publications, 2005).

[19] African and Asian Christians often repudiated western denominations through founding independent churches, or through regional church mergers, as in the creation of the Church of South India in 1947. During the 1950s and 1960s, Eastern church leaders often preferred to focus on regional ecumenical associations such as the East Asia Christian Conference, while Western church leaders preferred to work through international denominational groups such as the World Alliance of Reformed Churches, World Methodist Council, Lutheran World Federation, etc. D.T. Niles claimed this difference was an example of Western denominations attempting to retain control of resources during the devolution process.

[20] See, e.g. Bridston, *Shock and Renewal*; Lesslie Newbigin, *One Body, One Gospel, One World: The Christian Mission Today* (London: International Missionary Council, 1958).

conference after the merger of the International Missionary Council into the World Council of Churches was also the first mission meeting in which the Orthodox were full participants. The simultaneous gathering of Roman Catholic bishops for the Second Vatican Council (1962-1965) held out the possibility of even deeper missional unity in the future.

Lest it seem that the idea of 'whole church' to the 'whole world' represented shallow optimism, it is important to recognise it was also a cry of lamentation and call for repentance. Talk of the need for the 'whole church' to reach the 'whole world' recognised that previous mission efforts had been dominated by what Sri Lankan theologian D.T Niles called 'the westernity of the base'.[21] It also underscored that mission should pay greater attention to the 'other' global forces of politics and economics. For example, Communist victory in China, and its growing power throughout the world, seemed to some mission leaders the judgment of God against a divided colonialist church that had paid more attention to itself than to the needs of the world.[22]

The idea of 'witness to six continents', therefore, was a breakthrough in mission thought appropriate to a post-Christendom, post-geographic, global context. Henceforth missions should be multi-directional. They must include concern for God's work in the world and the eventual coming of God's kingdom.[23] The 'whole gospel' begins with the message of reconciliation with God through Jesus Christ. As the Mexico City report stated, 'The Christian mission is the proclamation of this message to the whole world: be ye reconciled to God'.[24]

---

[21] Sri Lankan Methodist D. T. Niles wrote the first broadly published treatment of mission theology by a non-Western theologian. See D.T. Niles, *Upon the Earth: The Mission of God and the Missionary Enterprise of the Churches* (New York: McGraw-Hill, 1962).

[22] This critique was sharply stated by Church of England missionary David Paton in 1955, 'If we must keep the Faith ever before us, we must keep the world ever before us, too; for it is God's world. It is God's world, and it is one. To it God's Church has one Mission ... The "wrath of God" is eminently a phrase we shall do well to live with... and this applies especially to us educated Protestants of the Anglo-Saxon industrial west who have such difficulty in understanding the world-wide revolt against our hegemony.' David M. Paton, 'World Events Reveal Our Weakness', in Bridston, *Shock and Renewal*, 29-30. See also Richard Shaull, *Encounter with Revolution* (New York: Association Press, 1955).

[23] 'The Christian message to men is not only concerned with individuals but also with the Kingdom of God as the destiny of mankind as a whole.' Orchard, *Witness in Six Continents,* 154.

[24] Orchard, *Witness in Six Continents*, 144. The report explored the ideas of mission as witness to persons of other faiths, witness in secular contexts (including the centrality of laity in mission), the witness of local congregations (including changing forms of church life), and witness across new mission 'frontiers' of the contemporary era. Because of its deepened commitment to visible unity, represented both by the merger of the IMC into the World Council of Churches and

And what of the Revelation vision of believers called from all 'tribes and peoples and languages' united in praise to Christ? What of the relationship between mission and unity? British mission leader Ronald Orchard wrote the clearest exposition of how the challenging transitions of the early 1960s related to the eschatological 'long view' in his perceptive book, *Missions in a Time of Testing*. To Orchard, the clearest expression of a postcolonial mission from and to all six continents was *doxology* – mission as praise of the risen Christ. Orchard wrote,

> Seen in the perspective of the 'last hour', the Mission of Christ is the establishment of the centre of the new humanity to which come God's people from the ends of the earth to worship. These are not two processes, but one: the sending is also the gathering. The one stresses the aspect of witness among men, the other God's use of that witness in the fulfilment of His purpose to gather his people into Christ... Mission is nothing else than this – to speak, to act, to live so as to 'cause his glory to be praised'.[25]

I find Orchard's analysis helpful because it reveals the deeper flow underneath the many problems, policies, and plans hatched by mid twentieth-century mission leaders. If 'common witness' means 'the whole Church bringing the whole Gospel to the whole world', then mission unfolds from the nature of the church itself, as a worldwide community both gathered and sent by God. Witness to Christ is rooted in the *missio Dei*, God's purpose for the world. And as the Message from the 1963 conference concluded, 'God's purpose still stands: to sum up all things in Christ'.[26]

Orchard's image of the mutuality of sending and gathering suggests that the process of unity in mission is like breathing. The church gathers in worship, inhaling the Holy Spirit. We gain strength from our gathering and centering of purpose, and then exhale in praise of the God who loves all creation. Emil Brunner famously stated that 'the church exists by mission as fire exists by burning'. Orthodox theologians like Ion Bria call mission 'the liturgy after the liturgy'. I would add that mission is the church breathing: we inhale in worship and exhale in witness.[27]

---

the participation of the Orthodox, the conference also invoked the centralising goal of sacramental unity as the ultimate witness to 'the final consummation of God's kingdom'. Orchard, *Witness in Six Continents*, 165-166. Thus despite the postcolonial mission theory implicit in the report, there was an inward ecclesial focus that symbolised a backtracking from evangelisation.

25 Ronald K. Orchard, *Missions in a Time of Testing: Thought and Practice in Contemporary Missions* (Philadelphia: Westminster Press, 1964), 195-198. Note that Orchard wrote his book before the 1963 conference, and he also edited the conference proceedings.

26 Orchard, *Witness in Six Continents,* 175.

27 I mention the image of mission as breathing in my study book for the United Methodist Church, Dana L. Robert, *Joy to the World!: Christian Mission in the Age of Global Christianity* (Women's Division, GBGM, United Methodist Church, 2010).

Mission in 2010

Now I come to the third and final section of my remarks. What has happened in the relationship between mission and unity that brings us to this place today? 1910 expressed hope for the church as worldwide fellowship.[28] 1963 deepened that reality by shifting the meaning of mission to multicultural, multidirectional, mutual 'witness in all six continents'. Now here we are in 2010 – another generation of living and breathing witnesses to Jesus Christ![29] How shall we live out the relationship between mission and unity for our generation?

Despite the high promises of 1963, fighting over mission mandates characterised the mid-1960s into the 1980s. Christendom mission was dying, and a new era of mutuality struggled to be born. The challenges remind me of the saying of Peter Maurin, a founder of the Catholic Worker Movement, who talked of creating 'a new society in the shell of the old'. In the early 1970s, the phrase 'missionary, go home' resonated to the ends of the earth, with calls for a moratorium on western missions coming from the South Pacific, Latin America, and Africa, and triumphant secularism in the West. Competing definitions of the mission 'frontier' split Protestantism asunder: liberation and evangelisation were pitted against each other, with each claiming God on its side. Today we are still dealing with the effects of the polarising mission theories and practices that characterised the mid to late twentieth century.

In my opinion, however, 1989 marked a symbolic turning point in the shared re-appropriation of the Revelation vision of the church as a worldwide community of believers, united in common witness. People took their faith into the public square in Eastern Europe and Russia, and the Berlin Wall came down. Stated one communist leader, 'We were prepared for everything, but not for candles and prayers'.[30] With students at Tiananmen Square, the cross appeared in public procession for the first time in many decades in China. The repression of dissent there led to new openness to the gospel among young people in what is now one of the fastest growing churches in the world. Lamin Sanneh's groundbreaking book *Translating the Message* appeared. Authored by an African convert to Christianity, this book single-handedly broadened the discourse on mission from colonial lament toward appreciation of the cultural diversity

---

[28] Of course Roman Catholicism already had a strong sense of itself as worldwide fellowship. But for divided Protestants, 1910 was a turning point in this direction.

[29] As we Methodists might sing with Charles Wesley, 'And are we yet alive, and see each other's face?'

[30] Quoted in Thomas Kemper, 'God is coming toward us', Address to Board of Directors General Board of Global Ministries The United Methodist Church, Stamford, Connecticut, April 13, 2010. http://gbgm-umc.org/global_news/full_article.cfm?articleid=5724. Accessed April 24, 2010.

unleashed by Bible translation.[31] Conviction about the mutual necessity of both evangelisation and social justice gained momentum at mission conferences sponsored in 1989 by the World Council of Churches in San Antonio, and the Lausanne Movement in Manila. Theological convergence increased with the papal encyclical *Redemptoris Missio* appearing the following year.

The events of 1989 opened the window to a fresh relationship between witness and unity. Recognition that Christian faith thrives in multiple cultural expressions has been gradually dawning since the 1990s.[32] A century ago, Elizabeth Northup, one of the missionary women who attended Edinburgh 1910, wrote of what she learned from the conference, 'Until the whole world can come together and interpret Christ, we shall never know him in his fullness'.[33] This necessity for all cultures to contribute to the fullness of Christ is also how historian Andrew Walls describes the theological necessity of our contemporary situation. Referencing Ephesians 4:13, Walls writes, 'The very height of Christ's full stature is reached only by the coming together of the different cultural entities into the body of Christ. Only "together", not on our own, can we reach his full stature'.[34]

And so we stand at a moment in history when multiple cultural streams of Christianity are renewing the Revelation vision. We honour our continuity with those who came before us in 1910 and 1963, and we anticipate that blessed day when persons from all nations, races, and tribes will be united in praise of Christ. Yet the urgent realities of 2010 must also guide how we witness to Christ today, and shape our dreams and hopes.

How does our context of 2010 differ from that of the twentieth century? For one thing, common witness has imbedded within it far more plurality than was recognised fifty years ago. Cultural, ecclesial, theological, and organisational diversity is greater than what could be imagined in 1963. Ours is no cookie-cutter faith, and since the 1970s the 'fourth self' of self-theologising has been increasingly affirmed by mission leaders across ecclesial and ethnic divides.[35] Seen in historical perspective, the

---

[31] Lamin Sanneh, *Translating the Message: The Missionary Impact on Culture* (Maryknoll, NY: Orbis, 1989).

[32] To put these changes into the context of one lifetime, when I was born in 1956, the 'average' Christian was a European. By the time I die, the 'average' Christian will be an African or a Latin American. When I received my doctorate from Yale in 1984, my dream to teach what I called 'comparative Christianity' was completely obscure and unusual. Now the recent proliferation of scholarship in the field of 'world Christianity' is so large I cannot keep up with it!

[33] Elizabeth C. Northup, 'Impressions of the World Missionary Conference – June 14 to 23', *Woman's Missionary Friend*, August 1910, 274.

[34] Andrew F. Walls, 'The Ephesian Moment', *The Cross-Cultural Process in Christian History* (Maryknoll, NY: Orbis, 2002), 77.

[35] E.g. in 1972, Taiwanese theologian Shoki Coe coined the term 'contextualization', and the Association for Theological Education in South East

multiplicity of 2010 celebrations (and critiques) around the world should be affirmed as signs of hope and opportunities for new forms of mission that must engage each other. The essence of worldwide Christian community must being reimagined as a more inclusive and broader 'global conversation' than was possible in the past.[36]

Secondly, the sorry state of the planet is shaping how we interpret the idea of 'the whole church taking the whole gospel to the whole world'. This phrase from 1963 is the theme of the Lausanne Congress in October, and the leadership of that movement is arguing that the 'whole world' includes stewardship of the earth as God's creation.[37] Focus by multiple 2010 partners on environmental mission, including the Edinburgh 2010 study process, contrasts sharply with the dominion theology present at the 1963 conference in Mexico City. Speaking personally, as a native of southern Louisiana and the grandchild of Gulf Coast fishermen, I am grieving the destruction of my homeland from Hurricanes Katrina and Rita, and now the massive oil spill inundating the marshes. To what extent may we speak of the 'repair' or the 'salvation' of God's creation when we conceptualise mission in the twenty-first century?

Thirdly, the reality of globalisation carries multiple implications for the meaning of mission. Today's macro context of globalisation has parallels to the macro contexts of colonialism in 1910, and secular modernisation/nationalism in 1963. Globalisation has stimulated migration as mission, the spread of world religions and the reinterpretation of local religions beyond their traditional borders, new levels of interdependent hostility between wealth and poverty, and the proliferation of new forms of mission such as international non-governmental organisations (INGO's) and short-term mission trips. Globalisation forces us to conceptualise missions beyond the boundaries of the nation state, and both to strategise and critique new forms.

Fourthly, the context of 2010 gives new meaning and urgency to the church's tasks of world evangelisation and forming disciples. A century ago the participants at Edinburgh 1910 complained that only one-third of the world was Christian. Today we rejoice that one-third of the world are

---

Asia adopted the Critical Asian Principle. On self-theologising from different ecclesial perspectives, see Catholic Robert Schreiter, *Constructing Local Theologies* (Maryknoll, NY: Orbis, 1985), and Protestant evangelicals William Dyrness and Veli-Matti Kärkkäinen (eds), *Global Dictionary of Theology* (Downers Grove, IL: Inter-Varsity Press, 2008).

[36] The term 'global conversation' is being used by the Lausanne Movement for its 2010 theological process. While a happy phrase, at the moment the term is used to include only 'Evangelicals'. The 2010 challenges that limitation by affirming a broader set of conversation partners.

[37] See statement by Lausanne theology director Christopher J.H. Wright, 'Whole Gospel, Whole Church, Whole World'. www.christianitytoday.com/globalconversation/october2009/index.html?start=1. Accessed April 15, 2010.

followers of Christ. What does this change in attitude mean for our commitment to sharing the Good News with all peoples? We must not allow difficult theological, socio-cultural, and political issues, or disagreements over theologies of religion, to discourage us from sharing God's love and salvation through Jesus Christ with all the world.

And finally, as did English and West African and German missionaries against the slave trade two hundred years ago, we must proceed in assurance that despite all odds, our united witness across multiple human boundaries makes a difference in the world.[38] As witnesses to Jesus Christ today, to take the 'long view' means that we stand on the promises that there will be no more hunger or thirst, that springs of living water will flow, and that God will wipe away the tears in the eyes of the world he loves. Even as we ask 'How long, O Lord, how long?', united in praise, we confidently embrace God's mission.

---

[38] Note that the first missionaries to West Africa sent by the CMS were German nationals, who met the African students in England prior to embarking for West Africa.

Perspective 1

Bishop Brian Farrell, Secretary of the Pontifical Council for Promoting Christian Unity, Holy See

The theme of this Conference, 'Witnessing to Christ today', not only affirms the evangelical faith that binds us together, but presents us and our churches with a burning challenge. The Spirit is surely asking us what we have done with the grace of 1910, and what we intend to do with it at the beginning of the third Christian millennium.

Mission in the Long Perspective

Catholics live by memory. They feel strongly that they are in continuity with the Church's mission from the beginning. In the Catholic tradition, mission is co-natural with being Christian: 'the pilgrim Church is missionary by its very nature'.[1] Responding to the 'great commission', which Catholics usually refer to as 'the missionary mandate', missionaries in every age have striven to bring the Gospel message to the four corners of the world. Beginning from Jerusalem, on through Samaria and to the ends of the earth, the apostles, in the words of St. Augustine, 'preached the message of truth and gave birth to churches'.[2] Down the centuries countless heroic and faith-filled women and men have witnessed to Christ, preaching the word and making disciples; the religious congregations and missionary societies carried the message to every land as it was discovered, and they continue to do so in that 'mission territory' that still today includes two thirds of the world's population. Today, lay missionaries and volunteers, lay ecclesial movements, are in the forefront of Catholic mission in all its forms.

In the hundred years since Edinburgh 1910 many things have happened. But above all, it is our outlook on 'the other' that has changed. The worth and dignity of every human being, human rights, including religious freedom and freedom of opinion, are becoming a shared consciousness of a large part of the human family. Mission must take into account that the Gospel cannot be imposed on anyone, and that it is only by persuasively

---

[1] Vatican II, Decree on the Missionary Activity of the Church (*Ad Gentes*), §2. Available at www.vatican.va.

[2] Augustine, *Exposition on Psalm 44*, §23. Available at www.newadvent.org.

and respectfully announcing the message of salvation that the world will come to believe. In this sense, for interreligious relations, the Code of Conduct on conversion being drafted in collaboration by the World Council of Churches and the Catholic Church, with the participation of the Evangelical World Alliance deserves keen attention.

The search for meaning, particularly in the West, has become more arduous, perhaps also because for many people it is often no longer the holistic panorama that accompanies religious experience, but the fragmented vista that goes with consumerism, social status, and political affiliation that defines personal self-awareness. The anthropological question – What does it mean to be human? – lies at the heart of our unease.

Two thousand years on, the mission continues within the flow of human history, as Professor Dana L. Robert has amply outlined. But it clearly stands in need of a fresh theological justification and a renewed spiritual impulse, if it is to meet the challenge issued in Luke's gospel (18:8): 'When the Son of Man comes will he find faith on the face of the earth?'

Some Aspects of Catholic Thinking on Mission in the Present

As you will know, many Catholic documents of reference have appeared in recent decades on the theme of mission. A certain pride of place belongs to Pope Paul VI's On Evangelisation in the Modern World (*Evangelii Nuntiandi*), and to the Decree on the Missionary Activity of the Church (*Ad Gentes*) from the Second Vatican Council. Equally substantive is Pope John Paul II's Mission of the Redeemer (*Redemptoris Missio*), with its examination of the today's new *areopaghi*, the new spaces where people meet. Pope Benedict recently took up this idea, calling on missionaries to give attention to 'the nerve centres of society in the third millennium'.

Recent debates in Catholic circles have focussed on a number of issues related to mission:

1) Fundamental is the discussion about the core question, the universal salvific character of Jesus Christ, the one mediator: 'No one comes to the Father except by me' (John 14:6). It is precisely this uniqueness of Christ which gives him an absolute and universal significance; he is history's centre and goal: 'the Alpha and the Omega, the first and the last, the beginning and the end' (Rev. 22:13). But is He the only one to have the words of life? That debate was at the heart of the document *Dominus Jesus*, which caused much discussion on various issues, but whose principal purpose was to uphold the very ground of the missionary mandate itself.

2) Secondly, Catholic missiology today is deeply involved in reflection on the precise relationship between evangelisation and inculturation of the Gospel, as well as on the impact of the Gospel on justice, peace and the safeguarding of creation, and on the need for a new evangelisation of the vast sectors of traditionally Catholic societies that have drifted away from

the Church. In the Catholic view, the transformation of the world is a constitutive dimension of the preaching of the Gospel; in other words, humanity's liberation from every oppressive situation is an indispensable part of the Church's missionary activity. It has been the proclamation of Christ together with the promotion of the human person through works of charity, justice and peace that has brought the power of the Gospel into the heart of human cultures and societies: building a civilisation of love.

Regarding human development, perhaps Edinburgh 2010 needs to remind us of two things. First, the primacy of the gratuitous efficacy of the universal saving action of the Risen Christ. Jesus himself said: 'And I, when I am lifted up from the earth, will draw all people to myself' (John 12:32). Human development does not derive primarily from money, material assistance or technological means alone, but rather from the formation of consciences and the gradual maturing of ways of thinking and patterns of behaviour. The Church forms consciences by revealing to peoples the God whom they seek and do not yet know, the grandeur of the human person created in God's image and loved by him, the equality of all men and women as God's children, with all the consequences of such a vision.

Likewise, Edinburgh 2010 needs to remind us that the contribution of the churches to the development of peoples is not only a struggle against underdevelopment in the South of the world, but should also be directed to the specific poverty of the North. An excess of affluence is as harmful as excessive poverty. A soulless development based on the idea that increasing wealth and the promotion of economic and technical growth is enough cannot satisfy human beings. And now this Northern development model is powerfully spreading to the South, where a wave of consumerism may replace important cultural and religious values with the emptiness and lack of transcendence already being felt in our Western cities. Pope Benedict has spoken about the missionary map of today not just as geographical and territorial, but also anthropological, made up of vast sectors of Western society which have drifted away from the Gospel.

3) Another important debate concerns how to proclaim the Gospel in the light of Christ's call to the unity of his disciples. Edinburgh 1910 initiated a journey of discovery of all that the churches had in common. It is true that a hundred years later churches are experiencing a re-assertion of difference, not just between them but also within themselves. Still, so much has been achieved and so much has changed! In his remarkable Encyclical Letter *Ut Unum Sint* (1995) John Paul II, after surveying the progress of the search for unity among Christians, concludes that the most significant ecumenical achievement has been 'brotherhood rediscovered'. The source of that brotherhood is not our subjective goodwill, but the objective bond of our common baptism. We have not yet become one with the oneness that Jesus prayed for, but we know that our divisions are a scandal and damage that most sacred cause, the convincing proclamation of the Gospel. The spirit of

this centenary celebration must serve to remind us that mission requires that the churches seriously undertake to eradicate every form of rivalry and competition in missionary engagement.

Mission in a Pneumatological Perspective

So, what will our future missionary outreach look like? I don't believe we have a blueprint. But a first simple but pregnant thought comes to mind. Near and far, our world is broken in infinite ways. And yet, Christians are bearers of the reconciling and healing power of the Spirit. We should retrieve and lift up the work and message of the Conference on Mission and Evangelism in Athens in 2005 as a key to understanding mission today. The theme of that Conference, 'Come Holy Spirit, heal and reconcile', opens up a vast horizon of guidance, motivation and practical proposals which we would do well to nurture. Throughout the Christian family there is a growing awareness that while mission centres on Jesus Christ, it is the Holy Spirit – bound up with and not separated from Jesus Christ – who sustains the Church in carrying out God's mission. For example, this pneumatological dimension of mission was the central part of Pope John Paul's encyclical on Mission (*Redemptoris Missio*), entitled 'The Holy Spirit, Principal Agent of Mission'. The Spirit gives the *parresia*, the boldness with which we confess and proclaim our faith in Jesus Christ (cf. Heb. 3:6; 4:16; 10:19-22).

Our young people in particular are demanding that we witness to Christ today with substance and in harmony. There are endless possibilities for common witness, if only we are bold enough to really seek God's truth together, and be converted to the One who still calls us his friends. If we become friends ourselves and walk the ecumenical miles of hope together, the Spirit of Christ will bring life to his people and mission will thrive and blossom, until 'all things are restored in Christ and in Him humankind can compose one family and one people' (*Ad Gentes*, 1).

PERSPECTIVE 2

Revd Dr Tinyiko Maluleke, Professor of Black and African Theology, University of South Africa

Brothers and sisters, I noticed that the first speaker's time was up after the second point, so I will stick to two points only. There is a limit to how much one can say, in a foreign language in less than ten minutes.

Let me start by thanking Professor Dana Robert for a magisterial paper that helped us and focused us on the long view of Christian mission. She managed to isolate the key moments, as well as to survey the major developments, during the past hundred years.

I will quickly summarise what I heard her say, because for me that is very important. The main focus of the paper is on the question of developing the right vision for mission. This is absolutely important. Professor Robert's paper starts with an elaboration of the importance of vision for mission and it ends with the same idea. In the body of the paper, she focuses on the major themes of Edinburgh 1910 and links some of these to the 1963 World Council of Churches mission conference.

At the end of her paper Professor Roberts raises a number of tantalising perspectives for mission in for our times. For this section, she builds on the 1989 work of the San Antonio mission conference, the Tiananmen Square march and the fall of the Berlin Wall, which was followed by the encyclical letter *Redemptoris Missio*. Now, my two points in response.

The Under-Representation of Africa and Africans

My first comment relate to a point on which Prof Roberts touches very briefly: the under-representation of Africa and Africans in 1910. At the Edinburgh conference, Africans and Africa were represented by missionaries. There was only one African representative at Edinburgh 1910. Indeed, we could argue that Edinburgh was only interested in Africa as missionaries saw and represented Africa and Africans. Has this tendency to see Africa only and mainly through the eyes of people other than Africans themselves come to an end? It has not actually. Even in our times Africans remain a people who are represented, spoken for and spoken about by others. This situation applies to this conference. Indeed Africans are today better recognized in circles other than church circles.

One of the most exciting developments in 2010 is the awarding of the

FIFA football world cup to an African nation, for the first time in the 80 year history of the competition. This event is a small and belated recognition of the significance of Africa in world culture and sport. Indeed, I would argue that the controversial instrument that is likely to dominate the FIFA World Cup 2010 – the Vuvuzela – symbolizes the cry of a continent long rendered invisible, dumb and dum. It is a desperate attempt by a people long misheard and mis-seen to be seen and heard more positively and more clearly.

I want to suggest that both the representation and under-representation of African and Africans continues to be a problem today. Christian Africa, despite the growing numbers of African Christians, continues to be *represented* rather than *presented*. The so-called 'shift of Christian gravity 'has not removed the hegemony of the West in theology and general leadership. Africa continues to be presented and treated as a 'mission field', as victim, as an object, as an illustration of what ought not to be. Indeed, the very fact that the plenary address

Vision for Mission

Professor Roberts bases her remarks on the importance of vision in mission on Revelation 7. In that chapter we get a picture of fully human and equally human tribes and peoples joined in worship and honour. Only people equal in their humanity can serve and truly worship God in mission. And yet, the African experience of the past century has been one of Dehumanization and disregard. It is time therefore for us to build a vision and quest for mission that is predicated on the restoration of the dignity and humanity of all, Africans included. The Revelation 7 vision is only realisable among and between fully and equally human people – men and women of all cultures and orientations. Until we can acknowledge that black is as human as white, that woman is as human as man, Palestinian is a human as Canadian, American as human as Iranian, we cannot hope to see the fulfilment of the vision of Revelation 7.

Nor can we brush aside the reality of the violent century we have just experienced – the 20th century: a century of two world wars, a century of countless civil wars, a century of several racist wars, a century of violence – the most recent examples of which include Kosovo, Bosnia, Rwanda, Iraq, Sudan, Afghanistan, and the ongoing conflict in the Middle East. The 21st century also started with the sounds of war – September 11th and the wars that followed ever since.

However, the vision of Revelation 7 vision is more than an anthropocentric vision. The multitudes depicted there are robed and they are carrying palm leaves in their hands.There is also a reference to the 'lamb', which I want to read literally at this time. The fact that they were robed suggests interaction between humans and the rest of creation. It suggests industry and creativity, and the fact that they were carrying palms is a recognition of created life-forms other than human beings. There is a hint of the human stewardship for creation. Such is the comprehensive nature of our vision for mission, it has to encompass all of creation. God has always intended to save the world – not just humanity. And so when we look back to this violent century, we have to ask ourselves in what ways has Christian mission been entangled and implicated in this.

It is not good enough for us merely to wish for a romantic vision of happy people combined in worshiping and serving God. We have to take cognizance of the vast inequalities between peoples, even peoples of the same country. The growing gap between rich and poor, the continued dehumanisation of others by some, the environmental degradation as well as the continuing wars must all become part of the agenda for mission.

PERSPECTIVE 3

Bishop Geevarghese Mor Coorilos, Malankara Syriac Orthodox Church, India

I greet you all in the name of the Holy Trinity! It is indeed a great honour for me and for the Commission on World Mission and Evangelism (CWME) of the World Council of Churches that I represent here, to be part of this historic moment when we together celebrate one hundred years of our ecumenical missionary journey which started right here in 1910. The leaders of the 1910 conference would not have anticipated the kind of sea changes in the global Christian landscape that we have witnessed over the years: crisis in Western civilisation, disintegration and collapse of colonial imperialism, emergence of new forms of colonialism (economic and cultural globalisation) and war ('war on terror'), growing secularisation, and the challenges of post-modernity are just a few aspects of the ever-changing global landscape. On the ecclesial front, the phenomenal growth of Charismatic and Pentecostal churches today is a major development. All of these, as Dana Robert has articulated in her key-note presentation, pose new challenges for conventional understandings of Christian unity and Mission and Evangelism.

For want of time, I should like to lift up only a couple of concerns here:

Mission as 'Liturgy Before Liturgy'

Dana Robert, in her presentation, has likened the process of mission in unity to the act of breathing. According to her, 'mission is the church breathing: we inhale in worship, exhale in witness'. She has also made reference to the classic Orthodox notion of mission as 'the liturgy after the liturgy', popularised by Ion Bria. Standing in today's context, marked by division amongst churches, lack of inter-communion even among members of same ecclesial family, exclusion of various sections of people within and without churches, brokenness of relationship between humanity and nature; my own sense is that it's time we also started talking about 'liturgy before liturgy' if we as churches are to be credible in our being and becoming. Perhaps it's also time we practised inhaling in witness and exhaling worship. How can we possibly claim to be a credible worshipping community if we are still far from being able to practise equality, sharing, justice and mutuality in our ecclesial and social engineering? How can we possibly call ourselves a liturgical community if churches continue to discriminate against people on the bases of caste, race, gender and so on even within their worship life? What is Holy Communion without social communion? To me, the challenge seems to lie in taking up 'liturgy after liturgy' (the ministry of healing and reconciliation) before liturgy. The actual practice of healing and reconciliation needs to be reflected in the liturgical life of the church. In fact, the Biblical tradition does take us in that direction: 'Therefore if you bring your gift to the altar, and there remember that your brother has something against you, leave your gift before that altar and go your way. First be reconciled to your brother, and then come and offer your gift.' (Matt. 5:23,24)

As the Conference on World Mission and Evangelism in Athens (2005) reminded us, we, as churches, are essentially called to be healing and reconciling communities. Our worship and liturgy will stand discredited, as Isaiah 1: 10-15 suggests, if we do not embody the values of equality, peace, justice and integrity of creation. Liturgy before liturgy, therefore, is just as important as liturgy after liturgy.

Mission as Contestation

Dana Robert has pointed out an important matter in her keynote presentation: that is the 1910 macro context of colonialism has now been supplanted with the current macro context of (economic) globalisation. The question of whether churches and mission agencies, in particular, are also being negatively influenced by the logic of globalisation and market imperialism needs to be addressed seriously, especially in a context where there is a growing concern that the prophetic voice has been gradually diminishing in ecumenical circles, including in the World Council of Churches. While it is true that the false dichotomy between evangelical and ecumenical strands is irrelevant, our attempts in widening the ecumenical umbrella should not result in diluting the prophetic dimensions of mission. Passion for evangelism and quest for social justice should be held together.

As David Bosch has written that our response to *missio Dei* should be to turn to God. And to turn to God is to turn to the world.[1] Differently stated, mission is the church's engagement with the world in a prophetic manner. In today's context of neo-colonialism, of systemic injustice and violence, manifested in increasing globalisation of poverty, economic and social marginalisation of people and exploitation of mother earth, mission as a quest for justice is not simply an option but a mandate. One hundred years since 1910, we need to underscore this affirmation in no uncertain terms. We must also recognise that the church is not the sole agent of the *missio Dei*, God's transformation of the world. She must witness to God in Christ

[1] David J. Bosch, *Transforming Mission: Paradigm Shifts in Theology of Mission* (Maryknoll, NY: Orbis Books, 1991), 389-93.

alongside all God's people, including people of other faiths and civil society initiatives. When the church engages the world, she is called to act like salt and get dissolved in it. Even after one hundred years of the missionary movement, I sense an obvious lack of courage and commitment on the part of the global church to address issues of global justice (social, economic and ecological justice) and religious pluralism, and their specific challenges, as fundamental mission concerns. While the 1910 mission conference was marked predominantly by a Western colonial missionary ethos, what seems to influence the global ecclesial and missionary context of today is a neo-colonial project of sidelining issues of global justice. The representation of the global South in this conference may have significantly increased from that of 1910, but the question is whether the pressing concerns of the global South, such as poverty, economic and social injustice, ecological violence and marginalisation of indigenous peoples, actually form the main mission agenda. For instance, it was quite appropriate that we decided to meet here in Edinburgh where the modern ecumenical movement was born one hundred years ago. But do we all share the same strong feelings about the place which is the very ground of our faith and of the ecumenical movement, the land where Jesus Christ himself was born? If we do not address the issues of the unjust and illegal occupation of Palestine and the continuing aggression of the State of Israel toward the people and land of Palestine, which world are we turning to in the *missio Dei*? If this conference does not have anything to say in missiological terms about the islands and their peoples, who are going to simply disappear due to climate change, which world are we turning to in God's mission? It is here that we need to highlight the importance of mission as contestation.

The miracle account in Mk 5:1-20 offers us some insights as to how mission can be perceived vis-à-vis contestation. Mission, here, can be understood in terms of exorcism, as 'casting out demons', confronting satanic forces. The most striking thing about the Markan story is that Jesus confronts the satanic forces by naming them. The name 'legion' (meaning 'a battalion of soldiers') is suggestive of the context of Roman military imperialism. The word 'legion' also is indicative of the fact that satan here is not an individual, but an army, a system, a structure of evil. In today's context of neo-colonialism, we are challenged by Jesus Christ to confront systemic demons and satanic forces that express themselves in the guise of economic globalisation, casteism, racism, patriarchy, ecocide and so on. Mission in this context is about calling them by name and casting them out. It is important that Dana Robert has lifted up the Revelation vision in her presentation. However, it is even more important to remind ourselves of the fact that this was a church daring to articulate alternative visions in a context of imperial domination. The early church's model of confronting the Roman Empire, as recorded in the Book of Revelation, is a classic example of how the mission of contestation is carried out in specific contexts. Revelation 18 is truly a prophetic passage on the doom of the then empire. This is how it is announced, proleptically: 'He cried with a loud voice saying: Fallen, fallen is Babylon the great. She has become a dwelling place of demons, and a stronghold of every unclean spirit...with the wealth of her wantonness.' (Rev. 18:2) John here speaks of the fall of the empire as if it had happened. This is the missionary spirit in which we need to contest the demonic forces of our times.

In sum, all mission conferences are meant to, as Wolfgang Gunther has put it, 'Make new discoveries of the grace and power of God for ourselves, for the Church, and for the world, to face the new age and the new task with a new consecration'.[2] Edinburgh 2010 is yet another opportunity to discover anew the grace and power of God for us, the Church, and for the whole created order. May the triune God help us discover that divine grace and power.

---

[2] Wolfgang Gunther, 'The History and Significance of World Mission Conferences in the Twentieth Century', in *The International Review of Mission* 92/367 (Oct 2003), 521-37, at 521.

PERSPECTIVE 4

Rev. Bertil Ekström, Executive Director, World Evangelical Alliance Mission Commission, Brazil

The Christian Church has been present and active in Latin America since the early sixteenth century and there is, of course, a lot to say about witnessing to Christ in our continent. However, I will concentrate on some practical aspects, giving a few examples of what happens in our days. In the statistics the continent is considered Christian with a majority of the population belonging to the many Christian traditions. In practice, however, regular church attendance is probably around 30 percent of the population.

The Church in Latin America

There is full religious freedom in most of the Latin American countries today, and a fertile soil for all kinds of religious beliefs and expressions. In Brazil we use to say that 'if something is established somewhere on the globe on Saturday evening, it will also be introduced in Brazil on Sunday morning'. It is possible to establish anything you want to, and the proliferation of sects and extreme movements – both those that call themselves Christian as well as others – is a concern to many of us.

Today Latin America has one of the largest and strongest Christian churches in the world, still with outstanding growth in many of the different denominations and traditions. We could talk about revival movements within the Catholic, the historic and traditional Protestant and Evangelical churches, and also among newer Charismatic and Pentecostal movements, particularly among lower middle-class and poor people.

Witnessing to Christ in Latin America

Here I note three characteristics of the church in Latin America which are related to the theme of 'witnessing to Christ today'. First, Christian witness in Latin America today is holistic, and basically all churches have the *kerygma* dimension walking hand in hand with *diaconia*. Credibility in society demands an integral approach to people where spiritual, emotional, physical, relational and social needs are met and taken seriously.

Second, we lack a united stand as Christians in many issues, and not having unity among the different Christian expressions is certainly a hindrance for greater impact on society and on our governments. We face high rates of corruption, violence and social injustice, and today also a tendency in some countries to dictatorial governments. A question we often raise is how can it be that the Church is so big and our influence on society, including different levels of leadership, media and governments, is so weak? There is certainly an important lack of discipleship and a dichotomy between life in Church on Sundays and life in the community during the rest of the week.

Third, in spite of earlier tensions between the different Christian traditions and the visible difficulty that we have had to work together there are signs of improvement and concrete steps to closer co-operation. One example is the Fraternity Campaign this year, focusing on financial issues and responsible stewardship, initiated by the Brazilian Conference of Catholic Bishops, but also supported by other Christian Churches. Another example is the Evangelical Alliances – that gather both 'Ecumenical' and 'Evangelical' churches, by the way – a distinction that does not make much sense for us in Latin America. Gary B. McGee summarises: 'Modern evangelicalism now encompasses an almost unbridgeable diversity of Christians, all loyal to the gospel message, but with varying theological and spiritual orientations. Major groupings consist of Lutherans, Presbyterians, Anglicans, Pentecostals, Baptists, Wesleyans, Mennonites, Brethren, Churches of Christ, and others of the Restoration Movement. To these can be added Messianic Jews, nondenominational Christians, and constituents of para-church agencies (e.g. Campus Crusade for Christ).'[1] There is also theological reflection in a dialogue between representatives from different ecclesiastical backgrounds – a theology *on* and *of* the road – well represented by the Latin American Theological Fraternity (FTL).

Jorge, one of my colleagues and friends in Fortaleza, in the northeast of Brazil, could be a good example of how witness to Christ happens in Latin America today. Born in a poor region of the country, he had a personal experience with Jesus Christ when he was a teenager and soon felt called to be a full-time minister. After theological studies he came to a small congregation in the slum area of Dois Irmãos ('two brothers') on the outskirts of Fortaleza. He realised soon that preaching the Gospel and making disciples of Jesus would not be successful without considering the entire situation of the people in the neighbourhood. There were no schools in the area, so he first started a pre-school in the backyard of the church and literacy courses for adults. The school started to grow and today the church offers quality education from pre-school to secondary level, with support from local authorities. Being a community of poor people, many of them without permanent jobs and living in sub-human conditions, a programme

[1] Gary B. McGee, 'Evangelical Movement', in A. Scott Moreau (ed.), *Evangelical Dictionary of World Missions* (Grand Rapids, MI: Baker Book House, 2000), at 338.

was also started, with help from the south of Brazil, to build and renovate houses, provide clean water and improve the sanitary system, giving people jobs and better living standards. The former slum area Dois Irmãos is not the same anymore. The witness to Christ continues with a holistic ministry, preaching the Gospel of salvation and transformation, praying for healing and for God's help and acting in different areas of community development, following the example of Jesus Christ and echoing his words in Luke 4:18-19: 'The Spirit of the Lord is on me, because he has anointed me to preach good news to the poor. He has sent me to proclaim freedom for the prisoners, and recovery of sight for the blind, to release the oppressed, to proclaim the year of the Lord's favour'.

Important Mission Developments

Is Latin America a Christian continent? Does it need missionary work? That was the question raised at the Edinburgh 1910 conference and the understanding of that conference was that Latin America did not need any further missionary investment from outside. The statement, however, was made without the participation of Latin American leaders; others decided on their behalf and the Latino voice was not heard. Six years later, Latin American leaders met in Panama to analyse the situation in the continent and contrary to the conclusion at Edinburgh, they considered Latin American was still a needy mission field. Panama 1916 was followed by two other conferences in 1925 in Uruguay and in 1929 in Cuba that reinforced the same conclusion.

It is important just to mention some of the conferences and consultations that have had a strong influence on the continent, such as the four CLADE conferences organised by the Latin American Theological Fraternity (1969, 1980, 1992 and 2003, the last two in Quito, Ecuador), and the Lausanne Conference of 1974 and the follow up conference in Curitiba, Brazil in 1976, hosted by the Intervarsity Movement (ABU). Regarding Evangelical churches, the COMIBAM conferences in Sao Paulo in 1987 and in Acapulco, Mexico in 1997 also had a decisive impact on the start and development of autochthonous mission movements, sending Latin American cross-cultural missionaries to other countries and continents.

What is the situation today? There are still many who have not yet been reached by the Gospel of Jesus Christ, such as around two hundred indigenous tribal groups, immigrants from many nations and a growing secularised middle-class who still need to hear a clear and living witness to Christ.

We celebrate the growth of the Christian Church in our continent, not so much in terms of numbers but with increasing desire to see the Kingdom of God coming to our countries, and the rest of the world, with an impact that has positive consequences for society, transforming individuals and communities, but also for participating in the multi-cultural choir that worship the Lamb and the King, according to Revelation, with hope of an eternity with the Lord. I finish with a quote from Orlando Costas, one of the leading Latin American theologians in the twentieth century:

> The issue seems to me to be not whether the church is growing, but whether it is authentically engaged in the mission of the triune God in its concrete socio-historical situations. It is a matter of efficacious participation in the ongoing life-struggles of society in a total witnessing engagement, which, more than a program or a method, is a lifestyle. For when this happens, the church is turned upside-down. It becomes a living organism, a dynamic training and research centre, and an effective team that is capable of leading multitudes to Jesus Christ. In such circumstances, the church is turned inside-out; its structures are put at the service of the kingdom and its missionary practice is transformed into a comprehensive endeavour, where the gospel is shared in depth and out of the depths of human life.[2]

[2] Orlando Costas, *Christ Outside the Gate* (Maryknoll, NY: Orbis Books: 1982), 54.

PLENARY 2: MISSION WORLDWIDE
FRIDAY, 4 JUNE 2010

CASE STUDY 1
CHRISTIAN SPIRITUALITY AND THE DIAKONIC MISSION OF THE YOIDO FULL GOSPEL CHURCH

Rev. Dr Lee Young-Hoon, Senior Pastor, Yoido Full Gospel Church, Seoul[1]

The History and Growth of the Korean Church

After Catholicism was first introduced in Korea in 1784, many Catholic believers suffered persecution and martyrdom partly because of the problems that had arisen from the cultural differences between the Korean society and the Western world. Protestant Christianity was introduced in 1885 and Protestant Christians experienced no less persecution. Robert J. Thomas, a Presbyterian missionary from Wales, arrived in Korea on board the General Sherman ship in 1866 with high hopes for evangelising the country. As soon as he approached Pyongyang, however, he was arrested and beheaded in Yanggak-do's Ssuk Island in Pyongyang. He was only twenty-seven years old, and he was not able to proclaim a word of the gospel before his death.[2] He was reported as saying to his slayer, '*Yaso, Yaso*' (Jesus, Jesus) and offered him a package. It contained many copies of the Bible. However, his martyrdom was not fruitless at all. In fact, the blood of the martyrs – either the Western missionaries, or early national believers – is the very secret of how the Korean churches have been able to grow so fast in such a short time, with 12 million believers today.

In the history of the evangelisation of Korea, there is a unique feature: Korea had voluntarily sought for the gospel, even before any missionary

---

[1] For further biodata, see Appendix 4.

[2] More detail on the martyrdom of Robert J. Thomas is available in many sources, such as Manyeul Lee, *A Study on the History of Acceptance of the Korean Christianity* (in Korean) (Seoul: Dooraesidae, 1998), 38; Kyungbae Min, *The History of the Korean Church* (in Korean) (Seoul: Yonsei University Press, 1993), 101-102, 136-139.

was able to set foot on Korean soil. By the time the first Protestant missionaries reached Korea, most part of the Bible had already been translated into Korean – either by Western missionaries, or by Korean believers who lived or studied abroad, such as in China, Japan or in the U.S. or who were international traders – so that the earliest missionaries to Korea were able to preach with Korean Bibles.[3] Evidence abounds to attest to the enthusiasm of the earliest Korean believers over the Christian faith with the attitude and fervour of inquirers.[4]

There is another important feature of the growth of the Korean Church: the attitude of humility found both among the missionaries and national believers. For example, Rev. Henry G. Appenzeller lived a simple life based on John Wesley's famous teaching, 'sanctification, justification, and one penny a week', and dedicated himself to be a missionary to Korea at the early age of 26.[5] He came to Korea as one of the first Western official Protestant missionaries in 1885.[6] Another remarkable characteristic of Appenzeller's missionary work was his respect for local culture and the situation of Korea as much as possible. For instance, he made every effort not to violate any rule that the Korean government had set for the foreign missionaries. Consequently he devoted himself primarily to educational activities for a considerable period of time.[7] He sat with his legs folded on the floor of the small sanctuary in Korean fashion at the first worship service at Chung-dong First Methodist Church in 1887. He powerfully demonstrated his adaptability to local Korean culture.[8] In summary, in the birth and development of the Korean churches, humility, devotion, and obedience were evident both among the missionaries and national leaders. Their resolute commitment to the scriptural teaching resulted in persecution and martyrdom.

---

[3] The Library of the British and Foreign Bible Society, *Historical Catalogues of Printed Editions of the Holy Scriptures* (London: The Bible House, 1903); M. Lee, *A Study on the History*, 38-44; K. Min, *The History of the Korean Church*, 165-167.

[4] M. Lee, *A Study on the History*, 458-68.

[5] William E. Griffis, *A Modern Pioneer in Korea: The Life Story of Henry G. Appenzeller* (New York: Fleming H. Revell Co., 1912), 70; M. Lee, *A Study on the History*, 202-49.

[6] Appenzeller, a formally appointed Methodist missionary to Korea, arrived in Korea on the Easter day (April, 5), 1885, with Horace Underwood, an appointed Presbyterian missionary. *Annual Report of the Missionary Society of the Methodist Episcopal Church*, 1885, 237; Tongshik Ryu, *A History of Chung Dong First Methodist Church, 1885-1990* (Seoul: Editorial Committee of Chung Dong First Methodist Church, 1992), 38.

[7] Jonghae Noh, *New View on the History of Korea Methodist Church* (in Korean) (Seoul: Poongman, 1988), 198-99; Tongshik Ryu, *A History of Chung Dong First Methodist Church*, 40-46.

[8] Henry G. Appenzeller, *Diary*, on October 11, 1887.

Brief History of the Pentecostal Movement in Korea

At the beginning of the twentieth century, God poured out the Holy Spirit simultaneously throughout the whole world. In 1904, God used a young man named Evan J. Roberts to spread the fire of the Holy Spirit in the United Kingdom centred on Wales.[9] In the United States, William Seymour, a son of an African American slave, was used by God to ignite the United States and Europe with the Holy Spirit from his humble Azusa Street Mission from 1906 to 1909.[10] Also in South America, countries like Brazil, Chile and Argentina experienced great Pentecostal outbreaks. India, influenced by the Wales revival movement, also experienced the flames of the Holy Spirit in the Khasa region and many other parts of India. The news of the Indian revival eventually reached the Korean Peninsula.

In 1903, Methodist missionaries invited Rev. M.C. White, who was ministering in China, for a revival meeting. White's spirituality had been shaped by the Keswick higher life movement, which emphasised the convention for the promotion of scriptural holiness.[11] In his Wonsan meeting, a strong manifestation of the Holy Spirit was felt by the participants. The revival in Wonsan had a direct influence to the Great Pyongyang Revival of 1907.[12] The Holy Spirit movement in the Korean churches started with repentance. On January 4, 1907, Pyongyang's Jangdaehyun Church, greatly inspired by the revival throughout the world, including Wales and India, held a revival meeting for two weeks.[13] People were not being changed until the end of the event. Sun-joo Gil, an elder who participated in the revival as a church leader, just led a prayer meeting. During the time of repentance, he publicly confessed his sins in front of the congregation as follows:

> I am like Achan, and because of me you could not experience the grace of God. Once my friend pleaded with me at his dying hour and said, 'I'm dying now and I want you to dispose of all my fortune. My wife cannot do anything because she is uneducated, so I plead with you', and with these words he passed away. While I was disposing of his fortune, I took 100 *Won* for myself

---

[9] Young-hoon Lee, *The Holy Spirit Movement in Korea: Its Historical and Doctrinal Development* (Oxford, UK: Regnum Books International, 2009), 27.

[10] Y. Lee, *The Holy Spirit Movement in Korea*, 66-67.

[11] 'Keswick Higher Movement', in Stanley M. Burgess & Eduard M. Van Der Maas (eds), *The New Dictionary of Pentecostal and Charismatic Movements* (Grand Rapids, MI: Zondervan Publishing House, 2002), 820-21.

[12] Y. Lee, *The Holy Spirit Movement in Korea*, 25.

[13] 1910 Edinburgh World Missionary Conference described the great revival in 1907 in Korea as a 'pure Pentecostal experience': World Missionary Conference 1910, *Report of Commission I: Carrying the Gospel to All the Non-Christian World* (Edinburgh and London: Oliphant, Anderson, & Ferrier; New York, Chicago, and Toronto: Fleming H Revell, 1910), 77-80.

and deceived God. Early tomorrow morning I will give that money back to the widow.[14]

Gil's public repentance challenged and inspired many others to follow his example in open confession of their sins. Missionaries also joined in their own public confessions.[15] The Holy Spirit's conviction of sins was the hallmark of the Pyongyang Revival. Other manifestations of the Holy Spirit also appeared: speaking in tongues, and being slain in the Spirit until the next morning by the power of the Holy Spirit. One child was under the conviction of the Holy Spirit and repented for stealing a Chinese pancake. Soon he went back to the store and paid for it. The revival from Pyongyang's Jangdaehyun Church spread throughout the country with the characteristic repentance.[16]

Korea had to go through an extremely difficult time until its independence in 1945, and so did the church. The revival brought an explosion of the church, and its flame was continued by several revival leaders in the next four decades, although the revival itself ran its own course. Christianity, once considered a vanguard of nationalism and independence spirit, became a formidable force for the transformation of individual life. The revival has brought a unique prayer life to the Korean church, beginning with the daily early morning prayer and unison prayer traditions. They were later followed by the prayer mountain movement, weekly (usually Friday) all night prayer, and mass prayer rallies. The revival tradition laid a firm foundation for the surge of the Pentecostal movement. Korean Christianity in general, but the revival tradition in particular, also contributed to social transformation, for example, by leading numerous campaigns to promote a biblical lifestyle, including the prohibition of alcohol and smoking,[17] and taking concubines, as well as promoting a prudent life, diligence, love for farming, the purchase of national products to support industries, and many other initiatives.

---

[14] William Newton Blair & Bruce Hunt, *The Korean Pentecost and the Suffering Which Followed* (Edinburgh: The Banner of Trust, 1977); Kwangsoo Kim, *The History of the People in Korean Christianity* (in Korean) (Seoul: Kidokgeomunsa, 1981), 140-141; for more detail on the ministry and the theology of Rev. Sun-joo Gil, see Y. Lee, *The Holy Spirit Movement in Korea*, 34-39.

[15] For instance, Rev. Hardie confessed his errors and arrogance in public and asked fellow missionaries and national Christians for forgiveness. All the participants then began to weep and repent altogether: Blair & Hunt, *The Korean Pentecost*, 71.

[16] Y. Lee, *The Holy Spirit Movement in Korea*, 29-33; K. Min, *The History of the Korean Church*, 276-81.

[17] International Theological Institute, *A Minister in Yoido: A Biography of Rev. Yonggi Cho* (in Korean) (Seoul: Seoul Logos, 2008), 232; K. Min, *The History of the Korean Church*, 266-267.

David Yonggi Cho and the Yoido Full Gospel Church

God had a plan for the Holy Spirit revival not only to impact Korea, but also to spread to many parts of the world. He took a nation which went through harsh colonial rule and the pains of the Korean War (1950-1953). God also raised up an unlikely individual and his tiny congregation on the outskirts of Seoul among the poor and marginalised. This young man was David Yonggi Cho, and his Yoido Full Gospel Church has now grown to be the largest congregation in the world.[18]

The basis of the growth of Yoido Full Gospel Church is the Pentecostal Holy Spirit movement.[19] Cho started his first church at Daejo-dong, a suburban area of Seoul in 1958.[20] This congregation was quickly known for claims of healing and miracles. First, an alcoholic was healed, and then two women who were deaf and blind. Even a shaman came to repent. Soon the congregation was known for speaking in tongues as the Holy Spirit gave utterance. The message was clear: sin and suffering comes from human separation from God's lordship, and thus the proper solution to any human problem is God's lordship in life. According to this belief, the gospel impacts not only the spiritual aspect of human life, but also the physical and material dimension of daily life. The Daejo-dong tent church grew to six hundred members in three years.[21]

In 1961, when the church moved from the impoverished Daejo-dong to Sudaemun, Seoul's central business district, and the work of the Holy Spirit intensified.[22] Initially people suspected a preference of the wealthy over the marginalised. However, soon the church proved to be a sanctuary from the poor, the sick, and the socially marginal. Once a woman missionary asked Cho, 'Reverend, why are there only sick people in this church? I can't stand the smell. How can our holy Lord come to this smelly place? Try not to gather these people anymore. And go out and preach the Gospel. Teach your congregation how to take a bath'. Cho's answer to the missionary reveals his view of the church's role to the poor and suffering:[23]

> Rightly said, missionary. These people are from heaven's first complex. Why is it the first complex? Because when Jesus comes, they will be the first ones

---

[18] Yonggi Cho launched a tent church with his five family members as church members on May 18, 1958 (Y. Lee, *The Holy Spirit Movement in Korea*, 95).

[19] Vinson Synan, *The Holiness-Pentecostal Tradition: Charismatic Movements in the Twentieth Century* (Michigan: William B. Eerdmans Publishing, 1997), 287; Myung Soo Park, 'David Yonggi Cho and the international Pentecostal/ Charismatic movement', *Journal of Pentecostal Theology* 12:1 (2003), 107.

[20] Y. Lee, *The Holy Spirit Movement in Korea*, 95-96.

[21] Y. Lee, *The Holy Spirit Movement in Korea*, 95; Frank J. Lechner and John Boli, *World Culture: Origins and Consequences* (Oxford: Blackwell Publishing, 2005), 173.

[22] Y. Lee, *The Holy Spirit Movement in Korea*, 96-97.

[23] Yonggi Cho, *A Commentary on the Gospel of Matthew* (Vol. 2) (in Korean) (Seoul: Seoul Logos, 2008), 240-42.

> to go to heaven. It is not that these people are not cleaning themselves because they do not know how to take a bath. During winter they have to go to a public bath for washing but they cannot afford to as they are poor. They can only clean themselves in the summer in the Han River. As a missionary, you must know this. Do you think that Jesus ever took a bath? Foxes have holes and birds have nests but Jesus had to sleep on the mountains and fields because He did not have a place to rest His head. Jesus could only take a bath in the Galilee beach when it rained. Jesus likes poor and smelly people because he belongs to them. Is there any greater news than healing the sick and helping the poor? Isn't this the gospel? Isn't God our healer, and healing the gospel?

Like the Daejo-dong Church, the Full Gospel Central Church was also a church for the poor and the sick. When the Holy Spirit started to work among them, their lives began to be transformed. First, there is regeneration, realising that what is visible in this world is not the full reality. People began to live with hopes of heaven, and naturally began to dedicate themselves to the Lord. They also began to live a sanctified life. Violent husbands became faithful to their wives and families, and those who always borrowed money from others started to lend and share their possessions with others. Church revival was the natural result of such dedication and service to the Lord.

In 1973, Cho made another move for his church to Yoido. In this new location, the church continued its growth, but this time, increased its influence on the wider Christian world. For example, from 1977 until today, the annual Church Growth International (or CGI) conference has been held with thousands of ministers from around the world.

To provide its members with clear identity of faith, vitality in faith and hope in life, Cho developed a theological framework later known as 'The Fivefold Gospel and Threefold Blessing'.[24] The 'Fivefold Gospel' is five principal themes of the Bible: (i) salvation (by faith); (ii) fullness of the Holy Spirit; (iii) (divine) healing; (iv) (divine) blessing; and (v) the second coming of Jesus Christ. His holistic theology of salvation found its expression in 3John 2: 'enjoy good health and that all may go well with you, even as your soul is getting along well'.[25] He tried to emphasise the fact that Jesus came to this world not only to save souls, but also to heal the

[24] Prof. Jürgen Moltmann succinctly summarises and analyses Cho's 'Fivefold Gospel and Threefold Blessing' in his article 'The Blessing of Hope: The Theology of Hope and the Full Gospel of Life', *Journal of Pentecostal Theology* 13:2 (2005), 149-150; Y. Lee, *The Holy Spirit Movement in Korea*, 100-102.

[25] Y. Lee, *The Holy Spirit Movement in Korea*, 97-99.

sick and resolve human suffering.[26] Cho even argued that in the Gospels Jesus often treated salvation and healing as synonymous.[27]

The significance of this theological thinking is not only the new interpretation of salvation, but also its close attention to the social context where the gospel is proclaimed. The message of the fivefold gospel and threefold blessing was a message of hope to the nation, which was suffering poverty, devastation and destruction after the Korean War. To Cho, Christian salvation is holistic, encompassing spiritual, emotional, relational, physical and material levels of human existence.[28] The work and intervention of the Holy Spirit is embodied in the message of hope, healing, miracle and blessing based on the fivefold gospel and the threefold blessing, and this has attracted the poor and marginalised to Yoido Full Gospel Church, which has eventually grown to be the largest congregation in the world.[29] The emphasis on holistic salvation was also expressed at a corporate level when Cho revolutionised church leadership by recruiting, training, empowering and appointing women lay leaders of the church's vast network of cell groups. Considering the male-dominant social culture of Korea, this was a radical decision, but theologically it is well traced to the Pentecostal theology of empowerment. Nonetheless, it is important to note that Cho's notion of salvation until the early 1980s was focused on the personal level.

Yoido Full Gospel Church's Missionary Engagement

Yoido Full Gospel Church's missionary engagement includes salvation, engagement with society and beyond. First, the Church has been strong in missionary engagement in the sense of saving souls. As a congregation committed to Pentecostal beliefs, in 1976 the church sent its first missionaries to minister to overseas Koreans. From 1993, the church has had a strong emphasis on cross-cultural mission.[30] Cho's highly publicised overseas crusades have also changed their focus from North American and European countries to Asia, Africa, Latin America and East Europe. YFGC missionaries have been establishing Bible schools throughout the world to

---

[26] Some references to the healing ministry of Jesus are Matt 4:23; 8:2-4, 14-17, 28-34; 9:1-8, 18-26, 27-31, 32-35, and so on; for Jesus' feeding ministry, see Matt 14:13-21; 15:29-39; Mark 6:34-44; 8:1-9; Luke 9:12-17; John 6:1-13.

[27] For example, Matt 9:21,22; Mark 5:23,28,34; 10:52; Luke 8:36,48,50; 17:19; 18:42; Acts 4:9; 14:9.

[28] Cf. David Yonggi Cho, *Salvation, Health and Prosperity: Our Threefold Blessings in Christ* (Altamonte Springs, FL: Creation House, 1987).

[29] As our church moved to the Yoido area in 1973, it was renamed from Full Gospel Central Church to Yoido Full Gospel Church.

[30] Yoido Full Gospel Church, *The Fiftieth Anniversary of Yoido Full Gospel Church*, 197. To date, our church has sent 727 missionaries in 65 countries; among them are 152 native missionaries in fifty countries.

train national workers and leaders. Today's annual World Missions Conference of the church celebrates its missionary work in many countries of the world.[31]

The cross-cultural missionary work of the church has a strong emphasis on the empowerment of national leadership. This approach is based on its reading of the Great Commission: 'Go and make disciples of all nations, baptising them in the name of the Father and of the Son and of the Holy Spirit, and teaching them to obey everything I have commanded you. And surely I am with you always, to the very end of the age' (Matt 28:19-20). The core of this commandment is 'making disciples'. This is understood as Jesus' disciples going to 'all the ethnic groups' and *making* their leaders *disciples* so that they may in turn take this mandate to their own country and people, and beyond.[32]

Second, the Church's mission vision includes the poor and suffering. As Korean society became politically stabilised and economically developed in the 1980's, the Church's ministries and the focus of its mission gradually started to change. Up to this point, much of the pastoral attention was focused on spiritual regeneration and empowerment to live a victorious Christian life. As theological maturity demanded that Christians reach for a higher purpose, there was a deep process of reflection. The faith of Threefold Blessing was clarified as not self-centred teaching, but a missional commitment to bring transformation to personal and corporate life by practising Christ's ethical teachings. This theological change has given rise to several distinct ministries as a concrete expression of the theological awareness.

The church began to serve the needy in society. An initial inspiration was drawn from Acts 2:44-47 which defines the church's impact to society. The church responded to disasters, both at home and overseas, with relief programmes. In 1982, the Church established a non-profit social programme called the 'Movement of Sharing', and it supported orphanages, nursing homes, the rural poor, impoverished slums and village churches. Support was offered in various forms: voluntary workers, finance, logistics, supplies and books. Free medical aid was given to orphans, seniors living alone, and social welfare recipients. A feeding centre was established to offer hearty meals to unattended seniors. This is a significant shift in the church's mission thinking and practice by bringing the social diakonic element into the existing mission emphasis on evangelism.

This ministry of serving is intensifying as Cho has created another instrument. Around Cho's retirement from his fifty-year pastoral ministry at the Church, the 'Sharing of Love and Happiness Foundation' was created in 2008. He is now devoting himself to a world-wide social relief and development ministry. This full-thrust ministry requires not only many

[31] Yoido Full Gospel Church, *The Fiftieth Anniversary*, 197-99.
[32] Yoido Full Gospel Church, *The Fiftieth Anniversary*, 197.

resources but a more fundamental theological realignment from self-centred faith to self-giving lifestyle. For this reason, the message of 'Threefold blessings' is now adapted with a godly purpose of blessing others. It is encouraging to see the wholehearted and enthusiastic support of, and participation of, the church in this ministry. As the new senior pastor, I publicly pledged my own commitment to fully support Cho's social ministry by equipping and empowering the church to be an instrument of God's transforming power of individuals and society.

Third, the Church has been nurturing the future of society. Among the various ministries of social service, the church's attention to children and youth is noteworthy. In December, 1982, the Church constructed and donated a building complex including a dormitory and a chapel to the Holt Children Services, Inc., a major institution caring for abandoned children and arranging foster families.[33] In 1987, the church also constructed the Elim Welfare Town to provide youth with skills training while caring for homeless seniors.[34] Since 1984, the Church has committed approximately 11 million dollars to underwrite the heart operations for 4,268 children. The church's role to serve society was formally recognised in 1996 by the Korean government which awarded Cho the 'Order of *Mugungwha*', the highest recognition offered to a civilian by the Korean government. This honour recognised particularly the Church's contribution to children's welfare through the heart operations programme for underprivileged children and ministry to orphans.

Fourth, the Church has taken an important decision to play a substantial role in the formation of public culture. This was an important theological shift on the Christian understanding of the world. Christianity is not called to stay isolated from the world, but to transform the world with the gospel teaching. In December 1988, the church began a massive media project by launching the *Kukmin Daily News*, a daily news paper with a distinct perspective drawn from the gospel teaching.[35] It requires enormous financial, personnel and logistical resources. Through the prayer and financial support of the members of the church, the newspaper today has a half million daily subscribers as one of the country's top five newspapers.

The YFGC's heavy investment in education ministries is also another platform for Christianity to make a contribution to the public platform of national life. To cultivate committed leaders to Christian faith, the church recognised the role of higher education. Conscientious Christian professionals can permeate Christian principle in their work places, thus, contributing to national life and global world. The church transformed the

---

[33] Yoido Full Gospel Church, *The Fiftieth Anniversary*, 181. The English website of Holt Children's Services Inc. is www.holt.or.kr/holten/main/main.jsp.

[34] Yoido Full Gospel Church, *The Fiftieth Anniversary*, 185.

[35] Yoido Full Gospel Church, *The Fiftieth Anniversary*, 189.

former Full Gospel Theological School into Hansei University, a reputable Christian liberal arts university.[36]

Fifth, Yoido Full Gospel Church works toward bringing churches together. Just as it is taught in the book of Ephesians to make every effort to keep the unity of the Spirit (Eph. 4:3), the Church has exerted every effort to create unity and agreement among the Korean churches. As Pentecostals are often blamed for creating divisions among Christians, this role is significant. Cho emphasises the personal experience of the Holy Spirit, but he seldom uses the Pentecostal term, 'the baptism of the Holy Spirit'. He prefers to use the term, 'the fullness of the Holy Spirit'. This is to prevent any theological disputes which may cause discord among denominations.[37]

I experienced the Holy Spirit of Pentecost when I was a child, and I am now here in this place to celebrate the centennial of the ecumenical movement because I share with the Holy Spirit the hope to achieve unity. Every year Yoido Church holds an international academic seminar and engages in various joint projects with churches from different denominations. I was a former director of the Theological Committee of The National Council of Churches in Korea (or NCCK), and am now serving as a co-chairperson of the Christian Council of Korea (or CCK), the national body for evangelicals. Furthermore, as the senior pastor of Yoido Full Gospel Church and as the moderator of the NCCK, I am actively involved in a various kinds of ecumenical events throughout the country. The pulpit of the Full Gospel Church accommodates a wide breadth of church traditions, while I am frequently invited to speak among wide variety of church bodies. For example, in 2009 I delivered the opening message at the general assembly of one of the largest Presbyterian denominations as it commemorated the centennial of its mission to Jeju Island, the southern providence of the nation.

---

[36] Yoido Full Gospel Church, *The Fiftieth Anniversary*, 191-93. Dr. Sunghae Kim, who is Rev. Yonggi Cho's wife, is currently the president of Hansei University (www.hansei.ac.kr/global/en/index.html).

[37] Dr. William Menzies, who is a theologian of the U.S. Assemblies of God, has often asked Rev. Yonggi Cho, who likes to use the term, 'the fullness of the Holy Spirit', to use the term, 'the baptism in the Holy Spirit' instead in public because the former is not the terminology of the Assemblies of God. However, Rev. Cho has thus far refused his request for the sake of the unity of the churches. Jack Hayford, who is a pastor of the U.S. Four Square Church suggested at the Lausanne Conference in Manila in 1989 to use the 'group of the Fullness in the Holy Spirit' instead of 'charismatic' or 'Pentecostal' churches (Russell Spittler, 'Perspectives on the Pentecostalism' in Harold Smith, *Pentecostals from the Inside Out* (Wheaton, IL: Victor Books, 1990). As long as the theological debate on the baptism in the Holy Spirit is still going on, we had better use the term 'the fullness in the Holy Spirit' for the pastoral intention to narrow the distance between denominations, and to be united as one in Christ.

Additionally, the YFGC has participated in, and provided leadership for, many interdenominational joint projects. Every year the church records the highest number of worshippers at the Joint Easter Service. I was invited as the main preacher at the 2010 Joint Easter Service, at which more than twenty thousand believers from all different churches and denominations gathered at the City Plaza in downtown Seoul early Easter morning.

As I look back on the past century, I find it regrettable that the Holy Spirit movement and ecumenism have been regarded as mutually incompatible. In the Pentecostal movement, there have been ecumenical heroes. Seeking to achieve unity and agreement in church, David du Plessis, who is called Mr Pentecost, preached a Pentecostal message to the Pope in Rome, even though he was threatened with losing his denominational affiliation if he did so.[38] The Holy Spirit, however, is the Spirit of unity. On the instruction of the Holy Spirit, Peter risked exposing himself to criticism by entering the house of Cornelius, the Gentile, and sharing the Gospel with him (Acts 10:1-11:18). The Yoido Full Gospel Church will continue to exercise its ecumenical leadership in the coming years not only within Korea but also at the global levels.

Sixth, love and peace-building is a unique gift that Christians can offer to divided society and broken relationships. One strong motivation for the care for the poor and marginalised is to bring reconciliation in society. Often the marginalised are the victims of unequal distribution of wealth or an unjust social structure. The victims are socially wounded, or people of *han* ('grudge'), according to Korean minjung theology. Therefore, without the practice of love and peace-building, restoration of harmony and justice is simply impossible. True people of God's blessing are those who embrace their neighbours and society with Christian love to foster peace and harmony.[39] This is the goal of Yoido Full Gospel Church's Sharing of Love and Happiness Foundation.

In spite of continuing social and economic development, the Korean society is currently facing numerous social challenges. The biggest is the current tension between North and South Korea, with the steady flow of North Korean refugees to South. Other social problems are labour-management disputes, ideological divisions, an increase in marital breakdown, unwanted and abandoned children, abortions, babies born out of wedlock, low birthrates, and so on. Some of these are symptoms of the steady slide of moral values, family life and increasing egoism, and they call for a strong role for the church. For example, the churches have a unique role in providing humanitarian support to lessen the food shortages of North Korea. Yoido Full Gospel Church's great investment in North

---

[38] Because of this, David du Plessis was deprived of his certificate of affiliation by the Assemblies of God in the USA.

[39] Yonggi Cho, 'Sharing of Love and Happiness'. Sermon at the thanksgiving worship service for the Fifty Anniversary of the Foundation of Yoido Full Gospel Church on 18 May 2008.

Korea in building a large-scale cardiac hospital is a visible expression of the church's commitment to this national agenda. Another area which demands the church's immediate missional attention is the increasing number of immigrant workers in Korea and the many problems which arise from this new social situation. Like many churches, the Yoido Full Gospel Church has developed not only an English-speaking congregation, but also services for various language groups. Often such spaces provide social networking among immigrant workers from a same country. Such a social change also provides unprecedented missionary opportunities. Many of the immigrant labourers return home now as Christians, and some with completed seminary education in Korea. Many Chinese Koreans and Taiwanese have experienced the transforming work of the Holy Spirit at Yoido Full Gospel Church. As they return, they often go home with a deep sense of the missionary mandates. Naturally the church makes efforts to support their ministries by providing training, prayer and financial support.

Finally, Yoido Full Gospel Church is experiencing another important mission paradigm shift. In 2005, during the church's opening service for the New Year, Cho confessed the shortcoming of his concept of holistic salvation. In his assessment, he said the message of personal salvation and social engagement is not sufficient to fulfil God's missional call. Interpreting John 3:16, he pointed out that 'God so loved the **world**' and the world is more than human beings.

> Just recently I found out many insufficiencies of my forty-seven years of ministry. The Bible says, 'For God so loved the world that he gave his only Son, so that everyone who believes in him may not perish but have eternal life' (NRSV). All these years, I had misinterpreted it. I understood that God so loved 'human beings', not 'the world', that he gave his only Son. What is the world? In the world, there are all things, including people, society, sky, land, ocean, plants, insects and animals. The Bible says that God so loved the 'world' that he gave his only Son; it does not limit the scope of the world to human beings, and say that God so loved them all. 1 John 5:19 also reads that the world is under the control of the evil one. I thought that the evil one only controlled human beings not the world, which is why my message and salvation ministry, up to now, have been restricted to human beings.[40]

He contended that his limited understanding of the scope of God's plan for salvation had kept him from participating in God's integral salvation ministry in personal, social and environmental dimensions. He believed, 'The fall of Adam is a universal event that became the origin of social evil and the decay of the environment. As result of Adam's sin, the devil took control not only of humankind, but also of the society as well as the environment. Therefore, salvation without including our commitment to care for the ecosystem cannot be considered a holistic salvation'. Cho declared, 'From this New Year [that is, year 2005], we will bring about salvation of our souls, get rid of social evils, and actively work toward

[40] Yonggi Cho, 'Sermon at the Opening Service for the New Year 2005'.

environmental protection'. This shift toward stewardship of God's creation has since had a strong impact on each member of the church, and its mission policies and practices. This message was welcomed by many scholars from within and without. Prof. Jürgen Moltmann, for instance, learned of Cho's message, and completely supported his 'shift in policy' by sending Cho an e-mail message. Moltmann said, 'If the Yoido Full Gospel Church can save souls, save society and restore the environment, then I can assure you that this church can be a church that will embrace the world'.[41]

The Best Way…

Having surveyed the formation of the Holy Spirit movement in Korea and the missionary engagement of the Yoido Full Gospel Church, several points deserve our attention. The shift in mission and pastoral ministry of the YFGC does not imply any change in the traditional Pentecostal understanding of the person and work of the Holy Spirit. Experience of the fullness of the Holy Spirit is all the more required to fulfil the church's mission to bring good news to the poor and the sick (Luke 4:18-19). The book of Acts teaches us that supplying one another's needs in the early church was a natural expression of hearts filled with the Holy Spirit. In fact, without the transforming work and power of the Holy Spirit, no true change can be possible, ranging from spiritual regeneration to behavioural change and social transformation. Without the Holy Spirit touching our hearts, we cannot even practise love. This is the true expression of the Spirit's empowering presence. The missionary work of the Church will continue to anchor itself on belief in the Holy Spirit.

When I look back on modern Pentecostal history, I cannot but acknowledge the criticism of Pentecostals' spirit of triumphalism. The glowing success in missionary work and the exponential spread of the Pentecostal movement may have contributed to this perception. However, the truth is that all missionary work is the work of the Holy Spirit and it has been done only through the grace of God. Thus, one should humble oneself and approach ministries with the spirit of *humility*. We must glorify God alone, and our confession should be 'We are unworthy servants. We have only done our duty' (Luke 17:10b). We are only messengers of the gospel of the cross and God's love. God empowered us to achieve his goal faithfully. We at Yoido Full Gospel Church well recognise this point and will do our best to bring God's message of salvation and love in the power of the Spirit with the heart of humility. So may God help us all to be faithful in our missionary call.

---

[41] The entire content of Prof. Moltmann's email is in the 13 February 13 2005 issue of the *Full Gospel Family Newspaper* (www.fgnews.co.kr/).

Case Study 2
Ecumenical Charity as Christian Witness

Dr Antonios Kireopoulos, Associate General Secretary, Faith & Order and Interfaith Relations, National Council of Churches USA[1]

As I begin, I wish to thank the organisers of this centenary commemoration of the Edinburgh 1910 World Missionary Conference. And let me also express my appreciation for being on this panel with these valued colleagues.

When I was a teenager, I belonged to a very active youth group in my local church. The group was led by a life-long member of the Greek Orthodox community, a good natured man whose religious experience included a kind of conversion of the heart that led to what I'd call an evangelical zeal, for both Christ and for Orthodoxy. His goal in our group, and thus his mission, was to help young people keep their faith at the centre of their lives.

One time in a private conversation, he told me that, in evangelising, if necessary to seal the deal with a potential convert, he would not hesitate to be less than honest, say about a particular biblical claim or an Orthodox doctrine, in order to win the person over to Christian faith. At the time, I was equally shocked and I must admit quite amused. I knew he was sincere in his concern for the spiritual life of his hypothetical interlocutor. But even at that time, when I was still a long way off from a theological vocation, I wondered if such a contradictory approach could lead to a genuine conversion.

Ecumenical Charity

Thinking about my remarks here today, I remembered this conversation from my past. And I believe it has significant relevance as we talk about mission. And I suggest that it begs questions about what makes for authentic mission, about the complex mix of sincerity of witness and church growth goals, and even about the genuineness of conversion. These

---

[1] For further biodata, see Appendix 4.

questions are made that much more urgent when we contemplate the extent to which churches favourably or unfavourably regard one another. This regard can be called 'ecumenical charity'.

'Ecumenical charity' is here defined as care, concern, and even affection of one church for another; a kind of relationship that is characterised by respect between the churches. These kinds of relations reveal an appreciation for the gifts of the other churches involved, and a willingness to share their respective burdens. In the presence of such relations, genuine evangelisation and authentic conversion can take place. In the absence of such relations, missionary efforts can clash rather than complement each other, they can introduce a denominational Jesus instead of the universal Christ, and they can lead to a diseased proclamation of the Gospel in place of the healing touch of the Good News.

The Roman Catholic – World Council of Churches working group addressed some of these issues. Particularly helpful was the delineation between what I like to call good (or appropriate) evangelism and bad (or inappropriate) proselytism. Proselytism gets a lot of attention these days when used in the context of missionary efforts in Muslim countries. But it's most harmful use is when Christians, while ostensibly seeking to make Christians from among people of other faiths, instead strive to make Christians from among people that are already Christians. What kind of evangelism is that?

I was asked to illustrate two contemporary cases studies that illustrate how various degrees of ecumenical charity impact mission. I will describe one negative example, and one positive example. I will also use examples of mission activity that stem from my own country, the United States. One example will illustrate mission understood in traditional terms, in which Christians go from one context to another in order to preach the Gospel; the other example will illustrate an expanded definition of mission, that of standing with the oppressed as a witness of the Gospel's message of justice that is inherently part of its message of salvation. It is important to note that I do not intend to generalise about a particular tradition or another, but to highlight sharply emblematic examples that are illustrative of intentional ecumenical charity and its opposite.

Mission Which Takes Advantage of the Weak

On the negative side, I could cite, of course, numerous examples of this kind of dubious behaviour. We are all familiar with the experience in Russia and other countries of Eastern Europe immediately after the fall of the Soviet system, when missionaries, generally but not only from evangelical or fundamentalist Protestant communities in the US, took advantage of the weak situation of the people, seeing them as 'heathens' who needed to be converted rather than as brothers and sisters whose Orthodox Christian self-understanding was just beginning to be resurrected after some seven decades in a virtual tomb. Even the unfortunate use of traditionally Orthodox ecclesiastical titles by the local Roman Catholic hierarchy in this same period and context could be understood in these terms. Likewise, I could lift up the example of Sri Lanka after the tsunami of 2004, when some apparently fringe missionary groups reportedly exploited the people's suffering in order to attract them to the Christ of certain material blessings, to their brand of Christ at the expense of the local Christians who were certainly suffering and in need of consolation from fellow Christians. Or, I could point to the Orthodox experience in the United States, which as a diverse immigrant community has often preoccupied itself more with 'protecting' a diaspora flock in a sort of self-satisfied isolation than with intentional critical engagement, and thus witness, alongside other Christian communities in social issues that confront all of us.

But I would like to focus in on one particularly egregious missionary effort, this one in Iraq. We all know the terrible suffering that has gone on in Iraq since the beginning of this current war of choice begun by the United States, and how much of this suffering has been borne by the Christian communities that have lived in that country since time immemorial. At the National Council of Churches USA, we have had visits from two of these communities, the Armenian Orthodox and the Chaldean Catholic.

One evening a few years ago, I was winding down in a hotel room after a long day at one of our annual general assemblies, and I was flipping channels on the television when I happened upon a religious programme about Christians in Iraq. I was pleasantly surprised – at first – because this was a channel owned by the ministry of one of the most famous, or infamous, televangelists on the religious right, and here was the announcer talking about the suffering, and even martyrdom, of Christians in these ancient communities. There was film of liturgical celebrations and social ministries being shown, and the speaker offered complimentary comments about these men, women and children, about their bravery, and he lamented the fact that so many of them nevertheless felt compelled to flee their country to escape the ravages of war.

So far, so good. But these charitable sentiments were not to last. The announcer immediately began to contrast these Christians with converts to a mission community supported by the televangelist. He praised the latter for not leaving, for sticking it out through the difficulties of war, basically characterising them as true Christians thus giving a robust witness to Christ and by implication not wavering in their faith like their apparently feckless neighbours. I don't doubt the sincerity of the Iraqis who made up this mission community; but it was dismaying to see these Christians set up as the faithful over and against other Christians as the faithless.

I do not know if the Iraqis in that particular mission community were converts from Islam – a logical conclusion, one would think, if watching this broadcast – or converts from one of the local Christian communities – probably the case here, and a common phenomenon across the last couple hundred years in every mission field, such as in the Middle East in the late nineteenth and early twentieth centuries, or Eastern Europe even until today. Nevertheless, in a land of other faiths, the focus of this story was on how one brand of Christianity was witnessing better than another brand of Christianity, even at the expense of the latter.

And yet, how much more powerful would the witness to Christ have been if the missionaries sent to Iraq were there in support of the local Christians, to work with the local Christian churches to foster reconciliation in their communities torn apart by war? In other words, where, my friends, was the notion that, instead of fragmenting the Iraqi Christian community by such divisiveness, it might have been a good idea to mount a missionary effort precisely to build up the Christians who were there already, as we are exhorted to do in 1 Thessalonians 5:11?

Ministering to the Needs of the People

Conversely, on the positive side, I could cite numerous examples of good behaviour in the mission field. For example, there is an American Jesuit engaged in building projects at a local Catholic parish in Ghana who, side-by-side with his Orthodox and Protestant counterparts, works to alleviate the suffering of the poor. I could also point to the example of the partnership of the Orthodox Christian Mission Centre (an American pan-Orthodox initiative) with the Orthodox Church in Albania, whose leader His Beatitude Archbishop Anastasios Yannoulatos is widely respected, and whose Christian vocation has nurtured the rebirth of the Church in Albania even as it has led to the betterment of the situation of all people, Christians and Muslims alike, after years of totalitarian oppression.

You will note in these two examples that, in proclaiming the Word of Christ, central to the proclamation is ministering to the needs of the people. In the Ghanaian example, digging water wells is as much a part of Christian mission as preaching in the church. In the Albanian example, Archbishop Yannoulatos, when asked once what he needed most to help in his ministry, is famously quoted in the US (and probably elsewhere) for answering, 'a tractor'. I could add to this list the ministry of the prominent American preacher, with his televised globe-trotting revivals which still serve as a positive template for mission. He sought to console people in their difficult circumstances – different in each context – even as he urged zealous converts to attend local churches – or to return to their own churches after answering his altar calls if they were already, although now reenergised, Christians.

But here I want to focus on a different type of mission, one that expresses itself in solidarity with the oppressed (which could be understood in any number of ways but is here understood in terms of the poor and politically downtrodden). And this is the work of the Friends community. Like, and along with, many mainline Protestant communities – and through ecumenical ties the Orthodox and Catholic communities – the Friends have a long history of advocating for peace in the Middle East. Today their work centres on development, primarily through the American Friends Service Committee.

The American Friends Service Committee's work in the Middle East today is primarily in development and peace-building. This takes the form of developing youth as bridge-builders in Palestine, of fostering dialogue between Muslims and Christians in Iran, and advocating (based on indigenous input from the region) for constructive US policy with regard to its peacemaking role throughout the region. This latter witness is generally done in partnership with other Christian communities. Their folks engaged in mission – certainly in mission more broadly defined than usually understood – seek to proclaim Christ through living out the Gospel they preach.

What does this type of witness say to the people of other faiths that live in the region? That being a Christian compels a believer, no matter their tradition or denomination, to seek peace and justice on behalf of the poor and oppressed. It may 'win' converts from other faiths; it may not. God is the director of all hearts. And this is the attitude that leads to genuine proclamation, and if God ordains, to genuine conversion.

Mission and Unity

These are just two examples, set within the context of many. These stories can be complemented by scores of others – good and bad in every tradition -- that are rooted in your own homelands. I offer them here today as fodder for discussion.

At the opening event of the conference, in one of the prayers we remembered that

> One hundred years ago in this city, men and women who were engaged in mission came together from every part of the globe. As they told their stories and prayed for each other, they were surprised by the Spirit with a moment of inspiration, when they glimpsed a vision of a united church speaking with one voice the name of Christ, and saw within grasp a world won for the gospel.

It is my hope that, at this conference, we would reflect upon what it means to be ecumenically charitable – to trust the witness of each church as good and pointing to salvation – which, my friends, is at the heart of the issue – and how our witness might contribute to this dream that we 'may all be one… so that the world may believe…' (John 17:21).

Again, I thank the organisers of this conference for giving us the opportunity to indeed converse about what it means to be engaged in 'mission worldwide'. I thank my colleagues up here on the dais with me for their important contributions. And I thank you for what I know will be a good discussion to follow.

CASE STUDY 3

A MISSING MISSION? THE 'BUDDING ECUMENISM' FORMATION PROJECT OF THE CENTRO PRO UNIONE

Dr Prof. Teresa Francesca Rossi, Associate Director, Centro Pro Unione, Rome[1]

The Budding Ecumenism Initiative

'*Ecumenismo in erba*' is a formation project of Centro Pro Unione, an ecumenical research centre and library founded and directed by the Franciscan Friars of the Atonement in Rome (*erba* means *grass*). The original Italian title in English can be translated into two different ways: 'Grass-root ecumenism' or 'Budding ecumenism': (i) 'Grass-root ecumenism' since it is an initiative of reception at a grass-root level; or (ii) 'Budding ecumenism' since it is directed to children; today's children will be tomorrow's faithful, and it is important that they can grow with a sense of the reconciling mission of the Church and what is the ecumenical movement. 'Budding ecumenism' aims at creating a Christian texture in which ecumenical awareness and dialogue, unity and common mission will no longer be considered secondary options for Christians. And it is fundamental that children experience all of this as they are still not taller than the grass!

The grass is also the place where children usually play and have fun. And this is probably the most important, maybe innovative, aspect of the initiative: the method that '*Ecumenismo in erba*' follows – or, as we will call it: the 'budding method' – is a *ludo-mathetic* one ('learning through the games' from the ethymological roots *matheo* – to learn and *ludus* – game), namely one where children are introduced to the principles and practice of ecumenism through an interactive, interdisciplinary, game-based methodology. 'Budding ecumenism' attempts to convey the content, methodology and spirituality of ecumenical dialogue into the life of the children, to the future generations, through mini-conferences, games and quizzes, videos, and so on, because by playing together children establish

[1] For further biodata, see Appendix 4.

relations among themselves, learn in a spontaneous way, are existentially involved.

The initiative addresses primary and secondary schools (5 to 13 year-old children), as well as groups from parishes, especially children preparing themselves to receive the Holy Communion or the Confirmation. The initiative started as a pilot project almost a decade ago. The preparatory process, from the very first inspiration to the finalisation of the standard session took about 2 years (2003-2005). Three years (2005-2007) have followed of testing the project; the current phase is the one in which we are producing the material in form of a booklet (2008-2010).

A Missing Mission

In the question posed in the title of my presentation – 'A missing mission?' – there is a twofold meaning to be grasped: missing is used in an effective as well as in an affective way: (i) In an effective way as something that should be there and it is not, something lacking. This refers mainly to the aspect of addressing children in ecumenical formation. In fact, Jesus' words concerning the children[2] remind us that children can be a privileged target even in ecumenical formation, and in an evangelisation which has the unity of the Church at its heart, because they have a quality that adults do not have, or have to conquer: they trust. One could deceive children very easily, something that is not possible with any other category of people. So children are quite suitable for ecumenical literacy. (ii) In an affective way as something that is missed in the sense of nostalgia for a unity that was there, that the Church of Christ once knew, that needs restoring and is strongly missed. A mission that bears nostalgia. For this reason, the project of 'Budding ecumenism' is by no means akin to the many projects concerning education for tolerance. Tolerance is definitely important, especially in the new pluralistic contexts, but here the purpose is another and different, for the matter at stake is conveying the idea of a unity to be restored, and of a story of how people of good will try to cooperate with the power of the Holy Spirit to restore it. In this sense it does not have to do with finding a way of co-existing for different cultures – somehow *ab extrinseco*, from the outside – but it has to do with searching for that *koinonia* that already unites in an invisible way and with making that explicit and visible – definitely *ab intrinseco*, from the inside.

Manifold competences have been at work to feature the initiative. The backstage work implies a team of people working basically in three fields, a team which had to submit itself to a quite accurate process of learning new dynamics and new languages before performing: psychology experts have outlined the mainlines of the learning process dynamics and potentialities

---

[2] Luke 18:16: 'Let the children come to me, and do not stop them, for it is to such as these that the kingdom of God belongs'.

in children according to the different ages of the children targeted, so that the best methodology in *ludo-mathetics* could be applied.[3] Experts in the fields of theology and ecumenism have selected the different issues to be presented to the children;[4] the biblical-catechetical framework, as well as the coordination of the liturgical celebration, were the task of a catechist and liturgist with four decades of experience.[5] And experts in the entertainment of children have helped us for the *ludo-mathetic* part: to play with the children, but also to select – under theological supervision – games, quizzes, prizes, simulations, dramatisation of Gospel, and competition according to the requirements of the ecumenical message to be conveyed. Although the core of the project is to link together fun and theology, pedagogically speaking, there must be a distinctiveness (not a separation) between the amusing part and the catechetical part in order to help the children perceive that, no matter how much fun they can have, the content they are dealing with is very serious.[6]

---

[3] One of these was Dr Prof. Antonella Pacini, Primary Physician of the Department of Neuropsychiatry of Ospedale San Giovanni-Addolorata in Rome, who is specialised in infant neuropsychiatry. She is a wonderful person, very talented as a woman, as a doctor, and as a faithful. I interviewed her several times on the whole process of infant learning as we had to structure into a concrete plan of session the ecumenical-theological contents, conveying the fundamental principles, guidelines and expectations of the learning process for each different age it was oriented to: from the 'magic thought' of 3 to 5 year-old children, toward the more conceptualized ideas of 6 to 8 and 10 to 12 year-olds.

[4] The contents of ecumenism were presented by myself and by the Director of the Centro Pro Unione, Rev. Dr Prof. James Puglisi, SA., who is Ordinary Professor in Liturgy at the Pontifical Atheneum St Anselm in Rome, and also Professor and Coordinator of the Department for Ecumenical Studies of the Pontifical University St Thomas Aquinas in Rome (as well as in other universities). I am professor of ecumenism at the Pontifical University St Thomas Aquinas in Rome and in some other universities and institutions. For that occasion, we both had to re-think our 'ecumenical package' in order to conceptualize it in a new way, accessible to children. It was an interesting journey for us as well.

[5] This was Mrs Elena Bellasina, for various decades responsible for the Catechetical Office and also Coordinator of the Liturgical Commission, at the Parrocchia Santo Nome di Maria in Rome, as well as a catechist herself. She has also cooperated with the Office for Catechism and the Cathecumenate for the Diocese of Rome. She has been an invaluable support, able to create an event-atmosphere less than ten minutes after the children had taken their seats.

[6] Among many candidates, I have chosen a team called 'Babytime', who usually spend time, for free, to entertain the children of the Bambin Gesù Hospital, a specialised hospital for children, and who also give a percentage of their profit to cooperate in a project to build a guest house for the families of children who are not resident in Rome yet are patients of the hospital.

Method and Message

Each session is arranged in different moments.[7] In general, classes and groups are invited to come to the Centro Pro Unione – two classes per time is the most suitable number – roughly for three hours.

The welcome is very important, and here the Franciscan spirituality which inspires the Centro proves to be very helpful. The whole Centro Pro Unione Staff is there to welcome the children to convey the idea that we take their presence very seriously, as an important visit for the life of the Centro. The entrance of the Centro has a welcome poster with the name of the school or parish. A guest book is open to invite student to leave their signature; a small, multicoloured badge is given to them to write their name on it, which will facilitate interaction, as a sociologically 'first group' has to be. The Conference room of the Centro Pro Unione is a beautiful old Library dating back to the sixteenth century – austere, brown and hung with bordeaux tapestries, which is meant to help concentration and silence. It is a fascinating room which, for the occasion, is transformed into a joyful, coloured welcoming space. Pillows and balloons are arranged in such a way as to suggest a virtual grass-root place. It is not an unanswered message: the children's reaction is attentiveness, receptiveness, enthusiasm, willingness to cooperate and to establish personal relationships with us.

The sessions include mini-conferences, presentations and videos. These lectures are *mini* because they are concept-focused; aiming at making them grasp a paradigm, not to be exhaustive. The theoretical journey of the children starts with the biblical framework, by recalling the history of some Israeli people, both from Old and New Testament; human stories of jealousy, fighting and division. Sometimes a reconciliation follows and a new path unfolds (Esau and Jacob; Paul and Barnabas – unlike Abel and Cain) and it produces sharing of gifts and riches, beside joy and peace of the heart. The journey continues with the ecumenical journey: they learn that the first Christians were united and that they have later been split into several denominations, which have been struggling one against the other. But children also learn about the many initiatives of the ecumenical movement to overcome those divisions. The goals achieved in the ecumenical movement are presented in their religious as well as historical or socio-cultural relevance (for example, the World Council of Churches 'Decade to Overcome Violence', the Popes meeting other religious leaders, and so on). Local belonging is an important element children have to learn: an ecumenical map of Italy is shown and explained.

The meta-message (namely what they learn without perceiving it) is, first, that division is an anthropological possibility as well as the paradigm

[7] See the video presented during the plenary at Edinburgh 2010, which is available at the Centro Pro Unione website: www.prounione.urbe.it. The video presents some moments of the different sessions in a snapshot way, as well as in a scattered sequences.

of human behaviour and weakness. Through the stories of these people, children learn that division has always been a great temptation (often we start the session asking the children about experiences of misunderstandings, fighting, division they might have had), but that it can be overcome and reconciled. Second, the meta-message is that *koinonia* is an anthropological need. The second stage is, in fact, to call for the necessary reconstruction of the broken relationships, on the anthropological as well as ecclesial level. Communion and sharing is shown to be the natural condition for human beings, whereas division bring loneliness, and loneliness goes nowhere. On the contrary, a multitude of people brings diversity and diversity brings complementarity and reciprocity. Being together is the condition to realise the big deal! This has to be felt as an experiential reality, and therefore it is presented through games.

Integral to each session are tests, quizzes and prizes. There is no commitment, without a personal achievement. The future of the information children receive (whether they will be kept and learnt or just forgotten) depends upon the emotions associated with it: personal effort, public recognition and an appealing reward is a good pedagogical companion to reach the goal of active learning and knowledge. For this reason, from the very beginning, while inviting them to relax and enjoy the morning, we also warn them to carefully listen to what will be explained to them! There will be, in fact, an *interrogazione*: a final test! And that, instead of a mark, they will get a prize! The test has been, in fact, carefully planned by us. It has to be a moment of real verification (also important for us, to taste the validity of the structure of the meeting and the fulfilment of its intentions) as well as testing the yield of the infomation given. Contemporary pedagogical theories are the basis for the verification part.[8] They emphasise the need to have different typologies of tests and exams in order to ensure that children, who have different talents and different ways of learning, can give their best in the format which is best for them.

Such tests are prepared according to various patterns: the most enjoyable and quick-to-catch are the team-test and the treasure hunt. Questions are precise and require either a write/wrong or yes/no answer, and also multiple-choice questions. Children are split into several groups; they are asked to name a leader charged with answering on behalf of the group; there is a time to reflect and a time to answer; time is counted. It is funny to see how children (and even teenagers) are creative in finding a good name for their team ('Fats and furious' [*sic*!], 'Tottiñe', 'Wolves', ...) and to see how, in a context like that, even simply answering the question 'How many churches belong to the World Council of Churches?' becomes a life-or-death issue! This is the wonder of the children's world! The purpose of having them split into teams is to have a mix of sharing and competition,

---

[8] Especially scholars such as: Ausubel, Bruner, Kirton, Kofka, Koheler, Kolbert, Marshall, Merrit, and Pavlov.

which is a good mix for learning. The setting for the treasure hunt is similar; usually it is only two teams. Indications on how to find the final treasure are given only after they have answered a question on ecumenism. It is chaos!

The result of the test is usually quite good: they have acquired some basic information regarding the ecumenical movement and the ecumenical map of Italy. Sometimes, an extraordinary schedule may include a short trip to Piazza Navona, with the whole group holding their balloons with a printed phase: '*Siamo piccoli ecumenisti!*' ('We are small ecumenists'). While walking through the piazza, we will throw the balloons away to symbolise the need to spread the good news about ecumenism.

Groups of children coming from parishes or private (Catholic) schools, can experience a moment of *prayer* for unity, prepared by the children under the guidance of experts. The basic idea of the whole project is that the children are co-subjects, therefore everyone is taking part to it; everyone has his/her own role. They all prepare the liturgy, under the guidance of the liturgist, often practising for a long time. Some sing, others prepare themselves for the lectures, while others write their own intentions of the faithful, and so on, and then they rehearse or refine their contribution according to the guidance of the liturgist. The atmosphere is now very quiet and concentrated, and when they are ready the short but intense celebration begins in an area separated from the rest of the room where games and fun were ruling, and appropriately prepared for the liturgy.

For most of the children being fully involved in the preparation of ecumenical acts, such as, blessing the water together with the priest, or recalling our baptismal call as Christians, is something they have never experienced. So the meta-message is important as (i) they attend their first *ecumenical* worship, in the sense that it is focused on unity, peace, reconciliation, common baptism; and (ii) they learn some principles of liturgical cooperation, and the ABC of dialogue (such as avoiding elements that are not shared by every confession, finding symbols to express their prayer for peace, and their commitment to grow as Christians). Through it they learn principles of dialogue, as well as the importance of spiritual ecumenism.

An Appraisal

The reception of the initiative has been very encouraging, though we are aware that, being simply a pilot project we have a limited feedback. I would like to make three remarks as an important evaluation of the initiative for us.

First, the project is an initiative of ecumenical reception and formation, attempting to put into practice the fundamental principles of ecumenical formation, as they are set in official documents of the churches –

particularly the Catholic Church – and by studies of experts in the field.[9] As ecumenists we are always very much concerned with reception issues and how to grant a future to our ecumenical efforts; how to turn ecumenism from professional/expert circles into church life. In particular, the pillar-principles are: (i) That ecumenical formation is for everyone as the 'concern for restoring unity pertains to the whole Church'.[10] Therefore, the Pontifical Council for Promoting Christian Unity, *Directory for the Applications of the Principles and Norms on Ecumenism* states that 'The objective of ecumenical formation is that all Christians be animated by the ecumenical spirit, whatever their particular mission and task in the world and in the society'.[11] There is a fundamental concept to support reception: ecumenical formation should be a priority in all levels of the Church, addressed accordingly to the different status and vocations in the life of the Church. (ii) That ecumenical formation requires a human maturity. The content conveyed by ecumenical programmes has to be both informative and formative as it is about equipping people with an ecumenical mentality. Ecumenism and the call to unity belong to very core of the Christian vocation, for Christ's prayer and will for unity must be made one's own by everybody. Ecumenism is not finding a Lutheran or a Waldensian to dialogue with, but providing a perspective on the Church, awakening a responsibility in the faithful and enabling to a more meaningful Christian witness to the world. This involves a human maturity that has to be acquired; a long-term process which has to be started as soon as possible. In this perspective it is important that the places for ecumenical formation should be: 'the places where human and Christian maturity, the sense of companionship and communion, grow step by step'.[12] The same passage of the *Directory* calls explicitly for an involvement of families, parishes, schools, educational agencies.[13] (iii) That ecumenical formation should be

---

[9] See the Pontifical Council for Promoting Christian Unity, *Directory for the Applications of the Norms and Principles on Ecumenism*, 1993 (available at www.vatican.va); Pontifical Council for Promoting Christian Unity, *The Ecumenical Dimension in the Formation of Those Engaged in Pastoral Work*, 1997 (available at www.vatican.va). See also: Joint Working Group between the Catholic Church and the World Council of Churches, 'Ecumenical Formation. Ecumenical Reflections and Suggestions', in the Joint Working Group, *Seventh Report*, 1998 (available at www.oikoumene.org).

[10] 'The attainment of union is the concern of the whole Church, faithful and shepherds alike. This concern extends to everyone, according to his talent, whether it be exercised in his daily Christian life or in his theological and historical research.' (*Unitatis Redintegratio*, n. 5). See also Pontifical Council for Promoting Christian Unity, *Directory for the Applications of the Principles and Norms on Ecumenism*, n. 55.

[11] Pontifical Council for Promoting Christian Unity, *Directory*, n. 58.

[12] Pontifical Council for Promoting Christian Unity, *Directory*, n. 65.

[13] Pontifical Council for Promoting Christian Unity, *Directory*, nn. 59-63.

interdisciplinary.[14] Ecumenism should be a concern that crosses all the disciplines, not only in theology but also in religious as well as in human education. The goal of 'Budding ecumenism' is to educate to dialogue, beginning with the very anthropological dimension; however, it is by no means something springing from a widespread sense of tolerance or with a purpose of education to respect to otherness; 'Budding ecumenism' deals specifically with the Christian call to this imperative. It is pastoral towards the Church as well as educative towards society. (iv) That the learning process has to be carried out on a doctrinal as well as on an experimental level.[15]

My second remark is that, though this is a narrow targeted initiative, it can be developed and spread in many different ways. It was a surprise that, although the initiative was meant primarily for the Catholic schools, it turned out that public schools were interested, as well as – as expected – parish groups. Also, we had fixed 5 to 12 years-old as the best target, but we also received requests for 13-15 years.[16] The initiative also reached the adults: parents as well as teachers. Some material prepared for them was given to the teachers – basic, though rigorous and full, with first-hand resources – to give them the possibility to continue the same discourse. Some teachers' feedback has been quite positive, especially since this is not a proselytising initiative, nor a 'politically incorrect' one. Ecumenism, in fact is self-explicatory and self-promoting in the sense that the audience was able, despite their religious belief, to understand and positively consider the value of a culture of dialogue to be presented to the children as well as the importance of the ecumenical movement from the historical, cultural, social and political viewpoints.

Concerning the future: an interesting – although not easily to realise experience – would be to take a sample-class to be followed in the long term, to see what kind of impact dialogue and ecumenism has had in the life of the *ecumenisti in erba*, and whether and how it has helped their process of formation.

---

[14] Pontifical Council for Promoting Christian Unity, *Directory*, n. 65.

[15] Pontifical Council for Promoting Christian Unity, *Directory*, n. 65.

[16] We were not ready to deal with the old age-group properly (we do the same kind of formation to high school students, though without the 'budding method'), though we do welcome classes of more adult high school students (14 to 18 years old) at the Centro, and we present to them a session – in a ordinary lecture style – about the reconciliation of memories process and the important theological agreements, as well on the World Council of Churches, the history of the Catholic Church commitment to ecumenism, and the relevance of some events which have taken place recently in the Catholic Church, such as the request of forgiveness on behalf of the Catholic Church which Pope John Paul II issued in year 2000. In our original format we also had guidelines for session for 3-6 year-old children, though we never really experienced it, as it would require a new, more specific learning process for the team itself.

Third, this programme could be a segment of longer ecumenical formation programmes. It is vital for the formation of the future generation of those who will form others in ecumenism at a grassroots level. My hope is that the Centro will in the future organise courses to help catechists, teachers and pastoral workers to educate children to ecumenism.

It would be possible to continue the initiative by having a co-opted staff from the Centro to go directly to schools and parishes and to have local sessions there. We could also open the initiative more specifically towards interreligious dialogue, though it would be a difficult and basically a different project. Journalists too reacted to the initiative, therefore articles and interviews have been published for the on-line Catholic magazine *Vidimus Dominum*, the *Live 105 Vatican Radio*, the Office for Cathechism of the Diocese of Rome, and other reviewers and journalists from the international milieu.

We are aware that, in a short time, the children will probably forget the right answers they gave on the meaning of the John Paul Encyclical *Ut Unum Sint*, or the number of Waldensians in Italy, but it is our hope that they will get the idea that divisions in the Church have happened, but also that there is a movement of people of good will working hard to overcome those divisions and heal this scandal for Christian identity; and that the children will associate this concept with a joyful, enjoyable morning spent in a nice place.

CASE STUDY 4

MISSION TO THE NORTH: OPPORTUNITIES AND PROSPECTS

Dr Fidon Mwombeki, Executive Director, United Evangelical Mission, Germany[1]

Edinburgh 1910 was a milestone, of course. Most countries in the world had been colonised by Europeans. Missions took advantage of colonisation to spread the gospel and the culture. That international conference was certainly mainly of Europeans and Americans trying to strategise how they would preach the gospel and convert the whole world to the Christian faith as quickly as possible. Christian and non-Christian worlds were clearly distinguished.

A generation later the reality was different. The 'mission fields' had become 'churches' and understood the need to further the gospel under their own initiative and management. After all, even under the leadership of 'missionaries' the main actors of mission had always been the native people. Without their participation, no missionary was successful. They taught the missionaries the language, they showed them what to do, they accompanied them, they gave them food and plots of land to build churches, and built churches by their own hands.

The Change in Theology of Mission in the North

The independence of the strong churches in the South forced the North to reconsider their theology of mission and their own role. The discussions in the International Missionary Council, the Commission for World Mission and Evangelism and the World Council of Churches had to respond to the independence and newly-acquired self determination of the Southern churches. The dominance of anyone in mission work was not wanted and should not be tolerated.

The development in missiological thinking can be observed through a look into the themes of the conferences of the international mission

[1] For further biodata, see Appendix 4.

conferences. At Edinburgh 1910, at the peak of colonisation Christians were optimistic of 'the evangelisation of the world in this generation'. At Jerusalem 1928 the mood was sombre, with the reality that other religions were not going to go away so fast. In the shadow of fascism in Europe (Germany, Italy, Portugal, Spain, and Japan) in Tambaram 1938 the strength of the Southern (younger) churches was felt, with more representatives than those from the North. At Whitby 1947 the Northern missions were suffering from the aftermath of World War Two and had discovered their limits. It was no longer possible to defend the notion of Europe as a 'Christian' and superior continent. New mission theology was developing with the concept of 'partnership' at the centre. Many churches began to negotiate their independence from missions. At Willingen 1952 a theological foundation was laid that has shaped missiology ever since: *missio Dei.* Not the church, nor the missions, nor the people, are indeed the actors in mission, but God! After New Delhi 1961 brought together the International Missionary Council and the World Council of Churches, the influence of missions would be felt in the churches. After this, missions in the North began slow processes of working closer with the churches at home, the idea of 'supporting churches' (*Trägerkirchen*) was established. However, in my view with the end of the International Missionary Council, the global church had lost a significant impetus in mission. The Commission for World Mission and Evangelism that was formed instead never filled the position of the International Missionary Council as it lacked the necessary independence from church structures.

In 1963 Mexico-City the conference on world mission and evangelism discussed in detail the concept of 'mission in six continents'. It was acknowledged that indeed all continents are mission fields. Statements were made that there is no church that is too poor to contribute in God's mission and there is no church that does not need others. This attitude was to continue at Bangkok 1972 which, after the formulation of a holistic approach to mission, was remarkable for discussion of just relations between churches. The following conferences continued in the same spirit, but the agenda from the South could no longer be peripheral. World mission started to be understood theologically as really global.

Changing Structures to Match Theology

Throughout these periods, the question of structures of churches and missions was being discussed. It was agreed that mission must be done ecumenically, and in all six continents. There was a good discussion at the Saint Antonio conference (1989) about the need to have new structures that make it possible for the churches globally to share their joys and tears, their gifts and their needs. In 1972 the former Paris Mission decided to restructure to reflect this theological understanding. It became CEVAA (Communauté Evangélique d'Action Apostolique), a community of forty-eight churches in sixteen countries in three continents. Later in 1977 Council for World Mission (CWM) was formed out of the former London Missionary Society into a community of thirty churches in five continents. Then in 1996 my own organisation, United Evangelical Mission (UEM) became a joint mission of thirty-three churches from Asia (15), Africa (12) and Germany (6), together with a diaconic institution, Bethel. In our statement on corporate identity we explain:

> How do we work together?
>
> Two are better than one, because they have a better reward for their toil. For if they fall, one will lift up the other, but woe to one who is alone and falls and does not have another to help. (Ecclesiastes 4: 9)
>
> Our members from Africa, Asia and Germany have equal rights in governance. Our decision makers –women, men and young adults– come from all three continents. All decisions about our work are taken on the basis of our common rules and regulations and our joint budget.
>
> We manage the resources entrusted to us transparently and conscientiously and account for them together in faithful stewardship. In working and living together we learn from each other and are willing to be transformed and renewed as we experience that our partaking in God's mission also changes our lives and our work.

The Present Challenges

I would say the structure has proven to work. The members of UEM, CWM and CEVAA cherish the communion among themselves as an example of living ecumenism. The communities are small enough that they can know each other and work together in trust unlike in larger global ecumenical settings. UEM especially is indeed ecumenical – with Baptists, Methodists, Lutherans, Reformed, United churches all accepting each other and sharing ministry with each other even before the controversies are resolved internationally.

Very significant in these communions is the exchange of co-workers or missionaries in all directions: North-South, South-North and South-South to serve as missionaries. In this exchange, I would like to highlight the challenges faced by the South-North missionaries.

First, the old convictions are not easy to get rid of. Many in the North still think their continent is not a mission field. It is Christian already with a few intruders of other religions. They do not understand the idea of a missionary coming from the South to serve in the North. For them mission is done by giving money to some mission organisation which does it on their behalf. And there are still too many people who regard mission as helping the poor, and therefore the people from the South have no mission in the North – no poor people they are in position to help. Therefore they are not missionaries. Instead they come to 'learn' something from the developed people which they should use for their benefit, and for that of their people when they go back home. On the other hand, it is difficult for those who have regarded mission as 'receiving' to accept that they are givers as well. They do not have something tangible like medicine or books to give to the Northerners anyway. They do not come with cash but they are paid with finances from the North. How could that be mission?

Second, in the sharing, it has been complicated for the North to say explicitly what they need from their Southern colleagues. The Southern churches many times know what they want from their Northern colleagues, most of the time in material or financial terms. They keep asking their colleagues to say what they need from the South, and that is a difficult question. Certainly exotic drumming and dancing is not enough. Some talk of 'spirituality', which is not easy to define. In UEM however, we are experiencing churches in Germany defining precisely what specific expertise and competences they want the co-workers from the South to bring.

Third, secularism is a challenge. The secularised culture of the North does not regard mission and religion as such as important for anyone at all. Liberal theology has not helped either. It is getting increasingly accepted that all religions are just the same and therefore there is no need to do Christian mission. Religion is simply an aspect of life and therefore free choice is necessary. We do not need even to educate our children in the Christian faith. They shall choose for themselves whenever they want. I have to say, after the shock of fundamentalistic religions, many people are making a new look at the need for mission in the North (for example, German President Köhler in May 2010).

Fourth, it is very difficult for anyone to break into the closed society of the North. It is particularly difficult for missionaries from the South, as foreigners, to penetrate the society. One of our co-workers in Germany told me of her shock as she read in the papers about the death of a member of the congregation. The widow of the fellow published a death announcement in that small village. The announcement ended with a note: 'Please, no visits'.

Sixth, stigma against foreigners is high. Foreigners in the North are generally stigmatised. They are not welcome. The most frequent question one hears from the native people when they get to know one is, 'When are you going back home?' The missionaries from the South are regarded as beggars and their gifts are not easily appreciated at the beginning. Most people in the North do not believe Southerners have a message to tell them, but that they are somehow trying to take advantage of the system to get access to wealth and services in the North. They are regarded as 'economic migrants' only. That means even those who feel indeed called to do mission are stigmatised. That makes it more difficult for them to penetrate the society.

Opportunities

Despite the challenges, I am encouraged by some opportunities that I can see. First, there is real hunger for the gospel in the North. The church members want to hear the gospel of Jesus Christ. I have talked to many people in the mainline churches who complain about sermons which are too much academic and abstract, from their own pastors,most of whom are employed until retirement however good or bad preachers they may be. I often hear the lay people say that most of the sermons have nothing to do with their daily lives or their real concerns. They are full of ideas and explanation of theological theories. People want to hear about Jesus. They want to know God is with them. They want to know about the forgiveness of sins. They want to be able to talk to their children about their faith. They want to learn how to pray. And these are the things people from the South are used to doing and can share if they have a chance. A growing interest in the mainline churches in such real basic Christian matters is also very much welcome.

I have to say that I see the churches in Germany officially being very serious about mission from the South. They are willing to hear and be enriched by the gifts of the people from the South. For me it is clear, through my election into the highest governing council of the Evangelical Church in Germany, which a sign of trust, that someone like me can, and is invited to, contribute their gifts and experience to the church life in Germany. There can be no bigger sign of trust of people like me.

Second, the reality of 'mission from the South' is settling in Europe through a variety of independent missionaries who are founding churches in Europe. It is a great phenomenon and, according to Claudia Währisch-Oblau, it is a factor to reckon with. These churches from the South are coming independent of the structures of the churches in the North and establishing churches here. They do start with the people from their own countries who are migrants, but they are slowly getting a footing in Europe with not a few European members and interested people. The European official churches do not yet know how to deal with this phenomenon. These missionaries solve the problem of finances by somehow getting access to the finances in Europe.

These migrant churches may play a role the Jewish congregations played in the early church. We read in the book of Acts that the apostles in every city always started their mission in the Synagogues. There they were welcome, even though their message was not easy to get through. But from the synagogues they moved into the wider society. Is it not possible to believe that these hundreds of migrant churches, though starting with their own kind, shall in some way break into the wider society? I hope God will use them to do exactly that, and that indeed God will assist the churches in the North to find ways to integrate them into their own churches and communities.

PARALLEL SESSIONS

THEME 1
FOUNDATIONS FOR MISSION[1]

The Mission of the Triune God

The central foundation for mission is the nature of the triune God, and how God works in the world. This was the central conclusion of Theme 1, 'Foundations for mission'.

The story of the 'Foundations for mission' study process began in 2007 when the conveners, Canon Janice Price and Revd Dr Deenabandhu Manchala, each began research projects related to this theme. Canon Price, then of Churches Together in Britain and Ireland, convened a group of UK and Ireland representatives, and Dr Manchala, of the WCC Just and Inclusive Communities, initiated the research project 'Mission at and from the margins' in India. Against the background of these research projects being progressed and developed, the Edinburgh 2010 study process organisers convened an international group to work on the chapter for the Edinburgh 2010 preparatory volume, *Witnessing to Christ Today*.[2] This comprised representatives from Argentina, Greece, India, Malaysia, South Africa, Switzerland, the United Kingdom, and the United States. Three areas were identified as the sources of foundations for mission by this group which were experience, the Bible, and theology. The group also outlined three approaches to mission as reconciliation, liberation and justice, and proclamation. This chapter was critical for the preparation for the study theme in the conference itself. Those who attended were asked to study the chapter prior to the conference and issues raised in it were reflected in the conference discussion.

The parallel sessions on Foundations for Mission were attended by over a hundred delegates and representatives from the conference, who joined together to consider the question 'What are our foundations for mission today?' We were led by the co-chairs, the Revd Dr. Clifton Kirkpatrick and Revd Dr. Ganoune Diop and they opened the session in prayer and outlined the process. Following contributions from the research studies, the session

---

[1] Report prepared by the conveners of this study theme: Canon Janice Price, Church of England, and Revd Dr Deenabandhu Manchala, World Council of Churches. The parallel sessions were chaired by Revd Dr. Clifton Kirkpatrick, World Alliance of Reformed Churches, and Revd Dr. Ganoune Diop, Seventh-day Adventist Church.

[2] Daryl Balia & Kirsteen Kim (eds), *Edinburgh 2010: Witnessing to Christ Today* (Oxford: Regnum Books International, 2010), 10-33.

used small groups to listen to the transversal contributors and to arrive at the ten areas they considered were essential Foundations for Mission. These were then gathered together in plenary. The chairs and convenors considered all the material and arrived at the summary statement below.

Mission is the Heartbeat of God

Mission is the heartbeat of God.

God's purpose for the world is to unite all creation under the Lordship of Jesus Christ.

The foundation for mission is the nature of God – the relational, self-giving, grace-filled nature of the triune God in which we are invited to participate.

The nature of God – and God's mission – is discerned through the work of the Holy Spirit in:

- the experience of a particular Christian community,
- the experiences of overcoming forces that work against God's will of life, justice and peace for all (Matt. 11:3-5),
- the experience of the apostolic community, most perfectly expressed in scripture,
- the experience of the ecumenical community in active dialogue with the cultural context in which mission is lived out, and,
- most importantly, in God's revelation in the life, ministry, death, and resurrection of Jesus Christ, which serves as the primary criterion for understanding and evaluating the various elements of mission.

The church, as a sign and symbol of the Kingdom of God, is called to share in God's mission through the transforming power of Jesus Christ and the empowerment of the Holy Spirit. We are called to

- witness to the love of God for the salvation of a fallen world,
- incarnate and proclaim the good news of the gospel for life in abundance,
- honour the wonderful diversity of the creation and all people,
- heal and reconcile in the way of Christ,
- love God and neighbour,
- work for liberation and justice in active solidarity with the poor and oppressed, and
- live and celebrate as one family in Christian community in such a way that we are a living demonstration of the love and justice that God intends for all the world.

Foundations for Mission

The statement above is the summary of the discussions of the Foundations for Mission study group, as agreed by the participants. It is in the nature of foundations that they provide a supportive structure from which a building can stand securely. Jesus' telling of the parable of the house built on the sand (Matt. 7:26) shows that without the appropriate foundations no building can stand securely and withstand stress. A further biblical image is of the cornerstone or capstone which holds a building together. Both the references in Ephesians 2:20 and 1 Peter 2:6 refer to Jesus Christ as the Cornerstone or Capstone. Jesus himself uses the image referring to Psalm 118 when he describes himself as the cornerstone once rejected by the builders (Mark 12:10 and parallels). The key question was 'as we follow God in God's mission in our complex and pluralistic world what are our foundations for mission?'

A key relationship in any understanding of a theology of mission rests upon the emphasis placed on each of the three foundational elements: the *missio Dei* (God's mission), the church and the Kingdom of God. The above statement is rooted firmly in the origin of mission being found in the triune God's mission which is manifested in creation through the Kingdom of God, and of which the church is a sign and foretaste. We want to be open to the work of the Holy Spirit beyond the church, seeing the church as being the vehicle for the Kingdom of God, but not exclusively or restrictively so. In a world which is complex, diverse and pluralistic we need to be sensitive to the action of God the Holy Spirit beyond the church. As well as sign and foretaste, the church is herald of the good news and the carrier of the story of Christ. We also want to proclaim with confidence and hope that the end or eternal purpose of God's mission is to bring all things together in Jesus Christ (Ephesians 1:10).

One of the most contested aspects of the Foundations for Mission chapter in the conference preparatory volume is the place of experience in the formation of mission theology. Some argued that how we experience God is prior to the formation of doctrine and the language of speaking about God, and is the source of new discernment of God at work by the Holy Spirit. Others argued that theology as articulated by the church is prior to experience of God as individuals or communities. This question remains open but experience in dialogue with Scripture and the tradition of the church can open new insights and practices. Foundations for mission, of which the central foundation is the witness to Jesus Christ in Holy Scripture, provide the framework through which authentic Christian mission is discerned.

The statement acknowledges that the nature of God and mission is discerned through the lived experience of Christian communities as they engage in mission in the world. Mission is contextual, embedded in community and expressed in relationship – as God the Trinity is relational and whose ultimate expression prior to the Second Return of Christ is through the Incarnation. This will be one of the distinctive marks of Christian mission – particular revelation in time and place. The experience of the local Christian community is also found in continuity with the Apostolic Community which is foundational and authoritative in mission, and which we see and learn from through Holy Scripture. Prior to the Apostolic Community is the witness of Jesus himself, witness to whom we find in the Gospels. The test of authentic mission is to be found in the process of discernment by the local and wider church together, between the needs of particular contexts and the witness of Jesus in the Gospels, between the Apostolic Community and the witness and fruit of the Holy Spirit in his work today. An important part of this process of discernment is the experience of the ecumenical community. The various denominations face similar issues in relating to contemporary cultures and therefore need to listen and learn from each other at all levels of the ecumenical community.

The statement reflects the contributions from selected Edinburgh 2010 transversal topics (healing and reconciliation, youth and mission, and ecological perspectives) and from particular Communions (Pentecostal and Orthodox), who were appointed to give presentations and input into discussions in the course of the study sessions. The transversal topics look to the current challenges in global mission. In a world of conflict, mission is understood as a process of healing and reconciliation between peoples, God and creation. Young people are the future of mission.

The study theme discussions began with presentations from the two convenors on the research projects which they had led in preparation for the conference. In effect these research studies acted like case studies giving the participants a place from which to engage their own experience in discussions on the study theme. Detailed discussion in plenary on the two research projects was not possible due to time restraints but the content was taken into small group discussion which sought to identify foundations for mission.

Rethinking the 'Colonial' Dimension of Mission

Revd Deenabandhu Manchala and Dr. Peniel Rufus Rajkumar described the research project 'Mission At and From the Margins'. This was an ethnographic, historical and theological study of the features of the mission of churches on the margins, with reference to the marginalised yet resilient Dalit[3] communities of India. The research was sponsored by the Just and

[3] 'Dalit' is the self-designation of the people of India formally known as 'outcaste' or 'untouchable'.

Inclusive Communities Programme of the WCC and conducted by the Collective of Dalit Ecumenical Christian Scholars (CODECS).[4]

The field study for the study project was undertaken at a village called Vegeswarapuram in the South Indian state of Andhra Pradesh. The primary purpose of the project was to recover the Dalit agency and agenda in Christian missions in Andhra Pradesh and draw the implications of this agency for the ecumenical imagination of the church's mission in the world today.

A presupposition of this research is that not all experience is foundational for mission. However the experiences of those at the margins were privileged as being foundational for mission theology in the context of this study project. To that extent, the study appeals to the biblical language of the rejected stone becoming the cornerstone. It resonates with the biblical subversion of rejection by making the rejected ones and their experiences the cornerstone of mission theology. It is hoped that from striking these 'rocks' or stones, fresh life-giving waters will spring forth which will rejuvenate mission theology today.

The orientation of the study is such that it questions the tendency in mission theology to think of mission in relation to marginalised communities as 'mission *to*' and opens space to think of mission in terms of 'mission *at*' and 'mission *from*'.

A key theme was '*Mission reforming the margins or margins reforming mission?*' One of the dominant notions that exists of the mission carried out by missionary organisations is that they transformed the margins. However, in our conclusions it was the Dalits who embraced the conditions and media of mission set up by the missionaries (access to education, health care, and employment) as avenues of renegotiating their social and economic status and for breaking away from the constraints of the caste system. It was the Dalit communities which humanised missions and gave them a humane face. They were the primary agenda-setters in 'converting mission' into concern for the marginalised.

By recovering the agency of the Dalits in reforming mission (and making mission an avenue for challenging the prevailing 'body politic') the study provided a new hermeneutical tool to interrogate the popular accusations about the 'colonial' dimension of mission. It also helped us to understand the importance of adopting a nuanced approach towards understanding the interplay between colonialism and the Dalit communities. Dalit relationships with missionaries are much more complex than patron-client or coloniser-colonised relationships. Dalit communities, which have no stakes in local power, viewed those in their own country who had power as 'colonisers'. In this context the conditions created by

[4] The full results of this project will be published as Joseph Prabhakar Dayam, Peniel Jesudason Rufus Rajkumar & I.P. Asheervadam (eds.), *Mission at and from the Margins* (Oxford: Regnum Books International, forthcoming in 2011).

mission were seen as a liberative-transformative space by Dalit communities for self-assertion and reclamation of their place in society, rather than as components of the colonising process.

One fundamental shift in perspective which emerged during the course of the study was to understand mission as creating *conditions* that facilitated the empowerment of people at the margins. A few specific illustrations drawn from the field study can clarify mission as '*the creation of conditions*' that facilitated empowerment and emancipation, and provide us with glimpses of the various patterns of mission which emerge from the margins.

The project drew two further conclusions. First, that mission is an *alliance*. Communities on the margins found in the establishment of the mission station, and in the missionary (the *Dora*), an advocate of their rights and used it as a springboard to further their own attempts for emancipation from the caste system. They saw in the *Dora* a possible ally because of the access that the missionaries had to the colonial administration. This colonial connection, coupled with missionary establishments like hospitals, schools and hostels, prompted the Dalit communities to shift their allegiance from their traditional landlords to these new *Doras*..

Second, there is a link between mission and *educational transformation*. Much of the transformative effect of Christian mission can be traced to the way the Dalits appropriated the educational ministry of the Christian missions. Appropriating the access to education was – for the Dalit communities, who were denied education under the caste system – a strategic intervention which fostered the empowerment of the Dalit communities.

Mission here can be understood as involving a midwifery role – a role which involves both *creating* those conditions which give birth to new realities as well as *eliminating* the various impediments which impose constraints on the flourishing of the communities on the margins. Understanding mission as having a midwifery role in a pluralistic context like India has significant implications because primarily mission does not become the monopoly of ecclesiastical Christianity. Mission transcends being an enterprise which can solely be in the service of the church. Rather, understanding mission as creating the conditions for liberation helps us to understand mission as a process, which offers itself to further the liberative agendas of other organisations, groups and bodies which may have their base outside the church but yet are involved in the issues of justice. It becomes a catalyst in forging alliances. Mission may be understood as hospitality – where the fruits of missional activity are offered to other partners in the service of their agendas in so far as they serve liberative purposes, and where other groups and forces are invited to partake in what has been achieved and give it further shape and direction.

Language, Theology and Praxis

The second piece of research which was presented was conducted among the churches and agencies of the United Kingdom and Ireland. It was devised by an ecumenical group comprising representatives of the ecumenical body Churches Together in Britain and Ireland, the evangelical Global Connections and the British and Irish Association of Mission Studies.[5] The question governing the research was 'what are the theological understandings and practice of mission among the churches and agencies of the UK and Ireland at the beginning of the twenty-first century?' In other words, the hypothesis for the research was that *what is **said** publicly about the theology of mission by UK and Ireland churches, agencies and institutions does not necessarily match up with the mission practice, understanding and outworking of those same bodies.* To test this hypothesis a three-stage approach involved a search of selected websites of the churches and agencies, a questionnaire distributed to churches and agencies at national and local level and in-depth interviews. The questionnaire rated people's responses to different statements about mission. It attracted a response rate of sixty-eight responses from the national survey of churches and mission agencies and ninety-three from the local survey in one region of England.

The conclusions of the research can be summarised as follows in the three categories of analysis: language, theology and praxis.

There was an openness to relational language with a high level of agreement on questions that concerned reconciliation and transformation. There was also a rejection of language that separated and seemed to harden attitudes such as 'confronting' or 'condemnation'. There was a high level of assent to the word 'mission' which was seen as positive but it was also likely that disagreement with the word mission was difficult given its high profile in current discourse. A significant number of respondents struggled with naming priorities in mission. This was particularly the case where the words 'primarily' 'most' and 'better' were used in the question which discouraged a general answer. Respondents struggled with these words largely because of a desire to embrace different concepts rather than prioritise. The survey showed some struggle with how and where mission happens. Questions relating to relationships with other faiths, who is best equipped to carry out mission and whether God works primarily through Christians all showed a high neutrality in the responses. The greatest divisions appeared with regard to mission and social justice. For some respondents mission and social justice are synonymous but for others social justice or social action is a means to mission which is seen as proclamation.

---

[5] The full report is published as Anne Richards *et al.*, *Foundations for Mission: A Study of Language, Theology and Praxis from the UK and Ireland* (London: SCM-Canterbury, 2010).

From the three models of mission adopted on the survey – proclamation, liberation and justice and *missio Dei*, it was found that proclamation was the most commonly described as the driver for mission in the local survey. The national survey was more concerned with integrating all three models. *Missio Dei* was found to be a weak driver for mission. Despite the prevalence of the language of *missio Dei* it was not found to be a prominent driver of mission in the interview stage. Matthew 28:18-20, the 'Great Commission', appeared to be the primary biblical driver for the local survey and interviews and this verse was also used in website texts. There was a tension in many answers between what mission ought to be and what it is in practice. Whatever the concepts or models in use, for many mission could not be separated from the reality of practice where mission was practical and embedded in everyday life.

There is an inconsistency between what is said and done which arises from the observation that mission does not exist as a concept but as embedded praxis. Respondents more often started describing mission from practice and then moved to theory. There is a need to root mission in experience and story. Websites do not demonstrate praxis but aim to be inspirational. Tensions between leadership and congregations were found in how mission is expressed at local level. Clergy often stressed that their views were not necessarily at the same place as their congregations. Tensions in national leadership were found in that some denominational mission departments were unable to complete the survey as a team because of sharp divergences in approach. Mission is varied and diverse. Holistic mission was found to be a helpful concept as it described mission across a spectrum that combined all three elements of proclamation, social justice and *missio Dei* among others.

Mission is not a neat concept. Christian mission today is a varied and diverse set of understandings and activities depending on context and discernment of God's work through the Holy Spirit and history. Discerning foundations for mission requires listening to the voice of God amidst the clamour for life and justice, to the church and to particular contexts using the tools of Scripture, and to spirituality and sources of the Christian tradition. It is a journey that the church makes together that holds many challenges as well as energising the very life of the church. At the heart of all this stands the triune God as the foundation and source of mission. God's activities are varied but his relational, self-giving, grace-filled nature is constant and defines our participation in what God is doing in the world.

THEME 2
CHRISTIAN MISSION AMONG OTHER FAITHS[1]

Building upon the work of the core study group that synthesised the theme's historical background, major approaches, and its contemporary challenges, the two sessions on Theme 2, 'Christian mission among other faiths' were organised in the afternoon of 3 June. The planning of the sessions presumed the knowledge of the work of the core group.[2]

Theory and Practice

A set of preparatory questions, originating from the study process, to prompt discussions were gathered and circulated especially among the resource persons. These were divided into theoretical and practical areas, as follows:

Questions relating to theoretical issues

1. How do we understand Christian mission in the religiously pluralistic context of today?
2. How has our understanding of other religious faiths and our relationship with people of other faiths been shaping and re-defining our understanding of mission?
3. How may churches in the West gain new insights from churches in the global South about witness and dialogue in a pluralistic setting?
4. Does the focus on the Holy Spirit in creation, culture and religion provide new avenues for a Christian theology of religion?
5. Can there be 'un-baptised' and/or 'churchless' Christianity (as some call it)? Should the church encourage un-baptised or churchless Christianity depending on the context?

Questions relating to priorities in mission

1. Is Christ the only way? Do other religions have ways of salvation?
2. What is the role of conversion in mission?

---

[1] Report prepared by the conveners of this study theme: Dr Lalsangkima Pachuau, Asbury Theological Seminary, USA, and Dr Niki Papageorgiou, Aristotle University of Thessaloniki with the kind help of Dr Eunice Irwin, Asbury Theological Seminary, who served as the recorder of the sessions. The parallel sessions were chaired by Rev. Doug Birdsall, Lausanne Committee for World Evangelization, and Dr Glory Dharmaraj, The United Methodist Church.

[2] See Daryl Balia & Kirsteen Kim (eds), *Edinburgh 2010: Witnessing to Christ Today* (Oxford: Regnum Books International, 2010), 34-60.

(a) How could Christians work together with people of other faiths?
(b) How can Christians avoid compromising their faith in/while working with people of other faiths?

3. Should Christians compete with people of other faiths in seeking new adherents?

The sessions both tried to draw from resource persons and to gather the opinions and ideas of the participants through small group discussions. They were focused on practical issues and challenges by identifying 'key issues' and 'priorities' of the theme. In addition to hearing the voices of all the proposed resource persons through panel interviews, two of the resource persons were selected to do presentations. Todd Johnson, Director of Center for the Study of World Christianity at Gordon-Conwell Theological Seminary, and co-editor of the *Atlas of Global Christianity* (a project of Edinburgh 2010),[3] did a presentation on 'Global religious demography and Christian mission' in the first session. In the second session, Dr Gwen Bryde of the University of Hamburg, and a youth representative in the conference, presented the findings of her empirical research in Germany on the experience of youth in the engagement of mission.

The first session (2:30pm to 4pm of 3 June 2010) was organised around 'key issues'. The session was chaired by Dr Glory Dharmaraj Director, Spiritual Formation and Mission Theology, the United Methodist Church, USA. After opening remarks and introduction of the resource persons and preliminary instructions to the sessions, co-convener Dr Kima Pachuau introduced and handed over to the chair of the meeting. Dr Dharmaraj introduced the theme. Through a PowerPoint presentation using statistical research, as published in *Atlas in Global Christianity,* Todd Johnson dealt with global religious demography and Christian mission. A summary of the presentation is to be found below. Johnson's presentation was followed by a panel interview of resource persons. Dr Knud Jørgensen interviewed four of the resource persons: Dr Marina Behara (India), Dr Hesdie Zamuel (Suriname/Tanzania), Dr John Azumah (Ghana/UK), and Fr Jan Lenssen (Belgium/Africa) on key issues of mission among other faiths. Each member shared their opinions and experience. The participants of the session were then divided into ten groups each of which were led by a resource person. The groups were asked to identify key issues in Christian mission among other faiths. The findings are outlined below.

The second session was chaired by Rev. Doug Birdsall, Executive Chair of the Lausanne Committee for World Evangelisation. Dr Gwen Bryde did a presentation on youth and mission with a focus on people of other faiths, pursuing the question, 'How should Christians relate with and witness to

---

[3] Todd M. Johnson & Kenneth R. Ross eds., *Atlas of Global Christianity, 1910–2010* (Edinburgh: Edinburgh University Press, 2009).

people of other faiths?' Byrde's was an empirical study among youth in the Lutheran Churches in northern Germany. A summary and findings is discussed below. As in session one, Dr Knud Jorgensen interviewed three resource persons: Rev. Ulrike Schmidt-Hesse (Germany), Revd Dr Philip Tye-Yau Siew (Malaysia), and Rev. Dr Ronald Wallace (Canada). Each of these resource persons shared their thoughts on 'priorities' in mission among other faiths today. The session then continued with small group discussion to identify priorities in Christian mission among other faiths. The findings are listed below. The diverse and rich background of the resource persons and the engaging participants enriched the sessions tremendously.

Global Religious Demography and Christian Mission

Todd M. Johnson dealt first with trends inside global Christianity. He made several observations: First, that Christianity has shifted dramatically to the South between 1910 and 2010. While 66 percent of all Christians lived in Europe in 1910, by 2010 only 25.6 percent lived there. By contrast, less than 2 percent of all Christians lived in Africa in 1910 skyrocketing to almost 22 percent by 2010. The global North (defined as Europe and Northern America) contained over 80 percent of all Christians in 1910 falling to under 40 percent by 2010. Second, simultaneous to the shift of Christianity to the South was the decline of Christianity in the North, but Christianity today is largely characterised by Western culture. Third, Christianity is fragmented. Christians are now found in 41,000 denominations. These range in sise from millions of members to less than a hundred members and are listed for each of the world's 238 countries in the World Christian Database. Fourth, Christians are experiencing unprecedented renewal. There are many forms of renewal within global Christianity including evangelical movements, liturgical renewal, Bible-study fellowships, and house church movements. The locus of Christian renewal is clearly in the global South where the majority of its practitioners live and where it is growing the fastest. Fifth, Christian resources are not evenly distributed. Christians of the global South, who represent 60 percent of all Christians, have only about 17 percent of all Christian income. This puts them at a disadvantage in many areas including health, education, communications, and overall quality of life. This imbalance is one of the great tragedies of global Christianity.

The second part of Johnson's presentation dealt with trends in global religions, where he pointed out, first, that the world is currently becoming more religious, not less, but the world of 2010 is less religious than that of 1910. However, closer examination of the rise of the nonreligious in the world reveals that since 1970, agnostics (and atheists) have experienced a drop in adherents. Second, countries are becoming more religiously diverse, not less. In 1910 nearly 80 percent of all Christians lived in a country that was 90 percent or more Christian. By 2010 this figure had dropped to only 33 percent. Third, Religious freedom is not a reality for many people. Restrictions on religious freedom are still a challenge for much of the world's population. The two most populous countries in the world, India and China for instance, have significant restrictions. Fourth, Christians are out of contact with Muslims, Hindus, and Buddhists. Research reveals that as many as 86 percent of all Muslims, Hindus, and Buddhists do not personally know a Christian.

Youth and Mission Among People of Other Faiths

Dr Gwen Bryde's presentation was based on an empirical study among youths from 18 to 29 years of age in Germany, none of them theologians, who had joined a programme by the German Lutheran Church mission organisation. These youth members, who had spent several months in a Lutheran partner church overseas, were asked:

1. What was your opinion on Christian mission before joining this programme? How did you experience Christian mission in your host church?
2. How should Christians and the church in Germany generally relate to people of other faiths?
3. What is so special about the Christian faith that others would miss a great deal if they didn't find out about it or experience it?

The results showed that most of those interviewed were ambivalent towards mission. Except for one person, they did not criticise mission among other faiths as totally outdated. On the whole, extremely little negative was said about the mission work of the partner churches where they stayed, quite to the contrary. They praised the practical help that was given to poor people by the partner churches and their expressive faith life. Upon asking them what they thought of the partner churches' mission among other faiths and the conversion of people to Christianity, almost all were in favour of it. But they could not imagine the church in Germany being involved in a ministry like this.

Based on the responses, the following points emerged: First, mission in practice is fine, but dialogue is favoured in theory. When asked about how Christians in general should relate to people of other faiths, they named the normally accepted theoretical ideas that Western Europeans favour such as dialogue, respectful behaviour, listening to each other instead of preaching. Second, the young people encountered a more expressive faith life and different approaches to Christian ethics. Many of those interviewed stated that they were challenged in their faith life in a positive way through encountering Christians in countries like Tanzania or India or Brazil. They were impressed by the outgoing faith of people and the churches. At the same time, they did not favour strict rules for Christians like no pop music or no alcohol. If we ask, how can young people in the German context be witnesses to the Gospel and make good use of their overseas experience? Then giving hope to people, openness to others and God's love for every creature were the main aspects that these young people shared as most meaningful about the Christian faith.

Issues and Priorities

The following is a compilation of the small group discussions in the two sessions where the groups were asked to identify key issues (in the first) and priorities (in the second) in Christian mission among other faiths. There are a number of unclear points and some could not be deciphered and were excluded.

Key issues

- *Dialogue* is a must especially in Muslim areas. Dialogue through witness is crucial. In connection with dialogue, the relevance of the 'Great Commission' needs to be reviewed. Closely connected to dialogue is to identify common accepted terms and their meanings in various religions. There is a fear of compromising one's own convictions in dialogue.
- In contexts where Muslims are the majority, the church has become apathetic and unready to *witness*, and Muslims have become suspicious of a 'conversionist' agenda. Concepts of witness are often too indirect; we need to engage consciously with hard questions and with real people. It is important not to fight about doctrine, instead we should promote common good.
- Mutual *education* among different faith traditions is a crucial issue today. In a similar vein, another group endorsed that we should fight against misunderstanding or prejudices of Christianity. In this it is important especially to Hindus to meet genuine Christians.
- Lack of *contacts* with people of other faiths (as the presentations showed) is appalling! It is an important issue for today.
- An instance of *power* manifestation of God causing the whole village to turn to Christ was reported in one group. Another group concurs and states: Do not discount the transformative power of miracles! They show the Truth – that God is powerful to heal and answer prayer.
- There can be a tension between *conversion* and *partnership*: To deal with many world challenges requires co-operation of many faith communities. There is continual tension between conversion and partnership, and between mission and dialogue.

- The role of the *Holy Spirit* in other faiths: If God is at work in other faiths, can mission be a joint discovery of the action of God? To discern where the Holy Spirit is leading the global Church is urgent. Is it leading the church to repentance?
- *Secularisation* may facilitate inter-religious encounter said one group; and another group said that a secular agenda is limiting religious interaction in England. For example, blasphemy laws limit speaking about religion for fear of offending others.
- Whether we approach other religions for dialogue, partnership, or encounter depends to a large extent on whom we meet. A *fundamentalist* may not be interested in mutual understanding. The reality of religious violence in the world testifies to this.
- The question of *salvation*: 'Must all people be Christian to be blessed/reconciled before God, or not?' This unsettling question within Christianity divides Christians, and prevents common witness.
- 2010 represents a *shift* from concern to rejoicing in our mission paradigm. As Dana Roberts rightly pointed out in her lecture at the conference, there is less anxiety in Christians comprising only one third of the world population today. We can have a firm sense of who we are, and a willingness to share what we have in Christ, rather than trying to conquer the world as a geographical space.
- Issues are different from continent to continent: Secularisation in Europe, religious freedom in Africa, and diversity in Asia, especially India. Each of these issues needs to be dealt with in *context*.
- Freeing Christianity from colonial *Christendom* and majority mentality continues to be a crucial issue in mission among other faiths.
- *Healing and reconciliation* in the world are essential in our encounter with other faiths.
- Tension between *truth* [or one's religious perception of it] and religious *liberty*. How to hold the two together and how to present truth without imposing it against the liberty of the other.
- *Violence* against Christians is caused by inflammatory comments/talks of Christians that show intolerance; enthusiastic evangelistic rhetoric can be damaging! It is also caused by wrong use of religious terms that incite reactions or tie the gospel to colonial past (in the Indian context): 'conversion' brings with it a political baggage, as does 'Christian mission'. 'Targeting' groups (such as by the 10/40 Window) has stiffened fundamentalism on both Christian and Hindu sides.

- There is a need to realise growing curiosity and interest of *young people* filling classes and taking programs in religious studies. These want to know about how religion relates to their lives and world.
- The Church must stand up for any who suffer *discrimination* (Dalits and others) of any religious groups. This is justice that Christians can bring.
- We should learn the power of '*testimony*' to the Truth in postmodern times. This is what we are left with in the postmodern era – the opportunity to 'tell our stories' and allow others to hear what we say. Invite storytelling!
- The '*uniqueness* of Christ' – does this have different meanings or one?
- The status of *Jerusalem* and advocacy of churches

Priorities

- *Key missiological terms* selected were: authenticity, relationality, dialogical, bold humility, vulnerability, and respectful witness. Authentic and relational life (more than doctrine) is called for in witnessing among other faiths. Witness involves prophetic, confident, and bold but humble and vulnerable sharing of faith (sharing but nor imposing), and addresses injustices prophetically. Respect is the first step for dialogue, and action is more important than words. Despising the religion of the poor is despising the poor.
- *Dialogue* is to be carried out respectfully, honestly, and with transparency. We should do so because people want to hear about what we really believe, and about who we are (more than our religion's doctrines). In doing dialogue, it is important to differentiate the goals of dialogue and evangelism.
- *Secularism*, taken by some as a theological rival, should be engaged. In the secular academy and beyond, atheism and agnosticism are 'faiths' which we must engage.
- '*Inculturation*' needs to be re-thought for the twenty-first century.
- *Clarity of message* to people of other faiths is a priority. Do we, for instance, have a message of reconciliation to Islam? Reconciliation must be a part of the way the Gospel is made known to others.
- *Understanding* of other faiths must increase. Christians need to understand the dynamics of other religions (such as Islam) and teach people how to befriend people of other faiths.
- *Addressing fear*. How do we make the Church less scared of Islam and help Christians in tough Muslim areas (Palestine, Iraq etc.)

not to leave but interact with Muslims and advocate religious freedom?

- *Inter-generational dialogue* is needed within Christianity on mission among other faiths.
- Crossing religious boundaries in *social ministry* among the poor. We should do holistic ministry among people of other faiths and create solidarity.
- Mission as *hospitality* with openness to learn from other religions.
- *Reading the Bible with Muslims*. Muslims are interested in the Bible as a holy book. The United Bible Society has produced a New Testament version for Muslims.
- Consciously *reframe language* for effective witness. For example, Christians do not do 'Christian mission', they are 'friends of faith in the mission of God'. Rehabilitate meaning of word 'conversion' in a positive sense. We should present evangelism as the core experience of a growing life. The idea here is that people in other religions would want to hear about this aspect of Christianity.
- *Encourage local churches* to communicate with other faiths. Stimulate conscious witness and dialogue while being firm in the faith conviction. Educate Christians about the inclusiveness (catholicity) of Christianity and the need to be welcoming.
- *Give higher profile to religious freedom*, freedom of conscience, and freedom of expression especially in contexts where Christians are in minority.
- Reconsideration of meaning of the uniqueness of Christ by bringing theologians and practitioners together.

THEME 3
MISSION AND POSTMODERNITIES[1]

The core study group, invited for Theme 3, 'Mission and postmodernities', in its statement submitted to the conference,[2] identified some of the key questions concerning mission in relation to postmodernities. Thus, for example, they questioned whether there is room for hope in postmodernity, whether the upholding of otherness is always beneficial, since encounters with the other may result in fear as well as understanding, whether conversion is necessarily legitimate, and whether Christians can witness to absolute standards of right and wrong in a society losing its belief in ethical absolutes. The consequences for mission in a postmodern context were discussed in relation to truth and evangelism – since claims to truth are generally unpopular, being deemed arrogant and imperialistic; in relation to the church – since belonging to a community of faith is unnecessary if faith is a matter of private belief; in relation to salvation, if there are allegedly many paths to God; and in relation to evangelism and witness, since being and doing are much more important than saying. What then should be the proper balance between word and deed? How do we combine bold proclamation with an attitude of humility? What does an integrated theology of mission require?

Areas especially recommended for further consideration were the exercise of leadership, particularly to perceive the need for encouraging and enabling servant leadership, theological education, particularly an insistence on spiritual formation as an integral part of theological education, understanding the Bible, especially the need to assess critically certain current influential hermeneutical trends, the environmental crisis and ecology, particularly welcoming constructive contributions from more holistic approaches, and reconciliation and healing, especially how they may be implemented in current conflicts.

One major weakness with the initial statement was that it was largely limited to Western voices. One reason for the scarcity of voices from the majority world may be that postmodernity is still often seen as a predominately Western issue and thus of less relevance outside the West, although the core group did not share this understanding. To some extent,

[1] Report prepared by the convener of this study theme, Revd Dr Andrew Kirk, formerly University of Birmingham, UK, and Rev. Rolv Olsen, Egede Institute, Norway. The parallel sessions were chaired by Dr Isabel Phiri, University of KwaZulu Natal, and Rev. Martin Breitenfeldt, Mission 21.

[2] Daryl Balia & Kirsteen Kim (eds), *Edinburgh 2010: Witnessing to Christ Today* (Oxford: Regnum Books International, 2010), 61-85.

this imbalance was rectified at the Conference, but sadly, far from overcome.

Perspectives on Postmodernity

After a brief setting of the scene, including DVD-presentations of postmodern architecture, the floor was given to the representatives of transversals and regional/confessional perspectives.[3] Revd Prof. Sebastian C.H. Kim, professor of theology and public life, York St John University, UK, and representing the International Peace and Reconciliation Conferences, reflected on the issue from the perspectives of healing and reconciliation, with emphasis on Korean experiences of despair and hope, through stories, poetry and visual images. Prof. Kim insisted that experience is pivotal for postmodernity; persuasion by argument is frowned upon but people respond to experiences conveyed in stories, poems and images. Thus, unless the church touches people's hearts and enters their experience, mission will be ineffective.

Dr Ernst M. Conradie, teaching at the University of the Western Cape South Africa and representing the Christian Faith and the Earth symposium, voiced ecological perspectives on mission, reflecting on the relationship of postmodernities to mission and ecology. He questioned whether the suggestion in the study group report that postmodernity is more in tune with environmental concerns than is the case with modernity is actually tenable. Referring to Zygmunt Bauman and his analysis of 'liquid modernity', Dr Conradi argued that what is taking place is a shift from a production-oriented to a consumer-oriented society, both of which are rather indifferent towards environmental concerns. Two implications for Christian mission were suggested: the danger of reducing churches to providers of consumer products, mainly vendors of religious services and goods, and the crucial need for boldly proclaiming and embodying a vision of a renewed earth in which God is coming to dwell.

Dr Claudia Währisch-Oblau, representing the 2009 United Evangelical Mission Theological Consultation on Mission ('Global Impulses for the Twenty-first Century'[4]), found three topics missing in the report, or rather three facets of the fundamental question of how the Gospel of Christ can be lived and preached in the market place without becoming a commodity. Firstly, the question of how we can phrase our Gospel message so that it speaks to the burning questions of our time. Secondly, to find ways to face the challenge to mission caused by the return of the irrational, whether as

---

[3] Unfortunately, the representative of Subaltern voices, Rev. M. P. Joseph, from India and Taiwan, working with the Christian Conference of Asia, was unable to attend the conference. He would have spoken on the subject of 'Revisiting mission from a colonised land'.

[4] Claudia Währisch-Oblau & Fidon Mwombeki (eds), *Mission Continues: Global Impulses for the Twenty-first Century* (Oxford: Regnum Books International, 2010).

esotericism in the West or the resurgence of witchcraft and magical practices in Africa and Asia. Thirdly, how churches in the North can properly receive the mission of African, Asian and Latin American Christians. Dr Oblau concluded by suggesting that mission today is first and foremost neither winning souls for Christ nor identifying the Spirit at work in world events, but rather trying to live as the body of Christ, a community which overcomes racial, social, economic and cultural borders and limits in an increasingly fragmented world.

Prof. Gianni Colzani, from the Pontifical Urbaniana University, Rome, responded on behalf of his institution's pre-Edinburgh 2010 conference. He began by outlining two radically different interpretations of postmodernity, and then discussed whether the church ought to respond negatively towards pluralism or rather take its place in this pluralism, as one of many possible choices. Prof. Colzani analysed the dual challenges of reducing knowledge to scientific knowledge and of the separation between politics and religion, arguing for an 'agapeic-kenotic' view of Christian revelation as a service of love, and for a theology capable of developing the prophetic role of the Church as a school of humanity.

A Pentecostal perspective was given by Rev. Dr. Harold D. Hunter from the International Pentecostal Holiness Church, USA. His response was rather critical towards the study group report, finding it often too conciliatory, indeed almost submissive, towards relativising Christian truth claims in a postmodern context, especially in the field of biblical hermeneutics, and insisting that engagement in interfaith conversations should not lead to affirming a ubiquitous salvific presence in all religions. Nevertheless, in the session, Dr. Hunter emphasised that Pentecostalism, in some aspects, is far from being incompatible with postmodernities. In particular, he emphasised that the hallmark of Pentecostal spirituality is the combination of 'word and deed' called for by the study group report. An Orthodox perspective was given by Ms Anastasia Vassiliadou, University of Thessaloniki, Greece.

Postmodernity in Many Contexts

The moderators decided to organise the small groups according to geographical and cultural lines rather than, as might have been expected when dealing with postmodernity, following fashion by allowing people to choose on their own. This was done to enable the groups to address more seriously the multifaceted nature of postmodernities by letting each group focus on the particular contextual challenges. The diversity within each group, however, was still sufficiently large to make genuinely context-based reflections and discussions difficult; nevertheless, the purpose was at least partially achieved. Each group was asked in the first group session to identify three issues relating to postmodernities, and in the second to outline three main priorities to be addressed by the church in its continuing mission. In what follows, a brief survey of the key issues and priorities addressed by the different regional groups is given. By such a methodology, a certain degree of repetitiveness is unfortunately virtually unavoidable, but we hope that is counterbalanced by the plethora of approaches and perspectives presented by the groups.[5]

The **Northern and Continental European group**, although probably having the smallest population base, was by far the largest, probably reflecting variations in the perceived urgency of the topic as well as the proportionally higher number of participants from the region in the conference as a whole. Thus, the group members decided to from two sub-groups, Continental Europeans in one group and 'Celts' in the other, with the Scandinavians being in a majority in both places. The group from Northern and Western Continental Europe identified as the three main issues: consumerism and market ideology; mistrust of grand narratives, truth claims, authorities and institutions; and individualism. The issues addressed were authenticity, especially in communicating one's faith, the need for a narrative rather than an argumentative approach to witness, storytelling and intercultural Bible reading, the development of an international missionary assistance programme, and the church as a social network in response to the alienation of consumerism.

The Nordic/Celtic Group (calling themselves 'the descendents of the Vikings group') perceived the main issues relating to postmodernities to be consumerism, individualism, social fragmentation and community without commitment, and diversity, plurality and relativism. The following are the most urgent issues the group thought should be addressed. Firstly, there is a thirst for authentic, committed community, since people in the context of de-industrialised societies long for community, but are largely unwilling to pay the price, and yet they do not necessarily see authentic relationships in the churches. Secondly, the challenge to live out the meaning of the good news in daily life has to be faced. This is to be interpreted as the way in which Christ brings freedom, showing that the Gospel is not merely a rational message about a legal transaction nor that the forgiveness of sins is somehow only related to sexuality and the life of individuals, but that the good news speaks to the whole of creation – the environment, the marginalised, the lonely, and those hungry and thirsty – and, thus, reflects perhaps something of the postmodern longing for a healing of the whole of life. Thirdly, there is a need to acknowledge the brokenness, limitedness and vulnerability of all human endeavours, including our witness as Christians, emphasising that the church is not the herald of the powerful and knowledgeable, but the work of the Holy Spirit through weak vessels.

---

[5] Unfortunately, parts of the notes received by the organisers were incomplete, making it impossible to reconstruct all group sessions as well as we would have liked.

This stance may be seen as a way of rejecting 'the juggernaut of modernity'.

The group from **Central and Southern Europe** listed the issues they addressed as life in community, focus on personal relations, the importance of listening and compassion, creating new ministries for lay people, recommending meditation, encouraging ways to reveal and discover beauty, openness to transcendence and silence, and the need for a prophetic voice that offers alternatives to current social pressures.

The issues perceived by the group from **Africa and of African Descent** were uncertainty, facing a liquid future, the fact that the forces that drive contemporary societies largely remain hidden and suspicious. They also thought that postmodernities are often ideologically loaded, that individualism alienates, and that consumerism is probably related to boredom. They touched on the big questions of neo-liberal capitalism and post-colonial reality, stressing that their agenda was to carve out opportunities for new generations, freedom to be what they are, the building of a capacity to resist the new empires, modernity, colonialism and cultural hegemonies, whilst continuing to live with uncertainty. The issues they addressed were a need for a prophetic vision, imagination and leadership to confront the structures and agendas of those that continue to dominate the postmodern scene, such as neo-liberalism, neo-colonialism, patriarchy and consumerism, a need to foster (liturgical) communities of character and discipleship, based on mutual recognition, respect and reciprocity amidst the forces of fragmentation, depletion and consumerist individualism, and a need for discernment of God's presence and the art of participatory theological reflection amidst the eroding of pre-modern worldviews and authoritarian, fundamentalist claims to truth.

The group from **East Asia and Oceania** perceived the main issues as disenchantment with progress and westernisation, combined with the pursuit of consumerism, a fragmentation of society among and between groups according to gender, age and class, and an integration and convergence in the search for meaning, common roots and cohesiveness in society. The issues the group addressed were the challenge of modernisation and westernisation, the picture of churches hardly able to counter the overwhelming thrust of consumerism, and sometimes even supporting or encouraging consumerism, and the emphasis on growth and numbers in some churches endangering their credibility. The group wished to see a rediscovery of a liturgical worship rich in symbolism, addressing the emotional needs of worshippers and enabling them to overcome the disenchantment with rationalism and modernism. They wanted Christians to be encouraged to develop new forms of spiritual interaction by providing more space for people of different languages or age groups to receive relevant spiritual enrichment. It recognised the tension between being relevant to the context and falling into the temptation of letting fashionable trends or new technology set the agenda. They believed that the postmodern climate created new opportunities for Christian voices to be heard, as long as they speak in a language which is acceptable in public discourse. Finally, they suggested that the Christian church has to relearn how to speak prophetically in ways that address social concerns of society in general in a relevant and acceptable manner, based on careful research and analysis of the context and expressed in a vocabulary that resonates with ordinary people.

In the group representing the **Asian Continent and the Middle East**, the discussion was influenced by the fact that postmodernity is scarcely a new phenomenon to the continent, but is an inherent part of the context. Asia may be regarded as already having been postmodern for thousands of years. Thus, the issues perceived were: just how 'modern' is postmodernity, why Asians have to identify themselves in categories defined by the West, and a suspicion toward all so-called meta-narratives. One issue the group addressed was defining and redefining the language Christians use, by recognising the context, considering whether the categories apply, and by realising that in Asia truth comes by discovery, being more experimental than propositional. Another issue was the challenge to the church to be a community that is an alternative to consumerism, paying attention to the doctrine of the body of Christ and to the doctrine of the Trinity, with one corollary being that different parts of the body need to be respectful of others. A third issue was to identify a proper balance between stability and change; each new generation brings change, so the church needs to be flexible and open to change, while at the same time maintaining some continuity and stability, recognising youth and elderly alike without catering to one group at the expense of the other.

The **Latin American and Spanish** group found one of the main issues and its consequences to be a 'melting pot' globalisation and a consequent search for identities (belonging to which groups and heritage, and identifying with what relevant references to the past?) that sometimes overlap and, by adapting to contemporary realities, create new identities. They pointed to the growing concern about loneliness, individualism and depression, expressed in migrations, virtual contacts, chats, and online dating, resulting in a loss of the notion of what is real and what is a simulacrum. Finally a relativisation of truth was seen as an issue. The group thought that the main issues to be addressed were a style of mission that was able to find a synthesis between rational and emotional approaches to human beings in an integral and contextual way, the avoidance of a 'market' or 'consumerist' mentality in the church, the building of communities of faith that make sense in people's lives, that integrate all kinds of people and where people learn to be interdependent. They also emphasised that the church must deepen the discussion of ethical responses to new challenges presented by postmodernity, addressing them with a prophetic voice.

The **Anglo Saxon Commonwealth** group perceived the main issues concerning postmodernities as the search for significance, diversity and pluralism, and consumerism and choice. Characteristics of postmodern approaches were further described as story and image in simultaneous coexistence, a dialectic between experience and truth, on both the virtual level and that of reality, and a practice of authority based on fluidity and relationship. The issues the group addressed were expressed as: first, to live an authentic Christian life is no easy task, but requires a community that both addresses fragmentation and is committed to a visible demonstration of fullness of life and hospitality; second, that mission requires an aesthetics of truth, that is that truth lived truthfully is attractive and the Gospel is beautiful; and third, that citizenship is increasingly lived in the dynamic tension between the global and the local.

The **Anglo Saxon North American** group saw the first cluster of issues to address as about how to enable people to experience church as people and not just a building, how to establish community when people want it on their own terms, and how to establish authentic community, making it possible to move from experience to commitment. A second cluster of questions centred on how to express the role of Christ, in order to convey the full meaning and extent of the freedom that he has promised to give. How is the meaning of the good news to be expanded, assuming that the forensic understanding of atonement alone is too narrow? In this context, the quest for authenticity was seen as crucial. Also, although sin is not understood, brokenness is, thus making it essential to show a radical love and hope that counters the fragmentation of relationships.

Key Issues and Priorities

It is tempting to conclude with this plethora of voices, imitating postmodernity in giving space to all viewpoints without giving any indications of preference. However, some key issues and priorities do emerge, and we will highlight these six:

- The longing for authenticity, whether in spirituality or in everyday life
- Experience being valued more than argument, and its implications for Christian witness; in life, worship and word
- The effects of fragmentation of society and life, and its implication for the church
- The suspicion towards authority, truth claims and other absolutes
- The need to give a constructive alternative to consumerism
- The church as a tool for empowerment or oppression

THEME 4
MISSION AND POWER[1]

This is the report of the 'Mission and power' parallel session which convened in Edinburgh on Friday, 4 June 2010 to build on the report of Theme 4, 'Mission and Power' as published in preparatory volume for the conference.[2]

To discuss this topic, in the tradition of North American indigenous peoples, approximately seventy conference participants from widely divergent ethnic, geographic, and ecclesiastical backgrounds were invited to gather in a circle around the edges of the meeting hall – the circle emphasising their coming together as equals in community. Terry LeBlanc – accompanying himself on a sacred drum – opened the session with a traditional Mi'kmaq welcome song, setting a fitting tone for the discussions to follow.

Ms Lori Ransom, co-convener of the mission and power study group, screened a ten-minute extract from a video-documentary entitled, *Where Are the Children? Healing the Legacy of Residential Schools*, produced by the Aboriginal Healing Foundation of Canada. And, her fellow convener, Dr Jonathan Bonk, summarised the key findings of the Mission and Power chapter, before turning the session over to the chairpersons. The Rev. Dr Mary Mikhael (President, Near East School of Theology, Lebanon) and Christoph Anders (Director, Evangelisches Missionswerk, Germany) shared chairing responsibilities, welcoming the delegates, reviewing with them the parallel session's aims and objectives, and keeping the processes moving throughout the tightly organised three hours. Eight individuals made five-minute summary presentations in response to the mission and power document on three 'transversal' themes and from five regional/confessional perspectives. Their trenchant observations inform this document; several of their presentations are found on the Edinburgh 2010 website.

Participants divided into ten table groups, led by designated facilitators, to engage the Mission and Power study in two thirty-minute sessions. They were asked to: (a) identify significant changes in mission thinking since 1910; (b) highlight key issues associated with this theme; (c) bring about

---

[1] Report prepared by the conveners of this study theme: Ms Lori Ransom, Presbyterian Church in Canada, and Dr Jon Bonk, Overseas Ministries Study Centre, USA. The parallel sessions were chaired by Rev. Christoph Anders, Evangelisches Missionswerk, and Rev. Dr Mary Mikhael, Near East School of Theology.

[2] Daryl Balia & Kirsteen Kim (eds), *Edinburgh 2010: Witnessing to Christ Today* (Oxford: Regnum Books International, 2010), 86–115.

interaction between this theme and the selected transversal topics; (d) include regional, confessional and other perspectives not yet considered; (e) propose key priorities for common action by the churches; and (f) encourage a new vision and common commitment.

Transversal Perspectives

The following interaction was noted between this theme and selected transversal, regional confessional voices.

From the perspective of women and mission, Dr. Atola Langumer (Baptist, NE India) commented that mission is **liberating yet limited**.

> 'The traumatic impact of residential schools among the Native people in Canada exemplifies powerfully Christian mission gone awry as a result of misconceived notion[s] of power.... The pain, social trauma, cultural dislocation, and the loss of identity that resulted... can be re-affirmed by other communities around the world.
>
> While not trivialising the traumatic legacy of the indigenous people in Canada... critical analyses of Christian mission reveal also a better side of the project. The power of the Gospel has initiated and wrought positive changes and transformations which can be exemplified from women's experience of mission.
>
> A case in point of mission being both a positive force and a limiting structure... is the experience of women in the northeast [of] India, particularly among the Mizo and Naga Christians.... To put it bluntly, the inherited Christian community has not challenged the patriarchal structures and the church has not been inclusive in its structure and function... The perils of being trapped in platitudes and tokenism are real and need to be addressed resolutely. The Christian community has the power to engender radical changes, and to follow a spirituality of 'hungering after what is right' (James Dunn).
>
> Mission historians inform us that the most vibrant Christian communities are in the global south, the erstwhile 'mission field'. Ironically this region is the area that poses most challenges for women, be it the raging epidemic of HIV/AIDS, women trafficking, violence against women, cultural practices that are oppressive to women, illiteracy, patriarchal structures, male-centric worldviews.
>
> Advocacy, support, courage to intervene, wisdom to direct, seek culture-sensitive knowledge and maintain critical/prophetic stance, mutually critical and deliberate involvement, not just funding but accompaniment, require women to be represented in consultations, make room for women at the decision making bodies, deliberate measures to equip and develop women leaders, encourage Christian communities to organise gender awareness liturgies/Bible studies, provide theological resources for gender inclusiveness.'

From the youth and mission transversal, Jec Dan S. Borlado (Philippines) said it was **time for repentance**:

'As Asians, our context is that of plurality and diversity. Most of the countries in this region have a colonial past... Asia is home to some of the world's living and reawakening religions that shape both culture and consciousness... in the Asian context, the Christian community is a minority.

It was 489 years ago when the first fleet of Spanish ships landed on the shores of my Motherland. And it has been said that they came holding the Cross in one hand, and a Sword in the other.

Some 333 years later, Protestant Christianity arrived in the Philippines introduced mostly by American missionaries.... After dividing the country up into seven parts, so as to delineate [one part] ... for each church, can it be said that ... they came with Bibles and scissors?

[Christian] missions have been very divisive, destructive and disempowering! If not among those we witness to, to those whom we witness with. The very opposite of what Jesus prayed for.

Today, we are at our crossroads as the global church representing our own respective local congregations. The fullness of God's time has come to pursue new and fundamentally better participation in God's mission in the world. And so I say, let us repent from our ways!

Essential to this road towards new and better things is the young person [who is] both a recipient and potential agent of The Mission.

As a young person, I say:

- through the prodding of the Holy Spirit: empower us to be reconciliatory to the divisions we did not start!
- through the prodding of the Still Small Voice: empower us to be restorative to the lives we did not destroy!
- through the prodding of the Sustainer of our Faith: empower us to re-empower others in reflecting God's will for the whole created world!

Dayam Joseph Prabhaka (Dalit, India) and Professor Dr Yi Su (Elder of Beijing Shouwang Church, China) spoke compellingly of the challenges and opportunities facing Christian minorities in these most populous countries in the world, and expressed **desire for solidarity** with Christians elsewhere. In India, the Dalits are doubly stigmatised and marginalised for caste and religious reasons. Photos revealed how opposition from civic powers drove house church members in China to worship outside in the winter snows.

The resilience and dynamism of these ostensibly powerless Christian communities confounds and distresses those who oppose them – a reminder to all of us that God's strength, exemplified in our Lord's life on earth, manifests itself in and through human weakness.

Regional and Confessional Voices

Veli-Matti Kärkkäinen (Pentecostal, Finland) commented on the power of the Holy Spirit:

> 'It seems to me Christian mission [from the Global North] in the beginning of the third millennium, differently from the past generations whose work has been under critical scrutiny in this document, suffers … more from the lack of divine empowerment than [from] the abuse of worldly powers….
>
> … the document is completely silent about the issue of *spiritual powers*…. In all cultures of the global South (Africa, Asia, and Latin America) and in many contexts of the global North, not only among Pentecostal-Charismatic communities but among all Christian churches, significant issues have to do with deliverance, healing, and similar *power encounters*. Neglecting the topic of *spiritual power(s)* … makes missiological discourse irrelevant in many contexts … [and] continues the Enlightenment-based modernist reductionistic discourse.'

Michael Biehl (Lutheran, Germany) reported on the work of the Association of Protestant Churches and Missions in Germany (EMW) related to Edinburgh 1910 and 2010:

> 'Looking back to Edinburgh 1910 we realised those present from Germany faced a comparable setting [to ours today]: [they] had power in relation to mission and mission churches overseas and they attempted to stick to this power, but they also complained about disinterest in mission in their society and the churches.
>
> We chose the theme 'Mission between power and powerlessness (*Ohnmacht)*'... denoting to be without command to the extent of being absolutely helpless.
>
> …to chose to become vulnerable... *Vewundbarkeit* which expresses both... being vulnerable and becoming sensitive to the vulnerability of others. What could it mean for instance to be attentive to the *charismata* of others? So-called migrant churches are often perceived as being in need of assistance, an object of *diaconia*... To become vulnerable could mean to take seriously that every woman and man can [share in the interpretation of the Bible]…
>
> …we also propose to explore the theme of hospitality. How do we live and express the hospitality we experience from God in the first place? By offering space to each other, by becoming willing to be changed by those to whom we offer or from whom we experience hospitality.'

Graeme Mundine (National Aboriginal and Torres Straight Islander Ecumenical Commission, Australia) drew attention to the power of Indigenous voices

> 'As Indigenous Christians we look to our Churches to walk with us as we throw off those things that oppress us.
>
> …
>
> We need to empower the local Indigenous church to live the life that Christ has called them to. But the Indigenous church needs support; don't

> presuppose that they can do it themselves without proper support and resources.
>
> We need to remember that the "White Western European Church" does not have all the answers... Indigenous peoples were once missioned to; now we are part of the mission force. We are equal partners in the creation of the community of church of the future.... Open your hearts and minds to what Indigenous peoples offer!'

Victor Rey Riquelme (Pentecostal, Ecuador) shared insights in the table group discussions. Anastasios-Elekiah Andago Kihali (Orthodox, Uganda) was prevented by British immigration from coming, but was represented by a designated spokesperson.

Questions and Key Issues

What follows is a distillation of the ten table group discussions which highlighted questions and key issues for ongoing consideration.

1. What are the criteria for differentiating between the transforming power of the Gospel and the deforming power of cultures (exerted internally or imposed externally)?
2. What about power within the Church itself – in its hierarchies, its traditions, its structures, its access to resources, its support and control of missions? The use and abuse of power within the Church is evident in scattered but recurring stories of financial corruption, sexual abuse, and racial, social, and gender discrimination.
3. How can we ensure the empowerment of women in both the church and society? How can western mission partners stress/require gender inclusive partnerships and networks? What would a missiology that is inclusive and gender-sensitive look like?
4. Despite the demographic shift of Christianity, the reality of economic and political dominance by the West remains. What powers do western Christians have to wield influence for a just and inclusive world?
5. What did Jesus mean when he promised that his followers would receive power to make them witnesses to the ends of the earth? Can this power, too, be corrupted and abused? We need to recognise empowerment by the Holy Spirit evident in God's gifts distributed throughout the global Church. Because abuse of power is a pervasive characteristic of all human societies, it must be challenged with the power of the Spirit, which is manifested in grace, love, compassion, and reconciliation.
6. Pentecostals have been quite successful in affirming people on the margins, bringing them into full participation in a grand story that gives them dignity and hope. Power encounter is a

phenomenon that is both common and hope-infusing throughout churches in the global South.

7. The church's alliance with military, economic and political power has been a temptation from the beginning – a temptation to which it has repeatedly succumbed ever since the fourth century. How can the Church extricate itself from such alliances, when often its identity and very survival are contingent on its perceived contribution to national identity and nationalist agendas? Can the Church retreat into the desert? Is there a way other than outright confrontation for the Church to be faithful to its identity and calling?
8. How can Church be an alternative – people-centred, rather than individualistic, market-centred – community, a light on a hill? Sadly, powerful people easily manipulate the Bible, using it as a self-justification mechanism to defend their greed, their comfort, and the unjust structures that perpetuate their privilege.

The Canadian example is one in living memory, but in other contexts, stories of oppression between peoples date back centuries. Time did not permit us to thoroughly consider the resulting questions that arise for Christians. Can any human being transcend the deep conditioning of his or her social milieu? Are the descendants of those who are retrospectively discovered to have done evil responsible for their ancestors' sins? If so, how can restitution or reparations be made? If not, how should we relate to the descendents of those wronged by our ancestors? How far back do we go in assuming responsibility for past oppressions? What is the responsibility of those who migrate into, and assume positions of power in, contexts of past oppression between peoples? What theologies of repentance can help us answer these questions?

Where does and where should the Church fit into all of this – in Africa, in Asia, in South America, in North America, in Australia? Emerging stories of restorative justice and healing and reconciliation processes around the world are signs of hope but they do not erase the damage that has been done. These questions need to be considered equally by those who are the beneficiaries if not descendents of those whose power, misapplied or brutally applied, resulted in the destruction or the marginalisation of peoples; it also applies to those who are the descendents of those whose vulnerability made them easy to bully and vanquish, marginalise, or even destroy.

It is difficult to imagine any resolution that would satisfy all parties, apart from living forward in hope, rather than backwards in blame and recrimination. The human story from the very beginning is the story of migration and the displacement or absorption of incumbent, weaker populations. The New Testament letters were written by and to people who were, if not disenfranchised, at the very least disenfranchised and powerless in homelands that were brutally occupied and ruthlessly governed by the military power of their day. There is little sense that the primary concern of Christian theology was to see that these injustices were redressed. The Good News is not that there can be justice in the here and now, but that a day is coming when all will be well; and that in the groaning-of-creation-meanwhile (Rom. 8:18ff), the followers of Jesus live as a 'peculiar people' – as strangers and pilgrims, citizens of a country whose ruler and maker is God. They are, furthermore, blessed with the palpable reality of God precisely because they are poor; they inherit the earth because they are meek. They do not take the earth by force, but inherit it by divine decree.

Power and Edinburgh 2010

A clear lesson from the past hundred years is the need to remain self-critical about how power is used in the church today. So it is appropriate to make some observations about Edinburgh 2010 itself. Some delegates expressed disappointment at the level of attention to Indigenous and global South voices at Edinburgh 2010. One observed that it took one hundred years for a woman (and presumably Dana Robert was meant) to be given a significant place, so perhaps at the bicentenary event other voices will be given prominence. Delegates valued the opportunity to reflect on questions of power in the parallel sessions and noted the efforts made to make the study process inclusive, but also noted that while the study groups were led by a good balance of men and women they came predominately from the global North. It is worth remembering, also, that a number of delegates, particularly from the global South, were prevented from adding their voices to the conference by the civil immigration powers in the United Kingdom.

Delegates also were saddened by the anguished communique, 'To steal a conference', circulated among principal organisers and study group facilitators by email on 5 May 2010 by Dr Daryl Balia, International Director Edinburgh 2010. This expressed his humiliation at being relieved of responsibility for the conference in the final weeks leading up to it. Since few of us are privy to the reasons for this, we sincerely trust that the silence of the principal organisers on this matter was pastoral in intent, with a view to protecting Dr Balia himself.[3] Nevertheless, this incident serves as a poignant illustration of well intended power at work.

[3] Daryl Balia entered into a dispute with his employer, the University of Edinburgh which was settled in November 2010. He did not attend the conference. Subsequent to the settlement, the General Council of Edinburgh 2010 initiated a process of reconciliation with Dr Balia.

New Vision and Common Commitment

Asymmetries of power – economic, social, political, military, gender, religious – trouble our world and our churches one hundred years after Edinburgh 1910, reminding us that we have not moved as far or changed as much as the inevitable or wilful limitations of our human understanding permit us to imagine.

The Holy Spirit continues to work through the weak, and the mission of the church today is chiefly implemented by those who are invisible from the distant vantage point of worldly power and privilege. Within the global church, the economically and socially *advantaged* are called to soul searching humility in the awareness that God resists the proud, that God in Christ stood outside the door of the affluent Laodicean church two millennia ago, and that God's power is made perfect in weakness. Within the global church, the economically and socially *disadvantaged* can take heart in the knowledge that God welcomes the poor, that it was the afflicted and impoverished believers in Smyrna before whom the great door of opportunity was opened two millennia ago, and that the meek inherit God's earth. Within the global church, collectively and individually, we are called to be disturbed by the asymmetries that divide and trouble us. We are called to repent, diligently, constantly, and actively seeking practical ways to live into the reality that we are members of One Body. They will know that we are his disciples by our love.

THEME 5
FORMS OF MISSIONARY ENGAGEMENT[1]

Church-Shaped Mission

It is an indisputable fact that in historical perspective, mission predates church. Whether we understand the genesis of mission as being in the eternal heart of God, or in the calling of the first Galilean disciples by Jesus, it always comes before the formation of those gathered communities that we call church. The life-blood of church is mission. In *Mission-shaped Church*,[2] a 2004 report to the Church of England, the authors challenge church leaders to re-imagine their ecclesial life as local and global expressions of the mission of God. In Edinburgh six years later a challenge was issued to mission leaders to also re-imagine their mission programs as expressions of church, as the church in mission. With the unquestioned 'success' of mission orders, agencies and movements in recent centuries there arises a real danger that 'church' and 'mission' exist in competition, and sometimes even opposition, with each other. Mission agencies see churches as competitors for finance and ministry, and churches resent the intrusion of agencies in ministry they regard as their own. One of the primary concerns of those who gathered in Edinburgh to consider Theme 5, 'Forms of missionary engagement' was to rid ourselves of this false dichotomy. Orthodox, Pentecostal, Catholic and Protestant participants alike were convinced that mission is primarily the vocation of, and the primary vocation of, the church. As churches must be shaped by, and for mission, so mission must be shaped by the churches that own it, and to which it will give birth.

This commitment to the struggle to hold together mission-shaped churches and church-shaped missions also led to a wider discussion of discipleship. Participants in the discussion came from very different Christian traditions where discipleship is expressed in diverse ways, but all were agreed on the importance of holding together the continuum of service, witness, conversion, nurture, disciple formation and ministry. We recognise that some agencies of mission (a church, agency or movement) might have particular expertise or ministry in one of these aspects of

---

[1] Report prepared by the conveners of this study theme: Canon Mark Oxbrow, Faith2Share, UK, and Dr Genevieve James, University of South Africa. The parallel sessions were chaired by Apostle Dr Opoku Onyinah, Church of Pentecost, and Rev. Dr Darrell Whiteman, The Mission Society.

[2] Graham Cray (ed.), *Mission-shaped Church: Church Planting and Fresh Expressions of Church in a Changing Context* (London: Church House Publishing, 2004) – available at www.cofe.anglican.org.

mission; they might be good apologists or strong in the nurture of the catechumenate, but as a whole church we need to ensure that the total mission of God finds full and faithful expression both locally and globally.

Modalities in Mission

The study group which prepared the preparatory material for the parallel session on *Forms of Missionary Engagement*[3] represented all major Christian traditions and were gathered from five continents. Participants in the Edinburgh 2010 Conference listened to presentations of this material by fourteen different people, using presentation styles that included interviews, video, story-telling and research reporting, and then responded through small group discussions, individual responses and plenary discussion. As a result ninety-four prioritised concerns and recommendations were produced together with seventy-six individual response cards. In totality these concerns, recommendations and responses represent the glorious diversity of God's mission in God's world. We reflected on the witness of those living with disability, the ministry of satellite broadcasts to Christians and enquirers in the Middle East, the benefits of collaboration in mission, the witness of children amongst their peers and to adults, the significance of migration for mission, the challenges of 'short-termism' in mission and much more. Our conviction was that there is no one-way to be engaged in mission but rather God calls us to participate in God's own mission in a myriad different ways. Although our callings may be very different, within the fellowship of the church, we are called to respect the calling and ministry of each other.

Summarising the most significant outcomes of our discussions we wrote,

> In contrast to 1910, today's forms of missionary engagement focus more on mutuality and reciprocity between those who are sent and those who receive. We stress the importance of understanding biblical foundations for our missional engagement, which include a call to risky collaboration with humility between churches and agencies in mission. A growing contemporary form of mission engagement is the use of short-term mission teams which we suggest might appropriately be seen as simply cross-cultural experience rather than as true mission. We call on the churches to recognise that God continues to use children and youth in furthering God's kingdom, but we need to employ appropriate and positive ways to engage them in mission. We also call on churches to rejoice in the fact that migrants from many nations are now bringing new and refreshing expressions of the gospel which have the power both to revive and create new Christian communities. We call on churches that both send and receive migrants to develop ways of equipping all God's people for more effective mission. In all these contemporary forms of missionary engagement we recognised that it is crucial to have a thorough understanding of the context in which mission is taking place.

---

[3] See Daryl Balia & Kirsteen Kim (eds), *Edinburgh 2010: Witnessing to Christ Today* (Oxford: Regnum Books International, 2010), 116-147.

Deep Discipleship

During one of the residential meetings of the study group prior to the conference, we had a challenging discussion about 'vulnerable mission'. Two of our members had written on this topic[4] and another had raised concerns about triumphalism in mission and the rise of the 'prosperity gospel' movement. Discussions during the conference returned to this theme, although time constraints had ruled out a presentation on this topic. There was a strong recognition that shifts in contemporary Christian demography mean that in the twenty-first century 'majority world' Christians (those resident in, or originating from, Africa, Asia and Latin America) will increasing take a lead in global mission and provide more missioners both locally and cross-culturally. Although there are exceptions, majority world Christians are typically characterised by being rich in relational and time/energy resources but lacking financial and material resources. Such situations, sometimes combined with governmental or societal opposition to missionary activity, can lead to very sacrificial and vulnerable mission engagement. In considering the prospects for sacrificial mission service in the present century we were reminded by Orthodox colleagues that across Eastern Europe the century between 1910 and 2010 had been a century of martyrdom with more Christians facing death as a consequence of witness than in the early centuries of the church. Looking to the future we were reminded that in China the church often regards mission service as a prelude to martyrdom – the witness and martyr being one.

Allied to discussions about vulnerability in mission are the concerns that were voiced about the superficiality of much of the evangelisation that has taken place since 1910. The phrase 'mile wide, inch deep' that has been used to describe Christian believing in Africa was honestly recognised to be an appropriate description of Christian communities in many parts of our world today. Participants discussed at some length the reasons for this prevalence of superficial discipleship and raised concerns about missional activities which focus exclusively on 'conversion' with inadequate attention given to nurture, theological education (informal as well as formal), and the formation and modelling of Christian life-styles. Deep discipleship is what is required.

These discussions were underpinned by a shared theological understanding that the call to discipleship is a costly call, involves vulnerability, and requires us to joyfully enter into the life of Christ which led to Gethsemane and the cross as necessary steps on the road to resurrection and glory. We challenge churches and agencies engaged in mission to be less concerned with numbers and more concerned with the depth and quality of the Christian discipleship being lived out in our world.

---

4 See papers by Monica Melanchthon and Joy Mindo available at www.edinburgh2010.org or from f2s@faith2share.net.

Short-Termism in Mission

Having recognised that mission is the work (and life-blood) of the local church, participants discussed many aspects of cross-cultural mission and the role of those who are sent out by the church, often through an agency, to share in the mission of a church or community in another culture and location. The two centuries preceding and following 1910 were recognised as the 'heyday' of the cross-cultural, professional, missionary – normally going from Europe or North America to other parts of the 'non-Christian' world.[5] The future of this particular modality in mission lies in the balance. Particularly in North America, but increasingly in Europe and even Korea and Brazil, the current century has been marked by a rise in the phenomenon of short-term mission. This ranges from cross-cultural engagements of two to three years to mission trips of a few weeks or less. We were presented with figures from North America which showed that in 1989 120,000 people where engaged in short-term mission, with this figure doubling by 1994 to 240,000 and then climbing very rapidly to an estimated[6] 1.6 million in 2005. On the one hand this increase in short-term mission means that a very large number of Christians are gaining first hand experience of another culture and some, rather limited, understanding of the life of the church in these cultures. However it remains questionable as to whether those engaging in such visits, typically of 2-3 weeks, contribute anything of lasting value to the witness of the churches in these contexts.

Two serious questions need to be raised about the stewardship of mission resources (personnel as well as finance) in relation to this rise in short-term mission. First, as each participant needs to raise significant support (typically US$3-5,000) these 1.6 mission visits represent a serious diversion of Christian funds which might otherwise have been available for other missional activities. Second, the help given to churches locally, typically through free labour, building and medical materials, can represent significant disruption to a local economy with churches being tempted to use free missionary labour rather than training their own members in ministry, and providing employment and income to local traders. It was suggested during our discussions that in general short-term mission trips, both for groups and individuals, should be understood primarily as a learning opportunity for the participant and the role of the 'receiving' church should be recognised as that of training facilitator. The need for adequate preparation and debriefing was also stressed. One argument often used in support of short-term mission is that participants then go on to offer for long-term cross-cultural mission at a later stage. This claim is not supported by empirical evidence. A very small number will later serve

---

[5] 'The non-Christian world' was the term used by the World Missionary Conference, Edinburgh 1910 to describe the rest of the world outside Europe and North America.

[6] Estimate produced by Robert Wuthnow of Princeton University.

long-term in another culture but most either engage in serial short-term mission or only make one trip. A stronger argument might be that those who engage in short-term mission go on to be more effective, and more missional, members of their local churches, strengthened by their cross-cultural exposure. For this to happen effectively a positive debriefing process is essential.

At a deeper level, concern was expressed during our discussions as to whether the rise in short-term mission is itself a reflection of endemic short-termism within Western society. Are North American and European Christians reflecting a culture in which three years is a long time to stay in one job, ten years of marriage is seen as 'long enough', and social networks are constantly fragmenting and reforming. What then might be the implications of this cultural shift for incarnational mission, particularly within cultures that value longevity of relationship, where language has to be learnt and where culture and religious backgrounds take many years to understand? We are convinced that God still has a mission for those who will acknowledge a calling to live cross-culturally for the rest of their lives, to learn language, culture and religious traditions, and to struggle over decades to enter the hearts and lives of those amongst whom they come to live. We challenge the churches to identify, call out, train, resource and constantly encourage such people.

Incidental Mission

Whilst recognising the major contribution made to world evangelisation by those who have served in mission full-time, as members of religious orders and as missionaries sent out by churches and agencies, particularly over the last four centuries, we also reflected on the fact that for much of the history of the church the gospel has been carried by 'voluntary' or 'incidental' missionaries. Space does not allow us to rehearse here the debate (held at one table during the parallel sessions) over terminology, but it is important to recall that the first cross-cultural Christian missionaries were refugees fleeing persecution following the martyrdom of Stephen (Acts 8:4), and that it was Nestorian traders and businessmen (mainly men) who took the gospel along the silk routes to China. Even today the vast majority of those who come to faith anywhere in the world do so as a result of the witness of a friend, a teacher, a business colleague or a member of their family. In our discussions this not only encouraged us to stress the first point made in this chapter – that the primary agent of mission is the local church – but also to recognise that God has in the past, and will in the future, use many different groups of people as gospel-carriers, as missionaries.

Some concerns were expressed that as a result of the success of the nineteenth and twentieth century missionary enterprise we may now over 'professionalise' the missionary vocation and fail to motivate and equip all members of the Body of Christ for their part in the mission of God. We welcomed the century old insights of Roland Allen into the role of the 'Voluntary Missionary'[7] and were encouraged to see renewed interest in such movements as 'Business as Mission'[8] and 'Tentmakers'.[9] We also wanted to recognise the missional impact of the professional environmental engineer, the diplomat, the campaigner for human rights and the family on holiday in Tunisia.

Migration and Mission

Of particular interest to participants in our discussions was the link between migration and mission. Throughout history migrants – Islamic, Buddhist and Hindu as well as Christian – have carried with them their faith commitments and planted new religious communities wherever they have settled. It is well recognised that we live in a world today that experiences more migration than ever before. People migrate for a vast range of reasons including hunger, persecution, environmental degradation and natural disaster, searching for employment, education, retirement and family reunion. In discussion we were reminded that the (temporary) migration of Chinese students to Europe and North America and their exposure there to Christian faith has been identified as a major factor in the growth of the 'third church'[10] in China today. Ethiopian migrants doing domestic work in the Gulf States have not been slow to share their Christian faith with their employing families, and the thousands of Filipino workers who find their employment outside the country are bearing witness to Christ in countless nations. The challenge we want to put before the churches is how they are preparing those members of their congregation who migrate, permanently or temporarily, to be effective witnesses to Christ in their new host culture. We heard good examples of mission agencies in the Philippines offering training to migrant workers pre-departure and of missional networks amongst Africans living and working in Europe but much more could be done. We also want to challenge churches to receive and welcome migrants as co-workers in mission and to offer them an effective induction into the challenges of mission in their new culture. One participant observed that the annual cost of sending one Norwegian family to work in Egypt is the

---

[7] Roland Allen *The Spontaneous Expansion of the Church* (London: World Dominion Press, 1927).

[8] See for example C.N. Johnson, *Business as Mission: A Comprehensive Guide to Theory and Practice* (Downers Grove, IL: IVP Academic, 2009).

[9] See for example J.M.M. Francis (ed.), *Tentmaking: Perspectives on Self-supporting Ministry* (Leominster, UK: Gracewing, 1998).

[10] The term 'third church' is used to describe the rapidly growing church amongst intellectuals and business entrepreneurs in China, as distinguished from the 'three-self' churches and the 'house church' movement. See Rob Moll, 'Great leap forward', in *Christianity Today*, 9 May 2008.

same as training over two hundred Filipino workers for mission across the Middle East.

Whilst migration offers many opportunities for mission, it also provides us with missional challenges in terms of human exploitation and damage to family life. At its worst migration is a result of human trafficking and results in sex- or trade-slavery. The mission of God requires that Christians engage with society to bring such practices to an end and to restore the image of God in the lives of persons broken by this evil.

The Mission of Children

One of the more controversial discussions during the conference was over the role of children in mission. The recent focusing of attention by several mission agencies on the '4-14 Window'[11] and a recognition that an increasing proportion of the world's population is under fourteen was coupled with the empirical evidence that most Christians begin their faith journey during childhood (up to eighteen years), or report childhood exposure to Christian communities as a significant factor in later coming to faith. Whilst expressing some enthusiasm for a fresh assessment of the role and potential of children in mission, participants also wanted to express concerns about the care of children, their potential for exploitation and a right recognition of childhood. We recalled that Jesus placed a child amongst his disciples and that several biblical children played key missional roles in the life of Israel and the early church. We recognised that children need to be freed and resourced to be witnesses to Christ in 'childish' (child-like) ways, and not expected to live and share the gospel as little adults. We challenge churches to review what resources and training they make available for children within their communities to witness to Christ in their own ways. The mission of children, we stressed, will be holistic, as it is for adults. We heard stories of children who have cared for the sick, advocated for the marginalised, proclaimed the gospel, prayed for the nations and seen God work miracles in their communities.

We also considered mission *to* children and stressed that this needs to be undertaken sensitively, within their family and community contexts, and address their levels of maturity and practical, psychological and spiritual needs. In considering the needs of children in contemporary society we particularly commend those churches and agencies that campaign to end the exploitation of children and foster healthy development through family, education and community.

This brief reporting of several hours of deliberations by almost one hundred experienced and well informed leaders from five continents and every Christian tradition inevitably omits key concerns and

---

[11] See www.4to14window.com and B. Budijanto, *Emerging Missions Movement : Voices of Asia* (Compassion/AEA, 2010), 23-49.

recommendations raised by many members. We had positive discussions about the role of the media and the arts in mission, we made pleas for more collaboration and coordination between churches and agencies, we shared the pain of neo-colonialism, we laughed with God at our small visions, and we fell silent when God spoke to our hearts. God reached out to us that week and we will continue to find a myriad ways of echoing that outreach of love in our world.

THEME 6
THEOLOGICAL EDUCATION AND FORMATION[1]

The parallel session on theological education on 4 June 2010 affirmed the general findings and recommendations of the international study report on theological education[2] which were summarised and presented by members of the international study group on theological education – Dr David Esterline, Dr Namsoon Kang, Dr Dietrich Werner and Dr Joshva Raja – in the beginning of the session.

Theological Education and Mission

Theological education – understood in broad perspective – supports the whole of Christian mission through education of:

- the ear to hear God's word and the cry of God's people;
- the heart to heed and respond to the suffering;
- the tongue to speak to both weary and arrogant;
- the hands to work with the lowly;
- the mind to reflect on the good news of the gospel;
- the will to respond to God's call;
- the spirit to wait on God in prayer, to struggle, and to be silent, to intercede for the church and the world;
- the body to be the temple of the Holy Spirit.

While the plea of Edinburgh1910 to develop contextualised forms of theological education in the Asian churches was partly answered by many indigenous models of theological education which were established in the twentieth century, Western patterns and concepts of theology continued to be exported throughout the global South, so that the task of Edinburgh 1910 was only gradually and very incompletely fulfilled. Therefore an

---

[1] Report prepared by the conveners of this study theme: Dr Dietrich Werner, World Council of Churches, ETE, Geneva, and Dr Namsoon Kang, Brite Divinity School, Texas Christian University. The parallel sessions were chaired by Professor Brian Stanley, University of Edinburgh, and Rev. Dr Desmond van der Water, Council for World Mission. The preparatory work of this study theme is summarised in Daryl Balia & Kirsteen Kim (eds), *Edinburgh 2010: Witnessing to Christ Today* (Oxford: Regnum Books International, 2010), 148-74.

[2] International Study Report on Theological Education: Challenges and Opportunities in Theological Education in the 21st century, WCC, ETE 2009, see also: Dietrich Werner, David Esterline, Namsoon Kang & Joshva Raja, *Handbook of Theological Education in World Christianity: Theological Perspectives, Ecumenical Trends, Regional Surveys* (Oxford: Regnum Books International, 2010).

urgent need remains in many places for culturally and linguistically appropriate programmes and resources of theological education.

The interlinkedness of Church, Christian mission and theological education was highlighted by many authors and studies in the twentieth century, but the concrete implementation of this vital interrelatedness remains a constant task for all churches and institutions of theological education. The process of theological education both reproduces and reflects existing ecclesial and denominational realities, but should also challenge the existing realities of both the church and the world from the perspective of the kingdom of God and his love for all creation.

New discourses in contextual theologies have also had a profound impact on the understanding and practice of theological education. These new discourses include feminist theologies, postcolonial perspectives, ecumenical perspectives, and theological responses to postmodernity, religious plurality, globalisation and ecology. The rise of Christian fundamentalism and the frequent lack of understanding of the values of the ecumenical movement present a serious challenge for theological education and its task to promote a proper and holistic understanding of Christian witness, service and unity.

Among the most important challenges for reshaping and strengthening theological education and missionary training for world Christianity in the twenty-first century are the following factors:

- Disparity in the availability of resources for theological education between the North and the South, and within several regions
- The tremendous rise in the number of higher education students in the South in general and the rise in applications for theological study programmes in particular
- The growing interest of Pentecostal churches in theological education programmes
- The urgent needs prevailing in many contexts to create more space for women in theological education, theological leadership and in the ministries of the church
- The lack of common quality standards and mutual recognition between theological schools of different contexts, denominational background and theological orientation
- Denominational fragmentation of the international landscape of theological education institutions
- The grave lack of scholarships and grants available for higher studies in theological education and the increasing difficulties of churches to fund their institutions of theological education
- Changing structural conditions of theological education (the move in some contexts away from church-related seminaries towards state-funded departments of religious studies)

- The fundamental implications of global migration movements and changing and increasingly diverse constituencies for programmes of theological education

The session listened to additional important perspectives from regional consultative processes and transversal themes by representatives coming from Roman Catholic, African-Feminist, Evangelical, Japanese and Australian backgrounds, including those offering perspectives on children's ministries and their relevance for theological education. Presenters included: Dr Fulata Mbano-Moyo, World Council of Churches; Dr Anthony Gittins, Catholic Theological Union, Chicago; Wendy Strachan, Scripture Union International Children's Ministry; Dr John Hitchen, Laidlaw College, New Zealand; Dr Ken Myamoto, Kobe Shoin Women's University, Japan; Dr Julie Ma, Oxford Centre for Mission Studies; and Rev. Mikhail Goundiaev, Moscow Patriarchate and Ecumenical Centre, Geneva. In discussing both the report and the additional inputs, the working groups of the parallel session affirmed some common issues and highlighted some additional perspectives which are summarised in the subsequent paragraphs.

Educating the Whole Church and the Whole Person

The concern for Christian education, theological education and ministerial formation which has been a key task throughout the history of Christian mission from its very beginning, needs to be reaffirmed and identified as a strategic task of common action for all Christian churches in the twenty-first century. We can say together: Educating the whole people of God is a key to mission and Christian mission should be the organising focus and reference point of theological education. As Christ's mission has had a deep concern for children, any mission-minded theological education in the twenty-first century needs to have concern for children's ministries and children's theology in order to give visible expression to the fact that children represent 30 percent of world Christianity while still being marginalised in theological curricula. We are called to an expanded definition of theological education as theological formation begins at a very young age, and does not happen only in schools and churches. Children should be seen at the centre both in church life as well as in programmes of Christian education and theological formation. As most theological education for children is still left to women, theological education institutions are called to support theologically-sound role models of both sexes today. The lack of properly trained Sunday School teachers is a very serious challenge for the future of all churches.

New ways of doing theological education are needed that encourage a holistic approach in methodology involving the entire human being, openness to interdisciplinary work and moving beyond compartmentalisation of theological disciplines. Theological educators should also aim for the integration of academic learning with spiritual growth and the development of pastoral identity, the development of gender sensitivity and inclusiveness towards marginalised groups, the contextualisation of teaching resources and language of instruction and an interaction between lay theological education and ministerial formation.

While the development in much of the twentieth century was towards institutional centres of theological education copying patterns of residential colleges of the West, new realities and challenges in the past decades have given emphasis to the strategic role of non-formal and non-residential forms of theological education and training for ordination which are often more viable and affordable to churches. To develop a proper balance between formal and non-formal, residential and non-residential forms of theological education is one of the key tasks for many churches in the early decades of the twenty-first century.

Bridging the gap between theory and practice, between serious theological work and critical reflection or reasoning and pastoral competences, spiritual and ministerial formation should form an undisputed goal of theological education in all Christian denominations as all affirm the holistic nature of theological education to serve the mission and pastoral work of the church in today's world. The spiritual life of the teacher often is the model which may influence students more than what is formally taught in the classroom. As the academy, college or university model of theological education appeared late within the history of Christianity it can learn from and be complemented by other models of theological learning and teaching which have an even longer history (wisdom model of theologising; discipleship model of learning theology; monasteries and worshipping communities as place of theological education).

Biblical, Ecumenical and Global Education

Reading and studying the Bible as the Word of God should form the basis and undisputed primary resource of any theological education. Immersing oneself into the rich treasures of its symbols, narratives, images and stories can serve as a common ground between different Christian traditions and also as an inspiration for alternative ways of theological reflection beyond critical reasoning. For all Christian traditions in the twenty-first century there is the challenge to re-evaluate the role of the Holy Spirit in both illuminating the Scriptures and also in seeing God at work in the lives of people and in this world. Theological education needs to be inspired by a new hermeneutic of the work of the Holy Spirit.

Both the ecumenical and the global dimensions need to be strengthened in theological education programmes so as to give sufficient attention and scope to burning issues of Christian unity and common witness in the rapidly changing landscape of world Christianity. The Gospel is a Public Truth and not a private matter, therefore theological education needs to equip people for reclaiming the public space for theology and for Christian witness by facing the burning issues of today's society.

While all theologies have a contextual nature and there is no universality of any type of theology which can be imposed on others, there is a universal and common basis of all theological education in the Holy Scriptures and Christian tradition. Therefore a balance needs to be maintained between the need for common standards and common criteria in quality of theological education and the need for contextualisation of its curriculum and content.

New spaces need to be created – both in physical and digital dimensions – for more interchange of resources for theological education, teaching staff and students, online-materials for theological education, curriculum models and courses between the continents and within regions. This will allow for more mutual benefit and strengthening of international partnerships in theological education. Text books for theological education which are often out-dated need re-editing with the help of persons assisting from other contexts. A worldwide online network among theological educators of diverse theological traditions could help to enhance open and frank discussions, to nourish mutual understanding and to correct theological perceptions and prejudices over against other traditions.

Theologies related to gender, children, minorities, refugees, marginalised people, and so on, often are not integrated into the core of systematic theology or biblical studies. There needs to be a clear understanding of how catholicity and contextuality in theological studies are balanced with each other in the definition of what belongs to core and compulsory or additional and voluntary courses of theological studies. Voices of the marginalised and subaltern populations need to be heard and have equal participation in theological education. 'Theological education in the presence of the other' is the key word for the future of theological education in the twenty-first century.

Access to and the Future of Christian Education

Churches should have more concern for the support and development of general Christian education both in universities and in private or public schools. The lack of basic Christian education which is spreading in many countries poses a serious challenge to the future of both the Christian presence in society as a whole and the future of theological education. Many people in secular universities in Asia, Africa and Latin America are open to the Gospel, but have few opportunities within these institutions to learn about Christianity. Many young people in urbanised and increasingly secularised regions do not have appropriate Sunday School education any more.

Increasingly candidates from Pentecostal and emerging churches join ecumenical and denominational theological training to obtain their theological degrees. This creates new ecumenical spaces for the Christian churches. The plea was made to include at least one representative from Pentecostal churches in the decision making bodies of ecumenical or interdenominational colleges to allow for mutually benefiting experiences. There is a need for strategic alliances with the Pentecostal and newly emerging churches in terms of ecumenical theological education without losing the theological, academic and contextual rigour.

Wherever politically possible, churches should engage with governments in order to secure the future of theological education in university settings. There is a move from denominational seminaries to studying in university faculties of religion. This means that many of the theological seminaries are at risk of closure or the dimension of ministerial formation has been weakened. This also risks a disconnect from the international communions of various Christian traditions. Also inter-denominational theological seminaries have been closed or are threatened in some contexts. While the insights of 'secular' education are of their own value to the theological enterprise and theological education should not be isolated from other realms of human knowledge, emphasis should be given to the need to bring theological perspectives to bear on the task of defining the distinctive goals and character of theological education. Increasing tendencies of universities to integrate theological education under philosophy and religion departments put pressure on churches to look for their denominational-oriented training centres. In some cases denominational houses of studies within university contexts have proved a good alternative and complement. Ecumenical institutions find it hard to survive both due to the monitory expectations of the universities and also due to the increasing secularisation of theological education in university contexts. While working under a lot of academic and financial pressure ecumenical theological colleges need to deliver the ministerial training expectations of the churches without losing their contextual emphasis. In this sense such ecumenical institutions of theological education need to be encouraged worldwide.

In much of Europe a general decrease of the number of students in theological education is evident, partly because the job market is constraining the usefulness of this type of education for future employment, and also because church membership in dwindling as a whole. Churches need to rethink how the study of theology can be attractive for future generations and how proper jobs for pastors, evangelists and missionaries can be maintained and financed. Churches might need also to think of a new kind of apologetics of Christian faith to be developed in facing highly secularised contexts. In European countries also the growing independence of the state in its role for funding, accreditation and general resourcing of theological education is a reality with which some churches have to come to terms with.

Across the diversities of the Church the need is felt for deep education and mentorship in spiritual as well as intellectual dimensions. The churches are called to prioritise such spiritual competence both among educators and among their students of all ages, both within the traditional settings of seminaries, universities, and churches, and also throughout all the life contexts in which learning takes place. Enabling continued theological education for its ministers is a strategic task for all churches.

There is also an urgent need to reconstruct the educational programme for theological educators. Who educates the theological educators? To whom are they accountable and how are they supported in their task? Theological educators need continued education, spiritual accompaniment and a reasonable time for new research and learning in their fields of competence so that they can grow in theological expertise and pedagogical skills as well as in spiritual mentorship.

New Partnerships Between South and North

As stated in the global study report the issue of language remains a strategic issue for the future and accessibility of theological education. The lack of proper indigenous resources for theological learning and instruction leads to exclusion of vast sectors of world Christianity from advancement in theological competence and Christian leadership. The hidden cultural factors involved in a situation in which mainly English materials and texts are recognised, published and circulated internationally need to be critically reflected.

We also need new and authentic models of international partnerships between institutions of theological education in the North and the South, East and West. As it is a known fact that most of the Christians are in the South and most of the educational resources are in the North, it is not acceptable that those who are in control of the inequity should attempt to solve this crisis with 'tokenism' by making unilateral decisions about who comes and who does not, rather than giving up some of their privileges and developing models of mutual sharing and decision-making. The richest seminaries of this world, rather than becoming the 'experts' on the communities of the South and importing select southern students to kneel at the altar of accredited education, should contribute to credible and authentic models of authentic partnership with theological colleges and faculties in the South.

Facing the rapidly growing needs for theological education in the southern hemisphere, a new global fund for promoting theological education in World Christianity should be considered as a visible expression of mutual solidarity between churches in order to continue the work which was started by the Theological Education Fund (TEF) in 1958.

An international working group for theological education should be considered – or explored as working group within the International Association for Mission Studies – which would bring together representatives of all Christian confessions beyond all present divides and which would serve as a continuation committee of this session of Edinburgh 2010 to explore common synergies and joint action in support of theological education for the mission of the Church.

The integrity and authenticity of all the diverse streams of World Christianity in the twenty-first century can be maintained and deepened only if we move beyond a situation in which Christianity seems to flourish where theological education does not and vice versa, but where instead innovative forms of theological education are emerging which are life-giving, renewing, participatory and relevant for the growing charismatic renewal movements in the South and for the renewing churches in the North.

THEME 7
CHRISTIAN COMMUNITIES IN CONTEMPORARY CONTEXTS[1]

Dr Marian McClure Taylor (Kentucky Council of Churches, USA) and Dr Walter Altmann (the Central Committee Moderator for the WCC) chaired the proceedings of Theme 7 Christian Communities in Contemporary Contexts on 5 June 2010. We began with words of welcome and introduction from Dr Afe Adogame, University of Edinburgh, convener of study group 7. He introduced the issues and priorities that had been the foci for this particular commission.[2] These priorities were: context/mission; service/*diakonia*; solidarity/advocacy and community (re)building; spirituality and youth. Some of the major issues addressed by the study group were: migration, HIV/AIDS, poverty, gender and reverse mission.

The study process accompanying the discussion of how Christian communities in contemporary contexts will carry out their task of witnessing to Christ today was presented in several formats, namely highlights from specific consultations that were held during the study process and presentations from various speakers.

Mission in Context

Dr Philomena Mwaura (Kenyatta University, Kenya), co-convener of theme 7 shared highlights from a consultation held at the Carmelite Conference Centre in Karen, Nairobi on 26-28 May 2009. This event included 46 participants from Eastern Africa (Kenya, Uganda, and Tanzania) from a variety of Christian traditions, and including scholars, clergy, youth, women, elderly and people with disabilities. Themes addressed during the one-year study process and at the conference reflected the pertinent issues of mission in the Eastern African context. It entailed a critical evaluation of the why, the what and the how of carrying out Christian mission in Eastern Africa. Some highlights from the consultation are as follows:

---

[1] Report prepared by the conveners of this study theme: Dr Afe Adogame, University of Edinburgh, and Dr Philomena Mwaura, Kenyatta University, Kenya with the support of Dr. Janice Maclean and Erica Dunmow. The parallel sessions were chaired by Rev. Dr Walter Altmann, World Council of Churches, and Dr Marian McClure Taylor, Kentucky Council of Churches.

[2] See Daryl Balia & Kirsteen Kim (eds), *Edinburgh 2010: Witnessing to Christ Today* (Oxford: Regnum Books International, 2010), 175-98.

1. The church is vibrant and alive in Eastern Africa and bears a youthful face. This is evidenced by its numerical growth, proclamation of the good news of Jesus Christ, prophetic witness and mission initiatives – justice and peace- building, reconciliation health care, education, media ministry, advocacy for democracy, humanitarian assistance, and many others.
2. Eastern Africa is a region largely characterised by poverty, disease, corrupt and unaccountable leadership, and ignorance amidst enormous resources. The mission of the church therefore has no alternative but to direct its engagement and proclamation towards redressing these anomalies.
3. Mission ought to be carried out in humility and guided by the principles of sharing, compassion, integrity, equity as opposed to charity, respect for the human person and cultures, and building community beginning with family values.
4. Women are increasingly accessing leadership in Pentecostal/Charismatic churches but this does not necessarily translate into empowerment of all women in the churches. Gender inequality and inequity as well as concern for youth and children are urgent concerns for mission in East Africa. The youth continue to feel marginalised in mainstream churches. While some have found a home in emerging churches targeting their needs and involving them in ministry, others are victims of militia groups that exploit their vulnerability. Children are an endangered community and there is need to develop a theology of childhood.

The second highlight of the study process was presented by Dr Janice McLean (City Seminary of New York, USA), a member of the steering group of theme 7. Her presentation was based on two consultations held in Edinburgh on December 2008 and June 2009 respectively. Some of the summary recommendations emerging from the themes discussed at these consultations were on the following concerns.

1. Regarding youth, the world church should acknowledge their full personhood in Christ; the liminal position that they inhabit within the society and celebrate the unique perspectives that such a position gives; and their need for space to grow in faith and equal opportunities in leadership within the contemporary church.
2. On the issue of gender, the church should strive to acknowledge and address the presence of the 'glass ceiling' phenomenon within contemporary churches and recognise that women are pivotal to the life and ministry of the church and should be given equal opportunities within leadership.
3. In relating to immigrants, the church should seek to acknowledge the perceptions that both the immigrant and the

people within the receiving country have of each other, and the lack of hospitality, restrictive access, racism, suspicion and disregard that regularly accompanies these perceptions. The church should live out the biblical mandate to welcome and to care for the stranger in our midst.

4. In urban contexts and situations of poverty, the church should strive to acknowledge the importance of urban ministry for the future – especially in regards to the needs existing in slums and *favelas* – and the need for creative, multidisciplinary, and culturally sensitive measures in dealing with the issues associated with poverty. The church has a responsibility to care for the poor and marginalised within the society, while also challenging the existing socio-economic and political world orders that undermine the dignity of all humanity.

These highlights and recommendations were followed by several regional presentations. A brief summary of these presentations are documented below.

Professor Nico Botha (University of South Africa, South Africa) outlined how, in the South African context, they have found that 'subverted hope' is a more sustaining concept that optimism. Even creative processes such as the Truth and Reconciliation Commission have not avoided the tendency to benefit the elite. Real transformation is much harder to achieve.

Dr Yong Cho (Tokyo 2010, Japan) spoke powerfully of how the delegates at the major mission Conference in Tokyo earlier in 2010 were challenged by a delegate from Sweden to pray for reverse mission to the First World as a primary mission need.

Rev. Dr Carlos Ham (WCC-Latin America and the Caribbean) gave a presentation on Latin American Council of Churches in which he outlined the complex inheritance of Christianity in South America since 1910. The Catholic, Independent and Pentecostal churches will need to work more closely to bring about a truly holistic mission, where there is both comfort for poor people and confrontation of the causes of poverty. Their history shows that 'mission without service (can) easily turn into violence and oppression' and that they are often tasked with sharing good news in the context of 'bad' news.

Dr Antonios Kireopolos (National Council of Churches, USA) spoke from the Orthodox perspective how after five generations in the US that church still has an essentially 'immigrant' self image, and that it is not mainstreamed within US society. This says powerful things about the impact of culture and ethnicity within churches.

Rev. Professor Kenneth Ross (The Church of Scotland, UK) gave an overview of the recently published *Atlas of Global Christianity*, co-edited with Dr Todd M. Johnson.

Poverty, Gender and Migration

The small group discussion that followed these regional presentations focussed on three theme clusters and three related questions as follows:

- Poverty, suffering and marginalised communities: How should the church disciple, work for justice, heal and witness in contemporary contexts of poor, suffering and marginalised communities?
- Identity, gender and power: In contemporary settings that are important to you, how do unequal gender relations in the church affect the integrity of church witness, and what can be done?
- The interface of migration, diaspora, ethnicity and reverse mission: What are the tensions in this interface? And what are some models for resolving these tensions?

During the discussion each group was asked to come up with three concise recommendations to be offered as our contribution to the 'Common Call'. The small group discussion was followed by a short video clip of the documentary *African Christianity* produced by James Ault. The afternoon session began with Walter Altmann giving a summary and feedback on the morning's proceedings. This was followed by four presentations addressing the application and practice of theme 7 concerns within Christian communities.

Rev. Laurie Hudson (Director, Edinburgh City Mission) highlighted some of the work of the City Mission within Edinburgh, giving particular attention to its work in West Pilton, a socio-economically deprived area of the city – a programme which incidentally is conducted by an African Christian immigrant.

Prof. Daniel Patte (Vanderbilt University, USA) gave a presentation on the Bible and mission, showing how attention to the context of New Testament teaching deconstructs a Western understanding of mission.

Ms Claudine Chinoh, an Asian migrant from Australia talked about the ongoing process of reconciliation within the churches with the indigenous peoples. However, only 12 out of 128 parishes in one Anglican Diocese have indigenous people in their congregations. There is an ongoing act of confession with the powerful church leaders saying 'sorry' to the less powerful. This makes some of the hurt of past actions bearable, but this needs to be followed up by real inclusion. Her presentation summarised the finding of a 'Towards Edinburgh 2010' gathering that was held in Melbourne in October 2009.

Rev. Dr Carlos Rodriguez Linera (SEDOS, Rome) spoke from a Catholic perspective about the need for the church to address our treatment of the planet and all its creatures, not just its human inhabitants, and how Genesis was being used as the starting point of a re-framing of the theology of mission.

One critique that was voiced during the afternoon session by Dr Antonios Kireopolos highlighted the absence of the Orthodox perspective during the presentations that occurred in the morning session. Following the critique, several minutes were given to a representative of the Orthodox Church to share with the participants some of the ways that the Orthodox Church was grappling with the themes addressed by the Commission.

The afternoon session concluded with a discussion by Walter Altmann and a Song/Psalm writing exercise, which was moderated by Ms Erica Dunmow (UK Urban Mission Congress), member of the steering group of theme 7. The idea for the Song/Psalm Writing exercise emerged out of the UK Urban Mission Congress, *JITC Belfast 2010*. As a way of responding to the thoughts that emerged, the attendees spent about 10-15 minutes simply reflecting on what they had experienced and bringing it to God. It was this reflection that was later offered to God and the community as a psalm/song.

Shalom as the Goal of Mission

During the conference, attendees came to the following conclusions:

Wholeness and *shalom* for the world as the goal of mission. Our mission is to serve and accompany communities and individuals on their journey to wholeness. Conversion can be an important part, of this journey. We must pursue wholeness for ourselves and others, for individuals, families and communities. This means *shalom*-healing for issues of mental health, sexual health, self esteem, unemployment, physical illness and in bringing reconciliation and justice. We seek a positive and healthy environment for all, challenging powers and authorities that do not bring *shalom*-wholeness.

The complexity of mission. Growing Christians in tough communities require the grace of God, prayer, unconditional love, long-term commitment and creativity. There is a false separation between taking social action to bless and social action to convert. The aim of our mission must be both personal and about society. We must be sensitive of the flows in and through our cities, and journey with the people who travel along them, creating community as we go. Above all we must show tenderness as we look upon people, and bring comfort by sharing in the suffering (2 Cor. 1:3, 4).

Leadership from within. We need to find ways of communicating the gospel in peoples' everyday language, and this may mean that people who have grown up in the community may be better placed to do this than us. This requires being willing to partner with others in recognition of all that God is already doing. Amidst all this we need to fix our eyes on Jesus, remembering that it is as we hope in the Lord and wait upon him that our strength will be renewed (Isa. 40:31).

The need for the church to change. We need to acknowledge that the church has been part of the problem, dividing, exploiting, disempowering and ignoring the wider issues. The church needs to surrender its power and strongholds, joining with the mission of God (*missio Dei*), the ministry of Jesus, to the world to bring the *shalom* of His upside-down servant kingdom. It means being an animator (not a catalyst) that is changed in the process of bringing about change. If the church is unwilling to change, the intervention can make the problem worse (the technical term for this is *iatrogenesis*).

The church as the whole body of Christ. The church is in danger of 'othering' – both finding a positive identity through the stigmatisation of others and a self-affirmation that depends upon the denigration of the 'other'. Instead the church must find its core identity by collaborating with partners who share kingdom principles, offering a prophetic voice to the city through our actions, working with God to bring His kingdom in the world.

'Messy truth about mission'. In this understanding of mission, 'messy' primarily means 'complex and diverse', but with an admission that it is not always as well-ordered or as positive in outcome as we would like it to be.

Change and Reversal in Mission

The following recommendations and summary sentences were initiated during the small group discussions, further deliberated upon by the core group and the moderators and then finally put forward as theme 7's contribution to the Edinburgh 2010 Common Call.

Poverty, suffering and marginalised communities. No system (in churches and agencies at all levels) favours the poor despite God's preference for poor, marginalised and suffering people. We need to identify and challenge this injustice. In light of this, people from poor, marginalised and suffering communities from all over the world need to be able to shape their own insights and theologies. Richer, more powerful parts of the Christian body need to support and recognise 'the ridiculous situation in North America [that the predominant style of church] means that Good News for the poor is unaffordable by the poor'. Mission in poor, marginalised and suffering communities should be from their standpoint. Mission agencies should work with indigenous/local/ neighbourhood churches, not primarily through national structures. Big, capital projects (schools, hospitals) do not address the causes of poverty. Financial support needs to be long-term. Where church leaders/missionaries are placed in poor, marginalised and suffering contexts from outside (North/West, richer) – that is where they are not indigenous leaders – they need to be better formed/trained/equipped in how to share faith and take actions of service and challenge, appropriately within context. Poor, marginalised and suffering people must be involved in shaping and delivering that training.

This should include good practical examples of places where it works, and short-course training events and materials including conscientisation, peace-building, and reconciliation strategies.

Identity, gender and power. The image of God in every person needs to be recognised through our own vulnerability and result in profound openness to every person. Christians should recognise the manner in which language can contribute to a marginalising identity – ethnic minority. This is a way of 'othering' especially by those who have power. We need to stop using a subject-object model of relations and adopt a subject-to-subject model which involves equity/equality, reciprocity and complementarity of personalities and gifts. We recommend the institution of programmes of gender equality training for the church; that men should partner with women to promote equal opportunities in the church; and that girls/women should be encouraged to accept positions in leadership, and remembering that Jesus Christ demonstrated respect for both men and women.

The interface of migration, diaspora, ethnicity and reverse mission. The quest for hospitality – sharing, accommodation, conversation, inclusion, friendliness – involves cross-cultural learning (because of mutual ignorance), mutuality in our relationship with each other (in the metaphor of the body), and realising that we are all immigrants, that is sojourners in the world. As an American permanent resident is called a 'resident alien', we are mundane but also extraterrestrial. When considering 'reverse mission', we need to ask: What do host Western churches stand to gain or lose? There is a mentality that the West does not need the gospel (mission) but the global church needs to reprioritise its mission to include the West.

One Body in Mission

To sum up: The God of mission sends us, vulnerable as we are, to witness by word and action for transformation as communities of faith. In the context of local needs and using available resources we will recognise the image of God in both women and men and bring them into the fullness of life in Christ.

Mission is encountering and discerning God in all human beings and all the created world. We call for a renewed understanding of holistic mission in the twenty-first century through empowered communities of local believers.

Mission in reverse mandates robust, mutual cross-cultural learning. In God's mission we are all sent to share God's love and to receive God's love from the other and in this mutual experience of God's grace we are all changed. There is a shared sense of relevance, urgency, and necessity of mission, especially in solidarity with the poor and marginalised, yet the call should not be read as a consensus about everything related to the purposes, strategies, and methods of Christian mission. In particular, the question of language and terminologies and 'who names what' needs to be critically looked at if Christian mission enterprise is to make significant difference in the world today.

The global church needs to be unified, standing as one bride in answering the call of Jesus to make disciples of all nations; reaching out to the poor, the wealthy, the marginalised, the ignored, the powerful, the young, and the old bringing reconciliation, showing love, demonstrating grace and speaking out truth. As a global church on a mission, our policies and academic work, our discussions and mission statements need to move off the page, out of the conference halls, into the streets, the offices, the homes, the schools – where our discomfort leads us to action.

THEME 8
MISSION AND UNITY – ECCLESIOLOGY AND MISSION[1]

Remembering a Future

The opening act of worship on Wednesday, 2 June 2010 in the Pollock Halls of Edinburgh University marked only one moment in a long process of study and reflection. Widely anticipated, yet momentous nevertheless, it opened a window onto the missional landscape of the early twenty-first century. Thus established, this vantage point allowed a brief opportunity to review at least one hundred years of prior commitment to mission and unity, understand its significance for the present moment, and draw collective lessons pointing the way forward to 2110. Many authors have detailed the developments in world mission and world Christianity following Edinburgh 1910 and study group 8's agenda was in part a direct reflection of some of these historical developments.

The success of Edinburgh 2010 may be seen in its commitment to facilitating the widest possible joint reflection, by representatives from every part of the worldwide Christian community, focussed on mission theology and practice. The presence of such a diverse selection of representatives was a wonderful testimony to the Holy Spirit's activity in drawing us into conference together. It was also a further reminder of the long journey that is yet to be made before the questions raised by Theme 8 are answered – questions that prompt heart-searching, theologically rigorous creativity, and even confession and repentance.

In 1910, Commission VIII was convened around the theme of 'missionary co-operation' and, although proscribed from discussing schemes of union between the various Christian churches, it has proven to have had a long-lasting impact on such issues. At no point has the search for the unity of the Church been able, for long, to avoid discussing questions of mission and unity. Equally, discussions of mission and unity have only begun to make complete theological sense when they have been joined by discussions of ecclesiology.

Throughout our discussions, the desire for the unity of the Church has been both our starting point and our assumed prerequisite and goal of

[1] Report prepared by the conveners of this study theme: Revd Dr Darrell Jackson, Redcliffe College, UK, Ms Kyriaki Avtzi, Churches in Dialogue, Conference of European Churches, and Rev. Dr Laszlo Gonda, Debrecen Reformed Theological University, Hungary. The parallel sessions were chaired by Revd Prof. Dr Viorel Ionita, Conference of European Churches and Sr Dr Geraldine Smyth, OP, Irish School of Ecumenics.

mission. We believe that Edinburgh 2010 stands apart from 1910 due to its exploration of mission and unity in their necessary relationship with ecclesiology. The presence of Roman Catholic and Orthodox missiologists and mission leaders as full participants in the 2010 conference and in the study group lent urgency to the task of ecclesiological dialogue. The presence of significant numbers of Evangelicals, Pentecostals, and independent indigenous churches points to the vertiginous nature of the challenge in the decades ahead. Their voices were joined by those of large numbers of women, young people, and representatives of socially marginalised groups whose priorities were reflected in the discussion and reflection of Theme 8 and are likely to prove vital to discerning a new vision for mission, unity and ecclesiology.

The Church in Relationship With and to the World

The Edinburgh Study Conference held during June 2010 was only one aspect of an ongoing study process. In March 2009 the conveners published a set of eight study questions intended to provide a framework for discussion of mission, ecclesiology and unity among and by the stakeholders as well as by ecumenical, theological and mission organisations with an interest in contributing to the study process. The study theme title, 'Mission and unity: Ecclesiology and mission' may have been taken to imply that there were two themes that did not wholly overlap. The conveners believe that theologically there is only one theme – that of the Church in its relationship with and to the World – but that it is a theme with three foci. Consequently, it framed the initial discussion of the theme with reference to the following eight questions:

1. The mission agencies of 1910 preferred to avoid ecclesiological discussion. Why has ecclesiology come to prominence in the contemporary discussion of mission and unity?
2. In the new landscape of world Christianity, what and where are the new or emerging missionary movements, missional ecclesiologies, and ecumenical missiologies?
3. Where are the biblical, theological, and contextual resources for a satisfactory discussion of 'mission, unity, and ecclesiology'?
4. What are the missiological and ecumenical implications of baptism (initiation), Eucharist, apostolicity, and ordination (ministry)?
5. What are the ecclesiological and ecumenical implications of mission focussed on healing and reconciliation?
6. Are evangelistic witness and prophetic witness compatible with the search for visible church unity?
7. What and where are the models of evangelistic witness undertaken ecumenically?

8. How might the coming century be one in which a journey towards one common commemoration in 2110 is charted and undertaken together by churches and mission agencies?

As the convenors – Revd Dr Darrell Jackson, Redcliffe College, UK, Ms Kyriaki Avtzi, Churches in Dialogue, Conference of European Churches, and Rev. Dr Laszlo Gonda, Debrecen Reformed Theological University, Hungary –prepared for the Edinburgh 2010 conference, and as they took soundings and consulted, it became clear that a number of emerging issues must be addressed by participants in Theme 8. In preparing for the parallel sessions at the conference, the conveners had at their disposal papers from Protestant, Evangelical, Pentecostal, Roman Catholic, Orthodox, younger missiologists, subaltern groups, and missiologists reflecting wide regional and confessional interests. These drew attention to the unavoidable theological dialogue that would be required if progress were to be made on the issues over coming decades. The convenors recognised from the outset that the Study Conference would not provide sufficient space for the necessary dialogue and consequently they drafted the following list of issues as a framework for focussing the discussion. The list summarised the most significant and remaining issues that still required urgent attention at the outset of the 2010 Study Conference:

1. How can we constantly renew the theological insight which understands mission as the responsibility of the whole church yet which guarantees the freedom to innovate in mission? How might we hold within the same concept of the *missio Dei*, for example, the Orthodox conviction that mission is exclusively the task of the Church alongside much Evangelical and Pentecostal practice that holds a special place for the autonomous missionary society?
2. There remains a need to give urgent attention to the missiological implications of baptism, eucharist, apostolicity, and ordination.
3. Mission engagement frequently raises questions of structural unity and this may be more remote today than at any point in the last one hundred years: 21,000 denominations globally in 1982 became 39,000 by 2001. Does a Roman Catholic theology of 'real if imperfect communion' sit comfortably alongside an Evangelical appreciation of missionary diversity, for example, even while the churches are engaged in a search for visible unity?
4. Contemporary discussions of mission, unity and ecclesiology continue to give inadequate attention to issues of equal partnership and sharing of power. Institutional centres of mission power are still in the North despite contemporary mission activity being predominantly an activity of the churches of the global South.

5. How to respond to an anti-mission mood, reinforced by the 1972 call for a moratorium on foreign missions, and reflect carefully on the implications of a growing inter-church relief and development presence in the very countries where missionary presence and involvement has been discouraged?

The convenors were also asked to distil key priorities that should be addressed in the foreseeable future by the Churches and their mission agencies. The convenors suggested the following priorities:

1. Churches are urged to give ongoing attention to the renewal of theological and missiological foundations for contemporary mission particularly, given our theme, those of 'reconciliation' and 'evangelism' as integral dimensions of the *missio Dei*. Specifically, churches are encouraged to discuss and adopt the World Council of Churches, World Evangelical Alliance and Roman Catholic 'Code of conduct' relating to evangelism and mission. At the very least, churches responsible for mission should underline their commitment to non-violent evangelism, disavowal of proselytism, and deeper appreciation for both missionary and canonical territory.
2. Commission Eight of Edinburgh 1910 highlighted joint action in Bible translation and joint conferencing. What new expressions of mission in unity might be stimulated by previous and current examples, particularly the laudable co-operation existing between Protestants and Orthodox with regard to the provision of study material for Orthodox youth and children across a number of Central European countries?
3. Churches are encouraged to renew their search for contemporary forms of co-operation in mission which centre around discussions and practice of 'mission(ary) spirituality'.
4. Churches should urge the global bodies to which they belong, including the Global Christian Forum, the World Council of Churches, the World Evangelical Alliance, the Lausanne Committee for World Evangelization, and other world confessional bodies, to renew their search for contemporary, credible and visible answers to the questions raised by mission, unity and ecclesiology.
5. The relatively recent and growing contribution of Pentecostal and charismatic movements to discussions of greater unity at world level should be communicated and devolved to regional and national ecumenical and missional movements and instruments.
6. Churches are called to confess mutual exaggerations, prejudice, ignorance and disrespect and support this generation of post-1961 church and mission leaders committed to repentance, mutual respect and prayer for the visible unity of the Church.

> This may necessitate a 'healing of memories' as they relate to the integration of the International Mission Council with the World Council of Churches, particularly in light of the fiftieth celebration of that event.

Rainbows and Hexagons

The study process on theme 8 at the conference was chaired across two sessions on Friday, 4 June by chaired by Revd Prof. Dr Viorel Ionita, Conference of European Churches and Sr Dr Geraldine Smyth, OP, Irish School of Ecumenics. Three-and-a-half hours were given to brief plenary presentations and a substantial small group process (in so-called 'Rainbow Groups') of discussion and deliberation.

Each session opened with a brief review of the issues and priorities that had been previously identified from the preparatory text produced for theme 8[2] as well as from pre-conference written contributions. Six self-selected small groups were addressed by presenters representing transversal, confessional and regional perspectives. Fifteen minutes of presentation was followed by forty minutes of group interaction reflecting, where possible, at least two transversal perspectives.

The final twenty minutes of small group discussion were spent in formulating short statements, questions, and observations in response to the issues presented and discussed in the small groups. Participants were also asked to keep in mind the issues and priorities identified previously, copies of which were presented to them at the outset of each session. Statements were written onto large hexagons that were subsequently mounted on the wall and arranged and re-arranged to allow the team of convenors to identify themes and relationships emerging from the statements written onto each hexagon. The arrangement was visible to participants throughout, formed the basis for further plenary discussion, and allowed the photographic capture of the work of each of the small groups.

Small group work in the study sessions allowed the discussion of the issues and priorities in the light of presentations representing the conference transversals. Contributions from the Asian region made reference to forms of Asian missiology that have arisen 'from the underside' and which therefore represent an impulse towards a wider unity that takes account of religious plurality, a unity or solidarity with the poor and oppressed, and a unity that eschews the perpetuation of eucharistic division. The contribution of such 'grass roots' missiology was also a particular feature of the Mission and Unity project of the World Alliance of Reformed Churches.

---

[2] Daryl Balia & Kirsteen Kim (eds), *Edinburgh 2010: Witnessing to Christ Today* (Oxford: Regnum Books International, 2010), 199-221.

The potential for unity to be discovered through the sharing of experiences, the seeking of 'common traces of the Spirit' was raised by the contribution from European theological educators. They stressed the need to see contextuality and catholicity as equally important influences upon our understanding of mission and unity. They posed the question 'Where does the unity of Christian faith lie?' and developed an understanding of unity to cosmic and universal conclusions in which the unity of the world is the unity towards which God is working.

Younger missiologists and theologians contributed a vision of ecumenical mission that is creative, contextual, communitarian, and compassionate, above all describing mission as the joyful sharing and service that leads to freedom and appreciation of the gift of life lived in God.

From Canada, subaltern perspectives emphasised narrative and mission. This perspective was shared by Pentecostal representatives, many of whom work within the predominantly oral cultures of the global South. They urged the global Christian bodies to give more space for Christian movements rooted in oral cultures and who consequently stressed narrative aspects of the Christian faith, in contrast with an emphasis on doctrinal statements.

For Pentecostals the unity of the church is a primarily pneumatological reality. They emphasise unity in the Spirit over 'one baptism' or even 'one eucharist'. In contrast to some approaches offered within the study session, Pentecostals argued that their eschatological outlook is a necessary antidote to seeing Christian mission as little more than human activism. For the Pentecostal, God's breaking into the present from the future is a hallmark of the missionary work of the Holy Spirit.

The work of the small groups was recorded using hexagons onto which were written short statements reflecting the questions and conclusions of each of the groups. The hexagons were displayed on a wall and arranged spatially to reflect common themes and contributions. Their ultimate arrangement was captured by digital camera and served as a point of reference for the final drafting of the Study Theme's submission to the drafting group working on the conference 'Common Call'.

Mission Flowing from Common Call and Sending

Addressing the theme of 'Mission and unity: Ecclesiology and mission' in small group presentations and discussions was a representative group of contributors. Dr. Jean-Daniel Plüss, a Swiss Pentecostal theologian, focused on the church as a Spirit-filled body of believers, the church as a business enterprise, and the church as God's instrument of reconciliation. Fr. Vineeth Koshy, Secretary of the Commission on Youth of the National Council of Churches in India, emphasised mission as liberation and located friendship at the heart of mission as healing and reconciliation. Pastor Julio

César López, minister of St. Andrew's Presbyterian Church in Buenos Aires, urged the restoration of the church in situations beyond human perception though not beyond God's ability. Rev Dr. Matthew Cook, a contextual theologian from the Faculté de Théologie Evangélique de l'Alliance Chrétienne in the Cote d'Ivoire, introduced the intercontextual audit as a means towards the goal of 'real though imperfect communion'. Ecclesial and missional unity have to be discussed with respect to contextual diversity. Virginia Beardy, a member of URM-Canada and part of a native Canadian community of 380 in the remote north of the country, told stories of marginalised networks of grassroots activists as a form of 'mission as accompaniment' participating in the 'struggle of the exploited, marginalised and oppressed for justice and liberation'. Dr Daniel Jeyaraj, Professor of World Christianity at Liverpool Hope University, addressed questions raised by reflections on the Indian context. Fr Baudouin Mubesala OMI, who works at the Institut African des Sciences de la Mission, Democratic Republic of Congo, was denied an entry visa to the UK but submitted a paper which described missionary community as *kenosis* and communion, a communion that unifies the *missio Dei* and the *missio ecclesiae* and inspires the Christian witness to life in the African context.

In responding to the presentations, study theme participants discussed questions of power and territory; 'baptism, eucharist and ministry'; healing communities; mission theologies rooted in context, experience and biblical faith; missionary spirituality; the missionary nature of the church; the centrality of dialogue to mutual learning from narratives of grassroots unity; the need to seek new dialogue partners; the need for repentance of disrespectful, violent, or ignorant attitudes towards others and the towards God's creation; a recognition that authentic mission expresses humility and vulnerability alongside a confidence in God's missionary presence; the need for more adequate ministerial formation; an essential emphasis on conversion understood in the light of the grace and love of Christ; and, the acknowledgement that unity in mission requires both institutional *and* organic structures.

Through a final, though brief, plenary session the study theme participants identified the following themes:

1. A core conviction that the Church is missionary in its very nature, but it is a mission flowing from God's call and sending. The 'body the Christ' metaphor reminds us of our need for common vision, the need to respect the diversity that exists among us, and our need for mutuality, partnership and networking in mission.
2. The failure of Churches to disavow the abuse of power and money, territorial exclusivism, individualism., and a surrender to secularism. The challenges of baptism, eucharist and ministry remain, and together we are urged to seek an

understanding and practice of unity-in-diversity in the global Christian community that emphasises hospitality, mutuality, missionary spirituality, love, and renewal in the Holy Spirit.

3. Mutual learning emerges through dialogue and the sharing of stories of historical and contemporary good practice of the church, united in experience of hospitality, evangelisation, healing, and the partnership of all God's people in witness and service.
4. We are already in communion, although it is not a perfect communion. Thank God for progress and give thanks for the excellent work towards unity achieved by various ecumenical and evangelical agencies and organisations. In this respect much might be learned from inter-contextual audits.
5. More networking in mission is needed, especially of networks engaged in mission practice at the grassroots level, and greater attention was urged to the concerns of young people about inadequate models of mission.
6. It was also agreed that discussions of mission and unity could not afford to ignore questions of young people, creation and ecology.

The Banquet of the Kingdom

In summarising the work on the study theme, the conveners and moderators presented the following submission to the conference working group, elements of which appeared in the 'Common Call':

> From across six continents and after one hundred years we come in praise and thanksgiving to God, Father Son and Holy Spirit, for those who have preceded us, and those who will follow us, as participants in the *missio Dei trinitatis* and for their commitment to that unity for which Christ prayed; so that the world might believe.
>
> As churches we acknowledge our failures; the abuse of power and money, territorial exclusivism, individualism, inadequate respect for other cultures and surrender to secularism. So too, recalling Christ the host at the banquet of the Kingdom and His super-abundant generosity towards the poor, the outcast, and the stranger, we have much of which to repent; particularly in our lack of hospitality towards one another.
>
> We invite churches, mission societies, ecumenical and evangelical bodies to a process of deep reflection on the meaning and call of mission as hospitality. In particular, we encourage, local and national councils and alliances of churches to take initiatives in welcoming churches in diaspora and in creating opportunities for mutual learning, exchange and common witness in the one Body of Christ.
>
> We also encourage closer co-operation and dialogue towards convergence in our respective and joint statements on mission and ecclesiology. We commend for further study, for example, the 'Code of Conduct on

Conversion', 'The Nature and Mission of the Church', 'The Whole Church', and the results of bi-lateral dialogues on relevant themes.

THEME 9
MISSION SPIRITUALITY AND AUTHENTIC DISCIPLESHIP[1]

Our report in the pre conference publication concluded that in our time we need 'a mission spirituality that recognises that God is already working, has been working within all cultures, revealing Godself'.[2] We affirmed that mission spirituality cannot exist without authentic discipleship and a discipleship that is holistic. We also called for a 'renewed discipleship that expects the unexpected in a spirit of humility and reconciliation'.[3]

We began our series of meetings at Edinburgh 2010 by wondering if we should rather be discussing mission spiritualities in the plural rather than just the singular. We affirmed that our spirituality must be shaped by our context and that this would influence our understanding and expression of spirituality as followers of Jesus. Our spirituality must be daily, local and lived. We also affirmed that God's call to mission is for every Christian and that we are called to live this out in community. We considered that for Christians, the staple food for our spiritual lives is: the Scriptures, prayer, confession and the Sacraments. These are important sources for our mission spirituality and discipleship. We also noted the importance of the Trinity in modelling a community.

This report covers activities during the conference week in Edinburgh, particularly the two sessions allocated to the commission theme: 'Mission spirituality and authentic discipleship'. As the study process began years prior to the conference, and will continue on toward the publication of a study volume, the conference discussions are considered as part of a larger study process. Like other study group meetings, the participants of our sessions had been pre-assigned to ensure diversity in confession, geography, gender and age.

---

[1] Report prepared by the conveners of this study theme: Dr Cathy Ross, Church Mission Society, UK, and Dr Wonsuk Ma, Oxford Centre for Mission Studies. The parallel sessions were chaired by Most Revd Mario Joseph Conti, Archbishop of Glasgow, and Rev. Bertil Ekström, World Evangelical Alliance Mission Commission.

[2] Daryl Balia and Kirsteen Kim (eds), *Edinburgh 2010: Witnessing to Christ Today* (Oxford: Regnum Books, 2010), 222-44, and 241.

[3] Balia & Kim, *Edinburgh 2010*, 242.

What Motivates and Sustains You in Mission?

During the conference, on the last working day (5 June 2010), two parallel sessions had been allocated for discussion and deliberation. The first session was chaired by Most Revd Mario Joseph Conti, Archbishop of Glasgow. In this session, participants were asked to sit in small groups, preferably among those of different ecclesial traditions and to answer the following question: What motivates and sustains you in mission? It was noted that at least two groups were language-specific: Spanish and French.

The records of the groups reveal lively interactions and discussions during the session. Some repeated keywords or phrases illustrate discussions around them in the groups, and some of them are: 'mission spirituality is Christian spirituality'; 'working for community motivates working in community of Christ'; 'focus on scripture for direction'; 'the Holy Spirit motivating in mission'; 'motivation of mission coming [found in] responses to injustice'; 'word of God, sacraments, and prayer'; 'love of God'; 'incarnation'; 'being and doing in Jesus' way'; 'mission sustenance [found] in the community in the Trinity'; 'cost of discipleship'; and enigmatic scribbles such as 'back stairs above dirty room'.

Each group then produced a paragraph to summarise their discussion. Against the original plan, time did not allow to share the small group discussions with the entire group. The group statements are as follows.

> Living mission is to be Spirit-filled, to respond to God's call, empowered to make Christ's love and justice visible; we do this as a community of disciples open to conversation and partnership with others.
>
> Mission spirituality is experience of God, lived out as persons in communities through the empowerment of the Holy Spirit for witness and service, following Christ's way in the hope of reconciliation with the whole of creation.
>
> Mission spirituality is daily commitment to Jesus Christ and obedience to the Holy Spirit that directs that our whole life in joyful service to God and creation.
>
> Mission spirituality is rooted in the work of God, going beyond the church, and we live this out through the humility, love and forgiveness of Christ and forming authentic relationships in community.
>
> Mission spirituality is the ongoing inspiration of the Holy Spirit that moves us to witness to the good news of God's love in Jesus Christ's life, suffering, death and resurrection with the aim to bring together God's family in a loving household, share a sense of God's call, live life in humility and fulfil God's will on earth.
>
> Mission spirituality is responding to Jesus' sacrificial love for us empowered by the Holy Spirit, in joyful obedience in crossing boundaries to live attentively to others in a shared search for the fulfilment of God's purposes.
>
> The Holy Spirit grounds us in mission and sustains us in living it out so that we see the fruits of the Spirit in ourselves and others.

> Mission spirituality means the urgency to love God and one's neighbours as oneself, through self-discipline, risk-taking, and cultivating relationships as in the parable of the Good Samaritan.
>
> Living mission is to be Spirit-filled, to respond to God's call, empowered to make Christ's love and justice visible; we do this as a community of disciples open to conversation and partnership with others.
>
> Mission spirituality [refers to] God's transformation of humanity and all creation through a daily relationship with his disciples to serve in the love and power of the Holy Spirit.

The second session was chaired by Rev. Bertil Ekstrom, Director of World Evangelical Alliance Mission Commission. The aim of session two was to give a clear articulation of what we mean by 'mission spirituality' and how we live it out. Participants were asked to do this in one sentence and to use, where possible, strong, active verbs to ensure our mission spirituality is a lived spirituality. These sentences, beginning with 'We believe we are called to…', formed the basis of our statement in the Common Call issued at the end of the conference. At the end of the process, each group statement was posted, discussed and questioned, and at the end, an initial group statement was reached:

> Remembering Jesus' way of witness and service, we believe we are called by God to follow it joyfully, inspired, anointed and empowered by the Holy Spirit, nurtured by Christian disciplines in community, to bring God's transforming and reconciling love to the whole creation.

Subsequently the statement underwent a revision process, as summaries from other groups were brought together to form an integral whole as the Common Call. The Call was read at the closing ceremony.

The *Missio Hominis*

As part of the group process, both sessions also included brief presentations, divided into two categories: transversals and regional/confessional presentations. Also given was a brief report on the Seoul Consultation of the study group 9.

Dr Wonsuk Ma (Oxford Centre for Mission Studies, Korean, Pentecostal) and Dr Cathy Ross (Church Mission Society, New Zealander, Anglican), conveners of study group 9, gave a report of the Group's planned consultation, which took place in Seoul, Korea in March 2009. About a dozen presentations were made at that event, representing mission experiences in different socio-cultural settings. Predominantly coming out of mission experiences, these stories illustrate how mission is understood in theory and practice, and what motivates and sustains mission. Christian spirituality is shaped not only through the understanding of a community, but also through its lively interaction with cultural and social context, and its response to human needs. Many studies agree that the main impetus for mission comes from the combination of the biblical call to serve others and the immediate needs presented by society, especially in the context of suffering. Worship, word, liturgy, and prayer are critical parts of Christian spiritual discipline which sustains mission, and they are practiced in a community context.

Short presentations were given on three of the seven Edinburgh 2010 transversal topics: Bible and mission, subaltern voices, and ecological perspectives. The Bible and mission report was presented by Rev. Nicolae Mosoiu of the Romanian Orthodox Church, who argued that, while the concept of *missio Dei* provides the foundation for Christian mission, God's people are called to actively participate in this in Christ's way. Thus, their role is to fulfil the *missio hominis*. The response of humans, created in God's image, to God's call for mission is illustrated in three particular ways: (i) God is omnipotent but he respects our will (Matt. 23:37-38); (ii) God is omniscient but we can surprise him because we really are free and spontaneous (Matt. 8:5-13); and (iii) God has total freedom, but he, somehow, feels obliged to answer to our repentance (Luke 19). Rev. Mosiou reflected that the ground of mission is love, and its goal is life. The Church is the aim of mission, not vice-versa. Mission is part of the nature of the Church, and mission is centripetal rather than centrifugal, organic rather than organised.

Furthermore, he stressed that the importance of 'the liturgy after the liturgy' cannot be overstated. Liturgical life nourishes the Christian not only in the personal realm but also in the social and political spheres. The liturgy nourishes the community gathered for worship and then sends the community out to the ends of the earth refreshed and sustained by the bread and wine of the Eucharist. A fresh appreciation of the life of the martyrs of our communities can also inspire and motivate us in mission and contribute to our mission spirituality.

Sister Sarah Newland-Martin (Protestant, Jamaica) of Ecumenical Disabilities Network (EDAN) issued a call for a theology of transparency – a challenge to live transparent lives with no hidden agenda. We were reminded that for our mission to be sustainable we must speak the language of the people so that our mission is indeed transformative. There was also a powerful call for our mission spirituality to therefore address the issues of the day (such as poverty, terrorism, HIV/AIDS and exploitation of creation) and so to model a different way – the way of the Cross.

Dr Rogate Mshana (Tanzania) reported on the World Council of Churches' project on economic justice. Through the report, we were challenged to a costly discipleship in the area of creation care, and to put justice and sustainability at the heart of our faith. We were called to a costly discipleship as we work for eco-justice. This means addressing the ongoing plunder of the earth and developing a theology that will sustain and encourage care for God's creation. We need teaching on just and fair stewardship so that we not only restrain ourselves from over-consumption but also learn to share freely. We need to learn to live an exemplary life modelling what it means to live a sustainable lifestyle. We could draw lessons from indigenous peoples whose spirituality is all-embracing and holistic. A final and more demanding task may be to advocate for the recognition of ecological debt where Christians challenge international institutions and governments to flesh out international and national regulatory and legal frameworks that oblige ecological debtors (whether a country, corporation or institution) to stop destroying sources of sustenance, to repair, and to pay for ecological damages. Dr Mshana concluded that a robust theology of creation is needed as part of our mission spirituality and discipleship.

Transformative Spirituality

A series of contributions was made from regional and confessional perspectives. Megan O'Callaghan (Anglican, New Zealand) presented the study process of the spirituality sub-group of the World Council of Churches' Commission on World Mission and Evangelism. The Commission has recognised the need to be spiritually grounded to inform and inspire Christians as we participate in God's mission. Its working group was called together intentionally to reflect on what the various elements of a 'transformative spirituality' might be and how this relates to mission in an ecumenical context. In its 2008 meeting, the group recognised that a transformative spirituality calls us into a relationship with the Trinitarian God through the experience of the Spirit. It involves seeking to bring healing to a wounded world, searching for a new relationship with God and God's creation and responding to Jesus' preaching of the kingdom of God. The 2009 meeting highlighted that spirituality by its very nature is something that cannot necessarily be defined because it is experienced and understood in many different ways, but a transformative spirituality requires naming the barriers that separate us and then breaking them down. The third meeting explored the issue of 'transformative spirituality, mission and care for creation'. Again, the method of the ecumenical conversation provided deep insights on how our spirituality as Christians in all our diversity calls us to a new way of seeing and relating to God's world that brings new life, sustains, heals and reconciles. Throughout its study process, Ms O'Callaghan reported, the workgroup was sustained and motivated by focused prayer and spiritual sharing.

Professor Calixto Salvatierra (Catholic) reported on the Edinburgh 2010 research project of Instituto de Misionología, Universidad Católica Boliviana, Bolivia. He reminded us of the extraordinary influence of the ecclesial base communities within that continent. The starting point of mission is the encounter with Jesus, and our spirituality is enriched by our engagement and solidarity with the poor. Professor Salvatierra reminded us that the church is in a permanent state of conversion. He challenged new movements to be transformed into small missionary communities that would love and radiate the life of Christ for the good of humanity. However, we also considered the importance of mass movements and were asked to reflect on the challenge of 'Ghandian Christianity'. Gandhi lifted the love ethic of Jesus above mere interaction between individuals to a powerful social force on a larger scale so that structures and society could be impacted.

Revd Dr Kwabena Asamoah-Gyadu (Anglican, Ghana) brought a summary report of the West Africa regional Edinburgh 2010 conference which took place at the Akrofi-Christaller Centre, Ghana in March 2009. Deliberations focused on the nature of African Christian spirituality not just as an academic enterprise, but as something that has been shaped by the encounters with indigenous or primal spirituality and other transnational church movements of the last century. In the African traditional cultural context, what is primarily real is the spiritual and this appears to be in some contrast to traditional western Christianity which tends to generally be a system of doctrinal ideas. The issues of culture, gender, and experiential Christianity, which have been at the heart of the growing presence of Christianity in Africa, thus featured prominently in the deliberations. The aim was to present African Christian spirituality as having much to say about the changing nature of Christian mission a century after Edinburgh 1910 and even beyond.

Dr J. Steven O'Malley, Professor of Methodist Holiness History, also Director of Revitalisation project of Asbury Theological Seminary, Kentucky, USA, presented a report of the second of three annual consultations of the Center for the Study of World Christian Revitalisation Movements, an interdisciplinary research center at the seminary. This took the form of a pre-conference event preceding Edinburgh 2010, and was held at the University of Edinburgh, on 30 May – 2 June, 2010. Sponsored by the Henry Luce Foundation, the consultation theme was 'Exploring the dialectic between revitalisation and church', and it included forty participants representing five continents and seventeen nations. Teams explored data on revitalisation from consultation one, supplemented by presentations of diverse models of revitalised churches, and they produced informed briefs on interpretive trends in Christian revitalisation for the early twenty-first century.

The last presentation was by Dr Joshua Kalapati, Associate Professor of Philosophy of Madras Christian College, Tambaram, India, who reflected on Indian Orthodox experience. One of the challenging tasks for Christians living in India today is to relate the message of Christ meaningfully and relevantly to the other religious communities, especially the Hindu community, which constitutes more than eighty percent of population. As a mission strategy in the Indian context, he suggested, one could think of utilising such secular, progressive, liberative ideas and voices which are not in conflict with the Christian gospel. Besides, he reported, there are several contemporary and contextual models of mission, which are emerging out of the economic and socio-cultural dynamics of the country, which could also serve as effective channels of spreading the Christian message.

Remembering Jesus' Way of Witness and Service

The statement produced from the group sessions has now been incorporated into the final paragraph of the historic Edinburgh 2010 Common Call, which reads:

> Remembering Jesus' way of witness and service, we believe we are called by God to follow this way joyfully, inspired, anointed, sent and empowered by the Holy Spirit, and nurtured by Christian disciplines in community. As we look to Christ's coming in glory and judgment, we experience his presence with us in the Holy Spirit, and we invite all to join with us as we participate in God's transforming and reconciling mission of love to the whole creation.

As mentioned earlier, the conference sessions were part of a longer study process which will culminate in the publication of a study volume. One paragraph of the listening group of the sessions captured the essence of the group discussions:

> At the conference we heard a call for a return to the classical Christian spiritual disciplines: the practice of daily scripture reading and meditation, prayer and solitude is a fount from which flows spiritual vitality for mission. But neither Christian spirituality in general nor mission spirituality in particular are solitary enterprises: they have to do with a spiritual life lived in community, rooted in common worship and sustained by the prayer and encouragement from our local Christian communities. Transformations that we are privileged to see in the lives of others grow out of the same source of sustenance. Today we are discovering anew the significance of spiritual direction or companionship, two persons walking and talking together in the presence of God, seeking his will and direction for their lives.[4]

At the end of the group sessions, we became aware that Christian spirituality, and hence mission spirituality, is an ongoing process of Christian life and experience. No one can claim to have reached the fullness of Christian and mission spirituality, as growing to the fullness of Christ cannot be achieved in this side of heaven. Furthermore, this process is also a series of encounters and interactions between Christian conviction and living contexts, all in a community setting. In spite of the critical role of the context, the group wishes to join the affirmation which the listening group made in its report: 'Discipleship and the call to discipleship are the gifts of grace from God, and from God alone, and mission spirituality recognises that God is already at work, and that we may join in on what he is doing'.[5] The participants have also realised that our mission shapes our spirituality and our spirituality is shaped by our mission so that our spirituality, mission and discipleship become an integrated whole.

---

[4] Edinburgh 2010 Listening Group Report. See Reports section of this volume.
[5] Edinburgh 2010 Listening Group Report. See Reports section of this volume.

Selected Papers from the Parallel Sessions

The Atlas of Global Christianity: Its Findings

Todd M. Johnson & Kenneth R. Ross[1]

Why an Atlas?

When marking the centenary of the 'Edinburgh 1910' World Missionary Conference, it would be remiss not to recall that one of its significant achievements was the production of the *Statistical Atlas of Christian Missions*.[2] This groundbreaking volume was produced at the behest of the flagship Commission I on 'Carrying the Gospel to all the Non-Christian World', chaired by John R. Mott. A sub-committee of its members, chaired by James S. Dennis, prepared the atlas as an appendix to the Report of the Commission. It was soon recognised as an authoritative and definitive work in terms of mapping the progress of Christian missions in the 'non-Christian world' as it was understood at that time.

As the centenary of the epoch-making conference approached, a plan to create a new atlas was adopted as an adjunct project of Edinburgh 2010. With a nerve centre at the Center for the Study of Global Christianity at Gordon-Conwell Theological Seminary near Boston and a worldwide network of contributors spanning the confessional spectrum, the atlas project got fully into gear during 2006.[3] Edinburgh University Press agreed

[1] Dr Todd Johnson is Research Fellow in the Study of Global Christianity and Director of the Center for the Study of Global Christianity at Gordon-Conwell Theological Seminary, USA; Rev. Prof. Kenneth R. Ross is former Council Secretary of the Church of Scotland World Mission Council and Honorary Fellow of the Edinburgh University School of Divinity.

[2] *Statistical Atlas of Christian Missions: Containing a Directory of Missionary Societies, a Classified Summary of Statistics, an Index of Mission Stations, and a Series of Specially Prepared Maps of Mission Fields. Compiled by Sub-committees of Commission I, 'On Carrying the Gospel to All the Non-Christian World', As an Integral Part of Its Report to the World Missionary Conference, Edinburgh, June 14–23, 1910* (Edinburgh: World Missionary Conference, 1910).

[3] See further Todd M. Johnson & Kenneth R. Ross, 'The Making of the *Atlas of Global Christianity*', *International Bulletin of Missionary Research* 34/1 (Jan 2010), 12-16.

to publish the volume. The atlas was set in the framework of 1910–2010, seeking to map the presence of the Christian faith worldwide during this period. Rather than replicating the 1910 atlas, produced in the heyday of Western missions, the *Atlas of Global Christianity* sought to take account of the entire presence of Christian faith on a worldwide basis.[4]

Christianity's Demographic Transformation 1910-2010

To understand the status of global Christianity and world evangelisation for the one hundredth anniversary of the World Missionary Conference held in Edinburgh in 1910 one can consider trends both within global Christianity and beyond global Christianity. First, trends within global Christianity:

Christianity has shifted dramatically to the South

For the entire one hundred-year period, Christians have made up approximately one third of the world's population. Yet this masks dramatic changes in the geography of global Christianity – a process stretching back to the earliest days of the world Christian movement. While 66 percent of all Christians lived in Europe in 1910, by 2010 only 26 percent lived there. The global North (Europe and Northern America) contained over 80 percent of all Christians in 1910, falling to under 40 percent by 2010. By contrast, less than 2 percent of all Christians lived in Africa in 1910, skyrocketing to almost 22 percent by 2010. In fact, the most dramatic difference over the one hundred years is in Africa – less than 10 percent Christian in 1910 but nearly 50 percent Christian in 2010, with sub-Saharan Africa well over 70 percent Christian.

The ten countries with the most Christians in 1910 and 2010 are presented below in Table 1, where the southern shift can be quickly perceived. Nine of the top ten countries in 1910 were in the global North, whereas seven of the top ten in 2010 are in the global South. Analysis of growth rates of Christianity by country from 1910 to 2000 to 2010 shows that the fastest growth both over the past hundred years and over the past ten years has all been in the global South. As further evidence of the shift, an examination of mother tongues with the most Christians worldwide shows that Spanish is first and Portuguese third – reflecting the numerical strength of Christianity in Latin America. Asian languages such as Mandarin Chinese (5) and Tagalog (10) are in the top ten while African languages such as Amharic (11), Yoruba (15) and Igbo (16) are in the top twenty.

---

[4] Todd M. Johnson & Kenneth R. Ross eds., *Atlas of Global Christianity, 1910–2010* (Edinburgh: Edinburgh University Press, 2009).

	1910	Christians	2010	Christians
1	USA	84,800,000	USA	257,311,000
2	Russia	65,757,000	Brazil	180,932,000
3	Germany	45,755,000	Russia	115,120,000
4	France	40,894,000	China	115,009,000
5	Britain	39,298,000	Mexico	105,583,000
6	Italy	35,330,000	Philippines	83,151,000
7	Ukraine	29,904,000	Nigeria	72,302,000
8	Poland	22,102,000	DR Congo	65,803,000
9	Brazil	21,576,000	India	58,367,000
10	Spain	20,357,000	Germany	58,123,000

Table 1.

Christianity is fragmented

Christians are now found in some 41,000 denominations. These range in size from millions of members to fewer than an hundred members and are listed for each of the world's 232 countries in the *World Christian Database*.[5] Moonjang Lee observes,

> Christianity has become too fragmented. Existing in a fragmented world, churches fail to show a united front. There are so many divisions within Christianity that it is an intriguing task to clarify a Christian identity. At the beginning of Christian history, the designation of a person as a 'Christian' was sufficient to tell about his or her social, religious and cultural identity. Today, however, we have to supply subcategories to tell about who we are as Christians, for there are many different and conflicting forms of church life.[6]

Note that the vast majority of denominations are found in the Independent and Protestant traditions. By 2025, there will likely be 55,000 denominations.

Christians are experiencing unprecedented renewal

Global Christianity encompasses many forms of renewal, including Evangelical movements, liturgical renewal, Bible-study fellowships and house-church movements. One of the most significant is the Pentecostal/Charismatic Renewal that coincides with the hundred-year

[5] *World Christian Database*, Brill Online, 2010.

[6] Moonjang Lee, 'Future of Global Christianity', in Johnson & Ross, *Atlas of Global Christianity*, 104-105, at 104.

period on which we have been reflecting. Over one fourth of all Christians are involved in this Renewal. Daniel Jeyaraj observes,

> Pentecostal Christianity… promotes the ideals of Spirit-filled holy life, apostolicity and catholicity. It incorporates practical ways of leadership, training and mission that draw much inspiration not only from Western business models, but also from local socio-religious customs, hierarchies and practices. Its emphasis on tithing of financial resources and time, using personal talents in mission, and accountability to the Holy Spirit make it mostly self-sufficient and self-propagating (although its view on material wealth and good health as symbols of God's blessings is critiqued).[7]

The locus of the Renewal is clearly in the Global South, where the majority of its practitioners live and where it is growing the fastest.

Christian resources are not evenly distributed

Christians of the Global South represent 60 percent of all Christians but live on only about 17 percent of all Christian wealth. This puts them at a disadvantage in many areas, including health, education, communications and overall quality of life. This imbalance is one of the great tragedies of global Christianity that could not have been easily predicted at Edinburgh in 1910.

Second, there are trends beyond global Christianity:

There is enough evangelism to reach everyone in the world

One might have the impression today that what is needed to reach the world for Christ is more evangelism. But, in sheer quantity, there is already enough evangelism in the world today for every person to hear a one-hour presentation of the gospel every other day all year long. This amounts to over 1,136 billion hours of evangelism generated by Christians every year, ranging from personal witnessing to television and radio broadcasting. Asia and Northern Africa have the least evangelism but the largest non-Christian populations.

Most Christian outreach never reaches non-Christians

85 percent of all Christian evangelism is aimed at other Christians and does not reach non-Christians. Part of the explanation is the unanticipated success of Christian missions in the twentieth century. Much Western missionary deployment is trying to sustain the growth of the churches in Africa, Asia and Latin America. Surprisingly, however, missionaries from the global South have also been drawn into mission primarily to other

---

[7] Daniel Jeyaraj, 'The Re-Emergence of Global Christianity, 1910–2010', in Johnson & Ross, *Atlas of Global Christianity*, 54-55, at 54.

Christians. Deployment studies in Nigeria and India have shown this to be the case, although there has been a perceptible shift in the past decade toward work among non-Christians.

Christians are out of contact with Muslims, Hindus and Buddhists

Recent research reveals that as many as 86 percent of all Muslims, Hindus and Buddhists do not personally know a Christian.[8] This must be viewed negatively in light of the strong biblical theme of incarnation that is at the heart of Christian witness. Christians should know and love their neighbours! In the twenty-first century it is important to realise that the responsibility for reaching Muslims, Hindus and Buddhists is too large for the vocational missionary enterprise. While missionaries will always be at the forefront of innovative strategies, the whole church needs to participate in inviting people of other faiths to consider Jesus Christ. It is significant that Muslims, Hindus and Buddhists are increasingly found living in traditionally 'Christian' lands.

Recurrent Themes in the Analytical Essays

Complementing the demographic material in the Atlas are 52 analytical essays that critically examine the geographical regions, ecclesial traditions and key themes featured in the maps. The essays were written independently by authors who are authorities in their respective fields. Therefore, points that recur in the essay collection represent significant indications of salient trends and issues in global Christianity today. Among them are the following:

The many and the one: Diversity and unity

Time and again, authors highlight the diversity that characterises the Christian faith today. Concluding his essay on African Christianity, Jesse Mugambi writes,

> Perhaps the greatest mistake we could make in assessing African Christianity today would be to generalise too much, for diversity is the order of the day. Among the churches wide differences can be discerned in cultural identity, doctrinal standpoint, social concern, pastoral approach, mission strategy and ecumenical commitment. Christians are among the wealthiest and the poorest, among the most politically conservative and among the most politically transformative, among the most ethically exemplary and among the most

[8] Todd M. Johnson & Charles L. Tieszen, 'Personal Contact: The *sine qua non* of Twenty-first Century Mission', *Evangelical Missions Quarterly* (Oct 2007), 494-502.

> scandalous, among the most Westernising in cultural values and among the greatest champions of African tradition.[9]

Diversity is the order of the day not only for church but also equally for mission. As Cathy Ross concludes her essay on Great Commission Christians, 'Christianity is now a faith of many centres, and mission is multi-directional – from anywhere to anywhere. Christians in various parts of the world engage in mission differently and in new ways. We are experiencing Christianity as a kind of multi-coloured and multi-layered quilt with many shapes, sizes, fabrics and textures'.[10]

The *Atlas* tells a story, however, not only of diversity but also of unity. Apparent in a bewildering variety of circumstances and in a dazzling diversity of cultural forms, Christian faith nonetheless is marked by an irreducible unity and coherence which demands that consideration be given to global or world Christianity. This commonality is affirmed by the atlas but also recognised as a pressing contemporary challenge, particularly in the essay on the future of global Christianity by Moonjang Lee: 'The question for global Christianity over the next century is how to restore the theological and ecclesial unity within the Christian faith and the spirit of love and tolerance in Christ.'[11]

Migration and mission

One factor making for diversity in the Christian faith is the large-scale migration that is a feature of today's world. As Jonathan Bonk comments in his essay: 'Much contemporary evangelisation is part of a vast migration surpassing in scale and potential import the one that saw Europeans sweep the globe. ... A great majority of [the migrants] are deceptively inconsequential, profoundly Christian and explicitly evangelistic.'[12] The effects of this are evident in many different parts of the world.

Commenting in his essay on the missionary impact of African Christianity, Jehu Hanciles observes,

> By the end of the [twentieth] century, African migrants were widely dispersed among the wealthy industrialised countries of the North, and everywhere they went they established new Christian congregations. In effect, African migrations have provided a vital stimulus for missionary expansion, for the simple reason that every Christian migrant is a potential missionary. In both Europe and Northern America, African immigrant

[9] J.N.K. Mugambi, 'Christianity in Africa, 1910–2010', in Johnson & Ross, *Atlas of Global Christianity*, 110-111, at 111.

[10] Cathy Ross, 'Great Commission Christians', in Johnson & Ross, *Atlas of Global Christianity*, 290-91, at 291.

[11] Lee, 'Future of Global Christianity', 104.

[12] Jonathan J. Bonk, 'Finance', in Johnson & Ross, *Atlas of Global Christianity*, 294-95, at 295.

> congregations have grown in unprecedented fashion and represent... the cutting edge of Christian growth.[13]

Roswith Gerloff and Abraham Akrong, in their essay on Independent Churches, refer to 'religions on the move' amidst 'processes of transmigration and transculturation, which unleash dynamic, reciprocal, transitory and multidimensional creations in shaping a "poly-contextual world"'.[14] They conclude that

> the overall scene on all continents, including the migration of African, Asian or Caribbean Christians to Northern white-dominated societies, displays a reticulate structure – the vast variety and pluriformity of Christian families including traditional elements which overlap denominationally, culturally and linguistically. ... Current trends suggest that this mobilisation of the masses in the South will be the driving force in Christian mission, with all promises and risks.[15]

Rise of Pentecostalism

Pentecostalism has proved to be a form of Christianity particularly well adapted to a world of large-scale migration. As Julie Ma and Allan Anderson comment, 'Pentecostalism has polynucleated origins, a global orientation and network and inherent migrating tendencies that, coupled with its strong individualism, made it fundamentally a multidimensional missionary movement'.[16] All these factors play a role in what is perhaps the greatest single change in the composition of world Christianity: the rise of Pentecostalism. In his essay on Eastern Asia, Edmond Tang states, 'It is estimated that over 80 percent of new conversions in Asia are Pentecostal or Charismatic, while the traditional denominations are declining or have reached their ceiling'.[17] Commenting on the rise of Pentecostal and Charismatic movements in India, Paul Joshua Bhakiaraj remarks that 'The resonance they found with local religious and social reality, particularly because of the immediacy of their spirituality and its close attention to existential questions and dilemmas, set them up as an attractive force and facilitated significant growth'.[18]

---

[13] Jehu J. Hanciles, 'Missionaries Sent and Received, Africa, 1910–2010', in Johnson & Ross, *Atlas of Global Christianity*, 264-65, at 265.

[14] Roswith Gerloff & Abraham Akrong, 'Independents', in Johnson & Ross, *Atlas of Global Christianity*, 76-77, at 76.

[15] Gerloff & Akrong, 'Independents', 77.

[16] Julie Ma & Allan Anderson, 'Pentecostals (Renewalists)', in Johnson & Ross, *Atlas of Global Christianity*, 100-101, at 100.

[17] Edmond Tang, 'Christianity in Eastern Asia, 1910–2010', in Johnson & Ross, *Atlas of Global Christianity*, 138-39, at 139.

[18] Paul Joshua Bhakiaraj, 'Christianity in South-central Asia', in Johnson & Ross, *Atlas of Global Christianity*, 142-43, at 142.

Examining the Latin American context, Ana Maria Bidegain recognises the growth of Pentecostalism and comments that 'one important characteristic of this new form of Christianity is the capacity to create new and adaptive forms of religion, which often have melded effectively with Latin American cultures'.[19] She also highlights the strict moral code of Pentecostal churches and suggests that

> Also significant is the prominent role women have played in the spread of this new Christian movement, particularly in starting new congregations. ... [T]he most important aspect from a female perspective is that Pentecostalism establishes a familial context in which women receive emotional and physical advantages. When husbands convert, they cease practising patterns of masculine behaviour associated with a *machista* lifestyle (such as alcohol/drug consumption, gambling and solicitation of prostitutes) and transform into more consistent, positive presences.[20]

This may help to account for Pentecostalism's extraordinary reach. As Cecilia Mariz and Eloisa Martin observe, 'In Brazilian *favelas*, slums that police, governments, and even census researchers are unable to reach because they are dominated by drug traffickers, there are Assembleias de Deus [Assemblies of God] churches'.[21]

Missionaries – not so foreign

'A century ago', observes Dana Robert in her essay on missionaries worldwide, 'India and China had the largest foreign missionary presence, with "foreign" defined as mostly European. Today their governments keep out foreign missionaries through visa restrictions. But within their borders tens of thousands of "home" missionaries evangelise other ethnic groups'.[22] The complicity of Christian mission with Western power in the twentieth century sealed its foreign character and made it unappealing as a faith option for most Asians. By contrast, Lalsangkima Pachuau reports the assessment of a Korean missionary in Thailand: 'We are easily accepted as one of their own, and we, on our part, understand better their situation and ways of thinking.'[23] To put this in historical perspective, Pachuau remarks, 'If the 1910 World Missionary Conference in Edinburgh represents the high point of the modern missionary movement from the West to Asia,

[19] Ana Maria Bidegain, 'Christianity in Latin America, 1910–2010', in Johnson & Ross, *Atlas of Global Christianity*, 174-75, at 174.

[20] Bidegain, 'Christianity in Latin America', 175.

[21] Cecilia Mariz & Eloisa Martin, 'Christianity in South America, 1910–2010', in Johnson & Ross, *Atlas of Global Christianity*, 186-87, at 187.

[22] Dana Robert, 'Missionaries Sent and Received, Worldwide, 1910–2010', in Johnson & Ross, *Atlas of Global Christianity*, 258-59, at 259.

[23] Lalsangkima Pachuau, 'Missionaries Sent and Received, Asia, 1910–2010', in Johnson & Ross, *Atlas of Global Christianity*, 268-69, at 268.

Edinburgh 2010 marks another high point, namely Christian missions from Asia, by Asians, in Asia and around the world'.[24]

Violet James gives the flavour of the missionary movement in South-eastern Asia: 'Many missionaries are entering countries as "tent-makers" or through "short-term missions". ... Indonesians, Filipinos, Malaysians and Singaporeans are part of a large missionary force in Asia today as educators, doctors, nurses, businesspeople and consultants in information technology. Some businesspeople have started various micro-enterprise projects to empower the poor'.[25] A similar pattern is observable in regard to Latin America:

> The first decades of missionary work on the continent relied heavily on the hundreds of devoted Northern American and European missionaries who dedicated their lives sacrificially for the sake of the gospel. Today foreign personnel are still active but not indispensable to the missionary task. What makes mission occur today are the thousands of local and national partners working every day as missionaries not only within their own continent but also all over the world.[26]

Integrity in discipleship

One important area where the essays complement the demographics is by offering analysis of the quality of the faith that is professed. Philomena Mwaura, writing on Eastern Africa, concludes trenchantly, 'The numerical growth is yet to be matched by deep, faithful commitment to the gospel. The faithful need to be aware that peace, justice and reconciliation are integral to evangelisation'.[27] Likewise with regard to the Pacific, Featuna'i Liua'ana notes the 'huge gap between religious principles and action' and observes, 'Churches that failed to address important theological, political , economic and social issues became compromised when they participated in corrupt politics and supported military coups which promoted ethnic separation'.[28]

Fohle Lygunda observes that

> In a context like the eastern [Democratic Republic of] Congo, where many people have been displaced through ethnically-based conflicts and civil wars, the credibility of the churches' witness will depend on how far they are able

---

[24] Pachuau, 'Missionaries Sent and Received, Asia, 1910–2010'.

[25] Violet James, 'Christianity in South-eastern Asia', in Johnson & Ross, *Atlas of Global Christianity*, 146-47, at 147.

[26] Marcelo Vargas & Antonia Leonora van der Meer with Levi DeCarvalho, 'Missionaries Sent and Received, Latin America, 1910–2010', in Johnson & Ross, *Atlas of Global Christianity*, 276-77, at 276.

[27] Philomena Mwaura, 'Christianity in Eastern Africa, 1910–2010', in Johnson & Ross, *Atlas of Global Christianity*, 114-115, at 115.

[28] Featuna'i Ben Liua'ana, 'Christianity in Melanesia, Micronesia and Polynesia, 1910–2010', in Johnson & Ross, *Atlas of Global Christianity*, 200-201, at 201.

> to provide a basis on which just and peaceful communities can be built. … Amidst sometimes catastrophic social breakdown, they face the question of whether they can uphold basic Christian values, faithfully announce the gospel of justice and peace, and offer healing and hope amongst a sorely afflicted people.[29]

Ambition and Achievement

The atlas offers a visual tour of the remarkable changes in global Christianity over the past one hundred years. The story of the Southern shift has been told in many other books and encyclopaedias over the past thirty years or so. But it has never before been depicted through a comprehensive set of maps and charts, presented in living colour.

The academic study of World Christianity has focused much of its attention, rightly, on particular forms of Christianity, especially in the non-Western world. This is a much-needed counter-balance to the false impression that Christianity is a Western religion. But Christianity is more than the sum of vastly different denominational, national and linguistic manifestations. This *Atlas* puts every Christian – Western and non-Western, black and white, man and woman, German and Papuan – in the same book under the unifying moniker 'global Christianity'. With the corrosive fragmentation the world experiences every day in conflicts and struggles, it is important for Christians to return frequently to the reality of the prayer of Jesus that 'they be one'. While giving full recognition to the diversity evident in many contexts, the *Atlas* also demonstrates the common belonging of Christians worldwide. It fulfils its ambition to take account of adherence to the Christian faith on a comprehensive, worldwide basis and hence to offer an assessment of global Christianity.

---

[29] Fohle Lygunda, 'Christianity in Middle Africa, 1910–2010', in Johnson & Ross, *Atlas of Global Christianity*, 118-119, at 119.

THE MISSION HAS A CHURCH: PERSPECTIVES OF A ROMAN CATHOLIC THEOLOGIAN

Stephen Bevans, SVD[1]

God is a Verb

A few years ago I began to realise that our God – the God revealed to us by Jesus of Nazareth through the power of the Holy Spirit – might be best described as a *verb*, not a noun. What I mean by this is that the God we know from revelation might be best imagined not as a static kind of 'person' – sort of like us but wiser and more powerful – who is 'up there' or 'out there'. Rather, in a way that is much more exciting and worthy of our adoration and love, God is a Movement – more personal than we can ever imagine – who is always and everywhere present in God's creation, present in the warp and woof of it, working for creation's wholeness and healing, calling creation to its fullness, and calling women and men on a small planet in a minor galaxy in this vast universe – billions of years old, billions of light years in extension – into partnership in God's work. These women and men, Genesis tells us (1:26-27), God created in the divine 'image and likeness'. They are to be, as Nigerian Old Testament scholar James Okoye tells us, stewards, caretakers, 'greeners', viceroys of God on earth.[2] We do not know, although it is surely possible, that other creatures – perhaps in a far-off galaxy and perhaps many times more intelligent than we – have been entrusted by God with the same task. What we do know from revelation is that *we* have been.

Nothing about our God is static. One of our greatest theologians, Thomas Aquinas, spoke of God as pure act.[3] And the equally great theologian Bonaventure speaks of God as self-diffusive goodness and love.[4] In the great Western Medieval tradition, Mechtilde of Magdeburg

---

[1] Dr Stephen B. Bevans, SVD is Louis J. Luzbetak, SVD Professor of Mission and Culture at the Catholic Theological Union, Chicago.

[2] James Chukwuma Okoye, *Israel and the Nations: A Mission Theology of the Old Testament* (Maryknoll, NY: Orbis Books, 2006), 33.

[3] See Thomas Aquinas, *Summa Theologiae*, Part I, Question 3, article 1.

[4] Bonaventure, *De Trinitate*, 3.16. See Ilia Delio, 'Bonaventure's Metaphysics of the Good', *Theological Studies*, 60, 2 (1999): 232.

spoke of the 'restless Godhead', an 'overflow... which never stands still and always flows effortlessly and without ceasing...'.[5]

God is not even static within Godself as such. God in God's deepest identity is a relationship, a communion. 'In the remotest beginning', Brazilian theologian Leonardo Boff writes of the Trinity, 'communion prevails'.[6] This life in communion spills out into creation, healing and sanctifying, calling all of creation, according to its capacity, into that communion, and once in that communion, sending that creation forth to gather still more of it into communion. It is though God as such is a dance – a great conga line, I like to imagine – moving through the world, inviting the world – material creation, human beings – to join in the dance. And the more that join the more attractive joining becomes.[7]

This self-diffusive, gathering, and sending nature of God hints at what the true nature of reality is. What is real is not what is concerned with itself or turned in on itself (this latter is Luther's definition of sin!). What is real is going beyond oneself, being in relation, calling others to relation. The British philosopher Alfred North Whitehead suggested that God, rather than being the *exception* to the laws of the universe, is really their greatest exemplar. And so God is perfectly related to the world – in fact God is relation itself. God is perfectly involved in the world, and rather than unable to change and suffer with the world, God is infinite in God's ability to be affected by the world and is, in Whitehead's famous words, the 'fellow sufferer who understands'.[8] Benedict XVI describes God in a way far from Platonic and Aristotelian thinking: God is 'a lover with all the passion of true love'.[9]

God is Mission

Another way of saying all this is that God is Mission. Not that God *has* a mission, but that God *is* Mission. This is what God is in God's deepest self:

---

[5] Mechtilde of Magdeburg, *The Flowing Light of the Godhead*, Book VII, Chapter 55, in *Classics of Western Spirituality*, Vol. 92, Frank Tobin, trans. (New York: Paulist Press, 1998). Seé Oliver Davies, 'Late Medieval Theology', in G. R. Evans (ed.), *The Medieval Theologians: An Introduction to Theology in the Medieval Period* (Oxford: Blackwell, 2001), 228.

[6] Leonardo Boff, 'Trinity', in *Mysterium Liberationis: Fundamental Concepts of Liberation Theology* (Maryknoll, NY: Orbis Books, 1993), 389.

[7] This idea comes from a play on the word *perichoresis*, from the Greek *perichoreo*, meaning 'cyclical movement or recurrence'. 'To dance around' or 'dance in a ring' comes from the Greek *perichoreuo*. See Elizabeth A. Johnson, *She Who Is: The Mystery of God in Feminist Theological Discourse* (New York: Crossroad, 1992), 220-221.

[8] Alfred North Whitehead, *Process and Reality: An Essay in Cosmology* (New York: Macmillan, 1929), 521, 532.

[9] Benedict XVI, Encyclical Letter *Deus Caritas Est*, §10. Available at www.vatican.va.

self-diffusive love, freely creating, redeeming, healing, challenging that creation. God, as my colleague Anthony Gittins once said in a lecture, is 'love hitting the cosmic fan'. Or, to be a bit more prosaic, God is like an ever-flowing fountain of living water, poured out on earth through the Holy Spirit and actually made part of creation through the Word-become-flesh. As the Decree on Missionary Activity (*Ad Gentes*) of the Second Vatican Council puts it, God 'generously pours out, and never ceases to pour out, the divine goodness, so that the one who is creator of all things might at last become "all in all" (1Cor. 15:28), thus simultaneously assuring God's own glory and our happiness'.[10]

God Inside Out

There has never been a moment when God has not been present to and in creation. From the first nanosecond of time, God has been there, in the fullness of God's Mystery, through the presence of the Holy Spirit. The Spirit is, as it were, God 'inside out' in the world. She is God's complete presence, palpable, able to be experienced, and yet elusive, like the wind. Or, as she is described in a best-selling book today, *The Shack*, she is perhaps best seen from the corner of our eye rather than visible straight on.[11]

In our own tradition, with its roots in the Old Testament, the Spirit is described as breath or wind, *ruach* in Hebrew. She broods over the primeval chaos in the first lines of Genesis, like a mother bird brooding over her nest. She is the breath that God breathes into the 'earth creature', *ha adam*, that we call Adam. She is the spirit that stirs up prophecy, that brings the dry bones in Ezekiel, chapter 37 to life. She is the water that pours out of the Temple in Ezekiel's great vision in chapter 40, the water that gives life to healing plants and abundant fruits. She is the ointment in Isaiah, chapter 61that brings good news to the afflicted, to bind the wounds of the broken-hearted, that proclaims liberty to captives, that frees those in captivity. US American feminist theologian Elizabeth Johnson beautifully sums up the Spirit's role in history: 'Whether the Spirit be pictured as the warmth and light given by the sun, the life-giving water from the spring, or the flower filled with seeds from the root, what we are actually signifying is God drawing near and passing by in vivifying, sustaining, renewing, and liberating power in the midst of historical struggle'.[12]

---

[10] Vatican Council II, Decree on Missionary Activity, *Ad Gentes*, §2. Available at www.vatican.va.

[11] William P. Young, *The Shack* (Newbury Park, CA: Windblown Media, 2007).

[12] Johnson, *She Who Is*, 127.

God is like Jesus

'In the fullness of time' (Gal. 4:4), the Word of God became flesh and gave the Spirit, God's complete yet elusive presence, a human face. Jesus continued the work of the Spirit, but now God is present in a visible, audible, and concrete way. Jesus was a man led by God's Spirit. All three synoptic gospels begin their narrative of Jesus' ministry with Jesus being led – or in Mark 'driven' – by the Spirit into the desert to prepare for his ministry (see Matt. 4:1, Mark 1:12, and Luke 4:1). Luke describes Jesus' inaugural sermon at Nazareth, as he read from the scroll of Isaiah: 'The Spirit of the Lord is upon me, because God has anointed me to preach the good news to the poor, ... to proclaim release to the captives and recovering sight to the blind, to set at liberty those who are oppressed, to proclaim the acceptable year of the Lord' (Luke 4:18-19). The work of the Spirit in Isaiah is now the work of Jesus, and this is the programme of his ministry.

In this ministry Jesus reveals the God who is a verb: God is a God who reigns, and God reigns by forgiving, healing, saving, reconciling, being in relation. 'God is like Jesus', Uraguayan liberation theologian Juan Luis Segundo writes.[13] Note that what Segundo says is *not* that Jesus is like God, as if we already know who God is; rather, it is Jesus who shows us what God is like. When we see the way Jesus taught and acted and suffered, we see the way God teaches and acts and suffers. Three hundred years later, when the church was embroiled in the controversy with Arius, this is what was at stake. If Jesus was not truly God (*homoousios to patri*), then we do not really know what God is like. The truth is, though, that we do.

Jesus taught, especially in parables. He taught about forgiveness in parables of the lost sheep, the lost coin and the lost son in Luke, chapter 15. He taught about God's generosity in the parable of the generous employer in Matthew, chapter 20. He taught about how all are called to salvation in the parable of the wedding feast in Matthew 22, and about God's persistent quest for justice as portrayed by a persistent widow in the face of an unjust judge in Luke 18.

Jesus' was a message of joy. It is too bad that Christian artists have for the most part portrayed Jesus as a serious, even sombre character. How could he have attracted children if he did not smile? How could he have held the crowds if his parables were not humorous – even though ultimately deadly serious? Recently one of my students in Chicago put me on to a wonderful Internet exhibition on the 'Laughing Jesus', sponsored by the Major Issues and Theology Foundation based in Queensland, Australia. Jesus portrayed as a dancer, a comedian, a juggler and in abandoned conversation with the disciples at Emmaus (where he appears as a woman)

---

[13] Juan Luis Segundo, *Christ in the Spiritual Exercises of St. Ignatius* (Maryknoll, NY: Orbis Books, 1987), 22-26.

has helped me visualise and better imagine the God of joy that Jesus revealed.[14]

Jesus healed and drove out devils. His healings and exorcisms were parables in action. Making the lame walk, the blind see, the deaf hear, the dead return to life, those caught in the grip of evil experience liberation – these were all ways of saying that God's salvation was not just something spiritual, but fully and completely involved with living in this world.

As Edward Schillebeeckx[15] and others have suggested, Jesus himself was a parable. His own personal freedom in interpreting the Law, his fun-loving lifestyle (e.g. drinking wine), and his scandalous, inclusive behaviour all pointed to the nature of a God who is a God of life, a God who cared for all, a God of freedom.

Of course, we know where all of this got Jesus. Although his message was deeply rooted in the Jewish tradition – particularly that of the prophets – it proved to be too much for the Jewish leaders of the time. They interpreted Jesus' joy and freedom and inclusiveness as an affront to their tradition, even a blasphemy to the God of Israel. And they intuited – probably correctly – that if people continued to take Jesus' message seriously it would prove a threat to the Roman occupation of their country. And so they killed him. But even here Jesus reveals the nature of God. God is vulnerable; God will not override human wickedness, but will suffer because of it. In many ways, the image of Jesus on the cross is the dearest image we have of God. God will go to such lengths to reveal a love that so deeply respects human freedom.

But you cannot kill God! You cannot stop the Movement that is overflowing life and love. The Mission continued. The disciples experienced Jesus as alive in their midst, especially when they gathered to break bread and share the cup of wine in his memory. They began to realise now that Jesus had been no ordinary man. Jesus had in one way been taken from them in death, but in another way – one that was even more real – he was still with them, guiding them by the Spirit to whom he gave a face. Gradually they began to realise that his mission – the mission of God – was their mission. The mission began to have a church.

The Mission Has a Church

Gradually, as Jesus' disciples experienced his living presence among them – and especially after the extraordinary experience that took place some fifty days after his death, on the day of Pentecost – they realised that they had been given the task to continue Jesus' mission of proclaiming, demonstrating and embodying God's Reign. But, most probably like Jesus

---

[14] See http://miatorgau.melbourneitwebsites.com/page/jesus_laughing_exhibition.html.

[15] Edward Schillebeeckx, *Jesus: An Experiment in Theology* (New York: Vintage Books, 1981), 156, 158.

as well, they understood this mission as (i) quite temporary, for Jesus would soon inaugurate the Reign of God when he returned in glory, and (ii) only for the Jews. Although Judaism had engaged in some mission to bring Gentiles into the covenant people, the prevailing understanding was that, once God's Reign had been inaugurated, the nations would stream toward Jerusalem and acknowledge the God of Israel as the God of all the earth (e.g. Is 2:2-5). The members of the Jesus community almost certainly thought that, after Pentecost, the Jews had been given another chance to accept Jesus' vision of God and the radical change of mind and heart that it entailed, and when the Jewish nation would change its mind and believe the good news (see Mark 1:15), the Reign would be established and the Twelve would be set up on the twelve thrones that Jesus promised to judge (i.e. rule, govern with righteousness) the twelve tribes of Israel that the coming of the Reign of God would reconstitute. The fact that they were having such success – three thousand converts here (Acts 2:41), five thousand there (Acts 4:4), people added every day (Acts 2:47) – probably convinced them that the time was very near.

But soon there began to be doubts about all of this. Stephen, with some Greek-speaking disciples perhaps, may have been the first to intuit that what Jesus meant went beyond Judaism. When he was killed for preaching such a radical, unthinkable doctrine and many Greek-speaking Jews had to flee the city lest they suffer the same fate, strange things began to happen. One of Stephen's companions, Philip, preached to Samaritans – derided as half-Jews, half-breeds – and they accepted the Lordship of Jesus, and his vision of God and of the world. Philip was also led to preach to an Ethiopian eunuch – by law excluded from becoming a Jew – and he was moved to admit him into the Jesus fellowship. Peter was amazed to be led to the house of a Roman centurion – a *good* Gentile but a Gentile nonetheless – and when he preached about the Lord Jesus the same Spirit that had fallen upon the disciples of Pentecost fell upon Cornelius and his household. This was unbelievable! Peter could only baptise them, even though he had to face the grave doubts of the Jerusalem community when he returned. When he explained they exclaimed 'even to the Gentiles has God granted repentance unto life!' (See Acts 11:18).[16]

What had started out as a movement *within* Judaism had become something much different. The Spirit was moving the community to another place, taking Jesus' vision to where perhaps even he had not imagined it would or could go. The climax came – according to Luke's theological/historical retelling in Acts – when some unnamed men and

[16] For a more detailed treatment of the movement of Acts, see Stephen B. Bevans and Roger P. Schroeder, *Constants in Context: A Theology of Mission for Today* (Maryknoll, NY: Orbis Books, 2004), 10-31.

women who had fled persecution after Stephen's execution,[17] arrived in the great urban centre of Antioch in Syria (the third largest city in the world at the time) and preached not only to Jews, but also to Gentiles. The result was that 'a great number turned to the Lord' (Acts 11:21).

My contention over the last several years has been that it was here in Antioch that the church was born. We often speak of the day of Pentecost as the 'birthday of the church', but I do not think this is true. I think it is here in Antioch, where the disciples were first called 'Christians' (Acts 11:26). My reasoning is that before Antioch – although the realisation was growing all through Acts up to this point – the disciples saw themselves as Jews, not as a separate, discrete religion. Now, however, at least in germ, they began to see that in Jesus something new had begun, that God's mission in the world – begun in the Spirit from the first moment of creation and continued concretely in Jesus – had been handed over to them. And now they were called to continue this mission to the ends of the earth – in every nation, in every culture, in every time period. Now it became clear – or at least they saw glimmers of it – that God had chosen a particular people to carry on the divine mission, to be the face of the Spirit, the bodily presence of Jesus in the world. At Antioch and thereafter, what began to become clear is that God's Mission has a Church.

Conclusion: The Mission Has Us

The church comes to be as the church engages in mission – as it crosses the boundary of Judaism to the Gentiles, and realises that its mission is the very mission of God: to go into the world and be God's saving, healing, challenging presence. This is why we can say, with Vatican II's document on missionary activity, that the church is 'missionary by its very nature'. Mission precedes the church. Mission is first of all God's: God inside out in the world through the Spirit, God in Jesus teaching, healing, including, suffering. Almost incredibly – as an act of grace! – God shares that mission with women and men. Mission calls the church into being to serve God's purposes in the world. The church does not have a mission, but the Mission has a Church.

---

[17] See Andrew F. Walls, 'Culture and Coherence in Christian History', in *The Missionary Movement in Christian History: Studies in the Transmission of Faith* (Maryknoll, NY: Orbis Books, 1997), 16.

CHRISTIAN MISSION AMONG OTHER FAITHS: 'GIVING ACCOUNT OF OUR HOPE'

Ulrike Schmidt-Hesse[1]

'How should we understand "Christian mission among other faiths"?' This was the question asked by the Study Group on Theme 2 in its report for the conference preparation volume, *Witnessing to Christ Today*. 'As a mission to non-Christians, as a mission among other faiths, or witnessing to Christ in the context of contemporary challenges in the mutually edifying fellowship of neighbours of living faiths and ideologies?'[2]

On this subject we read, 'To understand "Christian mission among other faiths" means to perceive Christians as believing human beings among other believing and non-believing human beings, sharing, facing or opposing each other in specific situations in which they live their faith and draw on their respective traditions'.[3] This understanding of mission 'among others' corresponds to the approach taken by the current priority programme of the Association of Churches and Missions in South West Germany (EMS), an international fellowship of twenty-eight churches and mission societies in Africa, Asia, the Middle East and Europe, which is entitled 'EMS Focus 2009-2012: Giving Account of our Hope – Christian Witness in a Pluralistic World.[4] I would like to share some of the experiences and insights we have gained in this programme, which is itself a contribution to the Edinburgh 2010 process.

Giving Account of Our Hope

The Focus Programme is based on the observation that due to the processes of globalisation and migration, all churches in the EMS Fellowship live in a pluralistic context – with people of other faiths and those without religious connections, as people and with people who differ not only in their culture,

---

[1] Rev. Ulrike Schmidt-Hesse, Head of Mission and Partnership Department and Deputy General Secretary, EMS, Germany.

[2] Daryl Balia & Kirsteen Kim (eds), *Edinburgh 2010. Witnessing to Christ Today* (Oxford, Regnum Books, 2010), 39.

[3] Balia & Kim, *Edinburgh 2010*, 41.

[4] For more information on the programme see: www.ems-online.org.

but also in their social and economic background. It aims to grapple consciously with these different contexts and to relate to the people living in them in order to witness to God's love for the world and to give account of the hope of the kingdom of God that has come near in Jesus Christ.[5] In 'Common Witness', the mission statement of the EMS fellowship, we read: 'Mission in the first instance is God's economy (*oikonomia*) for the world, in the act of creation, in the history with humankind, in Jesus Christ, and in the power of the Holy Spirit. Our witness means our response and our participation in God's compassionate and transforming love'. And later, 'In our witness we meet people of other faiths and ideologies with esteem, respect, empathy, the willingness to listen, and to live together as good neighbours in bold humility'.[6]

What we can further say in response to the initial question asked and thereby to the theological relevance of other religions and other world views, and what all this means for Christian witness, is to be further

---

[5] The objectives of the EMS Focus 2009-2012 'Giving Account of our Hope – Christian Witness in a Pluralistic World' with its motto 'Journeying towards Justice – Sharing Faith – Encountering the Other – Celebrating the Fullness of Life' read: 1. The EMS Focus 2009-2012 shall invite churches and groups in the EMS fellowship to embark on faith journeys together, thus exploring how to witness to the good news of life in fullness for all in pluralistic contexts, where people of differing faiths and worldviews, differing cultures as well as differing social and economic conditions are living together. 2. This programme shall foster experiences in inter-faith and inter-cultural co-operation which reflect the fact that our own spirituality may be enriched and renewed in encountering each other and living together. Congregations/Christians may see that distinct Christian witness and conviviality, identity and plurality are not contradictory. 3. This programme shall challenge and encourage persons to come to a better understanding of differing faith communities in their respective contexts, to realise the inter-connectedness of social, cultural and religious factors and to engage differing spiritualities respectively concepts of faith and life with each other. 4. The programme shall enable people to see that international ecumenical co-operation is essential regarding the concept and practice of Christian witness in a pluralistic society in our respective contexts. 5. Within this programme the projects of the year(s) shall foster international exchange/networking/learning from one another, as well as mutual support in times of crisis, respectively situations of conflicts between religious groups. 6. It shall provide spaces for the development and exchange of theological reflections among various contexts. 7. The programme shall promote interfaith co-operation in practical ways, particularly joint initiatives for the protection of human dignity and the development of just communities. 8. It aims at exploring and promoting concepts and practice of a spirituality of life. (Taken from a document approved by EMS Mission Council in June 2008).

[6] From the Mission Statement of the EMS Fellowship, available at www.ems-online.org. The statement also says: 'We witness to the Gospel of Jesus Christ at all our respective places in an inviting and faithful way. The experience of being strangers to each other in encounters and in exchange across borders helps us to rediscover the Gospel in new ways'.

explored in the EMS Focus Programme. In the process, it is important for us to keep in mind the interdependence of religious, cultural, political and social factors. We assume that churches in the North and in the South have a great deal to learn from each other, particularly with regard to Christian mission among people of other faiths and those without religious faith. In the EMS fellowship, as in the whole of the worldwide church, there are both churches that have always existed in the midst of other religions and those for whom this situation is relatively new. There are churches in majority and minority situations. There are experiences with different religions and life philosophies in various contexts as well as with the secular world and with the criticism of religion. Churches exist in social and political contexts that differ enormously in terms of religious freedom, respect for human rights as a whole and in their economic, social, political and cultural situation.

The main agents of witness are the churches living in a particular context. At the same time all churches, as parts of the worldwide body of Christ, are called to commit themselves to common witness by challenging, encouraging and supporting one another. In the EMS fellowship, joint programmes like the Focus have been instituted for this purpose. Personnel exchange and the sharing of financial resources serve the same end.

The EMS Focus with its international activities,[7] in particular a large intercultural Bible reading programme, a pilgrimage in the Middle East on

---

[7] International activities within the framework of the EMS Focus are: A. 'Reading the Bible through the Eyes of Another'. Groups discover the Bible through different eyes in intercultural exchanges with partners. This is based on biblical texts which speak about the witness of hope, about paths beyond cultural and religious boundaries and about respect for others. The method used is 'Bible sharing', which ensures that all group members participate in the exchange. Working materials for adults and children are provided. B. Pilgrimage 'Crossing Borders'. A group of participants from the world-wide EMS Fellowship is embarking on a journey of faith. Their joint pilgrimage towards Jerusalem will lead them through four countries in the Middle East, to holy and 'unholy' places in this region which is equally important to Christians, Jews and Muslims. They will meet people of different faiths who are committed to peace and justice and will support them in their joint commitment. C. 'Theological Training in the Presence of the Other'. Those who teach theology in the presence of people from different religions can and must formulate their statements with much greater precision. Members of theological institutions in different countries of the EMS Fellowship exchange their views on how to express their relationship to other religions in the content and teaching methods of theological training. Their aim is to obtain new stimuli to use in their own programmes. D. 'Appreciating Diversity – Sharing Life in Community': Church and Migration. Congregations and institutions in the international EMS Fellowship are encouraged to open up to the migrants living among them and to strengthen their rights. International trainings promote cross-cultural competence and explore new ways to live faith together as migrants and non-migrants, to co-operate in the shaping of just communities and to combat

the theme of 'crossing borders', exchanges between theological training centres on the topic 'theological training in the presence of the other', and support for interaction between locals and migrants by way of training in international workshops are some of the responses to one of the questions listed at the end of the report of the study group. This question reads as follows: 'How may churches in the West gain new insights from the churches in the global South about witness and dialogue in a pluralistic setting? What could churches in the global South gain from discussions on pluralism in the North?'[8] In what follows I would like to present responses to this question by way of sharing some of the experiences and insights that EMS has gained.

Learning from One Another North and South

Christians in Ghana help Christians in the West to see that evangelism and dialogue are not contradictory. In EMS Mission Council meetings as well as in seminars and encounters they emphasise that it is essential to proclaim the Good News and to invite people to believe in Christ. They continuously challenge Christians in the West to be more outspoken, to voice their faith in the workplace, in the neighbourhood, in the public realm. At the same time they urge them to live together and share daily life in families and communities with people of other faiths, and to work together for the prevention of conflicts or for non-violent conflict resolution. Thus churches in all continents are encouraged to engage in a 'dialogue of life' as well as a joint commitment to the common good. That all human beings are made in God's image is given as a basis for dialogue and co-operation with people of other faiths. As a Ghanaian theologian remarked in conversation: Christian witness can be given through service (Phil. 2), essentially through Christian health care and Christian schools, not only by proclaiming the word.

Christians from Indonesia, who often live among Muslims as a small minority, share their experiences with sisters and brothers from other parts of the world: In some regions they are confronted with fundamentalist Muslim groups who threaten individual believers and, indeed, churches. A pastor shares impressive and moving stories of courageous persons witnessing to Christ in frightening situations, and she asks her sisters and brothers for support, for prayers and their advocacy of religious freedom, emphasising that all human rights – religious and political rights as well as economic, social and cultural rights – need to be respected, for all persons, in all places. Churches in Indonesia develop programmes in which they cooperate with people of other faiths for the common good, for justice and

factors which force people to migrate. (From the Focus flyer, available at www.-ems-online.org.)

[8] Balia & Kim, *Edinburgh 2010*, 55.

peace, for health services and sustainable development. They stress that Christians and adherents of other faiths should oppose and prevent fundamentalism in all religions.

The participants of two international workshops on the role of religions in conflicts, taking place in Lebanon and in Indonesia, called upon the churches within the EMS Fellowship 'to promote interfaith dialogue wherever people of different faiths live together'. They explained:

> We learned from the experiences we shared in both workshops that dialogue in times of peace leads to a mutual trust, personal relationship and profound understanding of one another. This will not only help to sustain peaceful co-existence, but also in times of conflict, experiences of past encounters will make dialogue an effective tool to re-establish peace and achieve reconciliation.[9]

As the theological basis for this approach, they cited the call to bear witness to God's love to all people. Their call points to the need to have a clear understanding of one's own tradition and stresses that as peacemaking is a core value of Christian teaching, it should be reflected in the content and methods of Christian education.

The Schneller Schools in Jordan and Lebanon offer – as Protestant institutions – education and vocational training to Muslim and Christian children from poor families. Their work is being highlighted and supported as the EMS Project of the Year 2010. The children in the schools receive esteem and individual support as they learn to live together in peace. The schools and the churches sponsoring them emphasise an understanding of mission as witness through education and *diakonia* (Phil. 2). A pastor quoted St Francis of Assisi by saying, 'Preach the gospel at all times; if necessary, use words'.

Another essential part of their witness is the commitment to peace and reconciliation (2 Cor. 5; Luke 2). Many church leaders and members work for a just peace in the Middle East, thus cooperating with people of other faiths. It is very important for Christians in the West to realise that there is a great variety of Christian churches present in the Middle East, some of which have a tradition going back to the first centuries, and that these churches also have a long history of relations with Islam and Judaism. Accordingly, students from other countries studying at the Near East School of Theology (NEST) in Beirut, ecumenical co-workers and young volunteers serving the schools, and participants in the EAPPI Programme (Ecumenical Accompaniment Programme in Palestine and Israel of the World Council of Churches) benefit richly by becoming acquainted with the interconnectedness of religious, political, historic, cultural and economic factors. After returning to their home countries, many of them commit themselves to interreligious dialogue or to advocacy work.

---

[9] *Calling for Dialogue. Prayers and Texts from the EMS-Workshops on Religions in Conflicts in Lebanon and Indonesia*, brochure, Stuttgart 2007, 37-39.

At a Synod meeting, a pastor from South Africa reminded the EMS Fellowship of the fact that Christian witness in a pluralistic world must not sideline the quest for justice. He challenged the churches to leave their 'comfort zones' and walk with the poor. Referring to Luke 4 and Matthew 25, he emphasised God's preferential option for the poor and the need for the prophetic voice of the churches. He said, 'Let us witness to Christ and his reign and what it means – liberation, justice and healing – hope for new life!'

Through the witness of another brother from South Africa, the EMS Fellowship is reminded of the co-operation between Christians and people of other faiths in the struggle against apartheid. Today, co-operation is necessary in the struggle against poverty and HIV&AIDS. Currently an ecumenical co-worker in Germany, the brother stresses that in the North, the courage to speak out for justice is needed at least as much as new capabilities in speaking of the faith.

Bible Sharing Cross-Culturally

In order to open ourselves to persons of other religions, world views and cultures, it is important to develop a sense of certainty with regard to one's own faith. In our experience, reading biblical texts in groups is quite helpful in this regard. Reading the Bible is for one itself a characteristic feature of Christian identity. Secondly, Bible reading in groups helps to discern the 'content' of this identity, and provides clarity and spiritual nurturing. A form of identity is being strengthened which is not characterised by fear of the other. When groups read biblical texts by way of intercultural exchange, the participants learn that their partners really are different, that they live and believe in different ways. They are challenged to acquaint themselves with new methods of approaching biblical texts and they realise that intercultural exchange opens the richness of the Bible. My own understanding of being a Christian is further developed and strengthened.[10] In the Focus Programme 'Reading the Bible through the Eyes of Another', groups in various countries use a participatory method of Bible sharing, working together in tandems to share experiences and their insights. There are currently some ninety groups in sixteen countries involved in the project, using a workbook provided by EMS to work through suggested biblical texts which speak about the witness of hope, explore ways of overcoming cultural and religious boundaries, affirm the values of hospitality and uphold respect for others. Textual and

---

[10] Note: This approach needs support also *vis-à-vis* xenophobic positions in Western societies which consider it necessary to defend 'Christian civilization' over and against Islam, whereas they themselves are very much estranged from Christian values and perspectives.

hermeneutical 'fruits' of this exchange will be gathered in an international workshop in 2011 and presented in documentary form.

Among the groups involved in the Programme is a group in Tokyo. The members are Japanese-Filipino youth, living in irregular situations in jobs and schools. They grew up in the Philippines and it is hard for them to find their way and to be accepted in Japanese culture. Most of them are children of single mothers. Their participation in church life is low, but they believe in Jesus Christ and they are working together under the auspices of a mission programme of the Center for Japanese-Filipino Families (CJFF) called the 'Best of Both Sides' (BoBS). Together, they read Exodus 15 and other texts speaking about Miriam and Moses, and they sent their findings to their partner group in Germany. In the report we read that the group members compared their experiences to that of the child Moses sailing in the roughness of the river, bumping boulders and experiencing heavy downfalls. It took these young people long years to find an elder sister in Japan, a Miriam-like figure, who helps and guides them in times of darkness and joy.

> As Miriam is looking after the welfare and spiritual well-being of her younger brother, it is the same with the Best of Both Sides (BoBS) mission for the second generation migrants … BoBS started as a singing and dancing group and we did presentations to reflect on our situation as Japanese-Filipinos. … Only after the Bible reading did we realise that BoBS performances in the future have to be songs and dances of redemption.[11]

Discerning Faith Across Borders

A pastor from Lebanon with a great deal of experience living and working with Muslims took part in an international workshop in Frankfurt-am-Main. At the workshop, the concept for the EMS Focus was developed. As part of the programme there were visits and encounters in that multicultural and multi-religious city. This was later described as a journey of faith by some of the participants.[12] In Frankfurt, we visited churches, mosques, schools, church social welfare services and the university. The international Christian group was present at evening prayer in one of the mosques. At the end the pastor said: 'I have heard the call to prayer and the prayer itself many times and understand the words, of course. But here I was able to feel and appreciate the spiritual meaning and the beauty of the texts. I think that is because the call to prayer took place without the use of a loudspeaker and the group at prayer was relatively small.' This experience makes it clear, on the one hand, that the majority or minority situation plays an important part

[11] From an e-mail sent from the group in Japan to the partner group in Germany in July 2010.

[12] This concept now determines the whole of EMS Focus. We were also very much impressed to see how the motif of a common journey of faith became an essential part of the anniversary conference in Edinburgh in June 2010.

in our relationship to another religion, and that, on the other hand, an encounter in an unfamiliar context can open up new perspectives.

In Germany, many Christians live and work together with persons without religious affiliation or persons of varying world views and ideologies. 'By studying the Enlightenment, secularism and the criticism of religion I have learned that these have opposed Christian faith', a pastor says, 'but at the same time have contributed to the development of democracy and human rights. In some respects they have even helped the churches to reflect on their history, doctrine and praxis critically and to respond to the gospel more adequately'. Christians from the West share with their sisters and brothers in other regions their experience of collaborating with secular people in their work for the common good, in social work in the community, in self-help groups, in the peace movement, in the work with migrants and refuges and in initiatives for the preservation of creation. 'For me the work for an abundant life for all people and for all of creation is an expression of Christian witness', says a young woman in an ecumenical encounter. 'Secular people I work with do indeed ask me about the source of my commitment. There are many opportunities to give account of the hope that is within us. Actions often speak more strongly than words, but it is also necessary to be able to explain our actions verbally. This I learnt from Christians in the South.'

In view of the renaissance of religion in many places, even in the West, we have to discern the spirits, as not all expressions of faith, even within Christianity, are in the service of life. Reading the Bible together and listening to brothers and sisters is crucial in this respect. Secular traditions may help us in our discernment, as they ask critical questions and as not all secular attitudes and forces are in contradiction to Christian faith and values. In fact, it is necessary to cooperate with all persons of good will. And sometimes we see that God is at work outside the Christian community. Secular persons and movements may be actors in God's mission. Christian mission among people of other faiths – and no faith – may turn out to be mission with them as well as mission to them. And there are, indeed, forms of secularism which we have to challenge or even oppose as Christians.

Along this line there is another experience to be shared. When the EMS Focus was introduced in a celebratory service in Frankfurt-am-Main, representatives of other faith traditions participated as guests. During the reception, a Muslim representative said that dialogue should include challenging one another, pointing out each other's short-comings, failures and contradictions so that these can be corrected and the person can move towards further development. People of other faiths may also remind us of our strengths and treasures. There are Hindus in India who remind Christians in India and in the West that there were missionaries in India who pioneered intercultural relations and interreligious dialogue. In an EMS Focus seminar, a theologian from India emphasised the wideness of

God's mercy: 'Salvation belongs to God, not to us', she said. 'We are searching for God, as others also do, and on our journey we share our faith in Jesus Christ with them.'

In the framework of the EMS Focus we shall further explore the issues raised. This includes the discussion of our differing concepts regarding the theological meaning of other faiths as well as of secularity. Other issues to be addressed are the relevance and understanding of conversion and adequate forms of evangelism. It is necessary, indeed, to develop a code of conduct. Mission to the North is a further challenge requiring special attention. Christians in the North do need their brothers and sisters in the South to support them in their witness. At the same time it is important to challenge the presupposition that the church in the North is spiritually dead. In the EMS Focus, as well as in the Edinburgh 2010 process, it has become clear that Christians from all contexts have something to share – in bold humility. Over and against tendencies to focus either on the maintenance of the church as an institution or on individual salvation and well-being, we must emphasise in all places that Christian witness means to share the good news of God's love for the whole world. In view of increasing plurality in our societies and within Christianity itself, in the North as well as in the South, it is crucial to continue the reflection on criteria for authentic Christian witness. In doing so, we may draw on the statement of the Conference on World Mission and Evangelism in Salvador da Bahia in 1996 saying that Christ crucified and risen is the source and true measure of our faith and hope and that the gospel is life-affirming, inclusive, liberating and community-building.[13]

We very much hope that Christians in all continents will continue journeying together to challenge, encourage and support each other in giving account of our hope, in witnessing to Christ among people of other faiths today.

---

[13] See Report of Section IV of the Conference on World Mission and Evangelism, Salvador da Bahia, Brazil, 1996, in Christopher Duraisingh (ed.), *Called to One Hope: The Gospel in Diverse Cultures*. Report of the Conference of the CWME, Salvador, Brazil, 1996 (Geneva: WCC, 1998; German trans. Frankfurt-am-Main: Lembeck, 1999)

Towards an Arabic Political Theology: A Contextual Approach to Co-Existence and Pluralism

Andrea Z. Stephanous[1]

This paper will focus on the contextual role of Arabic Theology that promotes dynamic citizenship as a base for coexistence. It will present as well an Arabic Political Theology as a core theology for pluralism.

Political Christianity in the Middle East is developing as a result of specific trends: crises in personal identity and ideology; the decline of Arab nationalism; the emergence of Political Islam as an alternative political ideology; the imposition of 'democracy' as a foreign Western political concept; the lack of political legitimacy in existing regimes; authoritarian rule in most Middle Eastern countries; the lack of effective economic development; the re-Islamisation of existing institutions and political systems; the Islamisation of the media, economy, and culture; a weak civil society and the absence of a political theology that supports coexistence.

'Arab Christian': Not a Contradiction in Terms

'Arab Christian' is an important term, which will be used in this paper. Different groups in the Middle East and the West have debated a term which can imply contradiction. Some argue that to be an Arab is to be a Muslim because Arabism is equivalent to Islam. In the past, Caliph 'Umar Ibn 'Abd Al-'Azīz (717-720) declared that Arab tribes cannot profess Christianity, and in August 1980 Libyan President Qadhāfī declared that Arab Christians must convert to Islam because 'it is a contradiction to be both Arab and Christian'.[2] In an interview in 1985 Qadhāfī stated, 'Christians who live in the Arab World have closer links to the Vatican than to Mecca. They have a European spirit in an Arab body'.[3]

---

[1] Rev. Dr Andrea Zaki Stephanous is Vice General Director for Program Affairs of the Coptic Evangelical Organisation for Social Services, Egypt.

[2] Cited in Antonie Wessels, *Arab and Christian? Christians in the Middle East* (Kampen: Pharos, 1995), 1.

[3] Wessels, *Arab and Christian?* 1.

However, Arab Christians have existed from the earliest days of Christianity.[4] There are various stories about Christianity in Arabia, where Islam has its roots, showing that Arab Christians were in existence before Islam; there was no contradiction in being an Arab and being a Christian. Another important factor is that most of the inhabitants of the region have the same roots. There is a debate over the origin of the Copts as well as the Maronites. Some argue that the Copts are descendants of the Pharaohs and that the Maronites are descendants of the Phoenicians, both having no connection to the Arab race. However, it is suggested that all the inhabitants of this region are a mix of the Semitic, Hametic, and Caucasian peoples. So whether they are Arabs, or descendants of the Pharaohs or Phoenicians in terms of race, it is appears that in origin the inhabitants of the region are all Arabs. So the term 'Arab Christian' will be used in this paper; the words Arab and Christian are not mutually exclusive. Finally, one can argue that the term 'Arab Christian' summarises the core of the thesis of this paper. To be a part of this region, speak Arabic, be influenced by Arab-Islamic culture, to stand committed to the land and fight for its independence, and to live for its development and create its history is the ultimate goal of Arab Christians.

Political Theology for Civil Society

The development of civil society through the practices of democracy can contribute to flexible relationships between majorities and minorities. The dynamic concept of minority in the case of Arab Christians must be supported by a theological position that promotes citizenship and coexistence. The theology of minorities in the Arab world is characterised by either passive resistance or sectarian violence. Bībawī indicates that the dreams and the visions that occupy the mind of the minority are of the second coming of Jesus Christ and the establishment of his millennium. Such dreams reflect the desire of the minority to overcome current problems. However, insistence on a literal interpretation of Bible stories makes criticism difficult and reduces the possibility of developing a theology that can meet the needs of the community.[5] A theology that focuses on heavenly intervention does not encourage co-existence. Theologies that support sectarian politics – both Muslim and Christian –

---

4 Otto F.A. Meinardus, *Two Thousands Years of Coptic Christianity* (Cairo: American University in Cairo, 1999); Bishop Athanāsyūs, 'The Copts through Ages', *WSCF Journal Quarterly* (May 1986); Samīr Fawzī, *Al-Qidīs Marqus wa-Ta'sīs Kanīsa al-Iskandariyya* (Saint Mark and the Establishment of the Church of Alexandria) (Cairo: Al-Hay'a al-Mis}riyya al-'A<ma li-al-Kitāb, nd); and Victor Sah}āb, *Al-'Arab wa-Tārīkh al-Mas'āla al-Masīh}iyya* (Arabs and the Christian Issue) (Beirut: Al-Wihda, 1998).

5 George Bībawī, *The Mind of the Minority*. Handwritten document.

hinder the promotion of dynamic citizenship. Theological development that encourages pluralism, coexistence and citizenship is needed.

The theology that the Copts adopted was based on passiveness and implies fundamental contradictions. The Coptic Orthodox Church advocates a secular state while it promotes theocracy, seeing itself as the sole political alternative with the traditional view of the separation of the Kingdom of Heaven from the Kingdom of Earth and the eschatological expectation of God's intervention in the favour of His people. Practically, the Church becomes involved in the political struggle, not as a civil society institution, but as a political alternative. This results in the weakening of civil society and hinders the development of citizenship. Dynamic citizenship that is established as a result of common struggle; social, cultural and economic development; and political independence needs political theology that strengthens civil society and accepts comprehensive democracy.

The emphasis on Christian nationalism, the absence of the concept of citizenship, and the limiting of secularisation to the political level all create a theological contradiction. On one hand it sees the connection between the Kingdom of God and the current reality; on the other hand it considers politics as a secular concept achieved through sectarian policies. This contradiction confuses religion with politics at the level of identity formation, but not within government, which tends to have a secular appearance. Thus religious identities within secular government limit the development of citizenship.

Religious institutions need to develop an Arabic political theology that can contribute to the emergence of civil society, encourage democracy and realise dynamic citizenship. Such a task is crucial in developing the role of Arab Christians. A contextual theology that transcends the barriers of the past and contributes to the development of dynamic citizenship will enhance coexistence and affirm pluralism. Some ideas for such a contextual theology are suggested below.

Arabic Contextual Theology

For an Arabic contextual theology, the concept of the Church must be developed. As I have previously stated, religious institutions are considered an old structure of civil society. In that case, Church should not be a political alternative. Although there is no Arabic political theology that supports the notion that Church is a political alternative, the practices of the Church leaders and the instable policies of the state contribute to such a position. In that context, the Church is not part of civil society, but it becomes a political institution. However, if I consider the Church an old structure of civil society which must be integrated into the stream of the civil movement, it must have a theology that supports this role and takes it over to the heart of the developing civil society.

Arabic contextual theology must consider loyalty in its wider concept, replacing single religious obligations with multiple commitments. The problem with political Islam is its commitment to religion alone. Loyalty in its wider sense will encourage a contextual theology that accepts other ideas and sees the Kingdom of God as a way toward pluralism and diversity; thus pluralistic loyalty will contribute to the empowerment of civil society – instead of its Islamisation or Christianisation. Arabic political theology that introduces such a concept of loyalty will open the door for interaction between theology and society in a way that affirms citizenship. Citizenship is not a religion but religion will be a contributor to its formation. Multiple loyalties will contribute to dynamic citizenship.

Multiple loyalties will contribute to the restructuring of identity. Political theology that considers religious commitments as one component of identity structure is crucial. However, such a relative and flexible concept of identity needs a theology that believes that no one owns the absolute truth. In that context, pluralism will become rooted in the religious context, which hitherto tends to believe in a single truth. This notion of absolute truth is one of the root causes of theological problems in the Arab world. To encourage a theology that recognises multiple loyalties, pluralistic identity and transcends a single legitimate truth, multiple interpretations of the religious texts are required.

The pluralistic interpretation of religious texts is a key concept in developing a political theology that promotes pluralism that is the basis of dynamic citizenship. Arabic political theology also needs this tool to promote pluralism at different levels of the Church and society. Such pluralism will enhance the practice of the concept at the theological level as well as at the social and political levels. The church will accept the need for openness and involvement with other religious communities. Muslims will contribute to a diverse civil society that legitimises different opinions of the current reality and alternative visions of the future. Such pluralism affirms and establishes democracy that strengthens the civil society and leads to dynamic citizenship.

Arabic political theology considers solidarity as the basis of coexistence. Pluralism does not mean fragmentation. The theology that sees solidarity as a tool for common struggle and coexistence can contribute to the realisation of dynamic citizenship. Solidarity must be based on the doctrine of creation where all humans have an equal right to exist and to thrive. Equality and justice come before solidarity. Religious doctrines are selective by nature and tend to exclude those who are different. A political theology that can establish a concept of solidarity and go beyond the limitation of doctrine will contribute to the notion of unity and diversity that is essential for civil society and democracy. Solidarity as a theological concept will also contribute to the socialisation of the Church and encourage the religious institutions to become an active part of civil society.

Institutionalisation is a necessary component in developing a political theology that contributes to dynamic citizenship. The absence of the concept of social sin characterises an individualistic approach to society. This notion is clear in the current Coptic contextual theology that separates the Kingdom of God from the earth. However, political theology that promotes institutionalisation as a theological concept will encourage the church to have an institutional role that is independent of the state and contribute to building bridges between the Church and society. Institutionalisation will bring the Church to the heart of civil society and help it to overcome the isolation and alienation that the Church faces in the Arabic society. It will also establish the role of the Church as an institution, limit the role of individual to some extent and will encourage democracy. Institutionalisation will affirm the role of God's people as a community committed to equality, justice and full involvement and these are the essences of dynamic citizenship.

These are some ideas that are needed to develop a contextual theology that can respond to the social and political development of the Arab world and meet the needs of the Arab Christian as a catalytic in the process of achieving dynamic citizenship. An Arabic political theology that demonstrates the involvement of Arab Christians in the public life of the Middle East is an area for future research.

A piper welcomes the delegates to the opening worship at the Edinburgh 2010 conference

Dr Dana L. Robert gives the keynote speech 'Mission in the Long Perspective' at the opening plenary

Prof. Tinyiko Sam Maluleke blows the vuvuzela during his address at the opening plenary

Ms Adele Ngomedje speaks to the delegates at the reception at the Scottish Parliament

The youth delegation

Bishop John F White and Dr Elijah Jong Fil Kim during the parallel session on Mission and Unity (Theme 8)

Small group during the parallel session on Theme 6: Theological Education and Formation

Dr Michael Biehl addresses the parallel session on Mission and Power (Theme 4)

Ceilidh. Miss Heather Chester and Dean Hakan E Wilhelmsson

Press conference: (left to right) Rev Dr Olav Fyske Tveit,
The Most Reverend Brian Farrell and Rev Dr Geoff Tunnicliffe

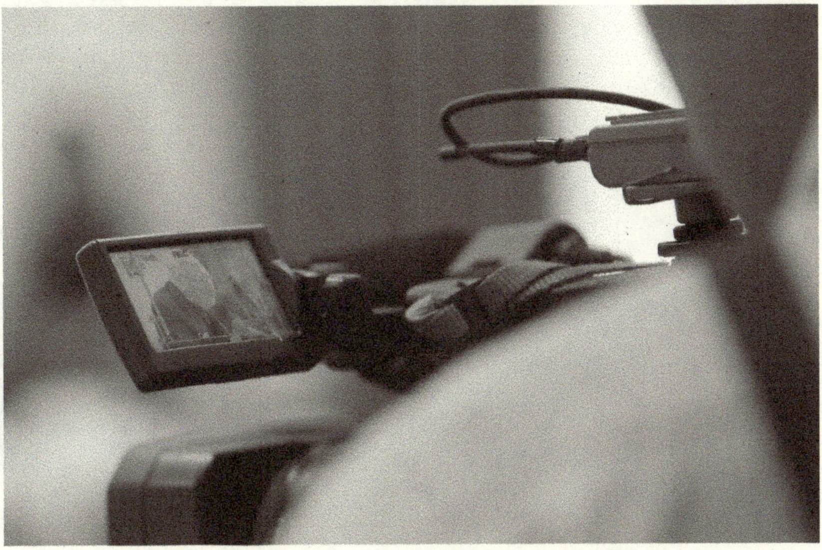

TV camera records the press conference:
The Most Reverend Brian Farrell on screen

Delegates take the Ecumenical Pilgrimage through the grounds of Pollock Halls. Dr Fulata Mbano-Moyo tries out an exercise bike at one of the stops on the pilgrimage.

Bishop Dr Geevarghese Mor Coorilos suggests changes to the first draft of the Common Call at the closing plenary

The congregation enjoy the sound of the Scotland African Mass Choir at the closing celebration in the Church of Scotland Assembly Hall, venue for the 1910 World Missionary Conference

Archbishop John Sentamu speaks at the closing celebration.

Delegates leave the Assembly Hall after the closing celebration past the statue of John Knox in New College, University of Edinburgh

POSTMODERNITY: A CATHOLIC PERSPECTIVE

Gianni Colzani[1]

I am a Catholic priest and I belong to the diocese of Milan, but for these past ten years I have been teaching theology of mission at the Pontifical Urbaniana University. As agreed with Professor Andrew Kirk, I have been entrusted the task of illustrating the Catholic position on postmodernity. From the beginning I must say that I have no other title than my competence; I do not belong to the Magisterium, and in the Catholic world, theology offers its reflections to the Christian community, but then it is up to the Episcopal or Pontifical Magisterium to agree with them or not.

The theme of postmodernity is a recent one. However, in 1950 R. Guardini had already predicted the birth of a new conception of life and of the world,[2] and it is J.F. Lyotard – in 1979 – who speaks about the 'postmodern condition'.[3] Postmodernity is understood in opposition to modernity, however not everybody agrees about its precise meaning and about the relationship between the two epochs. I understand modernity on the basis of the unlimited perfectibility of the person, on a conception of history as continuous progress and happiness as its ethical instance; the failure of this plan is evident to everybody, and drives J. Habermas to think modernity as an unaccomplished plan and to perceive postmodernity as a critical recommencement of the failed objectives.[4] Today, the most common idea perceives postmodernity as a new epoch: the fragmentation of identity, existential uncertainty and instability of life make it impossible to use the same categories which were formerly used.

---

[1] Dr Gianni Colzani is a Catholic priest of the Diocese of Milan and professor in the Faculty of Mission Sciences at the Pontifical Urbaniana University, Rome.

[2] R. Guardini, *La fine dell'epoca moderna. Il potere* [1950] (Brescia: Morcelliana, 1993). About his thought see A. Kobyklinski, *'Modernità e postmodernità'. L'interpretazione cristiana dell'esistenza al tramonto dei tempi moderni nel pensiero di Romano Guardini* (Roma: Pontificia Università Gregoriana, 1998).

[3] J.F. Lyotard, *La condizione postmoderna. Rapporto sul sapere* [1979] (Milano: Feltrinelli, 2002).

[4] J. Habermas, *Il discorso filosofico della modernità* (Roma-Bari: Laterza, 1987).

Postmodernity: Which? What meaning?

A lot depends on what one intends with postmodernity. I will recall two interpretations linking the first to the thought of G. Vattimo and R. Rorty and the second to the vision of Z. Baumann and of Charles Taylor. Vattimo abandons the traditional Christian vision of rationality as a way to truth about God and man and, in postmodernity, he perceives the attitude of whoever welcomes precariousness, multiplicity and the contradictory nature of an ephemeras reality;[5] according to him, in this weak thought he perceives the key for the decrease of violence and the democratisation of society with the spreading of pluralistic and tolerant attitudes. Rorty, instead, proposes an agreement with the community which the individual lives in.[6] In this logic, postmodernity is a post-metaphysic epoch which does not feel regret for the truths of the past, nor desire for new certainties; postmodern man is a person who is alone, who does not feel the need for the reassurance offered by God: 'half-truths' which enable him to live with himself and with his own lack of foundations, are enough for him. If there is something that he needs, this is lay ethics and not a faith. In this way postmodernity is a revolution of the West's spiritual world, a reorganisation of its cultural universe, a different mental coherence with the aim of a new social cohesion. A similar perspective cannot but question faith: it is a question of redefining the social and cultural meaning of its presence in history.

The position of Z. Baumann and of Charles Taylor is different, for they try to re-think Christian faith in a post-modern epoch. In 1993, Z. Baumann published *Postmodern Ethics*,[7] a text in which he argues that morality does not depend on society as both the above authors propose, but on the contrary, morality is the foundation of social life. According to Baumann, ethical judgement belongs to the person as such, and cannot be delegated to others; going back to Lévinas, he proposes that in encounter with the

[5] Vattimo's journey starts with G. Vattimo & P.A. Rovatti, *Il pensiero debole* (Milano: Feltrinelli, 1983); also by him, G. Vattimo, *Opere complete*. I/1-2: *Ermeneutica*, (Roma: Meltemi, 2007-2008); G. Vattimo, *Addio alla verità* (Roma: Meltemi, 2009); G. Vattimo, *Oltre l'interpretazione. Il significato dell'ermeneutica per la filosofia* (Roma-Bari: Laterza, 1994).

[6] Works by Rorty include: R. Rorty, *La filosofia e lo specchio della natura* [1979] (Milano: Bompiani, 1986); R. Rorty, *Verità e progresso. Scritti filosofici* (Milano: Feltrinelli, 2003); R. Rorty, *La filosofia dopo la filosofia*, (Roma-Bari: Laterza, 2008). On Rorty, see, G. Hottois & M. Weyemberg (eds), *Richard Rorty. Ambuigüités et limites du postmodernisme* (Paris: Vrin, 1994).

[7] Z. Baumann, *Postmodern Ethics* (Oxford: Blackwell, 1993) – Italian edition, *Sfide dell'etica* (Milano: Feltrinelli, 1996). Translated works: Z. Baumann, *Il disagio della postmodernità* [1997] (Milano: Mondadori, 2002); Z. Baumann, *La società dell'incertezza* (Bologna: Il Mulino, 1999); Z. Baumann, *La solitudine del cittadino globale* [1999] (Milano, Feltrinelli, 2000); Z. Baumann, *Una nuova condizione umana* [2003] (Milano: Vita e Pensiero, 2003).

'other', an unconditional responsibility is inherent, an original ethical instance that is in opposition with relativism. The meeting with the other is an experience that challenges the authority and the freedom of the individualistic I; putting into question the spontaneity of the person, the meeting with the other's countenance becomes the foundation of an original, ethical relationship with reality.

On his part, Taylor[8] has deeply analysed the history of secularisation where he pointed out the presence of an anthropological constant, which had substituted the preceding spiritual order centred on God with two immanent realities: the rational control of nature and the authentic and uninhibited expression of one's own subjectivity. According to his point of view, not only have these two anthropological constants acquired an absoluteness which are historically on a par with the Hebrew-Christian theism, but they have made people put the question of *fullness* in a new way, that is a kind of interior richness and fullness which are symbolic place of people's integral way of being-in-the-world. This humanism has maintained the dignity of the person but, instead of founding it on God, it is described according to an immanent conception which is, moreover, at the basis of the kind of fragility which accompanies our life today.[9]

These are the 'unquiet frontiers of modernity',[10] which are continually challenged by existential fragility, by the futility of everyday and by the mediocrity of our real life. Whilst Vattimo and Rorty totally adhere to this, and Baumann appeals to social ethics, Taylor retains that Christianity should not express an antagonistic conception that proclaims the truths of the faith and their metaphysic and natural foundation, but needs to accept to take its place in this pluralism, as one of the possible choices which the person could make. It is a position that can make sense under the social and public profile, but never the personal one; a political order that accepts human finiteness knows that this produces a plurality of positions rather than untouchable truth. In this pluralistic context, Taylor puts the question of *fullness*: this term refers to a kind of fullness of life, to an interior richness, to a deep reconciliation which believers relate to the meeting with God, while non-believers associate with a sort of authentic humanity. If faith can cultivate the dream of a rebirth, of being 'born-again', it is in this challenge that it needs to enter.

---

[8] Ch. Taylor, *A Secular Age* (Cambridge, MA: The Belknap Press of Harvard University Press, 2007) –Italian edition, *L'età secolare* (Milano: Feltrinelli, 2009). On the topic, see the extensive discussion in Italian: 'The Secular Age', in *Euntes Docete* 62 (2009/2), 5-123.

[9] Ch. Taylor, *A Secular Age*, 531.

[10] Ch. Taylor, *A Secular Age*, 711-727.

The Challenges of Postmodernity

More than to make list of problems, I would like to go to the core of the problem. One can say that postmodernity invests above all anthropology; it touches, even more, the whole of Christian soteriology and puts Christology and the role of the Church in question. In this immanent vision of salvation, our time pursues salvation without a Saviour, reconciliation without a Reconciler. It is possible to formulate such a perspective? Can a Christian love this world positively or must he go back to the Johannine warning, where one must be in the world but not of the world (John 17:11, 14-18)? Is the being-in-the-world a value or a hard necessity? Since, in this way, the discussion goes back to the revelation and to the event that confesses a God who 'so loved the world that He gave His only born Son' (John 3:16), the soteriological problem is widened to include the mission of the Risen one and of his community (Matt. 28:10-20; Mark 16:15.).

To face this problem one can start from Taylor's critique, which indicated the *turning point* in a 'theism characterised by providential traits'; in his point of view, this has led to an 'organic but impersonal conception of reality'. There where God is seen as an omnipotent Being and supreme Creator, the access to the design of God takes place through the world so that, in an immanent perspective, a road is open for a conception of the world and its truth which can do without God. Thus this poses the problem of relationships between the theological understanding of reality and the intellectual vision of the cosmos; the theological conception of the cosmos is destructured, to be then recomposed around reason and human freedoms as the centre of history. Still left to be known is the sense and value of the human search for truth in itself, as well as in order of democracy and of the rights of persons. Political theology and the theology of liberation cannot be set aside.

Even without mentioning historians of thought like K. Löwith [11] and H. Blumenberg[12] and sociologists[13] like P. Berger and A. Seligman, we find many questions here. There is an epistemological diminution that reduces knowledge to scientific knowledge, in this way forgetting that at the core of knowledge we do not find the 'experiment' but the totality of the human experience.[14] Besides, the separation between politics and religion, which

---

[11] K. Löwith, *Significato e fine della storia. I presupposti teologici della filosofia della storia* [1953] (Milano: Comunità, 1963).

[12] H. Blumenberg, *La legittimità dell'età moderna* [1966] (Genova: Marietti, 1992).

[13] On sociology refer to the general reconstruction made by H. Lübbe, *La secolarizzazione. Storia e analisi di un concetto* (Bologna: Il Mulino, 1970); U. Ruh, *Säkularisierung als Interpretationskategorie. Zur Bedeutung des christlichen Erbes in der modernen Geistesgeschichte* (Freiburg-Basel-Wien: Herder, 1974). Together with them refer to A.J. Nijk, *Secolarizzazione* (Brescia, Queriniana, 1973).

[14] G. Siegwalt, *Dogmatique pour la catholicité évangélique. Système mystagogique de la foi chrétienne*. III: *L'affirmation de la foi*. I: *Cosmologie théologique: sciences et philosophie de la nature* (Genève: Labor et Fides & Paris: Cerf, 1996), 137-146.

the West would hope is by now consolidated, is in reality more fragile than is normally thought; after the fall of the wall of Berlin and the explosion of fundamentalism, the reflection on the public role of religions is once again an arduous point and it oscillates between the private conception of the West, that looks upon religions as a person's right, and the Arabic-Asian conception which makes of it a criterion of people's unification and an orientation for custom.[15] One can say that Christology and soteriology, rationality and its anthropological importance, and sociability supported by the civil and democratic organisation are all involved in this problem.

A Working Hypothesis

The first problem is ontological and epistemological reductionism which expresses 'a widespread distrust of universal and absolute statements, especially among those who think that truth is born of consensus and not of a consonance between intellect and objective reality'.[16] Here we find a decline in absolute certainties where precariousness and what is provisional occupy a central position, a renunciation of the totality of sense and its fragmentation which lead to a life characterised by what is provisional and fleeting; the human and the humanising sense of faith is under discussion as well as the meaning of reason in the sphere of the act of faith. Without entering into the question, I would only like to say that the kind of reason that concerns revelation is that which is capable of understanding how revelation is a historic person, that is, a reality which is not to be subdued as an object but which, as an experience, questions intelligence and freedom. The background of faith and the theological reflection spring forth from here, from a gift that comes to us and urges us to assume our responsibility.

According to my point of view, this revelation is *agapic-kenotic*: therefore its content is found in the divine *agape* and in the *kenosis* which is the highest expression of it. Vibrant with the love of Christ and sent in service of this love, mission has its heart within the *agape*, in the openness towards the other and in its donation to the other. And this other, is primarily the non-Christian, above all the one who can also refuse the faith. Being a living and personal crystallisation of this love, the believer and the Church are at the service of a love which is addressed towards everybody. As Paul wishes himself, 'accursed and cut off from Christ for the sake of my own people' (Rom. 9:3), therefore love belongs to the Church on account of the reality which postmodernity understands as finiteness and multiplicity, and it is possible for Her to accept the challenge which Taylor indicated as the aspiration to *fullness* and to the experience of fragility.

---

[15] S. Ferrari (ed.), *Introduzione al diritto comparato delle religioni. Ebraismo, islam e induismo* (Bologna: Il Mulino, 2008).
[16] John Paul II, *Fides et Ratio* (1998), §56.

In accompanying the pathway of this concrete humanity, the Church cannot but call upon the dignity whose foundation lies 'only in the mystery of the Word made flesh' and cannot but proclaim that, on the basis of the universal love of Christ, the Holy Spirit gives everyone the possibility of coming into contact with the paschal mystery, in the way that God knows.[17] Mission needs to be understood against this background.

In this sense John Paul II speaks about faith as a 'convinced advocate and convincing in reason';[18] and Benedict XVI asks for 'a faith ally of intelligence' and argues that 'not acting according to reason, is contrary to the nature of God'.[19] It goes without saying that the kind of reason which is invoked here, is not any kind of knowledge, but one which is capable of establishing a relationship with God. In his comment about Pope Benedict XVI's speech in Regensburg, J. Habermas[20] asks for an alliance between 'the illuminated conscience of modernity' and the 'theological conscience of world religions', in view of a commitment that goes against the defeatism of reason which the author sees being carried out by 'positivistic scientism', as well as by the 'tendencies of a derailed modernisation that seem to obstruct more than favour the imperatives of its morals of justice'. This position is not acceptable because Habermas realises the separation between the Hellenistic heritage, that is the reason, and the Jewish inheritance, that is soteriology.

According to Christian Duquoc, this is the time for a theology where the solidity of faith does not match with the capacity of organic and global synthesis: for the postmodern theologian, the exchange with this culture functions as an opening for a search for truth which represents a further peculiar motive of faithfulness to the revelation.[21] According to Christoph Theobald, we instead need to re-understand in terms of wisdom, the work of reason in the bosom of this culture.[22] If there can be a theology, it needs to be a theology of this kind. Postmodern theology appears to be a theology

---

[17] Vatican II, *Gaudium et Spes* (1965), §22.

[18] John Paul II, *Fides et Ratio* (1998), §56.

[19] A cross reference to the famous speech held by J. Ratzinger at the University of Regensburg on 12 September 2006. In this passage Benedict XVI cites a passage of the 'Controverse VII 3b' (in A. Th. Khoury, *Manuel II Paléologue. Entretiens avec un Mussulman. 7 ᵉ Controverse* (Paris: Cerf, 1966), 144-145). It is the VII Controversy which the Byzantine Emperor Manuele II Paleologo had with a Persian expert on Christianity and Islam. These two meetings probably go back to winter of 1391 and their drafting in the form of a diary could be the work of the same emperor.

[20] J. Habermas, '*Contro il disfattismo della ragione moderna. Per un nuovo patto tra fede e ragione*', in *Teoria politica* 23(2007), n. 1, 5-10. The original text appeared on the edition of 10 February 2007 of *Neue Zürcher Zeitung*.

[21] Ch. Duquoc, *La teologia in esilio. La sfida della sua sopravvivenza nella cultura contemporanea* [2002] (Brescia: Queriniana, 2004), 95.

[22] Ch. Theobald, *Il cristianesimo come stile. Un modo di fare teologia nella postmodernità*. II (Bologna: Dehoniane, 2009), 147.

without global and definite solutions, but capable of understanding the providential sense of this difficult time which solicits the development of the prophetic role of the Church as a school of humanity, and to transform the deep sense of the limit in a need for spirituality and for transcendence.

Postmodern theology can open pathways where the multi-culture of Western societies should, and must, make use of the dialogue with the relational vitalism of the African world[23] and with the religious and spiritual sense of the Asian world. Perhaps it is not by chance that in a prophetic text at the end of his long pontificate, John Paul II spoke about the relationship with this world indicating to an 'enormously rich body of teaching and *the striking new tone* in the way it presented this content constitute as it were a proclamation of new times'.[24] For the mission, this is a time of sowing rather than one of fruits, a sowing in which the love of God has become the essence of an attentive and responsible love for human destiny.

---

[23] M. Nkafu Nkemnkia, *Il pensare africano come 'vitalogia'* (Roma: Città Nuova, 1995). See also the conception of P. Tempels who places 'vital energy' as the foundation of African philosophy: P. Tempels, *Filosofia bantu*[1946] (Milano: Medusa, 2005).

[24] John Paul II, *Tertio millennio adveniente* (1994), §20.

Mission and Power: A Comment from Germany

Michael Biehl[1]

I come from the global North, I am white, an academic, 53 years old, I am ordained and worst: I am male. Measured against the ecumenical arithmetics I am politically incorrect. As Ruth Padilla has put it: 'The face of mission and the face of Christian faith of today is young, southern and predominantly female'. The criteria by which I thus am characterised highlight my position in relation to others within a network of power relations in the field of mission and ecumenical relations of churches.

What does mission and power mean to you if you are considered to be in a position of power but at the same moment you face the fact that mission in your highly secularised society is almost powerless. A widespread understanding marginalises mission as something you do not do, especially within the mainline churches, although they value *diakonia*, for instance, highly. And again, other expressions of the Christian faith like charismatic migrant churches from Africa and Asia may challenge you as 'preaching persuasive words of wisdom' whereas they claim their mission to be 'a demonstration of the Spirit and the Power'. From this standpoint we chose the theme 'Mission between power and powerlessness (*Ohnmacht*)'. (Note that the German original term for powerlessness is a strong expression denoting to be without command to the extent of being absolutely helpless.) 'We' are staff and members of the EMW (the Association of Protestants Churches and Missions in Germany), of the Academy of Mission at the University of Hamburg and of the German Association for Mission Studies.

Looking back to Edinburgh 1910 we realised that those present there from Germany faced a comparable setting: Those assembled definitely had power in relation to mission and mission churches overseas, and they attempted to keep hold of this power, but they also complained about disinterest in mission in their society and the churches. Today, the main line churches in Germany – like the Lutheran ones to which I adhere – have integrated most of the former mission societies into the church. Furthermore, many of the so-called partner churches in the Southern hemisphere are the heirs of the former missions from Germany. So there are a lot of historic relations and deliberate attempts to journey together from a dependency situation to a partnership situation, exploring various

[1] Rev. Dr Michael Biehl is a Lutheran pastor and head of studies at the Academy of Mission at the University of Hamburg, Germany.

understandings of mission and activities in mission: mission and evangelism, mission and development, partnership. The mechanisms of organising the relations are sometimes questioned as tending to redirect control back to the North. This is not only to do with money, but also about knowledge, skills, education, the number of trained specialists. And it is not only about who has but about who is defining the focus, which approaches are taken and who is forging the instruments.

In this network of relations we proposed to study closer two themes. First, we proposed to explore in this situation our mission in the light of vulnerability. We can relate here to the report of Theme 5 Forms of Missionary Engagement, which also spoke about vulnerability. There are those who are vulnerable to the dangers of their contexts like poverty, violence, insecurity, racism, injustice, untimely death. To become vulnerable means here to really look and to become sensitive to those who are vulnerable.

There is a second theme: that is to choose to become vulnerable. What could it mean, for instance, to be attentive to the charismata of the others? So-called 'migrant churches' are often perceived of as being in need of assistance, an object of *diakonia*. Their insistence on the power of the Holy Spirit is often denied or ridiculed by the reproach that it is based on a premodern, unenlightened reading of the Bible. So where they are vulnerable, they are seen, but where they do have charismata, they are silenced because their way of doing theology does not fit the structures. One field where such a mission of becoming vulnerable can be explored is a very basic activity which everyone can join: the sharing of the Bible. To become vulnerable could mean here taking seriously that every woman and man can do this, instead of starting by exercising a hermenutical power of interpretation which rules out right from the beginning any other approach to scriptures. Where such a change of perspective takes place we really will be listening to the ocean of stories of those who as subjects in their own right became Christians, in history and today, like the impressive and touching testimonies we read about in the report of Theme 4 Mission and Power. To make ourselves vulnerable means to be willing to listen more closely to the voice of the other and their way of witnessing.

Engaging in this we also propose to explore the metaphor of hospitality as it was, among others, proposed in a study text of the World Council of Churches on 'Religious plurality and Christian self-understanding'. How do we live and express the hospitality we experience from God in the first place? By offering space to each other, by becoming willing to be changed by those to whom we offer or from whom we experience hospitality. If you take this approach seriously it ultimately questions if mission can identify objectives at all.

Vulnerability translates the German word *Verwundbarkeit*, which can express both the meaning of being vulnerable and of becoming sensitive to the vulnerability of others. *Verwundbarkeit* may be a category for perceiving a shared history in which wounds have been inflicted upon each other. Such an orientation could at least help to dress wounds if not heal them, and it definitely can help to avoid hurting each other further by looking at power differently.

Theological Education and Formation in Mission: An Evangelical Response

John M. Hitchen[1]

Evangelicals find much to appreciate and be grateful for in the preparatory report from Theme 6 Theological Education and Formation.[2] We endorse its analyses and confirm the survey of current trends. We recognise ourselves in some of the warnings and accept its appropriate criticisms. We will give serous consideration to the thoughtfully presented recommendations. Evangelicals share the study group's commitment to the priority of theological education at the heart of the mission task. This is not surprising, given the intertwining of the roots from which both Edinburgh 1910 and the evangelical Bible Schools movements grew in the late nineteenth century, not to mention earlier missionary and evangelical theological education confluences from the start of the modern Protestant missionary movement.[3] Moreover, many evangelical theological education centres today see themselves as inheriting and developing the heritage of Edinburgh 1910 in their mission education emphases. So we appreciate the opportunity to bring an Evangelical response to the Theme Six paper.[4]

---

[1] Dr John M. Hitchen teaches Mission Studies in the Laidlaw-Carey Graduate School of Theology, Auckland, New Zealand and served as a missionary in Papua New Guinea from 1965-79.

[2] Daryl Balia & Kirsteen Kim (eds), *Edinburgh 2010: Witnessing to Christ Today* (Oxford: Regnum Books International, 2010), 148-74.

[3] For just one example, consider the role of Trevecca College established by Lady Selina, Countess of Huntingdon, founded in 1768 in association with the revivals of George Whitfield, and moved to Cheshunt, Hertfordshire, England, in 1792 to become a leading theological, ministerial and missionary training college of the Congregational Church throughout the nineteenth century, before moving to Cambridge in 1905 to become Westminster College. See John M. Hitchen, 'Training Tamate: The Formation of the Nineteenth Century Missionary Worldview: The Case of James Chalmers of New Guinea', PhD Thesis, University of Aberdeen, 1984: 465-522.

[4] In accepting this invitation to respond, we note a potential problem in categorization. We can differentiate Evangelical, Charismatic and Pentecostal groups in some areas of theological discussion. We also accept that some Theological Education schools differentiate themselves by claiming to belong to one of those three 'camps', and by distinguishing themselves from one or both of the others. However, in some parts of the world, particularly Australia, New

Since Evangelicals are characterised by and approach theological education with a number of distinctive concerns, we shall use an adaptation of David Bebbington's distillation of the four distinguishing marks of Evangelicals as our lens through which to comment on the paper.[5]

Conversion and Mission Leading to a Holistic Life-Transforming Experience of Christ

Evangelicals focus on conversion and mission leading to a holistic life-transforming experience of Christ as we evaluate theological education. For us the Gospel is central, therefore we look first for theological education that promotes the growth and missional involvement of the Church, by giving due priority to evangelistic proclamation, prophetic engagement with society, and humble service to fellow-humans. We would like a sharper emphasis on such criteria as one goal of contemporary theological education.

Second, we expect programmes that value the spirituality of faculty and their commitment to Gospel priorities as crucial for quality theological education. So we evaluate theological education by asking:

- Does the theological education programme prioritise personal spirituality and involvement in active witnessing to the faith when recruiting faculty and allocating faculty loads?
- Does the programme foster the flame of the Spirit in faculty and students, along with their submission to the Word of God; and encourage modelling of a radical discipleship?
- How does the programme manage the tension faculty members face in balancing the responsibilities and expectations laid on them for teaching; researching; scholarly publishing; mentoring and pastoring students; spiritual sustenance, and involvement in missional witness?

Zealand, and Melanesia, many theological Colleges serve all three of these groupings without distinction. Thus, while this response comes from an Evangelical background, it is not set over against either Charismatic or Pentecostal groups. We see both Charismatics and Pentecostals as sharing most of our Evangelical distinctives, and we share many of theirs. In our part of the world we work together as much as the constituent groups will allow.

[5] David Bebbington, *Evangelicalism in Modern Britain: A History from the 1730s to the 1980s* (Grand Rapids, MI: Baker, 1989), 1-2; for discussion of the groupings and emphases within Evangelicalism, John Hitchen, 'What It Means To Be An Evangelical Today – An Antipodean Perspective' in Two Parts, *Evangelical Quarterly* 76/1 (Jan 2004), 47-64 and 76/2 (Apr 2004), 99-115; for an attempt to address current trends in the movement, Brian Harris, 'Beyond Bebbington: The Quest for Evangelical Identity in a Postmodern Era', *Churchman* 122/3 (Autumn 2008), 201-220.

- How does the theological education institution protect its faculty from succumbing to academic occupational hazards such as: (i) inappropriate desire for academic status, influence or power? (ii) Unwillingness or reluctance to be prophetic in stance and teaching? (iii) Failure to keep the warmth of the Spirit in teaching, in depth of relationship with students; in church involvement and in active missional outreach? (iv) Moving towards 'professionalism' and 'elitism' institutionally and personally as faculty? (v) Becoming a theological 'in group' discussing amongst ourselves the issues we define as important, and not heeding the issues, concerns or questions of church, wider ecclesiastical groupings, society and needy humanity?

The Theme Paper gives little attention to the spirituality and integrity of faculty as critical for quality Theological Education.

Next, we look for Theological Education that equips graduates with an in-depth grasp of the Gospel message, and provides the contextualisation and communication skills to effectively present this Good News in our pluralistic societies. The paper makes only passing reference to the tension inherent in theological education curriculum goals between academic formation and formation for practical ministries. This will require cross-cultural communication understanding and skills, translation competence to bridge from theological language to everyday life-situations, and bi-cultural relationship skills for effective witness to the Gospel in the multi-cultural and multi-faith twenty-first century worlds we inhabit. But building depth of theological appreciation of the Gospel and developing these communication skills need to be integrated into the whole curriculum, not left as optional 'field-work' extras. The helpful discussion of distance theological education and electronic learning in section 3.9 of the Report, could also be extended to include intentional formation of such ministry skills. Embracing multi-cultural relationships as cohorts of fellow students and creating partnerships with local churches may need to be incorporated as methods of achieving such better balanced academic and ministry-skill formation.

We would, as Evangelicals, commend the Report's rigorous questioning of the relationship between theological education and university control (section 3.4). We recognise there is a contribution to theological education to be made by secular university departments of religion and theology, particularly where mutually respectful partnerships exist between church and academy. But we are grateful for the Report's bold challenge for churches to take ownership of the theological education task and to ask the hard questions about the tone and goals of theological education offered outside church authorised institutions. An evangelistic cutting edge and prophetic, missional, and pastoral application can be lost by trusting the theological education task to non-church-related bodies.

The theological education curriculum needs adequate attention to missiological understanding of the processes of religious change, and therefore of conversion, as amply illustrated from the history of mission encounter in a range of cultural settings. An adequate theological education curriculum will investigate the reasons for Evangelical and Pentecostal schools in the South having been effective in addressing pre-Constantinian church situations, as the paper highlighted at section 2.3. One reason for this may be that Evangelicals and Pentecostals take seriously the ontological reality of the spirit world, as Theme 2 Christian Mission among Other Faiths acknowledges in the case of Pentecostals. In such primal religious and religious change situations, the traditional worldviews can retain their explanatory power and not be quickly replaced by an integrated biblical perspective. But historically, and this is the second reason for their effectiveness, Evangelicals and Pentecostals have presented the Gospel as a call for a change of basic religious loyalty – a conversion – so as to make Christ Lord of their cultural settings, not to withdraw from them. In such settings the Gospel is Good News indeed for those who have known the oppression of spirit powers, witchcraft and sorcery. For them the conversion call has focussed the choice between continuing to live under the power structures of the spirit world, or to discover the ontological reality of release and freedom in Christ. This level of loyalty transfer and subsequent life-style transformation is still fittingly described as conversion. Similar challenges now confront mission in Western post-Christendom settings, with secular ideologies and new spiritualities functioning as religious structures of domination. So the call for a radical transfer of basic religious loyalty is demanded there too, for re-evangelisation of secular post-Christian contexts.

Evangelicals look for theological education that leads to what Darrell Guder calls, 'The continuing conversion of the church',[6] requiring the established churches to maintain their spiritual vitality and missional heart in each new generation. Thus we would like to see a stronger emphasis on theological education enabling Western Christians to hear and heed the 'boomerang challenges' coming back to the Northern churches from the more vital Christianity of the fast-growing and persecuted churches of the South. Challenges about Western individualism, rationalistic dualism, intellectual scepticism in handling biblical texts, and questions like, Why is it that where theological education is flourishing the church is not, and where the church is flourishing theological education is not? Such ongoing renewal requires an emphasis on personal development for students and faculty through life-long learning, ongoing ministry enrichment, upgrading of both qualifications and competency of graduates; adequate care in

[6] Darrell L. Guder, *The Continuing Conversion of the Church* (Grand Rapids, MI: Wm B. Eerdmans, 2000).

faculty selection, and provision of professional development; mentoring, supervision; and pastoral care for faculty members in both North and South contexts. To facilitate this global cross-fertilisation and ongoing renewal of church life we welcome Theological Education which is committed to publishing and promoting South-South as well as South–North theological interchange. We would welcome greater emphasis in the Report on these, for us, foundational matters.

'Biblicism': Seeing the Bible as the Authority for Christian Faith and life

Evangelicals are known for their 'Biblicism', seeing the Bible as the authority for Christian faith and life and as central in the theological education curriculum. We would hope that the commitment to biblical authority that implicitly characterised Edinburgh 1910 might be addressed at this Centennial as an issue demanding serious theological attention in our theological education programmes. The discussion of Theme 1 Foundations for Mission in the preparatory volume fails to bring clarity regarding the place of the Scriptures in mission, thus highlighting the importance of this as a theological education issue.

We accept the Report's challenge and confess that despite our focus on Bible translation we, as Evangelicals, have not adequately addressed hermeneutical assumptions and contextualisation issues in mission. We want to bring a more richly nuanced Evangelical voice to the global hermeneutical discussion, particularly in shaping a 'missional hermeneutic' in exegetical methodology, and re-stating the role of the Spirit in 'illuminating' the supremely authoritative text where multiple theological authorities are treated as of equal value.

We would welcome deeper biblical undergirding and discussion of the Report's implicit and often explicit assumption that a certain kind of ecumenical unity ought to characterise theological education globally. Evangelicals will welcome and participate in more dialogue and cooperation when they sense a depth of mutual respect and appreciation for their perspective. This sense could be enhanced by a different tone in the proposal at section 3.2, for a 'global and regional forum on theological education' as a continuation from this Conference. The Report suggests that the proposed forum 'should cooperate with the World Council of Churches' programme on Ecumenical Theological Education', implying that other groups should automatically accept the direction of the World Council group. Or, again, the assumption that the forum 'can function as an enlarged framework of WOCATI' begs the question as to why Evangelicals have established their own alternative groupings, and whether they would want to be subsumed under WOCATI. As it stands, the proposal raises questions as to whether the chief body proposing the cooperation is only partially committed to it, or wants to dominate it, or has its own independent programme it expects the other cooperating bodies to support. Such less than open partnership proposals have not won Evangelical support in the past. A more respectful approach may well lead to precisely these outcomes, but it is not wise to assume them as a precondition of the proposal.

Similar open and more frank discussion is necessary to enable greater Evangelical participation in regional theological associations and accrediting agencies, as suggested at section 3.7. Evangelicals have both participated in and contributed to the strengthening of regional ecumenical Associations of Theological Schools, while at the same time they have also established their own parallel networks to more fully meet their needs. Evangelicals have valued Associations of Theological Schools' guidance in establishing criteria and developing standards for contextualised theological education and in developing study resources. We have, however, usually not encouraged the imposition of common curricula and still regard retaining control of the heart of the teaching content in theological education as vital to maintaining our priorities and ethos.

We note the way, at section 2.9, the Report laments the 'weakening of interdenominational cooperation and joint programmes in theological education' in ecumenical circles. Alongside that 'weakening', the Evangelical interdenominational Bible Colleges movement has, in many cases, matured in the past thirty years to become interdenominational theological colleges and /or universities, and may well have experience and insights which, if shared appropriately with ecumenical interdenominational theological colleges, could lead to mutual support and enrichment, as they each respond to financial restrictions in varying ways. Certainly, the disdain or lack of mutual respect which has characterised relationships between these two groups could be helpfully laid aside regionally and globally in our present context.

We recognise we have much work to do on biblical models for engaging with persons of other faiths in theological education in order to more adequately reflect the diversity and nuancing of biblical teaching on attitudes to other religions; to better reflect the 'justice, courtesy and love', which Edinburgh 1910 showed the Bible calls for in inter-faith relationships; to uphold with Christ-like courage and humility the uniqueness, supremacy and sufficiency of our Lord Jesus Christ as Saviour of all humanity; and to move beyond the caricaturing often inherent in categorising approaches under the terms: 'universalism', 'inclusivism' or 'exclusivism'. Thus we welcome attempts to present fresh paradigms for inter-faith relationships which keep in balance the integrity of the Gospel and proper respect for the beliefs of others. We also acknowledge the urgency of this work in the light of the new migration patterns in our globalising world.

'Activist' and Entrepreneurial for the Cause of Christ

Evangelicals are 'activist' and entrepreneurial for the cause of Christ. So, the Report has challenged us to confess that in theological education we have been quick to export our own methods, curricula and expectations of theological education in our mission enterprise, and slower to listen, learn from, and adapt to the local cultural setting in some of our theological education. We have been slow to equip, transfer responsibility to, and trust local leadership in theological education, but also adept in equipping entrepreneurial visionaries for new ministries in and from their local settings. We have sometimes been separatist and insular in theological education, but at other times we have established strong interdenominational colleges with proven track records over generations of service.

As Evangelicals we confess our 'activist' tendencies have meant we have sometimes contributed to the lack of depth, the lack of attention to contextualisation, and failure to develop adequate teaching and learning resources. We have too often stood apart from cooperation for common standards, and helped escalate the prevalent fragmentation and inappropriate duplication of theological education resources. But as our movement matures we also report that we have proven and developing skills in drawing fellow-evangelicals into alliances and cooperative ventures for improving standards and quality of theological education, as seen in the associations of Bible colleges and accrediting agencies, and theological education funding agencies working globally. We can also report that many Evangelical schools are now committed to and working for new levels of integrated and mutually enriching theological education in our regions by developing articulation relationships, mutual cross-crediting and seeking to pull our weight in accreditation agencies and processes where we are respected and welcomed.

For viability in Majority World theological education, we need to enhance the governance competency of board members (referred to in section 2.5) and the professional competence of senior faculty as well as addressing the financial viability issues raised at section 3.10 (p. 170). Part of the viability problem is that local board and faculty members are being called on to carry simultaneously too many roles for which they are not adequately supported. They are expected, with only or mainly local experience, to develop contextualised curricula (pp. 163-4), and at the same time lead institutions into mutually enriching regional, and international relationships; to bridge the gap between serious research-based theology and populist theologies in Christian literature, practical discipleship programmes, church worship styles and general standards of church life (section 2.8, pp. 164-5); to creatively develop new contextual theological education models as an institution with often only, or primarily, Western educational experience, while at the same time achieving or maintaining international parity and carrying heavy local administrative duties. This people development needs equal research, resourcing and global interchange and support, to match that being proposed to ensure financial viability.

We call for appropriate contextual criteria and competency standards for academic graduation qualifications with international recognition, as an aspect of affirmation 3.3 (p. 167): We need to break the Western hegemony on undergraduate and graduate criteria and standards for academic acceptability in theological education around the globe. We call on some courageous Western schools to break the mould and set new patterns of academic excellence which recognise and reward more culturally diverse learning methods, more communally oriented assessment criteria, and more contextually flexible means of assessment to allow international recognition of the academic equivalence of alternative epistemologies, pedagogies and assessment methodology. We seek not a less rigorous, but a more flexible approach. Feminist and Indigenous educationalists have made a start in this direction. The new developments in qualitative research suggest possibilities. Biblical teaching on the equivalence in value, but diversity of form and expression of spiritual gifts lays the theological groundwork. But we need further courageous experimentation for more globally contextualised theological qualification standards. As Evangelicals we would gladly cooperate in regional theological education association activities geared to implementing such better contextualised criteria and standards. The paper hints at this need with its comments at section 3.7 (p. 169) 'a system of assessment and institutional enhancement', and at section 3.9 (p. 170) 'common understandings of transferability and assessment of learning are still to be developed'.

'Cruci-centrism': Seeing Christ's Work in His Death and Resurrection as the Heart of the Gospel to Which we Witness

Evangelicals are committed to 'Cruci-centrism': seeing Christ's work in his death and resurrection as the heart of the Gospel to which we witness, and the pattern and measure of our Christian lifestyles and ministry standards. So we look for theological education which stresses consistency with the self-denying, self-sacrificing love of Christ expressed at Calvary, in our institutional ethos and in the administrative practices of our colleges; our teaching methodologies so that they genuinely serve, liberate and empower our students; our curriculum design, to ensure forgiveness and reconciliation flow from our learning and characterise our graduates' ongoing service; our patterns of student formation and practical ministry formation; so that cruciform self-sacrifice and service become the norm rather than exception in the lives, life-styles and ministries of graduates; and in our relationships between faculty, staff, and students. We look for theological education which not only focuses on the culturally and contextually most relevant biblical metaphors to open up the local significance of the Triune God's self-giving at the Cross, but also explores and explains the biblical fullness of diverse redemptive, reconciling and salvific metaphors expanding the meaning of the death and resurrection of our Lord Jesus Christ.[7] This kind of cruci-centrism in our Theological Education will enable us, like the Apostle Paul, and in line with the Edinburgh 2010 theme, to say we aim to 'make the word of God fully known' and thus fulfil our Lord's intention that 'repentance and forgiveness of sins will be proclaimed in his name to all nations … [As we become] witnesses of these things'.

These are emphases Evangelicals long to see enriching our theological education. Again we thank those who have prepared the Report which we shall continue to study and implement in our ongoing theological education for mission in the twenty-first century.

[7] See J.M. Hitchen, 'Culture and the Bible: The Question of Contextualization'. Paper presented at the South Pacific Association of Bible Colleges' Biennial Conference, Adelaide, 1-5 July 1991. Reprinted in *Melanesian Journal of Theology* 8/2 (Oct 1992), 30-52.

Christian Communities in Contemporary Contexts: A Latin American Perspective

Carlos Ham[1]

First of all, I want to thank the missionary God, who intends life in fullness for all creation through Jesus Christ, for the blessing of attending this historical gathering to commemorate the first centenary of the World Missionary Conference. I am particularly grateful for the opportunity to contribute to our theme 'Christian Communities in Contemporary Contexts' from a Latin American perspective. I would also like to greet at least three accompaniers in our missionary journey in our region, who are here this day: Rev. Dr. Walter Altmann, Moderator of the World Council of Churches and President of Evangelical Lutheran Church in Brazil, currently serving as one of the chairpersons of our theme; Bishop Julio Murray, from the Anglican Church in Panama and President of the Latin American Council of Churches (CLAI), and Rev. Nilton Giese, General Secretary of CLAI.

Latin America and Edinburgh 1910

The World Missionary Conference in 1910, which met under the theme 'the evangelisation of the world in this generation', marks the beginning of the contemporary ecumenical movement. Even though there were North American missionaries serving in Latin America among the delegates, the continent itself was excluded because it was considered to be already Christian or evangelised, due to the strong Roman-Catholic presence. Since these missionaries considered Latin America a pagan continent and therefore did not agree with this opinion, they organised a Conference of Foreign Missions in North America in March 1913 in New York. They founded the Committee of Latin American Cooperation (CLAC) which would take the responsibility to coordinate mission Congresses in Latin America. The first such congress was on Christian work in Latin America and took place in Panama in February 1916. It was still considered as 'foreign' since it was conceived and organised by missionaries and executives of the foreign mission boards. Afterwards CLAC planned two

[1] Dr Carlos Ham is World Council of Churches Programme Executive for Latin America and the Caribbean.

other congresses, one in South America and the other one for the Caribbean region. The former took place in Montevideo, Uruguay, in March 1925, but it did not really reflect an authentic Latin American identity since, again, it was sponsored by the North American mission boards. It was nevertheless a bridge between the Panama and the Havana Congresses.

The Havana Hispanic-American Evangelical Congress took place in June 1929, for the Caribbean churches as mentioned above. As the title suggests, this congress opened a new chapter in the search for a Protestant Latin American identity, since it was designed and organised by Latin American leaders. Therefore, the importance of the Havana Congress is that it gathered for the first time Latin Americans as protagonists of the Christian mission in the continent, without the North American tutelage, which took place in the previous congresses. Just as it occurred with the Edinburgh conference globally, the Havana Congress marked the beginning of the Latin American unity in mission, and laid the foundations for the Latin American missionary work present today.

From 22-26 June 2009, a group of Latin American leaders met in the Matanzas Theological Seminary in Cuba to commemorate the eightieth anniversary of this Havana Congress. It was a gathering co-organised by the World Council of Churches (WCC), the Latin American Council of Churches (CLAI), the Cuban Council of Churches (CCC) and the Matanzas Theological Seminary (MTS), and it convened representatives of Protestant, Evangelical and Pentecostal churches, confessional families, ecumenical organisations and movements, centres for theological formation and research of the region, theological institutions, and Protestant personalities and theologians. This event provided a space for reflection on the Latin American Protestant identity on mission, which is not limited to the past, but is also forward looking. It therefore took into consideration the current context of mission and evangelism in the Latin American continent in order to refocus this effort ecumenically. In fact, this gathering was intended to be part of the Latin American contribution to the 2010 Edinburgh centennial process. Although we are grateful for receiving the support of the Edinburgh 2010 project, and other churches and agencies, and are also appreciative of the opportunity for sharing these reflections with the churches globally, we would have hoped to have a bigger and more representative delegation from our continent in this commemoration.

In the meeting we accomplished the following objectives: performing an analysis of the Latin American context in which the Church fulfils its mission; continuing with the critical assessment of mission and evangelism in the Protestant tradition in Latin America, in the past eighty years; reflecting on the possibilities, the difficulties and the challenges of the Latin American churches in order to fulfil our evangelising and transformative mission; and contributing to the process of the Edinburgh centennial celebration in the year 2010 from a Latin American perspective. The participants produced a final document, which can be found in the

Edinburgh 2010 website.

Latin American Mission Ethos

Regarding our theme Christian Communities in Contemporary Contexts, from a Latin American perspective, and based on this event mentioned above and other experiences, I would like to highlight the following points, which reflect the Latin American *ethos*:

a) Sharing the good news in a context of 'bad' news.

There are increasing social, political and economic challenges in our continent resulting from neo-liberal globalisation, among other factors. Just to mention some: migrations (both internally and abroad); poverty, which has increased in the last two years in the region (to 36.5 percent of the population); unjust distribution of wealth; drug trafficking; human trafficking; insecurity in the region and the increase of US military bases; the exploitation of natural resources by foreign companies, at a high human and ecological cost; climate change and natural disasters; and domestic violence, among others. Some progressive governments are emerging in the region, but with little possibility of success due to corruption and structural deficiencies. This is the scenario of 'bad' news, where the Latin American churches share the good news of the gospel.

The Latin American churches proclaim the good news of the gospel comforting the poor and at the same time, confronting the power structures, which generate injustice and poverty. Dom Elder Camara (Brasil) has said: 'When I feed the poor, they call me saint; when I ask why they are poor, they call me communist'. We are urged to recover the values of God's kingdom and rebuild hope, through prophetic witness in the social and political arena. The Latin American churches say: 'a different world is needed and, by the grace of the Holy Spirit of God, it is possible'.

b) Proclaiming a holistic mission

The *missio Dei* starts with God, and therefore, it is not that the Church has God's mission in the world, but rather, God's mission in the world has the Church, in order to proclaim life in fullness for all. The efforts to accomplish mission and evangelism separated from *diakonia*, development, emergency aid and advocacy for justice, peace and integrity of creation are an offence against the integrity of the *missio Dei* as it was practised by Jesus in his proclamation of the kingdom to come. Therefore, we emphasise the need to acknowledge the unity and complementarity between *diakonia* and the proclamation of the good news as a concrete manifestation of the holistic mission as it is conceived and practised in Latin America and the Caribbean.

Reflecting on false dichotomies in the Churches' work, our Moderator, Rev. Dr. Walter Altmann in his address to the World Council of Churches Central Committee meeting held in Geneva on 26 August to 2 September 2009 said:

> I would like to reflect a little more on the importance of the diaconal ministry in the life of the church, because another false dichotomy which exists considers *diakonia* of lower value than mission, rather than seeing mission in a holistic way and *diakonia* as an essential dimension of mission itself. Mission without *diakonia* would easily turn into an arrogant and violent enterprise, not respectful of the culture, values and identity of the addressees of the Christian message. It would try to impose one's own faith upon others, instead of giving reasons for the hope that is within us (1 Pet. 3:15) and respecting the others' own faith decision.

c) Celebrating the gospel in unity

Our theologian of the liberation, Gustavo Gutiérrez has said: 'The Latin American people are poor and believers', and as a result of this we celebrate life joyfully and in community. Not that we have accomplished it, but we are committed to sharing the gospel in collaboration, rather than in competition against each other, so that the world may believe (John 17:21). We have a long way to go, but we aim to be inclusive communities, embracing women, children, youth, indigenous people and of African origin, disabled brothers and sisters, diverse minorities, sharing our spiritualities, cultures and traditions.

The charismatic and Pentecostal movement represents a creative challenge for the so-called 'historical churches', which have not always continued to be reformed, and which are rather stagnating in time by sacralising their ways and formulas and losing the capacity to adapt and give an effective response to the needs of the population. In this sense, it is important that, without renouncing biblical and theological precepts in the name of reaching to new people, the spiritual needs of our peoples, which are related to symbols, emotions and feelings rather than to extremely elaborate rational processes, should be taken into account.

One of our main challenges today in Latin America is, as former WCC general secretary Philip Potter said in a different context, at the Sixth Assembly held in Vancouver, Canada (24 July to 10 August 1983): 'to cooperate with God in making the *oikoumene* an *oikos*, a home, a family of men and women, through the crucified and risen Christ, by the living power of the Spirit'. Amen.

CONTEXTUAL UNITY FOR THE CHURCHES

Matthew Cook[1]

Unity is stated to be the theologically undergirded precondition for the credibility of the proclamation of the gospel.[2] Unfortunately, many types of unity have proven unacceptable to churches. Organisational, organic, or institutional unities are unwieldy. Theological unity (in the sense of uniformity) is unacceptable to many. Cooperational unity is pragmatic but hardly provides a theological precondition for credibility. Relational unity (in the familial sense – calling each other brothers and sisters) may even be difficult for some. Dialogical unity (which opens conversations) seems to me the most acceptable type of unity given the constraints of cultural, historical, and theological presuppositions. Any credibility we wish to attain cannot be won at the expense of our own integrity. We dare not abandon who we are. This credibility can be won by recognising the sources of our differences (be they cultural, historical, or theological... among other categories), yet continuing the journey toward understanding each other in the Christian tradition.

Theology as Contextual

This article is written with the presupposition that context influences who we are and how we view the world. It also, therefore, impacts our theological positions. In this perspective, 'there is no "theology" as such – no "universal theology" – there are only contextual theologies. 'Context', however, while it is a reality that allows one to see clearly from a particular perspective, is also something that can, if not blindfold one, then certainly cause one to wear blinders that severely limit vision'.[3] While I neither wish nor consider it acceptable to say that one culture cannot understand another culture, nor that one ecclesial tradition cannot understand the theological

---

[1] Dr Matthew Cook is Lecturer in Systematic Theology at La Faculté de Théologie Evangélique de l'Alliance Chrétienne, Abidjan, Côte d'Ivoire.

[2] Kyriaki Avtzi, László Gonda, and Darrell Jackson. 'Theme Eight: Mission and Unity – ecclesiology and mission', in Daryl Balia & Kirsteen Kim (eds), *Edinburgh 2010: Witnessing to Christ Today* (Oxford: Regnum Books International, 2010), 199-221, at 204.

[3] Stephen Bevans, *An Introduction to Theology in Global Perspective* (Maryknoll, NY: Orbis Books, 2009), 4.

assertions of another theological tradition, the 'blinders' of which Bevans speaks do create hindrances to the unity which we are trying to attain in the church.[4] Using this perspective and a particular idea of unity which must be rejected, Paul Hiebert penned the agonising question, 'How can we work toward the unity of the Church when people and their societies are so different?'[5] Indeed, we need to look for a different type of unity for the churches.

An acceptable unity must accommodate theological divergence. Accommodating divergence is easier or more difficult depending on how one defines that divergence. The early church had easy categories: either a theological statement was orthodox (conforming to the rule of faith and ecclesial teaching) or it was heterodox/heretical. There was a clearly bounded set of acceptable teachings.

The shift we see in the world today from a centralised model of unity to a polycentric one presents its own problems. If we picture the earlier centralised model as one circle which bounded all of the acceptable theology of the early church, then we are inclined to picture the contemporary polycentric model as a multitude of circles which define the acceptable theologies of the multitudes of ecclesial communities. Some of those circles may overlap – United Methodists, Free Methodists, and even the Church of the Nazarene share some theological affirmations. Others of those circles are almost completely distinct from any other – the Kimbanguist Church of the Democratic Republic of Congo offers many unique affirmations. The trouble is evident when one tries to make connections, see similarities, apply constraints, or search for the theological unity. This polycentric model allows a theological pluralism which affords the absence of an authoritative commonality. This model allows a situation where 'diversity may also lead to divisions, to discrimination, to intolerance, to animosity, and even to violence'.[6] Each circle needs justification and power to maintain its own boundaries.[7] The polycentric transformation to the old model of theological integrity is helpful, but insufficient. There have to be other changes to the model as well. In the

[4] For a refutation of incommensurability – the lack of ability to understand another culture or ecclesial tradition, see Harold Netland, *Encountering Religious Pluralism: The Challenge to Christian Faith and Mission* (Downers Grove, IL: IVP, 2001), 285-87.

[5] Paul Hiebert, 'Syncretism and Social Paradigms', in Gailyn Van Rheenen (ed.), *Contextualization and Syncretism: Navigating Cultural Currents* (Pasadena, CA: William Carey Library, 2006), 32.

[6] Andrew Walls, 'The Great Commission 1910-2010', paper submitted to the Edinburgh2010 consultation and available at www.edinburgh2010.org.

[7] See the Fundamentalism project for more discussion on the need to maintain boundaries. Martin E. Marty and R. Scott Appleby (eds.), *Fundamentalisms Comprehended* (Chicago: Univ. of Chicago Press, 1995).

following paragraphs I would like to improve this mental image for unity in the church.

Towards a New Model of Unity

First, we need to fuzzy-up the edges of each circle. Unity necessitates humility. Alister McGrath enumerates four functions of doctrine: (i) social demarcation, (ii) interpretation of narrative, (iii) interpretation of experience, and (iv) truth claim.[8] Even though I will be coming back to these ideas for other parts of this modified model, in this point we really are talking about truth claims. Although our doctrinal systems have specified in (sometimes overwhelming) detail what is true and what is false, it could be the case that not all that has previously been affirmed has the same justification as other parts. To say that Jesus has died and rose from the dead is more certain in most doctrinal systems than the date of his second coming (or even the form of that second coming). We should recognise which parts of our admissible (and inadmissible) doctrines carry more weight. Once that is done, our openness to listen to other options is indirectly proportional to the certainty allowed by the biblical witness. It could be that some of our fuzziness allows more overlap with other traditions than initially expected.

Second, we need to put a temporal axis in the graph. There is a wonderfully interesting website which puts a great deal of information on one graph and then puts that information in motion to indicate how it has changed with time.[9] It would be interesting to see a similar chart of doctrinal limits for ecclesial communities. In April 2010, I was conversing with several leaders of the African Inaugurated Church, Chrétien Celeste about the development of their doctrines and practices. One of the leaders admitted that it is possible that the rumours are true that in the past some forms of Voudou or traditional religion were practised among their believers. (What African church can categorically deny such a thing?) But the church is changing, cleaning up such practices, and developing in such a way that it is difficult to say how the church will think, look, and believe twenty years from now. While it is true that official doctrines are slow to change in established churches, popular theology moves more rapidly with the change of cultural expectations and political movements.

The addition of a temporal component puts extra value on convergence and divergence rather than simple identity. In this article, we are talking about similarity between movements. However, that convergence should normally be around a fixed standard: the text of scripture. Even though

---

[8] Alister McGrath, *The Genesis of Doctrine: A Study in the Foundation of Doctrinal Criticism* (Grand Rapids, MI: Wm. B. Eerdmans, 1997), 35-80.

[9] Software to view many charts offline is available at www.gapminder.org. Consulted July 15, 2010.

there are diverse interpretations of scripture (which will be addressed in the fifth element of this discussion), scripture has been the historic point of connection for Christianity.[10] So, one would hope that the various communities' fuzzy circles would rotate around that pole in ever tighter proximity to it. The point was not relation to other groups, but rather coherence with the teaching of the Bible when Hiebert explained two types of syncretism: 'In one sense syncretism is a message that has lost the heart of the Gospel. In another sense, it is moving in the wrong direction, away from a fuller knowledge of the Gospel.'[11] The unity we seek can be evidenced as the circles are all progressing toward a fuller knowledge of the Gospel, and, thus, toward a greater congruence.

The use and abuse of scripture (especially from the perspective of one or another group) is a particularly sticky point in the unity of the church. But if we are willing to view each other in diachronic perspective, we are more likely to see the efforts and progress in the use of scripture and a clearer understanding of willingness toward unity.[12]

Third, we must add dialogical arrows between circles. Unity demands interaction. As an example, let me use the Church of Christ – Harris Mission (as it is listed in the World Council of Churches membership directory).[13] In a recent interview with four preachers and half-a-dozen apostles of the local church in M'Badon, Cote d'Ivoire, I learned of the history of the theology of this church. When many of the faithful were illiterate, they held to the belief that William Wadé Harris (the charismatic preacher from Liberia who preached in Côte d'Ivoire in 1913[14]) was the messiah himself. A charismatic leader taking the role as spiritual intermediary closely coheres to what could be expected in the Anyi culture in which Harris was preaching. The present day preachers to whom I was speaking attributed a doctrinal change to the fact that more and more literate people became leaders and introduced what they saw as the biblical teaching that Jesus, not Harris, was the messiah. This example could serve for the previous point that we need to look at the movement of any particular church. I have reserved it for this point because of the context of

---

[10] Kevin Vanhoozer, 'Christ and Concept: Doing Theology and the "Ministry" of Philosophy', in John Woodbridge & Thomas McComiskey (eds), *Doing Theology in Today's World: Essays in Honor of Kenneth S. Kantzer* (Grand Rapids, MI: Zondervan, 1991), 99-146.

[11] Hiebert, 'Syncretism and Social Paradigms', 44.

[12] I harbour no illusions. This diachronic perspective may also cause some communities to lose hope in any ecclesial unity because the use of Scripture, viewed as fundamental, may be seen as diverging.

[13] www.oikoumene.org/member-churches/regions/africa/ivory-coast/church-of-christ-harris-mission-harrist-church.html, consulted 11 May 2010.

[14] David A. Shank, 'Wadé Harris, William', in *Dictionary of African Christian Biography*. www.dacb.org/stories/liberia/legacy_harris.html, consulted 11 May 2010.

this particular interview: I was not alone with these leaders of the Harrist church (as it is called in Côte d'Ivoire), but was surrounded by a dozen evangelical seminary students. These students had certainly heard of the Harrist church in the past. They thought it was a cult which glorified its founder and practised a syncretistic Christianity which had replaced key biblical truths with Anyi values. If our interview had been conducted fifty years earlier, these students may have been correct. But this interview was held in 2010 and these students were astonished to find their core beliefs about Jesus Christ in close agreement. The interaction between those students of traditional evangelical churches and this African Inaugurated Church produced a unity previously unknown. We need to keep our knowledge up to date and we need to do it in different ways: 'Intercultural theologising should take place at four levels: between churches of different cultures, between individuals of different educational and social levels within the churches of each culture, between different denominations and theological traditions, and between the church of each generation and the church of past generations.'[15]

Fourth, we need to re-examine the motivations which produced divisions in the past. Unity revisits the past, forgives, and eliminates baggage. Historic animosities foster a 'surface tension' on the circles to inhibit co-penetration with other communities. Admittedly, the phrase 'amicable church split' is used, but it seems a theological oxymoron unless the administration was just too large for efficient operation. Whenever there is a dividing of paths, the fuzziness of the doctrinal boundaries are polished into blinding clarity. That is not to say that the necessary faithfulness to the judgments of scripture are respected, but that both groups become very clear about why they split. We may refer once again to McGrath's function of doctrines. It could be that the difference between two groups at the time of their separation was more a matter of interpretation of narrative or experience than truth claim. When reading the accounts of the different movements' responses to the Azusa Street Revivals, it is not surprising that the Christian and Missionary Alliance (to which I am connected) and the Assemblies of God (a close sister organisation) decided to form different organisations. Their polishing of the edges on the criterion of 'tongues' as evidence of the fullness of the Holy Spirit made clear differences in interpretation. The suspicion which started long ago remains with some from one or the other group. It is those suspicions which need to be revisited, reconsidered, and reduced by interaction in the contemporary world... not the world of past animosities or misunderstandings.

Fifth, make visible the cultural layer. Each social location is different; a dynamic unity allows for cultural differences (within reason). In the movie

---

[15] Steve Strauss, 'The Role of Context in Shaping Theology', in Gailyn Van Rheenen (ed,). *Contextualization and Syncretism: Navigating Cultural Currents* (Pasadena , CA: William Carey Library, 2006), 119-120.

The Parent Trap (staring Hayley Mills in 1961 or Lindsey Lohan in the 1998 remake), twins were raised apart with different views on the world and different practices which must be learned before they make the switch into the other's context. Values (appreciation of the 'out-of-doors'), resources (capability at the piano) and vocabulary (notably a whole different register of speaking) are all obviously different.

The difference in ecclesial communities may be as liturgically specific as the use of feet: processions have never been a strong component in Evangelical Protestant churches as in Catholic churches. Physical response to music in conservative churches in America might (I said 'might') include clapping. In Africa, besides simple moving in place, processions ('dances') around the church are not uncommon. The difference may include a theological emphasis: the reality of God is important in secularising Europe and North America where Africa is more concerned with access to God. The difference may be ways of formulating theology: instead of a written discourse, a song or dance may communicate far more powerfully an interpretation of the Bible.

> Because no culture can understand all the traits of Scripture, and because each culture contains elements that will help it uncover what another culture might overlook, *intercultural theologising* is essential for the universal church. Intercultural theologising is the cross-pollination of many contextual theologies between churches and different contexts. Intercultural theologising plays at least two key roles in the process of doing theology. First, such sharing of theologies enriches the theology of the church in each context and the theology of the universal church... [by including] what they may have missed [and] preventing them from being blinded by their own cultural biases.... Second, intercultural theologising helps ensure that each contextual theology remains biblical and congruent with the theology of the universal church.[16]

The propositions offered here will certainly not produce unity among all the churches, but it is hoped that they will lighten unnecessary or inappropriate differences and barriers. Although I am unconvinced that an organic unity will be produced, my hope is that this dialogical unity, this model of fuzzy, historical, interconnected, baggage-free, cultural circles of churches will enable movement forward in the expansion together of the Kingdom of God. The crucial element is conversation which emphasises listening so as to hear what the Spirit is saying through the church(es).

---

[16] Strauss, 'The Role of Context in Shaping Theology', 119.

Pentecostal Perspective on Mission and Unity

J.D. Plüss[1]

The global growth of the Pentecostal movement within the past one hundred years raises questions as to why it has been so successful. At the same time, weaknesses can be seen that seem to have their origin in the same area as where their strengths lie, as if the two were flip sides of the same coin. Addressing these strengths and weaknesses has a direct bearing on ecclesiology and missions. The presentation will focus on spirituality (the church as a Spirit-filled body of believers), pragmatism (the church as a business enterprise) and on theology (the church as God's instrument of reconciliation) as key issues for Pentecostals. I will then identify key priorities in mission and unity for Pentecostals.

Spirituality: The Church as a Spirit-Filled Body of Believers

The Pentecostal movement has experienced a tremendous growth, especially in the urban areas of the Global South. We will be able to locate key issues in view of the Pentecostal understanding of the church: its nature, its mission and the implications for Christian unity, if we can recognise what factors contributed to this development.

Pentecostalism started as a renewal movement. Like other churches at that time, early Pentecostals were taken by the idea of restorationism, which basically claims that he church, in order to present herself as the bride before the second coming of Jesus Christ, had to renew herself through repentance and sanctification, so that it would again attain the character of the apostolic church as illustrated, for instance, in the Book of Acts. It was in this context, that the work of the Holy Spirit was rediscovered and appreciated. The charismatic nature of this revival led to a focus on the laity. First, the gifting by the Holy Spirit meant that the division between the clergy and lay persons became less pronounced. Second, 'if two or three are gathered in my name' (Matt. 18:20) meant, in a truly Reformed fashion, that believers were released to study the Word of

---

[1] Dr Jean-Daniel Plüss is Chair of the European Pentecostal Charismatic Research Association.

God on their own and were free to share the Gospel without strings attached.

Furthermore, restorationism also meant that the final days where near; that Jesus could come any time now and that the world had to be evangelised as much as possible before the Lord of Lords and the King of Kings would be coming in judgment and glory. This eschatological sense of urgency coupled with an awareness of the Holy Spirit's power propelled the missionary drive into all corners of the earth.

Pentecostals were truly experiencing empowerment, especially by the charismatic gifts of healing and prophecy as well as the ability to pray in an unknown language. They shared this experience with the people they met. Two things were particularly important, they shared their experiences through testimonies and they prayed for whatever need the other person had, expecting God to graciously intervene. As a consequence people from other cultures, regardless of their cultural or educational background, could understand them. In addition they experienced salvation as something that related to their whole existence and not just to their intellectual convictions. Jesus was real. Soon the converts would join in, with the same eschatological fervour.

One of the characteristics of Pentecostals is that they developed their convictions after they had acquired an understanding of the spiritual side of their faith. As a result their faith is not primarily analytical, but relational. This fact has great potential for the ecumenical mandate of the Church.

Pragmatism: The Church as a Business Enterprise

Another aspect that will inform our discussion on the mission and unity of the church relates to the pragmatic nature of Pentecostal missions work. As children of the early twentieth century, western Pentecostals were enamoured of a pragmatic attitude: 'If it works and does not stand against biblical teaching, do it.' To that they would add the desire to be led by the Holy Spirit.

This attitude brought about a number of consequences. First, it allowed for innovation; it could cut through much red tape of more structured missionary agencies. Secondly, it promoted the idea that any church had to be self-sustaining, self-governing and self-propagating. Consequently, churches will also be self-educating. It follows that they deserve full respect. Third, it also created a plurality of independent ecclesial bodies. The intention was to spread the Gospel as best as one could. This brought about an interpretation of New Testament ecclesiology that emphasised diversity rather than unity. Furthermore, many Pentecostals recognised the Charismatic renewal as move of God because of their pragmatic approach. If others shared the same experiences, then it must be the same Spirit that moves them, regardless of their church affiliation. In a similar vein, women were admitted to the ministry because there was evidence of blessing. They prayed for the sick and miraculous healings were reported, their preaching brought about a revival of the church, and so on. Later on, a fifth aspect began to influence Pentecostals due to pragmatic points of view. As the eschatological urgency to spread the Gospel waned, especially in the more affluent parts of the West, the vitality of the church began to be measured by numbers. Church growth was the issue and some churches began to run like business enterprises. Unfortunately, that meant in some cases that a sense of competition crept in that was not all positive.

Theology: The Church as God's Instrument of Reconciliation

Before we will look at key issues that need to be addressed allow me to add a theological reflection. For Pentecostals, evangelism is a priority. In fact, one could say that for them the church equals missions, which equals evangelism. To that one could add: which equals reconciliation. Countless are the testimonies of people having found peace with God, of animosity overcome and of families having been brought together. As Pentecostals can personally relate to reconciliation and as they want to walk in step with the work God's Spirit, they should be predisposed to understand that the church, in all its diversity, is one before God and should be one before mankind. After all, should we not all be keeping the unity of the Spirit through the bond of peace (Eph. 4:3)?

Based on reflections on spirituality, pragmatism and theology I would like to respond to the key issues mentioned by the study group on Theme 8 Mission and Unity.[2]. First, based on their desire to be attentive to the move of the Holy Spirit and their pragmatic attitude, Pentecostals are not afraid of innovative mission and new theological insights. It is important to remember that they hold to the principle that every new insight and every action has to be in line with the fundamental teachings of the Bible. It is not enough to feel the Spirit move.

Second, from a classical point of view, apostolicity, the practice of baptism and especially the celebration of the Eucharist have been corner points of Christian ecclesiality. For historical reasons this is a typically Western understanding of the Church. Pentecostals and many churches of the global South may wish to add another point of view, namely that it is the Holy Spirit that initiates, invigorates and unites the church as the temple of the Holy Spirit, the Body of Christ and the House of God. Again, the work of the Holy Spirit would always have to be discerned and interpreted in accordance with the Bible. And, this also needs to be mentioned: Pentecostals are encouraged to reflect on the value of traditional understandings of what makes the church in general and the role of the Eucharist in particular.

---

[2] Daryl Balia & Kirsteen Kim (eds), *Edinburgh 2010: Witnessing to Christ Today* (Oxford: Regnum Books International, 2010), 199-221.

Third, Pentecostals have oftentimes been concerned about the unity of the church when it related to their own ranks. The unity of the global Church was primarily seen as a spiritual unity. The coming of the charismatic renewal has brought a new dimension to the understanding of visible unity. The rise of independent churches creates a need for Pentecostals to develop an ecclesiology that can be called ecumenical, which at the same time honours their Pentecostal identity.

Fourth, the unity of the church has often been defended by episcopal models and safeguarded by institutional structures. Christians vitalised by the Spirit of God have experienced the gifts of the Holy Spirit, who emphasises responsible partnership and a sharing of power. The tension between institution and charisma is an issue that Christians have to live with. It is a fruitful tension between order and freedom and a way of keeping the institutions from petrifying and charismatic expressions from losing relevance.

Finally, due to the multi-cultural face of Pentecostalism and the fact that most Christians live in the global South, any form of mission activity has the potential to become more and more participatory in nature. The pragmatic strain and optimism with regard to the work of the Spirit within Pentecostalism may also lead to an increased participation in inter-church relief and government assisted development projects.

Pentecostal Priorities

Pentecostalism is a relatively recent phenomenon on the ecclesiastical sky of Christianity. Thus its churches and denominations experience the birth pains that are typical on any new religious movement. Many Pentecostal leaders feel the tension between assuming their proper identity and relating to other Christian churches. The fundamental challenge is that of fulfilling the Christian mandate to proclaim the Good News on one hand for the benefit of others, and on the other hand to relate to the global Body of Christ and thus responding to the prayer of Jesus (John 17:20-23) and the admonition of Paul towards unity (Eph. 4:3-6). How can one navigate in such a dilemma? The following priorities can be identified.

First, the mistrust displayed by and towards historic churches and the animosity experienced by many Pentecostals, have created tensions that often times revealed themselves in the context of evangelism and mission. The issue of proselytism is a key priority that needs our attention. There is an urgent need to live by of a code of ministerial ethics. This implies no illicit means for winning people to faith like the misrepre-sentation of others, dishonesty, coercion, intimidation, bribery etc. are acceptable. Evangelism in terms of proclaiming the Good News is not to be questioned; it belongs to the essence of every church. Rather, guidelines as to the integration of the person that has come to a living faith must be observed. These guidelines are to lead ministers to display a sensitivity to the unity of the Body of Christ (1 Cor. 12) and the love God has poured into the heart of the believer by the Holy Spirit (Rom. 5:5). Proselytism is challenged by ministerial communication on a local level. It could be communication that provides information pertaining to people who have considered changing church affiliation. But it could also be about the ministers own spiritual journeys. The events surrounding Acts 15 can serve as a paradigm on how to discuss issues between different ecclesial groups. The proclamation of the Word is to be Bible focused and is not to use disrespectful, deceptive or uncharitable remarks about others.

A second priority is to teach our communities to understand that God heals the person to come into the family of God. In other words, there needs to be a shift from the individual to the communal. Pentecostals often emphasise personal salvation, value baptism as a personal decision, strive for personal sanctification and seek individual blessings. Although God heals the individual and equips every person with gifts, the goal is to be part of the community of Christ, which is a local, regional and global reality.

As a third priority, expressions of Christian unity are to be fostered at the grassroots level by prayer for and with one another across denominational lines; by sharing testimonies of faith; by expecting the Holy Spirit to guide the household of God; and by engaging in works of love for the benefit of the larger community.

A fourth priority should focus on mission spirituality. Classical missionary activity often meant that the convert had to repent from idols. Today missionaries have to repent from their own idols such as religious values that reflect their own culture but are not related to the essence of the Gospel. Mission workers are to repent from prejudice and disrespect towards other workers in the vineyard of God (Luke 9:49-50). Mission spirituality means being aware that God has entrusted his people with the ministry of reconciliation of the world in Christ; reconciliation among Christians is to be a visible witness of God's grace (2 Cor. 5:18-20). A true mission spirituality not only has to be God-honouring and Christ-centred, but also Spirit-filled, in the sense that it is the Spirit of God who is the missionary in us, the one who empowers, the one who guides and the one who reveals Christ to the glory of God and the salvation of humankind and all creation (John 20; Acts 1; 2; Rom 8).

A fifth priority relates the experiences of unity with regard to global bodies. The traditional structures of ecumenical organisations usually emphasised doctrinal statements and analysis. In view of the fact that most Christians are at home in predominantly oral cultures, global bodies are invited to include narrative aspects of the Christian faith. Therefore meetings like the Global Christian Forum should be encouraged in order to allow all Christians to voice their joys and concerns in a way that is familiar to them. The inclusion of narrative communication such as testimonies and worship can also revitalise the more formal nature of many ecumenical bodies.

Issues that relate to mission and unity should be protected from drifting into manmade schemes and intellectual manoeuvrings. All our efforts are at best of penultimate value. In order to keep a sense of humility before God and humankind it is necessary to maintain an eschatological outlook. This outlook includes a sense of urgency to communicate the Gospel, but also that the church is on its way and that its mission will only be fulfilled in Christ at his return (Matt. 28:20; Eph. 1:7-14; Rev. 22). Finally, eschatology also relates to God's creation as a whole, when God's creative intent will find its fulfilment in a new heaven and a new earth. Christians, as those who have been touched by God's grace, are challenged to unite in witnessing to the hope they have and to speak prophetically wherever nature is selfishly exploited and people are taken advantage of.

In essence mission and unity fall together whenever a person finds peace with God and can express it in a communal context.

YOUTH ENVISIONING ECUMENICAL MISSION: SHIFTING ECUMENICAL MISSION PARADIGMS FOR WITNESSING CHRIST TODAY

Vineeth Koshy[1]

Today many 'movements' have become 'monuments'; however the 1910 World Missionary Conference, which was a starting point of the modern ecumenical movement, has made remarkable progress quantitatively and qualitatively, extensively and intensively. Ecumenism and mission activities have now moved away from the mere fringes of proselytising and baptising to greater and noble areas of work and study, thanks due to the engagement of many creative thinkers, enthusiastic ecumenists and committed missionaries. Ecumenism and mission receive an overwhelming barrage of responses. Initially and even now a large majority of population is negative, sceptical and pessimistic about the ecumenical and missionary enterprise and endeavours. Analyzing some of these unfavourable responses, I get the impression that many of these misunderstandings are due to insufficient knowledge of the nature of mission, its background, its working, its relevance and future prospects, or else we are too impatient. A well-informed, deeply-reflected and dispassionate study of the ecumenical and missionary movements will lead us to a balanced and positive assessment regarding the contributions of these movements. Therefore the centenary celebration of the World Missionary Conference, Edinburgh 1910, becomes a unique occasion to celebrate ecumenical unity, map the mission mandate and understand the challenges and opportunities faced by the churches and ecumenical movements in the contemporary world.

Youth is a state of life and mind when there is quality of thinking, predominance of courage and appetite for adventure. However, one of the alarming features of today's youth participation and leadership in the Church is that the younger generation is in the 'exit-phase' and there may be various reasons for justifying this exit. We are forgetting that the gifts of the Holy Spirit are distributed equally and widely in the Church. Therefore it is quite essential that the spiritual experience and expertise of every member must be recognised and drawn into the common spirituality of the

---

[1] Fr Vineeth Koshy belongs to Malankara Orthodox Syrian Church and is the Executive Secretary-Commission on Youth, National Council of Churches in India.

local congregations. Thus the concerns of the Church must be broad-based involving the youth, women, and children.

In interpreting the theme and mandate of the Edinburgh Centenary, the youth may ask, 'What does it mean to witness [to] Christ today?' Though the Church exists for mission, the basic question is: What type and kind of mission are we looking forward to? I may say that in this twenty-first century youth envision some major shifts of mission paradigms and the ecumenical mission must take future direction looking from four different perspectives: creative, contextual, communitarian and compassionate

Creative Mission

Creativity is a vital dimension of human existence. The true basis of our creativity is the belief that we are made in the image of God. Thereby God has shared God's creativity with us. Creativity is not some rare esoteric gift enjoyed by a few people like poets, musicians, actors, sculptors, artisans, and so on. Rather it has been gifted to all, something that comes with being alive, sensitive, caring, questioning, and open to the Spirit of God, willing to learn from the past, analyse the present and explore the future. To be creative is to be willing to grow and to encourage growth in others. The Church and the ecumenical movement is challenged to the sacred task of unfolding the possibilities of the mission in creative ways, and not merely being satisfied with the 'doing the minimum'. In the normal order of things, if only the conventional way is attempted, it may bring short term results but it may not bring desired outcomes. What the youth and society today really needs is a combination of both the ways, that is to be conventional and creative, whereby the problem is not merely solved but eliminated completely.

The call from the youth to the Church for being more effective and meaningful is to go beyond boundaries, beyond conventional approaches and to be open to the infinite potential stemming from God who is the source of all creativity and who himself is creative. This has been proved by the great thinkers and leaders of all ages, who responded creatively and did not just react prosaically to the prevailing situation. Today's youth thus envisions such a Church where they can dare to dream creatively and these creative dreams are transformed into actions. In these times the degree of change in society is accelerating, every new generation is radically different in culture from the earlier generation. This generation gap is growing larger and in different cultures, and surprisingly such differences are more than cosmetic or superficial changes in 'forms' of expression, such as clothing, music styles and mannerisms.

The task is to be creative without compromising the non-negotiable basic foundations of scripture and traditions. The changes required of a church to contain, integrate and communicate to their youth, effectively amount to adjusting their sights to be on target to reach their mission field of neighbours. The spiritual needs of youth cannot be met fully by our ordinary approach. What is needed is a new approach, an unusual way of responding to the situation, a creative style of encountering the problems and challenges. The gigantic problems of the youth of our church demand an unusual, imaginative and even fanciful response. That can be brought forward only by critical, constructive and creative thinking and working.

Contextual Mission

Classical science claimed that everything in nature is immutable and unchangeable. However modern science now proves through the theories of relativity, evolution, the uncertainty principle, and so on, that nothing in the universe is immutable and matter is changing constantly. However the mentalities and attitude of the church and society down through all ages remains constant. In this context the young people dream of a Church fully catering to the needs of the church in the new and evolving context of a 'common global culture'. The truth is that regardless of whether the youth live in village or city, they are all being influenced by the three great unifiers of global culture: movies, music, and especially the social networks through the Internet.[2] Recently someone asked me, What is the reason for the strong influence of the media and the Internet on this present generation? And I replied that, 'They don't influence them, rather they own them'. Today it seems to many that Church is the last one to catch up and own these changes, therefore church's mission needs to be tuned and adapting in accordance to the rising cultural revolutions.

The rate of change brought about by spreading global youth culture with all its modern distinctiveness renders traditional structures of religious expression obstructions in conveying their original meanings to the young people. The mandate of the contextualisation of the gospel requires that no unnecessary stumbling block be put in the way of young people in understanding Christian mission. For an effective mission, the Church must understand the soul and spirit of the today's youth. Today there is lot of discussion and debate going on about the matter of indigenisation and inculturation of the liturgy for a greater participation of young people. Unless Christ is truly incarnated, all these efforts would be fruitless and meaningless. Inculturation must be going beyond adapting to the contemporary cultures, traditions and attractive strategies to attract young people. Therefore the challenge is to complement and mutually enrich the diverse cultures but at the same time remember that there is One People of God adoring and worshipping Him. Thus it means bringing the mission,

[2] Nicholas Christakis & James Fowler, C*onnected: The Amazing Power of Social Networks and How They Shape Our Lives* (London: Harper Press, 2009), 10-17.

life and teachings of Christ into contemporary cultural situations without adulterating the culture, values and principles of Christianity.[3]

Culture is not a ready-made or finished product; every culture is in a process of becoming by continuous encounter with the present realities and the cultures of other people. The meeting of two cultures and the process of give and take between them may be called 'inter-culturation'. The process of inculturation is also a process of 'inter-culturation'.[4] The gospel or the Christian faith does not exist first in abstract form and then inculturated in every culture or context. On the contrary the original gospel and the original Church were embodied in a social-cultural form. Every apostle/missionary/believer has received the faith in a particular historical, context and socio-cultural form, and as a missionary s/he carries this inculturated faith to other peoples. Therefore it is the recipients or the people who have to respond to the Gospel and receive and translate the faith into their own contextual, historical and socio-cultural form.

Communitarian Mission

We can never refute that human beings are 'rational' and 'relational' at one and the same time. In fact, it is by being relational that we grow and come to be truly rational. We know that 'to-be-human' is 'to-be-with'. More precisely, we are related at all levels of existence, personal, social, universal and transcendental. If we turn to the biblical economy of creation and redemption, it is clear that the Bible supports a relational anthropology. God in the creation did not create human beings merely as individuals but as 'male and female' in his own image and likeness. Also it must be noted that Eve was not created from the man's feet to be his slave nor from his head to be his master, but from the middle showing clearly that they are partners and created in equality. This clearly showed women have equal rights and equal opportunity to serve God and humanity.[5] It means that God created us to be in relationship and God intended 'being-human' to be essentially be 'being-with-others'.

Furthermore, God's redemption of humankind was not individualistic. Only the understanding of humans are relational, interrelated and interdependent can help us to respond to some of the serious challenges facing humankind today. Alienation 'is the cry of men who feel them to be the victims of blind economic forces, social stigmas, political structures'

[3] M.M. Thomas, 'Towards an Indian Understanding of Jesus Christ', in Mathai Zachariah (ed.), *The Indian Church Identity and Fulfillment* (Chennai: CLS, ISPCK, LPH, 1971), 17-19.

[4] Raimundo Panikkar, 'Indic Christian Theology of Religious Pluralism from the Perspective of Interculturation', in K. Pathil, *Religious Pluralism: An Indian Christian Perspective* (New Delhi: ISPCK, 1991), 252-299.

[5] Gretchen Gaebelein Hull, *Equal to Serve: Women and Men in the Church and Home* (Grand Rapids, MI: Revell, 1987), 65.

and 'the frustration of ordinary people excluded from the processes of decision-making which are beyond their control'.[6] The challenges are precisely the structures of exclusion, marginalisation, oppression, on the one hand, and racism, gender discrimination, and suchlike on the other. Yet we hear of stories of building of counter structures promoting justice, praxis of inclusion, cohesion, fraternity, equality, liberation.[7]

Modern youth is now surrounded by technology which makes them alienated and isolated from the rest of the community. Because of the social changes of the past two decades, today's youth spend more time alone than any other generation, thus they miss a coherent sense of community feeling. In the disguise of the freedom of expression and information, youth are having a secret life or lost in cyber-highways seeking friends in social networking sites like Facebook, Orkut, and Twitter. Social networking aims to build online or virtual communities of people who share common interests or activities, or who are interested in exploring the interests and activities of others, or to reinforce established friendships and form bonds with new friends. Social networking has encouraged new ways to communicate, share information and make friends.[8] Today if the youth are lost or alienated, it is only because the Church refuses to enter into their lives. The responsibility is on Church and community to know what their youth are doing and not the other way around, blaming them for their lack of participation.

Towards the end of the high priestly prayer of Jesus, we hear Jesus calling his disciples as his friends (John 15:13-15). The model of relation between Jesus and his followers has been has shifted and now is characterised as 'friends'. The term 'friend' has deep and wide implications and meaning. As Christ himself shows, a friend knows everything, is equal and intimate. In daily human relations too we can find that friendly relations are deeper and more lasting than the blood relation. In our ordinary life also we find many people following closely the teachings of Christ in their life. However the common misconception is that the evangelised and baptised are the only true Christian disciples. Raymond Panikkar writes about the *Unknown Christ of Hinduism*.[9] In today's context our mission demands we identify also the 'unknown friends of Christ' in our surroundings, since we know ourselves that in our work place and

---

[6] Inaugural address of James Reid to the students when installed as Rector of Glasgow University, 1972. Available at www.gla.ac.uk/media/media_167194_en.pdf.

[7] Walter Rauschenbush, *Christianity and Social Crisis* (London: Macmillan, 1907), 11-14.

[8] Vineeth Koshy, 'Friendship: Online and Offline', *National Council of Churches in India Review,* 128/ 1 (Jan-Feb 2009), 41-42.

[9] Raymond (Raimundo) Panikkar, *The Unknown Christ of Hinduism,* 1st edn (London: Darton, Longman & Todd, 1964).

neighbourhood there are many living unknown friends of Christ, even though they do not know even an iota about Christianity.

It is common to hear about teenage circles: scholarly, religious, or other groups. The Christian circle is the group where the faithful live and celebrate, where they are supposed to transform their lives within the set of ideals and values of Christ. However there is a tendency to make the circle exclusively Christian or Church-centred, isolated and disengaged from the rest of the humanity. The modern mission and the call of the Christ today is to enlarge our inner circle and make it a cosmic circle, beckoning not only the human race but also the whole creation to become the participants and members of this circle. The term 'mysticism' means union, 'spiritual mysticism' means union with God or the ultimate reality. In the Eucharist we are united with Christ, the Body broken and shared for the life of the world, which speaks not only about the spiritual mysticism but also about a social mysticism. So Christ calls all partakers of Eucharist to share our food with the poor and hungry, and this sharing also has a Eucharistic dimension. In Orthodox tradition the bread and wine are the fruits of earth and the same are offered to God by humans and turn into the Body and Blood of Christ. This invites us to the 'production for sharing' and the 'sharing of resources'. This is contrary to the consumerism, hoarding of goods and profit motive which are characteristic of capitalist culture.[10]

As we approach in awe the Eucharistic Altar, we have One Paten of Body and One Chalice of Blood. The entire Church sings in one voice. This is certainly a call to oneness and community living. As a source of unity the Eucharist is able to bring us together more closely, to reconcile broken relationships and heal the many divisions in our lives. The Eucharist is the crucial symbol of sharing and social meaning; it speaks about the social wholeness and our table fellowship with social outcasts.[11] One of the primary objectives of the Millennium Development Goals is the eradication of poverty. However at global and local levels things could have changed if the resources were simply shared and distributed. In the corporate world the idea of production for sharing would be resisted, however the Eucharistic meaning of production is essentially for sharing among communities. The Eucharist that we celebrate tells us the sacrifice of Christ is for all and that it compels all who believe in him to become 'bread that is broken' for others.[12]

---

[10] Sebastian Painadath, 'Church as the Continuation of the Table-Fellowship of Jesus', in Rosario Rocha and Kuruvilla Pandikkattu (eds), *Dreams and Visions: New Horizons for an Indian Church* (Pune: Jnanadeepa Vidyapeeth, 2002), 79-81.

[11] Sebastian Kappen, *Jesus and Society* (New Delhi: ISPCK, 2002), 84-86.

[12] Mathew Jayanth, 'Body Spirituality: Incarnation as an Invitation to an Embodied Spirituality', *Jnanadeepa: Pune Journal of Religious Studies*, 7/ 2 (Jan-Jun 2004), 124-126.

Compassionate Mission

Compassion is a prominent biblical word and a spiritual virtue which can best understood in relation with God only, because the magnanimity and fullness of compassion was revealed in God alone. It is a derivative from a Latin word meaning 'to bear', 'to suffer', and so suffering with the sufferer. Therefore compassion does not mean mere emotional sympathy and pitying, but one who shows compassion lives compassion, accepting the responsibility to heal, bring hope and minister justice.[13] Hugo Rahner is of the view that the main cause of the persecution of the early church was not religious but social and political because Christians preached a God who came not to conquer but to serve and give justice to the oppressed. The core and essence of the Christ's teaching was administering justice, showing compassion and life-giving mission for the humanity. So Christ became a threat to the Jews and Romans who were both proponents of colonialism. In present context too the youth must challenge the Church to rediscover the lost and forgotten legacy of compassion and equality of the early Christian community.

The traditional model of mission had the mandate of service and martyrdom; however in today's context persecution and suffering has disappeared from the mission perspectives. Today many countries have become battle fields of missionary agencies and donors which are now causing strife among churches with their intervention of heavy monetary support.[14] Suffering and persecution is seen as something alien to Christianity; mission has become now more luxurious and comfortable. The challenge of modern mission is therefore to rediscover the diminishing ethos of sacrifice and life-giving mission.[15] All the teachings, life, work, signs, parables, miracles of Christ were showing and teaching of sacrifice, and importantly Christ as a life-giver. However the ultimate paradox is that life-giving is through the Cross which he taught through the parable of grain of wheat: unless it falls into ground to die, it cannot rise again to new life (John 12:24).

Charity derives from the Greek word *charis* or grace, meaning imparting gift that one possesses and shares with who does not. However the tendency of the Christian mission is now confined to the charity works only, and to serve this purpose we have now started innumerable charitable institutions and organisations. The point of the argument here is not that

---

[13] Ezamo Murry, 'Compassion and Care for the HIV/AIDS Infected and the Affected', in A. Wati Longchar (ed.), *Health, Healing and Wholeness Asian Theological Perspectives on HIV/AIDS* (Assam: ETE-WCC/CCA, 2005), 73-74.

[14] Keynote address delivered by Dr. Mathews George Chunakara, Director of International Affairs, World Council of Churches during the National Ecumenical Youth Assembly of Commission on Youth of National Council of Churches in India held in Kolkata on 6 January 2010.

[15] Hans Ucko, *Common Roots, New Horizons* (Geneva: WCC Publications, 1994), 80-81.

charity is not good; rather the argument is that mission should not end or be confined only to charity; it needs to journey beyond and transcend the mere walls of charity. True missionaries need to be promoters and agents of justice, peace and reconciliation with a prophetic and active role in the societal life. Mission also demands greater involvement in political life too. In the life of Christ also we could see that on various occasions he offers charity to the needy. At other times he questions the unjust structures and powers that oppress the poor, and all the time he never becomes part of these oppressive systems or structures.[16]

The mission is not to reach and change the world ideologically and dogmatically alone, rather it needs the extension of love, care and compassion. The problem of the marginalised and oppressed cannot be solved only through relief such as reservations and quota systems, although they are also required to some extent as a positive step to overcome the past violence and discrimination against them. We also need compassion, justice and harmony that are extended to broader communities crossing the narrow boundaries, including the animal and plant kingdom.[17] We are inevitably committed to work for God's justice in the face of oppression, for God's truth in the face of lies and deceits, for service in the face of the abuse of power, for love in the face of selfishness, for cooperation in the face of destructive antagonism, and for reconciliation in the face of division and hostility.[18] The world needs the touch of love, compassion and justice that could be concretely spelt out, in the light of the experience of interreligious relations, interfaith approaches, peace, justice, understanding, collaboration, forgiveness, compassion in times of calamities and tragedies. As before now too, human beings need humanity, heart over mind.

Youth envision ecumenical mission to be liberating individuals from the social conditioning that prevents them from living as free persons. It must enable them to develop inner freedom, so that they are not pressurised by the conditions and expectations of society, but enabled to decide freely on crucial issues that affect choice of life, of family and human love. In the words of Simon Oxley, Christian mission is no longer limited to the history of attempts to reunite churches or the growth of ecumenical organisations or individuals. It should aim to affirm life and relations (community), inspire rebuilding and reconstruction of community, inclusive of the different and diversities and importantly reach out beyond the future of church and society embracing God's entire creation.[19] It must conceptualise

---

[16] Edward Norman, *Christianity and the World Order* (London: Oxford University Press, 1979), 20-24.

[17] Walter Rauschenbush, *A Theology for the Social Gospel* (New York: Macmillan, 1917), 56-64.

[18] John Gladwin, *God's People in God's World: Biblical Motives for Social Involvement* (Leicester: Intervarsity Press, 1979), 125.

[19] Simon Oxley, *Creative Ecumenical Education* (Geneva: WCC Publications, 2002), 11.

a theology and culture from the experience and perspective of young people. Challenge and transform the structures that limit youth participation and leadership. Mission is to see life as a call and a gift that leads the individual into the sacred space and makes them aware of the inalienable human rights and their giftedness. It assists them to develop these to reach high levels of competence for life and living, by providing many opportunities to discover and develop their talents and turn them into strengths so they can grow in self-esteem and confidence. Edinburgh 2010 is not an ultimate answer on any of the present ecclesial, missiological or ecumenical issues and concerns, rather it is a humble attempt to reflect and pool together the perspectives and resources of youth, women, and subaltern voices, provide guidance, stimulate reflection, and encourage common action by the churches and ecumenical movements to think and act creatively towards God's mission.

Communities of the Spirit: The Missiology of Roland Allen in the Twenty-First Century

Andrew R.H. Thompson[1]

'I hate it', responded one disaffected seminarian. 'I hate the word "mission"'. The seminarians were preparing for a trip to El Salvador, and were discussing missiology and its various implications. All of the students were ambivalent about the idea of mission, and they discussed the various possible locutions to describe to others the purpose of their upcoming trip: 'service', 'volunteer', 'study', 'relationship-building'. Anything but 'mission'.

These students are not alone in their uncertainty. Conversations like this are occurring throughout the church, some with reactions every bit as adverse as that of the student above. Church groups on short-term visits wonder what it means to call such a thing 'mission'. A group of young adults preparing for their departure into the field struggles with the connotations of the term 'missionary', most opting for 'volunteer', or 'community development worker'.[2] These conversations reflect an understanding of mission primarily as an encounter between distinct cultures, usually characterised by inequality of wealth or power, and accordingly they express discomfort with the colonialist or imperialistic connotations and history of mission so conceived. Likewise, the choice of labels like 'service' points to a recognition that the church must attend to communities' material needs, and a belief (justified or not) that mission may not always include such attention. These sentiments are especially prevalent among young leaders in the church, such as the seminarians and missionaries above, who see mission as a relic of a less pluralist, less culturally-aware past, and yet struggle to reconcile this perspective with the mandate to 'go and make disciples of all nations' (Matt. 28.19).

Such a narrow view of mission, as primarily one-way, from 'developed' or 'advanced' societies to 'developing' or 'third-world' countries, with all

---

[1] Andrew Thompson is a doctoral candidate in religious ethics at Yale University and a teaching fellow at Yale Divinity School. This essay was the winning entry in the Edinburgh 2010 Writing Competition and is also published in Kirk Sandvig (ed.), *Edinburgh 2010: Youth Perspectives* (Pasadena, CA: William Carey International University Press, 2010), 9-23.

[2] These experiences are from my own time as a missionary in El Salvador with the Episcopal Young Adult Service Corps.

of its attendant implications, is inadequate to address the contemporary faith of Christians, young and old. It is also theologically impoverished, as I will argue. Christians need an understanding of mission that integrates the Great Commission with respectful pluralism, and evangelism with concern for material well-being. Ironically, a missiology that meets these twenty-first century needs is found in the writings of a missionary from the turn of the previous century, Roland Allen. Allen's challenge to the missionary practices of his time, with their dependence on what he called 'the modern Western spirit', and call for greater trust in the work of the Holy Spirit in mission communities, are as relevant to our current situation as they were a century ago.

Before turning to Allen's methods, though, I make the case for a conception of mission that is broader than the narrow view indicated above. A more theologically appropriate missiology views mission as the concrete witness of Christian communities in all places – 'the whole church bringing the whole Gospel to the whole world'.[3] The theology of John Howard Yoder presents a compelling call for just such a view, one that will subsequently be clarified by the methods commended by Roland Allen.

Expansion of missiology beyond a unidirectional conception is not novel, as Allen's writing shows. In my own tradition, leaders of the Anglican Communion called upon the church to 'rethink the whole idea of mission' in terms that reflect equality, interdependence, and mutual responsibility as early as 1963.[4] Yet as the discomfort of the conversations mentioned above indicates, careful consideration of mission that addresses the conceptual and theological needs of contemporary Christians remains necessary and urgent.

Proclaiming the *Missio Dei*

Mission is the concrete witness of Christian communities in the world. Christians have consistently affirmed that Christian mission is always a participation in the *missio Dei*, God's saving purpose for the world.[5] The core of mission, then, must be the faithful witness of Christians to the *missio Dei,* our testimony that God has a purpose for creation that embraces and subsumes and saves all other goals and acts. Mission is therefore central to the identity of the church itself, as the community of believers that exists as a sign, in the world, of God's mission. Conversely, the primary locus of Christian participation in God's mission is the church, or,

---

[3] David Bosch, *Transforming Mission: Paradigm Shifts in Theology of Mission,* (Maryknoll, NY: Orbis books, 1991), 10.

[4] Address by Rt. Rev. Stephen Bayne to Anglican Congress 1963, cited in Ian T. Douglas, 'The Exigency of Times and Occasions', in *Beyond Colonial Anglicanism*, eds. Ian T. Douglas & Kwok Pui Lan (New York: Church Publishing, 2001), 28.

[5] Titus Presler, *Horizons of Mission* (Cambridge, MA: Cowley Press, 2001), 30; Bosch, *Transforming Mission,* 10, 370; Douglas, 'Exigency', 42.

more specifically, the faithful communities that testify to that mission; in other words, the church is central to mission. The 'sending' to which the etymology of 'mission' refers is not the sending of individuals by one community to another, but rather the sending of God's people by God into the world. If mission is essentially a contact between two distinct societies, as the narrow view outlined above would have it, it is not between developed nations and the third world, but rather between the believing community and the world to which it proclaims God's own mission.

John Howard Yoder articulates a vision of this witnessing community.[6] Its mission is primarily a 'modelling mission', in that, 'the church is called to be now what the world is called to be ultimately'.[7] Because the God it proclaims is other than and beyond the world, the church's ability to carry out this modelling mission depends on its ability to stand against the wisdom and values of the world when necessary.[8] For Yoder, the believing community enacts values of reconciliation, peacefulness, and egalitarianism in the midst of a world that undermines or rejects those values. It thereby proclaims by example God's desire for human life in community as revealed by Jesus, and works toward some partial realisation of that desire.

The witness of Yoder's believing community is theologically founded. Its first and core commitment is to Christ's example, most fundamentally his cross. The believers' cross that is mandated in the New Testament is our imitation of Jesus in his disavowal of worldly ways of relating to others.[9] It is our willing acceptance of rejection and suffering as potential consequences of our testimony. Witnessing to God's mission necessarily places believers apart from – yet always in mission to and in service of, never purely against – the world to which they are sent.

Yet Yoder's vision is also culturally apt: it acknowledges and addresses contemporary concerns about pluralism. He argues that gaps between different cultures or beliefs are not bridged by some universal meta-language, but rather by our own particular witnesses proclaimed in the language of pluralism.[10] We are called to discern how to proclaim Christ's lordship in a way that is meaningful to a pluralist world, the same way the first Christians discerned how to proclaim it in new and different contexts.[11] Yoder refers to this as a 'missionary ethic of incarnation'.[12] The fact that the truth has taken on particularity in a particular time and place is the basis for our engagement with other ways of believing. We proclaim

---

[6] John Howard Yoder, *The Priestly Kingdom: Social Ethics as Gospel* (Notre Dame: University of Notre Dame Press, 1984).

[7] Yoder, *Priestly Kingdom,* 92.

[8] Yoder, *Priestly Kingdom,* 91.

[9] John Howard Yoder, *The Politics of Jesus* (Grand Rapids, MI: Wm. B. Eerdmans, 1994), 94-97.

[10] Yoder, *Priestly Kingdom,* 56.

[11] Yoder, *Priestly Kingdom,* 49-54.

[12] Yoder, *Priestly Kingdom,* 44.

this truth not by seeking to be less specifically Christian, but rather by working at every commonality and conflict to which our particularity leads us. The existence of Christian communities testifies to the fact that our truth, like all truth, is particular, and *because of this particularity*, it can be meaningfully communicated – universally – to other particular contexts: 'We report an event that occurred in our listeners' own world, and ask them to respond to it. What could be more universal than that?'[13]

Roland Allen: Communities of the Spirit

Roland Allen, an Anglican missionary in China at the turn of the twentieth century, criticises the missionary practices of that period. His challenges invite comparison with modern concerns and may suggest methods for realising Yoder's notion of a particular communal witness in a pluralist context. Allen argues that the 'modern Western spirit', suffers from a lack of trust in the presence of the Holy Spirit in mission communities, creates utter dependence on the missionary, and is inconsistent with the practices modelled by the most successful missionary in the history of the faith, St. Paul, who was able to establish viable Christian communities in four provinces of the Roman Empire in the ten years between 47 and 57 CE.[14]

Allen elaborates St. Paul's methods. He attends to Paul's use of miracles (they served primarily to manifest the Spirit and character of the new religion, not specifically to convert), financial arrangements (Paul never established financially dependent communities; financial matters were always means to the spread of the Gospel and the unity of the church), and his preaching (to be addressed below). In contrast to the methods of his modern-day successors, the key to Paul's success is 'that he founded churches whilst we found missions'.[15] That is, rather than gather dependent communities centred around a single missionary, usually sent and supported by an elaborate foreign organisation, who administers the sacraments and delivers the teachings of the faith, Paul, according to Allen, incorporated the local leadership, introduced the fundamental elements of the Gospel and Old Testament and basic sacraments, and, usually after five or six months, left behind a viable church in the care of local elders.[16] He taught in a context of mutual instruction, allowing 'local prophets' to speak, then withdrew from the community to enable local leadership. Of course, Paul maintained communication with the churches through his letters. Nonetheless, he consistently emphasised the importance of their freedom.[17]

---

[13] Yoder, *Priestly Kingdom,* 59.
[14] Roland Allen, *Missionary Methods: St. Paul's or Ours?* (Grand Rapids, MI: Wm. B. Eerdmans, 1962), 6.
[15] Allen, *Missionary Methods*, 83.
[16] Allen, *Missionary Methods*, 84-90.
[17] Allen, *Missionary Methods*, 91. Cf. Paul's letter to the Galatians.

Allen surveys the accounts of St. Paul's preaching, and discerns a characteristic recognition and understanding of the particular 'condition' of his listeners as regards their current beliefs, and a corresponding effort to address their own peculiar challenges to accepting the Gospel.[18] Underlying this approach is a frank acknowledgment of the general difficulty of such acceptance, as well as an unfaltering respect for the hearers' understanding and confidence in the message itself. These aspects portray a style of teaching that gave careful attention to the specific circumstances of the communities. Allen also points to Paul's working of miracles and teachings on charity (such as 1 Cor. 13:1-3) as illustrating Christian concern for 'doing good', a perspective that saw, 'in every case of trouble or disease... an opportunity for the revelation of grace and loving-kindness'.[19]

This latter point deserves more consideration than Allen gives it. Although mission cannot be reduced to social or economic development programmes, neither can it ignore the concrete realities of those to whom it is addressed. Indeed, one aspect of modern dissatisfaction with the idea of mission is based on a perception, noted above, that missions have neglected these realities in the past. Both Jesus and Saint Paul consistently attended to the material care of those with whom they shared the Gospel, in the form of miracles and, in Paul's case, the collection for the poor in Jerusalem; we, as their successors, must do so as well. Nor does it suffice simply to assert that teaching of the faith must be accompanied by care for material well-being, as two distinct parts of the church's mission. There is an intrinsic relation between the two. The Gospel is the 'good news to the poor' (Luke 4.18). With its message of hope and liberation, the Christian faith has concrete consequences in the life of the community.

These concrete implications are not strictly 'economic development' in the way it is often understood, with wealthier communities aiding those less fortunate (though they do not exclude this), any more than mission is necessarily a movement from more advanced societies to more marginal ones. They are, rather, an integral aspect of the concrete discernment of the Gospel in communities of all kinds. Allen recognises this: 'the activities of the Christians as individuals and as a body, the church in the place, should be the most clear revelation of the spirit... [W]hen [people] see a change in the lives of their neighbours... [t]hen the people are face to face with the Holy Ghost'.[20] If Christians have at times neglected the integral nature of this connection, it is nonetheless true that it has had real manifestations throughout the world. Christian faith has been an integral (rather than incidental) part of efforts at education, community development, human rights advocacy, and revolution (two examples are considered below).

[18] Allen, *Missionary Methods*, 62-64ff.
[19] Allen, *Missionary Methods*, 45.
[20] Roland Allen, *The Ministry of the Spirit: Selected Writings of Roland Allen,* ed. David M. Patton (Grand Rapids, MI: Wm. B. Eerdmans, 1960), 100.

Christian communities proclaim and participate in God's mission not simply or primarily in their words, but in their very lives.

The missiology that I propose, then, builds on Allen's insistence that the church follow the example of St. Paul in focusing on the communities in which mission takes place. The church must address its Christian formation to the actual social and material situations of communities themselves and empower these communities to advance this formation themselves; that is, it must discern the truth of the Gospel in those specific contexts. Discernment does not relativise or undermine the Gospel. Rather, as Yoder argues, it is precisely the particularity of the Gospel, of Christ's lordship, that is professed in all new contexts, spoken in the language of pluralism. And in all contexts, appropriate humility and dependence on God's self-communication lead us to acknowledge that God is already present in all places and communities, waiting not to be revealed *to* them, but rather *in* them. This realisation and the attendant goal of empowering communities themselves to witness to the Gospel in their own particular contexts together constitute the heart of Christian mission.

This requires us to approach mission with an attitude of faith in the power of God in the Holy Spirit. It was this faith that enabled Saint Paul to entrust the formation and guidance of the early church to the communities themselves. In doing so, Allen notes, he ran great risks, and at times the churches fell into error, as illustrated by Paul's intense concern for the purity of the Christian message at Galatia and the moral and Eucharistic controversies at Corinth.[21] Nonetheless, Allen argues, throughout his ministry Paul 'believed in the Holy Ghost, not merely vaguely as a spiritual Power, but as a Person indwelling his converts. He believed therefore in his converts. He could trust them. He believed that Christ was able and willing to keep that which he had committed to Him'.[22] God is active and revealing Godself in communities everywhere. The church is blessed with the opportunity to witness to and participate in this *missio Dei*, and to commend all of its efforts to God, trusting that God and God's people will together bring it closer and closer to fruition.

Examples of Missionary Community

As a missionary of the Episcopal Church, I worked in Sitio de los Nejapa, a poor community in rural El Salvador. It is a place of great need, and its residents have been grateful recipients of a small number of charity and development programs. Yet when the few community leaders try to mobilise support for their own efforts, or to encourage new leaders, they are met with indifference. Many community members, particularly women with little formal education, attribute this apparent indifference to, among

---

[21] Allen, *Missionary Methods,* 91.
[22] Allen, *Missionary Methods*, 149.

other things, feelings of inadequacy or lack of ability. They do not advocate on their own behalf, they say, because they are looked down on or ignored by local officials; they cannot be leaders because they lack the skills.

Yet in weekly Bible studies, these women are able to encourage one another to value their own voices. In reflecting on passages such as Matthew 11:25 ('I thank you, Father… because you have hidden these things from the wise and the intelligent and have revealed them to infants') they begin to overcome their self-doubt and recognise their ability to speak for themselves. This new self-awareness, in turn, empowers them to collaborate with leaders of the church and community to develop other programs, such as a weekly sewing class.[23]

The story of the women of Sitio de Los Nejapa is an example of discernment of the truth of the Gospel in the specific context of a community, and the concrete implications it may have. Another, perhaps more striking, example can be seen in the well-documented, real impact of Christian base communities in Latin America. Don Pablito, a Salvadoran in the town of Cinquera, recounts how regular Bible studies initiated by local priests empowered community improvement: drunks stopped drinking, men stopped beating their wives, and workers began to advocate on behalf of their rights.[24] The life of the community testified, however partially, to God's purposes for the world.

In both these examples, the material and social life of the community is one with its reflection on the truths of Christianity, and constitutes its witness to the world. This witness relies on the work of missionaries, persons sent to build up each community. Yet more fundamentally, the mission involved is the witness of the communities themselves, as their formation empowers them to proclaim to the world, through their common life, the *missio Dei*.

Mission as Participation in Christ

At its heart, Christian mission is participation in God's overarching mission for all of creation. This participation is enacted in the lives of Christian communities everywhere, lives that bear witness to the divine purpose. In following Christ's example and testifying to values other than those that dominate society, believers are set apart from the world, as he was, in mission to it. This mission is integral to the identity of the church. The life of the church witnessing to the world: this is the foundation of mission, 'the whole church bringing the whole Gospel to the whole world'.

---

[23] The mission in Sitio de los Nejapa is still relatively young, too young to point to more dramatic outcomes. The sewing class has, at the time of this writing, come to an end, and the community members are working with the missionary (a Salvadoran) to discern new possibilities for community engagement.

[24] Interview with Don Pablito in Cinquera, El Salvador, November, 2007.

The character of that proclamation will be determined by the practices we use to shape our communities. Roland Allen's methods, focusing on the formation of viable communities, leadership from within, teaching that addresses particular, concrete contexts, and trust in the communities themselves and the Spirit working in them, offer some initial suggestions, as do Yoder's values of reconciliation, peace, and egalitarianism. Mission so understood provides a theologically compelling corrective to the impoverished conception that still leads some Christians, especially younger ones, to question the relevance of mission or reject it altogether. Christian mission is not intrinsically colonialist or hegemonic, but is rather the proclamation of God's presence in particular communities everywhere. This is good news in a world that sorely needs it.

Welcoming Children: Reinstating Children in our Theological Reflections on Mission

Wendy Strachan[1]

There are around 7 billion people in the world. Almost a third of these are children under the age of 15. God defends children. Jesus welcomed children. Children have been chosen by God to play a significant role in His kingdom plan throughout history. Yet children have been marginalised in our mission thinking. The disproportionately small amount of time and energy devoted to children in theological institutions seems to parallel the reality that less than 20 percent of mission resources worldwide are spent on children despite their numbers and their receptivity to the Good News.

It's a scandal. As a result of this 'great omission', children have suffered and the church has been diminished. This paper presents a challenge to theologians and theological institutions to use their influence to reinstate children in missional thinking and to address with urgency and gravity, the issues that children and Christian childcare workers are grappling with.

Joining God at Work on Behalf of Children

In 2002, the United Nations declared that this world should be 'a world fit for children'. The church has been relatively slow to see its vital place in making this a reality. Yet God is at work, and recent years have seen some exciting child-centred initiatives at a global level. There are many examples of such initiatives. As early as 1996, Dr Dan Brewster, a missiologist, challenged the church in his paper, 'The 4/14 Window: Child Ministries and Mission Strategy'.[2] Since then, the Global Alliance for Advancing Holistic Child Development has challenged Christian theological institutions to develop high-level holistic child development training programs to equip Christian workers and professionals to care for children around the world. Viva has been instrumental in networking and equipping thousands of people, churches and agencies across the world who work

---

[1] Wendy Strachan is Children's Ministry Coordinator for Scripture Union International.

[2] Published in Dr Phyllis Kilbourn (ed.): *Children in Crisis: A New Commitment* (Monrovia, CA: MARC Publications, 1996).

among children at risk. *Understanding God's Heart for Children,*[3] a book that rose out of their grass-roots consultations with childcare practitioners, explores a biblical framework for ministry to children at risk. In 2004, a Lausanne Occasional Paper, *Evangelisation of Children,*[4] produced by thirty-five people representing every continent, implored the church and its theologians to take children as seriously as God does. Since 2008, the Global Children's Forum has been growing as a partnering network of global children's ministry agencies and leaders whose vision is to ensure that every child in every generation is given the opportunity to engage fully with Jesus, through God's word. Since 2009, the 4-14 Window Global Initiative has been drawing together thousands of people in a 7-year commitment to strategise together so that a new generation of young Christ Followers will be raised up who will transform the world. The Child Theology Movement formed in the early twenty-first century, has been challenging the church and its theological institutions to consider the significance of Jesus' action in putting a child in the centre of the disciples when they were having an argument about greatness in the kingdom of God. It asks the question: how might the child's presence among us and in Scripture re-shape our theology and practice?

The reality is that there are hundreds of thousands of practitioners in children's ministry who are engaging every day in mission among children. But with their very best efforts, there are millions of children every day who remain desperate for the hope that the words and the actions of the Good News will bring. The task of mission amongst children urgently needs theological reflection and research that will permeate the church and that will inspire the church beyond its existing paradigms so that children become an integral part of the life and mission of the church; inform and encourage those who are already working among children; sustain a model of mission to children that will create a 'world fit for children'.

Joining Children in Their World: Four Stories

How do we move forward? In the Edinburgh 1910 World Missionary Conference, there were groups that were largely absent: women and leaders from developing countries were among those. The Edinburgh 2010 conference has made deliberate efforts to redress the balance one hundred years later and we celebrate the attendance of large numbers of women and of those from the global South. Yet in the preparations and presentations

[3] Douglas McConnell, Jennifer Orona & Paul Stockley (eds), *Understanding God's Heart for Children: Toward a Biblical Framework* (Colorado Springs, CO: Authentic Media, 2007).

[4] Wendy Strachan & Simon Hood (eds), *Evangelization of Children*. Lausanne Occasional Paper # 47 (Lausanne Committee for World Evangelization, 2004). Available at www.lausanne.org/2004-forum/documents.html.

for the Edinburgh 2010 conference, it was hard to find more than a few fleeting references to children.

How do we start to redress the balance in favour of children? We start in their world and learn from their experiences. The following are four stories for theological reflection:

Latin America

About 40 boys live in a streetkids centre in Lima. They are tough and they have tough stories. These are boys who don't easily trust people. Nor do they believe you when you talk about God. Why would a God who is so good and pure have anything to do with boys like them who have come to believe they are worthless? You can tell them the stories of Jesus' miracles – but there's no connection. It just increases the distance between them, the insignificant, and God the all-powerful.

Each night, the staff simply read a passage of the Bible to the boys. There's little comment – just the Word of God, together with a silent prayer. Usually there's no response. But one night it was different. As the boys were listening to the Bible story, the adults realised that almost every boy was crying. 'This is our story', they sobbed. What had they heard? It was the story of Jesus' arrest and his silence in the face of the abusive questioning of powerful people: '… he was silent and did not answer' (Mark 14:61). The street boys understand this silence: if they are arrested, abused, pressured for information – no matter what is inflicted on them – they have a code of silence. When you own nothing except your thoughts and feelings you protect these with silence – no one can take these away from you. 'Our silence is our truth. This Jesus is one of us', they say.

These boys are *doing* theology. They are not biblically literate but they have discovered that in God revealed in his Word, there is someone who understands them – not just because he is God and knows everything but because He became one of them: vulnerable, abused, marginalised. How do we accompany these boys on that journey of discovery? How do we do that without manipulation or presumption given the power dynamic that exists between powerless children and adults? How do we as adults listen to and learn from children knowing that spiritual insight is not the sole domain of adults? And – as we journey with children – what is good about the Good News for children? How does a child experience the Holy Spirit?

Asia

A woman has worked among child prostitutes for several years. Some girls (and boys) are sold into prostitution as an economic measure by the parents. Most are now drug addicts. It's difficult work and encouragement is hard to come by. There have been times when a child seems to be well along the path of rehabilitation when she slips back into familiar ways – into a life with at least some certainty. If they grow older, they become less 'desirable' as prostitutes, so they start on a life of petty (or serious) crime. But many will

> not grow older: they will die of AIDS. In despair, this childcare worker asks: Are there some children who are so damaged they can never be restored?

These children are made in the image of God. But the image is so tarnished. Is it recoverable?

What is the status of the child before God? Is it possible for a child who has never experienced love to experience the love of God? Is our theology of hope robust enough to help this childcare practitioner? Is our theology of suffering and dying robust enough to help us accompany children who are suffering or dying?

Europe

> An 18-year-old university student tells the story of how she has come to be studying social work with a view to working with teenage prostitutes. 'When I was 12 years old', she says, 'my church took a group of us – all aged between 12 and 14 – down to the Red Light district in Amsterdam. That night I spent half an hour talking to a girl-prostitute – and that changed my life forever'.

Children are actively participating in the mission of God. What does it mean to 'empower children' to engage in mission in the Kingdom of God where power is clothed in humility – the opposite of its construct in the world today? How do we 'empower' children to be witnesses to Christ in ways that are authentic for children? What is a child witnessing to? How do we inspire courage to serve God amongst the vulnerable: courage on the part of parents, the Christian community and the child? How do we balance the God-given mandate to protect our children with the God-given mandate to accompany them in the real world?

Australia

> Joseph is from a church background and at the age of 5 has become captivated by the stories of the Bible. Excitedly telling his mother the latest things he has learned, he pauses for a moment and then asks thoughtfully: 'But Mum, when is God going to finish this story?'

Joseph's 5 year old experience had led him not only to appreciate the story of the moment, but to glimpse a bigger picture: that this story is part of a big story; that this big story is God's story; that some day this story will end – and that all this has something to do with him.

How do we open the Bible with children in a way that ignites their imagination and respects their integrity? How do we move away from our information-based or entertainment-based approach to the Bible to a more holistic approach, with confidence that children can meet the living God in his Word? How do we encourage children to respond to what God is saying to them? How do we explore biblical concepts with children in ways that are simple without being simplistic? How do we respond to the difficult questions that children pose in ways that encourage them to keep exploring? How can the Christian community be enriched by the insights and enthusiasm of children?

Building the Future

The Psalmist wrote: 'We will tell the next generation the praiseworthy deeds of the Lord' (Ps. 78:4; New International Version). We can do that in words; we can do that in actions. We need both. But this is the responsibility of the whole faith community. We can no longer expect that tired Sunday school teachers and catechists, exhausted childcare workers and busy parents must bear all the responsibility for mission among children whether they be found in our churches or outside them. If this is to be a reality, it will take a paradigm shift in the church. If the paradigm is to be shifted, it will require a change in theological thinking and commitment that will filter down from *every* theological institution through *every* part of the church. It cannot remain the domain of a few specialist seminaries. But imagine what might happen…[5]

Imagine theological institutions that allow theological thinking about children, by children and on behalf of children to inform all disciplines, that esteem children's ministers as highly as all others in ministerial training, that create a synergy between theory and practice that is rooted in the harsh realities of a child's world, and that are active in training and equipping children for mission. Imagine families whose parents or caregivers have confidence in their role as *spiritual* caregivers, are empowered to live out Christian values in their homes, and are equipped to create spiritual traditions in the home. Imagine a church that commits the necessary resources to help children to follow Christ, builds a 'good news' relationship with every child in their community. Imagine a church that believes that, like the biblical child Samuel, children can have a voice in their congregation and invites them to be in the midst of its teaching, worship, evangelism and discipleship, and where people of all generations work together to see 'God's Kingdom come' in their communities. Imagine a child who knows and experiences that Jesus is present with her and will never forsake her – even when the pain of her life never fully goes away. Imagine a child who finds that hope and the kingdom of God are not mere concepts but acts of love by those who gather her into a place of protection and care – away from fear, war, stigma, exploitation and abuse. Imagine a child who finds that Jesus can help her understand the difference between sinning and being sinned against, and that both of these are wrapped with the healing grace and constant love of God. Imagine a child with special educational needs who encounters Jesus' unconditional love among church friends – and becomes one of their worship-leaders. Imagine a child who is

[5] This section is adapted from Strachan & Hood, *Evangelization of Children.*

excited that he meets God in the Bible – because he has something of the Scriptures in a format he can understand, and whose experience of following Jesus is such that he shares it naturally among peers and family. Imagine a world where children are safe, well-cared for and living in hope, given many opportunities to know and respond to the love of Jesus Christ, encouraged to bring hope, healing, comfort and Jesus to one another, and able to be discipled no matter how diverse their family or faith background.

'A World Fit for Children' cannot only be the mandate of the United Nations. It is surely the mission of the church in the next decades. When the next Edinburgh Missions Conference is held to explore different ways of that mission is impacting our world, will children be prominent on the agenda? Will children be active and equal participants at the conference?

UBS Reborn? Scripture Engagement in a Glocalised World

Bill Mitchell[1]

The United Bible Societies (UBS) traces its beginnings to the founding of the British and Foreign Bible Society (BFBS) in 1804.[2] The organisation itself did not come into being until 1946, though there were earlier calls for such a 'World Federation of Bible Societies' in 1910, and much later at a conference in Woudschoten, Netherlands in 1939. Following the urgings of Hendrik Kraemer, it was resolved then to form a 'Council of Bible Societies'. The outbreak of war in Europe meant that was not implemented. However in Haywards Heath, Sussex in May 1946, in the first non-governmental international conference in Britain since the end of the war, representatives of thirteen national Bible Societies decided to form UBS.

The bicentenary celebrations of BFBS in 2004 gave UBS, by then a global fellowship of 145 national Bible Societies, an opportunity to reflect and celebrate the past, but equally to examine its role and ministry in a changed and changing world.

UBS in a Changed and Changing World

At the beginning of the third millennium these Bible Societies found themselves in a globalised world characterised by a 'loss of boundaries', namely: loss of identity, loss of certainty and loss of authority. All of those impacted on the religious, economic and social life of people across the world. Yet there was paradox in the midst of change. The loss of identity was paralleled by a search for personhood and community. The global was complemented by the local and individual. There was loss of certainty, yet equally there was a longing for meaning and significance. The loss of authority contrasted with a rise of authoritarianism, as seen, for instance, in the growth of fundamentalism, whether religious, ethnic, or nationalistic.[3]

---

[1] Dr Bill Mitchell, former Americas Area Translation Coordinator for the United Bible Societies.

[2] See Bill Mitchell & Fergus Macdonald, 'Bible Societies in Mission', in Daryl Balia & Kirsteen Kim (eds), *Edinburgh 2010: Witnessing to Christ Today* (Oxford: Regnum Books International, 2010), 253-259.

[3] Alexander Schweitzer, 'Fundamentalism: A Challenge for Biblical Pastoral Ministry', *Bulletin Dei Verbum* 70/71 (2005), 14-16.

New technology held out the promise of wealth, quality of life and safety – a promise that remained unfulfilled for the overwhelming majority of the world's six and a half billion people. Rather than enhancing life, technology had dehumanised people, reducing them to things rather than persons. Yet this technology had produced an inter-connected world – the communications revolution provided the driving force for globalisation.[4] This technology had become the preferred means of communication of youth culture. New communities existed on the web, internet-based tribes with neither accountability nor responsibility, networking through social media. Beyond the global youth culture, the media were the major resource for many people of spiritual information and exploration – a place for creating meaning, ritual, and religious and transcendent experience. Martín-Barbero sees the media 'as *the* place of resacralisation and re-enchantment of cultures today'.[5]

This challenges the churches and Bible Societies to intentionally engage the new culture, to express the faith in new media forms. Making the Word of God accessible on the Internet, as opposed to making it possible to access the standard text of the Bible via the Internet, requires understanding and use of a new 'media language'.[6] The Internet opens up a semiotic maze where meaning is built through multiple sign systems. The focus is not on notions of reading and writing linear text. Instead it is centred on the integration of semiotics and hypertext. David Crystal has noted 'nothing in traditional language remotely resembles the dynamic flexibility of the Web'.[7] Internet language is 'something fundamentally different from both writing and speech, as traditionally understood...it is a development of millennial significance'.[8]

The Bible Societies operate in cultures which may be pre-modern, modern or postmodern, or perhaps all three in juxtaposition. Yet increasingly they find themselves in a postmodern world characterised by 'the rejection of metanarratives, the loss of confidence in reason and the sciences, a sense of deception with the idea of sustained progress, and a

---

[4] Not a single phenomenon with a uniform impact, instead a reality that takes some powers from the nation state into the global arena, but equally pushes other aspects 'down' to a different level, promoting local identity. The global and the local are interdependent. Bill Mitchell, 'The New Media: Culture, the Christian Faith, the Church and Translation', *Journal of Biblical Text Research* 20 (2007), 155-176.

[5] Jesús Martín-Barbero, 'Mass Media as a Site of Resacralization of Contemporary Cultures', in Stewart M. Hoover & Knut Lundby (eds), *Rethinking Media, Religion and Culture* (Thousand Oaks, CA: Sage Publications, 1997), 102-116; see 107, 111-112.

[6] For instance, the new interactive *Basisbibel* project of the German Bible Society involves a new Bible translation designed for the screen, not for the printed page. www.basisb.de.

[7] David Crystal, *Language and the Internet* (New York: Cambridge University Press, 2006), 210.

[8] Crystal, *Language and the Internet*, 272.

frustration with unfulfilled promises of betterment.[9] This is producing relativism in ways of thinking and acting, together with the loss of a sense of values, the lack of commitment to institutions and anything permanent, the prevalence of the emotional over the rational, and fragmentation at personal and community levels. In this setting the Christian faith is not an important matter in people's lives – it has lost the evidence of its validity. Anything traditional has run out of steam, while the Church means less and less for people. Yet many of these same people have begun a spiritual journey, seeking coherence and integration to their existence. Their distrust in the 'big story' has not invalidated the personal story – the human story has immense validity (for example, blogs).

UBS Reborn?

This new reality required UBS to revisit its own identity and ethos. The UBS World Assembly held in Newport, Wales in 2004 reaffirmed the fraternity's nature and purpose in the following terms:

> The world fellowship of national Bible Societies joins together, as the United Bible Societies, for consultation, mutual support and action in their common task of achieving the widest possible, effective and meaningful distribution of the Holy Scriptures and of helping people interact with the Word of God. The Bible Societies seek to carry out their task in partnership and co-operation with all Christian churches and with church related organisations.

The Assembly theme was 'The Unchanging Word for a changing world' – the Word unchanging in truth, power and purpose – 'what the Bible wants of us, what it impels us toward… is agreement with the direction in which it looks itself. And the direction it looks is to the living Christ' (Karl Barth).

As the delegates looked to the past they remembered that 'the Word of God had been heard in all of this book and in all parts of it'. They looked to the future with conviction: 'we expect that we shall hear the Word of God again, even in those places where we have not heard it before. The Bible has a living dimension, because of encounter with the Living Word'.

The UBS response to the changing mission landscape meant recovering Biblical patterns for mission:

- God's mission is the source of mission
- Jesus Christ is the embodiment of mission
- The Holy Spirit is the power for mission
- The Church is the instrument of mission
- Cultures are the context in which mission takes place.[10]

---

[9] *Declaración de Barueri II*, UBS Americas Consultation held in Barueri, Sao Paulo, Brazil, 6-8 March 2007.

[10] United Bible Societies, *Strategic Challenges: The Mission Imperative.* Position paper, UBS 2004 World Assembly (Reading: UBS, 2004), 7.

The commitment to serve in cooperation with all churches raised issues of strategy and priorities. In part this came from the change in the global Christian community, whose centre of gravity had moved from the 'North' to the 'South'. What might serving *all* churches mean?[11] Without the Scriptures, there can be little 'Scripture engagement' and in affirming that 'translation remains at the heart of our task',[12] priorities and methodology needed to be established.[13]

Depending on the social context of a given Bible Society, issues such as availability, relevance and credibility of the Scriptures needed to be addressed. These in turn led to strategies for provision of the Scriptures, encounter with the Word and advocacy of the Word. This marked a move from dealing with Bible needs to developing mission strategies.

In the BFBS Bicentenary Celebration in St. Paul's Cathedral Archbishop Rowan Williams reminded those present that 'our history and our theology alike tell us that no human style or speech is finally impermeable to Scripture'.[14] The Bible Societies saw the need to move from distribution targets to engagement and encounter, from biblical illiteracy to transformational change, and from sales strategies to shared communication.[15]

Scripture Engagement

In UBS thinking, 'Scripture engagement' is a concept that emphasises making the Bible discoverable, accessible and relevant, that includes both making the Bible recoverable and discoverable *as Sacred Scripture*, and making Scriptures accessible as a place of life enhancing and life transforming encounter. The following examples from Latin America and the United Kingdom illustrate the creative implementation and localisation of global mission strategies.

a) Making the Word available in Brazil

The rapid growth of evangelical and pentecostal churches in Brazil – now representing at least 15 percent of the country's 190 million inhabitants –

---

[11] E.g. Roman Catholic, Orthodox, 'Mainline', Pentecostal/charismatic, Post-denominational, the 'emerging' church, Africa Initiated Churches, etc.

[12] United Bible Societies. *Newport Declaration* (UBS: Reading, 2004), 1.

[13] E.g. The so-called 'unreached' languages, 'new' languages such as creoles, sign languages, media languages; or the type of translation – formal, functional, liturgical, oral, etc.

[14] Rowan Williams, Service to celebrate the Bicentenary of the British and Foreign Bible Society, St Paul's Cathedral, 2004; see www.archbishopofcanterbury.org/1171.

[15] Bill Mitchell, 'Por um novo Pentecostes: A tradução da Bíblia no novo milênio', *Fórum de Ciências Bíblicas* 2 (2007), 13-22.

has created an ongoing demand for Bibles. The demand also comes from the Roman Catholic community. The implementation in the last forty years of the recommendations of *Dei Verbum*,[16] plus the role of the base communities, have led to biblical renewal in the Roman Catholic Church. A further impetus to this has come from Benedict XVI's call to Latin American bishops gathered in Aparecida, Brazil in 2007: 'As the missionary Church prepares… to begin a new stage in its life, a deep, experiential knowledge of the Word of God is essential… We must build our missionary commitment, and indeed our whole lives, on the rock of the Word of God.'[17]

The *Bíblia Almeida* is the 'classic' Bible of Protestants. The New Testament was first published in 1681 and the Old Testament in 1753, and it has been revised many times since then. Herculano Alves shows convincingly that this Bible is the 'most widely distributed book in the Portuguese language' (over 110 million copies of all editions).[18] Demand continues. The Brazil Bible Society has also developed the *Nova Tradução da Linguagem de Hoje*, the work of an interconfessional team, a Bible which is now used widely by Evangelicals and Catholics. Its translation style and its study notes facilitate not only access and understanding of the Scriptures, but its use in interconfessional community groups. Currently the Brazil Bible Society prints and distributes over 5 million Bibles each year for Brazil, and also publishes in Spanish and produces in African languages (for example, Yoruba, Igbo) to meet the needs of partner societies there.

b) Latin America's exploding youth population

Among the challenges facing the Church (and governments!) is the continent's high birth-rate. In many countries fully 40 percent of the population is under fifteen years of age. The average age in Mexico City, with more than 20 million people, is fifteen-and-a-half. When asked what his greatest challenge was, a Costa Rican priest immediately said 'how to catechise the cell phone generation'.[19]

In 2006 the Conference of Latin American Bishops (CELAM) and UBS began work on a *lectio divina* programme for young people and children using a variety of media – print, music, radio and Internet. This multimedia initiative would provide access for different strata of society – individuals, families, schools, churches, parishes and dioceses – to network together

[16] Vatican II, Dogmatic Constitution on Divine Revelation, *Dei verbum*, 1965.
[17] CELAM, *Documento Conclusivo: V Conferencia General* (Bogotá: Centro de Publicaciones del CELAM, 2007), §247.
[18] Herculano Alves, ‚Joao Ferreira D'Almeida, tradutor da Biblia'. Paper presented in the Fórum de Ciências Bíblicas, Barueri, Sao Paulo, Brazil. 8-9 June 2006; Herculano Alves, *A Bíblia de João Ferreira Annes D'almeida* (Lisbon: Universidade Católica, 2007)
[19] Personal conversation with Fr. Omar Solís, Bogotá, 1 June 2005.

throughout the continent. Technological and social networking developments since then moved the programme to a different level – as *Lectionautas*[20] for young people, and *Discipulitos*[21] for children show – with MP3 downloads, Facebook and My Space now also finding a place.

Already over 12,500 young leaders from parishes in a dozen countries have been trained in the programme. They are introducing it in their churches and forming groups of young people using cell phones, computers and other technology to access the biblical passages for their prayer, reflection and action. The young people themselves develop the programme in creative and innovative ways – texting has become a way of encouraging one another and sharing together their experiences of the Word. From its beginnings in Spanish, the programme is now available in other languages and is being accessed globally.

For this programme the Church's own language was one obstacle that had to be faced. The Aparecida document notes: 'evangelisation, catechesis, and pastoral ministry as a whole, are still speaking languages that mean little to contemporary culture, and to young people in particular.'[22] Here a new Spanish translation of the Bible for young people and children developed by a UBS interconfessional, inter-disciplinary team – the *Traducción en Lenguaje Actual* – has proved providential.[23]

c) Peru – responding to violence

Domestic violence, spousal abuse, and child abuse are major concerns in Peru. A World Health Organisation study carried out in 2000 of women in the 15-49 age range in the greater Lima area showed that 51 percent of women have suffered physical or sexual violence at least once from their partner.[24]

The Bible Society of Peru has developed Bible-based materials for use by churches – *Alto a la Violencia* – to create critical awareness and action on spousal abuse.[25] This has been extended to take into account the situation of sexual abuse of children and adolescents with materials for use in and by churches, as well as by a network of NGOs working in this area.

---

[20] www.lectionautas.com.

[21] www.discipulitos.com.

[22] CELAM, *Documento Conclusivo*, §100d.

[23] Edesio Sánchez C., 'Children, Theology and Translation in Latin America: *La Traducción en Lenguaje Actual*'. Paper presented at the SBL Annual Meeting, New Orleans, 21-24 November 2009.

[24] Rhoda E. Mitchell, *Empowering Women and Including Men: A Case Study of Gender-Based Violence in San Juan de Lurigancho, Peru.* Unpublished MSW thesis, University of Calgary, 2008, 13. www.ucalgary.ca/md/PARHAD/documents/2008-Empowering_Women_and_Including_Men.pdf.

[25] Sociedad Bíblica Peruana. 2009. *A la imagen de Dios: Alto a la Violencia.* Lima. www.casadelabiblia.org.

An agreement has also been signed with the *Ministerio de la Mujer* to develop together a programme using these materials in the nation's schools.[26]

d) Bible Society in England and Wales: Advocacy and encounter

In the dystopia that is the postmodern England, the Bible Society sums up its mission as 'making the Bible heard', so the Bible is 'available, accessible and credible'.[27] Bible Society initiatives therefore aim to connect different narratives – cultural, personal and biblical – with the aim of transforming culture through the Word. Their advocacy involves confronting contemporary paradoxes and working in open, uncertain environments. It sees the need for telling stories, and *the* story, with the purpose of changing the prevailing discourse, leading to transformational change in society. They identify the 'drivers' of change in society and aim to influence the change makers in order to bring something that is on the edges of society – that is the Bible – back into the centre. Their multi-faceted initiative of Scripture engagement has led to developments in the media, arts, politics[28] and education[29]. For them the nature of advocacy and encounter with the Bible involves wide-ranging research[30] and imaginative engagement initiatives to 'change the conversation' and re-tell the story.[31]

e) Scottish Bible Society: The Bible in religious education in Scotland

Scotland has a Christian heritage reaching back at least to the arrival of St. Ninian in Galloway in the late fourth century. Contemporary Scotland is, however, now a multicultural, multifaith society. Religion continues as part of the school curriculum, albeit in a pluralistic context. The Scottish Bible Society Bibleworld Centre in Edinburgh and the Bibleworld mobile unit introduce schoolchildren and students to the Bible as part of religious education's 'curriculum for excellence'.

The programmes have been designed to aid teachers and educationalists cover the religious and moral education curriculum. Each workshop intentionally deals with other areas including expressive arts, health and

---

[26] See 'Cartilla educativa para niños y adolescentes busca prevenir el maltrato y la violencia sexual', www.casadelabiblia.org.

[27] Bible Society CEO, James Catford. www.christianmarketplace.org.uk/engine.cfm?i=43&cma=1717

[28] E.g. The Bible Society public theology thinktank *Theos*.

[29] E.g. The BIBLOS Education and the Bible research initiative (with Exeter University).

[30] E.g. 'Bible in Pastoral Use' (with Cardiff University), 'Scripture and Hermeneutics' (with Cheltenham & Gloucester College of Higher Education).

[31] E.g. Interfacing with contemporary 'cultural icons' such as the soap opera *Eastenders*.

wellbeing, literacy and social studies. As the website states: 'We use Bible texts and historical events to help develop an understanding of Christian beliefs and practices and how they have been fundamental in the fabrication of our society in Scotland. We also examine social and religious values in context with Christianity and the message of the Bible.'[32] The wide use of the Centre and the mobile unit's visits by schools and the public in general underline the important role Bibleworld plays in contemporary Scripture engagement in Scotland.

Now at 'age 64' UBS perhaps evokes the Beatles' song 'will you still need me.... when I am sixty-four?' In answer, the changing strategies and mission priorities seen in UBS and the examples of how these are contextualised and implemented in specific countries, suggest that UBS can and does play a key role in contemporary mission, global and local.

---

[32] www.bibleworld.co.uk

Missio Dei or Missio Creator Dei?
Witnessing to Christ in the Face of the Current Ecological Crisis

Kapya John Kaoma[1]

Human attitudes towards the Earth will determine the future of life on planet Earth. Deforestation, air and water pollution, land degradation, uncontrolled population growth, global warming, and many other ecological predicaments that are adversely affecting our planet are some of the negative effects of irresponsible attitudes towards God's Earth. Since most of these attitudes are religiously conditioned, Christian mission can be instrumental in changing human perceptions of nature.

The belief that the natural world exists solely for human use is a product of modernity and, in some Third World countries, by Enlightenment influenced Protestant mission theories. Although this belief influenced how Christian mission was understood in the nineteenth century, the perception that Earth's natural resources (hereafter referred to as 'natural goods')[2] can be exploited indefinitely for human use is slowly becoming recognised as a fallacy. There is a compelling body of scholarly literature that documents the connection between contemporary policies inspired by this nineteenth century theory and the negative ecological effects wrought on much of the planet.[3] Unfortunately, this Western worldview (which is rooted in the Protestant Reformation, the Enlightenment, and eighteenth-century economic theories) still dominates our mission activities. Yet it is putting

---

[1] Rev. Dr John Kapya Kaoma teaches at St. John's Anglican Seminary, Zambia and is Project Director for Political Research Associates, USA.

[2] 'Resources' is the most common term for Earth's natural benefits that are available for human (and often for non-human) use, and are extracted by humans as individuals and industrial corporations. The usage here follows that of John Hart, who in *Sacramental Commons* uses 'Earth goods' or 'natural goods' in place of 'resources', without elaboration. John Hart, *Sacramental Commons: Christian Ecological Ethics* (Lanham, MD: Rowman and Littlefield, 2006), 150.

[3] Séverine Deneulin & Masooda Bano, *Religion in Development: Rewriting the Secular Script* (London and New York: Zed Books, 2009); Jeffrey Haynes, *Religion and Development: Conflict or Cooperation?* (New York: Palgrave Macmillan, 2007); Kirkpatrick Sale, *Dwellers on the Land: The Bioregional Vision* (Athens, GA: University of Georgia Press, 2000); Paul Hawken, *The Ecology of Commerce: A Declaration of Sustainability* (New York: Harper Business, 1993).

the planet in jeopardy.[4] While some effects of this theory are felt in the West, sadly, the poor and millions of nonhuman species suffer the most. For this reason, witnessing for Christ today demands addressing the pending ecological disaster!

Christian Mission as the Mission of the Creator God

The shift from an ecclesiocentric to a theocentric (*missio Dei*) conception of Christian mission should redirect missiological thinking to ecological liberation. Although it is tempting to consider humanity (*imago Dei*) as the sole beneficiary of *missio Dei,* God's mission is holistic. Indeed, the sidelining of nonhumans in God's mission is partially due to the twentieth century context in which the concept was born.

David Bosch's book, *Transforming Mission* is an excellent tool in understanding how the concept came about. Bosch argues that advancements in science and technology, the growing secularism of the West, the two World Wars, the growth of the Church in the global South, the spread of other religions, the subjugation of the poor and people of colour, the ever-growing global economic inequalities, and the birth of local theologies created a crisis for modern mission and led to a paradigm shift from church-centred to God-centred mission. Although the concept of *missio Dei* has dominated mission literature, Bosch warned that this shift 'is not the first shift the world (or the Church) has experienced. There have been profound crises and major paradigm shifts before. Each of these paradigms constituted the end of one world and the birth of another, in which much of what people used to think and do had to be redefined'.[5] If Bosch's observation about paradigm shifts is true, then the ongoing ecological crisis demands another shift in Christian mission. Just as the concept of *missio Dei* aided the advancement of human rights across the world, the new ecological paradigm of mission should address human responsibility towards creation, one another and future generations of life.

The emphasis placed on humanity (*imago Dei*) as the major focus of *missio Dei* underestimates the value of God's creation. No doubt humanity is the beneficiary of God's mission, but participating in the *missio Dei* implies sharing God's love towards every creature. In short, the mission of the Creator brings 'the good news of liberation or salvation for all creation'.[6] Theologically therefore, God's eschatological grace carries a universal or cosmic application (Rom. 8:21-22; Isa. 11:6-11). In this regard,

---

[4] Sallie McFague, *Life Abundant: Rethinking Theology and Economy for a Planet in Peril* (Minneapolis: Fortress Press, 2000), 117.

[5] David J. Bosch, *Transforming Mission: Paradigm Shifts in Theology of Mission* (Maryknoll, NY, Orbis Books, 1991), 4.

[6]Marthinus L. Daneel, *African Earthkeepers: Wholistic Interfaith Mission* (Maryknoll, NY, Orbis Books, 2001), 276.

the missional church should take ecological liberation and reconciliation as the expression of wholistic *missio Dei*.

In sub-Saharan Africa and other parts of the world, the on-going ecological crisis has a poor person's face. Eco-theologians have observed a direct link between the liberation of the poor and that of nature. Eco-feminist theologians have equally identified a direct link between the exploitation of nature and of women in the male-dominated world. Aside from countless species threatened with extinction, the ongoing destruction of the Earth is a death penalty for the people whose livelihoods depend on the land. Most of these people are pushed out of their indigenous lands or simply lose their land after it has become a dumping site for industrial and commercial wastes. In developing countries, however, women are the ones who have to walk long distances in fetch of firewood or drinking waters. In mission studies, the exploitation of the poor and women has received some missiological attention. However, the exploitation of nature is still understudied. But as Dana L. Robert argues, 'the vulnerability of God's Creation, combined with the vulnerability of the world's poorest people, together create a strong motive for cross-cultural mission in the twenty-first century'.[7]

Witnessing to Christ as Safeguarding the Integrity of Creation

The reality that the Earth is under threat due to human irresponsibility and the realisation that we might be the last generation to exist on Earth should force us into challenging human attitudes towards the cosmos. Witnessing to Christ would mean addressing population growth, pollution, species extinction, climate change and human responsibility towards future generations. In other words, the instrumental view of the natural world, which dominated early missionary activities and still influences our economic theories, should be replaced with 'holistic approaches' that honour the interconnectedness of creation.[8] In this case, the *missio Dei* should be understood as the mission of the Creator (*missio Creator)* revealed in the cosmic Christ, under whose authority, care and influence Earth and heaven now exist. Thus, all environmental issues are subjects of mission studies.

In addition, since the mission of God cannot be separated from the reign of God, ecological injustices are matter of critical importance to the missional Church. Of course, those who met in 1910 could not have seen the urgency of addressing the occurring ecological crisis. After all, the exploitation of the Earth was part of the modern era in which their

[7] Dana L. Robert, *Christian Mission: How Christianity Became a World Religion* (Oxford, Wiley-Blackwell, 2009), 112.

[8] Daryl Balia & Kirsteen Kim (eds), *Edinburgh 2010: Witnessing to Christ Today* (Oxford: Regnum Books International, 2010), 81.

missionary theories and activities were conceived. However, in the face of the ongoing ecological crisis and the exploitation of the poor by the capitalistic economic system, mission theology beyond Edinburgh 2010 can hardly advocate justice, love, and peace for the world without addressing the occurring ecological crisis. In his book, *Loving Nature*, ethicist James Nash argues that love and justice carry with them great ecological implications, which are essential for 'an adequate Christian ecological ethic.'[9] The same can be said about Christian mission.

Accepting experience as a foundation of Christian mission suggests that we seriously consider addressing the ecological context in which human experience occurs. The incarnation (an expression of mission of God in the person of Jesus) comes to us from a specific natural environment. Although there is a tendency to view mountains, trees, lakes, rivers, fish, snakes, wheat and many other natural phenomena in the Bible as of little value to the mission of the Creator, an ecological reading of the Bible suggests otherwise. In biblical terms, God's mission is not devoid of ecological relationships. Indeed the goal of God's mission is to bring about *shalom* to the entire created order. Although Darrell L. Guder argues that '*Shalom* envisions the full prosperity of a people of God living under the covenant of God's demanding care and compassionate rule', biblical witness also emphasises holistic peace and justice on Earth.[10] In fact, biblical *shalom* is inclusive: in the coming Kingdom, lions, humanity, snakes and other species will live in perfect harmony (Isa. 11:6-9; cf. 65: 25). Like any other biblical theme, the consummation of *shalom* carries strong ecological implications.

In addition to biblical arguments, human understanding of the origin of creation can compel ecological Christian mission. Across religious traditions, creation is said to be the product of the Creator Spirit. In most religious traditions, the Supreme Being and other spiritual beings can manifest in natural phenomena. In this regard, the sacredness associated with Earth in Native American religions, African Traditional Religions and Asian religions (which early missionaries dismissed as evil) can aid interfaith ecological initiative and dialogue. Although such understanding can be characterised as nature worshipping, Christian mystics and missiologists have related to nature in a similar manner. Despite sharing the tradition that valued the doctrine of *imago Dei*, Saint Francis of Assisi viewed nature as the vehicle of divine grace. For Francis, God's love was inclusive of all created order. Long before the ecological crisis gained momentum, Albert Schweitzer, a missionary to today's Gabon, argued that every creature has intrinsic value. In 1936, Schweitzer wrote:

---

[9] James A. Nash, *Loving Nature, Ecological Integrity and Christian Responsibility* (Nashville, TN: Abingdon Press, 1991), 179.

[10] Darrell L. Guder, *Missional Church: A Vision for the Sending of the Church in North America* (Grand Rapids, MI: Wm B. Eerdmans, 1998), 91.

> The important thing is that we are part of life; we are born of other lives; we possess the capacities to bring still other lives into existence. So nature compels us to recognise the fact of mutual dependence, each life necessarily helping the other lives which are linked to it. In the very fibres of our being, we bear within ourselves the fact of solidarity of life. Our recognition of it expands with thought. Seeing its presence in ourselves, we realise how closely we are linked with other.[11]

We should realise that we are part of Earth and like any other part of creation, we belong to the Creator God. An argument can therefore be made that human beings and nonhumans are equal audiences of the *missio Dei*. The occurring crisis demands that we abandon what Sallie Mcfague calls 'apartheid thinking': the falsehood that human life is more valuable than that of other species in the universe.[12] In fact, the argument that non-humans have intrinsic value is theologically sound; the Creator declared creation good (Gen. 1: 31). The goodness of creation, Christopher J.H. Wright notes, is theologically and chronologically 'affirmed before humanity was around to see it'.[13] Furthermore, if the goal of creation is to 'declare the glory of God' (Ps. 19:1), then creation is not just intrinsically good but a true witness of the Creator's glory.

The triune God is directly involved in Creation, hence God's mission encompasses the Earth. Therefore, protecting Earth from human abuse is a fundamental faith issue in which the Church is called to participate.

African Christology and Ecology

The Creator's glory revealed in creation can inform Christian Christology. Among Africans for example, 'nature is sacred' and 'wild animals are the most pure expression of God's power'.[14] Although ancestors and the Supreme Being manifest and sometimes reside in nature, they are also 'the guardians of the land'.[15] Africans believe that the Earth was originally given to the ancestors as a 'sacred trust'. Although the living can use the Earth's natural goods for their wellbeing, they also have a moral obligation

---

[11] Albert Schweitzer, 'The Ethics of Reverence for Life'. Originally published in *Christendom* 1 (1936): 225-39. Available at http://www1.chapman.edu/scheitzer/sch/reading4/html. Accessed 07/16/08. Schweitzer argues that our 'Solidarity for and sympathy with all life encourages sympathy with all life' and 'becomes engraved upon our hearts, and culminates in spiritual union and harmony with the Creative Will which is in and through all'. Schweitzer, 'The Ethics of Reverence for Life', 10.

[12] McFague, *Life Abundant*, 117.

[13] Christopher J.H. Wright, *The Mission of God: Unlocking the Bible's Grand Narrative* (Downers Grove, IL: InterVarsity Press, 2006), 398.

[14] Jacob Olupona, 'Comments on the Encyclopedia of Religion and Nature', *Journal of American Academy of Religion* 77/1 (Mar 2009), 63.

[15] J.M. Schoffeleers (ed.), *Guardians of the Land : Essays on Central African Territorial Cults* (Gwelo (Zimbabwe): Mambo Press, 1979).

to hand over this Earth to future generations. Destroying the Earth is an attack on the ancestors and by extension on the Supreme Being.

From this perspective, the African Christological title of 'Christ as our ancestor' carries ecological motifs. African theologians have generally accepted Jesus as an ancestor. John S. Pobee, writing from an Akan perspective, views Jesus as Nana, 'the Great and Greatest Ancestor'.[16] Charles Nyamiti views Jesus as 'our brother-Ancestor'. François Kabasélé adds that Christ is an elder brother-ancestor. For Bénézet Bujo of the Congo, however, Christ is the proto-ancestor, healer and master of initiation.[17] Of late, Gift Makwasha developed an ancestral Christology that links Jesus to family, tribal and national lands in Shona cosmologies.[18] Although these titles are indicative of the multi-functional roles of ancestors in African cosmologies, theologians have limited the role of ancestors to economic and socio-political issues. The ecological implication of these Christologies is still under-studied.

The cult of ancestors is an earthly cult with strong ecological overtones. The ecological ancestorship of Jesus is attested in the Bible, where Jesus is the 'origin' of creation and 'the first born of all creation' (Col. 1:17). In African cosmology, however, ancestors are considered to be the first born of the human lineage. Yet ancestors find their origin in the Supreme Being. Due to their ontological position, ancestors are by default 'guardians of the land'. Theologically, however, by being the source of all life including the ancestors, Jesus becomes the 'Supreme Guardian of the land.' The ecological significance of this Christology is immense. Aside from the fact that the crisis threatens Earth, which is the arena or mission field of God's mission, Earth belongs to Jesus who is both the Creator and the first born of all creation (ancestor) as proclaimed in the New Testament (Col. 1:15-20). The supremacy of Christ over all life does not only suggest the interconnectedness of life through Christ but also the ecological ancestorship of Christ.

Although ancestors are guardians of the Land, the Supreme Being is the Creator of the universe. This belief is also found in the Bible. According to the Bible, the first human being was created from the dust or clay of Earth (*adamah* – the Hebrew for clay, Gen. 2:9). This is reiterated in the story of

---

[16] John Pobee, *Toward an African Theology* (Nashville, TN: Abingdon, 1979), 94.

[17] There are as many African Christologies as they are African theologians. Jesus as our ancestor, elder brother, healer, liberator, chief, guest, proto-ancestor and Earthkeeper are among the African Christological titles proposed. Robert J. Schreiter, *Faces of Jesus in Africa* (Maryknoll, NY, Orbis Books, 1991); Donald J. Goergen, 'The Quest for the Christ of Africa', *The Journal of the Faculty of Theology, Catholic University of Eastern Africa*, 17/1 (March 2001), 5-51.

[18] Gift Makwasha, *The Repression, Resistance, and Revival of the Ancestor Cult in the Shona Churches of Zimbabwe: A Study in the Persistence of a Traditional Religious Belief* (Lewiston, NY: Edwin Mellen Press, 2010).

the Fall, at the end of which God reminds humanity of its relationship with Earth: 'For Earth you are, and to Earth you will return' (Gen. 3: 19).

The belief that Earth came into being by God's own love and care is, in fact, a biblical given. Biblical writers were careful not to treat Earth or humanity as above God. Doing so would be considered idolatry. Neither did they present Earth as something outside God's realm. It is for this reason that Yahweh's covenant at the end of the Flood story is not just with humans: it is with Earth and all living creatures, including humanity; it includes God's promise not to destroy Earth again (Gen. 9:11-13). Just as God cares for humanity, the Creator cares for every creature, big and small. In the Psalmist's words, 'The heavens are yours, Earth also is yours, the world and all it contains, you have founded them' (Ps. 89:11 cf. 1 Cor. 10:26). The Old Testament conviction that Earth is the Lord's is carried over into the New Testament, creation is viewed as the product of the Christ (John 1:1-2). The epistle to the Colossians identifies the Christ as the Creator of all things 'in heaven and on earth, visible and invisible' (Col. 1:16). Through the blood of the Christ shed on the cross, God was pleased to bring reconciliation to all creation on Earth and heaven (Col. 1: 20).

The Christ, who is the firstborn and redeemer of creation, is connected to creation by virtue of being one with the Creator. That said Christ becomes the ecological ancestor as well as a relative of all that exists on Earth. In other words, it is through him, in him, and for him that all things exist. In this regard, the interconnectedness of creation is founded on the power of Christ, who is both the Creator and the vital force behind creation. He is that link that connects the Earth community to the Creator Spirit. The eschatological *telos* (goal) of creation is also hereby pronounced. Whereas outside Christian thought (and sometimes, unfortunately, within Christian thinking) it is assumed that creation exists for humanity, in Colossians, creation exists for the Christ who is both the Creator and the *telos* of creation.

The declaration that Jesus Christ is both the source and goal of life finds expression in other biblical books as well. Writing to the Romans, Paul argues that 'For from Him and through Him and to Him are all things' (Rom. 11:36). Likewise, he argues that 'for us there is but one God, the Father, from whom are all things and we exist for Him; and one Lord, Jesus Christ, by whom are all things, and we exist through Him (1 Cor. 8:6). This biblical conviction is important in developing mission theology of Earth. Christ is not only the origin of human life; he is the life of all that exists (cf. John 1:4). Thus, the assumption that Earth exists solely for its instrumental value, fails to address the eschatological significance of creation in Christ.

Earth's Integrity as a Foundation of Mission

Missiologists should not abandon Earth to the environmental movement. Our conviction that 'The Earth is the Lord's' should propel us into ecological responsibilities and actions beyond our faith traditions. The tree-planting experiences of African Earthkeepers in Zimbabwe (led by a son of a missionary, Marthinus Daneel) that saw the planting of more than 3 million trees and conservation of wildlife in Zimbabwe can inform cross-cultural mission. To Earthkeepers, trees have intrinsic value accorded to them by the Creator.[19] African Earthkeepers applied *missio Dei* to encourage dialogue and ecumenism. For instance, despite the enmity and theological differences that characterise African traditionalists and African Independent Churches in Africa, the ecological crisis has acted as a catalyst to bring both parties together. Like any other crisis, addressing the occurring ecological crisis can aid missionary endeavours to dialogue with other faiths. After all, we are all agreed that Earth belongs to the Creator Spirit. In short, a well understood Earthkeeping theology can aid the mission of God in this broken world.

The worsening ecological crisis deserves missiological responses. The growth of the Church in the global South is celebrated as indicative of the success of *missio Dei*. Yet it is in the global South where the ecological crisis is worsening every passing day. This situation underscores the value of developing missiological reflections that address the growing numbers of Christians on one hand and the Earth's death on the other. Finally, as the occurring crisis continues unabated at both local and international levels, local initiatives such as African Earthkeepers can easily be dismissed as a drop in the ocean. But as Marthinus Daneel rightly argues, Christian ecological mission springs from a 'spiritual mandate' to heal, liberate and care for Earth after the pattern of the loving Creator. In this regard, the mission of the Creator compels us 'to reach out in mission regardless of the disheartening realities of the global situation'.[20]

---

19 Daneel, *African Earthkeepers*.

20 Daneel, *African Earthkeepers*, 277.

TOKYO 2010: ANALYSIS AND REFLECTION ON THE GLOBAL MISSION CONSULTATION

David Taylor & Yong Cho[1]

Over 880 mission leaders from 67 countries met together for the Tokyo 2010 Global Mission Consultation held on 11-14 May 2010. The gathering was sponsored by dozens of national, regional and global mission networks and associations, representing 100,000 cross-cultural missionaries. The purpose of the gathering was to celebrate the progress made in missionary efforts since Edinburgh 1910, assess what remains to be done in making disciples of all peoples, and develop plans for inter-mission cooperation to fully engage the remaining least-reached peoples in our generation.

Following the pattern of Edinburgh 1910, most of the delegates came as representatives of their mission sending structure. A good number were the CEOs or top decision makers of both large and small organisations from around the world. Beginning a process that will continue well beyond Tokyo, mission agencies were asked to make specific commitments to send church-planting teams to those people groups without any missionary work. A special listing called the 'Finishing the Task List' was distributed at the meeting, detailing the existence of 632 unreached people groups over 50,000 in population without any long-term missionary engagement. Specific commitments were made at Tokyo 2010 to engage 171 of these in the next three years with evangelism and church-planting initiatives. Mission organisations also signed up to send out 1,244 oral Bible teams, which will translate and dub Bible stories for priority language groups where the majority of the population are primarily oral learners. Eighty-five mission agencies also volunteered to help with national surveys in their country to document those areas without access to a culturally-relevant local church.

In addition to focusing on the least-reached peoples and places in the world – what was referred to at Tokyo 2010 as the 'breadth' of the Great Commission – the consultation also brought attention to the 'depth' of the Great Commission mandate, represented by the phrase 'teaching them to

[1] David Taylor was Co-Organizer of the Tokyo 2010 Conference and is a member of the Global Network of Mission Structures Task Force; Dr Yong Cho was Chairperson of the Tokyo 2010 Planning Committee Chairperson and is Director of the Global Network of Mission Structures.

obey all that I have commanded'. The Tokyo Declaration issued at the consultation underscored the importance of this dimension both at the individual level as well as at the social or national level. Under the category of transformation, the Declaration made the following affirmations:

> The new believer's worldview must be adjusted to a biblical worldview; his lifestyle changed to increasingly conform to the image of Christ; and his ethical conduct progressively marked by biblical morals. Ideally, this results in individuals applying the gospel of the kingdom to every sphere and pursuit of life – from government to economics, from education to health, and from science to creation care. As a consequence whole communities, cultures and countries benefit from the transforming power of the gospel.

The Tokyo Declaration's emphasis on the transformational dimension of the Great Commission added an element to the Edinburgh tradition that many mission leaders felt had been a glaring omission in previous gatherings. For this reason the theme and watchword for Tokyo 2010 was established as 'making disciples of every people in our generation'. This watchword built on the previous two watchwords of Edinburgh 1910 and Edinburgh 1980, which were 'the evangelisation of the world in this generation' and 'a church for every people by the year 2000'. The watchword of Tokyo 2010 thus took the 'generation' timeframe of Edinburgh 1910, and the people group emphasis of Edinburgh 1980, and added the discipling aspect of Matthew 28:19-20. In doing so, Tokyo 2010 sought to draw attention to an important progression over the last century that has led to greater depth as well as precision in defining how we measure success in fulfilling the Great Commission.

Background and Uniqueness of Tokyo 2010

Tokyo 2010 had the special privilege of being the first of four gatherings to be held this year commemorating the Edinburgh 1910 meeting. Each of these gatherings were designed to have a unique focus and delegation, the combined sum of which should well represent and touch virtually every church and mission tradition in the world – from Pentecostals to Roman Catholics to the Eastern Orthodox community.

The purpose and special contribution of Tokyo 2010 was to reproduce four elements of Edinburgh 1910 which made that gathering historically significant to the global mission community. Those four elements were as follows: (i) Delegates came as representatives of all the major Evangelical sending agencies and nations of the world; (ii) The specific focus was on the final frontiers of the Great Commission; (iii) Concerted effort was made to identify and fill in the gaps of inter-mission collaboration; (iv) Participating agencies continued to cooperate following the meeting on the national, regional and global level to reach the remaining 'unengaged' non-Christian peoples (today's terminology for what were called the 'unoccupied fields' in 1910).

The Tokyo meeting was first called for by the late Ralph D. Winter, convener of Edinburgh 1980. Though two other global meetings were planned in 1980, one sponsored by the Lausanne movement and the other by the World Council of Churches, Winter felt it was necessary to call a meeting that would follow the Edinburgh 1910 pattern, especially with regard to its emphasis on bringing together mission agencies to focus on reaching the final frontiers. Almost the exact same scenario would be repeated thirty years later, though unlike in 1980, the organisers of all the 2010 meetings met together in advance, exhibiting a spirit of cooperation and Christian unity not seen in previous decades.

The Edinburgh 1980 meeting is famous for encouraging mission agencies to focus on the year 2000 as a milestone for seeing a missiological breakthrough – or the birth of an indigenous church with national leadership – in every people group in the world. From out of the momentum of this meeting developed what would become known as the AD2000 & Beyond Movement, which for ten years became the largest frontier mission network of evangelical agencies and denominations ever assembled. Following the wake of the AD2000 movement, and as the centennial of Edinburgh 1910 approached, Winter called a meeting of non-Western mission leaders and challenged them to organise a global mission consultation that would follow the blueprint of Edinburgh 1910 and 1980. However, in keeping with the new realities of global mission, this third Edinburgh-type meeting would be held in the non-Western world, and would be organised primarily by non-Western mission leaders, networks and agencies. At the same time, the meeting was to be a global effort, meaning Western participation was welcome and encouraged, but would only represent a minority contribution.

The result of this challenging idea was that Tokyo 2010 became the first-ever global level meeting following the Edinburgh 1910 pattern that was planned, organised, led and funded primarily by the non-Western mission movement. In contrast, the Edinburgh 1910 meeting had just a handful of non-Western participants, none of which came as representatives of non-Western mission agencies, and none of which were part of the leadership team. Similarly, Edinburgh 1980 had just one non-Westerner on its executive team, although its delegations were made up of one third non-Western mission leaders – an achievement which was greatly celebrated.

As envisioned, Tokyo 2010 reflected almost the reverse of the Edinburgh 1980 meeting, with around 74 percent of its delegates coming from the non-Western world, and a similar percentage making up its leadership team. These percentages closely resemble the proportions of missionary sending today in the early twenty-first century. The percentages of delegates coming from various countries and regions also closely reflected their proportional contribution to the global missionary force.

Another unique contribution of Tokyo 2010 to the Edinburgh tradition was its inclusion and elevation of the 'secular peoples of Europe' as a 'frontier mission' priority for the global church. One of the most moving times during the consultation followed the presentation by Stefan Gustavsson, leader of the Swedish Evangelical Alliance, who described the dismal situation of both the society and church in Europe. After his presentation, the entire consultation (most of which represented the fruit of European missionary sending in past centuries) began to intercede for this once Christian continent that is now itself in need of pioneer missionary effort – a phenomenon being referred to as 'reverse mission'. At the same time, many non-Western mission leaders remarked that the very trends which contributed to the decline of the church in Europe are beginning to affect their countries as well. Such a realisation brought Tokyo 2010's theme of discipleship into even sharper focus, underscoring the reality that the Christian faith is just a generation away from extinction in every society.

Beyond Tokyo 2010

One of the visions of the Edinburgh 1980 meeting was to see an ongoing global networking structure for mission agencies that would function in a similar capacity to Edinburgh 1910's International Missionary Council. Although the AD2000 & Beyond Movement helped to facilitate this in part, the central office was disbanded as scheduled in the year 2000. In order to fill in this gap, Ralph Winter convened a small meeting of mission leaders from around the world in the year 2005 to discuss what it would take to bring into reality a global network that would facilitate inter-mission cooperation to finish the task of reaching all the world's remaining unreached peoples. From out of this discussion, the foundations were laid for what has become the Global Network of Mission Structures (GNMS). The first task and priority of this new network was to coordinate efforts for Tokyo 2010, and following this consultation, to help steward whatever visions and plans the Holy Spirit might generate from the gathering.

In the pattern of Edinburgh 1980, coordinating task forces and study groups at Tokyo 2010 were encouraged to think towards a specific milestone, in this case the year 2020, and to ask the question, 'What's it going to take to see a disciple-making movement among all the world's unreached peoples in the next decade?' The media task force, for example, set a goal to form a 20/20 Vision Partnership that would facilitate the development of contextualised media resources for every least-reached people over one million in population by the year 2020. (The significance of prioritising these larger ethno-linguistic groups is that most of the world's smaller unreached peoples are influenced by or can access media in one or more of the languages of these so called 'mega-peoples'.)

Altogether, there were eighteen coordinating task forces at Tokyo 2010, which focused on areas such as frontier mission training, unreached people intercession, crisis response, missiological research, next generation mobilisation, technology and mission, mission associations and networks, field partnerships and cooperation, and unreached people engagement. Each task force was encouraged to develop and discuss strategy papers that would examine the scope of the need in their particular area of focus, identify what is presently being done, and propose specific recommendations to mission agencies for how they might more effectively work together to bridge existing gaps.

From out of this study process, the Global Network of Mission Structures (GNMS) has begun to prioritise specific areas for development that will require central coordination over the next five to ten years. One of those priorities is the formation of national and regional task forces that will assess the progress of missionary deployment among the least-reached peoples and develop specific strategies to engage those population segments without any church-planting initiatives. Two large international agencies volunteered at Tokyo 2010's Global Coordination Task Force to help facilitate this process in every country and region that may require it. Another priority is the establishment of special forums to bring together on an annual basis the directors of major international missions, regional and national field leaders of expatriate missions, and coordinators of national mission associations. The latter group, which met together as part of the Mission Associations and Networks Task Force, has already set plans in motion to begin coordinating annual meetings.

Finally, the planning of Tokyo 2010 revealed the general lack of global mission intelligence in multiple areas, which the GNMS will begin to address over the next several years. There is still, for example, no existing directory of African or European mission agencies, no global registry for missionary deployment among unreached peoples, and more importantly, no unified listing of the world's priority unengaged peoples and population segments. In addition to addressing these intelligence gaps, the research department of the GNMS has begun to gather existing mission data into a global directory that will include information on all the world's known mission agencies, mission training centres, mission resources, and unreached peoples. Much of this data will be made accessible to the general public on the GNMS website. A more exclusive directory of mission leaders is also being developed which will be made available only to participating mission agencies. A similar private directory of mission resource people will also be maintained by the Global Network for the purpose of identifying consultants that have expertise in various critical areas, ranging from missionary care to accounting to relief and development.[2]

[2] More information about these projects, Tokyo 2010 follow up, and the Global Network of Mission Structures can be accessed at www.gnms.net.

Reports

Listening Group Report

The Song of Songs ends with the king saying to his beloved: 'Your friends listen to you. Let me hear your voice!' (Song of Sol. 8:13). In any encounter and gathering listening as well as speaking are significant. At Edinburgh 2010 a group of eleven persons was given the particular task of listening to what was said and observing what was happening in this worldwide gathering. The purpose was not only to provide a report of its findings, but in listening to detect how the many voices may contribute to and strengthen our common voice and witness to Christ.

The members of the Listening Group met each other for the first time in Edinburgh, and the group mirrored the composite participation in the conference (see the list of group members at the end of this report). During the conference we shared meals, met for group sessions and compared notes. After the three full days of the conference we gave a preliminary report to the plenary on Saturday evening, 5 June 2010. Based on the notes of the members and in communication with them after the conference, this more comprehensive report has been compiled and given its final form by the co-chair of the group.

The conference had been well prepared, and we tried to listen with the material of the conference book *Witnessing to Christ Today*[1] at the back of our minds. Edinburgh 1910 lasted for ten days; our gathering was for four days with only three days for deliberations. The limited time available did not allow for in-depth discussions of significant theological and missiological issues related to the nine themes covered by the conference book and the conference programme. It is our hope that this can be done in the follow-up of Edinburgh 2010 in the various regions of the world as well as in the Global Christian Forum, in the Commission on World Mission and Evangelism, and by the various stakeholders of the conference.

Paradigm Shift in World Mission

As an event Edinburgh 2010 demonstrated to us the paradigm shift that has taken place in world mission and in the global church since 1910 and particularly in the last decades. Hopefully the conference as such with the

---

[1] Daryl Balia & Kirsteen Kim (eds), *Edinburgh 2010: Witnessing to Christ Today* (Oxford: Regnum Books International, 2010).

study process in advance and the follow-up will foster and further develop this shift in focus for the worldwide church in its missional ministry:

- From mission as the church's mission to God's mission (*missio Dei*), and thus from a church-oriented mission to a mission-centred church.
- From world mission and a global church dominated by Western culture to a worldwide community with a major growth in the global south, with many colours and a multifaceted face.
- From competition among churches and missionary organisations to cooperation and unity.
- From a split between ecumenism and evangelism, dialogue and mission to a more united ministry with the Gospel.
- From a focus on verbal communication to a more holistic understanding of the Gospel and Christian ministry.
- From a power-exercising church to vulnerable communities and a church among and for the poor.
- From male-dominated ministries to full involvement of women, young adults and children in the life and ministry of the church.

In listening to the many voices that spoke and conversations that took place during the conference, we not only sensed an affirmation of this paradigm shift, but we also came to acknowledge that there still are many stumbling blocks on our way to achieve this common witness to Christ in our lives. In this report we highlight how we heard that this paradigm shift was affirmed, but also the challenges in front of us.

Foundations for Mission

The worldwide Church has been on a theological journey since 1910. Ecumenical discussion in the last decades of the twentieth century developed the understanding of mission as God's mission (*missio Dei*), and that the Church is called to participate in the mission of the triune God. This understanding of mission reverberated throughout the conference. Mission is the heartbeat of God, and its foundation is the very nature of God: the relational, self-giving, grace-filled nature of the triune God in which we are invited to participate.

The paper on 'foundations for mission' in the conference book[2] deals with experiential, biblical and theological foundations. The focus upon experience was appreciated, as a way of dealing honestly with the history of Christian mission in the last century and particularly its dark sides, but also as a significant signal to overcome the tendency to prioritise the so-called theoretical above the empirical approach. At the same time some expressed the desire that the biblical foundations always should have

[2] Balia & Kim, *Edinburgh 2010: Witnessing to Christ Today*, 10-33.

priority, and that both the theological and experiential approach and reflections must be rooted in Scripture.

In the last decades the uniqueness of Christ and the work of the Holy Spirit have been key issues in the missiological debate. The previously mentioned paper on 'Foundations for mission' in the conference book states: 'Linking Christology and pneumatology avoids exclusive christocentrism in our understanding of the person and work of Christ, neither neglecting the creativity of the Spirit in creation, mission and redemption, nor emphasising a false autonomy of the Spirit that displaces Christology and the Trinity'.[3] In this respect we heard references to the World Council of Churches Conference on Mission and Evangelism in Athens in 2005: 'Come, Holy Spirit, heal and reconcile', in which Orthodox and Pentecostals discovered common ground in their understanding of the work of the Spirit. At the conference in Edinburgh there was little time for a more in-depth discussion of the uniqueness of Christ and the work of the Holy Spirit with its implications for our participation in God's mission. We sense, however, not only that further study and reflection on these issues are needed, particularly with regard to the next topic – Christian mission among other faiths – but also that such reflection is a fertile ground for developing a dynamic and sound spirituality in our missional practice.

A trinitarian understanding of mission today has several implications, for missiological thinking as well as for our missional practice. It is participation in the incarnational life of Jesus Christ and following him on his way to the cross and the resurrection: walking alongside the poor, the oppressed and the abused. It also implies responsibility and concern for God's creation, particularly in view of the contemporary consumer culture and the current exploitation of earth, water and air. It calls for a more holistic witness to the love of God for the salvation of a fallen world.

Christian Mission Among Other Faiths

Also from a missional perspective the world in 2010 is significantly different from 1910. In 1910 80 percent of Christians were in Europe and North-America, today less than 40 percent of all Christians are in the same regions. In 1910 there was an urgency in the recognition that only one third of the world population was Christian. Today we rejoice in the growth of churches in the global South, and that with the growth in world population Christians still are one third. Today we live in a 'global village' with a plurality of cultures, languages and faith-traditions in our societies. It is in this new context that Christian mission among other faiths takes place. Mission used to be to 'the far', today it takes place in our local context, in our neighbourhoods. Today mission is about being good neighbours and

---

[3] Balia & Kim, *Edinburgh 2010: Witnessing to Christ Today*, 24-25.

faithful witnesses at the same time. Yet, as we were told, 86 percent of all Buddhists, Hindus and Muslims do not personally know a Christian.

With regard to the history of Christian mission in the last century, some asked about the place of the revitalisation of Islam in this story. When militant Islam often is focused by the media, and we acknowledge that Christians live under pressure in many Muslim countries, we also note that Muslim scholars today write on the duties of proximity and a theology of neighbourliness. In today's world this seems to us to be a key challenge: How to live with Muslims as neighbours and share the Good News of the Gospel with them?

In the conference we realised anew that the discussion about either dialogue or evangelism in the encounter with people of other faiths belongs to the past, although we still need to deepen our understanding of the uniqueness of Christ and the work of the Holy Spirit for these encounters. In every encounter with a fellow human being we need to listen intently and respectfully and to speak the truth with humility. In sharing the Gospel of Jesus Christ there can be no superiority.

It was challenging to listen to the story told about young adults in Germany as an illustration of the situation in much of Europe. Many young people there know little of the faith and even less about the mission of the Church. They are impressed by an expressive faith, yet are uncertain in matters of ethics and evangelism. Thus the question was asked: Have western Christians lost confidence in the Gospel? Is it possible to maintain confidence in the Gospel and respect for people of other faith traditions?

Mission and Postmodernities

Postmodernism and postmodernities are complex concepts, debated and criticised as well. We found it helpful to address postmodern culture as a way of analyzing the cultural context of which we ourselves are part, and in which mission takes place. Being a phenomenon significantly marked by western values, we also noted that postmodern culture expresses itself in different ways and poses varying challenges in different regions of the world. Common features that we noted, are possibly: an emphasis upon relations and experience rather than rationality; relativism rather than normativity, with mistrust of authorities; a search for autonomy and authenticity; an emphasis upon aesthetics more than ethics; fragmentation in the life of the individual as well as in society, with plurality and pluralism as a distinct mark of postmodern culture; a consumerist life-style in a society marked by market liberalism.

It is evident that mission in such a postmodern context has to be distinctly critical and countercultural, and we heard this particularly with respect to contemporary relativism, the fragmentation of life and consumerism. But this should not make us blind to sound elements in the reaction of postmodern culture to modernity, both in our own critical assessment of Christian mission and church life today, as well as in the acknowledgement of the genuine possibilities for Christian ministry in this context. The triune God, Christian faith and the Church's participation in the mission of God are if anything relational, and experience and aesthetics are distinct elements in the life of the believer and in Christian worship. In this regard we noted what was reported from North America that Orthodox and Pentecostal churches, with their emphasis upon non-verbal elements in worship and communal life, are growing.

In reflecting critically and constructively on postmodern culture as our current context in many parts of the world, we detect some priorities for the life of our churches and ministries: Now is a time for renewed telling of biblical and personal stories and for worship that provides space for the aesthetic and the experiential. Our current context also represents a call to authentic Christian living, to a proper emphasis upon the relational aspect of Christian faith and community, and to strengthen Christian unity and fellowship as a way to overcome fragmentation. Authenticity, however, is not the same as the perfect story. Our brokenness and vulnerability are as much part of authentic Christian living and have to be recognised. Finally, postmodern culture also challenges churches and Christians to uphold a prophetic voice in the encounter with consumerism in our own lives and societies.

Mission and Power

In reviewing the history of Christian mission in the twentieth century, Edinburgh 2010 for many of us became a humble conference, particularly with regard to the dark history with abuse of power by churches, missionary organisations and workers, sometimes manifest and wilful use of power, other times through abuse of power in the shadows of missionary ministry. The stories told in the conference book from indigenous communities and residential schools in Canada were also shared orally and visually at the conference, and we heard similar stories from other continents and countries. These are stories about physical harassment and sexual abuse of children in residential schools, as well as overt and more sophisticated suppression of indigenous cultures by churches and missionary organisations. We no longer live in the colonial era, but there are still people in our midst living with traumatic memories from such abuse of power in their personal lives and against the indigenous culture in which they grew up. There are still stories to be told, repentance to be made and restorative justice to be exercised. In many places there is still a need for healing.

But past history also challenges us to a fresh and more profound approach to the questions of power in our churches and missionary organisations, a conscious appreciation of indigenous cultures and particularly taking seriously the dignity of children and their rightful place in the Christian community. For a Church that consciously wants to be vulnerable and follow in the footsteps of its crucified Lord, this is also a challenge to lift up the voices of the marginalised and subjugated people of the earth. The question of power has also wider implications for the worldwide Church participating in God's mission. These implications concern the use of economic power in the relationship between the poor South and the richer North, and between churches and missionary organisations in these regions. These relations and questions we have only begun to address, and we need both humility and creativity in order to develop a stewardship that will mirror the unity we long for in our common ministry and witness.

Forms of Missionary Engagement

We received a lot of input and noted a wealth of issues from the discussions on 'forms of missionary engagement'. Criticism of insensitive evangelical missionary activities and particularly tele-evangelism was voiced, but unhappiness was also expressed with what some experienced as a caricature of evangelicals.

The paradigm shift from the Church's mission to God's mission, and from a mission to 'those far away' to 'those who are near', implies a renewed focus upon local context and the primary role of the local church in mission. The local church is always the actual expression of the worldwide church, the people of God in their local context. But this implies that the local church should never be seen and experienced as a static entity. On the contrary, renewal in mission depends on the continuing renewal of church communities, being sent and reaching out in a holistic ministry to their local communities and beyond.

This focus upon the local church is consequential. In most local contexts this calls for constructive and ecumenical cooperation as well as space for new and emerging churches, not overlooking the difficulties that this sometimes involves. Today we sense a new willingness and a common search for cooperation between the 'come' and the 'go' structures in the history of the church: the local church and the missionary team, or the institutional church and the missionary organisation, sometimes called 'para-church'. However, we also note a mushrooming of missionary agencies in several countries, presenting us with new challenges towards risky collaboration in humility. We listened to stories of missionary lay movements and communities within both the Roman Catholic and Protestant churches and recognise their significance in our common missionary endeavour.

At the conference we heard and watched a vivid presentation of the growth of churches in South Korea. Churches there have a strong missionary identity, and we were told that today there are more than four thousand Korean congregations in Europe and North America. This demonstrated another difference from one hundred years ago. Today there is mission from the east and the south to the west and the north and between all continents, and migrant communities have become a mark of a globalised society in most countries.

'No church is so rich that it does not need mission. No church is so poor that it cannot provide mission' (Fidon Mwombeki, United Evangelical Mission). Migrants from many nations and cultures today bring with them new and refreshing expressions of the Gospel to the countries where they settle. This has had and continues to have the potential of reviving and creating new Christian communities. With this potential it is not only important that the migrants are given a Christian welcome, which sometimes is lacking in the North because of a frequent stigma of foreigners. But there is a need to develop new ways of ecumenical cooperation with migrants and migrant congregations and to provide cross-cultural training so that unnecessary stumbling blocks are overcome for the sake of their integration into a new context and their participation in our common mission.

A new and refreshing concern was voiced in Edinburgh as well as in the preceding study process: the role of children as 'a new energy for twenty-first century mission'. Some critical remarks were heard. With past examples of abuse of power in the treatment of children, it is important that powerful and demanding language is avoided, and that there is a deep respect of their dignity – as children. But respecting their dignity and their full participation as members of the Body of Christ makes us realise anew that God has used children as his willing instruments throughout Christian history. At the conference stories were shared about children from eight to fifteen years in eastern and southern countries involved in discipling, reconciling and environmental ministries. From Rome we heard about the Catholic 'Centre for unity' with its interactive program for teaching children reciprocity and mutuality across confessional and religious boundaries. In many Christian communities children are mainly treated as passive recipients of verbal messages and passive participants in fellowships for grown-ups. It is time that both children and youth are taken seriously as active participants in our communities and in living out their Christian faith.

Christian Communities in Contemporary Contexts

Today more than half of the world's population lives in urban centres, and poverty is one of the major challenges in our societies. Although the church as such does not have the means to solve the problem of global poverty, it does challenge the identity and the ministry of the church. In many parts of the world, and particularly in the global South, the Church is a church of the poor. A key element in the ministry of Jesus was 'bringing good news to the poor' (Luke 4:18), and in his life this was not only about sharing a verbal message but life itself, and transforming it. In this we today hear a call to the Church and to Christians on all continents to live with the poor and for the poor.

Living missionally is to be context-oriented, rooted in the reality and experience of actual persons and communities, always marked by reciprocity and mutuality. This concern was voiced by people working on the study theme 'Christian communities in contemporary contexts', particularly with respect to migration, the new urban contexts and the mega-cities of today. Mission is never about being powerful, but rather about making oneself vulnerable and hospitable to others, so that we may share the Good News of the Gospel and our lives be transformed.

Theological Education and Formation

In most parts of the world there is today a growing demand for higher education, and there has been a proliferation of theological schools, Bible colleges and training institutions, particularly in the global South. The composition of student bodies has changed, with a richer diversity in gender, age, race and vocational goals. The current context of education is also marked by new forms of accreditation standards and the possibility of the electronic media in providing online models of delivery and resources. But there is also a disparity between the North and the South with regard to financial resources for educational institutions and programmes. How does this affect theological education and formation in mission?

At the conference we noted a strong affirmation not only of Christian faith as committed to education, but that mission should be a key, integrating element, and that we need a new vision for theological education within a missional model. This is particularly the case where growing tension is experienced with regard to ministerial and spiritual formation versus academic preparation. Teachers are to be spiritual mentors, and there still are needs to further develop education and training which are rooted in the local and regional context, resisting the impact of western models on a non-western context

In the current landscape of theological education and training we observed a paradox. In the global South and East, where there are fewer financial resources, Theological Education by Extension has become a major instrument for training, not only as a preparation for pastoral ministry, but for grounding lay people in their faith and equipping them for participation in Christian service. In the global North and West, however, there is in many countries less focus upon the training of lay people and a lack of recruitment to pastoral ministry. We believe this situation calls for new, cooperative and inventive partnerships between traditions, institutions and geographical regions in theological education.

Concerns that were voiced in other tracks, were also discussed with regard to theological education and formation. The changing financial conditions and difficulties for churches to support their institutions and programmes were noted, also because they lead to less support of interdenominational cooperation in education. But churches working together in theological education are a significant contribution to Christian unity and may strengthen our common witness. With the past and present abuse of children in our communities, a sound 'theology of children' should be developed, and the concern for children should be moved from the margins into the core of our curricula. Today grounding people in Christian faith and ministry also demands that they are equipped for engaging with persons of other faiths and are properly introduced to their faiths and traditions, and at the same time to sharing the Gospel as 'public truth'.

Mission and Unity

Edinburgh 2010 was in itself a signal of a growing unity among Christians, and we rejoiced in this fellowship with Orthodox and Catholic representatives, with Protestants from all streams, with Evangelicals and Pentecostals, African Initiated Churches and people from the charismatic movements as well as Adventists. But we still have a way to go, not only with regard to the differences among us, but in the way we express our unity when it comes to the participation of women and young adults. We also heard that today there are 41,000 Christian denominations in the world. Thus the growing unity that we experienced makes it more urgent to face the parallel development of increasing fragmentation within Christianity.

The study process of the World Council of Churches in connection with the document on *Baptism, Eucharist and Ministry* (BEM) has shown that confessional theology and practice of ecclesiology lie at the heart of our continued disunity, and the challenge of BEM is still relevant: to arrive at an understand and practice of unity-in-diversity based on hospitality and mutuality, love and renewal in the Holy Spirit. Perhaps the time has come to move away from attempts to forge some kind of uniformity which will force faith groups to become defensive, and rather explore new approaches and possibilities such as networking.

The notion of networking was emphasised as a way to seek and develop broader Christian unity. Networking provides a kind of mutuality that takes people beyond the formalities of organisations that tend to descend into misuse of power and domination. It also offers a potential to engage young adults who so far have had no interest in church or mission. There was some disappointment that the conference did not provide more ample space for young adults to be part of the revisioning of what future mission will be like. Any paradigms of unity in diversity will have to take seriously the language and methods of communication which young adults understand, embrace and promote. Young adults are uniting today and use innovative ways to do so, and we may learn from them and allow them to participate in leading the Church in the quest for unity.

Another recurring thread was the call for a movement toward unity to come from the grassroots rather than to wait for leaders to implement it. The irony was that this call came from leaders themselves, with whom the dismantling of unity seems to be tied up. There are also denominational structures in the West which not only sustain disunity in their countries, but which are imposed on the South. On the other hand, we should not overlook but highlight advances in dialogues that have taken and are taking place, so that members of churches may be aware of progress toward greater understanding and cooperation between traditionally conflicting communities.

Mission and work toward unity cannot be undertaken without an attitude of humility, but there should be confidence without arrogance. This was emphasised in connection with observations on proselytising activities from certain Pentecostal and Evangelical groups. It was felt that Christians can be confident in sharing their faith without promoting denominational structures, taking into consideration that we belong to the same Body of Christ.

The nature of Christian unity is and will be God-given. But divisions among us cause damage to the credibility of the Gospel, and inability to work together eclipses our common witness. On the other hand, unity across our confessional and other boundaries enables the beauty of our differences and gifts to impact our societies and communities with the Gospel. Unity is at the heart of Christian mission, as Jesus said when he prayed that 'all of them may be one... so that the world may believe' (John 17:21).

Mission Spirituality

'Mission spirituality is specifically concerned with what is necessary for the Christian to engage in mission'.[4] As in all Christian spirituality, spirituality in mission is intrinsically linked to the work of the Spirit: discerning and discovering the movement of the Spirit of God in the world and joining in with it.

In the conference book we read and at the conference we heard stories and descriptions of spiritual life and formation of Christians and communities in a missional context: from Africa and Asia, from Russia and migrant communities in North America. From South America we heard about the spiritual life of Base Ecclesial Communities and Pentecostal groups working together in mission. We realise that there cannot be one prescribed discipline for a missional spirituality. Our spirituality has also to be context-sensitive. Although critical analysis and reflection are always

[4] Balia & Kim (eds), *Edinburgh 2010: Witnessing to Christ Today*, 223.

needed, we still learn and share the riches of our diverse spiritual traditions and practices.

At the conference we heard a call for a return to the classical Christian spiritual disciplines: the practice of daily scripture reading and meditation, prayer and solitude is a fount from which flows spiritual vitality for mission. But neither Christian spirituality in general nor mission spirituality in particular are solitary enterprises: they have to do with a spiritual life lived in community, rooted in common worship and sustained by the prayer and encouragement from our local Christian communities. Transformations that we are privileged to see in the lives of others grow out of the same source of sustenance. Today we are discovering anew the significance of spiritual direction or companionship: two persons walking and talking together in the presence of God, seeking his will and direction for their lives.

In the classical tradition meditation and contemplation was combined with action. Today we also sense a renewal of this element in the classical tradition, a renewal rooted and shaped in our contemporary and regional contexts. Rene Padilla is quoted in the conference book: 'Contemplation without action is an escape from concrete reality; action without contemplation is activism lacking a transcendent meaning'.[5] Both contemplation and action take place in our various contexts. In Africa this implies addressing issues like the HIV and AIDS, and responding to conflict with biblical peacemaking principles, and in many regions it expresses itself in a concern for the environment.

Discipleship and the call to discipleship are the gifts of grace from God, and from God alone, and mission spirituality recognises that God is already at work, and that we may join in on what he is doing. Mission spirituality has to do with living a life oriented toward the fulfilment of God's purposes for all creation.

Witnessing to Christ Today

Many voices and narratives from different regional, confessional and other perspectives were heard at Edinburgh 2010. Arguments were articulated in an organic rather than a linear way, and the conference appeared to us more as an event than offering a set of conclusions. Nevertheless, it was a time for thinking together and doing missional theology in a new and different way, expressing itself in the concluding Common Call.

We note with joy that it was possible for participants from all parts of the world and from the various streams of the worldwide Christian Church to unite behind this Common Call, and we sensed throughout the conference not only honesty with regard to the past and to our present differences, but a willingness to let the many voices converge in a

[5] Balia & Kim, *Edinburgh 2010: Witnessing to Christ Today*, 241.

symphonic witness to Christ today. Modern symphonies are not without cacophonic elements, and so was the conference, but we definitely experienced it as a symphonic event.

The conference affirmed that we today have endless possibilities for common witness, if we are bold enough to seek God's truth together and are converted to the One who still calls us his friends. 'If we become friends ourselves and walk the ecumenical miles of hope together, the Spirit of Christ will bring life to his people and mission will thrive and blossom', as bishop Brian Farrell from the Pontifical Council for Promoting Christian Unity said at the conference. We were delighted by being given the task of listening. Now it is our hope that not only the Common Call from Edinburgh 2010 will be heard, but that our common witness may shape our lives and lead people to Christ, as we listen to one another and heed the call of our Lord: 'Let me hear your voice!'

Listening Group: Rev. Dr. Iain Torrance, President, Princeton Theological Seminary, USA (chair); Rt Revd Ole Chr. M. Kvarme, Bishop of Oslo, Norway (co-chair); Rev. Dr Daniel Buda, Romania and World Council of Churches programme executive for the Coordination of Church and Ecumenical Relations; Rev. Fr Gosbert Byamungu, Tanzania and the Pontifical Council for Promoting Christian Unity at the Vatican; Rev. Dr Gao Ying, Vice-president of the China Christian Council, Beijing; Rev. Dr Cheryl Bridges Jones, Professor of Discipleship and Christian Formation, Church of God Theological Seminary, USA; Mr Paul Joshua, Professor of Pastoral Theology and Counselling, South-East Asia Institute of Advanced Christian Studies, India; Rev. Marvia Lawes, Minister of the Jamaica Baptist Union, serving in Panama; Miss Claire-Lise Lombard, DEFAP Service Protestant de mission, France; Rev. Elizabeth Salazar Sanzana, Pentecostal Evangelical Church, Chile; Dr Antonia van der Meer, Latin American Theological Fraternity, Brazil.

@EDINBURGH2010: ONLINE ECUMENISM IN AN AGE OF PARTICIPATION

Aaron T. Hollander[1]

> 'I looked and there before me was a great multitude that no one could count, from every nation, tribe, people and language...' Revelation 7:9

'The old is passing away; the new is yet unformed.'[2] These words, written by delegates to the 1910 World Missionary Conference, serve as an encapsulation of these delegates' developing context at the start of the twentieth century. Many of these individuals found that they shared an experience of both instability and creative optimism when they considered the swift changes in the communities from which they came. Various technologies, including the telephone and improved telegraph systems, were opening new possibilities of rapid communication across large distances, and missionaries in formerly isolated lands could recognise a thirst for modernisation among their parishioners and neighbours. In Edinburgh, missionaries and theologians alike had the audacity to envision a world in which Christian witness would not be carved up along denominational lines and linguistic barriers, but rather, might breathe again in the exhilarating atmosphere of Pentecost, in which unprecedented comprehension could be achieved across inherited cultural boundaries. In such a light, it was not a warning but a celebration that 'we can never understand our own Holy Scriptures until they are interpreted to us through the language of every nation under heaven'.[3]

Today, reflecting on the centenary of Edinburgh 1910, we find that we are coming to terms with our own experiences of instability and creativity.

---

[1] Aaron Hollander (USA, Anglican) was a member of the Edinburgh 2010 communications team, and is currently a doctoral student in theology at the University of Chicago. Grateful acknowledgements are due to Miriam Haar, fellow media steward for Edinburgh 2010 and colleague at the Irish School of Ecumenics, who contributed insight and research support for this report.

[2] World Missionary Conference 1910, *Report of Commission I: Carrying the Gospel to All the Non-Christian World* (Edinburgh and London: Oliphant, Anderson, & Ferrier; New York, Chicago, and Toronto: Fleming H Revell, 1910), 26.

[3] World Missionary Conference 1910, *Report of Commission VI: The Home Base of Missions* (Edinburgh and London: Oliphant, Anderson, & Ferrier; New York, Chicago, and Toronto: Fleming H Revell, 1910), 296.

The turn of this present century has been characterised by cultural and technological shifts at least as dramatic as those of the last. In the foreground of these is the ascendancy of the Internet from a niche science project to a versatile and pervasive communications infrastructure. Alongside the technological development, no less, is the sociological impact of such a comprehensive increase in our potential for communication. Through the Internet, global civil society is in the process of constructing and reinforcing what Tim O'Reilly calls an 'architecture of participation',[4] in which everyday communication across spectra of national, ethnic, professional, and religious difference is at once facilitated, encouraged, and unregulated. The Internet, especially among the young who use it as instinctively as one might use a pen and paper, can be considered a communication tool for building this participatory society, albeit one of particular speed and scope. But it is also a critical part of the architecture itself: a change in context, an evolution of possibility, a development in the nature of community.

This chapter is, first, an *account* of the Edinburgh 2010 communications strategy, the real-time reporting and social media conversations surrounding sessions during the conference, and the 'user-generated' web of continued collaboration between the home networks of those who connected at the conference and then returned their separate ways – all of which have made not only pragmatic but theoretically and theologically robust use of the Internet. Second, the report addresses the *reception* of Edinburgh 2010's online elements, as they were considered both in conversations on online social networks and in the concerns of delegates at the conference. An Appendix is available – fittingly – on the Edinburgh 2010 website, in which the conference's incorporation of the Internet is analyzed from the perspective of the study process.[5] At the opening of the twenty-first century, the Church exists in a world that is rushing headlong towards the integration of physical and digital life; this brief report touches on the provisional, and open-ended, manner in which the mission of this Church can move in the unprecedented connectivity of this time.

Account

When documenting its strategy in the year leading up to the conference, the communications team of Edinburgh 2010 described its role in the proceedings as follows:

---

[4] Tim O'Reilly, 'The Architecture of Participation', O'Reilly Media. http://oreilly.com/pub/a/oreilly/tim/articles/architecture_of_participation.html (accessed July 2010).

[5] Since the Appendix is a brief analysis from the perspective of 'Mission and Postmodernities', it appears as a document under Study Theme 3, at www.edinburgh2010.org/en/study-themes/main-study-themes/mission-and-postmodernities.html.

- To promote the Edinburgh 2010 website as a global platform for Christians interested in mission related topics (www.edinburgh2010.org)
- To popularise what is at the moment mainly an academic project.
- To encourage communities and organisations all over the world to set up (ecumenical) events on or around 6 June 2010.
- To encourage young people to participate in the project.[6]

However, these practical goals were grounded in a more comprehensive perspective on the importance of communication between conference delegates and the global Church in its diversity: 'The aim of the project is a serious, in-depth interaction on both the *missio Dei* in general and on specific missiological themes. *It is hoped that this discussion will not just take place among conference delegates, but that it will develop into a global conversation about mission before, during and after the conference*' (emphasis mine).[7]

This intention to maintain an environment of open-ended interaction between the conference in Scotland and the many home communities of its delegates (along with the first professed communications goal, to strike a balance between academic and popular attention to twenty-first century mission) highlights a theme of Edinburgh 2010's mindset. Without in any way devaluing the dedication, experience, and expertise of the professional ministerial and academic establishment, the stakeholders of Edinburgh 2010 were committed to soliciting and incorporating lay voices from beyond this establishment, and to using Internet resources as the space for a vibrant conversation on the study process themes that would not be restricted to the nominated delegates. Especially because of the communications priority to promote awareness of and participation in Edinburgh 2010 among communities of the global South, both our website and our adjunct social networking hubs took on additional significance in the effort to include individuals who could not be present in Edinburgh.

It is in this light that Facebook (the dominant online platform for social networking in 2010) was exercised as a primary location for this international conversation that ran parallel to the formal study process. Facebook's value in this effort was threefold: its immense popularity and

---

[6] This text and the quote to follow appear in the internal Edinburgh 2010 Communications Strategy documentation, finalized as of September 2009.

[7] The utility of online communication had already been demonstrated through the global nature of the formal study process, in which deliberate and close collaboration was necessary among working groups in multiple continents, and in which materials (written drafts, videos, reference articles, etc.) could be shared instantaneously. The *efficiency* of such collaboration had increased radically – and so, use of the Internet as an in-between space accessible to all constituents was a clear boon to the ecumenical engine of Edinburgh 2010, even before the communications team had designed the space for the general public to participate.

visibility,[8] its egalitarian cost of participation (free), and its sophisticated group-management software, which allows nested conversations on many different topics to be linked together, so that any individual in any nation who wished to contribute could do so, with access to the whole, multi-directional conversation up to that point. Between September and November 2009, Kirk Sandvig[9] facilitated three 'online consultations' on the study process themes. Each two-week-long discussion could be as broad or as focused as the self-selecting online community chose to make it; indeed, each of the three consultations had a distinct character as participants came and went. Furthermore, the insights of each contributor were immediately available to the others – in addition to the questions that launched discussion on each study theme, many responses were themselves picked up and discussed in the open forum. Three examples:

- In our country… there was bold, audacious missionary expansion. Some pat each other on the back for the success… but it missed God's promptings, calls and cries... because we missed hearing his voice amongst the silenced, the victims of the expansion… Now, we are perhaps listening again, feeling, probing, learning… (South Africa)
- I imagine a kind of peer-to-peer friendship-based witness, rather than Crusade at Baseball Stadium? … I imagine a kind of community living in rural manner with self sustainable vegetable garden, rather than Mega Church? (Japan)
- One of the keys to many of the issues mentioned in this discussion is in language. As long as the language of discussion, as in this forum, is English, that is enormously empowering to the native English-speaking world. It can severely restrict the freedom and likelihood of initiatives being taken by churches outside of the Western world. … Much of East Africa has not only mother tongues available, but also a regional language; Kiswahili. Yet I would say that 99% or more of foreign missionary inputs into the region come through and are in English. (UK expatriate, living in Kenya)

Both the formal study process, undertaken among individuals who had come through a nomination process in their institutions and denominations, and the informal online consultations, characterised by unrestricted freedom to contribute, interpret, and direct conversation, had a vital place in the preparations for Edinburgh 2010. Since some of the formal Edinburgh 2010 delegates were also participants in the online social network, the conversation was two-way, and the insights of volunteer

[8] Current estimates put the 'population' of Facebook at more than 500 million individuals – if measured alongside physical nations, it would be the third largest, after China and India.

[9] Youth and Mission Coordinator for Edinburgh 2010.

contributors around the world were able to be a factor in the thoughts of participants leading up to (and during) the conference.

As the communications team shifted its focus from building international interest in Edinburgh 2010 to the task of making the speeches, workshops, and liturgies of the conference program itself accessible to all those who could not attend, it was decided to maintain this two-way character of conversation. The Edinburgh 2010 website continued to be a practical venue for sharing delegates' speeches and essays, and for live video broadcasting of sessions and celebrations – but the conversation migrated from Facebook to another online social networking hub that was better equipped to facilitate real-time reporting on the conference's concurrent themed sessions: Twitter.

Twitter's model of communication involves publicly visible posts of only 140-characters, but with a unique system of linking posts by many people on the same topics. Users create 'hashtags' (for example: the inclusion of the tag '#th1' signified a post's relevance to Theme 1 of the study process), which can be then employed by other users to make their own comments on the subject. We used the *edinburgh2010* Twitter account to share updates, as they were occurring, from each of the study process workshops at the conference. A member of the communications team was stationed in each of the concurrent sessions, sharing items of interest with those members of the global Twitter community who had chosen to 'follow' Edinburgh 2010 (i.e. to have our updates appear, in real time, on their own pages). Examples of insights and questions broadcast from the study process sessions include:

- Seminaries can too easily become cemeteries – theological hermeneutics must incorporate the freedom of Holy Spirit...' #th6
- 1910's urgency to conquer diversity has paradigm-shifted into 2010's reluctance to smother diversity... #th2
- Does mission only belong to the Christian Church? Or is it larger than we are? #th3 (#th2)
- If only the 1910 delegates could witness us at #e2010 importing video from YouTube to hear global voices on postmodern architectures... #th3

Simultaneously, the Edinburgh 2010 website was extracting these Twitter posts and filtering them by theme (using the simple hashtag system we had designed: #th1 for Theme 1, #th2 for Theme 2, #tr7 for Transversal 7, etc…), so that each study process page on the website would display running commentary from within the theme workshops at the conference itself.

Twitter, moreover, is set up to facilitate multi-directional conversation. By including the tag '@edinburgh2010', any user in the world could direct a comment or question to our media stewards at the conference – contributions which we could either respond to or pass on to the delegates to whom they were directed. One Twitter user (USA), in response to a delegate's discussion of mission spirituality during the Theme 9 workshop, suggests: '*@edinburgh2010* A spirituality of mission is outward focused. It contemplates God's presence in the world and not simply in my heart.' Another user (Germany), seeking clarification of a delegate's comment, asks: '*@edinburgh2010* What do you mean with Empire? What do you mean with Mammon? Is it the same? What can I do not to be a complice [sic] of Empire?' Many other users (in South Korea, Jamaica, El Salvador, etc), sensing that their own networks would gain value from the updates from Edinburgh 2010, 'retweeted' our posts so that anyone following them would see these selected posts from the conference. We see here, again, the symbiosis between the human interaction of delegates in a room together and the online community of interested parties, however remote they were.

Unlike in 1910, no 'continuation committee' is being established for Edinburgh 2010 – that is, the stakeholders of the event have chosen to leave the achievements and vision of Edinburgh 2010 in the hands and hearts of the delegates as they return to their own contexts. But, while there is no official long-term, institutional successor to Edinburgh 2010, a different sort of continuation has begun to flourish organically on the Internet.

Alongside the many fruits of the Edinburgh 2010 study process, liturgical creativity, and common call to the churches, surely we must name the bonds of friendship that were formed among delegates and staff in Edinburgh. In 1910, maintaining such bonds would require either geographical proximity or tremendous effort, but today's participants have gone their separate ways and rejoined their networks, confident that a new meta-network of ecumenical conversation and collaboration has come into being. Services like Twitter and Facebook are of great value in such an international community: for instance, a new Facebook group, 'Generation 2010', already serves as a blank slate in this regard, nothing more or less than a convenient space for assembly, discussion, sharing, and open-ended cooperation between those individuals who met at Edinburgh 2010 and their own local communities, now woven further into contact with one another. For this younger generation and those to follow it, the Internet is not so much a new technology as it is a natural habitat – and a Church that is fluent in online communication and community is neither a novelty nor a sideshow, but rather a visible, practical participation in mission 'from everywhere to everywhere'.[10]

[10] To dig down into the significance of this bountiful and 'viral' phrase of modern missiology, see (i) Michael Nazir-Ali, *From Everywhere to Everywhere: A World View of Christian Mission* (London: Collins, 1990); (ii) David Bosch, *Transforming Mission: Paradigm Shifts in Theology of Mission* (Maryknoll, NY: Orbis Books, 1991), 368-510, Chapter 12: Elements of an Emerging Ecumenical Missionary Paradigm; (iii) the Edinburgh 2010 study process documents, e.g. Theme 8: Mission and Unity: Ecclesiology and Mission, in Daryl Balia & Kirsteen Kim, ed., *Edinburgh 2010, Volume II: Witnessing to Christ Today* (Oxford: Regnum Books

Reception

Since our focus is on the use of the Internet as a collaborative medium in mission, it is necessary not only to present the manner in which online resources were used by the conference, but also to examine how they were *responded to* by individuals and churches around the world – indeed, 'Edinburgh 2010' is the sum of all these directions of communication and commitment, not only the physical coming together for five days in a single city.

Of the online consultations that he coordinated on Facebook, Sandvig writes:

> I was a bit surprised at the level of discussion and debate that was able to be conducted online. I usually prefer to discuss when I see people face to face, but I think the benefits of having these discussions online in such a way is that it allowed people to clearly articulate their well-thought points, without having to worry about being interrupted or cut off. People were free to post their ideas along with everyone else's.[11]

In the records of the online consultations, we see that four or five individuals tended to be the most consistent contributors, offering thoughts on every topic and question. In a communal discussion in person, this sort of enthusiasm would almost certainly come at the expense of less vocal participants, who might have trouble contributing their thoughts in the fast-paced environment. Online, however, this imbalance was evened out. Participants who only posted one comment were not beholden to the pace of the conversation, and could contribute what they wished, when they wished, confident that their posts would be visible to those reading the proceedings at a later time. Some of these isolated comments were taken up and discussed by others, since the agenda was flexible and informal. Likewise, although the conversation took place in English, participants were not penalised for untrained use of the language, as they might have been in a more formal setting of education or publication. The culture of such social networking websites prioritises content over polished form and grammar, and accordingly, native speakers communicated with non-native speakers without hierarchy.

On Twitter, as we reported live on the conference sessions and press conferences, other users responded directly to us, referenced our updates in their own musings, and shared insights from conference delegates with their own networks. Many of the direct responses were simply encouraging messages in support of the Twitter project[12] or particular questions about conference content. But we also received messages of criticism, which

---

International, 2010), 206; and (iv) the Edinburgh 2010 Common Call, §7.

[11] Kirk Sandvig, email to author (July 2010).

[12] For example, '*@edinburgh2010* Keep up the good work. We're getting a good flavour of what's going on'. Or, in one instance, '*@edinburgh2010* Thanks! I used this tweet in my sermon this morning'!

were frequently the most valuable as we endeavoured to use our Twitter account as a litmus test of international sentiment about the discussions in Edinburgh. One user challenged the notion that the conference delegates are capable of issuing a 'common call' to the churches: '*@edinburgh2010*. The Common Call isn't really common until it is entrusted to, challenged by, and embraced by the faithful people of the world'. Another user took issue with an admittedly glib post about understanding other religious traditions before making truth claims about them, and writes: '*@edinburgh2010* What?? The Qur'an in Sunday School? You have to be kidding. It's hard enough to teach Christianity there.'

Here we see one of the main shortcomings of using this otherwise useful tool for managing discussions on many topics simultaneously: the limitations of brevity and speed. By condensing the complex and thoughtful contributions of the delegates into 140-character bursts, much subtlety of the thought process that led to particular comments could be obscured, leaving the final product fragmented and seemingly shallow.[13]

Finally, an essential caveat: during the conference, the optimistic ideal of the Internet as an in-between territory with equal access for all was itself called into question. Despite the equalising factors discussed above, a delegate from Malawi, Fulata Mbano-Moyo pointed out that the availability and speed of online resources varies dramatically along lines of nationality and wealth. She argued that the extreme slowness and patchy accessibility of the Internet in Sub-Saharan Africa and elsewhere can make the hosting of educational or conversational communities online (or indeed, our proposed use of the 'website as a global platform') unintentionally but no less functionally stratified. It is telling that, although users from over 195 countries accessed the website's contents in 2010 alone, use was overwhelmingly concentrated in Europe and North America.[14]

So, does the Internet – a milieu that will only continue to evolve and integrate with daily life and culture – represent an unprecedented communicative and collaborative potential for human beings in an ever-more-connected society? Or, is it more akin to an attention-sapping, wealth-prioritising mall of endless distractions from the earthly and spiritual dimensions of the gospel? Or both simultaneously? These

[13] Moreover, there is a clear consequence to the real-time reporting model that we used to share the fruits of the conference sessions online: because updates were posted as they occurred at the conference, many comments that were intended only as thought experiments or rough proposals for later refinement could easily be misinterpreted as official stances on the issues. Where we had space, therefore, we tried to distinguish in our Twitter broadcast between prepared remarks and first musings – though such space was frequently lacking.

[14] Data were drawn from a report of the Edinburgh 2010 website analytics. India, Australia, and South Korea were exceptions to this trend, although, not surprisingly, these are nations with particularly developed Internet infrastructures – in their wealthier areas.

questions are taken up in more depth in the online Appendix, both from the perspective of computer scientists and from that of theologians with a particular interest in the conditions and cultures of postmodernity. Without historical distance, however, we see only the first sparks of the potential and pitfalls to which the twenty-first century Church will be subject, and we cannot fully comprehend (much less adequately respond to) these issues. They will need to be lived out, habitually discerned, and improvised in faith.

Conclusion

Without fluency in the many modes of online interaction, churches are increasingly isolated and mute relative to their neighbours; at the same time, churches can serve by providing sanctuary from the frenetic pace and noise of network culture. No context is free of perversity, nor empty of sublimity; the Internet, indeed, is awash in triviality and violence, and yet is filled with the multi-directional and unexpected currents of the Holy Spirit. I would suggest that on the Internet, like other settings of communal human flourishing, the gospel and its disciples have a presence that can affirm and defend the life abundant (John 10:10) of our *oikumene*, our one, co-inhabited Earth.

Edinburgh 2010 integrated online technologies and communities not only in its broadcast of conference proceedings but also in its very identity as a multi-denominational, multi-national, multi-ethnic, multi-directional conversation about the trajectory of the Church's witness in this century. In this sense, the use of our website and our social networking hubs is a development in both the tools of mission and the character of the ecumenical missionary community. This evolution is incomplete: It makes use of immature media for communication and incomplete systems for collaboration. Yet, we can be confident that even this modest innovation required of the agents of mission as we came together for Edinburgh 2010 is a confirmation that the mission of the Church continues to be discovered and lived into being.[15] We engage in mission, but never exhaust it.

[15] Cf. Bosch, *Transforming Mission*, 10 – 'The missionary task is as coherent, broad and deep as the need and exigencies of human life'.

REFLECTIONS

Mrs Anastasia Vassiliadou, Aristotle University of Thessaloniki, Greece[1]

We gathered this year in Edinburgh and in so many other places around the globe to celebrate the one hundred years from that first World Missionary Conference, to reflect and to pray together. We gathered to rejoice for what has been achieved all these years with the help and power of the Holy Spirit, to repent for things we have done when we failed to listen to and follow the Spirit, and to ask for a renewed energy, looking together for a renewed vision of the mission of the Church of the Triune God.

It is a common conviction that we have come a long way in the last one hundred years. We do live in a very different world; the face of Christianity is very different worldwide and our theology and practice of mission could not but change significantly. And the main aim of Edinburgh 2010 was indeed to reflect together on that changed reality in relation to God's ever unchanged call to participate in His love and our responsibility in response to it. It came out very clearly from the study process as well as from the Edinburgh conference itself that our understanding of mission can no longer be a triumphalistic one. Neither can it have an expansional character with imperialistic attitude and behaviour, as was the case in the past. The shift was clear, from *evangelisation* of the whole world, to *witnessing* to Christ in humility; from a tendency to *proselytise* to *reconciliation* and *dialogue* with people of other faiths and ideologies; from *triumphalism* and power, to *humbleness,* vulnerability and mutuality. As you all know, there were no Orthodox participants in 1910. In 2010 there were not many either, but I believe that the encounter with Orthodox theology in the last century played a role in that paradigm shift, especially in regard to the emphasis on the Holy Spirit, the understanding of mission as witness, and the relations with people of other faiths. It remains after all an Orthodox position that before and above all mission should not aim at the propagation or transmission of intellectual convictions, doctrines, moral commands, and so on, but at the transmission of the life of communion that exists in God.

---

[1] Anastasia Vassiliadou, MTh, is a theologian, working as a teacher of religious education in public school. She is a member of the Church of Greece (Eastern Orthodox) and a member of the World Council of Churches' Commission for World Mission and Evangelism. Reflection given in the final plenary.

Being an Orthodox myself and coming originally from the 'ecumenical' tradition (this is not a contradiction in terms as some may believe!), I found my home in mission and in the Commission for World Mission and Evangelism (CWME) of the World Council of Churches. It was in the light of mission that the search for unity and the struggle for justice made sense to me. And I cannot imagine mission but through unity and through justice. The Orthodox often like to refer to mission as a liturgy *after* the Liturgy, but also – as rightly underlined in Edinburgh by CWME moderator Metropolitan Geevarghese Mor Coorilos – there is a liturgy *before* the Liturgy, which is reconciliation. My understanding of the church can only be in the sense of a missional one. And by that I mean a church that is not closed to herself, but opening up to the world, reaching out to the entire cosmos, embracing the whole creation, giving witness to the Kingdom of God. I was pleased to see that holistic understanding of mission reflected in the Common Call, which, in spite of any criticism one might make is a great text in the sense that it covers a great range of issues and is at the same time affirmed by a great range of Christian Churches.

I am not here tonight to give you an account or an evaluation of this Conference that is ending tonight, or rather tomorrow with the worship. I am called to share with you my personal reflection on this event and invite you to do the same, here among ourselves, and back home in our communities. I wish to stay with one aspect of this Conference which is very important to me. That is the uniqueness of this event. And I would like to congratulate and thank the organisers, the stakeholders, the General Council, those who contributed to the Study process in one way or another, the hosting churches and the staff, for believing in this common celebration and working so hard for it, often against all odds. For the first time so many different churches and Christian traditions came together to help make this mission conference happen. And I see hope in that; I see an opportunity to heal the wounds of the past and hold together the call for mission and the call for unity – not just the one at the expense of the other. This is achieved not by softening the disagreements nor by hiding the burning issues, but by listening carefully to each other, engaging in genuine dialogue, disagreeing and challenging each other, but nevertheless staying together. We have been arguing for too long over the priority of evangelism versus unity, and hence over the authentic inheritance of Edinburgh 1910. In a world that is suffering from fragmentation, alienation and despair, our determination to continue staying and working together is more than anything else a sign that our witness is both a credible and an authentic one.

I do not know to what to what extent all of us (my Orthodox constituency and my ecumenical partners, together with the Evangelical and Pentecostal sisters and brothers) would at the end of the road feel comfortable with the enlarged constituency we find ourselves in after Edinburgh 2010 (although this process of reintegration has already started for CWME in Athens in 2005)? We probably would not all agree, but that is OK. Our human weakness and failure are scattered when we listen to 'what the Holy Spirit says to the Churches' (Rev. 2:7). It was after all when our churches felt comfortable that they failed to listen to the Spirit.

I personally very often struggle with the notion of *evangelism*, as well as with the *Great Commission,* as these terms are often understood – and at the same time revered – by the evangelical constituency. I might even feel uncomfortable with the spirituality and the mentality of the rising Pentecostal communities in Korea, in China, in Africa, in Latin America, and elsewhere. I might be confused by the practice and the theology of some of the African Instituted Churches. I am sure many of you also struggle to come to terms with, or even feel uncomfortable and confused by, the theology and the practice of the Orthodox Church! Especially when some quarters of her do not leave any ecclesial space to non-Orthodox! But I cannot hide my personal feeling that I am inspired by the zeal, the creativity, the enthusiasm and the deep and authentic faith of so many men and women from all over the world and from all spectrums of Christianity.

One may ask, 'Have we reached a common understanding or even a common language on issues of missiology, ecclesiology and anthropology?' The answer is definitely, no. It would be dishonest and superficial to say so. Does that mean we have failed? By no means! A great deal of progress has been made in the past one hundred years in the field of ecumenical dialogue – which in fact started as a necessity for mission itself – and this has shaped our mission theology and practice. It is true that in Edinburgh we did not really touch many difficult issues that remain controversial and divisive among us. Is this the price of being together? It should not be and it does not have to be. I believe that is the challenge lying ahead of us: to continue our journey together and include more partners on the way, no matter how uncomfortable and disturbing that might be, without compromising the truth and without hiding the divisions and disagreements. We have everything to gain by continuing to talk to each other, as Bishop Kallistos Ware reminds us. Only if we remain together, will we learn to appreciate and understand each other better. We will be mutually accountable and will be challenged, and even changed, in the direction of being faithful to the 'will of God'. But isn't that part of the new understanding of mission that we are advocating? Risking vulnerability, being humble, receiving the other instead of being powerful, self-sufficient, triumphant and imposing our perspective to the other.

Let us make sure that for the next centenary celebrations we (in fact our children or our children's children) will all be there as one to give praise, ask for forgiveness and seek enlightenment for the mission of the church, the mission of God.

Dr Vinoth Ramachandra, Secretary for Dialogue & Social Engagement, International Fellowship of Evangelical Students (IFES)[1]

It has been a great pleasure to participate in this centenary conference as well as in the study process leading up to it. I am impressed by the way we have worked hard to listen to each other and to be challenged by one another. In terms of representation by ecclesiastical traditions, I think this has been one of the most comprehensive held in the past hundred years. But in some other aspects we do not seem to have progressed far beyond Edinburgh 1910: the proportion of women here, for instance, has not increased greatly, young people are largely absent, and many of the Africans and Asians present here seem to have made their permanent homes in the global North. So can this gathering be considered truly representative of the world church? And, except for Dana Robert's opening address, I confess I haven't sensed the passion for the Gospel and the deep sense of accountability to God for the nations that resonates through much of the 1910 reports.

However, I want to highlight this evening one massive 'blind spot' concerning mission which prevails in many churches and which this conference has, in some ways, tended to perpetuate.

We seem to have forgotten that the primary way the church impacts the world is not through its programmes, or by multiplying religious professionals, or starting more mission agencies and ecumenical commissions; but, rather, through the daily work of Christian men and women in offices, schools, factories, village councils, research laboratories, company board rooms, and so on. These are the contemporary sites of Christian mission. Yet all the speakers who have addressed us during this conference have been Bishops and senior pastors, seminary professors or leaders of Christian institutions. We seem to talk only with one other and publish papers for one another to read. But are we listening to the millions of Christians who are following Jesus and witnessing to him in the secular world?

I was in Malaysia a few months ago and I spent a memorable morning with a handful of committed Christian politicians who were MPs representing different opposition political parties in that country. They came from a variety of church traditions, including Roman Catholic and Pentecostal. I asked them 'What is the biggest source of frustration you experience in your work?' I expected them to say something like 'The

[1] Reflection given in the final plenary.

compromises we need to make as party members', but instead they were unanimous in their answer: 'Our church'. They did not receive any support from their churches, whether in the form of regular prayer, financial assistance or volunteers to help in implementing social policies or just running their offices. One woman told me her church raised huge funds to send cross-cultural missionaries and young people on short-term 'mission trips' to other parts of Asia. But their work as politicians was not considered as 'mission'. The only time the church leaders showed any interest in what they did was when Christians themselves suffered political harassment.

This story is repeated all over the world. My wife and I work primarily with Christian in secular occupations, helping them to live out the Gospel and communicate God's truth and justice in the fields of science, business, the arts, medicine, education, and so on. These men and women who engage 'Christianly' with the public square are at the cutting-edge of mission. They face huge ethical challenges thrown up by, say, new medical technologies or new social networking media, genetic engineering, venture capitalism and hedge funds, anti-terrorist legislation, euthanasia, climate change and biodiversity loss. These all call for deep missionary engagement and missiological reflection. India and China together produce more science and engineering graduates every year than North America and Europe combined. But Asian mission studies dissertations and the bulk of articles in mission studies journals focus on historical studies of religious sects and denominations, traditional tribal cultures or exotic new religious movements.

It seems that we have been blinded by the neat divisions we have been drawn between theology, ethics and mission. Those boundaries need to be deconstructed. We have been reminded in recent years that all theology is mission theology, that the church does theology 'on the road' and not just in the library or the pulpit. But then theological education has to be re-oriented radically around the lives of 'lay' people, not the agendas of clergy and mission societies. Social and political ethics has become the locus of evangelical proclamation.

We need to go further and deconstruct the boundary between clergy and laity. Yes, the church needs leaders. But clericalism has crippled the witness of the church. There are many thoughtful people who are profoundly attracted to Jesus but frankly 'put off' by the church. They see a lack of integrity: a huge gulf between the message the church proclaims and the way its leaders behave, not least towards one another. How did a socially subversive, egalitarian movement centred in worshipping and following a crucified Jew change so quickly into a hierarchical, patriarchal and anti-Semitic religious institution? Whether we are Pentecostals, Eastern Orthodox or Roman Catholics we need to keep returning to and humbly pondering that old question. The younger churches seem destined to repeat the sins of the older churches. We in Asia and Africa cannot keep blaming

Christendom. I am amused by how many of our Southern bishops and clergy who bitterly condemn Western Christendom cling so tenaciously to titles and status honour and forms of address (and dress!) that they have inherited from Christendom.

In my experience, 'lay' men and women of different church backgrounds rarely have problems working together in facing common concerns. They have no sacred turf to protect. Remember that John R. Mott, the architect of the 1910 Edinburgh conference was himself a layman. It was his experience of working with the Student Volunteer movement and the YMCA that laid the ecumenical ground work for that conference. If left to church leaders and church-based mission societies, Edinburgh 1910 is unlikely to have happened.

And if, as Dana Roberts reminded us on the first morning of this conference, one of the unintended consequences of Edinburgh 1910 was the dismantling of the boundaries between so-called Christian nations and non-Christian nations, can we pray that one of the consequences of this conference will be the steady erosion of clergy-laity boundaries and the recovery of the priesthood of all believers? And also that the identifying labels 'ecumenical', 'evangelical', 'charismatic', and so on, will also be dissolved, because they are unnecessary hindrances to our common mission? But for that to happen, we may have to be more intentional than our forebears.

Rev. Dr Stephen B. Bevans, SVD, Louis J. Luzbatek, S.V.D. Professor of Mission and Culture, Catholic Theological Union, USA[1]

This evening I would like to share with you three things: A hope, a surprise, and a lament.

First, a hope. In the last several days I've been wondering who among the young people at this conference – the stewards, the young delegates – will emerge as the future leaders of the church in the next several decades of our twenty-first century. Who will be this century's William Temple? Who will be a twenty-first century John Baillie? Who will grow into the stature of a V. S. Azariah? A Pandita Ramabai?

We do not know, of course. We do know, however, that the leadership of the church in this century will almost certainly pass from the affluent global North to the poorer global South. We do know that many more women will assume leadership in our churches. My hope this evening is that the leadership of the future – many of whom are surely among us this evening – will lead with the conviction that the church, ultimately, is not important. Rather, they will realise that of ultimate importance is the Reign of God, and that the church exists only to serve that already-but-not-yet Reign by being a missionary church.

Second, a surprise. I remember the first evening when I went into the dining room to have dinner. I got my food, and saw a man sitting alone, so I asked if I could join him. At first he said no, that he was waiting for someone, but then he said yes – I could certainly join him and the person he was waiting for. When that person arrived, he introduced me to the general secretary of the Organisation of African Instituted Churches – Nicta Lubaale – and I was blown away. Here I was just a few hours at the conference and I had met someone who was trying to coordinate the churches that are the most vibrant and fastest growing in the world today. It was amazing. Throughout the Conference I saw Nicta here and there and really enjoyed talking to him. And in the subsequent days I met person after person who opened me up to ideas and experiences that I had never had, or ever thought about. We are a large, incredibly diverse, unbelievably rich, wonderfully joyful church. I kind of knew it – but I was surprised to find out just how true it actually is. Our God is a God of surprises – and God certainly was working these days to surprise me!

Third, a lament. I could actually mention a few laments. That the conference did not have more input. That it was still in many ways

[1] Reflection given in the final plenary.

dominated by white males. That we did not honour sufficiently Professor Andrew Walls at the Conference. But my lament is much more personal than all of these: it is that I did not dance at the ceilidh last night.

I lament this because I think that dancing is a really great image of both the ecumenical movement and Christian mission. In dancing, in mission, and in our quest for unity we have to take the risk of getting out on the floor. We have to in some ways make fools of ourselves, make mistakes, literally step on toes, accept the fact that we often do not know what we are doing. I have talked and written about how mission is about joining the dance of the triune God through the world. But last night I was too shy, too ashamed, too timid, and I lament this.

This has been an incredible few days. I have high hopes for the future, I have been wonderfully surprised, I lament that I did not dance as a symbol of what I very deeply believe. May all of us continue to hope, continue to be surprised, and not be afraid, like I was, to take the risk of the dance.

Dr Ken Christoph Miyamoto, Kobe Shoin Women's University, Kobe, Japan[1]

Dear Friends, Sisters and Brothers in Christ! I thank you for giving me an opportunity to offer you a brief reflection on this historic Edinburgh 2010 Conference. I am also very grateful to God and all of you for giving me a chance to be part of this great experience of Christian unity in mission.

Since I came to Edinburgh a few days ago, I have met so many brothers and sisters in Christ. Some of them are quite different from me. I have heard a variety of voices that came from various parts of the world and from various Christian traditions. I am now full of feelings, ideas and thoughts. I am sure it will take me a while to digest and organise them within myself.

What has amazed me most throughout the Conference was the repeated experience of convergence of ideas and thoughts. While they have their roots in very diverse and different contexts, cultures, and traditions, they have come together through discussions and produced the visions that are mutually similar and that most of us are eager to embrace in spite of the remaining differences and disagreements among us. In our daily lives, we seldom have such an extraordinary experience. Rather, we often find that even minor differences cause people to stay apart from each other. Thus, I could not help but sense the powerful operation of the Holy Spirit in the midst of our experiences of convergence here in Edinburgh.

It is indeed the Holy Spirit that has brought us here to Edinburgh. The Holy Spirit has united us in our common vision. And the Holy Spirit is now sending us back with the common call to a world full of conflicts, hatreds, sufferings, sorrows, despairs, and death. With God's help, I would like to respond to this call to unity and mission.

There is, however, one fact we should never forget nor take for granted. We have prayed together; we have shared together; we have worshipped together. But one important matter has still been missing. There has been no Lord's supper, no Holy Communion, no Eucharist shared in by all together during the Conference. We have celebrated the Eucharist in the confessional observances held every morning. However, we have failed once again to come together to celebrate the One Common Eucharist. We should not leave this sad fact behind in our euphoria over unity. We should remember that we are not truly one as long as we are unable to celebrate this divine sacrament together.

---

[1] Due to lack of time this reflection, which was prepared in advance for the Closing Celebration, was not actually delivered on 6 June.

In a country like Japan, where Christians constitute a tiny minority, the disunity around the Lord's Table is nothing but a scandal. While we as Christians invite our people to join us in the acts of love and compassion, we are in fact failing to love and embrace each other in the very presence of Jesus Christ. Isn't it an embarrassing irony that our divisions become most visible around the Lord's Table? How can we explain this grave failure to our people? Are we really qualified to tell them to love? Are we really followers of Christ?

This is the fundamental contradiction that still exists at the heart of our mission. We have to repent seriously and ask God to help us to overcome our own brokenness. Let's hope that we can make it better, with God's help, when we gather here next time. Thank you!

Ms Sarah Newland-Martin, Ecumenical Disabilities Network[1]

I was asked to share at the closing of the Edinburgh 2010 Conference what stood out for me during the period, and this was the importance of forgiveness.

In one of the small group sittings, there was a discussion on forgiveness. During the sharing, it was pointed out that when we forgive, someone suffers severe hurt and that it is not very easy to forgive. Examples of persons who were able to forgive for deeds that were done to them were suggested. These examples included persons such as Nelson Mandela, people who have been ostracised in their countries, and the list went on. I asked whether I could share with the group how I was able to let go and let God take control after meeting my mother.

I told the small group that when I met my mother at age 24, I encountered deep pain and asked myself how I could forgive someone who abandoned me in the hospital. It caused great pain and I did not know how to deal with it. There were many nights as a child growing up when my mind wondered about who was my mother and why I did not have a mother like all the children at the institution where I grew up. Their parents visited; I did not have any.

At age 24 when I met my mother I became very ill and almost died from shock. How do you forgive when you had no idea or knowledge of who mother was? I had to grapple with this question. But through it all, I knew I could depend on God and I had to find a way to get help to deal with the matter of forgiving my mother for what happened. My Pastor, the Rev. Dr Burchell Taylor gave a sermon series on forgiveness and I purchased the tapes. Every evening I would come home and listen to the tapes, crying my heart out and wanting to find out how I could let go of this pain of not being able to forget what I went through growing up in two institutions.

Several verses from the Bible helped me: 'Bear with each other and forgive whatever grievances you may have against one another. Forgive as the Lord forgave you' (Col. 3:13; NIV). I learnt that we forgive by faith, out of obedience. That since forgiveness goes against our nature, we must forgive by faith, whether we feel like it or not. We must trust God to do the work in us that needs to be done so that the forgiveness will be complete. I believe God honours our commitment to obey Him and our desire to please him when we choose to forgive. He completes the work in his time.

[1] Due to lack of time this reflection, which was prepared in advance for the Closing Celebration, was not actually delivered on 6 June.

We must continue to forgive (our job), by faith, until the work of forgiveness (the Lord's job), is done in our hearts: 'And I am certain that God, who began the good work within you, will continue his work until it is finally finished on the day when Christ Jesus returns' (Phil. 1:6; NLT). Corrie Ten Boom, a Christian woman who survived a Nazi concentration camp during the Holocaust, said, 'Forgiveness is to set a prisoner free, and to realise the prisoner was you'. We will know the work of forgiveness is complete when we experience the freedom that comes as a result. We are the ones who suffer most when we choose not to forgive. When we do forgive, the Lord sets our hearts free from the anger, bitterness, resentment and hurt that previously imprisoned us.

Most times, however, forgiveness is a slow process: 'Then Peter came to Jesus and asked, "Lord, how many times shall I forgive my brother when he sins against me? Up to seven times?" Jesus answered, "I tell you, not seven times, but seventy-seven times"' (Matt. 18:21-22; NIV). This answer by Jesus makes it clear that forgiveness is not easy. It is not a one-time choice and then we automatically live in a state of forgiveness. Forgiveness may require a lifetime of forgiving, but it is important to the Lord. One must continue forgiving until the matter is settled in our heart.

I have found that prayer is one of the best ways to break down the wall of unforgiveness in my heart. When I begin to pray on how to deal with what I went through, God gave me new eyes to see and a new heart to care for my mother. As I pray, I start to see her as God sees her, and I realise that she is precious to the Lord. I also see myself in a new light, just as guilty of sin and failure as her. I too am in need of forgiveness. If God did not withhold his forgiveness from me, why should I withhold my forgiveness from my mother?

Today, I have an excellent relationship with my mother and thank God for His enabling and giving me the courage to let go and let Him be. The conference provided the opportunity to share some of these deep needs we have as individuals which so often we do not get the chance to deal with. This parable of forgiveness may also help us as we try to heal the wounds of years of hurt in Christian relations.

Statements

A Statement by Pentecostal Participants

We acknowledge the historical significance of Edinburgh 1910 and rejoice that we have been counted among those gathered together in Edinburgh 2-6 June 2010 to mark the centennial.

The twentieth century gave clear testimony that although we were not in attendance at Edinburgh 1910, we have taken our rightful place on the landscape of contemporary Christianity. We would like to express our gratitude to those who prepared and participated in the Edinburgh 2010 conference and for giving us the opportunity to be able to affirm the significance of the global mission call joining a diverse fellowship of believers in Christ.

As Pentecostal delegates we participated at Edinburgh 2010 in the nine themes as well as on all levels of the study processes. We have shared issues and concerns. We listened, prayed and learned together, with an attitude of love and respect, building bridges rather than creating chasms, divisions and barriers. We affirm the divine mission mandate to reconcile the whole of God's creation in Christ and do this across denominational and confessional lines. We are to engage in effective witnessing [to] the Good News of Jesus Christ to all parts of the world, in the power of the Holy Spirit and to the glory of God. This vision reflects the heart of God and belongs to the very nature of the Church.

We appreciate that Pentecostals are recognised in a positive way. At the same time we leave with the challenge to find fuller expressions of global Pentecostalism in an ecumenical context. We also noticed a disparity of the language used and concerns expressed between the global North and global South. We must be careful that the academic voices of the North do not wash away the narrative claims of the South. As Pentecostals we are acquainted with both linguistic traditions, we realise that we can play an important role as bridge builders. This would truly benefit the whole Body of Christ. Furthermore, we are deeply aware that Christians need the help of the Holy Spirit. Through the Spirit's guidance and empowerment we will be able to answer God's mandate to the world.

We humbly acknowledge that it is God who has the last word. Issues that relate to mission and unity should not drift into intellectual manoeuvrings. It must be the prayer of all people of God, wherever they are, to hear what the Spirit has to say to the churches so that we can turn to God and our common call can be, 'Come, Lord Jesus!'

Pentecostal delegates: Rev. Dr.Miguel Alvarez, USA; Mr. Kenneth Ben, Cook Islands; Dr. Cheryl Bridges Johns, USA; Dr. David Daniels, USA;

Dr. Anne Dyer, UK; Mrs. Dynnice Rosanne Engcoy, Philippines; Dr. Samson Fatokun, Nigeria; Rev. Dr. Harold D. Hunter, USA; Rev. Dr. Veli Matti Kärkkäinen, Finland; Dr. Elijah Jong Fil Kim, USA; Rev. Steven K.L. Kum, Malaysia; Dr. Julie Ma, Korea; Dr. Wonsuk Ma, Korea; Rev. Rauno Mikkonen, Finland; Apostle Dr. Opoku Onyinah, Ghana; Rev. Philippe Ouedraogo, Burkina Faso; Rev. Dr. Tavita Pagaialii, Samoa; Dr. Jean-Daniel Plüss, Switzerland; Rev. Dr. Daniel Ramirez, USA; Dr. Elisabeth Del Carmen Salazar-Sanzana, Chile; Rev. Bal Krishna Sharma, Nepal.

STATEMENT BY INDIGENOUS PARTICIPANTS

Edinburgh 2010 – A 'Majority' Report

The Edinburgh 2010 Conference was impressive in many ways. To bring together a body representing such a broad cross section of Christian experience is worth noting in itself, regardless of the outcome or product of the gathering. Most who gathered were clearly committed to making the commemoration of Edinburgh 1910 a means to an enriched future for Christian mission. More could be said along these lines, but we would like to say that the greatest aspect of the conference was the simple act of gathering with such a multi-faceted community of worship. Those essential and basic acts of Christian faith are the moments when we most clearly perceive, if only for a twinkling, some of the manifold and ineffable goodness of our Creator's Living Word in Creation. To engage together with such a group was beautiful.

Unfortunately, no event is perfect. This is true even and, perhaps, especially when a gathering, like 2010, has such sprawling goals. When there is so much that can go wrong, there is always much that can be critiqued. But a Christian event of this scope and character demands to be evaluated by the inherent and insistent priority that God's promised presence places in our midst: being able to look beyond and through the event towards a compelling vision of the future; a vision that will do justice to the expansive horizon of the God promised future. It is that horizon that provides the only adequate basis for both critical and constructive valuations of the meaning of Edinburgh 2010.

It is from that conviction that we point to the closing of the conference as the moment that most adequately presented the breadth and depth of the missiological challenges before us. For it was there that many of us from the Indigenous and Global Southern Community saw the difficulties that still obscure God's horizon presented most clearly and honestly. In our view, the optics of Edinburgh 2010 until that moment had been plain and consistent – the majority church was still largely present as a minority. As one of our members put it, 'While in 1910 there were only twenty non-Europeans present – Bishop Azariah, the most notable – in 2010 we were now present but not presented!'

We hasten to say that conversations with the conveners made clear that this was neither the intent nor the desire of the 2010 leadership. And yet in the audible and visual representations of the conference, as in the organisation of the events and activities, the influence appeared to be largely Western. Whether this was or was not noticed by others, this was its appearance to us. And, as is true in so many of the endeavours of the human community, perception is reality. Only one voice of the three who reflected on the week's activities in the closing – a global southern voice – made this connection and spoke of it with urgency. Perhaps the ethnocentrism that so often distorts cross-cultural encounters makes it difficult to be otherwise.

And that is precisely why we, from the global South, felt obliged to offer something as our contribution to the closing of the conference. Hence our hastily constructed offering identifying our presence (as near as we could manage we sat as a block, we sang a song of solidarity, we placed a passage of scripture on the screen capturing our feelings, and we spoke words of confession of our angst) and that made plain our concern – or as nearly so as we could manage in that brief time. Allow us to explain some of the framing of our thinking.

As the Apostle Paul notes very pointedly, consciousness is a limited and misty veil, even in such a broadly based collection of experience and resources as we were in Edinburgh. Within human and institutional limitations, our capacity to discern the power and purpose of God's Living Word is constrained even at the best of times. One of the central paradoxes of our faith is the way the shape of our existence, both in our everyday lives and in the course of human history, simultaneously reveals and obscures the presence of the Living Word of God. Edinburgh 2010 was not exempt from the paradox but, in Christ, we are inheritors of a great promise: Truth and Light will be revealed to us as we seek God in faith, hope and love. Thinking, praying and acting, spiritually and biblically, we may begin to distinguish some of the currents of the future God is calling us to inhabit.

Discerning the Way Forward with the Living Word

Those who attended 2010 received a glimpse of the breadth of what Lamin Sanneh has called 'world Christianity' – the Christianity that is, in very new ways, being formed and shaped by its emergence in diverse places and cultures around the world. Global Christianity was also represented, being those churches that spread around the world from a Western cultural origin. The sheer range and diversity of this new world of Christian faith was certainly one of the most captivating features of the conference. But, if we explore some of the deeper, not so obvious, currents present at the meeting, we may find meaning that brings this all much closer to home by transforming our understanding of the mystery of God's work in our world.

Many of those present at 2010, whether they were from the West or not, had received significant training in the Western theological and academic systems. The Enlightenment shaped protocols, the habits and assumptions of the Western academy and 'global Christianity' were never too far from the surface of the event, even though organisers took pains to look beyond the theological and ecclesial borders of the West. The continuing influence of Western patterns of thought was evident even among many of those who had received their most significant spiritual formation in other cultural regimes.

This is not surprising. Those trained in the Western system were taught that the traditions and cultural patterns of the West hold a unique and privileged role in the communication of Christian truth. The trajectory of the Word of God in Western history was considered singular and normative. Western culture was thought to be uniquely designed to be a vehicle of the Christian message. Regardless of their context or culture, Christian leaders were obliged to learning the Western tradition as a preliminary for their service. The requirement that clergy be well versed in the Western tradition has remained even though that tradition is no longer able to claim a positive cultural correlation with active Christian discipleship in many Western societies, never mind non-Western cultures and contexts. A retrospective is important here then, in understanding what a way forward may be.

As many of us understand them, had the objectives of the 1910 conference been fully met, most of us in the Indigenous and global Southern contexts would not have been uncomfortable during much of the 2010 conference. An examination of the policies and practices that emerged from or, were otherwise sanctioned by the 1910 gathering, either directly or – through inaction – indirectly, would show that the intent of missionary efforts from that point forward was an intensification of the ongoing process of Christianising and civilising those of us in the global Southern and Indigenous communities. The inescapable reality, had this been completely successful, is that we would have become 'Europeanised' and therefore completely comfortable in a Euro-centric setting. Our cultures and languages would have been absorbed into the body politic of the church and its surrounding society – at best tactically assimilated, becoming 'window dressing' to the historic and more 'authentic' culture(s) of the church; at worst our uniquenesses in the Creator's economy would have been eradicated entirely. Sadly, for some of the peoples we represent, the latter became their current reality.

In contrast to this narrative, 2010 uncovered, without much fanfare, the reality and strength of a number of alternative trajectories of faith: the Koreans spoke of the role of Confucianism and Shamanism in the development of their unique and vibrant faith; Pentecostals were able to correlate pre-Enlightenment faith and cosmologies with the development of their vital and modern movement across the world; and in Orthodoxy, in all of its variety, we were reminded that some of the alternative vehicles for Christian faith and development have a history at least as long as the West – perhaps, in some senses, longer.

We may now speak of multiple trajectories of the Word of God in Creation – through different cultures, different languages, and even different values. With no apparent human coordination, with no joint human planning, and with precious little human cooperation, there has been what appears to be a multiplicity of spontaneous divine eruptions of Christian faith, each with their own unique cultural genesis and pattern. Though many of these trajectories of the Word are almost unrecognisable in correlation with the others, they are now joint witnesses of the indefinable wisdom and relentless power of God's Spirit throughout Creation.

The revelation of this new manifold reality goes hand in hand with another theological and spiritual current that ran through the gathering. We speak here of the renewal and deepening – involving, in some cases, a necessary rejection of alternatives – of a more holistic way of being through an affirmation of a biblical understanding of the presence of God in Creation. This too may be described as an identification of the trajectory of the Living Word of God in and through Creation. This recognition is evident in the growing dissatisfaction with the mechanistic and bifurcated cosmologies of Western modernity. We may note these trends in the revival of a deeper Trinitarian theology evident throughout the West, in the emerging Pentecostal, Global Southern and Indigenous theologies, and in the emergence of quite a few more ecologically sensitive expressions of Christian faith. These all resound with compelling affirmations of God's abiding presence in Creation.

Discerning these inter-related currents, we may then identify a profound shift in the missiology of World Christianity: we are moving from a missiology premised on absence (the divine is not present until duly authorised human agents bring its truth) to a missiology premised on presence (the divine is always present, but definitively revealed and fulfilled in the Good News of Jesus Christ). As Maximus the Confessor, echoing the confident theology of the first chapter of John's Gospel said, 'The Word of God, who is God, wills in all things to work the mystery of his embodiment'.

For Indigenous people and those from the global South these currents are vitally significant and clearly evident flowing, for example, through a vibrant renewal of Indigenous Christian faith and a liberating rise from the destructive currents associated with colonialism. Yet, even while we note the flowering of Indigenous faith, we must note, its contrast: the high profile role that the Western churches played in the misery of colonialism, much of it related to Indigenous and other people's captivity in the wickedly paradoxical hermeneutical boxes of Western modernity. Massive growth of information – without a corresponding advance in wisdom – and massive sophistication in technology – without a parallel advance in compassion – led the way. Some of these boxes are still powerfully present and expanding their reach in the globalising culture of money.

It will be a while before we all begin to understand the implications of this new world we live in. The churches of the West have yet to comprehend, much less repudiate, the effect, on themselves and on others, of the destructive aspects of a mission strategy that frankly acknowledged its goal was to make Indigenous peoples disappear while simultaneously gentrifying other peoples to roles of servitude according to Western ideals. Sadly, it must be admitted that this strategy is still active in many parts of the world. It is absolutely clear, however, that this strategy does not represent God's future for Indigenous and other peoples.

In our view what this should have meant in the planning priorities for Edinburgh 2010 was that it be a commemorative focused more on the needed change in regards to the above issues – and not what seemed, to most of us, to be the central concern of the conference: a pursuit of the temporally elusive ideal of Christian unity. What appeared to be true was that the organisers felt a greater burden for this other major concern that emerged from or evolved out of the 1910 gathering. In our view, unity in the absence of an actively embraced diversity – and not just in ecclesial terms – is moot, having no framing substance to provide a reason for its need. We are not suggesting that unity is irrelevant or, unimportant – it is vital. But to attempt to create or emphasise this in light of some of the outcomes of Christian mission of this past century (in particular with respect to Indigenous peoples and those of the global South) which clearly and compellingly repudiated the very basis for this unity – common grace at the foot of the Cross of Jesus – is to leave ourselves open, in our humble opinion, to a similar set of outcomes in the ongoing mission to which we are called.

Instead, perhaps representatives of the churches that were, for the most part, complicit in the attempts at eradicating or assimilating us culturally and spiritually, could have stepped aside. Their prominence as presenters, organisers and guides in the conference commemorated, by default, the intentions of the 1910 gathering to assimilate all those who did not belong to a Western cultural framework. Instead, more representatives – both philosophically and pragmatically – from the majority church could have made all the difference, not only in the quality of the conference, but in the expansiveness of its meaning and impact. That this did not occur seemed odd, to some of us even absurd.

Obviously funding was of concern given travel costs and other competing interests. But if it were simply a matter of funding (given that the majority church continues to have the smallest amount of resources) would it not have been a more expedient and missiologically significant thing to make arrangements for someone within the UK who originated from those places in question in the South and among Indigenous peoples to have been there in their place irrespective of their political position within the church. What is more, those of us who were there from the majority church might have played a greater role in the public presence of the sessions and collective worship. Would it not have been appropriate to use the available collective resource to have brought together a larger, dare we say more proportional, representation of the global Southern and

Indigenous church rather than ensure there was a unity representative from each tradition?

On a parallel point, it was curious that the facilitators of the track for which one of the authors was present (the people who had done all the work in researching and preparing the track as well as getting the materials together) were set aside, during the session's presentation, in favour of a pair of individuals who appeared to carry the church unity agenda but who had done none of the work and had little personal familiarity with the issues. This appeared to be true in several of the tracks and, while they served as adequate moderators, made the discussion awkward, wooden and less engaged than it might otherwise have been.

We must conclude, by observing the most subtle of the currents of 2010. We speak here of the surprising resiliency of the Word of God and its power to transcend the intent and limitations of those who use or misuse it. By our experience, we affirm that the Good News is the power of God unto salvation, even when human folly tries to manipulate it for oppressive ends. But this power should not be considered an excuse nor is it a free pass for prejudice. The grace revealed in God's triumph in human weakness is a call to repentance. It is a call to renewed endeavour and awakened hope so that we might, in all our diversity, discern the currents of God's Word in Creation and Scripture. We have fresh and encouraging experience of the astounding and manifold miracles of the trajectory of the Word in all of Creation and, especially, in the poor and marginalised. Our task, calling, and privilege, as it appears to be clarified in both the strengths and weakness of Edinburgh 2010, is to discern this trajectory of God's Living Word and to live in concert with its horizon for Creation.

Rev. Terry LeBlanc
The Rt. Rev. Bishop Mark MacDonald
With contributions from Graeme Mundine and Maria Chavez de Quispe

MISSION IN THE TWENTY-FIRST CENTURY

Kirsteen Kim[1]

Like its predecessor one hundred years before, Edinburgh 2010 was a landmark event – but for a different reason. Edinburgh 2010 brought together an unprecedentedly wide coalition of different Christian churches, through umbrella bodies, in its celebration of world Christianity and study of what it means to 'witness to Christ today'. The General Council of Edinburgh 2010 included official representatives of all the main strands of Christianity worldwide: Catholic, Evangelical, Orthodox, and Pentecostal (and other independent groups such as African Independent Churches) as well as Protestant. This show of confessional unity in mission was cemented by the willingness of the final plenary that there should be a Common Call to mission articulated on behalf of the delegates in the Closing Celebration on 6 June 2010.

In this concluding chapter, I would like to examine the understanding of mission that informed the Edinburgh 2010 project, highlight some ways in which the study process and conference pushed mission thinking further, and conclude by identifying priorities for the future.

Two Paradigms of Mission: Missio Dei and World Christianity

One of the 'transversal' topics of Edinburgh 2010 was 'Bible and mission'. As a transversal topic it was not a primary topic of investigation but a thread to be woven through the fabric of the Edinburgh deliberations. When Christians gather from so many different churches, the Bible assumes even greater importance because it is the only source for theological reflection which all Christians share whatever their denomination or region. So the authority for what was asserted in the study processes tended not to be the tradition of the church but the biblical text. In addition to this, certain academic theologians and missionaries who transcend ecclesial boundaries were also used to justify different points of view.

Edinburgh 2010 took a biblical theme. 'Witnessing to Christ today' comes most directly from the writings of Luke, especially Acts 1:8: 'But you will receive power when the Holy Spirit has come upon you; and you

---

[1] Dr Kirsteen Kim is Director of Programmes in Theology and Religious Studies at Leeds Trinity University College and served as Research Coordinator of Edinburgh 2010 from January 2009 to March 2011.

will be my witnesses in Jerusalem, in all Judaea and Samaria, and to the ends of the earth'. The nature of that witness is demonstrated in Luke's account of the lives of the apostles and the early church in the chapters that follow in the book of Acts, and also retrospectively in the ministry of Jesus Christ in the gospel of Luke, which is the basis of Christian mission. Acts 1:8 encapsulates two insights about the nature of mission that shaped the planning and execution of Edinburgh 2010 and are reflected in its Common Call: that mission is God's initiative and that Christian faith is for the whole world. In the twentieth century these insights have been expressed in a more particular way through two paradigms of mission thinking known respectively as *missio Dei* and world Christianity.

In the post-war and post-colonial period the global circumstances in which mission takes place were significantly altered, especially for Christians in Europe. By the 1960s the imperial world which had formed the context of Edinburgh 1910 was gone, the United States was the new global power and lots of newly independent nations were making their voices heard. As a result there was a great deal of reflection among mission agencies and churches about how to be faithful to the Great Commission in this new world order, especially in the newly constituted World Council of Churches, as Dr Dana Robert showed in her keynote address at the 2010 conference. This re-thinking in the ecumenical movement led to a new paradigm of mission which has become known by the shorthand *missio Dei*, God's mission. Not only did it become the paradigm of the mainly Protestant and Orthodox churches in the WCC but by the 1970s Catholics and Evangelicals had also come to use and own this broad approach. David Bosch's 1991 book *Transforming Mission* remains the best explication of the shift to the *missio Dei* paradigm.[2]

Missio Dei as a paradigm is multi-faceted and its dimensions are shown in a number of important practical consequences which are reflected in the way Edinburgh 2010 was organised. First, *missio Dei* puts mission at the very heart of the Trinity. It is a way of expressing the dependence of all human action on God's initiative so that human mission is merely a participation in God the Father's prior sending (mission) of the Son and the Spirit (John 3:16; 14:26). So mission is not only a practical task but also a theological matter. In 1910 the questions raised about mission were about its methods, efficiency and effectiveness. In order to get the different mission agencies to participate, such theological questions had been ruled out.[3] But the Edinburgh 2010 study process and conference explicitly explored the meaning of mission in order to recognise the mistakes of the past and discern what it means to 'witness to Christ today'.

Second, because mission God's, it is at the centre of what it means to be

---

[2] David Bosch, *Transforming Mission: Paradigm Shifts in Theology of Mission* (Maryknoll, NY: Orbis Books, 1991).

[3] Brian Stanley, *The World Missionary Conference, Edinburgh 1910* (Grand Rapids, MI: Eerdmans, 2009), 38.

a Christian and to be church. Instead of being a task added to the other activities of the church, and carried out by specialist missionaries and organisations, mission now appears as integral to church life and a natural part of participating in Christ. This puts the emphasis on the witness of the local church – each member in each place, rather than on sending missionaries, as the primary means of spreading the good news. Thus one consequence of the paradigm shift was that, whereas 1910 was organised by missionary societies, the stakeholders of Edinburgh 2010 were mostly church bodies which define themselves as missionary.

A third aspect of the *missio Dei* paradigm is that mission takes place everywhere. World War Two led to the breakdown of the old division between the Christian world (Christendom) and the 'non-Christian world' on which Edinburgh 1910 was predicated. In 1910 the focus was on the outgoing work of missions from Christendom, a message and way of life flowing from the West to the rest. Mission was an activity of enthusiasts in foreign countries which the churches needed to be persuaded to support. But Edinburgh 2010 primarily celebrated the worldwide presence and local witness of Christian churches themselves. At Edinburgh 2010 Christians from Europe, especially, who made up the largest group among the delegates, were acutely aware that their nations were also 'mission fields' in need of the renewing power of the gospel. In 2010 mission was understood as taking place in every continent primarily through the life of local churches.

Fourth, if mission is God's mission, then mission is one. *Missio Dei* stresses unity in mission not only for pragmatic reasons but as an integral part of witness to God. In the last one hundred years the ecumenical movement has reflected a great deal on the meaning and form that unity should take. No firm agreement has been reached but reflection on God as Trinity suggests that unity is not monolithic but differentiated and affirms that unity is bound up with the sending of the church into the world.[4] Edinburgh 2010 represented a recognition by all the churches that mission and unity are inseparable. Mission is centripetal as well as centrifugal: it is as much about calling the church and the world into one as it is about going out into the world.

Finally, the *missio Dei* paradigm affirms that God's concern is with the whole world and all life. Therefore mission is holistic and transformative of every area of human experience. In the middle years of the twentieth century the ecumenical and evangelical missionary movements were torn apart by the question of which took priority in mission: evangelism or social action. At Edinburgh 2010 both were able to agree on integral mission encompassing both. Furthermore, if the whole world is God's

---

[4] World Council of Churches, *Mission and Evangelism: An Ecumenical Affirmation* (1982), in Jacques Matthey (ed.), *'You are the light of the world': Statements on Mission by the World Council of Churches 1980-2005* (Geneva: WCC, 2005), 4-38, paras. 1-2.

concern, then mission reaches out to the whole creation. The 'transversals' of Edinburgh 2010 included 'ecological perspectives' because, although the human response to God's call to mission was an essential part of the theology of Edinburgh 2010, which issued in its Common Call to mission, human well-being and salvation is also inextricably linked to the liberation of the earth (Rom 8: 19-23).

The Edinburgh 2010 project also worked broadly within a second paradigm known as the 'world Christianity' paradigm, which has been developed especially by Andrew Walls and Lamin Sanneh,[5] and illustrated in the *Atlas of Global Christianity* edited by Todd M. Johnson and Kenneth R. Ross for the centenary.[6] Although it has theological implications, the paradigm is based on the sociological observation that since 1910, when seventy percent of Christians lived in Europe, the centre of gravity of Christianity has been shifting southwards so that now approaching seventy percent of the world's Christians are found outside the West. If present trends continue, within a decade or so the continent with the most Christians will no longer be Europe but Latin America or Africa. According to Walls, this 'serial expansion' is characteristic in the history of Christianity.[7]

Although the estimated proportion of the world's population which is Christian has stayed the same since 1910 – approximately one third – the paradigm portrays Christianity as more truly a world religion in the sense that it is at home in all parts of the world as 'the ultimate local religion'.[8] This ability of Christianity to root itself amongst the different peoples of the world is explained by Walls and Sanneh using the analogy of translation, although others have preferred the terms inculturation or contextualision as giving more emphasis to local initiative rather than missionary activity.[9] Edinburgh 2010 was intended to celebrate world Christianity both as the realisation of the vision of 1910 and the result of the faithful witness of believers in Africa and Asia especially.

Reference to the shift in the centre of gravity of world Christianity from the North to the South combines the world Christianity paradigm with the

---

[5] Andrew F. Walls, *The Missionary Movement in Christian History: Studies in the Transmission of Faith* (Maryknoll, NY: Orbis Books, 1996); Andrew F. Walls, *The Cross-cultural Process in Christian History: Studies in the Transmission and Appropriation of Faith* (Maryknoll, NY: Orbis Books, 2002); Lamin Sanneh, *Translating the Message: The Missionary Impact on Culture* (Maryknoll, NY: Orbis Books, 1989).

[6] Todd M. Johnson & Kenneth R. Ross, eds., *Atlas of Global Christianity, 1910–2010* (Edinburgh: Edinburgh University Press, 2009).

[7] Walls, *The Cross-cultural Process in Christian History*, pp. 27-48.

[8] Dana L. Robert, *Christian Mission: How Christianity Became a World Religion* (Oxford, Wiley-Blackwell, 2009).

[9] Ultimately none of these is adequate. See John Parratt, *An Introduction to Third World Theologies* (Cambridge: Cambridge University Press, 2004), 7-9.

division of the world into 'global North' and 'global South'. This is primarily an economic distinction but it also corresponds roughly to the line between the old colonising and colonised worlds, so that the advent of world Christianity can also be a way of talking about how there is now partnership between Western churches and former mission churches. Or it may be combined with post-colonial perception that the 'the empire strikes back' and mission goes into reverse, as the tables appear to be turned and those who were last are now first. In view of the North-South shift, a great deal of discussion in the 2010 General Council was given to whether if was appropriate to centre the commemoration in Edinburgh, or if it would not be more fitting to hold an event or events in the global South to signify this new reality. As a compromise, although the conference was held in Edinburgh, it was planned that it should include at least sixty percent of participants from 'the South' and the study process was polycentric; events were sponsored in other regions of the world, and the project website mapped as far as possible the many different activities worldwide.

The two paradigms of *missio Dei* and world Christianity complement each other in one important respect. *Missio Dei* was the result of theological considerations which brought together churches of different confessions. The world Christianity paradigm draws attention to the geographical spread of mission. In the twentieth century, the term 'ecumenical' has generally been applied to the former approach – the unity of churches. But its original meaning as it applied to the councils of the early church was more geographical: it brought together all the churches of the world.[10] These two dimensions of what it means to be 'ecumenical' – confessional and geographical – were in tension in celebrations of the Edinburgh 1910 centenary. In the end Edinburgh 2010 achieved a very high degree of confessional unity but was not as representative geographically as it might have been.

Beyond the Paradigms: Power, Plurality and Migration

The study process and conference discussions both affirmed the two paradigms of *missio Dei* and world Christianity and also pushed beyond them. Several issues emerged which challenged the received wisdom and suggested further developments in mission theology and practice. Here we will consider three: power, plurality and migration.

In retrospect the captivity of Edinburgh 1910 to colonial modes of operation is obvious and so participants at Edinburgh 2010 were especially mindful that mission has often been distorted and corrupted by its links with worldly power. The topic of 'mission and power', which was tackled Study Group 4, is the first new development to note. The group focused the discussion on a case study of the Canadian schools system that was so

---

[10] Cf. Stanley, *The World Missionary Conference*, 18-19, 36-37.

unjust to the Indigenous people. It was clear in the study that there are many parallel examples from around the world. Several of the 'transversal' topics also dealt with justice issues, aiming to redress past wrongs by including women, youth, and the marginalised or 'subaltern voices'. Theme 7 on 'Christian communities in contemporary contexts' dealt especially with the inequalities of poverty, gender and migration. Ecological perspectives also reminded the conference of the danger that mission is exploitative rather than empowering. As a response to such injustices, the conference called for repentance and wherever possible healing and reconciliation. Indeed in recent years healing and reconciliation has become an important new way of characterising mission.[11]

The study of 'mission and power' drew attention to the abuse of power in mission but if mission is done by local churches then it is not always done from a position of power. Not all Christians are in a position of power over others. Nevertheless the question of power underlay many aspects of the conference deliberations since mission takes place among the powers and principalities, prophetically speaking truth to power and bringing liberation to the oppressed. A Pentecostal delegate pointed out that there was a need to talk more explicitly about the biblical vocabulary of spiritual power(s) and power encounters – language which is readily understood in many parts of the global South especially.[12] Edinburgh 2010 also discussed the right use of power and the power of the Holy Spirit in mission. The prevalent discourse of Edinburgh 1910 about 'advancing the kingdom of Christ' no longer seemed appropriate in a post-imperial and post-Christendom age. Instead mission as 'joining in with the Spirit' would be a better way to describe the approach of Edinburgh 2010.[13] This phrase, which was picked up in the report of the Listening Group, both captures the Trinitarian understanding of mission from the *missio Dei* paradigm and also expresses the flexible and contextual nature of contemporary mission activity. Furthermore, mission as 'joining in with the Spirit' implies that mission is first and foremost a movement from below rather than an imposition from above.

'Joining in with the Spirit' as a definition of mission also suggests that mission is a spiritual endeavour. The question of 'mission and power' was also covered but under the heading of 'mission spirituality' (Theme 9). Here the focus of attention was the motivating and sustaining power of the Spirit of Christ in mission, which leads to transformation and revitalisation. Mission spirituality is grounded in the love of God and the way of Jesus

---

[11] See Jacques Matthey (ed.), *Come, Holy Spirit, Heal and Reconcile: Report of the World Council of Churches Conference on Mission and Evangelism*, Athens, May 2005 (Geneva: WCC, 2008); www.mission2005.org.

[12] Veli-Matti Kärkkäinen quoted in the report of Theme 4: Mission and Power in this volume, p. 145.

[13] Kirsteen Kim, 'Edinburgh 1910 to 2010: From Kingdom to Spirit', *Journal of the European Pentecostal Theological Association* 30/2 (2010), pp. 3-20

Christ. It involves authentic discipleship 'daily, local and lived' on the basis of the Scriptures, prayer, confession and the Sacraments in community. A recurrent theme across the project was the need for vulnerability in mission and the risks of suffering and persecution associated with 'deep' discipleship. Theme 6 reminded the conference that discipleship is supported by a holistic approach to theological education, which forms every Christian at the highest possible level in biblical, ecumenical and global ways.

The second issue to note was the question of mission in a plural world. The proportion of the world's population estimated to be Christians has not changed since 1910 but still stands at about one third. At Edinburgh 1910 this figure was regarded as too low because Christianity was regarded as 'the world's religion' and it was considered a realistic possibility that it could become universalised by 'the evangelisation of the world in this generation'.[14] Yet at Edinburgh 2010, it seemed accepted that Christianity is just one of the world's religions, and is likely to remain so, even while Christians continue to share the good news and invite a response. What was celebrated therefore was not the growth of Christianity at the expense of other forms of belief but the growth of Christianity in parts of the world where Christ was not known before and the worldwide spread of Christian witness. Despite this, it was pointed out that the majority of adherents to other religions do not know a Christian and that religious freedom is lacking in many parts of the world – the situation of Christians in Islamic states being a special concern.

The *missio Dei* paradigm can be used to secularise Christian mission for, if God's concern is with the whole world, it might be asked what is special about the church. Or, if God's Spirit is already at work in the whole creation why the need for evangelism and conversion to Christ? Since God created all peoples and cultures, are not their religions also valid paths to salvation? Some have suggested that 'dialogue' not 'mission' is the only acceptable approach in the context of different religious communities. In view of such questioning, the choice of 'Christian mission among other faiths' as the theme for the work Study Group 2 was controversial. As a result of the study process, the Edinburgh 2010 Common Call affirmed that dialogue, respect, friendship, reconciliation and hospitality are all integral to Christian witness in contexts of religious plurality as elsewhere, but confidence in the Christian gospel also demands testimony to the uniqueness of Christ and that the Christian invitation to salvation is for the whole world. Those Christians who have long lived in the context of other religions were able to share what it means to 'give an account of our hope' (1 Peter 3:15) in such circumstances.

The contemporary challenges to mission and evangelism were especially

---

[14] See, for example, John R. Mott, *The Decisive Hour of Christian Missions* (Edinburgh: The Foreign Mission Committee of the Church of Scotland, 1910).

brought to the fore by theme 3. Although postmodernity is often thought of as a feature of the West, the study group recognised in its title 'mission and postmodernities' that there are many forms that it takes and that these are experienced in other continents as well. In some cases this is because of the rapid spread of ideas in a highly globalised world but this is not always the reason. Asian participants, for example, pointed out that common features of what the West describes as 'postmodernity' – such as pluralism – have been present in their contexts for centuries. The emphasis on 'mission in six continents' since the 1960s has tended to regionalise mission as done in contextual ways in different places but here there was a recognition of the need for a concerted effort across continents to address the dominant philosophies of our age. Although historically Westerners have not had any hesitation about evangelising other regions, sometimes the impression is given that only those who have 'come of age' through the processes of modernity can understand and contribute to mission in the West. The participation of people of all continents in discussion of this theme demonstrated that mission and evangelism in the West is not a fundamentally different matter from anywhere else and that Christians from other places and cultures share a responsibility for the evangelisation of Europe and North America and are shedding new light on it.

The third issue which challenged the existing paradigms was the issue of migration and mission, which was raised especially by Themes 5 and 7. A world Christianity approach which divides the world into separate regions may play down the movements between them and the presence of migrant communities everywhere. And the *missio Dei* paradigm, which has emphasised mission as the role of each local church in its own region, has contributed to a view of churches as stationary, planted for ever in one place. The issue of migration has highlighted the interconnectedness and flows between different regions of the world and militates against the tendencies to regionalisation and compartmentalisation of the world into separate cultural blocks.[15] Today we see churches on the move, especially from poorer countries to richer ones in the West and in the Gulf. Churches exist very often in diaspora and in communities which have only recently migrated from one region to another. Although some complained that diaspora communities remain hermetically sealed off from the wider community and do not share their faith, others see the potential of diaspora movements for witness to Christ in parts of the world where Christianity is weak.

The increasing plurality of Christian expression caused by migration, especially in the world's cities, poses new challenges to unity, as Study Group 8 working on 'mission and unity' recognised. This is especially the

---

[15] See for example, Jehu J. Hanciles, *Beyond Christendom: Globalization, African Migration and the Transformation of the West* (Maryknoll, NY: Orbis Books, 2008).

case when the new churches are independent of the traditional denominations, such as many of those from sub-Saharan Africa, China and some other parts of Asia. One problem is that from the perspective of existing churches with a longer Christian tradition, the validity of such new expressions of Christianity is often questioned and so it is difficult to achieve the mutual respect that is essential for working together. Furthermore, when migrant communities are poor, they may be seen as targets of humanitarian aid rather than as partners in mission. Another problem is that newer churches may not respect the older ones, believing themselves to be the more vibrant and valid form of Christianity. In either case the unity of witness is impaired.

Some smaller-scale migration is the result of intentional missionary movements. The United States continues to send high numbers of missionaries overseas and so do some European countries but in recent years rising economic powers with large Christian populations – such as South Korea, Brazil and Nigeria – have also been sending missionaries around the world in large numbers. Some come to the North, to Europe especially, regarding it as a mission field, a phenomenon known as 'reverse mission' (because it is in the opposite direction to the mission sending of Edinburgh 1910). However, to label all missionary movements from the global South and East as 'reverse mission' is misleading because most missionaries are sent to the South – many offering educational, medical and other skills – and the main motive for such movements is not to turn the tables on former colonial masters. Nevertheless, the rise of intentional missionary movements from Africa, Asia, Latin America and Oceania is an example of the way in which mission 'comes back'.

In earlier generations mission tended to be seen as a one-way sending from the Christian to the non-Christian world, from the West to the Rest (although the extent to which it fed back into the life of Western churches even then is underestimated). Even in the post-colonial period, this pattern has been perpetuated by the high level involvement of churches in development activities and the unequal economic relations which divided churches into North and South. However, in the highly globalised world in which we live there are flows in multiple directions, and actions in one part of the world rebound in another. At Edinburgh 2010, being a gathering of Christians from many different regions in mutual respect, it was clear that it is no longer possible to do mission without any comeback, or without considering our endeavours from the recipients' point of view. This realisation impacts even on the foundations for mission, as Study Group 1 insisted when they included an experiential and empirical dimension to their work. Both research projects on which the group drew looked at grassroots experience of mission, in UK and Indian contexts. The way mission works out on the ground is the test of the theory. However finely articulated are the biblical grounds and mission theology, the real nature of the mission will be known by its fruits: by the extent to which lives are transformed into the likeness of Jesus Christ and communities experience justice and peace.

Witnessing to Christ Today: By the Spirit, to the World, in a Changing Landscape

Having seen some of the challenges to the paradigms of mission which we have from the second half of the twentieth century, there are some further insights from Edinburgh 2010 that we can draw for our mission practice in the twenty-first century. These concern the Spirit, the world and the changing landscape of global Christianity.

By thinking of mission as 'joining in with the Spirit' the Edinburgh 2010 discussions made explicit the pneumatological dimensions of *missio Dei* since the Spirit is the way God works in the world and the way we experience God. But if the mission thinking of Edinburgh 2010 is to have integrity then 'joining in with the Spirit' must be compatible with 'witnessing to Christ today'. This can only be the case if it is clarified that, because God is Trinity, 'the Spirit' shares a common source with the Son in God the Father. Being sent from the same Father, the Spirit and the Son work together in the economy of salvation. It is important to state this because it is what makes Christian mission distinctive. 'Spirit' is understood in many different ways and is not a specifically Christian term. Indeed it is the common awareness of the presence and activity of the Spirit that provides a point of contact with people of other religions, spiritualities, ideologies and philosophies – from Indigenous religions and Hinduism through Hegel and Marx to New Age and forms of postmodernism. But the criteria we use for defining the Spirit differs according to the worldview. It is the Christian confession that the Spirit of God descends and remains on Jesus the Christ, the Son of God, the Word Incarnate, 'the Lamb of God who takes away the sins of the world' (John 1). Therefore Jesus Christ, as testified to in the Bible and Christian tradition, is the key to discerning the work of the Spirit and joining in.[16]

'Joining in with the Spirit' expresses a profound insight about the nature of mission that was built into the structure of the Edinburgh 2010 conference: that mission is not merely a task but a spirituality – and not any spirituality but a way of life in the Spirit of Christ. Instead of worship sessions slotted in between the plenary and parallel sessions, attention was given instead to the whole 'spiritual life' of the conference, within which the meetings took place. This was a clear statement that the end does not justify the means in mission. Prayer and worship is not just a tool to motivate, inspire and make us more effective in a mission that is planned on other grounds. Rather, the spiritual life is the context which frames

[16] Kirsteen Kim, *The Holy Spirit in the World: A Global Conversation* (Maryknoll, NY: Orbis Books, 2007).

mission in every aspect. This non-instrumental understanding is also inherent in the word 'witness' in the conference theme. If mission is done in the Spirit then the process of mission is as important as its results. It cannot be done in ways that are unethical, unjust, underhand, aggressive, or otherwise incompatible with the Spirit of Jesus Christ.[17] Similarly, if mission is in the One Spirit, then it must be done in unity. In an era when the barriers to institutional unity between churches seem insuperable, nevertheless a spiritual unity such as that generated by Edinburgh 2010 is possible.

However, mission as a spirituality cannot mean it is other-worldly, remote or does not influence the world. The Holy Spirit, the Spirit made manifest in Christ cannot remain as an experience of international conferences. The spirituality of Edinburgh 2010 must be worked out in the material world governed by personalities, structures and institutions. Acts 1:8, from which the Edinburgh 2010 theme was drawn, makes it clear that witness to Christ is by power. However this was not a greater degree of power than others but a different kind of power, the power of the Holy Spirit. As recounted in Acts 2, the coming of the Spirit at Pentecost empowered the disciples and liberated them for bold preaching, humble service, barrier-breaking fellowship and boundary-crossing mission. They were 'turning the world upside-down' (Acts 17:6) as they bore witness – sometimes to death – to their Lord and Saviour. The Spirit of God is known not primarily as the Great Spirit which defeats all other powers of this world but as the Holy Spirit who exercises a quality of power different from any worldly spirit. Witness that is truly by the power of the Holy Spirit will change the world.

The Edinburgh 2010 had an added dimension not available a hundred years before: the online conference, which widened the participation and increased the modes of interaction with the project. In many respects the ideal of the Internet parallels the vision of Edinburgh: multi-cultural, poly-centric, multi-directional, interconnected. It expresses many of the hopes that Christian mission will foster exchange, understanding and mutual respect between peoples. However, the egalitarian, open access ideal of the Internet is far from the reality which is that many cannot participate at all, or if they do it is not on a level playing field. Similarly globalisation, which is often described as if it were a reciprocal interplay of forces, was condemned as inherently unjust by many from the global South who attended the conference. Confirmation of this was seen in the fact that several delegates from sub-Saharan Africa were denied visas to attend because of inequalities in a world in which those with the right passports are travelling further and more often than every before.

[17] See the *Code of Conduct on Conversion* being prepared by the World Council of Churches, the Pontifical Council for Interreligious Dialogue, with the participation also of the World Evangelical Alliance.

The close analogy between the ideals of the Internet and globalisation and the vision of Edinburgh 2010 suggests that the latter may in retrospect be as enmeshed in the prevailing norms of its world as was Edinburgh 1910. Certainly the project and event would not have been possible without electronic communications and air transport; nor could the conference have been so representative in the politically polarised situation that existed between nations for most of the twentieth century from the onset of war in 1914 to the fall of the Berlin Wall in 1989. Even the prevailing pneumatological understanding of mission seems to have come to the fore because it lends itself to a world in which power is exercised by force-fields, trade flows and cultural influence.[18] But although they are related – especially because Christian mission and movements for unity have been contributing to overcoming the barriers between nations, it would be unwise to link Christian mission too closely with globalisation. The driving spirit of each is different and so are their ends. There are many benefits of globalisation that Christian mission can affirm but it is also necessary to discern the darker forces at work.

A globalised world is one in which the world's communities are brought closer together, and this creates heightened possibilities both for conflict and for peace. Transversal 4, 'Contextualization, inculturation and dialogue of worldviews' was a reminder that as well as the rooting of the gospel in each culture, there is an increasing need to understand our differences through dialogue. Global communications make differences between Christians very obvious now and there is a particular need for understanding between churches of the global North and the South. Edinburgh 2010 and other truly global conferences can help to do this but 'knowing one another theologically' is something that needs to happen at the level of grassroots theological education. *The Handbook of Theological Education in World Christianity* produced in collaboration with Edinburgh 2010 was an attempt to achieve this.[19] Mission as mutual sending or exchange also becomes very important.

The same potential for conflict between communities applies to inter-religious differences. Christian-Muslim relations in particular have become a site of violence and clashes of worldview. In 2010 the memory of 9/11, the Gulf and Iraq Wars and Israeli-Palestinian conflict was very current and challenges to peaceful coexistence between Christian and Muslim communities were being felt in Europe, North America, Africa, West, South and South-East Asia, and many other parts of the world. Despite the

---

[18] Kim, 'Edinburgh 1910 to 2010',

[19] Quotation from John Mbiti, 'Theological impotence and the universality of the church', in Gerald H. Anderson and Thomas F. Stransky (eds), *Mission Trends 3: Third World Theologies* (Eerdmans 1976), 6-18 (at p. 17). Dietrich Werner, David Esterline, Namsoon Kang & Joshva Raja, *Handbook of Theological Education in World Christianity: Theological Perspectives, Ecumenical Trends, Regional Surveys* (Oxford: Regnum Books International, 2010).

celebration of world Christianity, the maps presented at Edinburgh showed a large patch in the middle with few or no Christian communities: much of the Muslim world. The proportion of Christians in the Middle East is lower now than it was in 1910, and the contemporary emigration from that region only accelerates a process that has been going on for centuries.[20] The pressure on these communities is not a problem that can be solved by courageous grassroots witness alone but which demands concerted efforts in interfaith dialogue and advocacy to change policies of both Western and Islamic governments.

Just as the map of the world has changed many times over the last one hundred years, so the landscape in which mission takes place continues to change. The rise in economic power of China, India, Russia, Brazil, Nigeria and others is benefitting their citizens but poses new challenges of resources, sustainability and peace. The shape of world Christianity is also changing. In many parts of the world rapid growth of Christianity has taken place in movements that are independent of the traditional denominations which the WCC brings together and even outside the networks of the Evangelical movement. Some of these wish to identify with the Christian tradition, although they may be critical of other churches. Those which do not will probably cease to be recognisably Christian. Many can be brought together under the label of Pentecostalism[21] but not all are less easily defined under that umbrella or resist such classification. Unity in mission is just as challenging now as it has ever been and new means need to be found to relate to these movements, especially as the constitute the fastest growing part of Christianity today. Too much attention to confessional unity may be to neglect the geographical dimension of large regions of Africa and Asia, and some parts of the USA, where the maps show that independent forms of Christianity predominate.

The new mission movements from South Korea, Brazil, Nigeria and other countries as another feature of the landscape suggest a renewed need to examine the role of mission agencies. In ecumenical but not evangelical circles, the settled model of *missio Dei* combined with that of world Christianity to suggest that, since mission was primarily the responsibility of each local church and the churches were widespread, the age of missions was over. Today we have a new wave of mission agencies being founded, many of them looking back to the models of mission by which they themselves were evangelised more than a century ago. If these churches have found a need to re-invent this pattern of Christian witness, perhaps it has biblical, theological and practical justification after all? At the very least there is a need for mutual discussion about mission activities that reach beyond church localities to another region with a willingness to

---

[20] See, for example, Anthony O'Mahony (ed.), *Christianity in the Middle East: Studies in Modern History, Theology and Politics* (Sawbridgeworth, Herts: Melisende, 2007).

[21] See Allan Anderson, *An Introduction to Pentecostalism* (Cambridge: CUP, 2004).

contemplate that this might be justified while also raising questions about how this relates to the missions of churches existing in that other region.

Mission in the twenty-first century is informed by the two twentieth-century paradigms of *missio Dei* and world Christianity. These are challenged by thinking which emerged at Edinburgh 2010 of mission as a power encounter, of mission taking place in plural societies, and of the links of mission with migration movements. The effect of these challenges is to emphasise that Christian witness is not fixed in a particular place but takes place on the move and in interaction with other movements in the world. Christian mission is a form of spirituality and deep discipleship which exercises the alternative form of power which Jesus Christ demonstrated. It is facilitated by – but not captive to – the forces of globalisation and it is responsive to a changing landscape, especially as new Christian movements emerge from different parts of the world. As the Common Call declares, witnessing to Christ today is 'sharing in God's mission of love through the transforming power of the Holy Spirit'. Ultimately it is judged not by the sophistication of its theory but by its faithfulness to Christ and actual mission practice (Matt 25:31-46).

BIBLIOGRAPHY

Allen, Roland, *The Spontaneous Expansion of the Church* (London: World Dominion Press, 1927)

Allen, Roland, *Ministry of the Spirit: Selected Writings of Roland Allen*. Edited by David M. Patton (Grand Rapids, MI: Wm. B. Eerdmans, 1960)

Allen, Roland, *Missionary Methods: St. Paul's or Ours?* (Grand Rapids, MI: Wm. B. Eerdmans, 1962)

Alves, Herculano, 'Joao Ferreira D'Almeida, tradutor da Biblia'. Paper presented in the Fórum de Ciências Bíblicas, Barueri, Sao Paulo, Brazil. 8-9 June 2006.

Alves, Herculano, *A Bíblia de João Ferreira Annes D'almeida* (Lisbon: Universidade Católica, 2007)

Anderson, Allan, *An Introduction to Pentecostalism* (Cambridge: CUP, 2004)

Athanāsyūs, Bishop, 'The Copts through Ages', *WSCF Journal Quarterly* (May 1986)

Aquinas, Thomas, *Summa Theologiae*, Part I, Question 3, article 1. Available at www.newadvent.org.

Augustine, *Exposition on Psalm 44*, §23. Available at www.newadvent.org

Balia, Daryl & Kirsteen Kim (eds), *Edinburgh 2010: Witnessing to Christ Today* (Oxford: Regnum Books International, 2010)

Baumann, Z., *Postmodern Ethics* (Oxford: Blackwell, 1993) – Italian edition, *Sfide dell'etica* (Milano: Feltrinelli, 1996)

Bebbington, David, *Evangelicalism in Modern Britain: A History from the 1730s to the 1980s* (Grand Rapids, MI: Baker, 1989)

Benedict XVI, Encyclical Letter *Deus Caritas Est*. Available at www.vatican.va.

Bevans, Stephen B., & Roger P. Schroeder, *Constants in Context: A Theology of Mission for Today* (Maryknoll, NY: Orbis Books, 2004)

Bevans, Stephen B., *An Introduction to Theology in Global Perspective* (Maryknoll, NY: Orbis Books, 2009)

Bībawī, George, *The Mind of the Minority*. Handwritten document.

Blair, William Newton & Bruce Hunt, *The Korean Pentecost and the Suffering Which Followed* (Edinburgh: The Banner of Trust, 1977)

Blumenberg, H., *La legittimità dell'età moderna* [1966] (Genova: Marietti, 1992)

Boff, Leonardo, 'Trinity', in *Mysterium Liberationis: Fundamental Concepts of Liberation Theology* (Maryknoll, NY: Orbis Books, 1993)

Bonaventure, *De Trinitate*, 3.16. Available at www.newadvent.org.

Bosch, David J., *Transforming Mission: Paradigm Shifts in Theology of Mission* (Maryknoll, NY: Orbis Books, 1991)

Bridston, Keith R. (compiler), *Shock and Renewal: The Christian Mission Enters a New Era* (New York: Friendship Press, 1955)

Budijanto, B., *Emerging Missions Movement: Voices of Asia* (Compassion/AEA, 2010)

Burgess, Stanley M. & Eduard M. Van Der Maas (eds), *The New Dictionary of Pentecostal and Charismatic Movements* (Grand Rapids, MI: Zondervan Publishing House, 2002)

CELAM, *Documento Conclusivo: V Conferencia General* (Bogotá: Centro de Publicaciones del CELAM, 2007)

Cho, David Yonggi, *Salvation, Health and Prosperity: Our Threefold Blessings in Christ* (Altamonte Springs, FL: Creation House, 1987)

Cho, Yonggi, *A Commentary on the Gospel of Matthew* (Vol. 2) (in Korean) (Seoul: Seoul Logos, 2008)

Christakis, Nicholas & James Fowler, C*onnected: The Amazing Power of Social Networks and How They Shape Our Lives* (London: Harper Press, 2009)

Crystal, David, *Language and the Internet* (New York: Cambridge University Press, 2006)

Costas, Orlando, *Christ Outside the Gate* (Maryknoll, NY: Orbis Books: 1982)

Cray, Graham (ed.), *Mission-shaped Church: Church Planting and Fresh Expressions of Church in a Changing Context* (London: Church House Publishing, 2004). Available at www.cofe.anglican.org

Daneel, Marthinus L., *African Earthkeepers: Wholistic Interfaith Mission* (Maryknoll, NY, Orbis Books, 2001)

Davies, Oliver, 'Late Medieval Theology', in G. R. Evans (ed.), *The Medieval Theologians: An Introduction to Theology in the Medieval Period* (Oxford: Blackwell, 2001)

Delio, Ilia, 'Bonaventure's Metaphysics of the Good', *Theological Studies*, 60/2 (1999)

Deneulin, Séverine & Masooda Bano, *Religion in Development: Rewriting the Secular Script* (London and New York: Zed Books, 2009)

Douglas, Ian T. 'The Exigency of Times and Occasions', in Ian T. Douglas & Kwok Pui Lan (eds), *Beyond Colonial Anglicanism* (New York: Church Publishing, 2001)

Duquoc, Ch., *La teologia in esilio. La sfida della sua sopravvivenza nella cultura contemporanea* [2002] (Brescia: Queriniana, 2004)

Duraisingh, Christopher (ed.), *Called to One Hope: The Gospel in Diverse Cultures*. Report of the Conference of the CWME, Salvador, Brazil, 1996 (Geneva: WCC, 1998; German trans. Frankfurt-am-Main: Lembeck, 1999)

Dyrness, William & Veli-Matti Kärkkäinen (eds), *Global Dictionary of Theology* (Downers Grove, IL: Inter-Varsity Press, 2008).

Fawzī, Samīr, *Al-Qidīs Marqus wa-Ta'sīs Kanīsa al-Iskandariyya* (Saint Mark and the Establishment of the Church of Alexandria) (Cairo: Al-Hay'a al-Mis}riyya al-'A<ma li-al-Kitāb, nd)

Ferrari, S. (ed.), *Introduzione al diritto comparato delle religioni. Ebraismo, islam e induismo* (Bologna: Il Mulino, 2008)

Fison, J. E., *Fire upon the Earth* (London: Edinburgh House Press, 1958)

Ford, Leighton, *One Way to Change the World* (New York: Harper & Row, 1970)

Francis, J.M.M. (ed.), *Tentmaking: Perspectives on Self-supporting Ministry* (Leominster, UK: Gracewing, 1998)

Gladwin, John, *God's People in God's World: Biblical Motives for Social Involvement* (Leicester: Intervarsity Press, 1979)

Goergen, Donald J., 'The Quest for the Christ of Africa', *The Journal of the Faculty of Theology, Catholic University of Eastern Africa*, 17/1 (March 2001), 5-51.

Griffis, William E., *A Modern Pioneer in Korea: The Life Story of Henry G. Appenzeller* (New York: Fleming H. Revell Co., 1912)

Guardini, R., *La fine dell'epoca moderna. Il potere* [1950] (Brescia: Morcelliana, 1993)

Gunther, Wolfgang, 'The History and Significance of World Mission Conferences in the Twentieth Century', in *The International Review of Mission* 92/367 (Oct 2003), 521-37

Habermas, J., *Il discorso filosofico della modernità* (Roma-Bari: Laterza, 1987).

Habermas, J., '*Contro il disfattismo della ragione moderna. Per un nuovo patto tra fede e ragione*', in *Teoria politica* 23(2007), n. 1, 5-10. The original text appeared on the edition of 10 February 2007 of *Neue Zürcher Zeitung*.

Hanciles, Jehu J., *Beyond Christendom: Globalization, African Migration and the Transformation of the West* (Maryknoll, NY: Orbis Books, 2008)

Harris, Brian, 'Beyond Bebbington: The Quest for Evangelical Identity in a Postmodern Era', *Churchman* 122/3 (Autumn 2008), 201-220.

Hart, John, *Sacramental Commons: Christian Ecological Ethics* (Lanham, MD: Rowman and Littlefield, 2006)

Hawken, Paul, *The Ecology of Commerce: A Declaration of Sustainability* (New York: Harper Business, 1993)

Haynes, Jeffrey, *Religion and Development: Conflict or Cooperation?* (New York: Palgrave Macmillan, 2007)

Hiebert, Paul 'Syncretism and Social Paradigms', in Gailyn Van Rheenen (ed.), *Contextualization and Syncretism: Navigating Cultural Currents* (Pasadena, CA: William Carey Library, 2006)

Hitchen, John M., 'Training Tamate: The Formation of the Nineteenth Century Missionary Worldview: The Case of James Chalmers of New Guinea', PhD Thesis, University of Aberdeen, 1984

Hitchen, John M. 'Culture and the Bible: The Question of Contextualization'. Paper presented at the South Pacific Association of Bible Colleges' Biennial Conference, Adelaide, 1-5 July 1991. Reprinted in *Melanesian Journal of Theology* 8/2 (Oct 1992), 30-52.

Hitchen, John M., 'What It Means To Be An Evangelical Today – An Antipodean Perspective' in Two Parts, *Evangelical Quarterly* 76/1 (Jan 2004), 47-64 and 76/2 (Apr 2004), 99-115

Hottois, G. & M. Weyemberg (eds), *Richard Rorty. Ambuigüités et limites du postmodernisme* (Paris: Vrin, 1994)

Hull, Gretchen Gaebelein, *Equal to Serve: Women and Men in the Church and Home* (Grand Rapids, MI: Revell, 1987)

International Theological Institute, *A Minister in Yoido: A Biography of Rev. Yonggi Cho* (in Korean) (Seoul: Seoul Logos, 2008)

Jayanth, Mathew, 'Body Spirituality: Incarnation as an Invitation to an Embodied Spirituality', *Jnanadeepa: Pune Journal of Religious Studies,* 7/ 2 (Jan-Jun 2004), 124-126

Joint Working Group between the Catholic Church and the World Council of Churches, 'Ecumenical Formation. Ecumenical Reflections and Suggestions', in the Joint Working Group, *Seventh Report*, 1998. Available at www.oikoumene.org

John Paul II, Apostolic letter, *Tertio millennio adveniente* (1994)

John Paul II, Encyclical Letter, *Fides et Ratio* (1998)

Johnson, C.N., *Business as Mission: A Comprehensive Guide to Theory and Practice* (Downers Grove, IL: IVP Academic, 2009).

Johnson, Elizabeth A., *She Who Is: The Mystery of God in Feminist Theological Discourse* (New York: Crossroad, 1992)

Johnson, Todd M., & Charles L. Tieszen, 'Personal Contact: The *sine qua non* of Twenty-first Century Mission', *Evangelical Missions Quarterly* (Oct 2007), 494-502

Johnson, Todd M. & Kenneth R. Ross eds., *Atlas of Global Christianity, 1910–2010* (Edinburgh: Edinburgh University Press, 2009)

Johnson, Todd M. & Kenneth R. Ross, 'The Making of the *Atlas of Global Christianity*', *International Bulletin of Missionary Research* 34/1 (Jan 2010), 12-16

Kappen, Sebastian,*Jesus and Society* (New Delhi: ISPCK, 2002)

Kemper, Thomas, 'God is coming toward us', Address to Board of Directors General Board of Global Ministries The United Methodist Church, Stamford, Connecticut, April 13, 2010. http://gbgm-umc.org/global_news/full_article.cfm?articleid=5724. Accessed April 24, 2010.

Kilbourn, Phyllis (ed.): *Children in Crisis: A New Commitment* (Monrovia, CA: MARC Publications, 1996)

Kim, Kirsteen, *The Holy Spirit in the World: A Global Conversation* (Maryknoll, NY: Orbis Books, 2007)

Kim, Kirsteen, 'Edinburgh 1910 to 2010: From Kingdom to Spirit',

Journal of the European Pentecostal Theological Association 30/2 (2010), 3-20

Kim, Kwangsoo, *The History of the People in Korean Christianity* (in Korean) (Seoul: Kidokgeomunsa, 1981)

Kobyklinski, A., *'Modernità e postmodernità'. L'interpretazione cristiana dell'esistenza al tramonto dei tempi moderni nel pensiero di Romano Guardini* (Roma: Pontificia Università Gregoriana, 1998).

Koshy, Vineeth, 'Friendship: Online and Offline', *National Council of Churches in India Review,* 128/ 1 (Jan-Feb 2009), 41-42

Lechner, Frank J., & John Boli, *World Culture: Origins and Consequences* (Oxford: Blackwell Publishing, 2005)

Lee, Manyeul, *A Study on the History of Acceptance of the Korean Christianity* (in Korean) (Seoul: Dooraesidae, 1998)

Lee, Young-hoon, *The Holy Spirit Movement in Korea: Its Historical and Doctrinal Development* (Oxford, UK: Regnum Books International, 2009)

Löwith, K., *Significato e fine della storia. I presupposti teologici della filosofia della storia* [1953] (Milano: Comunità, 1963)

Lyotard, J.F., *La condizione postmoderna. Rapporto sul sapere* [1979] (Milano: Feltrinelli, 2002)

McConnell, Douglas, Jennifer Orona & Paul Stockley (eds), *Understanding God's Heart for Children: Toward a Biblical Framework* (Colorado Springs, CO: Authentic Media, 2007)

McGee, Gary B., 'Evangelical Movement', in A. Scott Moreau (ed.), *Evangelical Dictionary of World Missions* (Grand Rapids, MI: Baker Book House, 2000)

McGrath, Alister, *The Genesis of Doctrine: A Study in the Foundation of Doctrinal Criticism* (Grand Rapids, MI: Wm. B. Eerdmans, 1997)

McFague, Sallie, *Life Abundant: Rethinking Theology and Economy for a Planet in Peril* (Minneapolis: Fortress Press, 2000)

Makwasha, Gift, *The Repression, Resistance, and Revival of the Ancestor Cult in the Shona Churches of Zimbabwe: A Study in the Persistence of a Traditional Religious Belief* (Lewiston, NY: Edwin Mellen Press, 2010)

Martín-Barbero, Jesús, 'Mass Media as a Site of Resacralization of Contemporary Cultures', in Stewart M. Hoover & Knut Lundby (eds), *Rethinking Media, Religion and Culture* (Thousand Oaks, CA: Sage Publications, 1997), 102-116

Marty, Martin E. & R. Scott Appleby (eds.), *Fundamentalisms Comprehended* (Chicago: Univ. of Chicago Press, 1995)

Matthey, Jacques (ed.), *Come, Holy Spirit, Heal and Reconcile: Report of the World Council of Churches Conference on Mission and Evangelism*, Athens, May 2005 (Geneva: WCC, 2008)

Mbiti, John, 'Theological impotence and the universality of the church', in Gerald H. Anderson and Thomas F. Stransky (eds), *Mission Trends 3: Third World Theologies* (Eerdmans 1976), 6-18

Mechtilde of Magdeburg, *The Flowing Light of the Godhead*, Book VII, Chapter 55, in *Classics of Western Spirituality*, Vol. 92, Frank Tobin, trans. (New York: Paulist Press, 1998)

Mitchell, Bill, 'The New Media: Culture, the Christian Faith, the Church and Translation', *Journal of Biblical Text Research* 20 (2007), 155-176

Mitchell, Bill, 'Por um novo Pentecostes: A tradução da Bíblia no novo milênio', *Fórum de Ciências Bíblicas* 2 (2007), 13-22

Mitchell, Bill & Fergus Macdonald, 'Bible Societies in Mission', in Daryl Balia & Kirsteen Kim (eds), *Edinburgh 2010: Witnessing to Christ Today* (Oxford: Regnum Books International, 2010), 253-259

Mitchell, Rhoda E., *Empowering Women and Including Men: A Case Study of Gender-Based Violence in San Juan de Lurigancho, Peru*. Unpublished MSW thesis, University of Calgary, 2008. www.ucalgary.ca/md/PARHAD/documents/2008-Empowering_Women_and_Including_Men.pdf

Netland, Harold, *Encountering Religious Pluralism: The Challenge to Christian Faith and Mission* (Downers Grove, IL: IVP, 2001)

Nkemnkia, M. Nkafu, *Il pensare africano come 'vitalogia'* (Roma: Città Nuova, 1995)

Min, Kyungbae, *The History of the Korean Church* (in Korean) (Seoul: Yonsei University Press, 1993)

Moll, Rob, 'Great leap forward', *Christianity Today*, 9 May 2008

Mott, John R., *The Decisive Hour of Christian Missions* (Edinburgh: The Foreign Mission Committee of the Church of Scotland, 1910)

Moltmann, Jürgen, 'The Blessing of Hope: The Theology of Hope and the Full Gospel of Life', *Journal of Pentecostal Theology* 13:2 (2005)

Murry, Ezamo, 'Compassion and Care for the HIV/AIDS Infected and the Affected', in A. Wati Longchar (ed.), *Health, Healing and Wholeness Asian Theological Perspectives on HIV/AIDS* (Assam: ETE-WCC/CCA, 2005), 73-74.

Nash, James A., *Loving Nature, Ecological Integrity and Christian Responsibility* (Nashville, TN: Abingdon Press, 1991)

Nazir-Ali, Michael, *From Everywhere to Everywhere: A World View of Christian Mission* (London: Collins, 1990)

Newbigin, Lesslie, *One Body, One Gospel, One World: The Christian Mission Today* (London: International Missionary Council, 1958).

Niles, D.T., *Upon the Earth: The Mission of God and the Missionary Enterprise of the Churches* (New York: McGraw-Hill, 1962)

Noh, Jonghae, *New View on the History of Korea Methodist Church* (in Korean) (Seoul: Poongman, 1988)

Norman, Edward, *Christianity and the World Order* (London: Oxford University Press, 1979)

Northup, Elizabeth C., 'Impressions of the World Missionary Conference – June 14 to 23', *Woman's Missionary Friend*, August 1910

Nurser, John, *For All Peoples and All Nations: Christian Churches and Human Rights* (Geneva: WCC Publications, 2005).

O'Mahony, Anthony (ed.), *Christianity in the Middle East: Studies in Modern History, Theology and Politics* (Sawbridgeworth, Herts: Melisende, 2007)

O'Reilly, Tim, 'The Architecture of Participation', O'Reilly Media. http://oreilly.com/pub/a/oreilly/tim/articles/architecture_of_participation.html (accessed July 2010).

Olupona, Jacob, 'Comments on the Encyclopedia of Religion and Nature', *Journal of American Academy of Religion* 77/1 (Mar 2009)

Orchard, Ronald K., *Missions in a Time of Testing: Thought and Practice in Contemporary Missions* (Philadelphia: Westminster Press, 1964)

Orchard, Ronald K. (ed.), *Witness in Six Continents. Records of the Meeting of the Commission on World Mission and Evangelism of the World Council of Churches held in Mexico City December 8th to 19th, 1963* (London: Edinburgh House Press, 1964)

Oxley, Simon, *Creative Ecumenical Education* (Geneva: WCC Publications, 2002)

Painadath, Sebastian, 'Church as the Continuation of the Table-Fellowship of Jesus', in Rosario Rocha and Kuruvilla Pandikkattu (eds), *Dreams and Visions: New Horizons for an Indian Church* (Pune: Jnanadeepa Vidyapeeth, 2002), 79-81

Panikkar, Raimundo (Raymond),*The Unknown Christ of Hinduism,* 1st edn (London: Darton, Longman & Todd, 1964)

Panikkar, Raimundo, 'Indic Christian Theology of Religious Pluralism from the Perspective of Interculturation', in K. Pathil, *Religious Pluralism: An Indian Christian Perspective* (New Delhi: ISPCK, 1991), 252-299

Park, Myung Soo, 'David Yonggi Cho and the international Pentecostal/ Charismatic movement', *Journal of Pentecostal Theology* 12/1 (2003)

Parratt, John, *An Introduction to Third World Theologies* (Cambridge: Cambridge University Press, 2004)

Paton, David M. 'World Events Reveal Our Weakness', in Bridston, *Shock and Renewal*, 29-30. See also Richard Shaull, *Encounter with Revolution* (New York: Association Press, 1955).

Pobee, John, *Toward an African Theology* (Nashville, TN: Abingdon, 1979)

Pontifical Council for Promoting Christian Unity, *Directory for the Applications of the Norms and Principles on Ecumenism*, 1993. Available at www.vatican.va.

Pontifical Council for Promoting Christian Unity, *The Ecumenical Dimension in the Formation of Those Engaged in Pastoral Work*, 1997. Available at www.vatican.va.

Presler, Titus, *Horizons of Mission* (Cambridge, MA: Cowley Press, 2001)
Ramsey, Michael, *Be Still and Know, A Study in the Life of Prayer* (London: Fount Paperbacks, 1982)
Rauschenbush, Walter, *Christianity and Social Crisis* (London: Macmillan, 1907)
Rauschenbush, Walter, *A Theology for the Social Gospel* (New York: Macmillan, 1917)
Reid, James, Inaugural address when installed as Rector of Glasgow University, 1972. Available at www.gla.ac.uk/media/media_167194_en.pdf.
Richards, Anne, *et al.*, *Foundations for Mission: A Study of Language, Theology and Praxis from the UK and Ireland* (London: SCM-Canterbury, 2010)
Robert, Dana L., *Joy to the World!: Christian Mission in the Age of Global Christianity* (Women's Division, GBGM, United Methodist Church, 2010)
Robert, Dana L., *Christian Mission: How Christianity Became a World Religion* (Oxford, Wiley-Blackwell, 2009)
Robert, Dana L., 'Faith, Hope, Love in Action: United Methodist Women in Mission Yesterday, Today, and Tomorrow', unpublished address delivered April 29, 2010, at the Mission Forward event, UMW Assembly, St. Louis, Missouri.
Rorty, R., *La filosofia e lo specchio della natura* [1979] (Milano: Bompiani, 1986)
Ryu, Tongshik, *A History of Chung Dong First Methodist Church, 1885-1990* (Seoul: Editorial Committee of Chung Dong First Methodist Church, 1992)
Sah}āb, Victor, *Al-'Arab wa-Tārīkh al-Mas'āla al-Masīh}iyya* (Arabs and the Christian Issue) (Beirut: Al-Wihda, 1998)
Sale, Kirkpatrick, *Dwellers on the Land: The Bioregional Vision* (Athens, GA: University of Georgia Press, 2000)
Sandvig, Kirk (ed.), *Edinburgh 2010: Youth Perspectives* (Pasadena, CA: William Carey International University Press, 2010)
Sanneh, Lamin, *Translating the Message: The Missionary Impact on Culture* (Maryknoll, NY: Orbis, 1989)
Schillebeeckx, Edward, *Jesus: An Experiment in Theology* (New York: Vintage Books, 1981)
Schoffeleers, J.M. (ed.), *Guardians of the Land : Essays on Central African Territorial Cults* (Gwelo (Zimbabwe): Mambo Press, 1979)
Schreiter, Robert J., *Faces of Jesus in Africa* (Maryknoll, NY, Orbis Books, 1991)
Schweitzer, Albert, 'The Ethics of Reverence for Life'. Originally published in *Christendom* 1 (1936): 225-39. Available at www1.chapman.edu/scheitzer/sch/reading4/html. Accessed 07/16/08.

Schweitzer, Alexander, 'Fundamentalism: A Challenge for Biblical Pastoral Ministry', *Bulletin Dei Verbum* 70/71 (2005), 14-16

Strachan, Wendy & Simon Hood (eds), *Evangelization of Children.* Lausanne Occasional Paper # 47 (Lausanne Committee for World Evangelization, 2004). Available at www.lausanne.org

Schreiter, Robert, *Constructing Local Theologies* (Maryknoll, NY: Orbis, 1985)

Segundo, Juan Luis, *Christ in the Spiritual Exercises of St. Ignatius* (Maryknoll, NY: Orbis Books, 1987)

Shank, David A., 'Wadé Harris, William', in *Dictionary of African Christian Biography*. www.dacb.org/stories/liberia/legacy_harris.html, consulted 11 May 2010.

Siegwalt, G., *Dogmatique pour la catholicité évangélique. Système mystagogique de la foi chrétienne*. III: *L'affirmation de la foi*. I: *Cosmologie théologique: sciences et philosophie de la nature* (Genève: Labor et Fides & Paris: Cerf, 1996)

Spittler, Russell, 'Perspectives on the Pentecostalism', in Harold Smith, *Pentecostals from the Inside Out* (Wheaton, IL: Victor Books, 1990)

Stanley, Brian, *The World Missionary Conference, Edinburgh 1910* (Grand Rapids, MI: Eerdmans, 2009)

Strauss, Steve, 'The Role of Context in Shaping Theology', in Gailyn Van Rheenen (ed,). *Contextualization and Syncretism: Navigating Cultural Currents* (Pasadena , CA: William Carey Library, 2006)

Synan, Vinson, *The Holiness-Pentecostal Tradition: Charismatic Movements in the Twentieth Century* (Michigan: William B. Eerdmans Publishing, 1997)

Taylor, Ch., *A Secular Age* (Cambridge, MA: The Belknap Press of Harvard University Press, 2007)

Taylor, John V., *The Go-Between God, The Holy Spirit and the Christian Missions* (London: SCM Press Ltd, 1972)

Tempels, P., *Filosofia bantu*[1946] (Milano: Medusa, 2005)

The Library of the British and Foreign Bible Society, *Historical Catalogues of Printed Editions of the Holy Scriptures* (London: The Bible House, 1903)

Theobald, Ch., *Il cristianesimo come stile. Un modo di fare teologia nella postmodernità*. II (Bologna: Dehoniane, 2009)

Thomas, M.M., 'Towards an Indian Understanding of Jesus Christ', in Mathai Zachariah (ed.), *The Indian Church Identity and Fulfillment* (Chennai: CLS, ISPCK, LPH, 1971), 17-19

Ucko, Hans, *Common Roots, New Horizons* (Geneva: WCC Publications, 1994)

United Bible Societies, *Strategic Challenges: The Mission Imperative.* Position paper, UBS 2004 World Assembly (Reading: UBS, 2004)

United Bible Societies. *Newport Declaration* (UBS: Reading, 2004)

United Bible Societies, *Declaración de Barueri II*, UBS Americas Consultation held in Barueri, Sao Paulo, Brazil, 6-8 March 2007

United Bible Societies, *Sociedad Bíblica Peruana, A la imagen de Dios: Alto a la Violencia* (Lima: United Bible Societies, 2009). www.casadelabiblia.org.

Vanhoozer, Kevin, 'Christ and Concept: Doing Theology and the "Ministry" of Philosophy', in John Woodbridge & Thomas McComiskey (eds), *Doing Theology in Today's World: Essays in Honor of Kenneth S. Kantzer* (Grand Rapids, MI: Zondervan, 1991), 99-146

Vatican II, Decree on Ecumenism, *Unitatis Redintegratio* (1964). Available at www.vatican.va

Vatican II, Decree on the Missionary Activity of the Church, *Ad Gentes* (1965). Available at www.vatican.va.

Vatican II, Constitution on the Church in the Modern World, *Gaudium et Spes* (1965)

Vatican II, Dogmatic Constitution on Divine Revelation, *Dei Verbum* (1965)

Vattimo, G., & P.A. Rovatti, *Il pensiero debole* (Milano: Feltrinelli, 1983)

Währisch-Oblau, Claudia & Fidon Mwombeki (eds), *Mission Continues: Global Impulses for the Twenty-first Century* (Oxford: Regnum Books International, 2010)

Walls, Andrew F., *The Missionary Movement in Christian History: Studies in the Transmission of Faith* (Maryknoll, NY: Orbis Books, 1997)

Walls, Andrew F., *The Cross-Cultural Process in Christian History* (Maryknoll, NY: Orbis, 2002)

Walls, Andrew, 'The Great Commission 1910-2010', paper submitted to the Edinburgh2010 consultation and available at www.edinburgh2010.org.

Warren, Max (ed.), *To Apply the Gospel: Selections from the Writings of Henry Venn* (Grand Rapids, MI: Eerdmans, 1971)

Werner, Dietrich, David Esterline, Namsoon Kang & Joshva Raja, *Handbook of Theological Education in World Christianity: Theological Perspectives, Ecumenical Trends, Regional Surveys* (Oxford: Regnum Books International, 2010)

Wessels, Antonie, *Arab and Christian? Christians in the Middle East* (Kampen: Pharos, 1995)

Whitehead, Alfred North, *Process and Reality: An Essay in Cosmology* (New York: Macmillan, 1929)

World Council of Churches, *Minutes and Reports of the Fourth Meeting of the Central Committee of the World Council of Churches, Rolle (Switzerland), August 4-11, 1951* (Geneva, Switzerland: World Council of Churches, 1951)

World Council of Churches, *Mission and Evangelism: An Ecumenical Affirmation* (1982), in Jacques Matthey (ed.), *'You are the light of the world': Statements on Mission by the World Council of Churches 1980-2005* (Geneva: WCC, 2005), 4-38

World Missionary Conference, 1910, *Report of Commission I, Carrying the Gospel to all the Non-Christian World* (Edinburgh and London: Oliphant, Anderson, & Ferrier; New York, Chicago, and Toronto: Fleming H Revell, 1910)

World Missionary Conference 1910, *Report of Commission VI: The Home Base of Missions* (Edinburgh and London: Oliphant, Anderson, & Ferrier; New York, Chicago, and Toronto: Fleming H Revell, 1910)

World Missionary Conference 1910, *Report of Commission VIII, Co-Operation and the Promotion of Unity* (Edinburgh and London: Oliphant, Anderson, & Ferrier; New York, Chicago, and Toronto: Fleming H Revell, 1910)

World Missionary Conference 1910, *The History and Records of the Conference together with Addresses Delivered at the Evening Meetings* (Edinburgh and London: Oliphant, Anderson, & Ferrier; New York, Chicago, and Toronto: Fleming H Revell, 1910)

World Missionary Conference 1910, *Statistical Atlas of Christian Missions: Containing a Directory of Missionary Societies, a Classified Summary of Statistics, an Index of Mission Stations, and a Series of Specially Prepared Maps of Mission Fields. Compiled by Sub-committees of Commission I, 'On Carrying the Gospel to All the Non-Christian World', As an Integral Part of Its Report to the World Missionary Conference, Edinburgh, June 14–23, 1910* (Edinburgh: World Missionary Conference, 1910)

Wright, Christopher J.H., *The Mission of God: Unlocking the Bible's Grand Narrative* (Downers Grove, IL: InterVarsity Press, 2006)

Wright, Christopher J.H., 'Whole Gospel, Whole Church, Whole World'. www.christianitytoday.com/globalconversation/october2009/index.html?start=1. Accessed April 15, 2010.

Yoder, John Howard, *Politics of Jesus* (Grand Rapids, MI: Wm. B. Eerdmans, 1994)

Yoder, John Howard, *Priestly Kingdom: Social Ethics as Gospel* (Notre Dame, IN: University of Notre Dame Press, 1984)

Young, William P., *The Shack* (Newbury Park, CA: Windblown Media, 2007).

Appendix 1: Edinburgh 2010 Project

The following statement was prepared in January 2008 by the stakeholders of Edinburgh 2010 to explain, promote and encourage involvement in the project.

Edinburgh 2010: Mission for the Twenty-First Century

A global initiative

The upcoming centenary of the Edinburgh 1910 World Missionary Conference is proving to be a suggestive moment for many people who are seeking direction for Christian mission in the twenty-first century. Several different constituencies within world Christianity have begun to plan significant events in the centenary year. Since 2005 a number have been working collaboratively under the aegis of 'Edinburgh 2010'. This initiative seeks to bring together representatives of many different strands of mission and church life for a well-focussed and well-organised process of preparation for the centenary. The memory of the 1910 Conference brings people together in a creative way and opens up new perspectives on mission today.

Council for World Mission • Churches Together in Britain and Ireland • World Alliance of Reformed Churches •Lutheran World Federation • World Evangelical Alliance • International Association for Mission Studies • Lausanne Committee for World Evangelization •Church of Scotland World Mission Council •Latin American Theological Fraternity •Seventh-Day Adventist Church • Pontifical Council for the Roman Catholic Church •Pentecostal World • Anglican Communion •Orthodox Church •African Instituted Churches • World Methodist Council •Baptist World Alliance •Commission on World Mission and Evangelism

Intended outcomes

The intercontinental and multidenominational initiative has the following intended outcomes:

1. The churches will be provided with an opportunity to celebrate what God has done in the growth of the Church worldwide over the past century and to prayerfully commit to God the witness of the churches in the twenty-first Century.
2. The biblical call to mission will be affirmed and articulated within our contemporary contexts in terms of mission in the world with particular focus on evangelisation.

3. A key conversation on mission will be initiated between e.g.
    - Mission leaders from the older mission movements of the North and the new mission movements from the South and East (on dynamics of new mission movements)
    - Church leaders and mission leaders (on who does what?)
    - Representatives of different Christian traditions (on defining mission theology).
4. Guidelines will be developed to help church and mission leaders evaluate for their own situation models of mission which are proving effective elsewhere.
5. Networks will be mobilized and alliances formed so as to develop greater strategic collaboration and greater synergy in fulfilling the mission mandate.
6. Based on a critical assessment of the status of the world, a new vision in terms of God's purposes for creation in Christ and a renewed spirituality and mission ethos will be developed in the life of the churches worldwide.

A decentralised study process

In important ways the celebration of Edinburgh 2010 and the process leading towards it will be different from the Edinburgh 1910 Conference and study process.

1. Rather than being centred in Edinburgh, a polycentric approach will be taken, both for the study process and for 2010 events which will take place in many locations around the world including Edinburgh.
2. Whereas 1910 was confined to mainline Protestantism, the participants in 2010 will be drawn from the whole range of Christian traditions and confessions.
3. Instead of being largely limited to the North Atlantic, there will be an intentional bias to the South, recognising that Christianity's centre of gravity has moved markedly southwards during the past century. The process will aim to be truly worldwide in its scope.

This chapter summarises some plans for reaching the intended outcomes. First, it outlines the major themes to be considered by the common study process. It will then describe how such a process could be envisaged. Finally, additional themes considered as 'transversals' will be presented. The approach should not be limited to an academic one only, but should – where applicable – seek to include non-formal ways of creating action-based learning. Pilot projects can be organised and/or encouraged in select countries, which will engage Christians in ecumenical mission in such action-reflection processes, focused on one of the nine study themes.

Decentralised study bases and a coordinating office

Recognising the worldwide character of the Church today, it is proposed that institutions, networks and agencies in different parts of the world be invited to contribute to the process in whatever way is best suited to their particular circumstances. Through a coordinating office and a central website, study of the mission themes will be developed through a diversity of contributions. Suggested ways of contributing are:

1. An institution, backed by its governing body, taking the main responsibility for one of the mentioned 2010 mission themes, including provisions for all needed personnel and financial resources. In that case, one can speak of a study commission on one of the themes.
2. Two or more institutions in different parts of the world could combine to form a study commission on one of the 2010 mission themes. Pooling resources, they could collaborate to bring a range of perspectives to the topic which no institution could achieve alone.
3. Existing networks, conferences, colloquia etc could devote part of their programme to consideration of one or more of the 2010 mission themes.
4. Churches and mission agencies could offer case studies of particular situations where significant mission engagement is taking place and which are of relevance to the 2010 mission themes.
5. Individual mission scholars and practitioners could contribute reports, essays etc which shed light on one or more of the 2010 mission themes.

It is hoped that through these different approaches, and perhaps others, many people with mission at heart will be able to contribute to the process. In order to give it coherence, there is a need for coordination. A plan is in preparation to establish a coordinating office in Edinburgh, at the site of the original 1910 Conference. In order to be as light as possible on resources, it is proposed to employ simply one coordinator. The Areopagos Foundation in Scandinavia has agreed to make staff time available to help support the common study process and the Commission on World Mission and Evangelism at the World Council of Churches in Geneva envisages a similar contribution. These centres will work closely together to provide informed and effective coordination.

In bringing together the diverse network of engagement with the mission themes, the attempt will be made to balance high academic standards, strong links to church life and missionary outreach, good communications infrastructure, and access to necessary financial resources. In order to allow the participation of a broad constituency, it was agreed that there would be a need to ensure the effective participation of Orthodox, Pentecostal and

Roman Catholic institutions, as well as the Protestant successors of the bodies which gathered at the original 1910 conference.

The 2010 Mission Themes

1. Foundations for mission

The task will be to explore how a Trinitarian understanding of God as Father, Son and Holy Spirit relates to the theory and practice of mission; how the confession that God has a missionary identity impacts Christian witness; how a discernment of the Trinitarian God's inner relationships and love impacts ecclesiology, community life and society. The meaning of salvation will be considered in its biblical witness and in relation to freedom from every form of slavery in every context and culture. The interfaces between the Trinity, mission, salvation and the interpretation of scripture (hermeneutics) will have to be explored.

2. Christian mission among other faiths

This study track will investigate ways of witnessing to Christ while acknowledging the religious and cultural plurality of a world experiencing a resurgence of religious belief and an escalation of conflict. It will explore the theological meaning of religious plurality reflecting on how it bears on Christian soteriology and missiology and address questions of conversion, proselytism, dialogue and encounter. It will explore issues such as religious fundamentalism, persecution, 'secret' and 'churchless' believers and the continuing growth of many different forms of religious conviction. Studies undertaken under this theme will as much as possible be conducted together with or in consultation with representatives of other faiths.

3. Mission and postmodernities

Work under this theme will concern issues raised by the new phenomena of postmodernity in its various forms in North and South and its significance for mission. This will involve an investigation of 21st century thought structures, religious beliefs and practices as well as ethical principles in a world of information technology. It will also require consideration of the influence of post-colonialism, economic structures, internationalism and engagement (or disengagement) with institutions and particularly with institutional religion. People involved in this study will discern commonalities and particularities in postmodern developments in different regions of the world.

4. Mission and power

The task will be to discern how mission is practised in a world shaped by various forms of power: spiritual, political, military, financial and international; raising issues of culture change, human rights, ecological sustainability and inequalities in the production, distribution and consumption of resources. This track will consider tensions and asymmetries resulting from the exercise of power and how these affect the sharing and communication of the Gospel message and life. It will assess the function of both power and weakness in our understanding and practice of Christian mission.

5. Forms of missionary engagement

Work on this theme will have to start by recognising and considering the huge variety of groups, organisations, trends, methods and new expressions of church life involved in mission today. The task will then involve seeking to discern where initiative lies in today's missionary movement. It will be forward looking in assessing patterns, initiatives and developments as they emerge and consider their implications for the future. It will treat issues of mission and evangelisation strategy, diversity and cooperation and identify problems of conflict and misuse of resources.

6. Theological education and formation

The need is to examine the connection between the catechetical and missional mandates of the Church, consider how to strengthen the missional aspects of the training and formation of every church member, as well as the ordained and lay leaders. Included in the study will be educational methodologies, theological curricula, character development, spiritual formation and the contemporary context. People involved in this theme will further examine the relation between academy and society, clergy and laity, local and global issues, resources, relevance and gifts.

7. Christian communities in contemporary contexts

The task is to examine the variety of Christian communities as they draw on different traditions and engage with specific contexts. It will take cognisance of such issues as urbanisation, immigrant communities, migrant workers, affluence, poverty and virtual worlds. It will note underlying forms of Christian expression including such concepts as world view, language, customs, traditions, inculturation, transformation, etc. It will examine ways in which churches can become holistic healing and reconciling communities, expressing both the welcoming and the transforming character of Christ's Gospel. It will explore what is involved in deep-level conversion.

8. Mission and unity – ecclesiology and mission

The 1910 Edinburgh Conference is considered the starting point of the contemporary ecumenical movement, due to its insistence on the importance of unity and cooperation in worldwide mission. Today, there is a need to revisit the intimate relationship as well as underlying tensions between a focus on mission and a focus on church unity. This track will deal with various interpretations of the link between ecclesiology and mission in theological and practical terms. Interface with the work on the history of mission and ecumenism in the last century (in particular as to the evaluation of 'integration' in 1961) will be key for this area.

9. Mission spirituality and authentic discipleship

Approaching mission spirituality will request to articulate a motivation and dynamic for mission that is rooted in God's Trinitarian identity and led by the vision of God's kingdom. The study will deal with both individual and community forms of spirituality, drawing on the experience of the early church, of Christians from all ages, of new Christian movements, as well as of the many new churches in the South. It will seek to understand mission in relation to such concepts as new creation, spiritual gifts, renewal, reconstruction, identity, holistic witness and service, but also suffering and martyrdom. It will explore the role of the Spirit and of the Church as signs and portents of the goal of all endeavours in the glory of God.

These themes have been developed through a wide-ranging consultative process during 2004-05 and have been affirmed by many mission leaders. However, the process is an open one and the common study programme may well lead to some of the mission themes being expressed in a different way or to entirely new themes being introduced.

Transversal themes

It was recognised that a number of 'transversals' will need to be developed, that is important themes which will run like a thread across all '2010 mission themes'. Several of these, such as Women and mission, Reconciliation and healing, or Bible and mission, may well be followed up by specially constituted groups to ensure that they take effect. This means that the distinction between the above-mentioned '2010 mission themes' and the 'tranversals' is somewhat artificial. Most mentioned themes are overlapping. For the time being the distinction is kept, but flexibility will be needed, as the processes move on. The following 'transversals' have been identified:

- Women and mission
- Youth and mission
- Reconciliation and healing

- Bible and mission, mission in the Bible
- Contextualization, inculturation (gospel and cultures) and dialogue of worldviews
- Subaltern voices
- Ecological perspectives

The kind of critical analysis which would be offered by each transversal is exemplified by the following proposal in regard to Women and mission:

> Women and mission is envisaged as a specific group that will observe the process of each of the study tracks with the brief of (a) ensuring that women's perspectives and issues are properly represented (b) effecting coordination among the individual studies on these issues and (c) dealing with issues of women and mission that do not find place elsewhere.

Fresh Perspectives on Mission: Historical, Geographical and Artistic

Three important additional approaches are being prepared by specialised groups:

1. A realistic look at where we have come from by means of a penetrating and critical historical survey of some specific moments in Christian mission since 1910 which impact the present at world or regional levels.
2. An informative look at where we are now by the creation of an Atlas of Global Christianity. This will show the global spread of present-day Christianity and its difference from the 1910 situation.
3. An international art exhibition, on the theme 'Who is Christ?', as an event for 2010. This will draw on Christian art worldwide and create an exhibition which will be accessible both physically and on the web.

Participation and Prayer

There still exists a high degree of flexibility in planning for 2010. The hope is to generate a unique resource for the worldwide Church through a cooperative and serious study work and dialogues between representatives of various mission efforts, and to feed the fruits of this process into the major 2010 events.

Prayer for this process is the primary form of participation that is needed and invited. Since it is an initiative which is seeking to engage with today's realities at a spiritual level it will only be as strong as its life of prayer.

APPENDIX 2: GOVERNANCE

Edinburgh 2010 General Council, 2007-2010

Church of Scotland: Rev. Andrew Anderson (Chair)
World Student Christian Federation: Rev. Michael Wallace (Co-chair)
African Independent Churches: Prof. Joseph Otubu
Anglican Communion: Rev. John Kafwanka
Asian Pentecostal Society: Dr Julie Ma
Baptist World Alliance: Revd Dr Alistair Brown (2007) / Revd Dr William Slack (2008-2009)
Churches Together in Britain and Ireland: Rev. Canon Edgar Ruddock
Council for World Mission: Dr Des van der Water
International Association for Mission Studies: Dr Cathy Ross
International Fellowship of Evangelical Students: Femi Adeleye
Latin American Theological Fellowship: Ms Ruth Padilla-De Borst
Lausanne Committee for World Evangelization: Rev. Blair Carlson
Lutheran World Federation: Rev. Roger Schmidt
Orthodox Churches: Prof. Petros Vassiliadis
Roman Catholic Church: Ms Maria Aranzazu Aguado Arrese
Seventh Day Adventist Church: Dr Ganoune Diop
World Alliance of Reformed Churches: Ms Jet den Hollander
World Council of Churches: Rev. Dr Jooseop Keum
World Evangelical Alliance: Mrs Rose Dowsett
World Methodist Council: Bishop Heinrich Bolleter

International Council, 2005

The following persons were involved in the initial planning meeting in St Colm's House, Edinburgh on 2-5 June 2005. This meeting formulated the study themes.

International participants

Kwame Bediako, Akrofi-Kristaller, Ghana
Steve Bevans, Catholic Theological Union, Chicago
Nico Botha, Southern African Missiological Association
Ruth Bottoms, World Council of Churches Commission on World Mission and Evangelism
Rose Dowsett, World Evangelical Alliance / Scotland
Tormod Engelsviken, World Council of Churches Commission on World Mission and Evangelism

Kofi deGraft-Johnson, Anglican Communion / Ghana
Michiko Kyoko Ete-Lima, Council for World Mission / Samoa
Sebastian Kim, York St John University / South Korea
Moonjang Lee, Trinity Theological College, Singapore
Carlos Rodriguez Linera, Service of Documentation and Study on Global Mission (SEDOS), Rome
Wonsuk Ma, Pentecostal Seminary, Philippines
Fergus MacDonald, Lausanne Committee for World Evangelization
Jacques Matthey, World Council of Churches / Geneva
Nestor Miguez, Instituto Universitario ISEDET, Buenos Aires
Philomena Mwaura, International Association of Mission Studies / Kenya
Birger Nygaard, Areopagus Foundation, Denmark
Lalsangkima Pachuau, United Theological College, Bangalore
Miguel Palomino, Pentecostal, Peru
Darrell Whiteman, International Association of Mission Studies / USA

Secretariat

David Kerr, University of Edinburgh
David Miller, International Christian College, Glasgow
Kenneth Ross, Church of Scotland
Jack Thompson, University of Edinburgh

Tony McLean-Foreman, Conference Administrator
Elizabeth Grant, Worship Coordinator
Alexis Cumming, Head Steward
Robert Anderson, Director, St Colm's International House

Stakeholders' Meeting, 2006

The following met as stakeholders at St Colm's House, Edinburgh on 4-5 July 2006 to set up the Edinburgh 2010 project.
Maria Arantxa Aguado, Pontifical Council for Promoting Christian Unity
Doug Birdsall, Lausanne Committee for World Evangelization
Jonathan J. Bonk, Overseas Ministries Study Centre, USA
Nico Botha, Southern African Missiological Association
Jet Den Hollander, World Alliance of Reformed Churches
Rose Dowsett, World Evangelical Alliance
Dr Jon Dybdhal, Seventh-day Adventist Church
Knud Jorgensen, Areopagos, Denmark
Fergus MacDonald, United Bible Societies
Jacques Matthey, World Council of Churches
Angus Morrison, Church of Scotland Mission Forum
Philomena Mwaura, International Association for Mission Studies

Kjell Nordstokke, Lutheran World Federation
Birger Nygaard, Areopagos, Denmark
Janice Price, Global Mission Network, Churches Together in Britain and Ireland
Ken Ross, Church of Scotland Mission Council
T. Jack Thompson, University of Edinburgh
Des Van Der Walter, Council for World Mission
Keith Warrington, Pentecostal
Andrew Anderson, Worship Coordinator
John Wylie, Conference Administrator

APPENDIX 3: PROJECT DONORS

The following corporate bodies donated toward the general budget of Edinburgh 2010. Donations by individuals are not included. Many other people and and organisations supported related activities directly, sponsored delegates or gave in kind.

ACTS (Action of Churches Together in Scotland)
Anglican Consultative Council
Areopagos, Denmark
Baptist World Alliance
Baptist World Mission
Church of England Archbishop's Council
Church of Scotland Ecumenical Relations
Church of Scotland Mission and Discipleship
Church of Scotland World Mission Council
Church of Sweden
Churches Together in Britain and Ireland
Council for World Mission
Evangelical Lutheran Church in America (ELCA)
Evangelisches Missionswerk (EMW), Germany
Finnish Evangelical Lutheran Mission
Lausanne Committee for World Evangelization
Lund Missionary Society
The Methodist Church of Great Britain
New College, Edinburgh
Norwegian Mission Society
Pollock Trust
Pontifical Council for Promoting Christian Unity
Presbyterian Church in Canada
Presbytery of Denver, USA
Protestantse Kerk in Nederland
Scottish (Catholic) Bishops Conference
Scottish Churches House
Scottish Episcopal Church
Scottish Journal of Theology
Seventh Day Adventist Church
Society in Scotland for Promoting Christian Knowledge (SSPCK)
Women's Missionary Society of the Presbyterian Church in Canada
World Alliance of Reformed Churches
World Council of Churches
Yoido Full Gospel Church, Korea
Youngnak Presbyterian Church, Korea

Appendix 4: Conference Programme

Time \ Day	Wednesday, 2 June	Thursday, 3 June	Friday, 4 June	Saturday, 5 June	Sunday, 6 June
7:00 – 9:00		Confessional Observances (optional)	Confessional Observances (optional)	Confessional Observances (optional)	**Breakfast**
		Breakfast	**Breakfast**	**Breakfast**	
9:00 – 9:40		Opening Celebration (SH)	Common Prayer (PS)	Common Prayer (PS)	Conference services in local churches with local families plus lunch; (see distributed lists)
9:50 – 10:30			Sharing Scripture	Sharing Scripture	
10:30 – 11:00		**Coffee/tea Break**	**Coffee/tea Break**	**Coffee/tea Break**	
11:00 – 13:00		Opening Plenary 'Mission in long perspective' (PS)	Plenary 2 'Mission Worldwide' (PS)	Parallel sessions: Themes 9, 7 & 3	
13:00 – 14:15		**Lunch**	**Lunch**	**Lunch**	
14:15 – 16:00	Arrivals and registration at JMCC, Pollock Halls	Parallel sessions: Themes 1, 5 & 2	Parallel sessions: Themes 8, 4 & 6	Parallel sessions: Themes 9, 7 & 3	

16:00 – 16:30		**Coffee/tea break**	**Coffee/tea break**	**Coffee/tea break**	**15:00 – 17:30** Closing Celebration General Assembly Hall of the Church of Scotland
16:30 – 18:00		Parallel sessions: Themes 1, 5 & 2	Parallel sessions: Themes 8, 4 & 6	Ecumenical Pilgrimage (optional) Local Events (optional)	
18:00	**Dinner**	Travel to Parliament	**Dinner**	**Dinner**	**Dinner (from 18:30)**
19:00 +		**19:00 – 20:00** Welcome by Scottish Parliament	**19:30 – 21:00** Local Events (optional)		
20:00 +	**20:00** Evening welcome and orientation (PS)	**20:30 – 21:15** **Serving Dinner**	**21:30 – 00:30** Ceilidh & Bar (SH)	**20:00** Closing Plenary 'Towards a common call' (PS)	
21:30		Night Prayer (optional)	Night Prayer (optional)	Night Prayer (optional)	

JMCC – John McIntyre Conference Centre, PS – Pentland Suite, SH – South Hall

APPENDIX 5: PLENARY SESSIONS

Plenary 1: 'Mission in long perspective'
Thursday 3 June 2010, 11.00am-12.50pm

Chairpersons

Dr Philomema Mwaura, Senior Lecturer in Philosophy and Religious Studies, Kenyatta University, Nairobi
Rev. Roger Schmidt, Youth Secretary, Lutheran World Federation

Contributors

KEYNOTE SPEAKER

Dr Dana Robert, Truman Collins Professor of World Christianity and History of Mission, Boston University School of Theology, USA

COMPLEMENTARY PERSPECTIVES

Bishop Brian Farrell, Secretary of the Pontifical Council for Promoting Christian Unity, Holy See
Revd Dr Tinyiko Maluleke, Executive Director: Research, University of South Africa
Bishop Geevarghese Mor Coorilos, Malankara Syriac Orthodox Church, India
Rev. Bertil Ekström, Executive Director, World Evangelical Alliance Mission Commission, Brazil

Plenary 2: 'Mission worldwide'
Friday 4 June 2010, 11.00am-12.50pm

Chairpersons

Dr Ruben 'Tito' Parades-Alfaro, Director of the Evangelical Center for Amazonian and Andean Mission(CEMAA), Lima, Peru
Ms Kyriaki Avtzi, Conference of European Churches, Churches in Dialogue Commission

Contributors

Rev. Lee Young-Hoon, Senior Pastor, Yoido Full Gospel Church, Seoul: 'Christian spirituality and the diakonic mission of the Yoido Full Gospel Church'
Dr Antonios Kireopoulos, Senior Program Director for Faith & Order and Interfaith Relations, National Council of Churches USA: 'Ecumenical charity as Christian witness'
Dr Prof Teresa Francesca Rossi, Associate Director, Centro Pro Unione, Rome: 'A missing mission? The "Budding Ecumenism" Formation Project of the Centro Pro Unione'
Dr Fidon Mwombeki, General Secretary, United Evangelical Mission, Germany: 'Mission to the North: Challenges and prospects'

Plenary 3: 'Towards a common call'
Saturday 5 June, 8.00-9.30pm

Chairperson

Rev. Dr Michael Kinnamon, General Secretary, National Council of Churches USA

Reflectors

Rev. Dr Stephen B. Bevans, SVD, Louis J. Luzbatek, S.V.D. Professor of Mission and Culture, Catholic Theological Union, USA
Dr Vinoth Ramachandra, Secretary for Dialogue & Social Engagement, International Fellowship of Evangelical Students (IFES)
Mrs Anastasia Vassiliadou, Aristotle University of Thessaloniki, Greece

Bio Data of Plenary Speakers

Dr. Dana L. Robert, Boston University School of Theology

Dr Dana L. Robert is the Truman Collins Professor of World Christianity and History of Mission at the Boston University School of Theology. In her twenty-five years of teaching she has directed approximately sixty doctoral dissertations in mission studies and the history of world Christianity. Former students hold teaching and ministry positions around the world. At Boston University, Robert also directs the Center for Global Christianity and Mission (www.bu.edu/cgcm) and is affiliated with the African Studies Center.

Robert's books include American Women in Mission: A Social History of Their Thought and Practice (1997), Christianity: A Social and Cultural History (co-author, 1997), 'Occupy Until I Come': A.T. Pierson and the Evangelization of the World (2003), African Christian Outreach: Vol. 2 Mission Churches (ed., 2003), Converting Colonialism: Visions and Realities in Mission History, 1706-1914 (ed., 2008), and Christian Mission: How Christianity Became a World Religion (2009). Her most recent book is the 2010-2011 mission study text for the United Methodist Church, Joy to the World! Mission in the Age of Global Christianity (2010). With her husband Marthinus L. Daneel, a leading scholar of African Indigenous Churches and African Traditional Religions in Southern Africa, Robert co-edits the book series African Initiatives in Christian Mission, published by the University of South Africa Press. She serves on the editorial boards of major journals, including the International Bulletin of Missionary Research, Church History, and Missionalia. In 2006 she launched the online History of Missiology website to provide resources in the history of nineteenth- and twentieth-century mission thought (http://digilib.bu.edu/mission).

Robert is a lifelong lay United Methodist from Baton Rouge, Louisiana. She serves on the Committee on Faith and Order for the denomination, and for many years has chaired the denominational professors of mission. She received her bachelor's degree in history from Louisiana State University, and her masters' and doctorate in religious studies from Yale University. In support of her husband's ministry among African Indigenous Churches, she travels regularly to Masvingo, Zimbabwe. She has two grown sons and lives mostly in Somerville, Massachusetts. As a visible reminder of the forgotten lay women who have supported missions over the past century, Robert is carrying a piece of her hundred year old grandmother's handmade quilt to all the 2010 events she attends.

Rev. Dr Young-Hoon Lee, Senior Pastor, Yoido Full Gospel Church

Rev. Young-Hoon Lee's great-grandfather was converted to Christianity by one of the first missionaries at Pyongyang, North Korea. Since then, each generation of his family has believed in Christ. Born in Seoul, Korea, on 19 November 19 1954, and raised by devout Christian parents, Lee learned how to please God and how to serve the Lord from his early childhood.

In April 1964, Lee joined the Full Gospel Central Church (now Yoido Full Gospel Church) in Seodaemun where Rev. Yonggi Cho preached. There, Lee had a personal experience with the living God by receiving the baptism in the Holy Spirit and speaking in tongues. Called to ministry, Lee went to Yonsei University to study theology. After graduation, he attended Full Gospel Theological Seminary (now Hansei University), and then on to United Graduate School of Theology, Yonsei University, graduating with a Master of Theology.

In 1977, Lee began his ministry at the Yoido Full Gospel Church in Seoul, Korea as the Editor-in-Chief for Youngsan Publishers (now Seoul Logos) and as the first editor of the Full Gospel Newspaper. He was also one of the founding members of the Institute for Full Gospel Education (now International Theological Institute). After his ordination in 1982, Lee completed a Master of Theology at Westminster Theological Seminary in Philadelphia. He received an MA and a PhD in Philosophy of Religion at Temple University. During this time of study, Lee served as Senior Pastor at Full Gospel First Church of Washington.

When Lee returned to Korea, he systematised and theologised Rev. Yonggi Cho's pastoral principles as the executive director of the International Theological Institute at Yoido Full Gospel Church. Lee has served as the Senior Pastor of Full Gospel Tokyo Church, as a professor at Hansei University (Korea), as the President of Bethesda Christian University (USA), as the President of Japan Full Gospel Bible College, as the Chairman of the Theological Committee for the National Council of Churches in Korea, as a Theological Committee member of Asia Pacific Theological Association (APTA), as the Senior Pastor of Full Gospel LA Church, and as the Vice-Chairman of the Council of Korean Churches in Southern California, and as the Co-President of Christian Council of Korea. Currently, Lee serves as the Senior Pastor of the Yoido Full Gospel Church, as the Co-President of Christian Council of Korea, and as the General Superintendent of the Assemblies of God of Korea, and as the Moderator of the National Council of Churches in Korea.

In 2008 he succeeded Rev. Cho as the Senior Pastor of the Yoido Full Gospel Church. Anticipating the second revival of the Yoido Full Gospel Church, he is now leading the Holy Spirit Movement and the Church Unity Movement. Lee's faith is characterised by the fullness of the Spirit, absolute positivity, Christ-centred life, and by a faithful life of early-morning prayer. He emphasises Christian sanctification, inner healing, and fruit-bearing life. He also urges his people to live by Spirit-filled faith, centred on the Cross of Jesus. Under the leadership of servant-hood within the church, he aims to steer the church in the direction of serving the underprivileged, bringing about change in society.

Lee and his wife, In-Ja Baik, have one daughter, Grace Sung-Eun.

Dr Antonios Kireopoulos, National Council of Churches in the USA

Dr. Antonios Kireopoulos is Associate General Secretary for Faith and Order and Interfaith Relations at the National Council of Churches of Christ in the USA. In this capacity he is responsible for the theological work done among both ecumenical and interfaith partners. Previously Kireopoulos directed the Council's work in international affairs. An Orthodox Christian theologian, he holds degrees from Georgetown University's School of Foreign Service, Thunderbird School of Global Management, St. Vladimir's Orthodox Theological Seminary, and Fordham University.

Kireopoulos' published works include: 'Theological Reflections on Security and Vulnerability', in *Arms Trade: Final Report from the 2nd Ecumenical Conference in Gothenburg* (2004); 'Witnessing the Peace of God in a Violent World', in *Violence and Christian Spirituality: An Ecumenical Conversation,* ed. Emmanuel Clapsis (2007); 'The US Response to *A Common Word Between Us and You*: An Affirmation of Theology as the Primary Rationale for Dialogue', in *Ecumenical Trends* 38 (3) 2009; and 'The State of Interreligious Affairs in the United States Today', in *Ecumenical Trends* 39 (1) 2010.

Kireopoulos' forthcoming publications include: 'Orthodoxy and Islam: An Uncommon Opportunity?' in *The Greek Orthodox Theological Review* (2007); 'Orthodoxy in the Public Square: The Contextual Reality and the Theological Challenge', in *Religious Pluralism in 21st Century American Public Life: the Challenges and Opportunities for Orthodox Christianity,* ed. Elizabeth H. Prodromou (2010); 'Papal Authority and the Ministry of Primacy', *The Greek Orthodox Theological Review* 42 (1-2) 1997; 'The Role of Ecumenical Charity in Christian Mission', in *Journal of Ecumenical Studies* (2010); 'Seeking Justice and Promoting Human Rights: Orthodox Theological Imperatives or Afterthoughts?' in *Sophia: Studies in Orthodox Theology, Vol. 2* (2010); *The Ecumenical Movement: An Anthology of Key Texts and Voices*, 2nd Edition, edited with Michael Kinnamon (forthcoming 2011); and *Some Ecumenical Directions in the US Today: Churches on a Theological Journey*, edited with Juliana Mecera (forthcoming 2011).

Dr Teresa Francesca Rossi,
Pontifical University of St. Thomas Aquinas

Teresa Francesca Rossi is Associate Director of the Centro Pro Unione, Rome (Franciscan Friars of the Atonement). Rossi received a Baccalaureate in Philosophy in 1988, a Baccalaureate in Theology in 1991, a Licence in Theology in 1994, and a Doctorate in Theology, with a specialisation in ecumenism, all from the Pontifical University of St Thomas Aquinas in Rome.

Rossi has served as Professor of Ecumenical Theology at the Pontifical University of St Thomas Aquinas in Rome since 1998; at the Pontifical Athenaeum St Anselm, Rome, since 2008; and at the Istituto Filosofico Teologico Viterbese since 1997. She teaches courses on ecumenism, the Pentecostal Movement, the World Council of Churches, and the question of lay ministry and women in ministry from an ecumenical perspective. She has lectured on ecumenism both in Italy and abroad extensively. Rossi's many publications include *Il Ministero della donna nella Chiesa* (Rome, 1998) and the revised edition of *The New Directory of Ecumenical Research Centres and Publication* (online at www.prounione.urbe.it).

Rossi has also served as Vice-Dean of the Faculty of Theology of the Pontifical University of St Thomas Aquinas in Rome (2001-2007); as a member of the 'Comitato di Referenti per il Master in Teologia Ecumenica' of the Istituto di Studi Ecumenici San Bernardino, Venezia, affiliated to the Pontifical University Antonianum, Rome (since 2009); and as author and coordinator of the project 'Ecumenismo in erba' (Budding Ecumenism), an initiative of Ecumenical Reception at grassroot level for children (3-13 years old) at the Centro Pro Unione, Rome (since 2003).

Rossi's many ecumenical responsibilities have included membership in the Joint Working Group between the Catholic Church and the World Council of Churches (mandate 1999-2006, reconfirmed for the mandate 2007-2013); membership in the International Baptist-Catholic dialogue (International Theological Conversations between the Pontifical Council for Promoting Christian Unity and the World Baptist Alliance for the mandate 2006-2011); and participation in the Edinburgh Study Group within the Edinburgh 2010 Study Process since 2008.

Rossi has also held a number of offices for the Diocese of Rome and for various ecumenical organisations such as the Permanent Joint Working Group on Petrine Ministry, a study project of the International Bridgetine Center in Farfa (2005-2010). She is involved at the pastoral level as former catechist and member of the Liturgical Group in the Parish Santissimo Nome di Maria alla Caffarelletta and as missionary for the Great Jubilee for the Diocese of Rome, among other activities and organisational responsibilities.

Rev. Dr Fidon R. Mwombeki, United Evangelical Mission

Fidon R. Mwombeki is General Secretary of United Evangelical Mission (July 2006 – present). He holds a Bachelor of Divinity (Makumira, Tanzania, 1987), a Master of Sacred Theology (Trinity Lutheran Seminary, USA, 1994), an MBA (California Coast University, USA, 1997), and a PhD from Luther Seminary, USA (1997). His dissertation was entitled 'Biblical Interpretation in a Current African Situation: The Case of Blood'.

Mwombeki's publications include 'Global Mission: An African Perspective', *Global Vision* 7 (1996); 'The Role of the Church in Development Work' in the *Report on Workshop on Capacity Building for Africa* (1999); 'Are We of the Same God?: A Pastor's Day Reveals Tanzania's Heavy Debt Burden', *The Lutheran* (2000); 'Ecology in the New Testament' in *Christian Theology and Environmental Responsibility*, edited by J.N.K. Mugambi and Mika Vahakangas (2001); 'The South Cries for "Fair" Trade, the North Wants 'Free' Trade', *Habari Tanzania Network.de* 1 (2002); 'Etikken i Partnerskab' in *Mission og Etik*, edited by Harald Nielsen (2003), 'Churches and the Vocation of Government in Africa', in *Communion, Responsibility, Accountability: Responding as a Lutheran Communion to Neoliberal Globalization*, edited by Karen L. Bloomquist (2004); 'The Theology of the Cross: Does it Make Sense to Africa?' in *The Gift of Grace*, edited by Nils Henrik Gregsen (2005); and 'Mission und Entwicklung: Ein Definitionsproblem' in *Mission und Entwicklung: Texte, Dokumente und Reportagen* (2009).

Prior to serving as General Secretary for United Evangelical Mission, Mwombeki served as pastor in Bukoba at the Evangelical Lutheran Church in Tanzania (1988); in Missionary Exchange in Sweden (1989), as Secretary for Communication and Literature, Evangelical Lutheran Church in Tanzania (1989-1992), as Pastor for the Swahili-speaking congregation in Minnesota, USA (1994-1997), as Secretary for Evangelism for Evangelical Lutheran Church in Tanzania for the North Western Diocese (1997-1998), as Deputy General Secretary for Evangelical Lutheran Church in Tanzania of the North Western Diocese (1999-2000), as General Secretary for Evangelical Lutheran Church in Tanzania for the North Western Diocese (2000-2004), and as Executive Secretary for Evangelism for United Evangelical Mission, Germany (2005-June 2006).

APPENDIX 6: PARALLEL SESSIONS ON STUDY THEMES

Theme 1. Foundations for Mission

Chairpersons

Dr Ganoune Diop, Director of the Global Mission Study Centers, Seventh-day Adventist Church
Rev. Dr Clifton Kirkpatrick, President, World Alliance of Reformed Churches

Study group representatives

Convener: Canon Janice Price, Church of England
Convener: Revd Dr Deenabandhu Manchala, World Council of Churches
Dr Peniel Rajkumar, United Theological College, Bangalore

Transversal contributors

2 YOUTH AND MISSION

Andrew R.H. Thompson, USA, Edinburgh 2010 Youth Essay Competition winner

3 HEALING AND RECONCILIATION

Dr Beate Jakob, German Institute for Medical Mission (Difäm) and Coordinator of WCC/Difäm project on mission and healing

4 BIBLE AND MISSION

Dr Marie-Hélène Robert, Francophone Association for Mission Studies (AFOM)

5 CONTEXTUALISATION, INCULTURATION AND DIALOGUE OF WORLDVIEWS

Dr Allen Yeh, Biola University, USA

7 ECOLOGICAL PERSPECTIVES ON MISSION

Rev. Dr John Kapya Kaoma, St. John's Anglican Seminary, Zambia /Political Research Associates, USA

Contributors from regional, confessional and other perspectives

PENTECOSTAL PERSPECTIVE
Rev. Dr Miguez Alvarez, Church of God, USA

ORTHODOX PERSPECTIVE
Dr Petros Vassiliadis, Aristotle University of Thessaloniki, Greece

CATHOLIC PERSPECTIVE
Dr Stephen B. Bevans, SVD, Catholic Theological Union, Chicago

Theme 2. Christian Mission Among Other Faiths

Chairpersons

Rev. Doug Birdsall, Executive Chair, Lausanne Committee for World Evangelisation
Dr Glory Dharmaraj, Director, Spiritual Formation & Mission Theology, The United Methodist Church, USA

Study group representatives

Convener: Dr Lalsangkima Pachuau, Asbury Theological Seminary, USA
Convener: Dr Niki Papageorgiou, Aristotle University of Thessalonki, Greece
Revd Dr John Azumah, London School of Theology, UK

Transversal contributors

2 YOUTH AND MISSION
Dr Gwen Bryde, University of Hamburg, Germany

3 HEALING AND RECONCILIATION
Revd Dr Philip Tye-Yau Siew, Malaysia Theological Seminary (STM)

Contributors from regional, confessional and other perspectives

UNITED THEOLOGICAL COLLEGE, BANGALORE, CONFERENCE ON INTER-RELIGIOUS RELATIONS
Dr Marina Behera, India

BOSTON STUDENT CONFERENCE
Dr Todd Johnson, Gordon-Conwell Theological Seminary, USA

WORLD COUNCIL OF CHURCHES' COMMISSION ON WORLD MISSION AND EVANGELISM

Dr Hesdie Zamuel, Moravian Church, Suriname/Tanzania
Rev. Dr Ronald Wallace, Presbyterian Church in Canada

CATHOLIC PERSPECTIVE

Fr Jan Lenssen M.Afr., Belgium/Africa

EVANGELISCHES MISSIONSWERK IN SÜDWESTDEUTSCHLAND, 'CHRISTIAN WITNESS IN A PLURALISTIC WORLD' PROGRAMME

Rev. Ulrike Schmidt-Hesse, Head of Mission and Partnership Department and Deputy General Secretary, Association of Churches and Missions in South West Germany (EMS)

AREOPAGOS, DENMARK

Dr Knud Jorgensen, Norway and Hong Kong

Theme 3. Mission and Postmodernities

Chairpersons

Dr Isabel Phiri, Professor in African Theology, University of KwaZulu Natal, South Africa
Rev. Martin Breitenfeldt, Director, mission 21, Switzerland

Study group representatives

Convener: Revd Andrew Kirk, formerly Senior Lecturer in Mission and World Christianity, University of Birmingham
Convener: Dr Kajsa Ahlstrand, University of Uppsala
Rev. Rolv Olsen, Egede Institute, Norway

Transversals

3 HEALING AND RECONCILIATION

International Peace and Reconciliation Conferences
Revd Professor Sebastian C.H. Kim, York St John University, UK

6 SUBALTERN VOICES

Christian Conference of Asia conference on 'Revisiting mission from a colonised land'
M. P. Joseph, Chang Jung Christian University, Taiwan

7 ECOLOGICAL PERSPECTIVES ON MISSION
Christian Faith and the Earth symposium
Dr Ernst Conradie, University of the Western Cape, South Africa

Contributors from regional, confessional and other perspectives

UNITED EVANGELICAL MISSION CONFERENCE ON 'GLOBAL IMPULSES FOR THE 21ST CENTURY'
Rev. Dr Claudia Währisch-Oblau, UEM, Germany

URBANIANA UNIVERSITY EDINBURGH 2010 CONFERENCE
Professor Gianni Colzani, Pontifical Urbaniana University, Rome

PENTECOSTAL PERSPECTIVE
Rev. Dr Harold D. Hunter, International Pentecostal Holiness Church, USA

ORTHODOX PERSPECTIVE
Anastasia Vassiliadou, University of Thessaloniki, Greece

Theme 4. Mission and Power

Chairpersons

Rev. Christoph Anders, Director, Evangelisches Missionswerk, Germany
Rev. Dr Mary Mikhael, President, Near East School of Theology, Lebanon

Study group representatives

Convener: Dr Jonathan Bonk, Overseas Ministries Study Center, USA
Convener: Lori Ransom, Presbyterian Church in Canada
Terry Leblanc, Canada First Nations

Transversal contributors

1 WOMEN AND MISSION
Dr Atola Longkumer, Leonard Theological College, India

2 YOUTH AND MISSION
ECHOS Commission on Youth in the Ecumenical Movement
Jec Dan S. Borlado, Philippines

6 SUBALTERN VOICES
'Mission at and from the Margins' project, Dalit voices, India

Rev. Dr Dayam Joseph Prabhakar, Andhra Evangelical Lutheran Church

Contributors from regional, confessional and other perspectives

LATIN AMERICAN THEOLOGICAL FELLOWSHIP CONFERENCES ON 'MISSION AND POWER'

Rev. Victor Rey Riquelme, President, LATF

NATIONAL ABORIGINAL AND TORRES STRAIT ISLANDER ECUMENICAL COMMISSION (NATSIEC), NATIONAL COUNCIL OF CHURCHES, AUSTRALIA

Graeme Mundine, NATSIEC Executive Secretary

EMW (ASSOCIATION OF PROTESTANTS CHURCHES AND MISSIONS IN GERMANY) AND MISSION ACADEMY HAMBURG STUDY DOCUMENT ON MISSION AND POWER, AND THE GERMAN ASSOCIATION FOR MISSION STUDIES (DGMW) CONFERENCE

Dr Michael Biehl, Academy of Mission at the University of Hamburg, Germany

PENTECOSTAL-CHARISMATIC PERSPECTIVE

Dr Veli-Matti Kärkkäinen, Professor of Systematic Theology, Fuller Theological Seminary, USA & Docent of Ecumenics, University of Helsinki

Theme 5. Forms of Missionary Engagement

Chairpersons

Apostle Dr Opoku Onyinah, Chairman, Church of Pentecost, Ghana
Dr Darrell Whiteman, Vice-President, The Mission Society, USA

Study group representatives

Convener: Canon Mark Oxbrow, Faith2Share, UK
Convener: Dr Genevieve James, University of South Africa

Transversal contributors

2 YOUTH AND MISSION

Jose Lopez Vasquez, Presbyterian, Mexico

4 BIBLE AND MISSION

Bible Societies 'Scripture engagement' work
Dr Bill Mitchell, Canada

5 CONTEXTUALISATION, INCULTURATION AND DIALOGUE OF WORLDVIEWS
Ujaama contextual Bible study project, University of South Africa
Dr Sarojini Nadar, South Africa

Contributors from regional, confessional and other perspectives

CATHOLIC PERSPECTIVE
Dr Francesca Teresa Rossi, Associate Director, Centro Pro Unione, Rome

ORTHODOX PERSPECTIVE
Minsk conference on 'Christian Mission in the 21st Century'
Olga Oleinik, Belarus

COUNCIL FOR WORLD MISSION (CWM)
Revd Dr Roderick Hewitt, United Church in Jamaica and the Cayman Islands

FJELLHAUG SYMPOSIUM ON 'MISSION AND GLOBALISATION', NORWAY
Erling Lundeby, Assistant Professor, Fjellhaug Mission Seminary, Oslo

CONFERENCE OF ASIAN THEOLOGIANS ON 'DOING MISSION FROM THE UNDERSIDE'
Dr Sung Kuk Park, Christian Conference of Asia

Theme 6. Theological Education and Formation

Chairpersons
Dr Brian Stanley, Professor of World Christianity, University of Edinburgh
Rev. Dr Desmond van der Water, General Secretary, Council for World Mission

Study group representatives
Convener: Dr Dietrich Werner, Ecumenical Institute, Bossey, Switzerland
Convener: Dr Namsoon Kang, Brite Divinity School, Texas Christian University, USA
Rev. Dr David Esterline, McCormick Seminary, USA

Transversal contributors

1 WOMEN AND MISSION

Dr Fulata Mbano-Moyo, Programme Executive, Women in Church and Society, World Council of Churches

2 YOUTH AND MISSION

Wendy Strachan, Scripture Union International Children's Ministry

Contributors from regional, confessional and other perspectives

CATHOLIC MISSION THEOLOGICAL EDUCATION

Dr Anthony Gittins, Catholic Theological Union, Chicago

EVANGELICAL MISSION THEOLOGICAL EDUCATION

Dr John Hitchen, Laidlaw College, New Zealand

PENTECOSTAL MISSION THEOLOGICAL EDUCATION

Dr Julie Ma, Oxford Centre for Mission Studies, UK

ORTHODOX MISSION THEOLOGICAL EDUCATION

Rev. Mikhail Goundiaev, Moscow Patriarchate and Ecumenical Centre, Geneva

NON-WESTERN MODELS OF MISSION THEOLOGICAL EDUCATION

Dr Ken Christoph Miyamoto, Kobe Shoin Women's University, Japan

Theme 7. Christian Communities in Contemporary Contexts

Chairpersons

Rev. Dr Walter Altmann, Moderator, World Council of Churches
Dr Marian McClure Taylor, Executive Director, Kentucky Council of Churches, USA

Study group representatives

Convener: Dr Afe Adogame, University of Edinburgh
Convener: Dr Philomena Mwaura, Kenyatta University, Nairobi
Ms Erica Dunmow, JITC UK Urban Mission Congress Executive
Dr Janice McLean, City Seminary, New York

Transversal contributors

4 BIBLE AND MISSION

Dr Daniel Patte, Professor of New Testament and Early Christianity, Vanderbilt University, USA

3 RECONCILIATION AND HEALING

Ms Claudine Chionh, Australia Edinburgh 2010 conference

7 ECOLOGICAL PERSPECTIVES ON MISSION

Rev. Carlos Rodriguez, Director, SEDOS Service of Documentation and Study, Rome

Contributors from regional, confessional and other perspectives

SOUTHERN AFRICA MISSIOLOGICAL SOCIETY (SAMS), CONFERENCE ON 'STORIES OF HOPE-GIVING COMMUNITIES IN SOUTHERN-AFRICA'

Dr Nico Botha, University of South Africa

GLOBAL MISSION CONSULTATION AND CELEBRATION, TOKYO 2010

Dr. Yong Cho, Tokyo 2010 Planning Committee Chairperson and Director of the Global Network of Mission Structures

CLAI (LATIN AMERICAN COUNCIL OF CHURCHES) CONFERENCE ON MISSION IN THE CONTEMPORARY CONTEXT

Dr Carlos Ham, World Council of Churches Programme Executive for Latin America and the Caribbean

ORTHODOX PERSPECTIVE

Dr Antonios Kireopoulos, National Council of Churches USA

ATLAS OF GLOBAL CHRISTIANITY PROJECT

Revd Professor Ken Ross, Church of Scotland

Theme 8. Mission and Unity – Ecclesiology and Mission

Chairpersons

Revd Professor Dr Viorel Ionita, Director of the Churches in Dialogue Commission, Conference of European Churches
Sr Dr Geraldine Smyth OP, Senior Lecturer in Ecumenics, Irish School of Ecumenics, Dublin

Study group representatives

Convener (Moderator): Revd Dr Darrell Jackson, Redcliffe College, UK
Convener: Ms Kyriaki Avtzi, Conference of European Churches
Convener: Rev. Dr Laszlo Gonda, Debrecen Reformed Theological University, Hungary

Transversal contributors

2 YOUTH AND MISSION AND 3 RECONCILIATION AND HEALING

Fr Vineeth Koshy, Executive Secretary, Commission on Youth, National Council of Churches in India

5 CONTEXTUALISATION, INCULTURATION AND DIALOGUE OF WORLDVIEWS

World Evangelical Alliance working group on contextualisation
Dr Matthew Cook, Faculté de Théologie Evangélique de l'Alliance Chrétienne, Cote d'Ivoire

6 SUBALTERN VOICES

Ms Virginia Beardy, Former Urban-Rural Mission, Canada

Contributors from regional, confessional and other perspectives

Institut Africain des sciences de la mission, Kinshasa
Rev. Baudouin Mubesala, Congo
Conference on Christian Unity in Mission and Service, Liverpool, UK
Professor Daniel Jeyaraj, Director of the University's Andrew F Walls Centre for the Study of African and Asian Christianity, Liverpool Hope University
World Alliance of Reformed Churches/Lutheran World Federation project 'Mission Today'
Mr Julio C. López, Argentina
European Pentecostal Charismatic Research Association
Dr Jean-Daniel Pluess, Switzerland

Theme 9. Mission Spirituality and Authentic Discipleship

Chairpersons

Most Revd Mario Joseph Conti, Archbishop of Glasgow, UK
Rev. Bertil Ekström, Executive Director of the World Evangelical Alliance Mission Commission, Brazil

Study group representatives

Convener: Dr Wonsuk Ma, Oxford Centre for Mission Studies, UK
Convener: Dr Cathy Ross, Church Mission Society UK
Dr Tom Harvey, Oxford Centre for Mission Studies, UK

Transversal contributors

4 BIBLE AND MISSION

Professor Nicolae Mosoiu, Romanian Orthodox Church

5 CONTEXTUALISATION, INCULTURATION AND DIALOGUE OF WORLDVIEWS

Rev. Dr Andrea Zaki Stephanous, Coptic Evangelical Organisation for Social Services, Egypt

6 SUBALTERN VOICES

Ecumenical Disabilities Network (EDAN)
Sarah Newland-Martin, Jamaica

7 ECOLOGICAL PERSPECTIVES ON MISSION

Dr Rogate Mshana, Director, Justice , Diakonia and Responsibility for Creation and Program Executive for Poverty, Wealth and Ecology, World Council of Churches

Contributors from regional, confessional and other perspectives

WCC COMMISSION ON WORLD MISSION AND EVANGELISM SPIRITUALITY GROUP

Megan O'Callaghan, New Zealand

PROJECT OF INSTITUTO DE MISIONOLOGÍA, UNIVERSIDAD CATÓLICA BOLIVIANA, COCHABAMBA

Rev. Calixto Salvatierra, Bolivia

WEST AFRICA REGIONAL E2010 CONFERENCE AT AKROFI-CHRISTALLER CENTRE, GHANA

Revd Dr Kwabena Asamoah-Gyadu, Trinity Theological Seminary, Legon

ASBURY THEOLOGICAL SEMINARY REVITALISATION CONFERENCE AND PROJECT

Dr J. Steven O'Malley, USA
Dr Joshua Kalapati, Associate Professor of Philosophy, Madras Christian College, India

APPENDIX 7: DAILY COMMON PRAYER SERVICES

Wednesday June 2: Songs and Welcomes

1. Gathering

Delegates gather in the Pentland Suite to the sound of drums

SONGS AS PEOPLE GATHER

'Bless the Lord' (Kenya)

Cantor My sisters ...
All Bless the Lord, there is no other God.
Cantor My brothers ... You children ... You elders ...
Together ... .

Text: derived from psalms. Music: Kenyan traditional song. Source: *There is One Among Us* (Glasgow: Wild Goose Publications); *Church Hymnary Four/Hymns of Glory, Songs of Praise* (Norwich: Canterbury); *Sing Glory* (Jubilate/Mayhew).

'God welcomes all' (South Africa)

God welcomes all, strangers and friends.
God's love is strong and it never ends.

'Themba Amen'. Words: John L. Bell © WGRG/Iona Community. Music: South African traditional. Source: *We Walk His Way* (Glasgow: Wild Goose Publications)

Introduction [given in all three languages]

One hundred years ago in this city,
men and women who were engaged in mission
came together from every part of the globe.
As they told their stories and prayed for each other,
they were surprised by the Spirit with a moment of inspiration,
when they glimpsed a vision of a united church
speaking with one voice the name of Christ,
and saw within grasp a world won for the gospel.
Now in a different age,
where violence and injustice still prevail,
where Christian witness is still fragmented,
and where secular forces mass against the gospel,
we gather to pray for a new moment of vision,
for new energy, fresh inspiration, and new resources
for witnessing to Christ today.

GREETING

We are invited to greet someone we have not yet met, telling them our name, country, church family, and sharing with them what we are looking forward to in the conference.

A SEQUENCE OF SONG

Americas '*Vamos todos al banquete*' (El Salvador)
Text: Misa Popular Salvadoreña. Music: Guillermo Cuéllar. Source: GIA Publications Inc., USA.

Europe '*Sfinte Dumnezeule*' (Romania)
Melody and text: Orthodox Liturgy of Romania. Source: *Thuma Mina* (Basileia Verlag, Basel; Strube Verlag, Műnchen-Berlin).

Asia, Pacific '*God, who made the earth*' (Korea)
Words: John L Bell. Music: Korean folk melody. Source: *One is the Body* (Glasgow: Wild Goose Publications); *Church Hymnary Four/Hymns of Glory, Songs of Praise* (Norwich: Canterbury Press).

Africa '*Munezero*' (Rwanda)
Text and melody: Leonidas Ntibimenya. Source: *Thuma Mina* ((Basileia Verlag, Basel; Strube Verlag, Műnchen-Berlin); *Worshipping Ecumenically* (Geneva: WCC Publications).

Scotland 'Sing to God with gladness'
Words: Fr James Quinn SJ. Music: Gaelic folk melody. Source: *Praise for All Seasons* (London: Chapman/Cassell); *New Songs of Praise 1* (Oxford: OUP); *Church Hymnary Four/Hymns of Glory, Songs of Praise* (Norwich: Canterbury Press).

2. The welcomes

Delegates were welcomed by representatives from the conference General Council, the Scottish Churches and the University of Edinburgh:

The Rev Andrew Anderson, Chair General Council

Prof. Larry Hurtado, Head of School of Divinity, University of Edinburgh

The Rt Rev John Christie, Moderator of the General Assembly of the Church of Scotland

His Eminence Keith Patrick O'Brien, Archbishop of St Andrews and Edinburgh

Rev. Dr. Fred Drummond, Scottish General Secretary, Evangelical Alliance

Other church leaders took part in the Epilogue:

Rev Lily Twist, Chair of the Synod of the Methodist Church in Scotland

The Most Rev. David Chillingworth, Primus of the Scottish Episcopal Church

Each welcome was greeted with:

Chant '*Laudate omnes gentes*' (France: Taizé Community)

3. Epilogue

Call to worship (using all three languages) with chant:

'Let all nations praise the Lord' (Taiwan)

Text paraphrase of Ps 117 and melody Hsiang-Chi Chang & I-to Loh. Source: *We Walk His Way* (Glasgow: Wild Goose Publications).

'You are my witnesses', says the Lord,
'and my servant whom I have chosen.'
'Before me, no god existed,
and besides me, there is no saviour.'
'Do not remember the former things.
I am about to do a new thing.
Can you not perceive it?'

Isaiah 43: 10-11, 18-19

Gospel John 15:1-11

Acclamation 'A ti, oh Seňor' (El Salvador)

Text and music: William O Ramirez. Source: *We Walk His Way* (Glasgow: Wild Goose Publications)

Prayer

We give thanks to God for the unique beauty
God has created in our motherlands:
their landscapes, their plant life,
their animal life and people.
Encourage, O God, a deep love
for the lands from which we come.
Preserve their water, air and soil;
keep their economies clean,
their trade fair, their politics healthy.
We give thanks to God
for the Churches to which we belong,
their centuries of worship and witness,
their service to those in need,
the potential in every member.
Keep them nourished, good Lord,
through your word and sacraments;
show them what to leave behind
and what to anticipate in hope,
so that they may attract others to Christ.
We give thanks to God
for calling us to be his ambassadors,
so that the Gospel may be shared
and shown throughout the world.
Let it take root in our time
as strongly as in the time of the apostles.
Give us discerning minds, O Christ,
so that we know when to speak,
what to say,

and when to be silent and trust your Spirit.
Give us courage to challenge beliefs and customs
which make people slaves,
and to proclaim the love which liberates and reconciles.
We thank you, eternal God,
for the World Missionary Conference of 1910,
and the good things which began there.
And we thank you for this moment, one hundred years later,
when, by your Spirit and with those around us,
we can prepare for the ever new future to which you call us.
Keep our eyes, our ears,
our hearts and our minds open,
for we do not know when your Holy Spirit
will confront us with a new thing.
May we all find new friends here,
and catch visions of your Kingdom
we have not glimpsed before.
And may those who speak find words to fire the faith
and shape the discipleship of all who listen,
so that we may become better witnesses to Christ today.

Silence is kept

Vesper 'Night has Fallen' (Malawi)

Malawian evening hymn adapted Tom Colvin. Source: *Come, Let us Walk This Road Together* (Carol Stream: Hope Publishing Co.); *Church Hymnary 4/Hymns of Glory, Songs of Praise* (Norwich: Canterbury Press).

Closing prayer *spoken in French*

The night is the cover of your peace, O God,
the rhythm of your rest for all your people.
The dark is the cloak of your gentleness, O God,
the warmth of your hand around the earth.
In its blackness is the sign of your eternity,
the never-ending living of your love.
In faith we go to sleep and leave our life to you.
In child-like trust we end our efforts of this day.
In our sleeping, be our company.
In our waking, be the gift of our new day.

Source: © Dorothy McRae-McMahon *Echoes of our Journey* (Melbourne: JBCE) and *Liturgies for the Journey of Life* (London: SPCK); aandd@bigpond.net.au.

The Blessing of the Conference

All sing Amen to the 'Themba Amen' which began the service as 'God welcomes all'.

Friday June 4: Gratitude

A senior class from St Mary's (Leith) RC Primary School took part.

Delegates were asked to sign the bookmark on their seat, with their name, country and church family, as they arrive. These were collected later in the service and given to the visiting children and others in their school.

Gathering song from children 'Here we are together' *Fischy Music.*

Source: www.fischy.com

Opening dialogue

Come and see what we have seen:
the lame dance for joy,
the blind see wonders,
the deaf hear music,
the voiceless given dignity and worth.
Come and see what we have seen:
the powerful are humbled,
the prisoners are freed,
women heard and honoured,
children grow in safety and love.
Come and see what we have seen:
the fearful find courage,
the brokenhearted find healing,
the addicted embrace freedom,
the indifferent find passion,
the superstitious find truth that is real.
Come and see what we have seen:
long-standing hatreds overcome,
sacrifices made across borders,
care and respect for the earth,
hope springing forth,
a new creation emerging,
God's praise rising from all nations.
Come and see –
See what God has done.

Song 'He came down' (Cameroons)
Words: traditional. Music: origin unknown, transcribed John L Bell. Source: *Many and Great* (Glasgow: Wild Goose Publications); *World Praise* (London: Jubilate/Harper Collins); *Sing Glory* (Jubilate/Mayhew); *Church Hymnary 4/Hymns of Glory, Songs of Praise* (Norwich: Canterbury) etc.

Scripture 2 Timothy 1:1-14 *read by children*

Music is played while the children distribute letters, highlighting parts of the epistle, to delegates.

Homily Prof. Dr. Metropolitan Nifon

Prayers with chant 'Glory and gratitude and praise' (Iona Community)
Source: *Come All You People* (Glasgow: Wild Goose Publications).

We give you thanks, gracious God.

You create the world.
You make us in your good image.
You declare all things good.
We thank you for Jesus
    who brings real hope
    and shows us how life is meant to be lived.
We thank you for your Holy Spirit
    who inspires and renews us
    and brings light to dark places.
Glory and gratitude and praise ...
We thank you, gracious God,
    that we have all been given gifts -
    some to create beauty,
    some to heal pain,
    some to speak the truth in love,
    some to think deeply in silence.
Thank you that you have made us
    to need each other's gifts and to share our own.
Glory and gratitude and praise ...
We thank you, gracious God,
    for the children who met with Jesus
    and for those who meet with us.
Thank you that he enjoyed the company of children,
    healed their pain, took their gifts,
    watched as they played and listened as they sang.
Thank you that he asked us to become like children
    and invited us to listen to them, learn from them,
    protect them and encourage them,
    so that we who are adults may enter your kingdom.
Glory and gratitude and praise ...
We thank you, gracious God,
    for those who – when we were small –
    showed us the love of Jesus
    and encouraged us to trust your Word.
We honour you for our lives in which we know
    you have saved and summoned us,
    not because of our merit but through your grace.
We treasure within us
    not our wealth
    but the riches of heaven,
    given to renew us at this time and on this earth.
We pray through Christ our Lord.
Amen.

Blessing and dismissal

Prof. Dr. Metropolitan Nifon

Song 'May you find peace, may you find hope' (*Fischy Music*)
Source: www.fischy.com

Saturday June 5: Repentance

Several settings of Kyrie eleison are used, from different parts of the world

1. Gathering

Song 'Mungu ni mwema/Know that God is good' (DR Congo)
Origin: unknown. Source: *One is the Body* (Glasgow: Wild Goose Publications).

Opening Sequence *from Psalm 33* (spoken in all three languages) with chant –

Kyrie eleison (Ukraine)
Traditional chant. Source: *Worshipping Ecumenically* (Geneva: WCC Publications); *Thuma Mina* (Basileia Verlag, Basel; Strube Verlag, Műnchen-Berlin), etc.

Rejoice in the Lord, you righteous;
praise is proper from those who are just.
Sing to God a new song,
make sweet music, raise a joyful song.
The word of the Lord is true;
the work of the Lord shows God's faithfulness.
The Lord loves justice and righteousness;
God's constant love fills the whole earth.
Let the earth stand in awe of the Lord,
its inhabitants reverence their Maker.
For God spoke and all came to be,
God commanded and all found its place.

2. Listening to Scripture

Scripture Reading 1 Corinthians 3:1-11 *read in languages other than the official languages of the conference*

Kyrie (Nepal) Setting by Chitra Karki. Source: *One is the Body* (Glasgow: Wild Goose Publications)

Homily Sister Elizabeth Moran S.S.C., Columban Sisters

Kyrie (Paraguay) As taught by Pablo Sosa. Source: *Sent by the Lord* (Glasgow: Wild Goose Publications)

3. Responding to Scripture

Prayer of penitence, with chant:
Kyrie (Ghana)

Setting: Dinah Reindorf. Source: *Worshipping Ecumenically* (Geneva: WCC Publications) etc.

Because God is merciful,
and because there is nothing we should hide from God,
let us express to our Maker regret which comes from our hearts.
Forgive us, gracious God, if – as your people –
we have tried to make heaven in the image of our church,
rather than making our churches resemble heaven.
And forgive us if we have looked with suspicion
on churches not of our tradition,
and especially if we have been unwilling to share the gifts
which your Holy Spirit brought to birth in other cultures.
Kyrie eleison
Forgive us, gracious God,
if we have called ourselves 'the Body of Christ'
but have refused to share the pain which others bear,
and have been jealous of the happiness others share.
Christe eleison
Forgive us, gracious God,
our abuse of power, personal and institutional,
if at any time we have approached with disrespect
the cultures and customs of those we are among,
and sought to impose our own interpretations
of the truth and love of Christ.
Kyrie eleison
Now, where penitence is real,
let your forgiveness, O Christ, be truly felt.
Say to us all, as you said to your first followers,
'Your sins are forgiven.
Go in peace.
Come and follow me.'

Silence is kept

4. Dismissal

Closing Responses *from Psalm 33* (spoken in all three languages)
God's eyes are on those who revere him,
on those who trust in God's faithful love.
God delivers their soul from death,
and keeps them in times of need.
Our soul waits for the Lord;
God is our help and our shield.
In God our hearts rejoice;
we trust in God's holy name.

Let God's steadfast love be upon us
as we put our hope in the Lord.

Recessional Song '*Mungu ni mwema*' (as at beginning)

Biodata of Revd Dr John Bell, Iona Community

John L. Bell is a native of Kilmarnock, Scotland, but has spent most of his life in Glasgow where he presently resides. He took degrees in Arts (MA) and Divinity (BD, 1st class honours) at Glasgow University, interspersed with three years of voluntary work in London and Amsterdam and a year as the president of the Students' Representative Council. He was subsequently elected as Lord Rector of the University for the triennium 1977-1980.

For ten years he worked in youth ministry with his colleague, Graham Maule, before transferring to concentrate on music and worship. He currently works with the Wild Goose Resource Group (WGRG), a semi-autonomous project of The Iona Community and an expression of its commitment to the renewal of music and worship. In association with colleagues and friends, the Group has produced a large range of music books, CDs and resources for worship with the aim of enabling lay and ordained leadership. Song collections include three short songbooks *Come All You People* (1995), *There Is One Among Us* (1998), *We Walk His Way* (2008), a compilation of seventeen songs for the time of grieving, *The Last Journey* (1996), and, more recently, eclectic collections for general use, *One Is the Body* (2002) and *I Will Not Sing Alone* (2004). In *The Singing Thing* (2000) and *The Singing Thing Too* (2007) John and the WGRG look at why people sing and how this can be encouraged and improved. *A Wee Worship Book* (4th incarnation 1999) has been used by worship planners, clergy and laity in public and private devotions for over fifteen years.

John's books of reflections and sermons include *10 Things They Never Told Me About Jesus* (2009), a beginner's guide to a larger Christ, *Hard Words For Interesting Times* (2003), biblical texts in contemporary contexts, *Wrestle And Fight And Pray* (1993, 2003), reflections on Christianity and conflict. *Thinking Out Loud* (2008) and *All That Matters* (2010) are collected Scripts from Radio 4's Thought for The Day. He lectures in seminaries and theological colleges at home and abroad and has conducted retreats and conferences for Anglican, Roman Catholic, Presbyterian, Lutheran, Baptist and Reformed church agencies in the UK and North America.

John is a hymn-writer, author and occasional broadcaster, but retains a primary passion for congregational song. He and the work he shares with his colleagues have been honoured by the Royal School of Church Music, the Hymn Society in the US and Canada, and the University of Glasgow. For five years, John convened the Panel on Worship for the Church of Scotland, overseeing the production of *Common Order* (its liturgy book) and editing two supplementary hymn books. He was appointed Convener and Joint Editor of the Church's new hymnal, and has been used as a consultant on worship by the World Council of Churches, World Alliance of Reformed Churches, and Christian Aid, amongst others.

APPENDIX 8: CONFERENCE PERSONNEL

Chaplains

Fr Gerard Hughes SJ
Pastor Festus Olatunde
Elspeth Strachan, Scottish Episcopal Church

Communications

Jasmin Adam, Edinburgh 2010
Fiona Buchanan, volunteer
Friedrich Degenhardt, co-opted writer
Gary Doak, photographer
Theodore Gill, World Council of Churches
Miriam Haar, volunteer
Martin Hoegger, co-opted writer
Aaron Hollander, volunteer
Nick Jury, Church of Scotland
Kyrie Kim, co-opted writer
Selaotswe Miranda Lerefolo, World Council of Churches
Manuel López, co-opted writer
Juan Michel, World Council of Churches
Anna Moyle, Evangelical Alliance
Antonio Carlos Ribeiro, co-opted writer
Olivier Schöpfer, World Council of Churches
Mark Taylor, volunteer

Conference Office

Margaret Clark, volunteer
Sandy Gemmil, volunteer
Sheilagh Kesting, Church of Scotland
Fergus Macdonald, Chair of Edinburgh 2010 Events Committee
Margaret Macgregor, volunteer
Amy Middlemass, University of Edinburgh
Ros Milne, Church of Scotland
Joan Pennicook, ACTS (Action of Churches Together in Scotland)
Gorden Ritchie, volunteer
Stephen Smyth, Edinburgh 2010
Rob Whiteman, volunteer
John Wylie, volunteer

Interpreters

Pilar Delaraye-Tosat, World Council of Churches
Carlos Sintado, World Council of Churches
Jane Stranz, World Council of Churches

SCOT (Scottish Organising Team)

Brother Stephen Smyth, ACTS – Action of Churches Together in Scotland
Major Alan Dixon, Salvation Army
Alistair Stevenson, Evangelical Alliance Scotland
Rev. Dr Brian Talbot, Broughty Ferry Baptist Church, Dundee
Sister Elizabeth Moran, Columban Sisters
Rev. Geoffrey Baines, Methodist Church
Helen Hood, Scottish Episcopal Church
Rev. Mitchell Bunting, United Reformed Church

Spiritual Life

John Bell, Convener of the Spiritual Life Committee
Claudio Carvalhaes, Spiritual Life Committee
Carol Ford, Spiritual Life Committee
Douglas Galbraith, Coordinator of the Spiritual Life Committee
Aftab Gohar, Spiritual Life Committee
Peter Gunstone, Spiritual Life Committee and music leader
Lim Swee Hong, Spiritual Life Committee
Carol Marples, Soul Marks Trust and Spiritual Life Committee
Margaret McLarty, musician
Jo Love, visuals
Elizabeth Moran, Spiritual Life Committee
Stuart Muir, musician
Mairi Munro, Spiritual Life Committee
Peter Okeno Ong'are, musician
Pastor Festus Olatunde, Mountain of Fire and Miracle Ministries and choir coordinator
Jesica Sinniah, choreographer
Mark Taylor, musician

Stewards

Divine Aguh, volunteer
Alicia Broggi, volunteer
Joshua Broggi, volunteer
Stephen Donoho, volunteer
Kang-Hee Han, volunteer
Jamie Hollis, volunteer

Dandan Hou, volunteer
Kathy Kim, volunteer
Martha Loewe, volunteer
Joyce Sun, volunteer
George Walsh, volunteer

Study Process

Afe Adogame, University of Edinburgh, Theme 7 convener
Maria Arantxa Aguado Arrese, Roman Catholic Church and Study Process Monitoring Group
Kyriaki Avtzi, Conference of European Churches, Theme 8 convener
Jonathan Bonk, Overseas Ministries Study Center, Theme 4 convener
Rose Dowsett, World Evangelical Alliance and Study Process Monitoring Group
Laszlo Gonda, Debrecen Reformed Theological University, Theme 8 convener
Darrell Jackson, Redcliffe College, Theme 8 convener and moderator
Genevieve James, University of South Africa, Theme 5 convener
Knud Jørgensen, Areopagos and Chair of the Study Process Monitoring Group
John Kafwanka, Anglican Communion and Study Process Monitoring Group
Namsoon Kang, Texas Christian University, Theme 6 convener
Jooseop Keum, World Council of Churches and Study Process Monitoring Group
Kirsteen Kim, Edinburgh 2010, Research Coordinator
Andrew Kirk, formerly University of Birmingham, Theme 3 convener
Wonsuk Ma, Oxford Centre for Mission Studies, Study Process Monitoring Group, Theme 9 convener
Deenabandhu Manchala, World Council of Churches, Theme 1 convener
Philomena Mwaura, Kenyatta University, Theme 7 convener
Mark Oxbrow, Church Mission Society, Theme 5 convener
Lalsangkima Pachuau, Asbury Theological Seminary, Theme 2 convener
Niki Papageorgiou, Aristotle University of Thessalonki, Theme 2 convener
Janice Price, Church of England, Theme 1 convener
Lori Ransom, Presbyterian Church in Canada, Theme 4 convener
Cathy Ross, Church Mission Society, Theme 9 convener
Kenneth R. Ross, Church of Scotland and Study Process Monitoring Group
Petros Vassiliadis, University of Thessaloniki and Study Process Monitoring Group
Dietrich Werner, Ecumenical Theological Education, Theme 6 convener

Technical Team

Matthew Bunting, volunteer
Mitchell Bunting, Edinburgh 2010
Stephanie Nicholson, volunteer
Kirk Sandvig, Edinburgh 2010
William Young, volunteer

Appendix 9: Conference Delegates

Title	Given name	Surname	Organisation	Denomination	Nationality	Residence
Prof	William	Abraham	Perkins School of Theology	United Methodist	Irish	United States
Bishop	Ivan	Abrahams	Methodist Church of Southern Africa	Methodist	South African	United Kingdom
Mr	Femi	Adeleye	International Fellowship of Evangelical Students	Anglican	Ghanaian	Ghana
Dr	Afe	Adogame	The University of Edinburgh		Nigerian	United Kingdom
Ms	Maria Aranzazu	Aguado Arrese	World Council of Churches	Roman Catholic	Spanish	Switzerland
Dr	Risto	Ahonen	Finnish Evangelical Lutheran Mission	Evangelical Lutheran	Finnish	Finland
Dr	Walter	Altmann	World Council of Churches	Lutheran	Brazilian	Brazil
Mr	Miguel	Alvarez	Church of God	Church of God	Honduras	United States
Prof Dr	James	Amanze	World Conference of Associations of Theological Education (WOCATI)	Anglican	Malawian	Botswana
Mr	Christoph	Anders	World Council of Churches and Association of Protestants Churches and Missions in Germany (EMW)	United Protestant	German	Germany
Rev	Andrew	Anderson	Church of Scotland	Church of Scotland	Scottish	United

						Kingdom
Mr	Antoine	Arjakovsky	Institute of Ecumenical Studies, Lviv	Orthodox (Ecumenical Patriarcate)	French	Ukraine
Prof	Kwabena	Asamoah-Gyadu	Trinity Theological Seminary	Methodist	Ghanaian	Ghana
Rev Dr	Martyn	Atkins	British Methodist Church	Methodist	British	United Kingdom
Ms	Kyriaki	Avtzi	Conference of European Churches	Greek Orthodox	Greek	Switzerland
Rev	Irene	Ayallo	Anglican Communion	Anglican	Kenyan	New Zealand
Rev Dr	John	Azumah	London School of Theology	Presbyterian	Ghanaian	United Kingdom
Mr	John	Baxter-Brown	World Council of Churches	Anglican	British	Switzerland
Ms	Virginia	Beardy	Urban Rural Mission Canada	Anglican	Canadian Native	Canada
Ms	Caitlin	Beck	Anglican Communion	Anglican Church of Canada	Canadian	Canada
Mr	Kenneth	Ben	World Council of Churches	London Mission Society / Cook Island Christian Church	Cook Islands	Cook Islands
Ms	Ulla	Bengtsson	Lunds Missionssällskap/ Lund Mission Society	Church of Sweden	Swedish	Sweden
Prof	Stephen	Bevans	Catholic Theological Union, Chicago	Roman Catholic	USA	United States
Dr	Michael	Biehl	Academy of Mission	Lutheran	German	Germany
Rev	Doug	Birdsall	Lausanne Committee for World Evangelisation	Presbyterian Church of America	USA	United States
Bishop	Heinrich	Bolleter	World Methodist Council	United Methodist	Swiss	Switzerland
Dr	Jonathan	Bonk	Overseas Ministries Study Center	Mennonite	Canadian	United States
Mr	Jec Dan	Borlado	World Council of Churches	Convention Baptist	Filipino	Philippines
Prof	Nico	Botha	University of South Africa	Uniting Reformed in Southern Africa	South African	South Africa

Rev	Martin	Breitenfeldt	mission 21	Lutheran	German	Switzerland
Prof	Cheryl	Bridges John	Pentecostal Theological Seminary	Church of God	USA	United States
Mrs	Shirley	Brown	Church of Scotland	Church of Scotland	Scottish	United Kingdom
Dr	Gwen	Bryde	Lutheran - Study Process	Lutheran	German	Germany
V Rev Dr	Daniel	Buda	World Council of Churches	Romanian Orthodox Church	Romanian	Switzerland
Dr	Bambang	Budijanto	Compassion International	Non-denominational	Indonesian	United States
Rev Fr	Gosbert	Byamungu	Pontifical Council for Promoting Christian Unity	Catholic	Tanzanian	Holy See (Vatican City State)
Bishop	Minerva G.	Carcaño	The United Methodist Church	Methodist	USA	United States
Prof	Carlos	Cardoza-Orlandi	Columbia Theological Seminary	Christian Church (Disciples of Christ)	Puerto Rican	United States
Sister	Janet	Carroll	Maryknoll Missionaries	Roman Catholic	USA	United States
Rev	Kwok Keung	Chan	The Anglican Communion	Anglican	Chinese	Hong Kong
Prof	Maria	Chavez Quispe	World Council of Churches	Methodist	Bolivian	Switzerland
Miss	Heather	Chester	Winner Youth Multimedia Contest	Missionic Church	USA	United States
Mr	Leiton	Chinn	WEA Missions Commission	Evangelical Free/Anglican	USA	United States
Ms	Claudine	Chionh	Melbourne Ecumenical Edinburgh 2010 Celebration	Anglican	Australian	Australia
Dr	Yong	Cho	Tokyo 2010	Presbyterian	Korean	Japan
Rev Dr	Song Mee	Chung	Sabah Theological Seminary	Lutheran	Malaysian	Malaysia
Rev Dr	Meehyun	Chung	Presbyterian Church of Rep. of Korea	Presbyterian	Korean	Switzerland

Mr	Luiz	Coelho	Episcopal Anglican Church of Brazil (Anglican Communion)	Anglican	Brazilian	Brazil
Rev Fr	Gianni	Colzani	Pontificia Universita Urbaniana	Catholic	Italian	Italy
Dr	Josias	Conradie	Church Mission Society	Dutch Reformed Church	South African	United Kingdom
Prof	Ernst	Conradie	University of the Western Cape	Uniting Reformed Church of Southern Africa	South African	South Africa
Most Reverend	Mario	Conti	Archdiocese of Glasgow	Roman Catholic	British	United Kingdom
Dr	Matthew	Cook	Faculté de Théologie de l´Alliance Chrétienne (FATEAC)	The Christian and Missionary Alliance	USA	Cote d'Ivoire
Bishop Dr	Geevarghese Mor	Coorilos	World Council of Churches	Orthodox	Indian	India
Prof	David	Daniels	McCormick Theological Seminary	Church of God in Christ	USA	United States
Rev Dr	Richard	Daulay	World Council of Churches	Methodist	Indonesian	Indonesia
Rev Dr	Joseph	Dayam	United Theological College, Bangalore	Lutheran	Indian	India
Ms	Jet	Den Hollander	World Alliance of Reformed Churches	Protestant Church in Netherlands	Dutch	Switzerland
Dr	Glory	Dharmaraj	General Board of Global Ministries	United Methodist	Indian/USA	United States
Mr	Ganoune	Diop	Seventh-day Adventist Church World headquarters	Seventh Day Adventist	French	United States
Dr	Cheryl	Doss	General Conference of Seventh-day Adventists	Seventh Day Adventist	USA	United States
Mrs	Rosemary	Dowsett	World Evangelical Alliance	Independent Evangelical	British	United Kingdom
Ms	Elizabeth	Duffy	Diocesan Centre	Roman Catholic	British	United

						Kingdom
Ms	Erica	Dunmow	UK Urban Mission Congress	Church of England/Methodist/URC	British	United Kingdom
Mrs	Linda	Dunnett	Church of Scotland	Church of Scotland	British	United Kingdom
Rev Dr	Huu Duc	Duong	Agape International Ministries		Vietnamese	China
Rev Dr	Andrew	Dutney	Uniting College for Leadership & Theology	United Church in Australia	Australian	Australia
Dr	Anne	Dyer	Mattersey Hall Christian College	Pentecostal/Methodist	British	United Kingdom
Rev	Bertil	Ekström	World Evangelical Alliance	Baptist	Swedish	Brazil
Mrs	Dynnice Rossanne	Engcoy	Asia Pacific Research Cntre	Assembly of God	Filipino	Philippines
Rev Dr	David	Esterline	McCormick Theological Seminary	Presbyterian (USA)	USA	United States
Bishop	Robert	Fannin	World Evangelism/World Methodist Council	United Methodist	USA	United States
Most Reveren d	Brian	Farrell	Pontifical Council for Promoting Christian Unity	Catholic	Irish	Holy See (Vatican City State)
Rev Dr	Samson	Fatokun	University of Ibadan	Pentecostal	Nigerian	Nigeria
Ms	Carmen	Fernandez Aguinaco	Commission for World Mission & Evangelism	Catholic	Spanish	United States
Mr	Frampton 'Frank	Fox	Centre for Mission Studies	Interdenominational	USA	India
Dr	H. Eddie	Fox	World Evangelism/World Methodist Council	Methodist	USA	United States
Rev	Norman	Francis	United Church in Jamaica & Cayman Islands	United Church in Jamaica and the Cayman Islands	Jamaican	United Kingdom

Dr	Bryan	Froehle	St Thomas University	Catholic	USA	United States
Rev	Bob	Fyffe	Churches Together in Britain and Ireland	Scottish Episcopal Church	British	United Kingdom
Rev Dr	Ying	Gao	China Christian Church	China Christian Council	Chinese	China
Rev Canon	John	Gibaut	World Council of Churches	Anglican	Canadian	Switzerland
Mr	Nilton	Giese	Consejo Latinoamericano de Iglesias	Lutheran	Brazilian	Ecuador
Rev Prof	Anthony	Gittins	Catholic Theological Union, Chicago	Roman Catholic	British	United States
Rev Fr	David	Glenday	Unione dei Superiori Generali	Roman Catholic	Scottish	Italy
Dr	Laszlo	Gonda	WCC Commission for World Mission and Evangelism	Reformed Church in Hungary	Hungarian	Hungary
Sister	Maria Victoria	Gonzalez de Castejon	International Union of Superiors	Catholic	Spanish	Italy
Rev Dr	John	Gorski	Maryknoll Fathers	Roman Catholic	USA	United States
Rev	Mikhail	Goundiaev	World Council of Churches/Russian Orthodox Church	Eastern Orthodox	Russian	Switzerland
Mrs	Åsa	Gustafsson	Lunds Missionssällskap/ Lund Mission Society	Church of Sweden (Ev. Luth.)	Swedish	Sweden
Rev Dr	Chung Yoube	Ha	Youngnak Presbyterian Church	Presbyterian Church of Korea	South Korean	South Korea
Rev Dr	Carlos	Ham	World Council of Churches	Reformed Presbyterian	Cuban	Switzerland
Dr	Thomas	Harvey	Oxford Centre for Mission Studies	Presbyterian	USA	United Kingdom
Dr	Kari Storstein	Haug	School of Mission and Theology	Church of Norway/Lutheran	Norwegian	Norway

Mr	Christoph	Haus	Baptist World Alliance	Baptist	German	Germany
Rev Dr	Roderick	Hewitt	Council For World Mission	United Church in Jamaica and the Cayman Islands	Jamaican	Jamaica
Dr	John	Hitchen	Laidlaw College	Christian Brethren	New Zealander	New Zealand
Dr	Pauline	Hoggarth	Scripture Union International	Scottish Episcopal Church	British	United Kingdom
Rev Dr	Pamela	Holmes	Queen's School of Religion/Society for Pentecostal Studies	Pentecostal	Canadian	Canada
Rev	Helena	Hooper	Organisation of African Initiated Churches	Church of Living God	Ghanaian	Ghana
Rev Dr	Vahan	Hovhanessian	Armenian Orthodox Church	Armenian Orthodox	USA	United Kingdom
Rev Dr	Harold	Hunter	International Pentecostal Holiness Church	International Pentecostal Holiness Church	USA	United States
Prof	Viorel	Ionita	Conference of European Churches	Romanian Orthodox Church	Swiss/Romanian	Switzerland
Prof	Eunice	Irwin	Asbury Theoloical Seminary	Christian Missionary Alliance	USA	United States
Mr	Noah Moses	Israel	Baptist World Alliance	Baptist	South African	South Africa
Rev Dr	Darrell	Jackson	Nova Research Centre	Baptist Union of Great Brotain	British	United Kingdom
Rev Dr	Michael	Jagessar	United Reformed Church	United Reformed Church	Dutch/Guyanese	United Kingdom
Dr	Beate	Jakob	WCC/German Institute for Medical Mission	Roman Catholic	German	Germany
Dr	Genevieve	James	University of South Africa	Interdenominational	South African	United Kingdom
Prof	Daniel	Jeyaraj	Liverpool Hope University	Church of South India	Indian	United

						Kingdom
Rev	Adelaida	Jimenez-Cortes	World Alliance of Reformed Churches - Presbyterian Church in Colombia	Presbyterian Church	Colombian	Colombia
Rev Dr	Joshva Raja	John Christopher	Selly Oak Centre for Mission Studies	Anglican	Indian	United Kingdom
Dr	Todd	Johnson	Boston Student Conference	Lutheran	USA	United States
Rev Dr	Beverly	Johnson-Miller	Asbury Theological Seminary	United Methodist / Assemblies of God	USA	United States
Rev	Mark	Johnstone	Church of Scotland	Church of Scotland	British	United Kingdom
Dr	M.P.	Joseph	Chang Jung Christian University	Church of South India	Indian	Taiwan
Mr	Paul	Joshua	Lausanne Committee	Brethren	Indian	India
Rev	McDonald	Kadawati	Church of Central Africa Presbyterian – Blantyre Synod	Presbyterian	Malawian	Malawi
Rev	John	Kafwanka	Anglican Communion	Anglican Church	Zambian	United Kingdom
Dr	Joshua	Kalapati	Madras Christian College	Church of South India/Lutheran	Indian	India
Prof	Namsoon	Kang	Texas Christian University	United Methodist Churches	Korean	United States
Rev Dr	John	Kaoma	Episcopal Church	Anglican	Zambian	United States
Prof	Veli-Matti	Karkkainen	Fuller Theoloical Seminary	Pentecostal Church of Finland	Finnish	United States
Mrs	Sarah S.	Kaulule	World Council of Churches/United Church of Zambia	United Church of Zambia	Zambian	Zambia
Ms	Norma	Kehrberg	Christian Unity Director, Hawaii United Methodist Church	United Methodist	USA	United States
Prof	Konstantinos	Kenanidis	Ecumenical Patriarchate	Orthodox	Greek	United Kingdom

Rev Dr	Jooseop	Keum	World Council of Churches	Presbyterian Church of Korea	South Korean	Switzerland
Rev	Vicentia	Kgabe	Anglican Church	Anglican	South African	South Africa
Rev	Lalhlmingliana	Khawbung	Aizawl Theological College	Mizoram Presbyterian Church	Indian	India
Most Revd	Elekiah	Kihali Andago	The Orthodox Church	Orthodox	Indian	Kenya
Rev Dr	Elijah Jong Fil	Kim	Gordon Conwell Theological Semiary, Emmanuel Gospel Center	Assemblies of God	South Korean	United States
Rev Dr	Dong Sung	Kim	World Council of Churches	Presbyterian Church of Korea	Republic of Korea	Republic of Korea
Rev	Dong Sun	Kim	Council For World Mission & Evangelism	Presbyterian Church of Korea	South Korean	South Korea
Prof	Sebastian	Kim	York St John University	Presbyterian Church of Korea	South Korean	United Kingdom
Dr	Roberta	King	Fuller Theoloical Seminary	Baptist/Congregational	USA	United States
Dr	Michael	Kinnamon	National Council of Churches	Disciples of Christ	American	United States
Dr	Antonios	Kireopoulos	WCC/National Council of Churches USA	Greek Orthodox	USA	United States
Rev	Andrew	Kirk	Formerly University of Birmingham	Anglican	British	United Kingdom
Rev Dr	Clifton	Kirkpatrick	World Alliance of Reformed Churches	Presbyterian Church (USA)	USA	United States
Miss	Taryn	Knibbs	Youth With A Mission	Presbyterian/Free Church	SouthAfrican/British	United Kingdom
Fr	Vineeth	Koshy	National Council of Churches in India	Malankara Orthodox Syrian Church	Indian	India
Ms	Maria	Koutatzi	Roman Catholic Church	Roman Catholic	Greek	Greece
Dr	Judith	Kubicki	Fordham University	Roman Catholic	American	United States

Rev	Kwok-Leong	Kum	Calvary Church Kuala Lumpur	Assemblies of God	Malaysian	Malaysia
Prof	Abraham	Kovacs	Reformed University of Debrecen, Hungary	Reformed	Hungarian	Hungary
Bishop	Ole Christian M	Kvarme	Oslo Diocese, Church of Norway	Evangelical Lutheran	Norwegian	Norway
Miss	Karyn	Lasei	Council for World Mission	Congregational Union of New Zealand	New Zealander	New Zealand
Rev	Marvia	Lawes	First Isthmian Baptist Church	Baptist	Jamaican	Panama
Rev Dr	Terry	LeBlanc	North American Institute for Indigenous Theological Studies	Fellowship of Canadian Assemblies	Mi'kmaq	Canada
Rev Dr	Young Hoon	Lee	Yoido Full Gospel Church	Yoido Full Gospel Church/AG	Korean	South Korea
Rev	Chul Shin	Lee	Youngnak Presbyterian Church	Presbyterian Church of Korea	Korean	South Korea
Rev Fr	Jan	Lenssen	Centre Amani	Roman Catholic	Belgian	Belgium
Rev Dr	Guy	Liagre	United Protestant Church in Belgium	Eglise Protestante Unie de Belgique	Belgian	Belgium
Very Rev	Peter	Lindvall	Church of Sweden	Church of Sweden	Swedish	Sweden
Rev Dr	Carlos Rodriguez	Linera	Pontifical Council for Promoting Christian Unity	Roman Catholic	Spanish	Italy
Rev	Anna	Ljung	World Council of Churches	Swedish Mission Council	Swedish	Sweden
Miss	Claire-Lise	Lombard	DEFAP - Service protestant de mission	Reformed Church	French	France
Miss	Margaret	Long	Roman Catholic Church in Scotland	Roman Catholic	Irish	United Kingdom
Dr	Atola	Longkumer	Leonard Theological College, India	Baptist	Indian	India
Mr	Julio César	López	Iglesia Presbiteriana San Andrés	Presbyterian	Argentinian	Argentina

Rev Fr	Nicta	Lubaale Makiika	Organisation of African Instituted Churches	African Independent	Ugandan	Kenya
Ass Prof	Erling	Lundeby	Fjellhaug Mission Seminary - NLM	Lutheran	Norwegian	Norway
Dr	Wonsuk	Ma	Oxford Centre for Mission Studies	Korean Assemblies of God	South Korean	United Kingdom
Dr	Julie	Ma	Oxford Centre for Mission Studies	Korean Assemblies of God	South Korean	United Kingdom
Bishop	Mark	MacDonald	The Anglican Church of Canada	Anglican	Canadian	Canada
Rev Dr	Duncan	MacLaren	Scottish Episcopal Church/ ACTS	Scottish Episcopal	UK	United Kingdom
Rev	Jonas	Maina	World Alliance of Reformed Churches	Lutheran	Cameroon	Cameroon
Prof	Samuel	Maluleke	University of South Africa	Presbyterian	South African	South Africa
Rev Dr	Deenabandhu	Manchala	World Council of Churches	Lutheran	Indian	Switzerland
Mgr	Urszula	Marek	Center for Missions and Evangelism	Silesian Evangelical Church of the Augsburg Confession in Czech Republic	Polish	Poland
Mrs	Jennifer	Martin	World Council of Churches	United Church in Jamaica and the Cayman Islands	Jamaican	Jamaica
Rev	Jacques	Matthey	World Council of Churches	Reformed	Swiss	Switzerland
Dr	Fulata	Mbano-Moyo	World Council of Churches	Reformed Presbyterian	Mozambique	Switzerland
Rev	Patrick	McGuire	Society of African Missions	Roman Catholic Church	British	United Kingdom
Mr	Iain	McLarty	The Church of Scotland	Church of Scotland	Scottish	United Kingdom
Dr	Janice	McLean	City Seminary New York	Episcopal	Jamaican/Ameri	United States

					can	
Dr	John	McVay	Walla Walla University	Seventh-day Adventist	USA	United States
Rev Dr	Alex Roy	Medley	American Baptist Churches USA	Baptist	USA	United States
Mrs	Mary	Mikhael	Near East School of Theology	Presbyterian	Lebanese	Lebanon
Mr	Rauno	Mikkonen	Fida International	Pentecostal	Finnish	Finland
Dr	Bill	Mitchell	United Bible Societies	Iglesia Evangelica Peruana	Scottish	Canada
Dr	Ken	Miyamoto	International Association for Mission Studies	Anglican Church in Japan	Japanese	Japan
Ms	Sunitha	Mortha	Evangelical Lutheran Church in America	Lutheran	Indian	United Kingdom
Rev Dr	Nicolae	Mosoiu	Romanian Orthodox Church	Orthodox	Romanian	Romania
Dr	Rogate Reuben	Mshana	World Council of Churches	Lutheran	Tanzanian	Switzerland
Mr	Graeme	Mundine	National Aboriginal and Torres Strait Islanders Ecumenical Commission (NATSIEC)/National Council of Churches in Australia	Catholic	Australian	Australia
Bishop	Julio	Murray	CLAI (Latin American Council of Churches)	Anglican	Panamanian	Panama
Miss	Clara Minoo	Muthuka	World Council of Churches	Baptist	Kenyan	Kenya
Rev	Mande	Muyombo	Saint Paul School of Theology	United Methodist Church	Congolese (DRC)	United States
Dr	Philomena	Mwaura	Commission Seven Co-Convenor	Catholic	Kenyan	Kenya
Rev Dr	Fidon	Mwombeki	United Evangelical Mission	Lutheran	Tanzanian	Germany
Dr	Sarojini	Nadar	University of KwaZulu-Natal	Lutheran	South African	South Africa

Mrs	Sarah	Newland-Martin	World Council of Churches	Baptist	Jamaican	Jamaica
Dr	Zakaria J.	Ngelow	World Alliance of Reformed Churches	Protestant	Indonesian	Indonesia
Ms	Adele	Ngomedje	World Student Christian Federation	Evangelical Church of Cameroon	Cameroonian	United Kingdom
Dr	Marina	Ngursangzeli Behera	The United Theological College	Presbyterian	Indian	India
Licenciado	Nicolas Schneider	Iglesias	World Lutheran Federation	Iglesia Evangelica del Rio de la Plata (IERP)	Uruguay	Uruguay
Prof	Nelus	Niemandt	Dutch Reformed Church South Africa	Dutch Reformed Church	South African	South Africa
Mr	Birger	Nygaard	Areopagos	Lutheran Church of Denmark	Danish	Denmark
Rev Dr	Setri	Nyomi	World Alliance of Reformed Churches	Reformed	Ghanaian	Switzerland
Ms	Megan	O'Callaghan	World Council of Churches	Anglican Church of Aotearoa, New Zealand and Polynesia	European New Zealander	United Kingdom
Dr	Mercy	Oduyoye	Institute of Women in Religion & Culture	Methodist	Ghanaian	Ghana
HE Metro	Prof Dr Nifon	of Targoviste	Romanian Orthodox Church	Orthodox	Romanian	Romania
Mrs	Oluyinka	Olatunbosun	World Council of Churches	Methodist Church in Nigeria	Nigerian	Nigeria
Miss	Volha	Oleinik	Belarusian Orthodox Church	Christian Orthodox	Belarusian	Belarus
Rev Dr	Rolv	Olsen	Egede Instituttet	Evangelical Lutheran	Norwegian	Norway
Ms	Harriett	Olson	Women's Division/GBGM/United Methodist Church	United Methodist	USA	United States
Prof	Steven	O'Malley	Asbury Theological Seminary	Evangelical United Brethren/United Methodist	USA	United States
Apostle	Opoku	Onyinah	Church of Pentecost	Pentecostal	Ghanaian	Ghana

Dr						
Ms	Alejandra	Ortiz	Latin American Theological Fraternity	Methodist	Mexican	Mexico
Rev Canon	Mark	Oxbrow	Faith2Share	Anglican	British	United Kingdom
Rev Dr	Lalsangkima	Pachuau	Asbury Theological Seminary	Presbyterian Church of North East India	Indian	United States
Dr	John	Padwick	Organisation of African Instituted Churches	Holy Spirit Church of East Africa	UK	United Kingdom
Rev Dr	Tavita	Pagaialii	Assemblies of God	Assemblies of God	Samoan	Samoa
Prof	Niki	Papageorgiou	Aristotle University of Thessaloniki	Orthodox	Greek	Greece
Dr	Ruben	Paredes-Alfaro	World Council of Churches	Non-Denominatonal	Peruvian	Peru
Rev Dr	Sungkook	Park	Christian Conference of Asia	Presbyterian Church of Korea	Korean	Thailand
Rev	Raj Bharat	Patta	National Council of Churches in India	Lutheran	Indian	India
Mrs	Aline	Patte	Vanderbilt University	Presbyterian Church USA	French	United States
Prof	Daniel	Patte	Vanderbilt University	Presbyterian Church USA	French	United States
Rev.	Ouedraogo	Philippe	Assemblies of God	Pentecostal	Burkinabe	Burkina Faso
Prof	Isabel Apawo	Phiri	University of KwaZulu Natal	Presbyterian	Malawian	South Africa
Rev	Viviana	Pinto	CLAI Consejo Latinoamericano de Iglesias	Methodist	Argentinian	Argentina
Mr	Jean-Daniel	Plüss	European Pentecostal Charismatic Research Association	Pentecostal	Swiss	Switzerland
Canon	Janice	Price	Church of England	Church of England	British	United Kingdom

Rev Dr	Peniel	Rajkumar	The United Theological College	Anglican/Church of South India	Indian	India
Dr	Vinoth	Ramachandra	International Fellowship of Evangelical Students	Anglican	Sri Lankan	Sri Lanka
Dr	Daniel	Ramirez	University of Michigan	Non-denominatonal	USA	United States
Ms	Lori	Ransom	The Presbyterian Church in Canada	The Presbyterian Church in Canada	Canadian	Canada
Rev	Victor	Rey Riquelme	Latin American Theological Fraternity	Baptist	Chilean	Chile
Dr	Anne	Richards	Churches Together in Britain and Ireland	Church of England	British	United Kingdom
Rev Dr	Seppo	Rissanen	Finnish Evangelical Lutheran Mission	Evangelical Lutheran	Finnish	Finland
Dr	Simon	Ririhena	World Alliance of Reformed Churches	Reformed Church of Netherlands	Dutch	Netherlands
Prof	Marie Hélène	Robert	AFOM Association francophone oecuménique de missiologie	Catholic Church	French	France
Prof	Dana	Robert	Boston University School of Theology	United Methodist Church	USA	United States
Dr	Catherine	Ross	Church Mission Society	Anglican	New Zealander	United Kingdom
Dr	Kenneth	Ross	Edinburgh 2010	Presbyterian	British-Scottish	United Kingdom
Prof	Teresa Francesca	Rossi	Centro Pro Unione	Roman Catholic Church	Italian	Italy
Canon	Edgar	Ruddock	USPG – Anglicans in World Mission	Anglican	British	United Kingdom
Bishop	Mano	Rumalshah	Church of Pakistan	Church of Pakistan (United)	Pakistani/British	Pakistan
Dr	Michael	Rynkiewich	Asbury Theological Seminary	United Methodist Church	American	United States
Dr	Elizabeth	Salazar-Sanzana	World Council of Churches	Iglesia Evangelica Pentecostal	Chilena	Chile

	Del Carmen					
Rev Dr	Calixto	Salvatierra Moreno	Istituto Latinoamericano de Misionologia	Roman Catholic Church	Bolivian	Bolivia
Rev	Roger	Schmidt	The Lutheran World Federation	Lutheran	German	Switzerland
Rev	Ulrike	Schmidt-Hesse	Association of Churches and Missions in South West Germany (EMS)	EMS Protestant	German	Germany
Rev	Bal Krishna	Sharma	Assemblies of God	Assemblies of God	Nepalese	Nepal
Rev Dr	Philip TY	Siew	Seminari Theoloji Malaysia	Methodist	Malaysian	Malaysia
Dr	Geraldine	Smyth	Irish School of Ecumenics, Trinity College Dublin	Roman Catholic Church	Irish	Ireland
Prof	Howard	Snyder	Tyndale Seminary	Free Methodist	USA	United States
Rev	Eric	So	The Hong Kong Council of The Church of Christ in China	The Church of Christ in China	Chinese	China
Rev	Hoon	Song	Youngnak Presbyterian Church	Presbyterian Church of Korea	Korean	Korea
Archbishop	Malkhaz	Songulashvili	Baptist World Alliance	Baptist	Georgian	United Kingdom
Prof	Brian	Stanley	University of Edinburgh	Baptist	British	United Kingdom
Rev Dr	Andrea	Stephanous	Coptic Evangelical Organization for Social Services (CEOSS)	Protestant Church	Egyptian	Egypt
Ms	Wendy	Strachan	Scripture Union International	Brethren	Australian	Australia
Dr	Yi	Sun	Peoples University of China	House Church	Chinese	China
Rev Dr	Brian	Talbot	Broughty Ferry Baptist Church	Baptist Union of Scotland	British	United Kingdom
Rev Dr	Marian	McClure Taylor	Kentucky Council of Churches	Presbyterian Church (USA)	USA	United States

Dr	Timothy	Tennent	Asbury Theological Seminary	United Methodist	USA	United States
Mr	Andrew	Thompson	Winner Youth Writing Contest	Episcopal	USA	United States
Very Rev Prof	Iain	Torrance	Princeton Theological Seminary	Church of Scotland	British	United States
Rev Dr	Geoff	Tunnicliffe	World Evangelical Alliance	World Evangelical Alliance	Canadian	Canada
Rev Dr	Olav Fykse	Tveit	World Council of Churches	Lutheran	Norwegian	Switzerland
Ms	Tonica	van der Meer	Latin American Theological Fraternity	Emmanuel Chapel	Brazilian	Brazil
Rev Dr	Desmond	van der Water	Council for World Mission	Council for World Mission	South African	United Kingdom
Mr	Wout	van Laar	Netherlands Mission Council	Protestant Church in Netherlands	Netherlands	Netherlands
Rev	David	Vargas	Disciples Ecumenical Consultative Council	Christian Church (Disciples of Christ)	USA	United States
Rev Dr	Timo	Vasko	Evangelical Lutheran Church of Finland	The Evangelical Lutheran Church of Finland	Finnish	Finland
Prof	Petros	Vassiliadis	University of Thessaloniki	Church of Greece/Eastern Orthodox		Greece
Mrs	Anastasia	Vassiliadou	World Council of Churches	Church of Greece/Eastern Orthodox	Greek	Greece
Mr	José	Vázquez	ISCC	Presbyterian Church of Mexico	Mexican	Germany
Rev Dr	Claudia	Waehrisch-Oblau	United Evangelical Mission	Evangelical Church of the Rhineland	German	Germany
Mr	Burkhard	Wagner	Lutheran World Federation	Pomeranian Protestant Church (PPC)	German	Germany
	Wafik	Wahba	Tyndale Seminary, Toronto	Presbyterian	Egyptian	Canada
Rev Dr	Ronald	Wallace	World Council of Churches/The Presbyterian Church in Canada	The Presbyterian Church in Canada	Canadian	Canada
Rev	Michael	Wallace	World Student Christian Federation	Anglican Church of New Zealand, Oceania & Polynesia	New Zealander	New Zealand

	Andrew	Walls	Centre for African & Asian Christianity	Methodist	British	United Kingdom
Bishop	Hope Morgan	Ward	United Methodist Church	United Methodist	USA	United States
Rev	Ge	Wen	China Christian Church	Postdenominational	Chinese	China
Rev Dr	Dietrich	Werner	World Council of Churches, Ecumenical Theological Education	Lutheran	German	Switzerland
Bishop	John F	White	African Methodist Episcopal Church	African Methodist Episcopal Church	USA	United States
Dr	Darrell	Whiteman	The Mission Society	Methodist	USA	United States
Dean	Hakan E	Wilhelmsson	Lund Mission Society	Church of Sweden (Lutheran)	Swedish	Sweden
Prof	Philip	Wingeier-Rayo	Pfeiffer University	United Methodist Church	USA	United States
Dr	Allen	Yeh	Biola University	American Baptist (ABC-USA)	USA	United States
Rev Dr	Hesdie	Zamuel	World Council of Churches Commission on World Mission and Evangelism	Moravian	Surinamese	Suriname
Dr	Olga	Zaprometova	Eurasian Theological Seminary-Moscow	Pentecostal (Church of God)	Russian	Russian Federation
Rev Monsignor	Blaise	Zubuor	Congregation for the Evangelisation of Peoples	Roman Catholic Church	Ghanaian	Holy See (Vatican City State)

Appendix 10: Other 2010 Statements

Summary of The Cape Town Commitment[1]

The Cape Town Commitment (CTC) is a masterful and comprehensive document, faithfully reflecting the proceedings of The Third Lausanne Congress on World Evangelization, which took place in Cape Town, South Africa (October 2010). It is impossible to capture the spirit of Lausanne III in a three-page summary, so this synopsis should be read in conjunction with the full CTC.

The CTC is rooted in the conviction that 'we must respond in Christian mission to the realities of our own generation.' The mission of the Church must take seriously both the unchanging nature of God's word and the changing realities of our world. The CTC reflects the Lausanne call for the whole Church to take the whole gospel to the whole world; it is framed in the language of love - love for the whole gospel, the whole Church, and the whole world. The Commitment has two parts: a confession of faith and a call to action.

PART I For the Lord We Love: The Cape Town Confession of Faith

The opening sentences set the framework, 'The mission of God flows from the love of God. The mission of God's people flows from our love for God and for all that God loves.'

The first five points deal with our love for God himself. We love the living God, above all rivals and with a passion for his glory. We love the triune God: Father, Son, and Holy Spirit. With respect to the Father, the CTC calls for a renewed appreciation of God's fatherhood. Concerning the Son, it highlights our duty to trust, obey, and proclaim Christ. Of the Spirit, it says, 'Our engagement in mission, then, is pointless and fruitless without the presence, guidance and power of the Holy Spirit. … There is no true or whole gospel, and no authentic biblical mission, without the Person, work and power of the Holy Spirit.'

The last five points cover our love for God's Word, world, gospel,

[1] *Prepared by Kevin Smith from the South African Theological Seminary.* This summary document is saturated with the actual language of the CTC, for which reason quotation marks are not used for every phrase lifted from the CTC. Only longer quotations and key phrases are marked by quotation marks. This document serves as a précis of the CTC. To read the full CTC, please go to www.lausanne.org/ctcommitment.

people, and missions. (a) We reaffirm our submission to the Bible as God's final revelation, and affirm our love for the Person it reveals, the story it tells, the truth it teaches, and the life it requires (while admitting we often confess to love the Bible without loving the life it teaches, a life of costly practical discipleship). (b) We love God's world, all that he has made and loves. This includes caring for creation, loving all peoples and valuing ethnic diversity, longing to see the gospel embedded in all cultures, loving the world's poor and suffering people, and loving our neighbours as we love ourselves. It does not mean loving or being like 'the world' (i.e. worldliness). (c) We love the gospel - the story it tells, the assurance it gives, and the transformation it produces. (d) We love all God's people, recognising that such love calls for unity, honesty, and solidarity. (e) We love the mission of God. 'We are committed to world mission, because it is central to our understanding of God, the Bible, the Church, human history and the ultimate future. … The Church exists to worship and glorify God for all eternity and to participate in the transforming mission of God within history. Our mission is wholly derived from God's mission, addresses the whole of God's creation, and is grounded at its centre in the redeeming victory of the cross.' We are called to *integral mission*, which is the proclamation *and* demonstration of the gospel.

PART II For the World We Serve: The Cape Town Call to Action

The call to action uses the six Congress themes, which are linked to the six expositions of Ephesians.

A. *Bearing witness to the truth of Christ in a pluralistic, globalized world.* The Congress affirmed belief in absolute truth, and particularly in Jesus Christ as *the Truth*. Christians, therefore, are called to be people of truth, to live and proclaim the truth. We must face the threat of postmodern relativistic pluralism with robust apologetics. We must promote truth in the workplace and the global media. We must harness the arts for mission, promote authentically-Christian responses to emerging technologies, and actively engage the public arenas of government, business, and academia with biblical truth.

B. *Building the peace of Christ in our divided and broken world.* Christ has reconciled believers to God and to one another; the unity of God's people is both a fact and a mandate. The Church, therefore, has a responsibility to live out its reconciliation and to engage in biblical peace-making in the name of Christ. This includes bringing Christ's truth and peace to bear on racism and ethnic diversity, slavery and human trafficking, poverty, and minority groups such as people with disabilities. It also means our missional calling includes responsible stewardship of God's creation and its resources.

C. *Living the love of Christ among people of other faiths.* Our 'neighbours' include people of other faiths. We must learn to see them as neighbours and be neighbours to them. We seek to share the good news in *ethical evangelism*, and we reject unworthy proselytizing. We accept that our commission includes a willingness to suffer and die for Christ in reaching out to people of other faiths. We are called to embody and commend the gospel of grace in loving action, in all cultures. We need to respect 'diversity in discipleship', and encourage one another to exercise cultural discernment. We recognise global diaspora as strategic for evangelization: scattered peoples can be both recipients and agents of Christ's mission. While being willing to sacrifice our own rights for the sake of Christ, we commit to uphold and defend the human rights of others, including the right to religious freedom.

D. *Discerning the will of Christ for world evangelization.* Six key areas are identified as strategically important for the next decade: (a) unreached and unengaged people groups; (b) oral cultures; (c) Christ-centred leaders; (d) cities; (e) children; all with (f) prayer. The focus on Christian leaders is to prioritize discipleship and address the problems that arise from 'generations of reductionist evangelism'. Within this, key priorities are Bible translation, the preparation of oral story Bibles and other oral methodologies, as well as eradicating biblical illiteracy in the Church. Cities are home to four strategic groups: future leaders, migrant unreached peoples, culture shapers, and the poorest of the poor. All children are at risk; children represent both a mission field and a mission force.

E. *Calling the Church of Christ back to humility, integrity and simplicity.* The integrity of our mission in the world depends on our own integrity. The Congress called Christ-followers back to humble, sacrificial discipleship, simple living, and moral integrity. We need to be separate and distinct from the world (morally). Four 'idolatries' were singled out: disordered sexuality, power, success, and greed. Disciples of Christ must reject these. (The prosperity gospel is rejected under the banner of 'greed'.)

F. *Partnering in the body of Christ for unity in mission.* Paul teaches us that Christian unity is a creation of God, based on our reconciliation with God and with one another. We lament the divisiveness of our churches and organizations, because a divided Church has no message for a divided world. Our failure to live in reconciled unity is a major obstacle to authenticity and effectiveness in mission. We commit to *partnership* in global mission. No one ethnic group, nation or continent can claim the exclusive privilege of being the ones to complete the Great Commission. Two specific aspects of unity in mission are the partnership of women and men and the recognition of the missional nature of theological education.

TOKYO 2010 DECLARATION: MAKING DISCIPLES OF EVERY PEOPLE IN OUR GENERATION

Preamble

We affirm that mission is the central theme of Scripture, through which God reveals Himself to be a God who communicates and works through us by action and word in a world estranged from Him. Furthermore, we recognize that fulfilling and bringing completion to Jesus' Great Commission (Mt. 28:18-20; Mk. 16:15; Lk. 24:44-49; Jn. 20:21; Acts 1:8) has been the on-going responsibility of the Church for 2000 years.

In this era of missions, we of the Tokyo 2010 Global Mission Consultation value and commemorate the 1910 Edinburgh World Missionary Conference, a hallmark event which stands out as an inspiration and impetus to the modern global mission movement. We celebrate a legacy of 100 years of mission that has transpired since that first world missionary conference.

However, the world has dramatically changed since that conference was convened a century ago. Missions is no longer the predominant domain of Western Christianity. Rather, the preponderance of mission activity today is being engaged by Majority World Christians outside of the West. Christ's ambassadors are coming from everywhere around the world and going to anywhere and everywhere in the world. We rejoice that today's mission force is global in composition, bearing a diversity of thought, practice and resources that enriches and energizes Christ's global Cause as never before.

Yet, the corresponding reality is that the present day mission task is so large and complex that no one church, agency, national missions movement, or regional mission block can take it on alone or independently. Also, the understanding of the essence of what is entailed in the remaining task has altered considerably in recent years.

Declaration

We, representatives of evangelical global mission structures, being intent on fulfilling the ultimate objective of the Great Commission, have gathered in Tokyo May 11-14, 2010 at this Global Mission Consultation to make the following declaration. We set forth this declaration in obedience to Christ's final command, as a means of calling Christ-followers everywhere to whole-heartedly embrace and earnestly engage in "making disciples of every people in our generation."

Mankind's Need

We affirm that all people are lost apart from faith in Christ. The clear statements of Scripture reveal that every individual, without exception, is a sinner by nature, choice and practice (Rom. 3:9-18, 23). As such, all are under God's wrath and condemnation (Jn. 3:18) because their sin is an affront to the perfect and holy nature of God (Rom. 1:18; 2:2-5). The tragic result of sin is man's alienation from God, leading to everlasting death (Rom. 6:23), and creation's bondage to corruption, subjecting it to futility (Rom. 8:18-21).

God's Remedy

We further affirm that out of love, God sent His only Son, Jesus Christ (Jn. 3:16), to reconcile the world to Himself, so that mankind's sin will not be counted against them (2 Cor. 5:19). God's justice for the penalty of sin was satisfied by the atoning death of Christ as a sacrifice on man's behalf. Through Jesus' vicarious death and victorious resurrection, mankind is brought into a restored relationship with God. God offers forgiveness and salvation to all who, through faith, repent of their sin and believe solely in the redemptive work of Christ on the cross on their behalf (Rom. 1:5,16,17; 3:21-26; Eph. 1:7; 2:8-10). Therefore the message of the Great Commission is that —repentance and forgiveness of sins will be preached in His name to all peoples (Lk. 24:47). Salvation is found in none other (Acts 4:12), nor in any other way (Jn. 14:6).

Our Responsibility

Because of the reality of mankind's dire need and God's gracious remedy, Jesus left with His followers the missional priority of making disciples of every people (Mt. 28:18-20). By this mandate we acknowledge both the breadth of the unfinished task – *all peoples* – and the depth of the task – *making disciples*, as its focus.

We recognize the breadth of our task as geographical, by going —into all the world‖ (Mk 16:15); as ethnical, by engaging —all peoples (Mt. 28:19; Lk. 24:49); and as individual by proclaiming the gospel to —every creature‖ (Mk. 16:15).

Furthermore, we recognize that the depth of the task contains three essentials that comprise aspects in discipling peoples (Mt. 28:19-20):

> **Penetration** ("go"): making a priority of going to those who have had little or no exposure to the gospel. Messengers go and encounter non-believers by way of personal encounters, broadcasts, podcasts, printed material, recordings, electronic communications, or any other innovative means used as a channel of penetrating witness. Thus, the importance of the ministry of evangelizing.

Consolidation ("baptizing"): gathering new believers into a relationship with Jesus and other believers, which is evidenced by the identifying rite of baptism. To conserve the fruit of evangelism and then be able to systematically disciple believers takes a local body of believers living in corporate harmony. Thus, the importance of the ministry of establishing churches.

Transformation ("teaching to obey"): teaching Christ-followers to observe His commands with the outcome of transformed lives. The new believer's worldview must be adjusted to a biblical worldview; his lifestyle changed to increasingly conform to the image of Christ; and his ethical conduct progressively marked by biblical morals. Ideally, this results in individuals applying the gospel of the kingdom to every sphere and pursuit of life – from government to economics, from education to health, and from science to creation care. As a consequence whole communities, cultures and countries benefit from the transforming power of the gospel. Thus, the importance of the ministry of teaching.

Finishing the Task

Although none dare predict when the task of making disciples will be brought to completion, we leave Tokyo cognizant of two realities:

1. We are closer now to finishing the task than at any time in modern history.
2. God has entrusted this generation with more opportunities and resources to complete the task than any previous one. We have more mission-minded churches, more sending structures and bases, more missionaries, more material resources, more funding, more and better technology, more information and data, a deeper understanding of the task, and a clearer focus of our responsibility than previous generations. God will require much of our generation.

However, we caution that all these advantages must be matched with a corresponding *will to serve and sacrifice*, coupled with genuine reliance upon the Holy Spirit. We acknowledge that we are engaged in spiritual warfare in which the presence and empowering of the Holy Spirit is essential (Acts 1:8). We give evidence of our reliance on God and His Spirit through frequent and fervent prayer on behalf of the world, the work and the workers (Jn. 17:20-21; Col. 4:3-4; 1 Th. 5:17).

Our Pledge

Therefore, as representatives of this generation's global mission community, we pledge to obey the Great Commission. We covenant together to use all that God has entrusted to us in this obedience. We will seek to know where people are unreached, overlooked, ignored, or forgotten. We will pray for the Holy Spirit to give strength and guidance as we join with others in changing that neglect, to love and make disciples in the way of the Cross.

We confess that we have not always valued each other or each other's work. We repent of those wrongs and will endeavor to bring an end to competition where it exists, and reconcile where there is hurt, misunderstanding and mistrust. Furthermore, we will endeavor to recognize that each part of the Body has its very own purpose, whether risking their very lives to show God's passion for the salvation of others, or supporting those who lead us forward, or caring for those who quietly support, or fervently pray that His will be done throughout the whole earth. We will respect all mission-engaging individuals and groups as special vessels for God's glory, each endowed with abilities that extend His Kingdom in multiple ways.

Finally, we recognize that finishing the task will demand effective cooperative efforts of the entire global body of believers. To facilitate cooperation and on-going coordination between mission structures worldwide, we agree to the necessity of a global network of mission structures. With this in mind, we leave Tokyo pledging cooperation with one another, and all others of like faith, with the singular goal of —making disciples of every people in our generation.

Signatories of the Tokyo 2010 Declaration

Global Mission Structures

Ethne to Ethne
Global Network of Mission Structures
Globe Serve
Lausanne Committee For World Evangelization
Muslim Unreached Peoples Network
Nomadic Peoples Network
Third World Mission Association
World Evangelical Alliance – Theological Commission
World Evangelical Alliance – Mission Commission

Regional Mission Structures

Asia Mission Association
Association of Christians Ministering among Internationals (ACMI)
COMIBAM International (pending ratification)
Evangelical Association of the Caribbean
Evangelical Missiological Society of US and Canada
CrossGlobal Link of North America
MANI (Movement of African National Initiatives)

SAMA Link
SEA Link
SEA Net

National Mission Structures

AMTB - Associação de MissõesTransculturais Brasileiras (Brazil)
Ghana Evangelical Missions Association
India Missions Association
Japan Evangelical Missionary Association
Japan Overseas Missions Association
Korean World Missions Association
Nigeria Evangelical Missions Association
Philippine Missions Association
Singapore Centre for Global Mission
Swedish Evangelical Alliance
The Mission Exchange, USA
AFCM-OWM (USA)

REGNUM EDINBURGH CENTENARY SERIES

David A. Kerr, Kenneth R. Ross (Eds)
Mission Then and Now
2009 / 978-1-870345-73-6 / 343pp (paperback).
2009 / 978-1-870345-76-7 / 343pp (hardback)

No one can hope to fully understand the modern Christian missionary movement without engaging substantially with the World Missionary Conference, held at Edinburgh in 1910. This book is the first to systematically examine the eight Commissions which reported to Edinburgh 1910 and gave the conference much of its substance and enduring value. It will deepen and extend the reflection being stimulated by the upcoming centenary and will kindle the missionary imagination for 2010 and beyond.

Daryl M. Balia, Kirsteen Kim (Eds)
Witnessing to Christ Today
2010 / 978-1-870345-77-4 / 301pp (hardback)

This volume, the second in the Edinburgh 2010 series, includes reports of the nine main study groups working on different themes for the celebration of the centenary of the World Missionary Conference, Edinburgh 1910. Their collaborative work brings together perspectives that are as inclusive as possible of contemporary world Christianity and helps readers to grasp what it means in different contexts to be 'witnessing to Christ today'.

Claudia Währisch-Oblau, Fidon Mwombeki (Eds)
Mission Continues
Global Impulses for the 21st Century
2010 / 978-1-870345-82-8 / 271pp (hardback)

In May 2009, 35 theologians from Asia, Africa and Europe met in Wuppertal, Germany, for a consultation on mission theology organized by the United Evangelical Mission: Communion of 35 Churches in Three Continents. The aim was to participate in the 100th anniversary of the Edinburgh conference through a study process and reflect on the challenges for mission in the 21st century. This book brings together these papers written by experienced practitioners from around the world.

Brian Woolnough and Wonsuk Ma (Eds)
Holistic Mission
God's Plan for God's People
2010 / 978-1-870345-85-9 / 268pp (hardback)

Holistic mission, or integral mission, implies God is concerned with the whole person, the whole community, body, mind and spirit. This book discusses the meaning of the holistic gospel, how it has developed, and implications for the church. It takes a global, eclectic approach, with 19 writers, all of whom have much experience in, and commitment to, holistic mission. It addresses critically and honestly one of the most exciting, and challenging, issues facing the church today. To be part of God's plan for God's people, the church must take holistic mission to the world.

Kirsteen Kim and Andrew Anderson (Eds)
Mission Today and Tomorrow
2010 / 978-1-870345-91-0 / 450pp (hardback)

There are moments in our lives when we come to realise that we are participating in the triune God's mission. If we believe the church to be as sign and symbol of the reign of God in the world, then we are called to witness to Christ today by sharing in God's mission of love through the transforming power of the Holy Spirit. We can all participate in God's transforming and reconciling mission of love to the whole creation.

Tormod Engelsviken, Erling Lundeby and Dagfinn Solheim (Eds)
The Church Going Glocal
Mission and Globalisation
2011 / 978-1-870345-93-4 / 262pp (hardback)

The New Testament church is... universal and local at the same time. The universal, one and holy apostolic church appears in local manifestations. Missiologically speaking... the church can take courage as she faces the increasing impact of globalisation on local communities today. Being universal and concrete, the church is geared for the simultaneous challenges of the glocal and local.

Marina Ngurusangzeli Behera (Ed)
Interfaith Relations after One Hundred Years
Christian Mission among Other Faiths
2011 / 978-1-870345-96-5 / 338pp (hardback)

The essays of this book reflect not only the acceptance and celebration of pluralism within India but also by extension an acceptance as well as a need for unity among Indian Christians of different denominations. The essays were presented and studied at a preparatory consultation on Study Theme II: Christian Mission Among Other Faiths at the United Theological College, India July 2009.

Lalsangkima Pachuau and Knud Jørgensen (Eds)
Witnessing to Christ in a Pluralistic Age
Christian Mission among Other Faiths
2011 / 978-1-870345-95-8 / 277pp (hardback)

In a world where plurality of faiths is increasingly becoming a norm of life, insights on the theology of religious plurality are needed to strengthen our understanding of our own faith and the faith of others. Even though religious diversity is not new, we are seeing an upsurge in interest on the theologies of religion among all Christian confessional traditions. It can be claimed that no other issue in Christian mission is more important and more difficult than the theologies of religions.

Beth Snodderly and A Scott Moreau (Eds)
Evangelical Frontier Mission
Perspectives on the Global Progress of the Gospel
2011 / 978-1-870345-98-9 / 312pp (hardback)

This important volume demonstrates that 100 years after the World Missionary Conference in Edinburgh, Evangelism has become truly global. Twenty-first-century Evangelism continues to focus on frontier mission, but significantly, and in the spirit of Edinburgh 1910, it also has re-engaged social action.

Rolv Olsen (Ed)
Mission and Postmodernities
2011 / 978-1-870345-97-2 / 279pp (hardback)

This volume takes on meaning because its authors honestly struggle with and debate how we should relate to postmodernities. Should our response be accommodation, relativizing or counter-culture? How do we strike a balance between listening and understanding, and at the same time exploring how postmodernities influence the interpretation and application of the Bible as the normative story of God's mission in the world?

Cathy Ross (Ed)
Life-Widening Mission
2012 / 978-1-908355-00-3 / 163pp (hardback)

It is clear from the essays collected here that the experience of the 2010 World Mission Conference in Edinburgh was both affirming and frustrating for those taking part - affirming because of its recognition of how the centre of gravity has moved in global Christianity; frustrating because of the relative slowness of so many global Christian bodies to catch up with this and to embody it in the way they do business and in the way they represent themselves. These reflections will - or should - provide plenty of food for thought in the various councils of the Communion in the coming years.

Beate Fagerli, Knud Jørgensen, Rolv Olsen, Kari Storstein Haug and Knut Tveitereid (Eds)
A Learning Missional Church
Reflections from Young Missiologists
2012 / 978-1-908355-01-1 / 218pp (hardback)

Cross-cultural mission has always been a primary learning experience for the church. It pulls us out of a mono-cultural understanding and helps us discover a legitimate theological pluralism which opens up for new perspectives in the Gospel. Translating the Gospel into new languages and cultures is a human and divine means of making us learn new 'incarnations' of the Good News.

Emma Wild-Wood & Peniel Rajkumar (Eds)
Foundations for Mission
2012 / 978-1-908355-12-6 / 303pp (hardback)

This volume provides an important resource for those wishing to gain an overview of significant issues in contemporary missiology whilst understanding how they are applied in particular contexts

REGNUM STUDIES IN GLOBAL CHRISTIANITY

David Emmanuel Singh (Ed)
Jesus and the Cross
Reflections of Christians from Islamic Contexts
2008 / 978-1-870345-65-1 / 226pp

The Cross reminds us that the sins of the world are not borne through the exercise of power but through Jesus Christ's submission to the will of the Father. The papers in this volume are organised in three parts: scriptural, contextual and theological. The central question being addressed is: how do Christians living in contexts, where Islam is a majority or minority religion, experience, express or think of the Cross?

Sung-wook Hong
Naming God in Korea
The Case of Protestant Christianity
2008 / 978-1-870345-66-8 / 170pp (hardback)

Since Christianity was introduced to Korea more than a century ago, one of the most controversial issues has been the Korean term for the Christian 'God'. This issue is not merely about naming the Christian God in Korean language, but it relates to the question of theological contextualization - the relationship between the gospel and culture - and the question of Korean Christian identity. This book demonstrates the nature of the gospel in relation to cultures, i.e., the universality of the gospel expressed in all human cultures.

Hubert van Beek (Ed)
Revisioning Christian Unity
The Global Christian Forum
2009 / 978-1-870345-74-3 / 288pp (hardback)

This book contains the records of the Global Christian Forum gathering held in Limuru near Nairobi, Kenya, on 6 – 9 November 2007 as well as the papers presented at that historic event. Also included are a summary of the Global Christian Forum process from its inception until the 2007 gathering and the reports of the evaluation of the process that was carried out in 2008.

Young-hoon Lee

The Holy Spirit Movement in Korea

Its Historical and Theological Development

2009 / 978-1-870345-67-5 / 174pp (hardback)

This book traces the historical and theological development of the Holy Spirit Movement in Korea through six successive periods (from 1900 to the present time). These periods are characterized by repentance and revival (1900-20), persecution and suffering under Japanese occupation (1920-40), confusion and division (1940-60), explosive revival in which the Pentecostal movement played a major role in the rapid growth of Korean churches (1960-80), the movement reaching out to all denominations (1980-2000), and the new context demanding the Holy Spirit movement to open new horizons in its mission engagement (2000-).

Paul Hang-Sik Cho

Eschatology and Ecology

Experiences of the Korean Church

2010 / 978-1-870345-75-0 / 260pp (hardback)

This book raises the question of why Korean people, and Korean Protestant Christians in particular, pay so little attention to ecological issues. The author argues that there is an important connection (or elective affinity) between this lack of attention and the other-worldly eschatology that is so dominant within Korean Protestant Christianity.

Dietrich Werner, David Esterline, Namsoon Kang, Joshva Raja (Eds)

The Handbook of Theological Education in World Christianity

Theological Perspectives, Ecumenical Trends, Regional Surveys

2010 / 978-1-870345-80-4 / 800pp

This major reference work is the first ever comprehensive study of Theological Education in Christianity of its kind. With contributions from over 90 international scholars and church leaders, it aims to be easily accessible across denominational, cultural, educational, and geographic boundaries. The Handbook will aid international dialogue and networking among theological educators, institutions, and agencies.

David Emmanuel Singh & Bernard C Farr (Eds)

Christianity and Education

Shaping of Christian Context in Thinking

2010 / 978-1-870345-81-1 / 374pp

Christianity and Education is a collection of papers published in *Transformation: An International Journal of Holistic Mission Studies* over a period of 15 years. The articles represent a spectrum of Christian thinking addressing issues of institutional development for theological education, theological studies in the context of global mission, contextually aware/informed education, and academies which deliver such education, methodologies and personal reflections.

J.Andrew Kirk

Civilisations in Conflict?

Islam, the West and Christian Faith

2011 / 978-1-870345-87-3 / 205pp

Samuel Huntington's thesis, which argues that there appear to be aspects of Islam that could be on a collision course with the politics and values of Western societies, has provoked much controversy. The purpose of this study is to offer a particular response to Huntington's thesis by making a comparison between the origins of Islam and Christianity.

David Emmanuel Singh (Ed)

Jesus and the Incarnation

Reflections of Christians from Islamic Contexts

2011 / 978-1-870345-90-3 / 245pp

In the dialogues of Christians with Muslims nothing is more fundamental than the Cross, the Incarnation and the Resurrection of Jesus. Building on the *Jesus and the Cross*, this book contains voices of Christians living in various 'Islamic contexts' and reflecting on the Incarnation of Jesus. The aim and hope of these reflections is that the papers weaved around the notion of 'the Word' will not only promote dialogue among Christians on the roles of the Person and the Book but, also, create a positive environment for their conversations with Muslim neighbours.

Ivan M Satyavrata

God Has Not left Himself Without Witness

2011 / 978-1-870345-79-8 / 260pp

Since its earliest inception the Christian Church has had to address the question of what common ground exits between Christian faiths and other religions. This issue is not merely of academic interest but one with critical existential and socio-political consequences. This study presents a case for the revitalization of the fulfillment tradition based on a recovery and assessment of the fulfillment approaches of Indian Christian converts in the pre-independence period.

Bal Krishna Sharma

From this World to the Next

Christian Identity and Funerary Rites in Nepal

2013 / 978-1-908355-08-9 / 238pp

This book explores and analyses funerary rite struggles in a nation where Christianity is a comparatively recent phenomenon, and many families have multi-faith, who go through traumatic experiences at the death of their family members. The author has used an applied theological approach to explore and analyse the findings in order to address the issue of funerary rites with which the Nepalese church is struggling.

J Kwabena Asamoah-Gyada
Contemporary Pentecostal Christianity
Interpretations from an African Context
2013 / 978-1-908355-07-2 / 238pp

Pentecostalism is the fastest growing stream of Christianity in the world. The real evidence for the significance of Pentecostalism lies in the actual churches they have built and the numbers they attract. This work interprets key theological and missiological themes in African Pentecostalism by using material from the live experiences of the movement itself.

REGNUM STUDIES IN MISSION

Kwame Bediako
Theology and Identity
The Impact of Culture upon Christian Thought in the Second Century and in Modern Africa
1992 / 978-1870345-10-1 / 507pp

The author examines the question of Christian identity in the context of the Graeco–Roman culture of the early Roman Empire. He then addresses the modern African predicament of quests for identity and integration.

Christopher Sugden
Seeking the Asian Face of Jesus
The Practice and Theology of Christian Social Witness in Indonesia and India 1974–1996
1997 / 1-870345-26-6 / 496pp

This study focuses on contemporary holistic mission with the poor in India and Indonesia combined with the call to transformation of all life in Christ with micro-credit enterprise schemes. 'The literature on contextual theology now has a new standard to rise to' – Lamin Sanneh (Yale University, USA).

Hwa Yung
Mangoes or Bananas?
The Quest for an Authentic Asian Christian Theology
1997 / 1-870345-25-5 / 274pp

Asian Christian thought remains largely captive to Greek dualism and Enlightenment rationalism because of the overwhelming dominance of Western culture. Authentic contextual Christian theologies will emerge within Asian Christianity with a dual recovery of confidence in culture and the gospel.

Keith E. Eitel

Paradigm Wars

The Southern Baptist International Mission Board Faces the Third Millennium

1999 / 1-870345-12-6 / 140pp

The International Mission Board of the Southern Baptist Convention is the largest denominational mission agency in North America. This volume chronicles the historic and contemporary forces that led to the IMB's recent extensive reorganization, providing the most comprehensive case study to date of a historic mission agency restructuring to continue its mission purpose into the twenty-first century more effectively.

Samuel Jayakumar

Dalit Consciousness and Christian Conversion

Historical Resources for a Contemporary Debate

1999 / 81-7214-497-0 / 434pp

(Published jointly with ISPCK)

The main focus of this historical study is social change and transformation among the Dalit Christian communities in India. Historiography tests the evidence in the light of the conclusions of the modern Dalit liberation theologians.

Vinay Samuel and Christopher Sugden (Eds)

Mission as Transformation

A Theology of the Whole Gospel

1999 / 978-18703455-13-2 / 522pp

This book brings together in one volume twenty five years of biblical reflection on mission practice with the poor from around the world. This volume helps anyone understand how evangelicals, struggling to unite evangelism and social action, found their way in the last twenty five years to the biblical view of mission in which God calls all human beings to love God and their neighbour; never creating a separation between the two.

Christopher Sugden

Gospel, Culture and Transformation

2000 / 1-870345-32-0 / 152pp

A Reprint, with a New Introduction,

of Part Two of Seeking the Asian Face of Jesus

Gospel, Culture and Transformation explores the practice of mission especially in relation to transforming cultures and communities. - 'Transformation is to enable God's vision of society to be actualised in all relationships: social, economic and spiritual, so that God's will may be reflected in human society and his love experienced by all communities, especially the poor.'

Bernhard Ott

Beyond Fragmentation: Integrating Mission and Theological Education

A Critical Assessment of some Recent Developments in Evangelical Theological Education

2001 / 1-870345-14-2 / 382pp

Beyond Fragmentation is an enquiry into the development of Mission Studies in evangelical theological education in Germany and German-speaking Switzerland between 1960 and 1995. The author undertakes a detailed examination of the paradigm shifts which have taken place in recent years in both the theology of mission and the understanding of theological education.

Gideon Githiga

The Church as the Bulwark against Authoritarianism

Development of Church and State Relations in Kenya, with Particular Reference to the Years after Political Independence 1963-1992

2002 / 1-870345-38-x / 218pp

'All who care for love, peace and unity in Kenyan society will want to read this careful history by Bishop Githiga of how Kenyan Christians, drawing on the Bible, have sought to share the love of God, bring his peace and build up the unity of the nation, often in the face of great difficulties and opposition.' Canon Dr Chris Sugden, Oxford Centre for Mission Studies.

Myung Sung-Hoon, Hong Young-Gi (eds.)

Charis and Charisma

David Yonggi Cho and the Growth of Yoido Full Gospel Church

2003 / 978-1870345-45-3 / 218pp

This book discusses the factors responsible for the growth of the world's largest church. It expounds the role of the Holy Spirit, the leadership, prayer, preaching, cell groups and creativity in promoting church growth. It focuses on God's grace (charis) and inspiring leadership (charisma) as the two essential factors and the book's purpose is to present a model for church growth worldwide.

Samuel Jayakumar

Mission Reader

Historical Models for Wholistic Mission in the Indian Context

2003 / 1-870345-42-8 / 250pp

(Published jointly with ISPCK)

This book is written from an evangelical point of view revalidating and reaffirming the Christian commitment to wholistic mission. The roots of the 'wholistic mission' combining 'evangelism and social concerns' are to be located in the history and tradition of Christian evangelism in the past; and the civilizing purpose of evangelism is compatible with modernity as an instrument in nation building.

Bob Robinson

Christians Meeting Hindus

An Analysis and Theological Critique of the Hindu-Christian Encounter in India

2004 / 987-1870345-39-2 / 392pp

This book focuses on the Hindu-Christian encounter, especially the intentional meeting called dialogue, mainly during the last four decades of the twentieth century, and specifically in India itself.

Gene Early

Leadership Expectations

How Executive Expectations are Created and Used in a Non-Profit Setting

2005 / 1-870345-30-4 / 276pp

The author creates an Expectation Enactment Analysis to study the role of the Chancellor of the University of the Nations-Kona, Hawaii. This study is grounded in the field of managerial work, jobs, and behaviour and draws on symbolic interactionism, role theory, role identity theory and enactment theory. The result is a conceptual framework for developing an understanding of managerial roles.

Tharcisse Gatwa

The Churches and Ethnic Ideology in the Rwandan Crises 1900-1994

2005 / 978-1870345-24-8 / 300pp

(Reprinted 2011)

Since the early years of the twentieth century Christianity has become a new factor in Rwandan society. This book investigates the role Christian churches played in the formulation and development of the racial ideology that culminated in the 1994 genocide.

Julie Ma

Mission Possible

Biblical Strategies for Reaching the Lost

2005 / 978-1870345-37-1 / 142pp

This is a missiology book for the church which liberates missiology from the specialists for the benefit of every believer. It also serves as a textbook that is simple and friendly, and yet solid in biblical interpretation. This book links the biblical teaching to the actual and contemporary missiological settings with examples, making the Bible come alive to the reader.

Allan Anderson, Edmond Tang (Eds)

Asian and Pentecostal

The Charismatic Face of Christianity in Asia

2005 / 978-1870345-94-1 / 500pp

(Published jointly with APTS Press)

This book provides a thematic discussion and pioneering case studies on the history and development of Pentecostal and Charismatic churches in the countries of South Asia, South East Asia and East Asia.

I. Mark Beaumont
Christology in Dialogue with Muslims
A Critical Analysis of Christian Presentations of Christ for Muslims from the Ninth and Twentieth Centuries
2005 / 978-1870345-46-0 / 227pp

This book analyses Christian presentations of Christ for Muslims in the most creative periods of Christian-Muslim dialogue, the first half of the ninth century and the second half of the twentieth century. In these two periods, Christians made serious attempts to present their faith in Christ in terms that take into account Muslim perceptions of him, with a view to bridging the gap between Muslim and Christian convictions.

Thomas Czövek,
Three Seasons of Charismatic Leadership
A Literary-Critical and Theological Interpretation of the Narrative of Saul, David and Solomon
2006 / 978-1870345-48-4 / 272pp

This book investigates the charismatic leadership of Saul, David and Solomon. It suggests that charismatic leaders emerge in crisis situations in order to resolve the crisis by the charisma granted by God. Czovek argues that Saul proved himself as a charismatic leader as long as he acted resolutely and independently from his mentor Samuel. In the author's eyes, Saul's failure to establish himself as a charismatic leader is caused by his inability to step out from Samuel's shadow.

Richard Burgess
Nigeria's Christian Revolution
The Civil War Revival and Its Pentecostal Progeny (1967-2006)
2008 / 978-1-870345-63-7 / 347pp

This book describes the revival that occurred among the Igbo people of Eastern Nigeria and the new Pentecostal churches it generated, and documents the changes that have occurred as the movement has responded to global flows and local demands. As such, it explores the nature of revivalist and Pentecostal experience, but does so against the backdrop of local socio-political and economic developments, such as decolonisation and civil war, as well as broader processes, such as modernisation and globalisation.

David Emmanuel Singh & Bernard C Farr (Eds)
Christianity and Cultures
Shaping Christian Thinking in Context
2008 / 978-1-870345-69-9 / 271pp

This volume marks an important milestone, the 25th anniversary of the Oxford Centre for Mission Studies (OCMS). The papers here have been exclusively sourced from Transformation, a quarterly journal of OCMS, and seek to provide a tripartite view of Christianity's engagement with cultures by focusing on the question: how is Christian thinking being formed or reformed through its interaction with the varied contexts it encounters? The subject matters include different strands of theological-missiological thinking, socio-political engagements and forms of family relationships in interaction with the host cultures.

Tormod Engelsviken, Ernst Harbakk, Rolv Olsen, Thor Strandenæs (Eds)
Mission to the World
Communicating the Gospel in the 21st Century: Essays in Honour of Knud Jørgensen
2008 / 978-1-870345-64-4 / 472pp (hardback)

Knud Jørgensen is Director of Areopagos and Associate Professor of Missiology at MF Norwegian School of Theology. This book reflects on the main areas of Jørgensen's commitment to mission. At the same time it focuses on the main frontier of mission, the world, the content of mission, the Gospel, the fact that the Gospel has to be communicated, and the context of contemporary mission in the 21st century.

Al Tizon
Transformation after Lausanne
Radical Evangelical Mission in Global-Local Perspective
2008 / 978-1-870345-68-2 / 281pp

After Lausanne '74, a worldwide network of radical evangelical mission theologians and practitioners use the notion of "Mission as Transformation" to integrate evangelism and social concern together, thus lifting theological voices from the Two Thirds World to places of prominence. This book documents the definitive gatherings, theological tensions, and social forces within and without evangelicalism that led up to Mission as Transformation. And it does so through a global-local grid that points the way toward greater holistic mission in the 21st century.

Bambang Budijanto
Values and Participation
Development in Rural Indonesia
2009 / 978-1-870345-70-4 / 237pp

Socio-religious values and socio-economic development are inter-dependant, inter-related and are constantly changing in the context of macro political structures, economic policy, religious organizations and globalization; and micro influences such as local affinities, identity, politics, leadership and beliefs. The book argues that the comprehensive approach in understanding the socio-religious values of each of the three local Lopait communities in Central Java is essential to accurately describing their respective identity.

Alan R. Johnson

Leadership in a Slum

A Bangkok Case Study

2009 / 978-1-870345-71-2 / 238pp

This book looks at leadership in the social context of a slum in Bangkok from a different perspective than traditional studies which measure well educated Thais on leadership scales derived in the West. Using both systematic data collection and participant observation, it develops a culturally preferred model as well as a set of models based in Thai concepts that reflect on-the-ground realities. It concludes by looking at the implications of the anthropological approach for those who are involved in leadership training in Thai settings and beyond.

Titre Ande

Leadership and Authority

Bula Matari and Life - Community Ecclesiology in Congo

2010 / 978-1-870345-72-9 / 189pp

Christian theology in Africa can make significant development if a critical understanding of the socio-political context in contemporary Africa is taken seriously, particularly as Africa's post-colonial Christian leadership based its understanding and use of authority on the Bula Matari model. This has caused many problems and Titre proposes a Life-Community ecclesiology for liberating authority, here leadership is a function, not a status, and 'apostolic succession' belongs to all people of God.

Frank Kwesi Adams

Odwira and the Gospel

A Study of the Asante Odwira Festival and its Significance for Christianity in Ghana

2010 /978-1-870345-59-0 / 232pp

The study of the Odwira festival is the key to the understanding of Asante religious and political life in Ghana. The book explores the nature of the Odwira festival longitudinally - in pre-colonial, colonial and post-independence Ghana - and examines the Odwira ideology and its implications for understanding the Asante self-identity. Also discussed is how some elements of faith portrayed in the Odwira festival can provide a framework for Christianity to engage with Asante culture at a greater depth.

Bruce Carlton

Strategy Coordinator

Changing the Course of Southern Baptist Missions

2010 / 978-1-870345-78-1 / 268pp

This is an outstanding, one-of-a-kind work addressing the influence of the non-residential missionary/strategy coordinator's role in Southern Baptist missions. This scholarly text examines the twentieth century global missiological currents that influenced the leadership of the International

Mission Board, resulting in a new paradigm to assist in taking the gospel to the nations.

Julie Ma & Wonsuk Ma
Mission in the Spirit:
Towards a Pentecostal/Charismatic Missiology
2010 / 978-1-870345-84-2 / 312pp
The book explores the unique contribution of Pentecostal/Charismatic mission from the beginning of the twentieth century. The first part considers the theological basis of Pentecostal/Charismatic mission thinking and practice. Special attention is paid to the Old Testament, which has been regularly overlooked by the modern Pentecostal/Charismatic movements. The second part discusses major mission topics with contributions and challenges unique to Pentecostal/Charismatic mission. The book concludes with a reflection on the future of this powerful missionary movement. As the authors served as Korean missionaries in Asia, often their missionary experiences in Asia are reflected in their discussions.

S. Hun Kim & Wonsuk Ma (eds.)
Korean Diaspora and Christian Mission
2011-978-1-870345-91-0 / 301pp (hardback)
As a 'divine conspiracy' for Missio Dei, the global phenomenon of people on the move has shown itself to be invaluable. In 2004 two significant documents concerning Diaspora were introduced, one by the Filipino International Network and the other by the Lausanne Committee for World Evangelization. These have created awareness of the importance of people on the move for Christian mission. Since then, Korean Diaspora has conducted similar research among Korean missions, resulting in this book

Jin Huat Tan
Planting an Indigenous Church
The Case of the Borneo Evangelical Mission
2011 / 978-1-870345-99-6 / 363pp
Dr Jin Huat Tan has written a pioneering study of the origins and development of Malaysia's most significant indigenous church. This is an amazing story of revival, renewal and transformation of the entire region chronicling the powerful effect of it evident to date! What can we learn from this extensive and careful study of the Borneo Revival, so the global Christianity will become ever more dynamic?

Bill Prevette
Child, Church and Compassion
Towards Child Theology in Romania
2012 / 978-1-908355-03-4 / 377pp
Bill Prevett comments that ¨children are like 'canaries in a mine shaft'; they provide a focal point for discovery and encounter of perilous aspects of our

world that are often ignored." True, but miners also carried a lamp to see into the subterranean darkness. This book is such a lamp. It lights up the subterranean world of children and youth in danger of exploitation, and as it does so travels deep into their lives and also into the activities of those who seek to help them.

Samuel Cyuma

Picking up the Pieces

The Church and Conflict Resolution in South Africa and Rwanda

2012 / 978-1-908355-02-7 / 373pp

In the last ten years of the 20th century, the world was twice confronted with unbelievable news from Africa. First, there was the end of Apartheid in South Africa, without bloodshed, due to responsible political and Church leaders. The second was the mass killings in Rwanda, which soon escalated into real genocide. Political and Church leaders had been unable to prevents this crime against humanity. In this book, the question is raised: can we compare the situation in South Africa with that in Rwanda? Can Rwandan leaders draw lessons from the peace process in South Africa?

Peter Rowan

Proclaiming the Peacemaker

The Malaysian Church as an Agent of Reconciliation in a Multicultural Society

2012 / 978-1-908355-05-8 / 268pp

With a history of racial violence and in recent years, low-level ethnic tensions, the themes of peaceful coexistence and social harmony are recurring ones in the discourse of Malaysian society. In such a context, this book looks at the role of the church as a reconciling agent, arguing that a reconciling presence within a divided society necessitates an ethos of peacemaking.

Edward Ontita

Resources and Opportunity

The Architecture of Livelihoods in Rural Kenya

2012 / 978-1-908355-04-1 / 328pp

Poor people in most rural areas of developing countries often improvise resources in unique ways to enable them make a living. Resources and Opportunity takes the view that resources are dynamic and fluid, arguing that villagers co-produce them through redefinition and renaming in everyday practice and use them in diverse ways. The book focuses on ordinary social activities to bring out people's creativity in locating, redesigning and embracing livelihood opportunities in processes.

Kathryn Kraft

Searching for Heaven in the Real World

A Sociological Discussion of Conversion in the Arab World

2012 / 978-1-908355-15-7 / 1428pp

Kathryn Kraft explores the breadth of psychological and social issues faced by Arab Muslims after making a decision to adopt a faith in Christ or

Christianity, investigating some of the most surprising and significant challenges new believers face.

Wessley Lukose

Contextual Missiology of the Spirit

Pentecostalism in Rajasthan, India

2013 / 978-1-908355-09-6 / 256pp

This book explores the identity, context and features of Pentecostalism in Rajasthan, India as well as the internal and external issues facing Pentecostals. It aims to suggest 'a contextual missiology of the Spirit,' as a new model of contextual missiology from a Pentecostal perspective. It is presented as a glocal, ecumenical, transformational, and public missiology.

REGNUM RESOURCES FOR MISSION

Knud Jørgensen

Equipping for Service

Christian Leadership in Church and Society

2012 / 978-1-908355-06-5 / 168pp

This book is written out of decades of experience of leading churches and missions in Ethiopia, Geneva, Norway and Hong Kong. Combining the teaching of Scripture with the insights of contemporary management philosophy, Jørgensen writes in a way which is practical and applicable to anyone in Christian service. “The intention has been to challenge towards a leadership relevant for work in church and mission, and in public and civil society, with special attention to leadership in Church and organisation.”

For the up-to-date listing of the Regnum books see www.ocms.ac.uk/regnum

regnum

Regnum Books International

Regnum is an Imprint of The Oxford Centre for Mission Studies
St. Philip and St. James Church, Woodstock Road, Oxford, OX2 6HR
Web: www.ocms.ac.uk/regnum

REGNUM EDINBURGH CENTENARY SERIES

David A. Kerr, Kenneth R. Ross (Eds)
Mission Then and Now
2009 / 978-1-870345-73-6 / 343pp (paperback)
2009 / 978-1-870345-76-7 / 343pp (hardback)

No one can hope to fully understand the modern Christian missionary movement without engaging substantially with the World Missionary Conference, held at Edinburgh in 1910. This book is the first to systematically examine the eight Commissions which reported to Edinburgh 1910 and gave the conference much of its substance and enduring value. It will deepen and extend the reflection being stimulated by the upcoming centenary and will kindle the missionary imagination for 2010 and beyond.

Daryl M. Balia, Kirsteen Kim (Eds)
Witnessing to Christ Today
2010 / 978-1-870345-77-4 / 301pp (hardback)

This volume, the second in the Edinburgh 2010 series, includes reports of the nine main study groups working on different themes for the celebration of the centenary of the World Missionary Conference, Edinburgh 1910. Their collaborative work brings together perspectives that are as inclusive as possible of contemporary world Christianity and helps readers to grasp what it means in different contexts to be 'witnessing to Christ today'.

Claudia Währisch-Oblau, Fidon Mwombeki (Eds)
Mission Continues
Global Impulses for the 21st Century
2010 / 978-1-870345-82-8 / 271pp (hardback)

In May 2009, 35 theologians from Asia, Africa and Europe met in Wuppertal, Germany, for a consultation on mission theology organized by the United Evangelical Mission: Communion of 35 Churches in Three Continents. The aim was to participate in the 100th anniversary of the Edinburgh conference through a study process and reflect on the challenges for mission in the 21st century. This book brings together these papers written by experienced practitioners from around the world.

Brian Woolnough and Wonsuk Ma (Eds)
Holistic Mission
God's Plan for God's People
2010 / 978-1-870345-85-9 / 268pp (hardback)

Holistic mission, or integral mission, implies God is concerned with the whole person, the whole community, body, mind and spirit. This book discusses the meaning of the holistic gospel, how it has developed, and implications for the church. It takes a global, eclectic approach, with 19 writers, all of whom have much experience in, and commitment to, holistic mission. It addresses critically and honestly one of the most exciting, and challenging, issues facing the church today. To be part of God's plan for God's people, the church must take holistic mission to the world.

Kirsteen Kim and Andrew Anderson (Eds)
Mission Today and Tomorrow
2010 / 978-1-870345-91-0 / 450pp (hardback)

There are moments in our lives when we come to realise that we are participating in the triune God's mission. If we believe the church to be as sign and symbol of the reign of God in the world, then we are called to witness to Christ today by sharing in God's mission of love through the transforming power of the Holy Spirit. We can all participate in God's transforming and reconciling mission of love to the whole creation.

Tormod Engelsviken, Erling Lundeby and Dagfinn Solheim (Eds)
The Church Going Glocal
Mission and Globalisation
2011 / 978-1-870345-93-4 / 262pp (hardback)

The New Testament church is… universal and local at the same time. The universal, one and holy apostolic church appears in local manifestations. Missiologically speaking… the church can take courage as she faces the increasing impact of globalisation on local communities today. Being universal and concrete, the church is geared for the simultaneous challenges of the glocal and local.

Marina Ngurusangzeli Behera (Ed)
Interfaith Relations after One Hundred Years
Christian Mission among Other Faiths
2011 / 978-1-870345-96-5 / 338pp (hardback)

The essays of this book reflect not only the acceptance and celebration of pluralism within India but also by extension an acceptance as well as a need for unity among Indian Christians of different denominations. The essays were presented and studied at a preparatory consultation on Study Theme II: Christian Mission Among Other Faiths at the United Theological College, India July 2009.

Lalsangkima Pachuau and Knud Jørgensen (Eds)
Witnessing to Christ in a Pluralistic Age
Christian Mission among Other Faiths
2011 / 978-1-870345-95-8 / 277pp (hardback)

In a world where plurality of faiths is increasingly becoming a norm of life, insights on the theology of religious plurality are needed to strengthen our understanding of our own faith and the faith of others. Even though religious diversity is not new, we are seeing an upsurge in interest on the theologies of religion among all Christian confessional traditions. It can be claimed that no other issue in Christian mission is more important and more difficult than the theologies of religions.

Beth Snodderly and A Scott Moreau (Eds)
Evangelical Frontier Mission
Perspectives on the Global Progress of the Gospel
2011 / 978-1-870345-98-9 / 312pp (hardback)

This important volume demonstrates that 100 years after the World Missionary Conference in Edinburgh, Evangelism has become truly global. Twenty-first-century Evangelism continues to focus on frontier mission, but significantly, and in the spirit of Edinburgh 1910, it also has re-engaged social action.

Rolv Olsen (Ed)
Mission and Postmodernities
2011 / 978-1-870345-97-2 / 279pp (hardback)

This volume takes on meaning because its authors honestly struggle with and debate how we should relate to postmodernities. Should our response be accommodation, relativizing or counter-culture? How do we strike a balance between listening and understanding, and at the same time exploring how postmodernities influence the interpretation and application of the Bible as the normative story of God's mission in the world?

Cathy Ross (Ed)
Life-Widening Mission
2012 / 978-1-908355-00-3 / 163pp (hardback)

It is clear from the essays collected here that the experience of the 2010 World Mission Conference in Edinburgh was both affirming and frustrating for those taking part - affirming because of its recognition of how the centre of gravity has moved in global Christianity; frustrating because of the relative slowness of so many global Christian bodies to catch up with this and to embody it in the way they do business and in the way they represent themselves. These reflections will - or should - provide plenty of food for thought in the various councils of the Communion in the coming years.

Beate Fagerli, Knud Jørgensen, Rolv Olsen, Kari Storstein Haug and Knut Tveitereid (Eds)
A Learning Missional Church
Reflections from Young Missiologists
2012 / 978-1-908355-01-1 / 218pp (hardback)

Cross-cultural mission has always been a primary learning experience for the church. It pulls us out of a mono-cultural understanding and helps us discover a legitimate theological pluralism which opens up for new perspectives in the Gospel. Translating the Gospel into new languages and cultures is a human and divine means of making us learn new 'incarnations' of the Good News.

Emma Wild-Wood & Peniel Rajkumar (Eds)
Foundations for Mission
2012 / 978-1-908355-12-6 / 303pp (hardback)

This volume provides an important resource for those wishing to gain an overview of significant issues in contemporary missiology whilst understanding how they are applied in particular contexts.

Wonsuk Ma & Kenneth R Ross (Eds)
Mission Spirituality and Authentic Discipleship
2013 / 978-1-908355-24-9 / 248pp (hardback)

This book argues for the primacy of spirituality in the practice of mission. Since God is the primary agent of mission and God works through the power of the Holy Spirit, it is through openness to the Spirit that mission finds its true character and has its authentic impact.

REGNUM STUDIES IN GLOBAL CHRISTIANITY

David Emmanuel Singh (Ed)
Jesus and the Cross
Reflections of Christians from Islamic Contexts
2008 / 978-1-870345-65-1 / 226pp

The Cross reminds us that the sins of the world are not borne through the exercise of power but through Jesus Christ's submission to the will of the Father. The papers in this volume are organised in three parts: scriptural, contextual and theological. The central question being addressed is: how do Christians living in contexts, where Islam is a majority or minority religion, experience, express or think of the Cross?

Sung-wook Hong
Naming God in Korea
The Case of Protestant Christianity
2008 / 978-1-870345-66-8 / 170pp (hardback)

Since Christianity was introduced to Korea more than a century ago, one of the most controversial issues has been the Korean term for the Christian 'God'. This issue is not merely about naming the Christian God in Korean language, but it relates to the question of theological contextualization - the relationship between the gospel and culture - and the question of Korean Christian identity. This book demonstrates the nature of the gospel in relation to cultures, i.e., the universality of the gospel expressed in all human cultures.

Hubert van Beek (Ed)
Revisioning Christian Unity
The Global Christian Forum
2009 / 978-1-870345-74-3 / 288pp (hardback)

This book contains the records of the Global Christian Forum gathering held in Limuru near Nairobi, Kenya, on 6 – 9 November 2007 as well as the papers presented at that historic event. Also included are a summary of the Global Christian Forum process from its inception until the 2007 gathering and the reports of the evaluation of the process that was carried out in 2008.

Young-hoon Lee
The Holy Spirit Movement in Korea
Its Historical and Theological Development
2009 / 978-1-870345-67-5 / 174pp (hardback)

This book traces the historical and theological development of the Holy Spirit Movement in Korea through six successive periods (from 1900 to the present time). These periods are characterized by repentance and revival (1900-20), persecution and suffering under Japanese occupation (1920-40), confusion and division (1940-60), explosive revival in which the Pentecostal movement played a major role in the rapid growth of Korean churches (1960-80), the movement reaching out to all denominations (1980-2000), and the new context demanding the Holy Spirit movement to open new horizons in its mission engagement (2000-).

Paul Hang-Sik Cho
Eschatology and Ecology
Experiences of the Korean Church
2010 / 978-1-870345-75-0 / 260pp (hardback)

This book raises the question of why Korean people, and Korean Protestant Christians in particular, pay so little attention to ecological issues. The author argues that there is an important connection (or elective affinity) between this lack of attention and the other-worldly eschatology that is so dominant within Korean Protestant Christianity.

Dietrich Werner, David Esterline, Namsoon Kang, Joshva Raja (Eds)
The Handbook of Theological Education in World Christianity
Theological Perspectives, Ecumenical Trends, Regional Surveys
2010 / 978-1-870345-80-4 / 800pp

This major reference work is the first ever comprehensive study of Theological Education in Christianity of its kind. With contributions from over 90 international scholars and church leaders, it aims to be easily accessible across denominational, cultural, educational, and geographic boundaries. The Handbook will aid international dialogue and networking among theological educators, institutions, and agencies.

David Emmanuel Singh & Bernard C Farr (Eds)
Christianity and Education
Shaping of Christian Context in Thinking
2010 / 978-1-870345-81-1 / 374pp

Christianity and Education is a collection of papers published in *Transformation: An International Journal of Holistic Mission Studies* over a period of 15 years. The articles represent a spectrum of Christian thinking addressing issues of institutional development for theological education, theological studies in the context of global mission, contextually aware/informed education, and academies which deliver such education, methodologies and personal reflections.

J.Andrew Kirk
Civilisations in Conflict?
Islam, the West and Christian Faith
2011 / 978-1-870345-87-3 / 205pp

Samuel Huntington's thesis, which argues that there appear to be aspects of Islam that could be on a collision course with the politics and values of Western societies, has provoked much controversy. The purpose of this study is to offer a particular response to Huntington's thesis by making a comparison between the origins of Islam and Christianity.

David Emmanuel Singh (Ed)
Jesus and the Incarnation
Reflections of Christians from Islamic Contexts
2011 / 978-1-870345-90-3 / 245pp

In the dialogues of Christians with Muslims nothing is more fundamental than the Cross, the Incarnation and the Resurrection of Jesus. Building on the *Jesus and the Cross*, this book contains voices of Christians living in various 'Islamic contexts' and reflecting on the Incarnation of Jesus. The aim and hope of these reflections is that the papers weaved around the notion of 'the Word' will not only promote dialogue among Christians on the roles of the Person and the Book but, also, create a positive environment for their conversations with Muslim neighbours.

Ivan M Satyavrata
God Has Not left Himself Without Witness
2011 / 978-1-870345-79-8 / 260pp

Since its earliest inception the Christian Church has had to address the question of what common ground exits between Christian faiths and other religions. This issue is not merely of academic interest but one with critical existential and socio-political consequences. This study presents a case for the revitalization of the fulfillment tradition based on a recovery and assessment of the fulfillment approaches of Indian Christian converts in the pre-independence period.

Bal Krishna Sharma
From this World to the Next
Christian Identity and Funerary Rites in Nepal
2013 / 978-1-908355-08-9 / 238pp

This book explores and analyses funerary rite struggles in a nation where Christianity is a comparatively recent phenomenon, and many families have multi-faith, who go through traumatic experiences at the death of their family members. The author has used an applied theological approach to explore and analyse the findings in order to address the issue of funerary rites with which the Nepalese church is struggling.

J Kwabena Asamoah-Gyada
Contemporary Pentecostal Christianity
Interpretations from an African Context
2013 / 978-1-908355-07-2 / 238pp

Pentecostalism is the fastest growing stream of Christianity in the world. The real evidence for the significance of Pentecostalism lies in the actual churches they have built and the numbers they attract. This work interprets key theological and missiological themes in African Pentecostalism by using material from the live experiences of the movement itself.

Isabel Apawo Phiri & Dietrich Werner (Eds)
Handbook of Theological Education in Africa
2013 / 978-1-908355-19-5 / 1110pp (hardback)

The *Handbook of Theological Education in Africa* is a wake-up call for African churches to give proper prominence to theological education institutions and their programmes which serve them. It is unique, comprehensive and ambitious in its aim and scope.

Hope Antone, Wati Longchar, Hyunju Bae, Huang Po Ho, Dietrich Werner (Eds)
Asian Handbook for Theological Education and Ecumenism
2013 / 978-1-908355-300 / 675pp (hardback)

This impressive and comprehensive book focuses on key resources for teaching Christian unity and common witness in Asian contexts. It is a collection of articles that reflects the ongoing 'double wrestle' with the texts of biblical tradition as well as with contemporary contexts. It signals an investment towards the future of the ecumenical movement in Asia.

REGNUM STUDIES IN MISSION

Kwame Bediako
Theology and Identity
The Impact of Culture upon Christian Thought in the Second Century and in Modern Africa
1992 / 978-1870345-10-1 / 507pp

The author examines the question of Christian identity in the context of the Graeco–Roman culture of the early Roman Empire. He then addresses the modern African predicament of quests for identity and integration.

Christopher Sugden
Seeking the Asian Face of Jesus
The Practice and Theology of Christian Social Witness
in Indonesia and India 1974–1996
1997 / 1-870345-26-6 / 496pp

This study focuses on contemporary holistic mission with the poor in India and Indonesia combined with the call to transformation of all life in Christ with micro-credit enterprise schemes. 'The literature on contextual theology now has a new standard to rise to' – Lamin Sanneh (Yale University, USA).

Hwa Yung

Mangoes or Bananas?

The Quest for an Authentic Asian Christian Theology

1997 / 1-870345-25-5 / 274pp

Asian Christian thought remains largely captive to Greek dualism and Enlightenment rationalism because of the overwhelming dominance of Western culture. Authentic contextual Christian theologies will emerge within Asian Christianity with a dual recovery of confidence in culture and the gospel.

Keith E. Eitel

Paradigm Wars

The Southern Baptist International Mission Board Faces the Third Millennium

1999 / 1-870345-12-6 / 140pp

The International Mission Board of the Southern Baptist Convention is the largest denominational mission agency in North America. This volume chronicles the historic and contemporary forces that led to the IMB's recent extensive reorganization, providing the most comprehensive case study to date of a historic mission agency restructuring to continue its mission purpose into the twenty-first century more effectively.

Samuel Jayakumar

Dalit Consciousness and Christian Conversion

Historical Resources for a Contemporary Debate

1999 / 81-7214-497-0 / 434pp

(Published jointly with ISPCK)

The main focus of this historical study is social change and transformation among the Dalit Christian communities in India. Historiography tests the evidence in the light of the conclusions of the modern Dalit liberation theologians.

Vinay Samuel and Christopher Sugden (Eds)

Mission as Transformation

A Theology of the Whole Gospel

1999 / 978-18703455-13-2 / 522pp

This book brings together in one volume twenty five years of biblical reflection on mission practice with the poor from around the world. This volume helps anyone understand how evangelicals, struggling to unite evangelism and social action, found their way in the last twenty five years to the biblical view of mission in which God calls all human beings to love God and their neighbour; never creating a separation between the two.

Christopher Sugden

Gospel, Culture and Transformation

2000 / 1-870345-32-0 / 152pp

A Reprint, with a New Introduction,

of Part Two of Seeking the Asian Face of Jesus

Gospel, Culture and Transformation explores the practice of mission especially in relation to transforming cultures and communities. - 'Transformation is to enable God's vision of society to be actualised in all relationships: social, economic and spiritual, so that God's will may be reflected in human society and his love experienced by all communities, especially the poor.'

Bernhard Ott

Beyond Fragmentation: Integrating Mission and Theological Education

A Critical Assessment of some Recent Developments in Evangelical Theological Education

2001 / 1-870345-14-2 / 382pp

Beyond Fragmentation is an enquiry into the development of Mission Studies in evangelical theological education in Germany and German-speaking Switzerland between 1960 and 1995. The author undertakes a detailed examination of the paradigm shifts which have taken place in recent years in both the theology of mission and the understanding of theological education.

Gideon Githiga

The Church as the Bulwark against Authoritarianism

Development of Church and State Relations in Kenya, with Particular Reference to the Years after Political Independence 1963-1992

2002 / 1-870345-38-x / 218pp

'All who care for love, peace and unity in Kenyan society will want to read this careful history by Bishop Githiga of how Kenyan Christians, drawing on the Bible, have sought to share the love of God, bring his peace and build up the unity of the nation, often in the face of great difficulties and opposition.' Canon Dr Chris Sugden, Oxford Centre for Mission Studies.

Myung Sung-Hoon, Hong Young-Gi (eds.)

Charis and Charisma

David Yonggi Cho and the Growth of Yoido Full Gospel Church

2003 / 978-1870345-45-3 / 218pp

This book discusses the factors responsible for the growth of the world's largest church. It expounds the role of the Holy Spirit, the leadership, prayer, preaching, cell groups and creativity in promoting church growth. It focuses on God's grace (charis) and inspiring leadership (charisma) as the two essential factors and the book's purpose is to present a model for church growth worldwide.

Samuel Jayakumar

Mission Reader

Historical Models for Wholistic Mission in the Indian Context

2003 / 1-870345-42-8 / 250pp

(Published jointly with ISPCK)

This book is written from an evangelical point of view revalidating and reaffirming the Christian commitment to wholistic mission. The roots of the 'wholistic mission' combining 'evangelism and social concerns' are to be located in the history and tradition of Christian evangelism in the past; and the civilizing purpose of evangelism is compatible with modernity as an instrument in nation building.

Bob Robinson

Christians Meeting Hindus

An Analysis and Theological Critique of the Hindu-Christian Encounter in India

2004 / 987-1870345-39-2 / 392pp

This book focuses on the Hindu-Christian encounter, especially the intentional meeting called dialogue, mainly during the last four decades of the twentieth century, and specifically in India itself.

Gene Early

Leadership Expectations

How Executive Expectations are Created and Used in a Non-Profit Setting

2005 / 1-870345-30-4 / 276pp

The author creates an Expectation Enactment Analysis to study the role of the Chancellor of the University of the Nations-Kona, Hawaii. This study is grounded in the field of managerial work, jobs, and behaviour and draws on symbolic interactionism, role theory, role identity theory and enactment theory. The result is a conceptual framework for developing an understanding of managerial roles.

Tharcisse Gatwa

The Churches and Ethnic Ideology in the Rwandan Crises 1900-1994

2005 / 978-1870345-24-8 / 300pp

(Reprinted 2011)

Since the early years of the twentieth century Christianity has become a new factor in Rwandan society. This book investigates the role Christian churches played in the formulation and development of the racial ideology that culminated in the 1994 genocide.

Julie Ma

Mission Possible

Biblical Strategies for Reaching the Lost

2005 / 978-1870345-37-1 / 142pp

This is a missiology book for the church which liberates missiology from the specialists for the benefit of every believer. It also serves as a textbook that is simple and friendly, and yet solid in biblical interpretation. This book links the biblical teaching to the actual and contemporary missiological settings with examples, making the Bible come alive to the reader.

I. Mark Beaumont

Christology in Dialogue with Muslims

A Critical Analysis of Christian Presentations of Christ for Muslims from the Ninth and Twentieth Centuries

2005 / 978-1870345-46-0 / 227pp

This book analyses Christian presentations of Christ for Muslims in the most creative periods of Christian-Muslim dialogue, the first half of the ninth century and the second half of the twentieth century. In these two periods, Christians made serious attempts to present their faith in Christ in terms that take into account Muslim perceptions of him, with a view to bridging the gap between Muslim and Christian convictions.

Thomas Czövek,

Three Seasons of Charismatic Leadership

A Literary-Critical and Theological Interpretation of the Narrative of Saul, David and Solomon

2006 / 978-1870345-48-4 / 272pp

This book investigates the charismatic leadership of Saul, David and Solomon. It suggests that charismatic leaders emerge in crisis situations in order to resolve the crisis by the charisma granted by God. Czovek argues that Saul proved himself as a charismatic leader as long as he acted resolutely and independently from his mentor Samuel. In the author's eyes, Saul's failure to establish himself as a charismatic leader is caused by his inability to step out from Samuel's shadow.

Richard Burgess

Nigeria's Christian Revolution

The Civil War Revival and Its Pentecostal Progeny (1967-2006)

2008 / 978-1-870345-63-7 / 347pp

This book describes the revival that occurred among the Igbo people of Eastern Nigeria and the new Pentecostal churches it generated, and documents the changes that have occurred as the movement has responded to global flows and local demands. As such, it explores the nature of revivalist and Pentecostal experience, but does so against the backdrop of local socio-political and economic developments, such as decolonisation and civil war, as well as broader processes, such as modernisation and globalisation.

David Emmanuel Singh & Bernard C Farr (Eds)

Christianity and Cultures

Shaping Christian Thinking in Context

2008 / 978-1-870345-69-9 / 271pp

This volume marks an important milestone, the 25th anniversary of the Oxford Centre for Mission Studies (OCMS). The papers here have been exclusively sourced from Transformation, a quarterly journal of OCMS, and seek to provide a tripartite view of Christianity's engagement with cultures by focusing on the question: how is Christian thinking being formed or reformed through its interaction with the varied contexts it encounters? The subject matters include different strands of theological-missiological thinking, socio-political engagements and forms of family relationships in interaction with the host cultures.

Tormod Engelsviken, Ernst Harbakk, Rolv Olsen, Thor Strandenæs (Eds)

Mission to the World

Communicating the Gospel in the 21st Century:
Essays in Honour of Knud Jørgensen

2008 / 978-1-870345-64-4 / 472pp (hardback)

Knud Jørgensen is Director of Areopagos and Associate Professor of Missiology at MF Norwegian School of Theology. This book reflects on the main areas of Jørgensen's commitment to mission. At the same time it focuses on the main frontier of mission, the world, the content of mission, the Gospel, the fact that the Gospel has to be communicated, and the context of contemporary mission in the 21st century.

Al Tizon

Transformation after Lausanne

Radical Evangelical Mission in Global-Local Perspective

2008 / 978-1-870345-68-2 / 281pp

After Lausanne '74, a worldwide network of radical evangelical mission theologians and practitioners use the notion of "Mission as Transformation" to integrate evangelism and social concern together, thus lifting theological voices from the Two Thirds World to places of prominence. This book documents the definitive gatherings, theological tensions, and social forces within and without evangelicalism that led up to Mission as Transformation. And it does so through a global-local grid that points the way toward greater holistic mission in the 21st century.

Bambang Budijanto

Values and Participation

Development in Rural Indonesia

2009 / 978-1-870345-70-4 / 237pp

Socio-religious values and socio-economic development are inter-dependant, inter-related and are constantly changing in the context of macro political structures, economic policy, religious organizations and globalization; and micro influences such as local affinities, identity, politics, leadership and beliefs. The book argues that the comprehensive approach in understanding the socio-religious values of each of the three local Lopait communities in Central Java is essential to accurately describing their respective identity.

Alan R. Johnson

Leadership in a Slum

A Bangkok Case Study

2009 / 978-1-870345-71-2 / 238pp

This book looks at leadership in the social context of a slum in Bangkok from a different perspective than traditional studies which measure well educated Thais on leadership scales derived in the West. Using both systematic data collection and participant observation, it develops a culturally preferred model as well as a set of models based in Thai concepts that reflect on-the-ground realities. It concludes by looking at the implications of the anthropological approach for those who are involved in leadership training in Thai settings and beyond.

Titre Ande

Leadership and Authority

Bula Matari and Life - Community Ecclesiology in Congo

2010 / 978-1-870345-72-9 / 189pp

Christian theology in Africa can make significant development if a critical understanding of the socio-political context in contemporary Africa is taken seriously, particularly as Africa's post-colonial Christian leadership based its understanding and use of authority on the Bula Matari model. This has caused many problems and Titre proposes a Life-Community ecclesiology for liberating authority, here leadership is a function, not a status, and 'apostolic succession' belongs to all people of God.

Frank Kwesi Adams

Odwira and the Gospel

A Study of the Asante Odwira Festival and its Significance for Christianity in Ghana

2010 /978-1-870345-59-0 / 232pp

The study of the Odwira festival is the key to the understanding of Asante religious and political life in Ghana. The book explores the nature of the Odwira festival longitudinally - in pre-colonial, colonial and post-independence Ghana - and examines the Odwira ideology and its implications for understanding the Asante self-identity. Also discussed is how some elements of faith portrayed in the Odwira festival can provide a framework for Christianity to engage with Asante culture at a greater depth.

Bruce Carlton

Strategy Coordinator

Changing the Course of Southern Baptist Missions

2010 / 978-1-870345-78-1 / 268pp

This is an outstanding, one-of-a-kind work addressing the influence of the non-residential missionary/strategy coordinator's role in Southern Baptist missions. This scholarly text examines the twentieth century global missiological currents that influenced the leadership of the International Mission Board, resulting in a new paradigm to assist in taking the gospel to the nations.

Julie Ma & Wonsuk Ma
Mission in the Spirit:
Towards a Pentecostal/Charismatic Missiology
2010 / 978-1-870345-84-2 / 312pp

The book explores the unique contribution of Pentecostal/Charismatic mission from the beginning of the twentieth century. The first part considers the theological basis of Pentecostal/Charismatic mission thinking and practice. Special attention is paid to the Old Testament, which has been regularly overlooked by the modern Pentecostal/Charismatic movements. The second part discusses major mission topics with contributions and challenges unique to Pentecostal/Charismatic mission. The book concludes with a reflection on the future of this powerful missionary movement. As the authors served as Korean missionaries in Asia, often their missionary experiences in Asia are reflected in their discussions.

Allan Anderson, Edmond Tang (Eds)
Asian and Pentecostal
The Charismatic Face of Christianity in Asia
2011 / 978-1870345-94-1 / 500pp
(Revised Edition)

This book provides a thematic discussion and pioneering case studies on the history and development of Pentecostal and Charismatic churches in the countries of South Asia, South East Asia and East Asia.

S. Hun Kim & Wonsuk Ma (eds.)
Korean Diaspora and Christian Mission
2011 / 978-1-870345-91-0 / 301pp (hardback)

As a 'divine conspiracy' for Missio Dei, the global phenomenon of people on the move has shown itself to be invaluable. In 2004 two significant documents concerning Diaspora were introduced, one by the Filipino International Network and the other by the Lausanne Committee for World Evangelization. These have created awareness of the importance of people on the move for Christian mission. Since then, Korean Diaspora has conducted similar research among Korean missions, resulting in this book

Jin Huat Tan
Planting an Indigenous Church
The Case of the Borneo Evangelical Mission
2011 / 978-1-870345-99-6 / 363pp

Dr Jin Huat Tan has written a pioneering study of the origins and development of Malaysia's most significant indigenous church. This is an amazing story of revival, renewal and transformation of the entire region chronicling the powerful effect of it evident to date! What can we learn from this extensive and careful study of the Borneo Revival, so the global Christianity will become ever more dynamic?

Bill Prevette

Child, Church and Compassion

Towards Child Theology in Romania

2012 / 978-1-908355-03-4 / 377pp

Bill Prevett comments that "children are like 'canaries in a mine shaft'; they provide a focal point for discovery and encounter of perilous aspects of our world that are often ignored." True, but miners also carried a lamp to see into the subterranean darkness. This book is such a lamp. It lights up the subterranean world of children and youth in danger of exploitation, and as it does so travels deep into their lives and also into the activities of those who seek to help them.

Samuel Cyuma

Picking up the Pieces

The Church and Conflict Resolution in South Africa and Rwanda

2012 / 978-1-908355-02-7 / 373pp

In the last ten years of the 20th century, the world was twice confronted with unbelievable news from Africa. First, there was the end of Apartheid in South Africa, without bloodshed, due to responsible political and Church leaders. The second was the mass killings in Rwanda, which soon escalated into real genocide. Political and Church leaders had been unable to prevents this crime against humanity. In this book, the question is raised: can we compare the situation in South Africa with that in Rwanda? Can Rwandan leaders draw lessons from the peace process in South Africa?

Peter Rowan

Proclaiming the Peacemaker

The Malaysian Church as an Agent of Reconciliation in a Multicultural Society

2012 / 978-1-908355-05-8 / 268pp

With a history of racial violence and in recent years, low-level ethnic tensions, the themes of peaceful coexistence and social harmony are recurring ones in the discourse of Malaysian society. In such a context, this book looks at the role of the church as a reconciling agent, arguing that a reconciling presence within a divided society necessitates an ethos of peacemaking.

Edward Ontita

Resources and Opportunity

The Architecture of Livelihoods in Rural Kenya

2012 / 978-1-908355-04-1 / 328pp

Poor people in most rural areas of developing countries often improvise resources in unique ways to enable them make a living. Resources and Opportunity takes the view that resources are dynamic and fluid, arguing that villagers co-produce them through redefinition and renaming in everyday practice and use them in diverse ways. The book focuses on ordinary social activities to bring out people's creativity in locating, redesigning and embracing livelihood opportunities in processes.

Kathryn Kraft

Searching for Heaven in the Real World

A Sociological Discussion of Conversion in the Arab World

2012 / 978-1-908355-15-7 / 1428pp

Kathryn Kraft explores the breadth of psychological and social issues faced by Arab Muslims after making a decision to adopt a faith in Christ or Christianity, investigating some of the most surprising and significant challenges new believers face.

Wessley Lukose

Contextual Missiology of the Spirit
Pentecostalism in Rajasthan, India
2013 / 978-1-908355-09-6 / 256pp

This book explores the identity, context and features of Pentecostalism in Rajasthan, India as well as the internal and external issues facing Pentecostals. It aims to suggest 'a contextual missiology of the Spirit,' as a new model of contextual missiology from a Pentecostal perspective. It is presented as a glocal, ecumenical, transformational, and public missiology.

Paul M Miller

Evangelical Mission in Co-operation with Catholics:
Pentecostalism in Rajasthan, India
2013 / 978-1-908355-17-1 / 256pp

This book brings the first thorough examination of the discussions going on within Evangelicalism about the viability of a good conscience dialogue with Roman Catholics. Those who are interested in evangelical world missions and Roman Catholic views of world missions will find this informative.

REGNUM RESOURCES FOR MISSION

Knud Jørgensen
Equipping for Service
Christian Leadership in Church and Society
2012 / 978-1-908355-06-5 / 168pp

This book is written out of decades of experience of leading churches and missions in Ethiopia, Geneva, Norway and Hong Kong. Combining the teaching of Scripture with the insights of contemporary management philosophy, Jørgensen writes in a way which is practical and applicable to anyone in Christian service. "The intention has been to challenge towards a leadership relevant for work in church and mission, and in public and civil society, with special attention to leadership in Church and organisation."

GENERAL REGNUM TITLES

Vinay Samuel, Chris Sugden (eds.)
The Church in Response to Human Need
1987 / 1870345045 / xii+268pp

Philip Sampson, Vinay Samuel, Chris Sugden (eds.)
Faith and Modernity
Essays in modernity and post-modernity
1994 / 1870345177 / 352pp

Klaus Fiedler
The Story of Faith Missions
1994 / 0745926878 / 428pp

Douglas Peterson
Not by Might nor by Power
A Pentecostal Theology of Social Concern in Latin America
1996 / 1870345207 / xvi+260pp

David Gitari
In Season and Out of Season
Sermons to a Nation
1996 / 1870345118 / 155pp

David. W. Virtue
A Vision of Hope
The Story of Samuel Habib
1996 / 1870345169 / xiv+137pp

Everett A Wilson
Strategy of the Spirit
J.Philip Hogan and the Growth of the Assemblies of God Worldwide, 1960 - 1990
1997 /1870345231/214

Murray Dempster, Byron Klaus, Douglas Petersen (Eds)
The Globalization of Pentecostalism
A Religion Made to Travel
1999 / 1870345290 / xvii+406pp

Peter Johnson, Chris Sugden (eds.)
Markets, Fair Trade and the Kingdom of God
Essays to Celebrate Traidcraft's 21st Birthday
2001 / 1870345193 / xii+155pp

Robert Hillman, Coral Chamberlain, Linda Harding
Healing & Wholeness
Reflections on the Healing Ministry
2002 / 978-1- 870345-35- 4 / xvii+283pp

David Bussau, Russell Mask
Christian Microenterprise Development
An Introduction
2003 / 1870345282 / xiii+142pp

David Singh
Sainthood and Revelatory Discourse
An Examination of the Basis for the Authority of Bayan in Mahdawi Islam
2003 / 8172147285 / xxiv+485pp

For the up-to-date listing of the Regnum books visit www.ocms.ac.uk/regnum

Regnum Books International

Regnum is an Imprint of The Oxford Centre for Mission Studies
St. Philip and St. James Church
Woodstock Road
Oxford, OX2 6HR
Web: www.ocms.ac.uk/regnum